PRAISE FOR
ANOTHER LIFE

"[An] engaging memoir." —*The New York Times*

"This is a memoir about the publishing business and the people who
swirl through it. For writers or serious readers or frivolous readers
who just love books, this is a delicious find. [Korda] knows how
to tell a wonderful story."

—*The Washington Post Book World*

"A triumph . . . so diverting, so lively, and so well-intentioned (even in
its wickedest characterizations) that it calls for a new classification:
a Book of Fabulous Beasts. What makes his book not only amusing and
instructive but appealing is that his close and canny observations are
conveyed with a writer's glee, never with sour resentment or envy."

—*New York Observer*

"Interesting, readable, and truly informative . . . reading *Another
Life* . . . is like taking a walk through a gallery of portraits of the
eccentric and famous with a guide who got to see them at their best and
worst and remembers with precision what those encounters were like."

—*The Atlanta Journal-Constitution*

"Gloriously funny, charming, and ultra-readable . . . A more candid,
engaging and warmly knowledgeable survey of the past 40 years of
publishing cannot be imagined. Nobody who loves the book business
with Korda's hopeless and enduring passion can fail to be delighted
and touched by this endearing saga."

—*Publishers Weekly*

"A wry, lively, informative, and wonderfully written chronicle that puts
to the lie any idea that publishing is a stodgy business."

—George Plimpton

Please turn the page for more extraordinary acclaim . . .

"A page-turner . . . a good read . . . [Korda] has an impressive memory, a good eye for telling moments, and surely knows how to pen a story. His instinct for what keeps pages turning has kept him in business all these years and serves him well here. As Korda might put it, this book *works*."

—*The Seattle Times*

"Full of delicious gossip . . . full of such vivid recollections, written with zest and intelligence . . . a good read."

—*Daily News* (Los Angeles)

"Once—before the telephone, television, and Internet—the village elder gathered people round the fire and told mesmerizing stories. None told stories better than Michael Korda does in this enthralling memoir about publishing and squeezing the most out of life. Your jaw will drop listening to this village elder tell wise and comical tales about the great and nongreat, about a publishing industry convulsed by change, about his own vivid, and admirable, career."

—Ken Auletta

"Charming and compulsively readable."

—*Detroit Free Press*

"Korda describes the people in his life in vivid and delightful detail . . . a relaxing, enjoyable book loaded with funny and quirky stories."

—*The Denver Post*

"A witty, pithy, and sometimes caustic look at some of the best-known names in the world of publishing and the movies."

—*Houston Chronicle*

I always had the idea that when I was

old I'd get frightfully clever. I'd get

awfully learned, I'd get jolly sage.

People would come to me for advice.

But nobody ever comes to me for anything,

and I don't know a bloody thing.

—RALPH RICHARDSON

Delta
Trade Paperbacks

MICHAEL KORDA

Another Life

A MEMOIR OF OTHER PEOPLE

A Delta Book
Published by
Dell Publishing
a division of
Random House, Inc.
1540 Broadway
New York, New York 10036

Cover design by Gabrielle Bordwin
Cover photo by Daniel Bordwin

Dell books may be purchased for business or promotional use
or for special sales. For information please write to: Special
Markets Department, Random House, Inc., 1540 Broadway,
New York, NY 10036.

Delta® is a registered trademark of Random House, Inc., and
the colophon is a trademark of Random House, Inc.

ISBN: 0-385-33507-5

Reprinted by arrangement with Random House

Manufactured in the United States of America

Published simultaneously in Canada

May 2000

RRH/ 10 9 8 7 6 5 4 3 2 1

For Margaret—

WHO EMBODIES

"COURAGE, LOVE

AND JOY"

(John Gay)

CONTENTS

PART ONE

The Creative Juices

CHAPTER 1

I WAS TWENTY-THREE before it occurred to me that my future might not lie in the movie business.

Until then, I had always taken it for granted that I would follow in my family's footsteps sooner or later. Admittedly, I did not seem to have those gifts that had made my father, Vincent, a world-famous art director, nor did I flatter myself that I had the monumental self-confidence that had made my Uncle Alex a successful film director at the age of twenty-one and a legendary producer and film entrepreneur before he was thirty. As for my Uncle Zoltan, the middle of the three Korda brothers, the steely determination to have his own way that was at the very heart of his genius as a film director had not, I had guessed even as a child, been granted me in my cot. The brothers were, in any case, each unique and inimitable, with their strange accents, their many eccentricities, and their uncompromising (and unself-conscious) foreignness.

Still, throughout my childhood and youth I clung to the notion, without much in the way of encouragement, that I would eventually make my living in the film business, if only because it was the only adult world about which I knew anything. It was not just that my father and his brothers were in it; my mother and my Aunt Joan (Zoli's wife), as well as my Auntie Merle (Oberon, Alex's wife), not to speak of Alex's ex-wife, Maria (a great star until talkies put an inglorious end to her career), all were actresses. It could not have been more the family business had we been shopkeepers living above the shop, and in fact all this often seemed just like that, except on a grander scale.

I was not unrealistic enough to suppose that "all this"—the mansion at 144/146 Piccadilly (once the residence of King George VI when he was Duke of York, now the headquarters of London Films), the sprawling film studio at Shepperton, the London Films offices in New York, Paris, Hamburg, and Rome—would one day be mine, but I anticipated, more modestly, a place for me somewhere there, doing *something*, though exactly what was never clear to me.

I learned French and Russian because Alex had remarked casually that his command of many languages had proven useful to him in the movie business. I took up photography because my father always carried a Leica in his pocket and believed taking photographs improved his eye for a scene or a detail. I labored at learning to write because Zoli believed that no movie was ever better than its script, and until you got it right it wasn't worth thinking about anything else. He himself labored for seven years on the script for a movie of Daphne du Maurier's *The King's General* without ever bringing it to the point where it satisfied him, or, more important, Alex. As a schoolboy on holiday, I cut my teeth as a writer trying to make the dialogue of this Restoration drama read more like English than Hungarian, at half a crown a page.

Even history, my first love at school, I studied largely because it seemed likely to be useful in the movie business, at least as it was practiced by the Korda brothers. Alex's favorite subjects for movies tended to be drawn from history and biography—*The Private Life of Henry VIII; I, Claudius; That Hamilton Woman; The Scarlet Pimpernel*, for example—while most of Zoli's great successes were drawn (improbably for a Hungarian) from British colonial history: *Elephant Boy, The Four Feathers, Drums, Sanders of the River*. My father mostly read history and art history, rather than fiction, and could produce depictions of a Roman bedroom, the drawing room of the king of Naples, or Henry VIII's throne room on demand, mostly from memory, and pretty much overnight when required, without getting a single detail wrong.

If the Korda brothers believed deeply in anything, it was the value of education. The Austro-Hungarian Empire might have been a ramshackle house of cards, but it had had a remarkably efficient educational system, with perhaps the highest standards in Europe. Even though they were Jewish, Alex, Zoli, and Vincent had had mathematics, ancient and modern history, foreign languages, and Latin beaten into them, like every other boy who attended the Gymnasium. These lessons were not forgotten, if only because of the blows that accompanied them. Nothing one learned was ever truly useless, my father liked to say—however nonsensical it seemed when one was young, it would sooner or later come in handy.

I clung to this belief throughout my school days, and even through university, though it went against the evidence of my eyes. I could see no way in which studying the poetry of the French Symbolists, for example, was likely to prove useful to me, still less the early roots of the Russian language—a suspicion that subsequent life has proven to be only too well founded. Increasingly, I came to feel that I was being educated to no purpose at all, that three years as an undergraduate at Magdalen College, Oxford, were just an expensive way of putting off the day of reckoning when I would finally have to make a choice and *do* something—but what?

I had spent two years in the Royal Air Force doing intelligence work in Germany before going up to Oxford and had enjoyed it as a kind of enforced pause in which nothing very much was expected of me except to keep my boots and buttons shiny and to not destroy any expensive pieces of radio equipment. If there was one thing to be said for the RAF, it was that in it I could be sure of being kept busy every hour of every day, without a moment's leisure to worry about my plans for the future—or the lack of them.

Since I was due to be graduated in the summer of 1957, the new year of 1956 provoked much thought: the future was closing in fast; all my friends already knew *exactly* what they were going to do after graduation, while I was still waiting fecklessly for the family summons to the motion-picture industry. As it turned out, the summons was never to arrive. On January 23, Alex died, and it was very shortly apparent that his film "empire," however solid it looked on the outside, was not going to survive him—indeed, that he had never intended it to.

PERHAPS AS a reaction to this dose of reality, perhaps because I felt a desperate need to join in *something*, however exotic, or perhaps simply because I needed, if nothing else, an escape from having to make up my mind about a profession or a job, I left Oxford in the late autumn of 1956. With three companions, I set off for Budapest at the first news of the outbreak of the revolution there, carrying medical supplies and helping out in the besieged city's hospitals. Like so many others throughout modern history, I thought better a uniform or the barricades than a lifetime of boredom as a clerk—a sentiment which to this day provides the French Foreign Legion with more recruits than it needs. In something of the same spirit, my friends and I drove a decrepit, borrowed Volkswagen convertible to Vienna, ready to do battle.

I did not speak a word of Hungarian, I did not feel myself to be in any way Hungarian, and the little I knew of Hungarian history and politics filled me with dismay rather than with any pride or sympathy. I went because I was looking for adventure, because it seemed like a good opportunity to be a part of history in the making (as so many of my father's friends had done in Spain, not to speak of in World War Two), and perhaps because it looked fairly clear which side was the right one. It was David and Goliath, with the Hungarian Communist Party and the Red Army playing the role of Goliath.

My years of RAF service, plus my obligatory annual summer stint in the RAF Reserve, were enough to give me the illusion that I might prove useful to the insurgents. I knew a lot about radios, there was hardly a weapon in the British arsenal that I could not strip and reassemble blindfolded, I was a good shot, I knew Russian. I saw myself perhaps playing the role in the streets of Budapest that the hero of *The Four Feathers* had played in the Sudan, or that T. E. Lawrence had played in Arabia. I would then, I thought, even more improbably, return home to woo Alexa, my Uncle Alex's young widow, with whom I had been hopelessly in love for years, to the annoyance of my family.

My decision to go to Hungary brought tears to the eyes of Alexa (who had agreed to buy the medical supplies) and to those of my father, who, having survived two earlier Hungarian revolutions by the skin of his teeth, had a good idea of exactly what we were getting ourselves into. Except for Alexa, the only adult who seemed enthusiastic about this adventure was the writer Graham Greene, an old friend of my father's and something of a mentor to me, who believed that young men had the right, if not the obligation, to seek danger anywhere, however remote. The cause, as such, did not seem to him important—the main thing was to be "in the thick of things," with the heady sound of bullets whistling past one's ears.

In the spirit of his later spoof of the British Secret Intelligence Service, *Our Man in Havana*, Greene introduced me to a member of MI6 over drinks at the Ritz Hotel bar, on Piccadilly. Greene himself had been a wartime spy for SIS, as well as one of Kim Philby's oldest (and most loyal) friends. Intrigue was second nature to him, and he reveled in mystery, so it was not surprising that I never learned the name of his companion, a military-looking gentleman with a Brigade of Guards tie who urged me to photograph the unit markings on any Soviet vehicles I saw, as well as the collar and shoulder flashes of the troops.

What, I asked, should I do with the exposed film? "Place the film cartridges in a French letter and insert it into your rectum," the gentleman from SIS whispered. "Vaseline helps," he added delicately, sipping at his pink gin.

He also told me the telephone number of a man in Budapest who might be able to help me in case of need, although, he warned, I was to use it only in the direst of emergencies. I must memorize the number, right then and there, since it was far too secret to write down.

"You'll see," Greene said contentedly, as we watched the SIS man stroll down Piccadilly, merging into the evening crowd with his neatly furled umbrella and his bowler hat—no doubt on his way back to the SIS building on Shaftesbury Avenue, which was supposed to be top secret, but was in fact so well known that London taxi drivers pointed it out to tourists—"they always look after their own."

More sensibly, my father gave me the telephone number of Zoltán Kodály, the famed composer—who would be respected, he said, by any regime—and promised to call the new prime minister, Imre Nagy, on my behalf, if necessary. Resigned to the inevitable, he advised me that the important things in a revolution were to wear plenty of warm clothes, to carry a street map, and to take as much food with me as possible. Alexa worried about my keeping warm too and gave me the heavy fur-lined jacket that Alex had used during the war to keep him warm on his journeys back and forth across the Atlantic in unheated bombers. I was going back to the city in which he had first become famous, wearing his coat. I wondered if there was any symbolism to this, and, if so, what it was.

I FOLLOWED my father's advice, loading up the car in Munich with as much delicatessen as could be crammed into what little space remained, and very good advice it turned out to be. Most roadblocks and barricades were manned by Hungarians who carried bottles of *baracs*, a peach brandy with a faint aftertaste of turpentine and the kick of jet fuel, in one coat pocket and spare ammunition or a grenade in the other. Cans of sardines and salamis were useful in calming tempers.

Driving around Budapest at night was to experience all the thrills of danger, even during the brief truce when the Russians weren't shelling the city. At every street corner, armed civilians stuck their heads—and more important, their guns—into the car, punctuating their questions with clicks of their safety catches. On the discovery that my friends and I were British, we were usually offered a drink and often needed it. The empty bottles were gathered neatly beside the barricades to be made into Molotov cocktails. In that sense, drinking could be seen as yet another way of supplying the revolution with additional firepower, as well as keeping everybody's spirits high, but the result was a high level of nervous anxiety and a lot of unnecessary shooting.

The Hungarians had won the first round of the revolution. The departing Russian troops looked even shabbier than the Hungarian civilians, at least by the spit-and-polish traditions of the British armed services. But what the Russians lacked in spit and polish they made up for in numbers and sheer ferocity. The first time I tried to photograph a column of tanks, an officer shouted a warning at me from the open cupola of his tank's turret, and when I didn't put the camera away fast enough, his machine gunner pointed his weapon straight at my head for emphasis. The expression on his face—he had the thickest, blackest eyebrows I had ever seen on a man, and was a dead ringer for Leonid Brezhnev—made it plain that nothing would give him more pleasure than putting a burst right into my chest. I decided then and there that SIS would have to do without any photographs from me.

The few days after the Hungarian insurgents appeared to have fought the Red Army to a standstill were at once euphoric and unsettling. We felt we were living in the calm before the storm, as the new Hungarian government struggled for international diplomatic and military support, neither of which was forthcoming. There were ominous rumors that the Russians were gathering reinforcements from the Ukraine to retake the city. In the meantime, the bodies in the streets were being picked up at last. They lay there, Russian and Hungarian, sprinkled with lime to mask the odor of death, faces covered with brown wrapping paper or old newspapers, sometimes with a few fading flowers at their feet. Many of the dead Russian soldiers lay on their backs, their hands frozen in positions of supplication or anger, their heavy greatcoats spread around them on the pavement; most of the Hungarian corpses were laid out with more care, the arms folded neatly across the chest, one hand over the other. Not a few had a piece of shirt cardboard tucked under the hands with a name written on it in big block capitals.

The Russians announced their return in force early on November 4, with a massive artillery barrage that began at three in the morning, lighting up the sky all around the city. There had been plenty of signs that they were coming, but nobody had wanted to believe them. Long-distance calls produced no reply or were answered in Russian, while radio stations all over the country closed down one by one, and trains that left Budapest failed to return. In the streets, the feeling was one of fatalism, a Hungarian national character trait even under the best of circumstances. The only optimism to be found was among the American correspondents lined up at the bars of the major hotels.

My own spirits were not exactly buoyed by the sight of barricades of cars, street-lamp poles, trams, and tram rails going up in the streets. I did not think they would hold back the Russians for very long, which shortly proved to be the case. The constant rolling thunder of the big guns, the scream of incoming shells, and the deafening crash as they hit some apartment building or monument seemed exciting at first but soon began to oppress. The cold, gray, cheerless sky of *Mitteleuropa* in late autumn was obscured by a low-hanging pall of greasy black smoke from fires and explosions, and the air smelled of cordite, burning gasoline, diesel fumes, clogged drains, and death. Clouds of gritty plaster and cement dust rose from each hit. Shards of broken glass, chunks of masonry, and pieces of white-hot shrapnel hissed and whizzed past my ears. All too soon, however, noises began that made the artillery barrage seem comforting by comparison: the sharp hammering of machine guns, the high-pitched crack of rifles, the thud of an occasional hand grenade, the rapid pop-pop-pop of automatic small arms, and worst of all the ominous roar of diesel engines and the squeal of metal treads on cobblestones that indicated the approach of tanks. The rumor was that the Russians were not taking prisoners

As the city burned and shook around me—the old streets seemed to heave with each detonation, as if rocked by earthquakes—I began to think about my future, if there was one, in clearer terms. A number of my illusions faded during the siege and fall of Budapest, some of them having to do with fear and courage, others to do with the future. It became clear to me in the harsh, cold, grubby, and dangerous reality of Budapest—the city to which Alex had come as an impoverished enfant terrible in 1908, and where he had directed his first movie in 1914—that Alex's death had in fact meant the end of any easy way for me to enter the movie business. For the first time, I thought about that with relief. Why, after all, enter a business in which Alex and his brothers had succeeded beyond their wildest imaginations?

Given my interest in history, my father had hoped that I would teach it eventually, but having seen history in the making, I didn't think that trying to make tidy sense of it would be the profession for me. In any case, I couldn't see myself settling into a comfortable life as an Oxford don, even assuming I could improve my academic record enough to make such a career possible.

Had I nurtured any fantasies about working for the British intelligence services, they would have evaporated when I saw the Red Army in action. This particular fantasy was not as far-fetched as it sounds. This, after all, was in the years before an endless number of Oxford- or Cambridge-educated traitors were exposed, discrediting the idea of recruiting young men over a glass of sherry during tutorial sessions. Many an Oxford or Cambridge don was a talent scout for the spymasters, and those undergraduates who, like myself, were fluent in Russian and seemed to be on the right side of the class barrier were likely to receive a carefully phrased offer from one of them—I certainly had. (Oddly enough, an attempt had also been made to recruit me for the other side while I was in the RAF.)

I had no interest in the more traditional "professions"—law, medicine, et cetera—and recognized that I was not at all the type for a career in the British diplomatic services, nor for the stock market or banking—like my father and my uncles, I was interested in spending money, not in dealing with other people's. There was always journalism, of course, but I had tried that during a brief spell with the *Financial Times* the summer before and hadn't liked Fleet Street much. Besides, the British journalists in Budapest were for the most part a poor advertisement for their craft, hard drinking, given to reporting even the wildest and most short-lived of rumors as truth. They seemed to me straight out of the pages of Evelyn Waugh's *Scoop*. "This is a second-rate profession," one of them said to me glumly, as we sat drinking in a bar, surrounded by bits of broken glass and pieces of the chandelier, which an explosion had brought down from the ceiling. "I mean, what can you say in five hundred words or less about all this? Anyway, what they want back in London is human-interest stories. And who wants to go out into the bloody streets and risk getting shot just to find some poor sod of a freedom fighter who understands English well enough to ask him how it feels to be shot at?"

Who indeed? I said sympathetically. Still, it was a big story, surely, exactly the kind of thing people wanted to read about?

"Don't you believe it. They want to read about pools winners and American film stars. This is foreign politics, that's all. The moment these people have lost, they'll be off the front page."

Truer words, I was very soon to learn, were never spoken.

THE FACT was, as it was gradually beginning to dawn on me while I sleepwalked through the last few days of the revolution, I didn't really seem to fit in anywhere in England. I didn't belong there any more than I belonged in Budapest. I was "mid-Atlantic"—as much a product of America, where I had lived as a child from 1941 to 1946, as of England; more at home in Switzerland, where I had gone to school at Le Rosey, or in France, where my father spent most of his time, than anywhere in the United Kingdom. During my service in the RAF, people had assumed that I was on some kind of Anglo-Canadian exchange program, while most people at Oxford mistook me for a Rhodes or a Fulbright scholar. I had lost most of my English accent while I was in America and made no effort to regain it once I was back in England. As a result, hardly anybody believed I was English—starting, unfortunately, with myself.

Not being thought of as English gave me a great advantage in that it removed me altogether from the British class system, in which the most obvious identifier is accent. But since the class system is central to life in the United Kingdom, it also left me adrift. I had none of the cozy companionship with my peers or the sense of belonging that constitute the real advantages of a class system. I had always felt myself to be an outsider except when at school in Switzerland, where *everybody* had been an outsider, except the Swiss.

So the problem wasn't what kind of a career I should pursue, it was where I was going to live, which was much easier to resolve. I felt a great sense of relief at reaching this conclusion, one that sustained me through many days of unpleasantness as the Russians "mopped up" after their victory, restoring the Hungarian Communist Party to power with a brutality that was to keep it there for more than thirty years. The streets were empty now of everything but burned-out tanks, smoldering barricades, corpses, and the omnipresent, expressionless Soviet soldiers. The enforced calm of defeat, oppression, and terror descended on the city.

I tried the secret telephone number that Graham Greene's friend had made me memorize, but it turned out to be that of the British Embassy, which you could find in any Budapest telephone book. I was eventually hustled out of Hungary in a long convoy of foreigners who had managed to annoy the Hungarian communists or their Soviet masters. As I crossed the border into Austria, I saw that man from MI6, dressed in the uniform of a British army doctor. He cut me dead— actually turned his back on me when I waved at him.

IT WAS a portent. I did not return home as a hero.

My friends and I got rather more attention than we wanted in the British press, but most of the papers treated our journey to Budapest and back as an escapade by high-spirited Oxford students, although the French press described us as if we had been adventurers in the John Buchan tradition. "Vacances en prison!" one Paris headline blared inaccurately, above a photograph in which we appeared unshaven and scowling, like Balkan bandits.

In fact, we had plenty to scowl about. We had left Oxford midterm, without permission, on the very sensible grounds that we would have been refused, and neither the university nor our colleges were pleased or in a forgiving mood. At last, at the cost of a long and serious lecture from the college dean warning me in no uncertain terms to apply myself to my studies more seriously in future and to avoid adventures, foreign or domestic, I was allowed back again, though not quite forgiven—I had committed the unpardonable sin of getting Magdalen College mentioned in the newspapers.

AS I struggled through that winter to catch up on my studies, lost in the poems of Stéphane Mallarmé (my tutor's specialty), I felt, for the first time, a certain discontent with my life at Oxford. It was not, I recognized, the fault of the university or of Magdalen College. They had not changed, nor were they ever likely to, but I had.

When spring came, I surprised my father—and myself—by taking a job as a waiter in a Chelsea espresso bar owned by the father of a girlfriend instead of joining him on the Cap d'Antibes. My father put it down to love (a possibility that struck him as far more dangerous than the Hungarian Revolution), while Alexa, who knew a thing or two more about love than my father, dismissed it as an ostentatious act of "slumming"—after all, I didn't need the money. The truth, however, was that I *liked* the noisy, late nights, the easy camaraderie with total strangers. It was a pleasure to be too busy to think. It was 1957, and Chelsea was at the forefront of that great cultural sea change in English life that was to take place in the sixties.

Besides, I was trying to stay out of my father's way, and Alexa's too, for what neither of them knew was that I had already decided to go to America—and that I wasn't planning on coming back.

CHAPTER 2

IN THE SUMMER of 1957, I returned to New York, which I had not seen since 1946. My father saw me off at Heathrow, dry-eyed and for once with no advice. I had already said good-bye to Alexa, with tears on both sides, and was never to see her again—she committed suicide some years later, after an unsuccessful second marriage and a difficult love affair.

New York is not like London, most of which changes slowly (many of the changes having been wrought by the Luftwaffe rather than by builders and planners). The New York I returned to was a radically different place from the one I had left. Then, the Third Avenue El had divided the East Side of Manhattan, its noisy trains rumbling and screaming above innumerable outdoor markets. Then, air-conditioning was quite unknown, except for the "air-cooled" movie houses, in which people took refuge during the summer. Offices were equipped with big, noisy standing fans, roaring like airplane propellers, that stirred the hot air to a gale, sending papers and cigarette ashes flying. Then, Fifth Avenue buses were double-deckers, like those of London, except that the top deck was open. Now, air-conditioning had tamed the summer, the El was gone, as were the double-decker buses, and everywhere glass-fronted skyscrapers were rising.

Television sets had been a scientific curiosity then, with postage stamp–size screens—a thick magnifying glass was placed in front of the screen by those who could afford to buy one, creating a picture that it was just possible to watch from a distance of a few feet, though everything looked as if it were being photographed in the dim waters of an aquarium. Now, in 1957, television was everywhere, most of it emanating from New York.

As a child, I had been taken to the BBC studios to watch my mother appear on a primitive television set. My nanny and I stared with amazement at the tiny screen, on which we could just make out my mother—or a miniature, black-and-white version of her—doing an old number from *Charlot's Revues*. Since then, television had played a very small role in my life. It simply did not *exist*, for all practical purposes, and for many years I was one of the few people in England who had ever even seen a television set in action. In France, in Switzerland, there was no television—in the evening people still sat in the café, read newspapers, and played cards, without even dreaming that their lives were about to be changed by a box with a glass screen in the front. In America, however, television had caught on while I was away. Everywhere I went there was a set, already changing people's lives, as it was about to change mine.

In that innocent age, moreover, there was still such a concept as "*quality* network television," though it was already beginning to die on the vine. *Playhouse 90* had been instrumental in bringing serious original drama to television, introducing talented playwrights such as Paddy Chayefsky. CBS was the undisputed leader in the culture stakes. So determined were they to produce quality original drama on television that they had signed very substantial contracts with some of America's leading playwrights, including Sidney Kingsley, the Pulitzer Prize–winning author of *Dead End*, *Men in White*, and *Detective Story*. Kingsley was married to Madge Evans, former Hollywood child actress; Madge, as it happened, was my mother's cousin.

It was my mother's intervention that procured me a job on the fringes of television almost as soon as I arrived in New York. Sidney, it turned out, was writing a play for CBS about the Hungarian Revolution and was stalled for want of "background." My qualifications for any job were nebulous, but if there was one thing I had to offer it was background about the Hungarian Revolution; more of it, actually, than most people wanted to hear.

Sidney and I met for lunch in the dark and gloomy Oak Room of the Plaza Hotel, a few yards from his office on Central Park South. I saw before me a short, powerfully built man with broad shoulders, a big head, and rough-hewn features that made him look like a bust by Sir Jacob Epstein. He had a deep, almost self-consciously "musical" voice and a strange accent—stage British lightly painted over New York Jewish—intended, I suspect, to disguise his Lower East Side background. He spoke slowly, articulating each word very clearly, as if talking to the village idiot, keeping his voice low, so that I was obliged to lean close to hear him. His method of writing, he explained, was to do meticulous, thorough research until he knew everything there was to know about a subject—not so much in his head (he tapped that organ for emphasis) but deep down in his gut. He patted his stomach forcefully. When you had that, the writing was easy—it was getting to that point that was hard. Research and facts, then more research and more facts, was what he needed. He would steep himself in them, soak them up, and demand still more. The story would come out of the research, eventually—there was no hurrying the process of creation. Eventually, the creative juices would reach the boiling point and flow.

I nodded vaguely. Even then, perhaps because of my friendship with Graham Greene, I knew that on no subject more so than their own writing are writers more likely to be self-deceived or, in conversation, more boring. Graham, perhaps for just that reason, never discussed how he wrote books and made savage fun of writers who did, but Sidney was of a more old-fashioned, self-taught school. His plays always had big social themes and "realistic" dialogue, very much in the spirit of the thirties, when he had had his big successes. He was now somewhat out of fashion and deeply resented the fact.

Sidney took the process of creation seriously and expected others to. He talked about it long into the afternoon, puffing on his pipe, slumped reflectively in his big leather chair, as the room grew darker and the waiters began setting the tables around us for dinner. My job, he emphasized, was to provide him with all the facts, the background, the raw material.

Apart from shoveling information at him, I was to play devil's advocate and tell him—frankly and ruthlessly—when he was full of shit. Above all, I should not spare his feelings. He could take it—he was a *stage* writer, not some cloistered novelist; he was used to arguments, objections, suggestions, pitched fights. He was not, in short, the kind of guy who bruised easily.

I promised to keep that in mind. My Uncle Alex's view had been that all writers had to be protected carefully from the harsh realities of the movie business, like children or sensitive plants, but I reasoned that perhaps the stage was different. Certainly Sidney looked like a tough guy. There was something of the boxer about him, with his heavy brow, his powerful chest, and his strong, muscular hands. (He had taken up sculpture as a hobby late in life, to my father's scorn, for when it came to art, he despised amateurs.) Sidney had, surely not by accident, the hunched-up stance of a fighter too, though there was, in fact, nothing particularly pugnacious about him. Indeed, his eyes, pale, deeply expressive, rimmed with long, pale lashes, seemed to be those of a man who was sensitive, withdrawn, perhaps easily hurt.

Did I want the job? Sidney asked. Absolutely, I said—after all, it was the only one I had been offered, as well as a foot in the door of serious television. We shook hands—Sidney's handshake was the kind that made you wince in pain—and parted on an amicable note. I was to start work on Monday.

ON MONDAY morning, promptly at nine, dressed as if for a funeral in a sober, dark suit, I turned up at Sidney's office, only to be told by Casey, his attractive young secretary, that he never arrived before eleven. The office was in fact a duplex apartment. Sidney had the downstairs part—a huge, two-story living room overlooking the park, together with a bedroom and the master bathroom—while Casey and I shared two small, windowless rooms, a bathroom, and a kitchen upstairs. A circular flight of stairs descended to Sidney's quarters, which, I was warned, I was never to visit unless he invited me to. I sat myself down at a desk in one of the small rooms and started to call around for material on the Hungarian Revolution.

For a couple of days, Sidney did not come in, so Casey and I were left alone, when I was not out of the office accumulating books, magazine articles, and documents. From her telephone conversations I was able to gather that Sidney was enormously late with his script and that CBS had not, so far, seen a word of it. I also deduced, without much difficulty, that this whole elaborate office was being paid for by CBS, as were Casey's salary and mine.

My growing pile of research was transferred down to Sidney's floor while I produced more. The Hungarian Revolution had been productive of paperwork, if nothing else. The United Nations had produced bulky white papers documenting every event, speech, and eyewitness report, as if the amount of paper would somehow make up for its complete inactivity in the face of brutal aggression. Various émigré groups had produced volume after volume of documents, too. If Sidney's dearest wish was to have plenty of research material, he was going to be delighted.

It was Wednesday before Sidney showed up at last. I had already been warned that he did not like to be spoken to or interrupted except for emergencies. Indeed, when he appeared, he emerged out of the elevator, hands behind his back, eyebrows contorted in a pensive frown, rather like paintings of Napoleon after 1812, and went downstairs without talking to either of us. He stayed down there all morning, sending for Casey from time to time to take down a note or a letter or to fetch him a cup of coffee. At lunchtime, he left for his usual table at the Oak Room. He returned about three, burying himself downstairs for the rest of the afternoon.

Promptly at six, Sidney reappeared, still apparently lost in thought, and left for home. The next day and the day after, this pattern repeated itself exactly. Sometimes, if he noticed me on his way in or out, he would smile and say, "Hello, my boy"; more often, he ignored my presence.

He did not mention the gathering pile of my research, all of it neatly organized in black binders, with notes. I had drawn up what I hoped would be a useful chronology, showing what had happened day by day and, where possible, hour by hour. I had even found the pathetic messages broadcast by provincial radio stations as they signed off for the last time. If all this, I thought, wasn't enough to start Sidney's creative juices flowing, I couldn't imagine what would.

From CBS came daily appeals for a "progress report" and, more boldly, "a face-to-face meeting." I have no idea exactly how much money CBS had invested in Sidney Kingsley, but to judge from the apprehension this extended period of silence from Central Park South caused among the higher executive ranks of CBS, it must have been a considerable amount. This was, in any case, not the kind of relationship that television executives were used to having with a writer. In television, the writer was just about the lowest man on the corporate totem pole. Jim Aubrey, a major CBS executive of the time, was in the habit of calling writers to his office for meetings, then leaving them in his waiting room for hours, only to have his secretary tell them, at the end of the day, to come back tomorrow. The notion of a writer who didn't take telephone calls and remained sequestered in his luxurious inner sanctum, as remote and silent as the Dalai Lama, had at first impressed CBS but was now beginning to cause alarm.

Eventually, some weeks after my arrival, Sidney, with great reluctance, agreed to a meeting to discuss his progress. The meeting would be held, naturally, in his office—the mountain would have to come to Mahomet—despite many attempts to lure him out of his retreat and into the CBS building, where he had never set foot.

The day of the meeting, Sidney put his hand on my shoulder in an avuncular fashion as he came in. "Let's talk about your work, my boy," he said, and led me downstairs for a chat. He made himself comfortable and lit a pipe.

The room was enormous, with a certain air of *la vie de bohème* but with money. It was half artist's studio, half expensively furnished "study," like the ones favored by major producers in Bel Air, with leather-bound books bought by the yard—just the kind of room, I reflected, that my father would surely have disliked as being neither one thing nor the other.

Sidney's big leather chair was placed so he could look out at the park comfortably, with his feet up; around it were placed chairs for visitors, all of them rather nice, well-worn English antiques. On a low table beside him was his Dictaphone, his pipes, a cigar humidor, and a tobacco jar. His desk—a big, antique, leather-topped *bureau plat,* a piece even my father would have admired—was bare of papers or any sign of work. Against one wall, facing the fireplace, was a majestic leather sofa, with a lot of pillows and a boldly patterned Indian blanket thrown over one arm—the ideal place, it looked to me, for an afternoon siesta.

One corner of the room was set up for Sidney's sculpture workshop, with a drop cloth on the floor. He appeared to be working on a life-size head of a man (unknown to me), in the style of Epstein, the clay layered on with deliberate roughness, and a small nude torso, much smoother, in more or less the style of Maillol—like so many amateur artists, Sidney did not appear to have a style of his own. The nude was not particularly graceful and was obviously giving Sidney a lot of trouble—patches of darker, fresh clay showed where he had recently scraped off what had been there and started all over again. I wondered if he used a live model, and if so, who?

Sidney's enthusiasm for sculpture, I decided, was greater than his skill—indeed, his status as an art lover, while he took it seriously himself, was disputed by my father, who was an unchallenged expert, a gifted painter in his own right and a serious figure in the world of art collecting. On one memorable occasion, he had unwillingly been obliged to have dinner at Sidney's apartment in the Dakota and found himself unable to avoid a guided tour of Sidney's collection, which included a large Rubens, of which Sidney was extremely proud. My father stood before it in the trance that came over him whenever he looked at a painting, until Sidney finally got up the courage to ask what he thought. My father looked at it skeptically, ran his hands over the surface, and sighed deeply, like a doctor attending a dying patient. He shook his head sadly, having recognized it as a forgery. "Vat the hell, Sidney," he said. "Vat it matters if it was painted by Rubens or not by Rubens? All vat matters is it gives you pleasure, no?"

I lit my own pipe, and we puffed silently for a few minutes. Sidney didn't require conversation, or impose it at any rate; he was content to sit in silence, nor did he expect to be amused. Eventually he spoke. "That's quite a pile of paper you've put together there," he said. My binders, I noticed, were piled neatly on the floor near his desk and showed no sign of having been opened.

I wasn't sure whether his comment was meant to be praise or criticism. Winston Churchill once remarked that anything worth knowing could be put on one piece of paper, and by this standard I had certainly failed Sidney. Still, he was the one who had asked me to pile it on him, I reminded myself. "I hope it's all going to be useful?" I said.

Sidney chuckled. "Oh yes," he said. "I think so."

"A good starting point for the play?"

"Maybe. The fact is, my boy, I haven't read any of it yet."

I tried to conceal my disappointment, but Sidney could tell that my feelings were hurt. He glanced at me shrewdly through a cloud of tobacco smoke. "You can't hurry the creative process," he reminded me sternly.

We sat in silence for a few minutes. "I want you to sit in on the meeting with these guys from CBS," Sidney said, to my astonishment. I could think of no good reason why he would want me present and said so.

"You're going to present what we've got," he said. "After all, you know what's there. I don't."

"Do you think they'll be interested?" I asked dubiously. There was an awful lot of material there.

"No. But they'll go back to CBS convinced that this is a mine of industry. I want you to bore the shit out of them, my boy. Don't disappoint me."

The two executives from CBS arrived on time and were shown downstairs. They had that combination of bland WASP good looks and a ruthless manner that was the style of the period in the television business. Both wore tailored, pinstripe English suits, white shirts, dark ties, glossy, expensive shoes—the CBS look.

Sidney greeted them amiably, every bit the artist, in a tweed jacket and a wool shirt open at the neck, offered them coffee, which they refused, introduced me as his assistant, and puffed on his pipe while they gradually worked their way up to asking him when he expected to have a first draft.

He listened to them in silence, nodding sympathetically. They should not think he wasn't just as concerned as they were, he said. He was anxious to get the play out of his system and move on to other things, but the creative process didn't run in a straight line, they should understand, it zigged and it zagged. He gestured with his hand.

"Is there anything in writing yet?" the more aggressive of the two executives asked.

Sidney smiled benevolently. Was there anything in *writing*? You *bet* there was! He signaled to me. I should show them what he had so far, he told me. While I placed the black binders full of research material on the desk, he explained, in a low whisper, as if I couldn't hear him, that I was a veteran of the revolution myself, a freedom fighter, and that my job was to give him the firsthand material that made the difference between fake theater and real theater: the *human interest*.

"Human interest," they understood. The one thing everybody in the television business knew was that "human interest" was the key to success. News had to have it (i.e., fires in Harlem or lost children, as opposed to commentary and facts), quiz shows had to have it (thus the need to rig them so the more appealing contestants won), drama had to have it, which is to say that it had to be about people the audience understood and, if possible, identified with. Television was an extension of the home, and the people who appeared on the screen had to be like family, not remote, glittering, and improbably good-looking, like movie stars, but familiar and unpretentious. All this the CBS executives knew by instinct; it was gospel, bred into their bones. If Sidney was pursuing human interest, he was on the right track.

It was my turn now to put them at their ease. I read to them highlights from the binders, now displayed on Sidney's desk. They didn't look particularly interested, but it wasn't my job to interest them. A veil of polite boredom settled on their faces, interrupted by one or the other of them glancing at his wristwatch. After about half an hour, they exchanged looks and stood up. Sidney, who had been listening to my recitation of facts, figures, and news items with Buddha-like contentment, looked concerned. Were they sure they had to leave? he asked. There was much, much more, all of it riveting.

No, no, they protested, they would love to stay, but they had to be getting back.

Sidney stood up and looked them in the eyes. What they had to understand, he said gravely, was that *this*—he made a sweeping gesture toward the binders—was the hard part; *this* was what had taken all the time and effort and—yes, let's be frank about it—money.

He stood in front of the window and pointed at the trees. Writing a play was like clearing a forest, he explained—a long, backbreaking job that made the plowing and the harvesting of the crops seem like nothing. He had now cleared the forest, his land was ready to be plowed, the harvest would soon be theirs.

I recognized that these homey agricultural metaphors derived from *The Patriots,* a play Sidney had written about the Founding Fathers, which had disappointed the critics and his investors. He also owned an estate in New Jersey about which he had squirearchical pretensions, as if he had planted every tree and strand of poison ivy himself.

Sidney accompanied his guests to the spiral staircase. "Go back and tell them," he said in a commanding voice, "that the play is right here."

He slapped his forehead hard. "It's just a question of getting it down on paper now," he went on, beaming with confidence and goodwill.

One of the executives cleared his throat. Will there be a love story? he asked. Television viewers, especially the women, were a whole lot more interested in love stories than in revolutions.

Sidney positively beamed at him, as if he had just made a critical comment worthy of F. R. Leavis in *Scrutiny*. He was glad that the question had been raised, he said. A love story was *exactly* what they were going to get, he assured them. *All* good theater was about love. Look at *Romeo and Juliet*! Look at *Othello*! Look at his own plays! This would be a love story, of course, played out against the drama of a city on fire, besieged by the communist hordes, about a man and a woman who find each other in a moment of supreme drama, and who end up making the ultimate sacrifice. . . . But no, he didn't want to spoil the play for them by giving away the ending now. They would read it, and, even if he said so himself, it would knock their socks off.

They went up the stairs, apparently happy, while Sidney breathed a long, low sigh of relief. He poured himself a drink and sat down in his chair, brooding over his view. I put the binders back on the floor quietly. "*Is* it going to be a love story?" I asked. Sidney hadn't said much about the play, but I had the impression that what he was aiming at was something more like Arthur Koestler's *Darkness at Noon*, a strong, dramatic denunciation of communism. As a matter of fact, if there was one element missing from most of Sidney's plays, it was a strong love story. He was an old-fashioned 1930s social realist, a dramatist who worked in the tradition of the novelist John Dos Passos (and who, like Dos Passos, had moved from mild left-wing opinions to strongly held right-wing ones as he grew richer). Each of his plays dealt above all with a single issue; the fate of slum children in *Dead End*, young doctors in *Men in White*, crime and punishment in *Detective Story*. Nobody would have claimed that the love story was his métier.

He didn't look up. "If that's what they want, that's what they'll get," he said. "Or that's what they'll turn it into, more likely."

"I thought the meeting went well. I mean, they seemed to go away happy."

"Mm. It will keep them off my back for another few months. With any luck." He clicked the ice in his glass and drank. "There's a lesson here for a writer, you know."

"Is there? I'm not sure that I'm going to be a writer, though."

Sidney laughed. "Oh, you will be, you will be, my boy. Trust me. I can tell. I know more about you than you do. What *kind* of writer, I don't know. Not a very serious one is my guess. And not a playwright. A journalist, perhaps," he said with some contempt. "Or a popular novelist." He sighed deeply. "Your father will be disappointed. He'll think you've wasted all that expensive education."

That was true enough, I thought, though not very nice of Sidney to say. "What's the lesson?" I asked.

"Ah, the lesson. Never forget that the people who pay a writer always have much, much more money and power than he does, whether it's a publishing house, a movie studio, or a television network. With that in mind,"—his voice changed to a fair imitation of W. C. Fields— " 'Never give a sucker an even break.' You can go now."

I THOUGHT about Sidney's lesson long and hard that night. I finally knew what I was looking for, and I already knew I wasn't going to find it sitting behind a desk and writing. Though I wasn't what anybody would call a "team player," I wanted to belong to a team—anybody's team.

As for Sidney's comment about writers, I realized, even then, that there was considerable wisdom in it. Writers are always outsiders and probably ought to be, since only outsiders see things clearly: the people who publish them, or make movies, or produce plays *are* always richer and more powerful, however successful the writer is. As I was soon to discover, there's a tendency among book publishers, especially when making speeches on public occasions, to boast that the writer and the publisher are both part of the same team. This, of course, is pious nonsense. Nobody in the book business really believes it, and no writer is ever taken in by it. A lot of people start out in book publishing believing that it's true, or at least that it ought to be true, then have to waste time learning otherwise, but I had the good fortune to know better, thanks to Sidney's insight.

DESPITE SIDNEY'S optimism, CBS eventually pulled the plug on his Hungarian project, which would have left me jobless, except that Sidney felt obliged, out of family feeling for my mother, to get me a job as a freelance reader in the CBS story department.

This was, at the time, about as low as you could get in the hierarchy of television, and indeed only one or two steps above being unemployed. First of all, the networks were already beginning to abandon the whole idea of doing original "quality" drama, even by established playwrights like Sidney or Paddy Chayefsky. Further, though we didn't know it at the time, they were planning to eliminate their story departments altogether. (Why own a cow when you can buy milk?)

It had never made much sense to have a whole department just to read books and scripts; the only reason CBS still had one was that it was too small and powerless to draw much attention from the cost cutters in the top brass. There was perhaps also some vestigial guilt feeling among the older television producers that the networks *ought* to consider original material, much as book publishers used to feel an obligation to read "the slush pile" of unsolicited manuscripts, rather than mailing them back unopened, as is now usually the case. Then, too, in television as in the book business, senior executives were always promising to look at somebody's novel or TV script, which then got sent down to the story department for a reading.

The script readers were a mixed bunch, mostly young writers for whom this was the equivalent of waiting on tables for aspiring thespians. They were paid twenty-five dollars apiece for each report, so it wasn't exactly a good way to get rich—still, neither was waiting on tables, and I'd already tried that.

The good part about the job was that I discovered I had a natural talent for putting the gist of a book or a script into a couple of paragraphs—no report could be longer than one page, which presumably represented the maximum attention span of a television producer. The bad part about it was that nobody who mattered at CBS paid the slightest attention to any of the reports.

The other bad part was that we weren't really CBS employees at all. It was piecework, like an old-fashioned garment sweatshop. Work was handed out to us in a big, empty room at the CBS studio on West Fifty-seventh Street by means of a kind of daily shape-up. You never knew whether or not you were going to get a book or a script to read, so there was no way to guess how much money you were going to make a week. Some weeks I got lucky and was assigned five or six books; other weeks

I got only one or two. Of course, there was no health coverage or employee benefits, and I worked at home.

Nevertheless, being paid to read seemed like money for jam. It had simply never occurred to me that anybody would pay money, however little, for something that was as natural as breathing to me. The only problem was that I wasn't being paid enough to live on and didn't have any structure on which to build a life for myself.

Freelancers are generally not a clubby lot, but I had made one friend, Leslie Davison, and we sometimes met for coffee or a sandwich after we had picked up our work for the day. Her brother, Peter, she told me, was the editor of the Atlantic Monthly Press in Boston, a fact that did not deeply impress me, since I knew nothing about book publishing. Books appeared somehow, but the process by which they did so was a mystery to me.

The only writer I knew well was Graham Greene, and his relationship with his publisher seemed distant, to put it mildly. Once he had finished writing a book, his secretary typed it, sent it off to Max Reinhardt, the beaming and affable chairman and managing director of the Bodley Head, in London, and that was that. Apart from Reinhardt, the only book publisher I knew was George Weidenfeld. Just as the British film industry seemed to be run by Hungarian Jews, the British book-publishing business seemed to be run by German Jews.

Leslie Davison made it her task to persuade me that I should be working in book publishing. She had no wish to work for a publisher herself, but she thought I was ideally suited to be in the same business as her brother. I was not so much resistant as baffled—in all the fantasies I had had about my future, the one business I had never considered was book publishing. Still, I had to admit that there was something in what she said. I was a fast reader in three languages who liked books, after all.

Of course, I was too innocent at the time to realize the fatuousness of this reasoning. The fact that one likes good food does not carry with it any promise that one would make a good chef or be a competent restaurateur. A taste for wearing good suits does not make one a tailor. As it happens, many of the most successful people in book publishing hardly like books at all and very seldom read one, but I did not know this at the time.

There were, at the time, a lot of new and unfamiliar pressures on me. I was anxious to prove to my father that I could exist on my own in

New York (or anywhere else) and even more anxious to get out of the no-man's-land of freelance work into something more secure. Moreover, I was now living with Casey, whom I had started to date when I was working for Sidney and who seemed likely to lose her job fairly soon, since Sidney had a feudal sense of property about her and apparently felt that he should have been consulted. When we decided, shortly afterward, to marry, he took even greater offense, and no wedding gifts were forthcoming from him or Madge.

At this time of my life, I was still haunted by my experience in Hungary, which was becoming harder to deal with the more it receded into the past. Apparently, the Hungarian Revolution had seeped down to my unconscious, along some hidden, Freudian pathway, emerging at night in my dreams. I slept restlessly—my head full of violent scenes and hidden dangers, not vague or fantastic ones but horribly realistic and familiar—with a sense of dread that wouldn't go away. Often I kept a loaded pistol under my pillow, as if I expected the AVO (the Hungarian secret police) or the Soviet military police to kick in the door at any moment. It was not a good frame of mind in which to begin a relationship, nor for job hunting, but I felt that regular employment at something I enjoyed might help get rid of the nightmares.

I began to make a few tentative calls.

CHAPTER 3

*B*OOK PUBLISHING, IT turned out, was not by any means easy to enter. The first difficulty was that it appeared to be rather like one of those English institutions—certain clubs and regiments, the Life Guards, the Grid or the Bullingdon at Oxford, Lloyd's of London—that you couldn't join unless you not only knew the right people but also understood all the unwritten rules. The second difficulty was that starting salaries were appallingly low. It seemed likely that I would actually be earning *less* money as a full-time editorial assistant than I was making freelancing for CBS, which hardly seemed possible.

Nor did book publishers seem like a particularly friendly lot. After responding to an advertisement in the help-wanted section of *The New York Times*, I was interviewed by the publisher of Henry Holt, an impressively suited and aggressive executive type who read my résumé with deep mistrust. "It says here you went to Oxford," he said.

I nodded.

"Can you prove that?"

The question startled me. I suppose Oxford does hand out diplomas of some kind, but I had certainly never bothered to collect mine, nor had anybody else I knew. It had never occurred to me that anybody would lie about things like that—or, perhaps more important, that anybody would suspect me of doing so. Besides, in England, one's accent, one's tailoring, one's haircut, not to speak of a thousand other small and subtle class distinctions, make it almost impossible to fake things like that successfully.

With some embarrassment, I conceded that I couldn't prove it. Could I prove the other stuff? he asked accusingly, thrusting a firm chin in my direction. School in Switzerland? Service in the RAF? I shook my head, feeling like an impostor. At any moment, I thought, he is going to ask me if I can prove that I'm Michael Korda. He stared at me darkly. "It says here you can speak French and Russian. That true?"

I said it was, a little defensively.

He looked at me with deep suspicion, and for a moment I wondered if speaking Russian might have made me seem like a subversive or a fellow traveler to him. Those were the days of the John Birch Society, the height of the cold war, with Ike and Nixon in the White House and Khrushchev in the Kremlin, perhaps not the ideal time to claim a knowledge of Russian. Even the English seemed subversive to many right-wing Republicans, on the grounds that we didn't take the cold war seriously enough.

My interviewer picked up his telephone and whispered into it. Was he calling for the police, I wondered, or for security guards to eject me from the building? We sat tensely for a moment, then the door opened and an attractive young woman entered. "Say something to her in Russian," he said to me, with a smile of satisfaction. We spoke in Russian for a minute or so. She nodded at her boss.

A look of gloom settled on my interviewer's face. He had clearly expected to catch me out in a lie. He waved her away, gave me a thin smile, and made a steeple with his fingers. "You can't be too careful these days," he said. He stood up, to show the interview was over. "You'll hear from us," he said.

I did not think that was likely, which proved to be correct. After quite a few similarly depressing and unsuccessful interviews, I decided that something must be wrong with my résumé, though I couldn't think of anything I could change. Would it be better *not* to admit to knowing foreign languages? Was it a mistake to say that I loved reading? Did the combination of Le Rosey and Magdalen College, Oxford, sound too frivolous or snobbish? Did my curriculum vitae lack the common touch? The few people who were willing to give me an explanation for turning me down said that I was overqualified to be an assistant editor, but one or two said that I was too inexperienced. They did not suggest how I was to gain experience, however.

Just as I was about to give up on the whole idea, I was saved by an old friend of my father's, Morris Helprin (father of novelist Mark Helprin, who would eventually be my assistant). He had run the London Films office in New York during and after the war, and I had called him in case he had any suggestions. He had a friend, Herbert Alexander, who was a vice president at Pocket Books. Paperback publishing might not be what I was looking for, of course, but it might be a way to get my foot in the door, if I wasn't too fussy to go into a business where sales meant more than literature. I denied any fussiness or snobbish love of literature, and Morris, the kindest of men, soon called me back to say that I had an interview with Alexander.

"By the way," Morris added, as he was about to hang up, a note of warning in his voice. "Herb is a real down-to-earth guy."

I said that I would bear that in mind, wondering just exactly what Morris meant.

"His bark is worse than his bite, just remember that. Don't let him bully you, that's all."

Oh God! I said to myself and put down the telephone receiver with a sense of dread.

So FAR book publishing had seemed to me a pretty staid business, so I was not prepared to find Herbert M. Alexander, vice president of Pocket Books, lying back in a barber's chair while being shaved. Beside him, an attractive young woman in a smock was buffing his nails. At his feet, an elderly black man was on his knees, shining Alexander's shoes.

The shoes, like Alexander himself, were outsize, resembling shiny black rowboats turned upside down on the beach. He was apparently a big man, with the build of a wrestler, broad shoulders, a massive chest, and a full belly. He had a big head, too, crowned with a crew cut, and wore tinted aviator goggles. He looked, in fact, just like the Americans in Gilles's famous cartoons in the London *Daily Express,* an Englishman's idea of what an American ought to be, right down to the button-down shirt, the narrow bow tie, and the massive class ring of God only knew what school or college. He had a big man's voice, too, low and rumbling, though rendered somewhat indistinct by the fact that he was speaking through a thick layer of shaving cream.

He waved me over to sit down next to him and reached out to shake my hand hard. "Call me Herb, kid," he growled brusquely, and immediately launched into convoluted narrative having to do, I dimly perceived, with the genesis of the mass-market paperback industry, in which Pocket Books had played a decisive role. Unfamiliar names rumbled by—Leon Shimkin, Jimmy Jacobson, Ian Ballantine, "Doc" Lewis, Robert De Graff—as Herb talked on and on about paperback publishing as if I were familiar with every moment of its history and everyone of consequence in it. As if to justify Morris Helprin's warning about his bark, Herb's theme seemed to be that I thought I was too good for the mass-market business. He did not say how he had reached that opinion, since he had not given me an opportunity to open my mouth.

For a big, tough-looking man, his speech was precise and even slightly academic in tone, like that of a college lecturer, though laced with the occasional profanity, presumably to show that he was a down-to-earth man at heart and not some bleeding-heart intellectual like me. From time to time he veered off into startling non sequiturs, weaving strange theories about the effect of history or economics or politics on book publishing. When he was off on a tangent, he sounded, in truth, a lot like one of those harmless cranks who believe that the Welsh are the lost tribe of Israel, or that the earth is flat, or that all world history is controlled by a secret cabal of Masons; at other times he sounded fairly sane. He had a fondness for baseball and football metaphors, which, since I didn't play or follow either game, were entirely meaningless to me.

Through the torrent of his words I discerned, however dimly, the outlines of a story: In the beginning, all books had been published in hardcover form, at a relatively high price, until, in the mid-thirties, Robert De Graff conceived of selling paperback reprints in a small or "pocket" size for a quarter, thereby bringing culture to the many instead of only the few. De Graff got nowhere with his idea, since every book publisher pooh-poohed it. Besides, it was a well-known fact that bookstores wouldn't stock cheap paperback books, hardcover publishers wouldn't sell the right to reprint their titles at any price, and anyway there was no unfilled demand for books out there in the marketplace. Books were a luxury item, and book buyers represented a small, educated market that wasn't particularly price conscious.

Similar arguments had been made against book clubs, Herb pointed out, until Harry Scherman had founded the Book-of-the-Month Club and proved them wrong, but at least the book clubs still sold the ur-product, albeit in a slightly schlockier form sometimes. In any event, Leon Shimkin—a former part-time bookkeeper at Simon and Schuster who had risen to wealth and power as the protégé of the late Marshall Field III—somehow managed to wrest De Graff's idea away from him, founded Pocket Books, and proceeded to prove that there was indeed a huge, untapped market for books at a quarter.

The key to Shimkin's success lay in his experience as business manager for *P.M.*, the liberal New York City afternoon daily into which Field had poured a fortune in a forlorn attempt to prove that a left-wing newspaper could survive in a big city. Shimkin had no sympathy with Field's political ideas, Herb pointed out quickly—this was still America of the fifties—but he very quickly learned everything there was to know about newspaper and magazine distribution.

That bookstores wouldn't carry mass-market books turned out to be true, but Shimkin hadn't been dismayed. The price of a paperback book meant that it could be treated like a magazine and displayed in racks in the same places where magazines were sold—newsstands, candy stores, drugstores, railway stations, and bus depots—thus reaching a whole new readership. The idea of linking books to the newspaper and magazine distribution business launched a whole new industry, which came of age suddenly in World War Two, when troops read paperbacks by the millions.

The clear outlines of a massive inferiority complex, combined with an outsize chip on his shoulder, were beginning to appear in Herb's lecture. Hardcover publishers, he went on, had accepted the mass-market paperback book grudgingly but still looked down their noses at those who worked in that end of the business. This was bound to change, he believed, and soon. Paperback people were just as cultured and well educated as hardcover people but had their feet planted more firmly on the ground. There was a lot more to publishing than bringing out a whole lot of unreadable first novels or new translations of the complete works of Gide or Proust.

I should not misunderstand him, he added hastily—there was a place for Gide, for Proust, even for the kind of snot-nosed little first novels your typically effete hardcover editor bought and that nobody else ever read, but mass-market publishing was attuned first and foremost to the needs of the marketplace, to what people *really* wanted to read. Pocket Books gave them what they wanted, even if that was Harold Robbins. What was so fucking bad about reading a Harold Robbins novel, anyway, he wanted to know? If they wanted to read Shakespeare, well, by Christ, Pocket Books *did* Shakespeare; if they wanted to read Pearl S. Buck, well, God damn it, Pocket Books did Pearl S. Buck too—in fact *The Good Earth* was Pocket Books' all-time, number-one best-seller. What did I think of *them* apples?

I wasn't sure what I thought of them apples, since I had never read Pearl S. Buck, nor, for that matter, Harold Robbins, but I kept my mouth zipped on the subject, rightly guessing that the question was rhetorical. Herb had me typed, I realized, as an effete snob, but before I could find a polite way to tell him that I wasn't the Gide/Proust type, he was off and running with a long list, recited from memory, of all the distinguished books and classics that Pocket Books had published over the years.

He seemed to be under the mistaken impression, thanks to Morris Helprin I felt sure, that I was a person of a scholarly nature, prodigious learning, and refined taste. He paused frequently to roll his head sideways so he could see me and say, about whatever arcane point he had reached in his narrative, "Of course, being an Oxford man, you already know all that," or, "Being an Oxford man, you've already guessed what I'm getting at."

It seemed best to nod wisely rather than argue, in the hope that silence would be taken for wisdom. In any case, Herb took care not to give me a chance to interrupt his flow of words—he apparently intended to talk until hoarseness or sheer exhaustion silenced him. In the event, the barber eventually silenced him with a hot towel, though not before Herb had explained to me that he was the kind of guy who needed to shave at least twice a day, hence the barber's chair. I felt my own cheeks, for which one shave a day was sufficient, and wondered if

I was cut out for the mass-market business. Apparently it was a manly undertaking, on the order of lumberjacking.

While the hot towel was doing its work, I managed to ask Herb if he thought he had a job for me.

Herb launched into a new tirade as the barber splashed him with bay rum. His beard seemed to be growing back already—he had the kind of five-o'clock shadow that used to make Richard Nixon look so sinister in photographs. The best thing for me, frankly, Herb thought, would be to throw me into the mass-market business, right up to the goddamn neck, and get rid of all my fucking Oxford, Limey intellectual pretensions and prejudices once and for all, so I could get a grip on what real people did in the real world. It would do me no harm to go out at dawn with "the guys in the trucks," carrying cartons of mass-market titles and arranging them in the racks. That's how you learned the business, the *only* way, if I wanted his opinion, and if I didn't, what the hell was I doing here? (I was later to discover that this was something of a romantic illusion in the mass-market business—neither Herb nor any of the other Pocket Books senior executives and editors had ever gone out with the trucks, nor served their apprenticeship by handing a druggist a five-dollar bill so he would turn his back while you threw all your competitor's titles out of the racks and replaced them with your own. There *were* people who did this, of course, but they did not as a rule get to the company's offices at Rockefeller Center.)

Herb paused for breath, while my heart sank. I wasn't fussy when it came to a job, but I didn't like the sound of starting off my career in book publishing at dawn in a delivery truck. It wasn't, as Herb seemed to feel was the case, that I thought this kind of thing was beneath me— I just didn't believe then, and don't now, that you can learn much about a business by carrying cartons.

If it depended solely on him, Herb went on, that's what I'd be doing, and who knew? It might even make a man of me. But he had two problems, when it came to me: One was that he just didn't have any jobs available at Pocket Books; the other was that he had sort of promised Morris Helprin that he would take good care of me, and he felt that Morris would be happier if I started out at a somewhat classier level. As it happened, there *was* a job available upstairs—he rolled his eyes heavenward—at Simon and Schuster, which was owned partly by Leon Shimkin, so the two companies had a relationship of sorts. Henry W. Simon (as I was beginning to discover, almost everybody of any importance in book publishing used a middle initial), the editor in chief, one of cofounder Richard L. Simon's brothers, was looking for an assistant even as we spoke.

Henry Simon, Herb went on, with a certain invisible sneer in his voice, was a former Columbia University professor, a Shakespearean scholar of some note, and a classical musician. I would probably feel more at ease upstairs with him than downstairs in the rough-and-tumble world of Pocket Books, though he hoped that when I'd found my feet I might realize where the action really was and transfer my allegiance to the mass-market business. In the meantime, I should go upstairs and see Henry, who was expecting me.

I thanked him, but he cut me off abruptly.

"Don't worry about it, kid," he said, examining the manicurist's work carefully. "If it doesn't work out with Henry, you come on back down here, and I'll find something for you, even if it's in the warehouse, you have my word on it."

The barber removed the towel, and Herb got out of his barber's chair and moved back to his desk. I had imagined he would tower over me, but to my surprise he wasn't any taller than me—he was broad in the beam, all right, but short, built rather like a Dutch barge.

"Tell Henry from me he's wrong about Harold Robbins," he said, and dismissed me.

HERB ALEXANDER'S secretary led me to a stairway that took us up to the Simon and Schuster offices on the floor above. The stairway had been opened only recently, she told me. It had been bricked up for some years, on the orders of Mr. Simon and Mr. Schuster, but Mr. Shimkin had recently had it opened again, so people could go back and forth between the two floors more easily. It took very little imagination on my part to guess what the relationship was between the owners of Simon and Schuster if they had been struggling for years over whether their employees could get from Pocket Books to Simon and Schuster and vice versa by the stairs.

Indeed, my guide looked nervous on the floor above her own, as if we had ventured into Indian territory, and seemed relieved when she handed me over to Henry Simon's secretary, who showed me right in. Seated behind a pale wood desk in a large corner office, Henry Simon was an impressive figure. It was easy enough to guess that he had once been a very handsome man indeed, almost theatrically so in fact, but age and what I imagined was ill health had given him a ghostly look. His pallor was alarming, and his long, thin hands—the hands of a musician, with narrow Giacometti-like fingers—trembled noticeably. I guessed him to be in his sixties (he was, in fact, then in his late fifties, but the young are never good at guessing older people's ages). His hair was silver, there were dark circles under his eyes, and his face was hollow-cheeked and deeply lined, as if all the cares of the world were on his shoulders. When he rose, I could see that he was tall, six foot or more, but painfully thin and slightly stooped. He came around from behind his desk and shook my hand, a quick, dry, whispery handshake, unlike Herb Alexander's, which had felt like being squeezed hard by a pipe wrench. Henry slipped behind his desk like a shadow, sat down again, and lit a cigarette.

Even in those innocent days when almost everybody smoked—as I did—Henry's consumption of tobacco was remarkable. There were two racks of pipes on his desk, all of them well used, and a huge, round ashtray the size of a pie plate that contained too many cigarette butts to count. His desktop was littered with cigarette packages, matchbooks, and tobacco ash, and his fingernails had a nicotine stain so dark that it seemed baked on. Not surprisingly, his voice, though soft and melodious, was a hoarse whisper. He spoke slowly, with the slightly prissy exactitude of the university professor he had once been, and it all seemed to me very much like an Oxford tutorial, except that neither of us was wearing a gown and he didn't offer me sherry.

If Herb Alexander had considered me to be rather too much of a hothouse flower for the world of mass-market paperback publishing, Henry's suspicion, perhaps because Alexander had sent me to him, appeared to be that I was an ignorant yahoo from the movie business, unsuitable for the refined world of hardcover publishing. My family's fame—then very much greater than it is now—had seemed to Alexander something I would have to overcome but not otherwise of any concern. At worst, he had feared it would prevent me from being "one of the guys" and make me a poor bet for servicing the racks. Henry Simon, to my consternation, was deeply suspicious of it. Why wasn't I working in the movie business? he wanted to know. How could he be sure I wouldn't rush off to Hollywood at any moment, if he hired me?

It would have been helpful if I had understood then that Henry's whole adult life had been a tug-of-war between his own inclinations as a teacher, writer, and musician and his older brother Richard's determination to find a place for him at Simon and Schuster. The phrase *love-hate relationship* might have been coined for Henry's feelings about his glamorous, dashing, wealthy, brilliantly talented brother, whose unerring instinct for commercial books and riverboat gambler's skills Henry lacked totally. Henry had been pulled out of a respected academic career by his brother and given a job at Simon and Schuster where he would always be in his shadow. Not unnaturally, he saw in me somebody who had similar problems, and it made him nervous.

We chatted briefly, and with a certain embarrassment (in those innocent days, I didn't know how hard this kind of job interview is from the other side of the desk), about my studies at Oxford, my languages (Henry was fluent in German but knew no French), my aspirations. Henry was, in fact, the first person I had met so far in book publishing who could actually be described as cultured and well-read in the European sense, who had read the same books I had, could talk about them like an Oxford don, and seemed to feel they mattered. I felt at home. He had traveled widely in England with his first wife, Margaret Halsey, and knew Oxford well.

Henry had edited the complete works of Shakespeare for the Pocket Books edition that Herb Alexander was so proud of and had published an edition of Beethoven's piano sonatas. That his was not a donnish job, however, was made clear by how his telephone rang constantly. From time to time, his secretary, Nancy, appeared to say that the call was from an important agent or author. Henry grimaced, lit a fresh cigarette, and, cradling the receiver between his shoulder and his ear, leaned back in his leather desk chair, placed his feet on the desk, closed his eyes, and engaged in what appeared to be difficult discussions, each of which seemed to depress him deeply. Once we were interrupted when a stranger, his face puffy and contorted with rage, strode briskly into the room, flung a piece of artwork down on Henry's desktop, shouted, "You tell your goddamn author he doesn't know what the fuck he's talking about!" then turned on his heel and stalked out. Henry winced. His gray face looked suddenly weary, and he shook his head. "That was our art director," he explained. He held up a sketch for a book jacket. It showed a man in what looked like a Roman helmet, set against a scene of mild Attic debauchery. The title was *Dara, the Cypriot,* by Louis Paul.

"What do you think?" Henry asked. "It's a historical novel set in ancient Greece and Crete."

"The helmet is all wrong."

He sighed and put it back on his desk. "That's what the author said." He lit a fresh cigarette and inhaled deeply. "I think you and I would get along," he said, breathing out two plumes of smoke. "On the other hand, you've had no experience at editing."

"I'm a quick learner."

"I don't have time to teach you, frankly. And I'm even not sure that it's a skill that can be taught. It really requires *Fingerspitzengefühl*—a certain instinct which you've either got or you don't. . . . Would you mind very much if I gave you a manuscript to read, as a kind of test?"

I said it was fine with me. Henry got up and walked over to his couch, which was awash with manuscripts, boxes, and bulky, rubber-banded, tattered, and dog-eared piles of paper. It struck me that if this was his backlog, Henry Simon really *needed* an assistant. He rooted around in the pile, letting loose a cloud of dust, and chose one manuscript, seemingly at random. "I won't tell you whether we're publishing this or not," he said. "Just read it, see what you think, and write me a report, all right? Take your time."

I grasped the manuscript. Henry showed me to the door. As we shook hands he gave me a small, embarrassed smile. "It's a shame you didn't come to see me a day or two sooner. . . . There's, ah, one *little* problem, I should tell you. There *is* another candidate, some fellow from New Jersey, to whom I more or less promised the job yesterday."

My spirits sank. What did "more or less" mean, I asked? Henry thought about this. "I told him I wanted to sleep on it. He seemed very qualified but not at all experienced, just like you. If you don't mind being in a two-horse race for the job, just read the book I've given you, bring me your report, and let me make up my mind. That's the best I can do."

Fair enough, I said, though in fact I was disappointed and walked home as fast as I could to read the book. Clearly, this was like an examination, and if there was one thing I was good at, it was examinations. I had always been able to cram for them successfully at the very last minute, in school, in the RAF, and at Oxford. I decided that the sooner I handed in my report, the better—speed had to count for something, even in a business as slow as book publishing—and got right down to it.

The manuscript was a study of the British press called *The Sugar*

Pill, by T. S. Matthews. Fortunately, it was short, hardly more than an extended essay. It distinctly failed to impress me. Matthews was apparently an American journalist of some distinction and clearly an Anglophile—one of those expatriate Americans who, in the long tradition of Henry James, found it more comfortable to live in England than at home and felt himself to be *plus anglais que les anglais.* The trouble was, I thought, that Matthews simply didn't understand the subtle nuances of the English class system and therefore often missed the point of the newspaper stories he was criticizing. On a more practical level, I couldn't see who would buy the book. English readers would resent being criticized by an American, and American readers were unfamiliar with the problems of Fleet Street and surely not very interested. I read the book quickly, wrote a blistering brief urging its rejection, and went back to Rockefeller Center to leave it for Mr. Simon.

The next morning I was summoned back. Henry was waiting for me, his high, noble forehead creased in a frown, a look of deep suspicion on his face, even of distaste, as if he smelled something offensive. "Did you *really* read the book?" he asked accusingly. "I expected it to take you a couple of days."

I explained that I was a natural speed reader and volunteered to take a quiz on the book's contents, but Henry waved the offer away impatiently. "Never mind that," he said. "You say here that the book is inaccurate and unpublishable, right?" I nodded. "Would it make any difference to your assessment of it if I told you that Tom Matthews is the former editor of *Time* magazine and one of my closest friends? Or if I told you that I've already bought the book and that I'm publishing it next spring?"

I thought about this unwelcome news quickly, wondering how I had managed to fall into Henry's trap so easily, and decided candor was the only way out. It made no difference to my opinion at all, I said—I would stick to my guns.

Henry put my report down with a sigh. "It's funny," he said. "The other fellow, the one from New Jersey, feels the same way about the book that you do. He didn't phrase it quite as elegantly as you do, not having been educated in England, but his advice was to turn it down, too. It just shows that you've both got a lot to learn about publishing. Well, I suppose you'll learn . . ."

"Does that mean I've got the job?" I asked incredulously.

He nodded glumly. "The other young man accepted an offer from

Doubleday first thing this morning." Henry stood up, and we shook hands across his desk. "I'll have Nancy get you a shopping bag and you can take some of those manuscripts over there on the sofa home to read, since you're such a fast reader."

Henry paused and handed me the jacket sketch we had looked at yesterday. His expression showed a certain cunning, as if he had found a way out of an unpleasant task. "While she's doing that and filling out the forms for hiring you, you might take this down to the art department. Ask for the art director. A fellow called Frank Metz. Somebody will show you the way. Tell him you're working for me—and that he's wrong about the goddamn helmet."

As I left his office, he called out, "If he throws something at you, *duck!*" and laughed.

PART TWO

File Under Grief

CHAPTER 4

*T*HE FIRST THING I found on my desk when I came to work officially on August 11, 1958, was a cast bronze plaque bearing the words: "Give the reader a break."

These, it appeared, had been designed by Dick Simon and had been placed on every editor's and assistant's desk. It was, in his view, our job to make things as easy and clear for the reader as possible. Left unsaid was how to perform this miracle. It was Henry Simon's method, I quickly observed, to painstakingly correct his authors' punctuation, grammar, and spelling with a precisely sharpened pencil and to write queries in a minuscule hand in the margins. Perhaps the first, and most important, difficulty of our relationship was Henry's discoveries, on day one, that I punctuated by feel and instinct rather than by rule, had a shaky command of grammar, and couldn't spell worth a damn. (On the other hand, I turned out to be a natural at the kind of picky, know-it-all comment in the margin that drives authors crazy, such as "Surely the Treaty of Utrecht was earlier than this?" or "Are you certain Wellington was a Field-Marshal at this point of his life?")

Right from the beginning, I felt that Henry was interested in only the kind of small details that somebody else could have fixed (though not me), while I was more concerned with the big picture—that is, whether the book *worked* or whether it needed massive cutting, could use a better title, or contained characters whose motives and actions made no sense. In short, it was as if our roles were reversed, perhaps not the best way to start out as an assistant.

It didn't help that I wasn't ashamed of my shortcomings. I spelled and punctuated badly in three languages, and it had never made any difference to me or anybody else. At Oxford, the dons cared more about the originality of the student's ideas and his grasp of the fundamentals of a subject than about spelling—indeed, in England, a certain aristocratic contempt for the rules of grammar and an idiosyncratic approach to spelling (the more daring, the better) were marks of culture.

Perhaps sensing right from the beginning that I was more eager to find out everything I could about Simon and Schuster than to spend the day penciling in commas or changing semicolons to colons, Henry had found for me a small, windowless cubicle with a desk that faced a blank wall, so that my back was turned to the hallway. Here I sat reading through the endless piles of manuscripts that had been submitted to him and occasionally editing the manuscripts of those of his authors whom he did not feel obliged to edit himself. It was not so very different from my work at CBS, except that I was no longer a freelancer. Modest my job might be, but I was an employee at last! It did not escape my attention, however, that Henry was anxious to keep me separated from the other members of the editorial department, or that his relationship with them was touchy and marked by mutual suspicion.

As it happened, I had stumbled into my job at a particularly interesting time for S&S and for the book-publishing industry. S&S was a hotbed of thwarted ambitions and intrigue, much of it swirling around Henry Simon. To me, it appeared that Henry was a powerful executive, with his corner office and his list of important authors, but the truth was that he was surrounded by enemies and hanging on by his fingernails. S&S had gone through several years of upheavals, all of which could be traced back to Richard L. Simon and M. Lincoln Schuster's decision to sell their company to Marshall Field III in 1944. After Field's untimely death, they managed to persuade his widow to sell it back to them. She agreed, on the condition that they admit Leon Shimkin as a full partner.

This was the proverbial camel's nose in the tent. Shimkin had been close to Field and also owned Pocket Books, which gave him a certain leverage. Without Shimkin's support, his connection to the Fields, and his access to capital, Simon and Schuster would have been unable to buy back their company; *with* it, they were beholden to a man who had little in common with the scholarly Schuster or the ebullient, risk-loving Simon.

It was not a partnership made in heaven. While Max Schuster retreated to his office to plan further volumes of philosophy and of Will Durant's *The Story of Civilization,* Dick Simon chafed at having to deal with the cautious and often nay-saying Shimkin. Simon was a handsome, chain-smoking, hard-drinking man with an eye for a pretty woman and a sense of fun and wit that made him a vast number of friends, most of them brilliantly talented. He played tennis with a terrifying will to win, turned his interest in photography into a multimillion-dollar business, had a passion for music that made him such friends as George Gershwin and Jerome Kern and helped establish one of his daughters as an opera singer and another as a pop superstar. His energy level was such that even after he had been diagnosed with heart disease and ordered to slow down by his doctor, a friend saw him running back to his house as fast as he could after a brisk tennis game. "What's your hurry, Dick?" he asked. Panting heavily, Dick shouted an explanation over his shoulder. "My doctor told me to take an afternoon nap," he gasped, "and I'm late for it."

He liked to be surrounded with men like himself, congenial spirits who knew how to sell books (without necessarily having any inclination to read them), and gradually built up a group of loyalists who came to be known as "Dick's men," among them his editor in chief, Jack A. Goodman; Albert R. Leventhal, his sales chief; and Richard L. Grossman, his assistant. Like him, they were men who worked hard and played hard, stayed late at the office, and hired as their assistants and secretaries attractive young women who didn't want to go home at five-thirty. Like him, they tended to view Shimkin as the enemy, if for no other reason than he was so unlike them. This group did *not* include Dick Simon's brother, Henry, who was "too serious" for them, neither congenial nor cut in their swashbuckling, reckless mode—in addition to which he had the misfortune of having married, in his former secretary, a woman with a notoriously sharp tongue.

Yet at the core, something was missing in Dick Simon. He was simply unable to recover the intensity of enthusiasm, the exuberant love of life, and the sure touch for best sellers that had distinguished his career before he sold out to Marshall Field. Although he was only in his mid-fifties, he was already running on dry; his health was breaking down—the cigarettes, the booze, the stress were taking their toll. A failing heart and severe episodes of depression made it necessary for him to retire in 1957, at the early age of fifty-eight.*

Simon and Schuster was therefore a house divided. Marketing and promotion were controlled by Dick Simon's loyalists, the editorial department was more or less controlled by Max Schuster, with the help of Henry Simon and Peter Schwed, the former rights director (the two were like cheese and chalk), while the financial side was firmly in the hands of Leon Shimkin, who like the Prince of Darkness ruled from the floor below, at Pocket Books, and never came upstairs.

Perhaps more important, Simon and Schuster, so often the leader and innovator, was a precursor of the troubles that were soon to face the rest of the book-publishing industry, most of which had to do with the fact that the era of private ownership was drawing to an end.

BOOK PUBLISHERS in those days liked to refer to themselves with a certain pride as "a cottage industry," by which they meant that most publishing houses were privately owned, many by the men who had founded them, others by a single family.

They also meant that it was a business that didn't require much in the way of capital. New publishing houses were easy to found, even in the 1950s—all you needed was an office somewhere, a telephone, somebody with a sharp eye for a book that would sell, and a rudimentary sense of marketing. One big best-seller and you were on your way. After all, S&S had been launched when Max Schuster, editor of an automotive trade magazine, and Dick Simon, a piano salesman, pooled their $8,000 savings and published the world's first book of crossword puzzles. (Henry Simon's first job in publishing was buying the pencils that were attached to each book by a string.) This Horatio Alger formula was perhaps the core myth that drew people into the business. After all, Atheneum, Ticknor and Fields, and Clarkson N. Potter were all founded in 1959—proof, it seemed to some, that a book-publishing company could be started with not much more capital than it would take to buy a new car.

---

* In the same period, Leon Shimkin also suffered episodes of depression so severe that he was sometimes found in tears in his bedroom closet in the morning, unable to face the task of choosing a tie for the day; unlike Richard Simon, he underwent successful shock treatment to overcome the problem.

But the age of the cottage industry was already coming to an end. The Wall Street wolf was already at the door, impressed by the growth of textbook and educational publishing and eager for a new industry to take public, while book publishers themselves were already trying to figure out how much they would be worth if they opened that door.

THE BUSINESS I had entered was more complex and divided than I could possibly have understood at the time. To begin with, there were still two separate worlds of book publishing, though the barrier between them was beginning to break down. The older, family-owned publishing houses of New York City and Boston were still dominated by Gentiles, while most of the newer houses that had been founded in the twenties were dominated largely by Jews. This distinction matters so little now that it is hard to believe how much it mattered in the 1950s, let alone how much it had mattered before World War Two.

At that point in my life, it was not a distinction that mattered to me at all. In fact, the subject was never mentioned in my family, so much so that my mother to this day refuses to believe that my father was Jewish. The truth is that the three Korda brothers, when they arrived in England in 1932, were so exotic, with their thick Hungarian accents and their extravagant behavior, that it never occurred to anybody to ask if they were Jewish or not, and since they themselves did not feel particularly Jewish, they simply never alluded to the subject. Their children, therefore, grew up unaware that they were half Jewish. (One of them stubbornly denies the fact to this day and had his father buried conspicuously as a Protestant.)

Having been born in England of an English mother and baptized and confirmed in the Anglican Church, I had no idea that I was half Jewish. Moreover, I had been educated in places where anti-Semitism was almost unknown. So far as I was concerned, Jews were people such as Sir Isaiah Berlin, Lord Rothschild, and the Warburg family, or Hollywood moguls such as David Selznick and Sam Spiegel, or artist friends of my father's such as Marc Chagall and Jacob Epstein. It never occurred to me to feel anything other than admiration for them.

I was, however, not totally unaware of anti-Semitism in the United States, which was far more widespread and more socially acceptable in the 1940s and 1950s than people are able to imagine today. In the winter of 1942, my father had flown over from England to see me and took me down to Palm Beach. He had booked a suite at a most luxurious hotel, and the manager himself showed us around. "You'll be very comfortable here," he told my father with a wink. "I need hardly say that you'll be among your own. The hotel is restricted, naturally."

My father glared at him from beneath fiercely bushy eyebrows. In his inimitable Hungarian accent, he asked, "Vat means *restricted?*"

The manager give him a knowing smile. "Well, Mr. Korda," the manager whispered, "I'm not supposed to say this, but we don't take people of the Jewish faith."

I had seldom seen my father angrier or move faster. Within an hour, we were in Miami, but the incident had soured him on Florida. After only one night there, we went back to New York, despite the sun and fresh food, both of which my father craved after two years in wartime England.

In retrospect, that would have been a good time for him to have told me that he was Jewish, or for me to have intuited it, but unfortunately, neither happened. Still, my father never left me in any doubt that anti-Semitism was wrong, and I was therefore constantly surprised to find evidence that there was so much of it in America. When I went to school in New York City, I had friends on the East Side and on the West Side. I did not perceive that there was any difference, and it came as something of a shock to discover that my friends on the West Side lived there because they were Jewish and envied the fact that I lived across town, where most of the older and more luxurious buildings were still restricted.

BOOK PUBLISHING, in fact, had always been one of the most restricted of professions—"an occupation for gentlemen," as publishers once liked to describe it. Culture and literature, it was felt, needed to be kept in the right hands—namely, those of white Anglo-Saxon Protestants who knew the difference between what was shoddy and meretricious and what was genuinely important and uplifting and who did not engage in "sharp" business practices.

Until the 1920s, book publishing in America was dominated by old, "respectable" houses that, for the most part, didn't hire Jews—certainly

not at an executive level—and published Jewish writers only with reluctance. In Boston, there were Houghton Mifflin, Little, Brown, the
Atlantic Monthly Press; in New York, Harcourt, Brace, Harper and
Brothers, Scribner's, G. P. Putnam, Doubleday, and Macmillan. Many
of these firms were still owned by descendants of the men who had
founded them in the mid-nineteenth century. Going from Harvard,
Yale, or Princeton into book publishing was a little bit like entering a
rather stuffy and self-important club. It was hard to make a real killing,
but you had job security and the satisfaction of being among well-
educated gentlemen of your own persuasion, pursuing an old, even
noble profession.

The one exception to this rule was the house of Boni and Liveright,
founded in 1917 and dominated by the mercurial figure of Horace Liveright, who had almost immediately driven out the peaceful Boni. Not
only was Liveright the first Jew to break into book publishing in any
significant way, he also single-handedly brought about a revolution in
the way books were published. He broke every tradition by publishing
daring, even shocking books, and he set out to make books into *news*,
becoming the first publisher to plan out an active publicity campaign for
each title. Liveright was an enthusiast, with a huge appetite for anything
that was new or controversial. Above all, he wanted to have a good time
publishing books, and, by and large, he did.

Liveright himself eventually died impoverished and disgraced, but
his example inspired others who had come under his spell. Dick Simon
had been a salesman at Boni and Liveright, Bennett Cerf not only
worked at Boni and Liveright, but bought the Modern Library, the
crown jewel of Liveright's ramshackle empire. Even Alfred A. Knopf,
though he deeply distrusted Liveright, was inspired by Liveright's example to found his own publishing house.

Thus, in the late twenties and thirties, there emerged houses that
were owned by Jews who were willing to take risks, knew how to promote and market books, and, however seriously they might take themselves, thought that publishing ought to be *fun*. That is not to say that
they weren't serious businessmen, nor that the profit motive wasn't important to them, but they brought a more flamboyant and adventurous
approach to publishing than any of the older WASP firms had ever considered. What is more, they prospered. World War Two not only increased the number of readers—as every soldier knows, a lot of service

life is spent waiting, and books filled in the time—it brought Jews and Gentiles together in large numbers for the first time, the common experience of war erasing many of the differences that had separated them.

When the war was finally over, book publishing had changed dramatically. Random House, Simon and Schuster, Viking Press (founded by Harold Guinzburg, in 1925), and Alfred A. Knopf were now mainstream houses, more interesting places to work than the old-line firms, and rapidly approaching them in size and influence. By the 1950s, there were Jews working in positions of power in the old-line houses and Gentiles working in the firms owned by Jews—the line separating them had not exactly vanished, but it had been blurred. Still, a Jewish CEO at, say, Harper, was as unlikely as a Gentile one at S&S or Random House.

To all these distinctions I was entirely blind. I was, as well, completely ignorant of Jewish holidays and of Yiddish, which was enjoying a kind of renaissance in publishing circles—at least as a language of insult—partly as a means of reaffirming one's Jewishness, partly because it had certain tough-guy connotations. Even non-Jews were using words such as *putz, schwartze, yenta,* et cetera, albeit with a certain self-consciousness and unreliable pronunciation. Yiddish was suddenly "in," to the surprise, not to say shock, of an older generation that had always looked down on Yiddish speakers.

People like Henry Simon, Dick Simon, and Max Schuster never used Yiddish words, even in anger. That was perhaps something their parents or grandparents had done, but to those who came from German-Jewish families that had long since been assimilated, the use of Yiddish was unspeakably vulgar. It was the kind of thing that Russian Jews were looked down upon for doing—back in those days, the distinction between the older, more assimilated German Jews and the less assimilated Russian Jews was almost as sharp a divide as the one between Jew and Gentile. It did not pass without notice that Leon Shimkin was of Russian-Jewish origin and that Max Schuster and the Simons were not.

I had, in taking a job at S&S, unintentionally chosen sides. There was still at Random House and at S&S very much a feeling of us against them, an underlying assumption that the older WASP publishing houses were, to use the title of Jerome Weidman's best-selling novel appropriately, "The Enemy Camp." Very shortly, however, the newer firms were to overtake and eventually subsume many of their old-line competitors, and within a decade the division between Jews and Gentiles in book publishing had simply vanished, as if it had never been there. But in 1958, eroded as it might have been, it was still something people thought about, even talked about from time to time, and it mattered.

IT TOOK me a while before I could steel myself to mention to Henry Simon Herb Alexander's message about Harold Robbins.

Henry sniffed disdainfully. "Robbins *belongs* downstairs," he said.

What exactly was the problem? I asked.

With a certain reluctance, Henry explained that Harold Robbins was a popular novelist who had been published for years by the distinguished house of Knopf. At one time, it had seemed that Robbins might be a serious writer. Robbins's second book, *A Stone for Danny Fisher* (his first was *Never Love a Stranger*), was one of those tough novels about poor Jews that occasionally succeeded and even became classics. Since then, though his sales rose, Robbins's writing had gone downhill with the speed of an avalanche, becoming more and more sexy—so much so as to make Alfred and Blanche Knopf nervous. His latest, of which Henry had only read the first part, was a long novel about the movie business that contained, quite frankly, a good deal of outright pornography. The Knopfs would almost certainly have turned the book down in horror after reading the first hundred or so pages, but they were never given the opportunity, since Robbins's new agent, a lawyer named Paul Gitlin, had made demands that neither they, nor anybody else in their right mind, could possibly meet.

Subsequently, Leon Shimkin's attention had been drawn to Harold Robbins—Henry's expression made it clear that this was no surprise to him—and Shimkin was neither horrified nor unwilling to come up with a generous, and in many ways unprecedented, offer. His original intention had been to publish the hardcover edition of the book at S&S and then do the mass-market edition at Pocket Books. With that in mind, he had asked Henry to read the pages.

Henry, to do him justice, thought the pages made pretty good reading, if you liked that kind of trash, and would probably make a lot of money. But he also thought they posed some tricky moral problems, so he gave them to Max Schuster, who took them home and returned the next day badly shaken and in a state of high indignation. This was emphatically *not* the kind of book that he wanted his name on, he told

Henry. Schuster had shown a few pages to his wife, Ray, and she had been deeply shocked. Was this, she had asked Max, the kind of *dreck*—Mrs. Schuster, I gathered, was not above the use of Yiddish where it hurt—that he wanted to publish at S&S? What would their friends think? What would people say? What was Henry thinking of? If Leon Shimkin wanted to grovel in the dirt, let him do it at Pocket Books, where nobody would be surprised.

Shimkin was not about to give up on the prospect of publishing Harold Robbins, whatever Max and Ray Schuster might think, and came up with the then-novel idea that Pocket Books would create a separate company, Trident Press, just to publish Robbins in hardcover. Robbins would then receive 100 percent of the paperback royalties instead of sharing them with his hardcover publisher in the usual way. This was unheard of, as well as an enormous amount of money spread over several as yet unwritten books. Thus was the "hard/soft" multibook contract born, ensuring that the face of book publishing was about to be changed in a very dramatic way. It was soon to be a case of *après nous le déluge,* as agents sought to emulate Robbins's coup and New American Library, Bantam, and Dell woke up to the notion that they didn't really need to play second fiddle to the hardcover publishers or bid themselves silly over the rights to "major" fiction from them.

Although neither Henry Simon nor Max Schuster were aware of it at the time, they had deprived S&S of a major source of income—for Harold Robbins's novel was to become *The Carpetbaggers* and was to be followed by several more enormous best-sellers—while the decision to let Pocket Books publish the novel in hardcover was to haunt every hardcover publisher, as the paperback houses one after another went into the hardcover business. Shimkin had doubled the number of competitors in a relatively small pond, with the inevitable result that the big ones would be obliged to eat the smaller ones until there were only a few giants left, warily eyeing each other.

None of this was clear at the time, least of all to me, though everybody except Henry had already guessed that Shimkin would use Trident Press as his Trojan horse in his war for complete ownership of S&S. Unfortunately for Shimkin, Trident Press boomeranged in the end. In order to give Trident some measure of respectability, Shimkin decided that it would also have to publish books by other authors. Even Harold Robbins could see that a publishing house with only one author lacked cachet—he wanted to be surrounded by other writers, albeit less successful than himself. Trident therefore went out and bought a lot of manuscripts in a hurry to give the imprint plausibility, and—no surprise—lost almost as much money on these acquisitions as was made from publishing Robbins.

In the meantime, quite unfairly, poor Henry soon became known as the man who turned down *The Carpetbaggers*. In the end, even Max Schuster couldn't forgive Henry for letting such a hugely profitable book go, and Ray Schuster was heard to say that her husband was too softhearted for keeping on Dick Simon's *nebbish* brother, who had been unable to recognize a gold mine when it was right before his eyes.

IT IS amazing how much one can learn from somebody who is not generally thought of as successful. In the first place, Henry looked down on what he thought of as "the popular taste" and despised himself for pandering to it. Nothing is more doomed in book publishing than an editor who tries to publish "popular" books without really enjoying them himself. Then, too, everybody who mattered at S&S had been under the sway of one or two magnetic personalities: Dick Simon, who had retired, and Jack Goodman, his editor in chief, who had died recently of a heart attack. Henry had been promoted to editor in chief because nobody else was available, but his promotion offended both those who thought that he was only a shadow of his brother and those who thought he wasn't fit to sit in Goodman's office. Merely by accepting an unlikely promotion, Henry had alienated many people at S&S, right down to the assistants and the mail-room boys. Worse, Henry was deeply embittered by all those years in his brother's shadow, and he nursed an endless list of resentments and grudges; at the same time, he was too old to recognize that a new era in book publishing was just beginning. Very shortly, S&S would publish Rona Jaffe's *The Best of Everything*—the very prototype of the hot "women's novel" that would eventually reach its climax with Jacqueline Susann's *Valley of the Dolls*—and Joseph Heller's *Catch 22*, which was to start a whole new school of black humor in American literature. Neither of these books was Henry's, nor was Henry even given an opportunity to read them in manuscript.

The Best of Everything would be a landmark in a number of ways: It had been bought as a movie by Jerry Wald before the manuscript had even been edited, so the movie company would be involved from the beginning in marketing the book; and it would begin, as well, a new tradition in popular fiction of using the author as a marketing tool. Philippe Halsman's haunting, full-color jacket photograph of Rona Jaffe took as much time to get right as the jacket itself and cost a good deal more. Until then, it had been thought sufficient for writers—particularly first novelists—to send in an old snapshot to appear on the back flap of the jacket; *The Best of Everything* was to usher in the new era in which the author's potential for glamour, real or faked, mattered almost as much as the writing, and the photographer's fee often exceeded what the average first novelist was likely to make from his or her book.

It was as if there were a whole separate, parallel publishing house operating on the same floor, with the express intention of keeping the older generation from finding out what was going on. At its center was the late Jack Goodman's former assistant, Robert Gottlieb, with Phyllis S. Levy, Goodman's former secretary, and Nina Bourne, the S&S advertising director. In uneasy alliance with them was Richard L. Grossman, nominally in charge of marketing, who was determined to carry on Dick Simon's tradition of photographic books, which had led to the publication of such successes as Henri Cartier-Bresson's *The Decisive Moment* and Edward Steichen's *The Family of Man*. Nevertheless, a nucleus of bright, ambitious youngsters had acquired just enough power to do what they wanted to do, and what they wanted to do was to change the face of book publishing.

OF COURSE book publishing, like any other business, needs to be shaken by a revolution from time to time. The last big one had been in the late 1920s, but the war had since then delayed any further major changes in the zeitgeist of publishing, sending the young men who might have taken over from Max and Dick, or Bennett Cerf and Donald Klopfer, or Alfred and Blanche Knopf, off to fight. When these men returned after 1945, they were happy to publish the same old safe books in the same old safe way as they and the whole country slipped quietly toward the Eisenhower years. It was the era of the suburban house, the six-o'clock cocktail shaker, and the regulation suit, a world defined by S&S with the publication of *The Organization Man* and *The Man in the Gray Flannel Suit*. The revolution was now overdue and not only at S&S.

There had been a brief flurry of excitement when the men who had gone to war came home with their novels—among them Norman Mailer, James Jones, and Irwin Shaw—and there had been a seismic tremor when the Beats became sufficiently commercial, like Jack Kerouac, who made that typically American jump from penniless outlaw to book-club selection and bookstore celebrity in one leap, with *On the Road*. But for the most part, publishing, like literature, slumbered on. It had upset many people when Mailer wrote the first war novel in which the troops swore the way they have always sworn in all armies since the beginning of warfare, but nobody in American publishing was prepared for a novel like *Catch-22* that made savage fun of war, had a hero who was proud to be a coward, and ridiculed both our side and the enemy's alike. It was all very well for that kind of thing to have been done in a Czech book like *The Good Soldier Schweik*, but it was unthinkable in this country.

Rather like the Manhattan Project, *Catch-22* (which was called *Catch-18* until it was discovered that Leon Uris's forthcoming novel was called *Mila 18*) was hatched in secrecy and on a strict "need to know" basis. It was Heller's first novel, and he had been rewriting it for nearly two years, following Gottlieb's suggestions. An aura of myth hovered around the book, all the stronger since nobody but Gottlieb and his acolytes had read it. He had shrewdly stage-managed a sense of expectation that grew with every delay, in part by allowing a few bits and pieces of the manuscript to appear in places such as *The Paris Review* from time to time, just to whet the appetites of reviewers.

I had already heard a good deal about this wunderkind (much of it cautiously negative) from Henry Simon before I actually met him, about a week after having been hired. One morning, a tall young man, looking rather like one of those penniless perpetual students in Russian novels, squeezed his way into my office and sat down on the edge of my desk. He wore thick glasses with heavy black frames, and his lank, black hair was combed across his brow rather like the young Napoleon's. The eyes behind the glasses were shrewd and intense, but with a certain kindly, humorous sparkle that I had not so far seen at S&S. He wore worn tan corduroy trousers, scuffed penny loafers, and a button-down shirt without a tie: the uniform of a graduate student rather than a young publishing genius. Gottlieb looked to be about my age, but he projected a certain deep wisdom, as well as layers of publishing experience. We shook hands and he introduced himself. "How do you like working for Henry?" he asked genially.

I said I liked it fine. He nodded. He did not look as if he believed me. "Henry showed me a couple of your reports," he said. "They weren't bad. If you like, you can read some of my submissions. I do some French fiction, you know. Not a lot, but there's some very interesting stuff being published there. You read French, don't you?"

I said I did, happy to have found, at last, somebody in book publishing who apparently wanted to take advantage of my knowledge of languages. I already guessed that Bob Gottlieb's submissions, whatever language they were in, would be very different from Henry's—much more literary and avant-garde, which suited me fine, since Henry's tended to be rather old-fashioned novels or on nonfiction subjects that didn't interest me.

My current task—which seemed likely to keep me busy for months, if not years—was to "fine-tune," as Henry put it, the revision of an interminable history of religion by an elderly Unitarian minister, Dr. Charles Potter. Dr. Potter's views on religion seemed to me so benign and ecumenical as to be meaningless. Dr. Potter's prose style, unlike his theology, was thickly convoluted and erratic, so I had my work cut out for me. Henry had made it clear, however, that even when time was lying heavy on my hands, it was *his* time. "Won't Henry mind?" I asked Gottlieb cautiously.

Gottlieb had a nervous habit of flipping back the lock of hair that crossed his brow with one hand, after which it immediately fell back into its former position. His glasses, I noticed, were so smeared with fingerprints that it was a wonder he could see through them. "Well, he might," he said cautiously. "You'd have to do it on your own time. He can't possibly object to *that*. If you like, I'll talk to him."

I said that would be great.

The legend was that Gottlieb had been rejected by his parents because he married a Gentile girl—a story that might have come straight out of a Philip Roth novel. His wife, Muriel, had given up her career as an actress to work as a waitress, so that Gottlieb could complete his studies at Columbia and go on to Cambridge, where he had dazzled everyone with his knowledge of literature and his enthusiasm for the criticism of F. R. Leavis. (His only treasured possession was one of the few complete sets of Leavis's magazine, *Scrutiny*, outside a library; he kept it in milk cartons under his bed and read himself to sleep with them.) All this had done him, at first, no good. On his return to America—Muriel was by then pregnant—he was obliged to take a job selling

Christmas cards at Macy's, whence he had been rescued when he was hired as Jack Goodman's assistant at S&S, and rose from that lowly position like a rocket. If I knew the story by heart already, it was because it represented just what I was hoping would happen to me, sooner rather than later.

"Call me Bob," he said, rising to his feet. One of the many inconveniences of an English education is the difficulty in getting on a first-name basis with anyone. Americans always seemed to expect that I would address them by their first name on sight, just as many of them called me "Mike," which I hated but didn't know how to correct. I still hadn't found a way of addressing my boss as "Henry," however often he invited me to.

Bob and I shook hands ceremoniously. He paused and looked at my desk critically. "You'll never meet anybody if your back is all they see," he said. He grasped one end of my desk. "You take the other side." Together, we lifted the desk and turned it around, so it faced outward. Now I could see down the whole length of the corridor. Anybody coming in or going to the bathroom would pass in front of me.

Bob nodded with satisfaction, though whether at the change in my position or at the discomfiture Henry would feel, I wasn't sure. Henry said nothing when he saw that my desk had been turned around. He merely sighed, his face paler and grayer than ever, went into his office, and lit another cigarette, followed by a dry, racking cough.

I knew that I had disappointed him, and I felt bad about it. I already understood that my loyalty was going to be deeply, sometimes painfully divided. More than anything else, I wanted to be part of that tight little circle that revolved around Bob, where, for the moment, the real excitement was.

CHAPTER 5

BY THE END of my second week at S&S, Bob and I were friends. He was also a mentor—a role in which he reveled—at a time when I badly needed one. I had two mentors, in fact: Bob, who taught me the importance of enthusiasm and imagination in publishing, and Henry, who taught me the importance of paying attention to details and of long hours of laborious, slow work over unrewarding manuscripts. *Sitzfleisch*, he called it, a German word signifying the ability to put one's ass down on a chair for many hours of uninterrupted work at a time. A plodder Henry might be, but he was indefatigable, a martyr to his own fussy perfectionism, as he sat lighting cigarette after cigarette, eyes red with fatigue, making tiny alterations in sentence after sentence with a succession of sharpened pencils.

I soon fell into the habit of working for Henry like a medieval monk toiling patiently over a piece of parchment; when I'd finished, I read manuscripts for Bob, with a sense of relief that kept me going until the small hours of the morning. Gradually, I became accepted in the group that centered around Bob, and took to joining them in his office, early in the evening, after the "grown-ups" had gone home. Almost everything that involved editorial decisions, advertising, jackets, and marketing was discussed here. The group also made by no means gentle fun of Max Schuster, from whom they tried to keep as far away as possible. Little did I know that Henry had already volunteered my services to him and that I would soon get to know him better than I could possibly have imagined.

SHORT, BALDING, bent over with cares and burdens, a-twitch with a kind of demonic nervous energy, Max was prey to such a veritable frenzy of tics, tremblings, stutters, and rapid blinks so startling that most people who met him assumed that he suffered from some kind of nervous disease, Tourette's syndrome, perhaps.

The truth was quite other: Schuster was an obsessive-compulsive workaholic, afflicted with an extreme case of shyness. In the right circumstances, he was a man of considerable charm and erudition, but he was also complex to a degree that would have baffled a Freudian analyst. At times, he seemed to those around him like a kind of secularized *yeshivah bokher*, one of those scholarly Jews who were content to *daven* for hours at an end over a text, rocking back and forth as he repeated it to himself and sought its meaning. Certainly Schuster read even the most innocuous memo as if it were a fragment of the Dead Sea Scrolls, his lips moving as he mumbled it aloud to himself, his eyes behind thick, old-fashioned, perfectly round horn-rimmed glasses, giving him a certain owl-like look as he searched for hidden meanings, ballpoint pen at the ready, twitching in his right hand ready to scrawl corrections, emendations, and second thoughts in the margin.

I had seen him jogging breathlessly down the corridor, a nervous, worried figure, bent over crablike, his mouth open in an *O* as he gulped for air like a fish, wearing a blue suit with sleeves far too long for his arms and round glasses with lenses as thick as the bottoms of Coke bottles, a bulging briefcase under each arm, while scribbled notes fluttered from his pockets like autumn leaves and his secretary ran stooped behind him, picking them up. Yet other times, he radiated the kind of worldly self-confidence that tends to settle upon the owners of publishing houses when they have all the money they will ever need and the right to publish anything they want to, however dismal or self-indulgent.

When he was seated in his office, he constantly pecked away with a pen held in his right hand, a palsied, nervous tic that drove everyone else mad and left the arms of his chair and his sofa and the surface of his desk pitted as if a destructive child had been let loose with an ice pick. Though normally he spoke with a certain old-fashioned and formal courtesy, when he wanted something in a hurry, he pushed the buzzer on his desk rapidly, over and over again, like a man sending Morse code, until one of his long-suffering minions appeared, eyes agog like the victim of some kind of Pavlovian experiment. As soon as he or she had left to perform whatever task Schuster had in mind, Schuster would start buzzing again for something else. One of his assistants, it was rumored, had thrown himself out of a window, twenty-eight floors down to Fifth Avenue, driven mad by the constant buzzing from the "inner sanctum" (as Schuster called his office), as well as by Schuster's passion for filing everything under a maddening variety of headings, most of them in coded initials known only to him.

Everybody at S&S soon learned to decipher the easier of these, invariably written in a firm hand with a thick black Chinagraph wax crayon marker and signed "M.L.S.": "PAAIMA" meant "Please Answer As In My Absence," "DTN," "Do The Necessary," "UYOJ," "Use Your Own Judgment," "RARB," "Read and Report Back," but these were merely the tip of the iceberg. Schuster rose early every morning and breakfasted alone at the Oak Room of the Plaza, and during these hours he devoted himself to clipping articles from the morning papers with a pair of folding scissors. These clippings usually represented ideas for books, which he would send to one or more of the editors, with cryptic instructions scrawled at the top of the clipping. They were also filed, under some arcane system, by any number of headings and cross-references, so that if you ignored one of them, it came back again and again, the thick black exclamation marks proliferating until you did something about it. I remember one of them, a front-page photograph from the *Daily News* showing a mother held back by two policemen, screaming, her hands covering her eyes, as her children burned to death in some tenement fire. Schuster had written boldly at the top: FILE UNDER GRIEF.

"FILE UNDER GRIEF" became a phrase that described anything Max Schuster involved himself in. Schuster was an indefatigable *nudge* and *kibitzer,* sending endless memos about meaningless details, with cc's or bcc's to everyone at S&S, all of which had to be answered before they started coming back again and again like the tide, defaced with cryptograms of ever-increasing urgency.

It would be easy to dismiss Max Schuster as a comic figure—or at any rate, a case from the files of Dr. Sacher-Masoch—but he was at the same time exceedingly shrewd, as in the famous quote from Archilochus: "The fox knows many things—the hedgehog knows one big one." Like the hedgehog, whom Schuster seemed to resemble in weak-eyed, hunchbacked timidity, he knew, if nothing else, how to curl up in a ball and survive. Odd he might look, with his curious round *yeshiva bokher* spectacles, his guileless expression and goggling eyes, his lips pursed like those of a goldfish blowing bubbles in an aquarium, but he was no fool. Not only had he survived the efforts of Dick Simon, Marshall Field III, and Leon Shimkin to oust him, in the end he outlived both Simon and Field.

On the whole, Schuster preferred to see the younger editors as little as possible. He avoided anything that might lead to argument or disagreement and painstakingly timed his arrival and departure from the office to give him the maximum possibility of not seeing anyone in the elevator or the halls. You could tell whenever he was about to arrive or depart by the presence of his staff in the halls, making sure that the coast was clear. He tried very hard *never* to see Bob Gottlieb, which suited Bob just fine. Most people at S&S tried to keep out of Schuster's sight, not because they necessarily feared or disliked him, but because he seemed irrelevant.

. . .

I WAS drawn into Schuster's orbit because of my background in history and my English upbringing. Henry had made my services available to Max without telling me; no doubt he thought it might do him some good with Schuster, and it could certainly do my career at S&S no harm. The opportunity arose from the fact that Justin D. Kaplan, who had worked closely with Schuster for many years on some of Schuster's more difficult books, was planning to leave. The reasons for Kaplan's departure were many. On one level, there was a certain rivalry between Bob Gottlieb and Kaplan, and it was apparent enough that Bob was going to be a force at S&S for the foreseeable future. Their dislike for each other was mild but visceral, a blend of envy and the slight contempt of a well-dressed, urbane Harvard man for a scruffy bohemian nonconformist with a dislike for stuffy academics—oil and water, in brief.

On another level, Kaplan—who was married to Anne Bernays, and thus son-in-law to the fabulously wealthy public-relations genius Edward Bernays, himself the son-in-law of Freud—was tired of being a junior editor, apparently doomed forever to worrying about Will Durant, Nikos Kazantzakis, Bernard Berenson, Bertrand Russell, and the rest of Schuster's worthies. Kaplan was anxious to carve out a bit of fame for himself as a writer (which he shortly did, with a Pulitzer Prize–winning biography of Mark Twain).

Schuster was a snob of a gentle, old-fashioned kind. He liked the people who worked closely with him to be "connected" to somebody—Kaplan had been Eddie Bernays's son-in-law; I was Sir Alexander Korda's nephew. He also, not unnaturally, liked people who were interested in the kind of books that he liked: history, philosophy, new editions of the classics. Whenever Max Schuster was interviewed, he said that his favorite way of spending an evening was to sit at home reading Spinoza, though since he also said that the only form of exercise he took was to go to the office every day and exercise his options, it was hard to know whether he was serious. I had not read history at Magdalen, but I had attended lectures by Alan Bullock, Hugh Trevor-Roper, and A. J. P. Taylor and was a protégé of Sir John Wheeler-Bennett, official biographer of King George VI, and had mentioned this in my job application. Schuster had apparently read it closely, even if nobody else had bothered, and what he saw there he had liked.

Kaplan's impending departure eventually moved me toward the enviable position of being more or less independent of any real authority.

I worked for Henry, to be sure, but since I was also going to be working for Max, I could pretty much set my own priorities. A man with two bosses effectively has none. In addition, I was to take over Kaplan's role as "secretary of the editorial board." The editorial board of S&S met on Thursday mornings in Max's office and at that time consisted of Max, Henry, and Peter Schwed. On very rare occasions, one of the other editors might be called in to describe a book he or she wanted to buy, but Schuster's shyness and his determination to have eye contact with as few people as possible meant that most editorial business was based on written reports and memos. It was a source of some bitterness in the company that the editors, however successful they might be, were excluded from the weekly meeting, but Schuster clung to the tradition stubbornly.

It was my job to attend the meeting and take the minutes, but there was no vow of silence involved. Schuster, I at once discovered, was as likely to ask me for my opinion as anyone else's. Since the minutes of these meetings were central to his claim that he was truly running the business, the person who took the notes and drafted the minutes played an important role, from his point of view (though not from anybody else's).

MY FIRST serious meeting with Max (he put us almost immediately on a first-name basis) had been interesting but unsettling. Henry and I sat facing his desk, as his right hand tapped out a speedy rhythm with the business end of a ballpoint pen. On close inspection, Max's toilette left something to be desired: There were bristly patches on his neck and cheeks that he had missed while shaving, small tufts of Kleenex clung to a couple of places where he had cut himself with his razor, he had neglected to put stays in the collar of his shirt, and several of his buttons were unbuttoned. He looked ever so slightly unkempt, despite the expensive, tailored, three-piece blue suit and the Sulka shirt and tie. One of his eyes strayed toward the side—he was a bit walleyed, as if searching, like a flounder, for danger on the periphery of his sight. His whole demeanor, for a man sitting in his own office in a company he half-owned, was remarkably nervous and edgy. In fact, I toyed with the notion that it was I who was making him nervous, but that didn't seem to be the case. His desk was littered—quite literally—with clippings, memos, notes, three-by-five index cards in various colors, bulging files full of Thermofaxes (those pale pink, curly, shiny precursors to xerography) and smudged carbon copies, all of them marked with his energetic, restless pencil.

On the walls hung a number of framed photographs, obviously designed to impress: Max and Ray at I Tatti with Bernard Berenson; Max and Ray in Jerusalem with David Ben-Gurion; Max and Ray with Bertrand Russell at Plas Penrhyn, his Welsh castle; Max and Ray with Sir Max Beerbohm at Rapallo; Max and Ray with Nikos Kazantzakis somewhere in the Mediterranean. In all these photographs Ray Schuster—a firm-jawed, compact, stylish, and good-looking woman of a certain age—stood close by the famous personality, sometimes even touching, smiling directly into the camera, while Max stood shiftily to one side, as if he suspected that his presence was an intrusion. In most of them the famous personality looked old and bewildered, as if uncertain about why he was being photographed with this energetic American woman. Beerbohm looked positively senile.

Max's handshake was trembly and damp and offered rather unwillingly, not, I felt sure, from any aversion to me but rather from a desperate need to keep a desk width between himself and any stranger. As I let go of his hand, he sighed with relief and collapsed back into his chair. The leather on the right arm of the chair had been holed so that the stuffing was emerging in unsightly gray clumps.

"Welcome to the inner sanctum," Max said. He had a resonant voice, spoiled by a tendency to stutter and by long pauses while he gathered his strength for the next consonant. "Have you read Will Durant's *The Story of Civilization?*" he asked, pointing to his bookshelves, where the first six volumes of Durant's life's work stood together. They were massive, each one of them a veritable *Missouri*-class battleship of a book, formidably bulky and armed with every possible footnote, index, and bibliography.

I indicated that I had not yet had the pleasure.

"No matter," Max said breezily. "It's never too late to start, is it, Henry?"

Henry nodded glumly.

"Will has just sent in the latest volume," Max went on, his face aglow with enthusiasm. "Wonderful stuff! I sat up all night reading the manuscript. It's called *The Age of Reason Begins*. A work of monumental importance. I cabled Will this morning telling him how proud I was to be his publisher." He shuffled through the papers on his desk, sending pieces of paper flying in all directions, looking for a copy of the telegram, but failed to find it. "I only wish I had the leisure to go through the manuscript in detail, but of course I don't." Max waved his hands at his desk and the piles of clippings that were waiting to be filed. He sighed. "History is an adventure," Max said. "A *voyage*. Will Durant sails the seas of history and time like a Columbus, discovering new continents of knowledge."

At first I thought that Max must surely be making fun of me, but since Henry wasn't laughing—if anything, he looked gloomier than ever—I assumed that Max often spoke like this, and I was right. He could spout advertising copy like Moby-Dick surfacing for air, some of it not half bad. In his time, Max had written—or dictated—any number of groundbreaking advertisements for books. He was at his best with the breathless style of mail-order book advertising, which S&S had practically invented, and had a gut instinct for great headlines such as YOUNG FOREVER! for a book about vitamins or FAT NO MORE! for a diet book. An ad for an anthology of the wisdom of the ages began, "Last night I walked hand-in-hand with Jesus by the Sea of Galilee." His prose was unmistakable and over the years became the S&S house style, a heady, oracular mash of superlatives, puns, and one-liners that most people at S&S could write by the yard but that only Max actually *spoke*.

"Will needs to have his hand held by someone," Max said. "Someone who cares about history." I nodded earnestly, to show my love of history, but Max was off on a riff of his own and didn't notice. "Ariel— Mrs. Durant—is still after me to get him the Nobel Prize," Max said plaintively. "It's not as if I haven't *tried*, but of course she just doesn't understand how difficult that kind of thing . . ." He paused and mopped his forehead with a handkerchief. "Ariel is very much part of the picture. . . . Did you know that Will was trained as a priest, and when Ariel made up her mind to marry him she was so young that she actually went to the marriage bureau on her roller skates? He renamed her 'Ariel,' and she called him 'Puck.' " Max paused for breath again, eyes goggling. "Of course, all that was a long time ago. She's no longer young. But they remain a very devoted couple, wouldn't you say, Henry?"

Henry shrugged. "You bet," he said glumly.

The two men sat for a few moments, apparently contemplating the state of marriage in a spirit of mutual gloom. Max, it was said, lived in fear of Ray Schuster's piercing voice, while Henry's bride was allegedly disliked by everyone at S&S, as well as by the rest of the widespread Simon family. She was reputed to make small dolls of those whom she disliked and stick pins in them.

"Ariel sits by Will's side and turns the pages as he reads," Max said. He did not say it with envy. His own ambition, it was said, was to lock himself in the library with his favorite books where Mrs. Schuster couldn't get at him. "Well, you get the idea. You have to include her, listen to her ideas, treat her as if she were Will's partner. Walk on eggshells, yes?"

I got the idea.

"It's a great opportunity for a young man like yourself," Max went on, more upbeat. "This is a monumental project, you know. Each volume is a Main Selection of the Book-of-the-Month Club, and a guaranteed best-seller. Why, Harry Scherman often calls the Book-of-the-Month Club 'the house that Will Durant built.' . . . This is commerce, you see, as well as culture. You'll be working with one of the great thinkers of our time. . . . I envy you. Of course, you'll have to be careful not to take too much time away from the work you're doing for Henry," Max added hastily. "We have a contract with the Book-of-the-Month Club, and I promised Will and Ariel we'd have the book out in September, so you'll have your work cut out for you. Come to me with any problem. My door will always be open to you." He paused. "Within reason."

Max's buzzer was keening noisily before we were out the door. On his assistant's desk was a huge stack of manuscript, neatly tied with string. It showed no sign of having been opened by Max. I looked at it with a certain degree of awe mixed with apprehension. It was almost unimaginable that any living human being could have written this number of pages without going blind. "If Durant is such a prize, why is he getting a junior editor?" I asked Henry.

Henry lit a cigarette and coughed. "The Durants are a little . . . ah . . . *difficult*," he said cautiously.

"How difficult?"

"On a scale of one to ten, ten. They won't work with me because they hate academics. They feel that everybody in the academic world looks down on Will as a popularizer. Which, of course, he *is*. Nothing wrong with that, really, but it gives them a monumental inferiority complex, as well as a chip on the shoulder. . . . It's not that Will's books need a lot of editing, by the way—it's just that he and Ariel are very fussy about details. My advice is to keep them away from Max as much as you can."

"I thought he liked them."

Henry grimaced. "Oh, Max likes them all right," he said. "He just doesn't want to *see* them."

FULL AS S&S was of odd people, Max Schuster was far and away the oddest. Office legend had it that because of Max's shyness when faced with a member of the opposite sex, he had married the wrong woman. Max had been a bachelor until well into his middle age, living a fairly hermitlike existence except when he was obliged to entertain authors or agents and apparently content with his lot. At some point in the thirties, he had apparently rented a house for the summer in Sands Point, on the North Shore of Long Island—Gatsby territory. His next-door neighbor turned out to be a well-preserved recent widow named Ray Levinson, who had three daughters. The late Mr. Levinson had been a local land-scape and nursery czar, and his widow was wealthy, but with social am-bitions that went beyond gardens and pools. At some point during that summer, Max fell in love with one of the daughters. Max's courtship was pursued so timidly that the young woman might not even have been aware of the feelings of her ungainly suitor, but at some point he finally got the nerve up to talk to her mother and seek her permission to pro-pose to her daughter.

Max visited the widow Levinson and haltingly managed to ap-proach the reason for his visit. He was, he told her, in love, and felt he had to unburden himself of his feelings. Ray put her fingers to his lips and in a sharp, piercing voice, strongly marked by a Russian-Jewish ac-cent, cried out: "Shush! Not another word!" Alarmed, Max fell silent. "I know just what you are going to say, Max," Ray went on. "I accept."

Whether from sheer timidity or the undeniable fact that Ray Levin-son's willpower and determination were positively Nietzschean, Max stayed silent and soon afterward married her, no doubt going to the altar in something of the sprit of a condemned man mounting the steps to the gallows.

An emotional predicament more calculated to drive Max to his beloved files can hardly be imagined—all the more so since Ray was a ruthless domestic tyrant, of whom poor Max lived in fear, desperate to please her but apparently unable to. She was a pint-size, Eastern European Jewish version of the Queen of Hearts in *Alice in Wonderland*, and her occasional visits to the office threw not only Max but everyone else into a state of panic, since she was quite likely to insist on having him fire any attractive young woman who happened to cross her path. Ray was apparently under the illusion that Max's appearance made him a magnetic attraction for women, or, even more improbably, that Max himself might lust after them.

MAX'S FORGETFULNESS was well noted by his colleagues and spawned many stories, some of them true—indeed, it was one of the bonds he shared with Dick Simon, who lost manuscripts, contracts, letters, and his personal possessions so frequently that everyone who worked for him knew the phone numbers of the major lost-and-found offices in New York City and the surrounding counties. Max usually managed to hang on to his coat, hat, and briefcase, but he was unreliable when it came to names and faces.

At one point before the war, S&S became the publisher of Gypsy Rose Lee's mystery novel, *The G-String Murders*. Gypsy had always fancied herself to be an intellectual (hence the song in *Pal Joey* in which one of the supporting players does a Gypsy Rose Lee imitation and sings, as she strips, "Zip!—I'm an intellectual") and writing a book had long been her dream. Her long-term lover Billy Rose took on the task of getting the book published, and when S&S bought the rights it was major news. Gypsy was by then well past her stripping days but was still a formidable woman, tall, voluptuous, and somewhat overpowering. Billy was tiny (he came up to about her waist), so they made an odd couple.

Rose got his start as a boy by taking shorthand from the famous financier and presidential adviser Bernard Baruch, made his fortune in show business, and inspired a good many other short, dark, energetic, and ambitious Jewish boys to follow in his footsteps, including Mike Todd. He was enormously wealthy by the time Gypsy plunged into authorhood—he was perhaps the only man in New York to have a malachite urinal in his downstairs guest bathroom (and a malachite sink to match it, too)—and made it clear that he expected Gypsy to get first-class treatment, which Max and Dick agreed happily to give her, given Gypsy's celebrity status.

Alas, like most publishers, they were more interested in Gypsy *before* they bought her book than they were afterward. In publishing as in love, the really heady period is during the courtship, when the author is still being wooed. Once the deal is consummated, the love affair ends, a certain indifference sets in, and the marriage begins. Since neither Dick nor Max were greatly interested in murder mysteries, Gypsy was handed over to S&S's mystery editor and promptly forgotten by the two owners.

As the publication date approached, Gypsy became more and more anxious about the big party that she assumed would be given to launch her book and increasingly upset to hear nothing about it from her publishers. When it became evident that no party was planned, she was distraught, but Billy Rose cheered her up. Fuck 'em, he told her, if the lousy cheapskates weren't going to give her a party, he would take her out to dinner to celebrate instead. So Rose booked a table upstairs at "21" and took Gypsy there for dinner. About halfway through the meal, Gypsy looked up and realized that Max Schuster was sitting a few tables away with his wife Ray and another couple. Should she get up and say something to him? she asked Rose. Rose was against it, but finally he could see that nothing was going to hold Gypsy back.

Embarrassed and a little nervous, she walked over to Max's table and interrupted the conversation to say hello and ask Max how her book was doing. Max beamed up at Gypsy, and before she could say a word, stammered out to her: "Gypsy, how nice to see you! You know, I've been thinking about you a lot lately." He paused. "One of these days, you ought to write a book."*

IN MY own small way, I soon had direct contact with the manic-compulsive side of Max's personality. The notes I took once a week at the editorial-board meeting had to be typed as a draft on dark yellow paper, triple-spaced, so that Max could rewrite and expand upon them,

---

* This probably explains why Billy Rose gave me a fishy look when I was introduced to him as an S&S editor and also why June Havoc, Gypsy's younger sister and rival, chose S&S to be her publisher when, in a successful attempt to outshine Gypsy, she wrote her autobiography, *Early Havoc.*

often until they bore no relationship at all to what had actually been said or decided. This was, to put it mildly, an eye-opener, first to the fact that Max was living at least part of the time in a dream world, and second, that what passed for facts at S&S were often not facts at all. I knew what had been said and by whom, I had even written it down pretty much verbatim, so it was odd to see how it changed under Max's relentless blue marks as he expanded his comments, downplayed Schwed's, and often eliminated Henry's altogether. Anybody reading the minutes would have supposed that Max talked nonstop throughout the meetings, whereas, in fact, he was usually silent, lips pursed as if blowing bubbles, while Schwed and Henry argued things out between themselves. Max's revisions gave him a certain statesmanlike air, though for a long time I had some difficulty in deciding why he cared enough to go to this trouble. Most people who got the editorial-board minutes merely looked to see which books we had bought and how much we had paid for them; it was a practical tool, not intended to leave S&S. When I mentioned this to Henry he sighed deeply, his face looking paler and more world-weary than ever. "The only copies Max cares about," he said, "are the ones that go to Leon Shimkin and to Ray Schuster."

Shimkin, of course, I could understand. Max was anxious to show his partner that he was in charge of things. Since Shimkin had known Max since the mid-1920s, I doubted that he was taken in by Max's mild and harmless deception, but it was really Ray whom Max was trying to impress. Having chosen Max over any number of other suitors (at least if she was to be believed), Ray was obliged to present her Max to the rest of the world as a "genius"—an *eccentric* genius, perhaps, but a genius all the same. Seldom have two people worked so hard to appear devoted to each other.

More than anybody else, Ray had been responsible for the hostility between Max and Shimkin. Many years ago, before the war, Max had prevailed upon Ray to invite Shimkin and his wife, Rebecca, to one of their parties in their apartment at the old Pulitzer mansion. In Ray's eyes, Shimkin was still "the bookkeeper." Deeply resentful of being obliged to invite him, she deliberately neglected to tell the Shimkins that it was a black-tie affair, so that they were the only couple not formally dressed, to their great embarrassment. Shimkin never forgave this insult (particularly to his beloved Rebecca), and it went far toward dividing the ownership of S&S into two implacably hostile opposite camps.

By making it obvious that her husband was terrified of her, Ray succeeded in making him seem foolish to his own employees—particularly the more talented and ambitious among them. This is not to say that she was a stupid woman—on the contrary, there was a side to her that was notably shrewd and smart—but her energy and ambition exceeded her husband's. Unfortunately, she had been brought up in an age when there was no outlet for those qualities except through poor Max.

This was, in those days, a far more common phenomenon than it is now. Indeed, the model on which Ray based herself was that of Blanche Knopf. Alfred and Blanche Knopf presented themselves as something of a publishing team. Elegant and sharply intellectual, Blanche Knopf was what Ray would like to have been seen as, the loving and equal partner of a famous husband, but unfortunately for her, she had neither the education nor the taste for such a task, nor did Max's choice in books and authors lend themselves to the kind of literary nurturing that the Knopfs were famous for as a couple.

In the contest for book publishing's most famous couple, the Knopfs remained light-years ahead in class, and there seemed nothing the Schusters could do about it. While the Knopfs were being photographed with André Gide or publishing the definitive translation of Proust, the Schusters were stuck with the Durants. Max and Ray fought back with what weapons they could, not always with happy results. When, in 1958, after years of labor by Justin Kaplan, Max finally published Kimon Friar's translation of Nikos Kazantzakis's monumental epic poem, *The Odyssey: A Modern Sequel,* he sent a copy to all his major publishing colleagues. Alfred Knopf, who had once referred to people like Max and Dick, among others, as "fresh young Jews," responded with a personal note: "Welcome, at last," he wrote, "to the ranks of the real publishers." Since S&S had been in business since 1924, this praise was rather faint; however, Max put on a good face and sent copies of the letter to everyone, as if there were no sting in it.

A further attempt to emulate the Knopfs was the publication of a small book by Max and Ray entitled *Home Thoughts from Abroad,* intended to memorialize one of the Schusters' yearly transatlantic visits to the great and near great, culminating with a pilgrimage to see "B.B." (Bernard Berenson) and his constant companion, Nicky Mariano, at I Tatti. Unfortunately, Max was obliged to cut short his trip, while Ray went on undaunted. As a result, their letters to each other make up the bulk of the text. In one, Ray (who was traveling with her daughter Beattie) wrote to Max that they had dined with B.B., that B.B. had placed her on his right and told her that her visit was like a ray of sunshine in his life and that if he had been a younger man he would have asked her to come and live with him. (What Nicky Mariano thought of this conversation, if it ever took place, is not recorded.) "The next day," she added, "we went shopping in Florence and bought several thousand dollars worth of antiques, which I am sending home, and which you should clear through customs."

Another letter was from Israel, where she recorded that Ben-Gurion asked her to sit on his right and drank a toast to her, calling her "his little American ray of sunshine" and saying that Israel would not be complete until she came to live there. The next morning, she told Max, she and Beattie combed Jerusalem buying antiques, which she would send home by air and which should be cleared through customs as quickly as possible. These letters were eventually bound up in a small book, with many photographs of Max and Ray, or Ray alone, with their famous hosts, and was sent out, signed by both of them, to Max's enormous "celebrity list," including all his fellow publishers. The copy sent to the Knopfs came back as if it had been a submission, with a card turning it down as unsuitable for the Knopf list. When the Knopfs found out about this, they apologized, but Ray never forgave them, suspecting that it had been a deliberate slight.

Ray was in the habit of dropping in at unpredictable moments during the day, often with one of her daughters, presumably in the hope of catching Max doing his dictation with a buxom secretary in his lap, like a tycoon in a Peter Arno cartoon.

Shortly after being made responsible for the Durants, I was called into the inner sanctum by Max to be introduced to Ray. She was a small, formidable woman, elegantly dressed, her fur coat thrown over the back of her chair. She reminded me of a certain kind of French or Hungarian older woman, indestructibly chic down to the smallest accessories, the kind of woman one used to see boarding the wagon-lit of the *Train Bleu*, bound for Monte Carlo, followed by two porters bent double under the weight of her matching Vuitton suitcases. She had the look of someone who never appeared in public without every hair in place and who believed that the best place for her good jewelry was on her hands and wrists, not in a safe.

I shook her gloved hand. "So you're Max's new young man?" she said, eyeing me up and down skeptically. Her English was heavily accented but hard to place exactly. She managed to squeeze a couple of extra vowels into Max's name, which took some doing. I felt obscurely as if I were back in school again, being examined.

"I met your uncle once," Ray went on, giving me a look that suggested that I did not compare favorably with him. "In London, at one of Weidenfeld's parties. Do you remember, Max?"

Max shook his head and stuttered something.

"He doesn't remember anything," she said, dismissing Max with a shake of her head. She continued, "Max tells me that you're going to be the Durants' editor."

I said that I was honored to be and that I was reading *The Age of Reason Begins* even now and making copious notes.

"Notes," she said contemptuously. "What do they need with notes, the Durants? Their whole lives are spent buried in paper, those two. Better they should buy some decent clothes instead of reading more notes." Ray's voice fell to a kind of piercing whisper, as if she were confiding something to me that she didn't want Max to hear, though judging by the martyred look on his moon face, he had heard it all before. "She's a *peasant*, that one. She wears men's shoes. She doesn't wash enough." Ray wrinkled her nose in distaste. "You're working for Henry, I hear?"

I said that I was.

She rolled her eyes and sighed. "Well, you have to start somewhere," she said. "You'll come to the house one day—we'll talk again." She dismissed me with an imperious wave of the hand.

As she went on, I noted that Ray spoke about Dick Simon in the past tense, even though he was still alive, and with a certain relish, which made Max shake his head in silent protest. Although Max and Dick had once been so close that, like Bennett Cerf and Donald Klopfer at Random House, they worked in one office with their desks facing each other, I intuited that their wives had not shared that closeness—and had perhaps even resented it. In Ray's case, she had done everything she could to bring it to an end, with the result that when S&S moved to new and more glamorous quarters in Rockefeller Center, the two partners got separate offices for the first time. The inner sanctum had once been their shared office, then it became the book-lined meeting room between their offices, then finally the phrase referred only to Max's office.

"Learn from Max," she called out to me as I opened the door. "It's a great opportunity for a young man to work alongside a genius." It was curious, I thought, that she was quite capable of treating Max like an idiot while insisting that he was a genius.

Max stared at me across his desk. It was hard to read his expression, beyond the embarrassment natural to any man who has just been called a genius by his wife, but whatever he looked like—a trapped animal begging for release without any hope of getting it, perhaps—it wasn't a genius.

THAT IS not to say that Max didn't *have* a genius of a kind. Whenever I read the purple prose of a certain kind of mail-order advertising, I close my eyes and can see Max Schuster writing it. Max understood, as very few people in publishing have, the power of simple ideas. Nobody was ever better at inventing books that filled a *need*, or at describing them with the kind of enthusiasm that sold them in quantity, or at breaking down the reasons for buying them into punchy, one-line sentences.

It was a shame that by the time I came to S&S Max had degenerated into a parody of what had once made him successful and that what he had invented other people could by then do as well, or better. There was a whole subindustry based on "words to live by" or "words of wisdom," of books on self-improvement, etiquette, self-enrichment, even sex, most of it born from Max's passionate belief that you could learn anything, change anything, help yourself ahead in any way merely by reading the right book. With an instinct based on his own bookwormish shyness and a childhood of reading Horatio Alger and Julius Haldeman's famous Little Blue Books (cheap digests of all the world's great philosophers), Max made S&S and himself rich. The key to it was the little rectangular order form at the bottom of each advertisement, which you could fill in and send, with your check, to "Dept. SM" at S&S to receive the book that would get you a better job, make your marriage happier, teach you the wisdom of the ages and the sages (as Max, with his love of puns, would have written), or make you rich or healthy.*

---

* Department SM was, in fact, a charming gentleman named Sam Meyerson, who was hired as the office boy when S&S was founded and who eventually rose to head the mail-order department. When well into his eighties, he still personally picked up the mail from the post office early every morning. The one thing that Max and Leon Shimkin shared was that the first thing each of them wanted to know each morning was how many orders Meyerson had received and for which books.

Still, whatever it was that Max knew, he didn't see it as his task to teach it to me. It was from Henry that I was to learn the most valuable lesson about book publishing, though at second hand. One evening, as I was heading for home, burdened down with several manuscripts and a sizable chunk of the Durants', Henry told me that years ago he had once met his brother Dick in the elevator, going home. Henry was carrying a heavy briefcase, buckled straps and handle straining with the weight of manuscripts, while Dick was nonchalantly carrying a thin leather portfolio under one arm. Dick stared at Henry's load and chuckled. Pointing to Henry, he said, in mock Indian, "You, editor." Then, pointing to his thin portfolio, he said: "Me, publisher."

CHAPTER 6

$\mathcal{A}$LMOST THE FIRST thing I learned about being an editor was that it was hard work. To be sure, ditchdiggers and miners have it worse, but for sheer, numbing, endless (I do not, deliberately, say *mindless*) work, editing books is hard to beat.

First of all there's the sheer *quantity* of reading. From behind an editor's desk, it sometimes seems as if the entire population of the United States is writing a book or sending in long, cramped, single-spaced letters, eccentrically typed, proposing to write one. Every mail delivery brings a fresh load of bulky, shapeless, poorly wrapped packages, many of them leaking that unpleasant gray stuffing that is impossible to get off your clothes, not to speak of rubber-banded piles of letter proposals, ranging from the insulting to the heartbreaking, and outlines for improbable books.

Many people in book publishing ignore this tide of flotsam and jetsam or return most of it unopened (a chore in itself), but it goes almost without saying that Max Schuster had devised a complicated and difficult procedure for numbering and tracking each of these unwelcome submissions. No matter how dog-eared, tatty, or unpromising the manuscript, it had to be logged in, a reader's report form ("R.R.F.") had to be attached to it, after which it was read, rejected, logged out, and the report filed. A very pleasant though much harassed elderly lady, Molly Singer, was responsible for this vast overload of paperwork, which was one of Max's favorite management achievements and which absorbed a good deal of his attention.

Editors senior to myself (which was almost everybody) were always arriving back from lunch with a "hot" manuscript they had received directly from an agent, which they then took home and read without bothering to log it in. If these made their way to the editorial board for further readings without the proper form, they were sent back again to be entered properly into the system. As for the unsolicited manuscripts, the infamous "slush pile"—those that came to us unagented, from total strangers—only Molly Singer knew by what arcane numerology of Max's they were divided up among the junior editors for reading. Seniority obviously had something to do with it, since my pile filled every square foot of space in my cubicle, including the space under my desk. Like mushrooms, the manuscripts seemed to sprout overnight.

The sheer volume of material that had to be read was daunting, but the task was essentially extracurricular, a built-in, routine burden of the profession, like getting up to go to mass in the middle of the night for a monk. Night after night, those of us who read—it was regarded as a kind of badge of honor that set us apart from people in marketing or sales, who were also, by the way, making more money than us— dragged home shopping bags full of manuscripts, always hoping to find buried somewhere in the pile a literary pearl, and morning after morning we wearily dragged them back to the office to reject them. The rejection letters ran to form and, having all been drafted by Max, were as unalterable as the Holy Writ. It was soul-destroying work, apt to turn anyone cynical, for the sad, awful truth was that there was hardly any evidence at all of talent in the slush pile and plenty of proof, for those who needed it, that the country was full of crazy people armed with typewriters—far more of them even than of crazy people armed with guns.

The worst of it was one could never get ahead of the flow—it was the lesson of King Canute, applied to paper instead of water. Perhaps even worse, nobody paid the slightest attention to these labors, which went totally unrewarded. You could read yourself blind and it wouldn't add a penny to your paycheck.

Still, compared to editing, the reading was easy work. At least with the reading, you were buoyed, however implausibly and against all evidence, by hope. The next manuscript might, after all, prove to be a work of genius, or at any rate talent, the discovery of which can make an editor's career overnight. Such things *do* happen; Bob Gottlieb *had* discovered Joseph Heller, after all, and *Catch-22* was about to change both their lives. The element of chance is as important as that of choice. Everybody in book publishing knows that if Macmillan's editor had not been overcome by a cold while visiting Atlanta, he wouldn't have stayed in bed and read the huge manuscript a lady had given him in the hotel lobby, which was to become, after much editing and renaming, *Gone with the Wind*. Miracles *do* happen.

Editing a manuscript is, however, a whole different story. To begin with, the publishing house already *owns* the manuscript, so the basic decision has been made. Far from hope entering into it, the question is: How can we fix this? And, of course, less usefully, How on earth did we get into this in the first place, and why? There is a kind of Don Juan—like quality to reading manuscripts—the next one, or the one after, might be the love of one's life—but editing them is a slow, painstaking effort to patch up and make presentable what has already been botched and fudged. It is possible to spend hours unraveling someone else's prose or trying to decide what he or she was trying to say and finding some way to make the words express it without starting from scratch in one's own words.

In editing, time becomes meaningless. A single page can sometimes absorb hours, like the most infuriating kind of puzzle. For most editors, there is no time to edit in the office, where they are caught up dealing with the problems of real live authors, talking to agents, being called to meetings, or trying to explain to the marketing people or the business people or the publicity people just what this or that book is about and why it's important to buy it or print fifty thousand copies of it or reject it. This in turn means that editors do most of their serious work at night and over the weekends and explains why so many of the better ones eventually become publishers, if only to have some kind of social or personal life.

It *is* possible to simultaneously overwork and underachieve—indeed, for an editor, nothing is easier. You can spend weeks—months, even—lovingly rewriting a manuscript that was never worth anything in the first place. You know it's somebody else's mistake, even as you sit up late every night with half a dozen sharpened number-two pencils, long after your partner has gone to bed with a martyr's sigh and a strong hint that he or she won't be responsible for what happens if this kind of thing doesn't stop so the two of you can have a normal marriage in which a person doesn't get pushed aside in favor of a manuscript every night of the week and gets fucked like a normal person every once in a while, not to speak of taken to the movies every once in a blue goddamn moon. Still, you just *have* to unravel another hundred pages or so before tomorrow, knowing that in the end nobody will thank you, there won't be a miracle that will make the book become a best-seller, nobody will know or care how awful the manuscript was before you began to work on it, none of your colleagues will thank you for the work you've done, nor will the author, who will think either you destroyed his book or that any improvements were his or her own work. . . .

WELL, I HAD nobody to blame but myself. Nobody had ever promised me that editing was glamorous work. Of course, there's a more glamorous, comparatively well paid side to editing or nobody would do it at all. Successful editors discover important authors, come up with original ideas for books (assuming there's such a thing in book publishing as an original idea, a very open question indeed), get to eat at expensive restaurants at company expense with famous people, travel to London to visit our English cousins (those at any rate who remain after the best of them have come over here to run American publishing houses and spend their summers in the Hamptons), fly to Frankfurt for the book fair, even to L.A. to see celebrities who might write a book (if somebody will pay enough money and get the right person to do the writing for them), and have lunch with movie agents who have seven-figure salaries and movie stars who make eight figures. But the rub is that first they have to learn to edit, at least until they have reached that blessed state where others do their reading and their editing while they sit in a four-window corner office, schmoozing with major agents as they sip their morning espresso and try to decide where to have lunch today.

When you come right down to it, real editing is a profession, unlike publishing, which is merely a business. A publisher, however good, is merely a businessperson, but an editor has a profession, like a doctor, a lawyer, an engineer, or a teacher. And like all the better professions, editing is something of an art, too, if it's done well, and something of a mystery as well. Nobody teaches it, of course; you're born to it, the way a good surgeon is born with the right hands; it's something you either can or can't do, though apprenticeship doesn't hurt. There are still plenty of people who call themselves editors who don't have a clue how to edit at all, and some of them are right there on top, with regular tables at their favorite restaurants and a whole string of best-sellers to their credit, and more power to them, say I, but I don't think of them as the real thing.

There are others—Henry was one of them—who work like a dog on every manuscript that comes before them, laboriously dotting the *i*'s and crossing the *t*'s, but that isn't editing, either. It is for this that publishing houses employ *copy* editors, a whole different species, who prepare the manuscript for the printer and never have regular tables at The Four Seasons or Michael's. Real editors don't necessarily have to spell or articulate the rules of grammar, and not all of them make their living over expensive lunches. The ones who know how to do it are a curious combination of cheerleader and story doctor, fixers-up of lame prose, inventors of the dramatic ending to a scene (instead of the one that fizzles out), ruthless cutters, the kind of people who don't hesitate to challenge everything the author has done in the attempt to make the book *work* the way it could, or the way it was supposed to, and who can sometimes guess what the author was *trying* to do and show him or her how to get there.

To a real editor, cutting a manuscript from seven hundred pages to four hundred, inventing a new title, reshuffling the chapters to give the book a drop-dead beginning and a surprise ending, is all in a day's work, a bravado challenge, like a difficult operation for a surgeon. Real editors, if they're any good, also know—more important still—when to leave well enough alone. "If it's good, don't touch it" might be the first rule of our oath, if we had one.

Because it's a long, painstaking job, largely unrewarded as compared to acquiring the right book or the right author by good luck or shrewdness, real editors are rare and getting rarer still. A certain amount of ego is involved, as well as the skill—the necessary belief that you *know* what will work—and the energy to do it. The best editors slash, cut, change, and rewrite boldly, in ink.

Right from the start, to Henry's shock and indignation, I used ink. Bold self-confidence was the trick, I surmised, watching Bob Gottlieb work. He used a thick, black, felt-tip pen, leaving no possibility for second thoughts or doubts. Between them, Bob and Nina Bourne not only edited in great, slashing strokes, but they also put whole pages of manuscript through their own typewriters, rewriting them completely, and used scissors and Scotch tape to cut pages into ribbons and paste the sentences back together in a different order. The manuscript of *Catch-22*, endlessly retyped, looked at every stage like a jigsaw puzzle as they labored over it, bits and pieces of it taped to every available surface in Gottlieb's cramped office. *That,* I thought, is editing, and I longed to do the same.

NEEDLESS TO say, Will and Ariel Durant did not lend themselves to this kind of slash-and-burn approach. Every one of their words was precious to them, and they did not give up a single one without a long-distance struggle. In any event, their prose, while rather more serviceable than inspiring or stylish, did not require major surgery. I clashed with them from time to time over their interpretation of historical facts. The Durants were masters of that old-fashioned form of history that centers on "great men," and like H. G. Wells they presumed that life is getting better and better with every scientific and philosophical advance. They seemed to have ended their study of how to write world history with Thomas Macaulay, which is just where most modern historians begin, but I was in no position to enlighten them and incurred a good deal of ill will by my marginal notes.

Fate, however, soon brought me better material on which to try out my skills. At some point, Max Schuster had given a contract to William L. Laurence to write a history of the atomic bomb, for Max dearly loved to publish books by major reporters from *The New York Times*, whether they could write or had anything to say or not, the latter being all too frequently the case. Laurence had once been the *Times*'s science reporter and in that capacity had written the first account of the atomic bomb to appear in the paper and had actually seen the Nagasaki bomb explode from one of the chase planes. Now retired and considerably aged, Laurence had waited too long to tell his story, which was sufficiently well known to appear in school textbooks. His manuscript, *Men and Atoms,* suffered from other problems more serious than being ten years too late: He had absolutely no interesting recollections or anecdotes and was unable to write English at all. It turned out that Laurence was a Polish Jew who was self-schooled in science and came to the *Times* in the twenties when science reporting was very small beer indeed. Since most scientific discoveries in those days were made by people who spoke German, Polish, or Hungarian, Laurence's ability to talk to them was more important than his inability to write English, so layers of *Times* copy editors struggled to turn his prose into something approaching the English language as it is understood at the *Times*.

Alas, in his retirement, the *Times*'s famous copyediting desk was no longer at his disposal, and much of his manuscript made hardly any sense. Working with such raw material was a pleasure in its way, particularly since Laurence didn't appear to mind or even notice that I was rewriting his book from stem to stern. The fact was that I had at last found something I could do at least as well as anybody else, and maybe better, even if it was something nobody else really wanted to do at all. Besides, I was taking the first stumbling steps toward becoming a writer. What I was doing was perhaps the lowest form of writing—or at least the most unremunerative—but I still felt a sort of dim creative pride, a foretaste of writing my own material.

Editors, of course, are not supposed to become writers, or at any rate they're not supposed to practice both professions at once, thus crossing over the invisible but very distinct barrier that separates the two. There had been exceptions, but most editors with a yen to write traditionally retired to do so, as Justin Kaplan, Ed Doctorow, Cass Canfield, and Richard Kluger, among others, did, with varying degrees of success.

My next task was to Simonize the prose of a much tougher nut than Bill Laurence: none other than Robert Moses, New York's "master builder" and one of those with whom Max claimed a close friendship—one not, so far as I could tell, reciprocated by Moses himself, who was then at the height of his power as New York City's parks commissioner and head of the Triborough Bridge and Tunnel Authority, which he ruled like a czar, only more so.

Moses had written—or caused to have written for him by his minions—a slim biography of Governor Alfred E. Smith, his mentor in public service. Thanks to years of begging the great man to write a book and promises to publish it, Max Schuster was stuck with it when Moses sent it to him. Of course, what Max had been hoping for was an autobiography, not what amounted to a monograph on a man whose memory (and reputation) FDR had all but eclipsed, but Moses was shrewd enough to take Max up on his promises, and poor Max was too deeply committed to them to object. This particular hot potato was a good learning experience, if only because it taught me that pursuing the great, the near great, or the once great is fraught with peril, the worst of it being the possibility that they will actually deliver a book. Most presidential memoirs—and virtually the entire lists of certain publishers—can be explained this way.

As I was soon to discover, the real difficulty of dealing with Robert Moses was not his vast ego, nor even his abrasive manner, but the fact that his staff had ghosted the book for him, which Moses couldn't bring himself to admit. It was hard enough to deal with the ordinary author's ego, but dealing with the ego of a man who hadn't even written the prose he was defending was a new experience (though one that was to eventually pay dividends when it came to dealing with the memoirs of presidents and CEOs).

Accustomed to dealing with the world as if he were a potentate and responsible to nobody but himself—though his wings were shortly to be clipped—Moses responded to even the smallest editorial question as if it were a challenge to his authority, and he frequently complained about me to Max. Max was a master at soothing hurt feelings, though Moses was no more easily soothed than his patriarchal namesake. At one point, he actually wrote Moses a fulsome letter apologizing for my rewriting the great man's prose and wrote at the top of the copy he sent me: "MVK—Pray pay no attention to this at all. Proverbs, 15:1. Go on with the good work. MLS."

I looked up the reference and it read, "A soft answer turneth away wrath," which was actually as good a formula for a publisher's letter to an irate author as I know and the kind of note that made it hard not to like Max. Max was well aware that Leon Shimkin suspected that he was running something of a vanity press for his friends and that Robert Moses's book was a perfect example, since it was being published only to satisfy the author's ego and could not possibly earn its way. Max, however, deftly persuaded Moses to buy copies for the New York City Parks Department and the Triborough Bridge and Tunnel Authority to give away to important politicians. To Shimkin's dismay, no doubt, the book thus earned a tidy profit.

Shimkin was always on the prowl for ways of proving that Max was playing fast and loose with his money, and he frequently took editors out for lunch to grill them on the subject—even editors as junior as myself. Fortunately, Shimkin was only dangerous as an inquisitor until he had downed the last of his first vodka martini of the lunch. After that, he was voluble, indiscreet, and easily misled. The trick was to avoid seeing him before noon, when his mind was still focused.

Of course, a lot of people suffered from the same problem in those days. Book publishing and drinking had gone hand in hand ever since Horace Liveright kept an open bar in his offices during Prohibition and put a good part of his profits, not to speak of his authors' royalties, into the pockets of bootleggers. Writers have always been notorious drinkers, and those who want to be their editors all too often learn to drink with them.

But it was not just writers and editors who drank. Publishers drank, advertising people drank, in the Christmas season a flood of liquor poured into the production and art departments from grateful printers and suppliers, the sales reps drank (which made the twice-a-year sales conferences of most publishing houses seem like drunken bacchanals), and office parties were occasions of awesome drunken revels. The whole industry sometimes seemed to be kept afloat on a sea of booze.

AS MY first year at S&S came to an end, I felt a certain sense of achievement. I had edited two complete books for Max, however boring they might be, and several for Henry, I was attending editorial board meetings, and I felt myself, at last, to be *part* of something, as if S&S were my home. I had actually, after a good many false starts, been permitted to buy a couple of books myself—a serious *rite de passage* for any editor, since you can only go so far by working on other people's books.

The first I owed to Bob Gottlieb, who taught me the value of buying contemporary French novels as a way of getting started. In the first place, nobody at S&S except Bob and me read French, so there was no objective way in which his claims or mine for a French book could be put to the test; in the second, French books could be bought cheaply, since hardly anybody else in American publishing read the language or took even the slightest interest in the French literary world, which was in any case then at its most hermetic, as if intentionally repelling any possible American interest. As a sideline to his career as a teacher of French literature at NYU, Georges Borchardt acted as the agent for most of the French publishers. He worked out of the living room of his apartment on Sixth Avenue, and since most of his wares were returned to him unread, he was happy to add me to his mailing list. Bob had already bought a series of avant-garde French detective mysteries and an intriguing novel by Michel Butor, then all the rage in Paris, in which the pages, packed in a box instead of bound, were printed on one side only and without page numbers, so that the reader could shuffle the pages like cards and read a novel with a different narrative every time, though the characters stayed the same.

Once Bob had introduced me to Borchardt, I managed to buy a slim, elegant novella by a Spanish nobleman about the Spanish Civil War that had been published in Paris to acclaim. Like most French fiction, it failed over here, but in the meantime I had edited and published a novel of my own, and with that I was content. Success in terms of sales would hopefully come in its own sweet time. In the meantime, I felt myself to be an *editor* in the full meaning of the word.

I also succeeded in buying a more conventional book, for one of my old friends from Oxford, Colin M. Turnbull, had turned up in New York having spent a couple of years in the Ituri Forest of Rwanda-Burundi, living with the Pygmies. Colin, a tall, handsome, and engaging young man who reminded many people of T. E. Lawrence, had already created something of a stir in anthropological circles as the first white man to have lived with these small, secretive people. He had emerged from his stay with them convinced that they had a richer culture than the surrounding tribespeople who had always despised them and passed these attitudes on to the white colonialists. On the basis of a few articles Colin had written for *Natural History*, I persuaded S&S to give him a book contract for $5,000 and started to work with him on an account of his experiences that we eventually called *The Forest People* and which is still in print as of this writing, nearly forty years later.

The atomic bomb, Governor Alfred E. Smith, French fiction, and Pygmies—it did not occur to me at the time, but I was beginning to set a pattern for my future as an editor, which was to have no pattern.

CHAPTER 7

EDITING IS A skilled profession, but it is not one that publishers have ever particularly respected or well rewarded. Ultimately, the big money goes to those who bring in big books. Even if they can't edit worth a damn, somebody can always be found to do the editorial don-keywork needed to make the book publishable. In extreme cases, a free-lance editor can be brought in to get the manuscript in shape, and it is not an accident that most of them are thin, pale, and wear thick specta-cles, since the only jobs in the publishing industry that require more ed-ucation, absorb more hours of painstaking drudgery, and pay less well are copyediting and indexing.

To buy books it is necessary to cultivate agents, but that is easier said than done. Relationships with agents are treasured and closely guarded by senior editors, particularly when it comes to the agents with major clients and a track record of commercial success. It is not that agents themselves are inaccessible—for the most part they are willing to be taken to lunch by just about anyone—it's just that no sensible junior editor wants to step on his superior's toes by poaching. Editor/agent re-lationships have often been forged by years of friendship and mutually shared success, so it's hard for a young and ambitious editor to get to the major agents without giving deep offense to the very people who decide on his or her raise.

This was even more true in the 1950s, when book publishing was a tighter, more "clubby" business, a small world in which everybody knew each other and in which personal relationships counted for every-thing. It was well known and understood that certain big-time agents such as Harold Matson, Sterling Lord, and Scott Meredith submitted their books to Peter Schwed, while others, such as Harold Ober and Paul Reynolds, sent their submissions to Henry Simon. Agents who specialized in more "literary" fiction, such as Candida Donadio and Phyllis Jackson, as well as the more showbiz-oriented agents such as Robert Lantz, Helen Strauss, and Irving Lazar, worked with Bob Gott-lieb. Indeed, Donadio was so close to Gottlieb that some people thought they were the same person. One simply could not pick up the phone and call one of these people to say, "Hi, I'm new at S&S, but I'm looking for some good books, so why don't you send me a manuscript?"

The *Literary Market Place* (*LMP*), the book industry's bible, lists in-numerable agents, but a great many of them are only one or two steps removed from the slush pile. I sent off fulsome letters to any number of them and got back a small avalanche of manuscripts, most of them so dog-eared that they had obviously made the rounds of every publisher in New York, not a few of them even containing previous rejection let-ters. Clearly, it was going to take more than this.

In the end, my first connection to an agent came about through an old Oxford friend, Bob Livingston, who called to say that a friend of *his* on the West Coast had had some dealings with a literary agent in New York who was complaining that he no longer knew anybody at Simon and Schuster. That sounded fishy to me, but Livingston brushed my doubts to one side. "This guy is no *schlepper*," he said. "He's Somerset Maugham's agent."

Having paid homage to Maugham myself at the Villa Mauresque with my Uncle Alex and Alexa, I could hardly fail to be impressed. Maugham was the butt of many stories—most of them, unfortunately, true—but he remained, even in extreme old age, one of the most successful English writers of the twentieth century, as well as one of the century's wittiest and most acerbic misanthropes. Maugham was to grow bitter in his old age and finally lapsed into precarious senility, but in 1959 his was a name still to be reckoned with, so I hastened to call Jacques Chambrun as soon as Livingston had hung up.

The voice that greeted me was low, rich, obviously French in origin, and full of grave courtesy. He said he would be delighted to meet me, all the more so since my family was one he respected deeply as a European and a man of culture. "We Europeans must stick together, *n'est-ce pas?*" he said with a sigh, and we chatted briefly in French, in which he was even more impressive.

I suggested lunch, but after consulting his calendar, lunch proved to be impossible for some time—his engagements were, I must understand, unfortunately unbreakable, since they were with many of the most important people in publishing and the cinema. I suggested that we meet for drinks, but Chambrun, it appeared, did not approve of the American cocktail hour.

I mumbled my agreement. Dinner seemed like a rather big deal to suggest to an agent as important as Chambrun, particularly since I must be small fry from his point of view. What about tea? he asked.

We agreed to meet at the Alhambra Room in a midtown hotel the next afternoon. I had happy visions of good china, polished silver, and many plates of gingersnaps, Bath biscuits, and seedcake, so I was surprised when the hotel turned out to look like what the French call *un hôtel de passe*—that is, one in which rooms are rented by the hour and in which the lobby is full of furtive gentlemen and heavily made-up *filles de joie*.

The Alhambra Room was off the lobby, past a stygian bar, and its name seemed to have influenced the rest of the hotel's decor, which was a combination of early Beverly Hills Spanish and Moorish Gothic. At the entrance I asked the maître d'hôtel—an ancient and poorly shaved European of some kind, dressed in tails so old as to have a shiny green phosphorescence to them—for Mr. Chambrun's table. He lowered the huge red flocked-velvet menu with faded gold tassels that he had been holding in front of him like a shield, as if I was about to attack him with one of the spears from the wall, and bowed, with a faint air of disapproval. "Monsieur le comte vous attend," he said in what was clearly not his native tongue.

Nobody had mentioned to me that Chambrun was a count. I seemed to recall that a Comte de Chambrun had been an eminent diplomat in France at the time of World War One, probably this one's father, I decided.

My mind was therefore not on my surroundings as my Bela Lugosi look-alike led me through the gloom to a tiny table set for two. My host was not in sight, so I sat down and looked around. Only now did I notice that there was an orchestra on a platform decorated with immense ferns. On a small dance floor, a number of elderly citizens were, in fact, dancing a spirited tango. Around me, the people taking their tea were older still. Some of the men actually wore spats, and not a few of the ladies rested their heavily beringed and arthritic hands on silver-handled canes.

The music stopped and one of the dancers, a short, rotund gentleman in a well-cut double-breasted suit, made for my table. He had a bald head and the well-fleshed features of a gourmand. It was an ugly face, pendulous and lumpy, as if molded from plaster that had sagged before drying, but the ugliness had a certain charm and elegance to it. Like many fat men, Chambrun moved gracefully on small feet. His shoes were unusual: narrow, expensive, and well polished, with high-buttoned tops to them in some kind of black stretch material, the sort of thing that Proust might have worn. Everything about him gave off an aura of prosperity and good-natured joie de vivre.

I rose, and we shook hands. I apologized for not having used his title. He waved the matter aside with one hand. The heat of his exertions on the dance floor had sharpened the odor of his eau de cologne and brought a slight beading of perspiration to his brow. He dabbed at it with a silk handkerchief. "We are here in America," he said pleasantly, with an air of noblesse oblige. "One does not bother about such things. I am perfectly happy to be *Monsieur* Chambrun, plain and simple." (I was eventually to discover that he was not even remotely related to the French noble family and as much entitled to be called "Count" as I am.)

Over a pot of tea—brewed with tea bags—and a plate of rather dry-looking petits fours, Chambrun told me of the many sales he had made for Maugham over the years, of his passion for new and exciting novelists, and of his close connections with the leading magazines. Certainly working with a great writer like Maugham was an honor—and a profitable one—but the real pleasure lay in discovering new young talent. He kissed his fingertips. He was discriminating, as he could see that I must be—after all, were we not both Europeans? The kind of books he liked were often *special*, I must understand, not for everyone. He himself was a passionate reader of fiction, in love with the written word. Even so, only if a work of real quality caught his eye did he send it on to a few favored editors who shared his tastes.

That sounded good to me. I did not aspire to be Maugham's publisher yet, after all. New young talent was exactly what I was looking for. Would I like to dance with any of the ladies? Chambrun asked. I declined. Chambrun clearly wanted to get on with his dancing—his feet were tapping in time to the music—so I made my *adieux*, and he promised to send me the work of a few of his very best writers. We should do business together, he hoped, very soon.

Shortly afterward, a steady stream of manuscripts began to arrive from Jacques Chambrun. Strangely enough, they did not seem very different from the ones in the slush pile; some of them, in fact, I even *recognized* from the slush pile. Most of them showed signs of having been mailed out many, many times, despite being accompanied in every case by a letter assuring me that I was the first editor to have the pleasure of reading the book. I had, in fact, the ungenerous impression that he might simply be passing along manuscripts without reading them at all.

There is hardly anything more depressing for a young editor than turning a book down when it has been sent to him by an agent. Chambrun took no offense at all at my sending his books back with long, apologetic letters explaining exactly what was wrong with them. In fact, he even called and invited me to lunch with him at the bar of the Sherry Netherland Hotel, where, apparently, he ate every day. I happened to mention where I was going to Henry Simon, and he raised an eyebrow in surprise. "Chambrun?" he asked, with an unpleasant chuckle. "The so-called Count? Is that charlatan still in business?"

He was not only in business, I said with some heat, but he was sending me manuscripts. Besides, he was Somerset Maugham's agent, which surely counted for something. Henry shook his head gravely, like a doctor confronting a terminal illness. "He *was* Maugham's agent for a while—God knows how. Maugham fired him eventually. It turned out that Chambrun was selling magazine rights to Maugham's stories all over the world without telling Maugham and kept the proceeds for himself. And that's not all . . ."

"Not all" involved a long discussion of agents who actually *charged* writers for reading a manuscript. This custom had been invented by Scott Meredith, who eventually had a stable of poorly paid readers working for him, busily sending back form letters that purported to tell the writer what to do to make his or her book salable to a publisher, for a fee. This practice was anathema to conventional agents, who felt that it was roughly tantamount to stealing pencils from a blind man's cup. Many publishing houses simply refused to do business with Chambrun, Henry said.

I took all this with a grain of salt. Most of the really interesting people one meets in life are rogues, and it did not shock me that Chambrun might be one of them—indeed, it was part of his charm. At the Sherry Netherland bar, where Chambrun was ensconced in a corner banquette, I chose not to bring up the unflattering portrait that Henry had drawn of him. After all, the man was sending me manuscripts, even if they were unpublishable. Other agents might have a better reputation for honesty, but I wasn't getting anything from them.

Whatever else might be phony about him, Chambrun was at least genuinely French. A fastidious eater who did not believe in the American ideal of the light lunch, he ordered elaborate dishes, sent them back to the kitchen when he wasn't happy with them, and took his time over dessert. He did not stint himself on the petits fours that were served with coffee and even wrapped the remaining ones frugally in a paper cocktail napkin to take home. When the check came, we both stared at it for a while, then Chambrun pushed it toward me firmly and without apology and popped a digestive mint into his mouth. He had taught me a basic rule of book publishing, never since forgotten: When an editor has lunch with an agent, the editor always picks up the check.

The flow of manuscripts continued, until one day, to my astonishment, I read one that actually excited me. I was so surprised that I had to read it twice. Even on a second reading, the novel still held my attention. What saved it from being an automatic reject was the fact that the author, Dariel Telfer, was a natural storyteller, with a real subject that she cared (and knew) a lot about: nursing in a big city hospital.

Henry wouldn't want S&S to buy a book from Chambrun, and it was just the kind of novel he hated: unformed, unpolished, raw, and full of sex scenes. It would have to be rewritten, replotted, and reconstructed to make it work, and that was just the kind of thing Henry didn't approve of. Not knowing what else to do with it, I gave it to Bob Gottlieb to read.

Bob had a kind of split personality as an editor: He pursued high culture and low culture with equal intensity and seemed to enjoy both. More extraordinary, he was *good* at both. Apart from skill, shrewd judgment, complete confidence in his own taste (and willingness to submerge it in the interests of commerce when necessary), what Bob had above all was *enthusiasm*. When he liked something, he wanted the whole world to like it, which is what publishing is really about.

Like me, Bob was a fast reader, and the next day he appeared in my windowless cubbyhole cradling the manuscript in his arms, dark eyes blazing with excitement, Napoleonic forelock plastered low on his noble brow. "It's just *great*," he said. "We have to buy it."

I noted, with pleasure rather than dismay, the *we*. I had been longing to work with Bob on something, rather than just looking on, my nose pressed against the windowpane. Bob had much the same effect on me as Irving Thalberg had had on F. Scott Fitzgerald when Fitzgerald went to work as a screenwriter in Hollywood: His energy, boldness, attention to detail, chutzpah, and intelligence set him apart from anyone else at S&S.

Where had the book come from? Bob asked. When I told him, his face darkened a bit, and he bit his lip thoughtfully. "Not so good," he murmured. Then he brightened. I would deal with Chambrun, while Bob would take care of getting the book past Henry and Max.

It needed a lot of work, I suggested. Bob beamed. It needed *everything*, of course, but it had the two things that really made popular fiction sell: energy and sincerity. Dariel Telfer's prose was often muddled and always verbose, but she cared about the nurses and patients in her book and somehow knew how to make the reader care along with her. "If a novel *doesn't* have that, you can't fix it, and if it does, the rest is easy to fix," he said, with the intensity of a real teacher. "It needs to be shorter, of course. And clearer. And it needs a new beginning, and a new end. . . . And of course a *title*."

The title came, almost immediately, from Nina Bourne—*The Care-takers*—but it took a good bit longer for Bob to persuade the editorial board of S&S to let us buy the book. It wasn't just that Jacques Chambrun was the agent, it was more a question of the book itself. Dariel Telfer was as forthright and frank about sex as Grace Metalious had been in *Peyton Place,* though in a slightly more clinical way, inclining one to believe that she was a nurse herself. Nobody but a nurse, in fact, could have written in such detail about what goes on in a big hospital with such authenticity. Still, nurse or not, her sex scenes, tame as they would soon seem in popular fiction, were a source of much concern and heartburn among our elders. Max was deeply opposed to censorship and a passionate defender of the First Amendment, but when push came to shove, he wanted no part of sexually explicit books himself and retreated into mumbling, trembling paralysis when asked to read one. Like his colleagues, he fell back on Voltaire's famous aphorism, "I disapprove of what you say, but I will defend to the death your right to say it." A fine sentiment, but from the mouth of a publisher the equivalent of Pontius Pilate washing his hands. What, after all, is the use of backing the First Amendment, if you haven't got the guts to *use* it? Bob and I found ourselves asking this more and more often as publishing moved with many misgivings into the era in which books such as *The Story of O, Lolita,* and *Portnoy's Complaint* were to become big, popular bestsellers.

Frightened as the older generation was by the kind of language that Telfer used in her novel, they were more frightened still of being thought out of touch with the modern world. Enthusiasm—however ill placed—has always been the currency of book publishing, and Bob's was irresistible. He did not exactly erase the doubts in the minds of those who supposed that he reported to them, but they gave him conditional approval, not quite daring to refuse it. We were to proceed cautiously, he and I, and offer Chambrun a $5,000 advance, on the promise that we would tone down the graphic sex scenes and keep S&S at an arm's length from her agent. Normally an agent receives all the money that comes in, keeps his 10 percent, and forwards the balance to the client. In this case, given Chambrun's reputation, we were to insist that S&S would pay the author directly and send Chambrun his commission separately.

I had anticipated difficulties from Chambrun over this, but he didn't seem at all concerned when I told him, over another luncheon, nor were his feelings hurt. "*Très bien,*" he said. When could he have the contract and his check? It occurred to me that his sangfroid might come from the simple fact that he had no shame.

Up until then I had mostly edited nonfiction. With nonfiction, there was only so much that you could do. You could rewrite it, cut it, sometimes reshape it, but the book was essentially defined by the subject, which you couldn't change without destroying the whole thing. With fiction, however, the only limits are set by the editor's energy and the author's willingness to live with big changes. Character, motivation, and plot can be changed, subplots and minor characters can be thrown out, whole scenes eliminated or created from scratch. After all, why not? It works in the movie business, where stories go through countless metamorphoses and countless hands before reaching the screen. Apart from his shrewd judgment and his ability to know the difference between salable trash and real quality (something that often gets hopelessly blurred in editors' minds), Bob's real talent was that he had no compunction in applying to a novel the methods of the movie business.

Telfer turned out to be a plump, gentle woman from Colorado who had fallen into Chambrun's hands by accident and was willing enough to let Bob and me tear her manuscript apart and to write endless new scenes to replace the ones we had cut. It is, I discovered, always much easier to do this with first novelists, whose major anxiety is whether or not their book will ever get published at all. Step by step, we reconstructed Telfer's book into what it ought to have been in the first place: a strong, shocking "commercial" novel with a simple story line and a lot of sex. The key, as I learned from Bob during many evenings in his apartment working on the manuscript, was to keep what was best about the book— its obvious sincerity and the author's righteous anger about the way the system treated decent nurses and patients—and eliminate what wasn't needed or didn't make sense. I had admired from afar the way he had revamped *Catch-22,* but now I was doing it myself, at his side, and could see that what was emerging, draft after draft, was a much stronger book. Since then, I have done this, with others or by myself, a hundred times and always found that nothing in publishing gives me more satisfaction if the book works. Some of these editorial reconstructions led to enormous best-sellers such as Shirley Conran's *Lace* or Jacqueline Susann's *The Love Machine,* others—many—were a lot of work for no result, but the fascination has never worn off. It is my substitute for Scrabble or crossword puzzles and perhaps explains why I do neither.

Of course there is nothing new to this. Maxwell Perkins's total reconstruction of Thomas Wolfe's sprawling novel *Look Homeward, Angel* is something of a publishing legend, but Perkins was forgiven because he was working on *literature*. What irked our colleagues at S&S was that Telfer wasn't a "serious" writer in their eyes and that we were therefore helping somebody who didn't *deserve* to be published in the first place. Henry, particularly, felt strongly that we were somehow prostituting the profession. In fact, by the time we had finally finished rewriting and retyping *The Caretakers*, it had become something of a symbol of the generational clash at S&S and perhaps the most disliked book the house had ever published. Naturally, we saw all this as mere sour grapes, old-fashioned fuddy-duddy thinking by people whose idea of a good read was Will Durant (Max Schuster), Henry Morton Robinson, the author of *The Cardinal* (Henry Simon), or P. G. Wodehouse (Peter Schwed).

The truth is that this kind of intergenerational fight is normal in book publishing, even healthy—indeed, its absence is usually a sure sign that an editorial group is ready to be certified brain-dead. Younger editors always want to publish books that trouble their elders for one reason or another, and this is normal, even desirable, or the book industry would still be chugging along happily publishing nothing more shocking than Marjorie Kinnan Rawlings's *The Yearling* or Felix Salten's *Bambi*. It is equally axiomatic that once the Young Turks have pushed their elders out of their corner offices into pasture and taken power themselves, they are likely to become as cautious and conservative as their predecessors were. At S&S, for example, the very same people who had fought to publish books by Jerry Rubin (who caused a seismic stir in the publishing industry by urging high school students to burn down their schools) or the Venceremos Brigade's account of their adventures in Castro's Cuba, or Bob Woodward and Carl Bernstein's *All the President's Men*—all books that seemed to wiser, older, more cautious heads dangerous, subversive, or irresponsible—found themselves twenty years later making headlines by turning down Bret Easton Ellis's novel *American Psycho*.

The Caretakers was not the kind of book that was likely to have any real effect on the culture or on history—though it *was* the first to portray the lives of nurses, doctors, and patients in a realistic light—but it had a decided effect on S&S. In the hands of Bob Gottlieb and Nina Bourne, the book was talked up outside the house while it was still in manuscript, a process that I had not yet witnessed at first hand, and that I now realized for the first time was a question of focus. Not a phone call or a letter went out from them that did not mention *The Caretakers*. Extraordinary efforts were made to get the advance bound-galley proofs into sympathetic hands for its first prepublication review in *Publishers Weekly*. Long before the book was out, people in the trade were already talking as if they had read it.

As things turned out, not even all these combined efforts could float *The Caretakers* onto the *New York Times* hardcover best-seller list (the Holy Grail of book publishing), but to everybody's astonishment the mass-market paperback rights were bought before publication by Victor Weybright of New American Library for $90,000. It would be as if someone were to pay over a million dollars for the paperback rights of a first novel today, perhaps even more. Anybody might have thought that we had somehow upset the balance of nature by selling the book for such a lot of money. It was as if we had opened the gates and let the Vandals into Rome.

It was my first experience with being criticized for having succeeded. Within S&S, the general feeling was that selling a sexy first novel for this kind of money was somewhat disgraceful, even shameful. When Henry heard about it, he shook his head sorrowfully and wondered what the world was coming to. Max seemed too embarrassed to talk about it at all, while Leon Shimkin merely wondered why we hadn't let Pocket Books have *The Caretakers* if it was so valuable. Inadvertently, we had changed the rules. All of a sudden, first novels seemed potentially valuable, the slush heap a potential gold mine.

More important, perhaps, the sale of *The Caretakers* ushered in the age of the high-stakes paperback auction. Up until then, mass-market paperback sales had represented a nice windfall for the hardcover publisher, but the sales of *The Caretakers* set off a long period in which popular fiction (and even some nonfiction) was sold to paperback publishers for ever larger amounts. We had not only hit the jackpot but raised the stakes for everyone else. Worse still, from the perspective of the old guard, we had drawn the attention of the media and of Wall Street. A business in which an unknown author's first novel could sell for $90,000 overnight—before it was even available in the stores— sounded to many people more like the movies than their traditional idea of book publishing, and not everybody thanked us for what we'd done.

Dariel Telfer, far off in Pueblo, Colorado, was grateful, of course (unlike a good many authors, she remained graceful and kind under the pressure of success, although, to our regret, she never managed to write another book like *The Caretakers*, despite many tries), though slightly puzzled by the fuss. For Bob, this was another step on his way to confirming his reputation as a major publishing figure. He had proven he could publish groundbreaking literature successfully with *Catch-22* and "commercial" women's fiction with *The Best of Everything;* now he had turned an unpublishable first novel into a record-breaking paperback sale. He seemed to the publishing world like a miracle worker, though inside S&S this new triumph merely hardened the rivalry between himself and his elders. For myself, the paperback sale of *The Caretakers* had a whole host of consequences. For the first time, my salary was raised to a point where we could actually *live* on it—up until then, I had been making less money than my wife, who was still working as a secretary. I was moved out of the windowless cubbyhole in which I had been placed as Henry's editorial assistant and given an office of my own, with a window, though I would continue to work on Henry's books. Perhaps most important, it moved me firmly over into Bob's camp and ushered in one of the happiest periods of my career. Bob was not only a natural and gifted mentor, he soon became a close friend with a wonderful capacity for making even the most difficult problem seem like fun and a sense of humor that saw him through even the darkest of publishing crises. If I had felt any secret regrets at not having gone into the movie business, I lost them now in the warmth of being accepted into Bob's band of friends and admirers. Even without my new office and more money, I would have been happy.

The only person, in fact, who didn't do well out of *The Caretakers* was Jacques Chambrun. At first, he was happy enough—even astonished—that a submission of his should have made so much money, but then he began to brood, no doubt on the fact that all he was getting from us was his 10 percent. It must have seemed to him unjust that we had given him a great success and at the same time taken away his chance to exploit it.

He invited me to his apartment for a drink—a strange place in which the elevator, run by an elderly man in shabby livery who looked as if he might be an extra in a horror movie, took me straight up to Chambrun's apartment. The elevator opened with a crash, depositing me straight into his living room, which seemed to have been furnished with leftovers from a theatrical warehouse. Chambrun was on his feet, as nattily dressed as ever, opening a bottle of champagne; lounging on his sofa was a lush young woman—young, at any rate, in comparison to Chambrun—dressed in a kind of kimono or wrapper and smoking a cigarette in an ivory holder. Chambrun introduced her as his secretary, though from the length of her lacquered fingernails I judged this to be a euphemism.

We toasted our mutual success, but there was an air of sadness to the proceedings. Now that *The Caretakers* was making so much money, Chambrun said, perhaps we would like to reconsider our arrangement and return to the conventional author/agent relationship? I said no as politely as I could. Chambrun was not surprised, but there was a certain lowering of the temperature in his voice, a sense that between one gentleman and another I had somehow disappointed him.

I left sooner than I had expected to and never got another manuscript from him again.

CHAPTER 8

I WAS SOON getting them from other agents, however. Success breeds success, in book publishing as elsewhere. One book that works encourages other agents to send books—a process that is reversed when failure sets in. I was beginning to put down roots at S&S—framed photographs on the wall, pipe rack and tobacco humidor on the desk, just the kind of domestic touches that I had always despised in other people's work spaces. Indeed, I was inadvertently in the process of doing what so many other people my age were: I was making my work the center of my life.

The process was so gradual and natural that I scarcely noticed it; like so many others, I told myself that I was working to make a living, putting in long hours to jump-start my career, doing it all for Casey's benefit in the long run, but of course none of that was really true. S&S simply seemed to me a far more exciting and fulfilling place than home; I dreaded weekends and holidays when the office was closed and put aside as much of Saturdays and Sundays as I could to read manuscripts and edit, missing the camaraderie, impatient to get back to the office on Monday morning.

The word *workaholic* had not yet been invented, but the phenomenon was almost as widespread in publishing as alcoholism, and only too frequently (though not in my case) the two went hand in hand. But the people I liked and admired most were those who stayed in the office the latest, and I simply fell into the habit of being one of them. I very often found myself walking home with Bob, who lived about two blocks away from us, after the cleaners had driven us out of our offices. Our standing joke revolved around S&S's treasurer, Emil Staral, who had been appointed by Shimkin and was in the habit of walking around the office at five-thirty every afternoon to make sure the lights were turned out. If you weren't in your office and the lights were on, he turned them off and left a little note on your desk so you would know he had been there. If you were in your office, he would pause at your door and with a frown explain that almost no work done after hours was likely to be worth the amount it cost in terms of wasted electricity—he knew, he had done the calculation. Staral, like Shimkin, was of the old school: A penny saved was a penny earned, and no expenditure, however necessary it might seem to others, was ever a good idea. If it had been up to him, we would have bought no books at all.

Looking back now, I am not so sure that Staral, who was in every respect a character straight out of the pages of Molière, was not right after all. Most of the people I knew in the late fifties and sixties ended up divorced in the seventies, and by the time the eighties rolled around they were busily trying to find in a new marriage the domestic happiness they had fled from when they were just starting up the career ladder. I was no exception.

It was, in retrospect, a strange period, the sunset of the Fifties, before rock and roll, Vietnam, the sexual revolution, and women's liberation changed all the rules we were living by. One's own photograph from that time now seems to be one of a complete stranger. It is hard to summon up a world so different in so many ways from the present and yet so close, a world where manual typewriters were still in use, in which the orders were counted by a couple of gray-haired ladies, the accountants still used ledgers, and there was a real, live telephone operator with a switchboard on the premises. In the age before the photocopy machine, carbon copies still reigned supreme, and everybody in the editorial department had black smudges on their fingers and shirt cuffs, the proud badge of the profession, like a coal miner's blackened skin.

Wives still stayed home while their husbands went off to work, and they went away with the kids for the summer while their husbands stayed in town during the week, and everyone tried as hard as they could to lead the same kind of lives their parents had, or at least one of which their parents might *approve*. Rebellion was unthinkable, and what little there was of it took place furtively, in the form of heavy drinking and the office affairs that often accompanied it. Men still ran the world, unquestioned (except at home), and although there were more women executives in book publishing than in most other businesses, real power remained in the hands of men. There were exceptions—a couple of the more powerful agents were women: Helen Strauss of the William Morris Agency, Phyllis Jackson and Kay Brown at the Ashley-Famous Agency (eventually to become International Creative Management), as well as a handful of important publishing executives.

S&S had a few of what were then known as "ballsy" women, including the head of the production department, who, when Emil Staral's even more penny-pinching deputy tried to end an argument with her by stepping into the men's room, followed him in and continued it, while he stood in the urinal, fly halfway unzipped, shocked into silence. On the whole, though, it was still thought of as a man's world, even though much of the useful work in it was done by women.

A publishing firm like S&S or Random House or Knopf was still small enough physically that all its major components except warehousing and shipping could be contained in one place, sometimes, as in the case of S&S, on one floor. This meant that every department was within reach, and that department heads were constantly in and out of each other's offices. In the days when Dick Simon had been active at S&S, he liked to open his door and shout when he wanted to call his troops together for a quick meeting, and Max could still have done so, had he been of a mind to, which he wasn't, being more concerned with hiding from his troops than gathering them. The advent of big news—a Book-of-the-Month Club selection, a new best-seller, the delivery of an important or eagerly awaited manuscript—was signaled by a sudden burst of noise and activity in the hallway, which brought everyone running to find out what was going on. When Bob had something in hand that he really liked, he would read aloud from it in the hall and was quickly surrounded by people urging him to buy the book or, on some occasions, to turn it down. Enthusiasm not only was held to be the life force of book publishing but also was instantly available and rapidly communicated to everyone in the company, right down to the clerks, accountants, typists, and mail-room boys.

The sales conference, at which the sales reps (who were then referred to, altogether accurately, as "the men") were introduced to the next season's list of books by the editors, was held in a New York hotel in one day, as opposed to the present custom of spending the best part of a week at some lush Florida resort hotel. Back then, the sales force of a major publisher consisted of perhaps a dozen men, most of them grizzled veterans of weeks on the road touting the list to skeptical small-town bookstore owners who mostly wanted new editions of the Bible.

PROGRESS IN book publishing sometimes seems erratic and accidental, perhaps because book publishers are almost always surprised by their own successes. None of us could have guessed that one of the biggest books in S&S's history would come from one of our fellow editors, Joseph Barnes. Once a speechwriter for Wendell Willkie, editor of *P.M.*, and former foreign editor of the New York *Herald Tribune*, Barnes was editing a long and much-delayed history of Nazi Germany. Barnes himself was something of an exercise in deliberate obscurity. In the days of his association with Willkie, the Republican presidential candidate nominee who was referred to in the Democratic press as "the barefoot boy from Wall Street," Barnes had been in the limelight, but his leftist views, mild as they had been, eventually made him unemployable, except in book publishing, which had not seemed like an important enough industry to merit the attention of the witch-hunters during the McCarthy era. Since Shimkin had been Marshall Field's éminence grise during the period when Field was launching *P.M.*, it is possible that Barnes's job as an S&S editor represented the payment of an old debt, or perhaps some residual guilt on Shimkin's part at the abrupt closing of *P.M.*, but whatever the reason, Barnes sat in his small office every day, chain-smoking as he went over galleys with a skeptical eye. He was a tall, well-dressed, debonair, and deeply dignified figure, full of old-fashioned but rather remote courtesy and richly cynical in the manner of newspapermen the world over. Every day he sauntered off to lunch at the Overseas Press Club, a dashing brown fedora cocked over one eye, and a well-worn foreign correspondent's trench coat draped over his

arm. He returned at three, his cheeks slightly rosier from the two martinis he invariably drank before lunch, for another afternoon of silent ab-
sorption in his galleys. He did not attend meetings or join in the noisy
commotions that exploded from time to time in the hallway, nor join the
group of Young Turks in Bob's office. He was like a man who carried
some dark tragedy on his shoulders that separated him from ordinary
mortals, which was, in fact, not very far from the case, for Barnes had
been close to power until Willkie's defeat and the rising tide of
McCarthyism washed him up in a small office at S&S, with a part-time
secretary he shared with another editor.

The book that Joe Barnes was working on with such monastic devotion—and which was growing larger and larger every day—was
being written by his old friend and colleague William L. Shirer, who had
been a noted foreign correspondent for CBS until his leftist ideas and
connections made him as unemployable as Barnes. From time to time,
Emil Staral would bring Shimkin's attention to how late the manuscript
was, and Shimkin would order Staral to cancel the contract and get the
company's $25,000 back, but every time this happened, Barnes put on
his jacket, went downstairs to see Shimkin, and returned with a reprieve
of six months for Shirer. Whatever Barnes had on Shimkin, it was
enough to keep Shirer writing the book that would eventually become
The Rise and Fall of the Third Reich.

At the time, however, the book was not only several years late but
was called *Hitler's Nightmare Empire,* planned for a first printing of five
thousand copies and treated pretty much as a relief project for Shirer,
whom most people correctly saw as having been spinelessly abandoned
by CBS. The jacket for *Hitler's Nightmare Empire* had already been designed and appeared in the catalog while Shirer was still trying to finish
the book. It was dark bloodred, with the title spelled out in spiky letters
of barbed wire. The subtitle, appearing in small letters at the bottom,
was "The Rise and Fall of the Third Reich."

Being something of a student of German history and of World War
Two, I was one of the very few people at S&S apart from Barnes himself who had actually read Shirer's book. Barnes had loaned me the galleys, painstakingly corrected by him in his small, tidy hand. He had
apparently decided to act as his own copy editor and fact checker, perhaps as some kind of penance. Unlike Bob, Barnes did not exactly communicate enthusiasm. He was obviously aware that Shirer's book was
something special, but he seemed to have erected an invisible wall of re-

serve, self-imposed, between himself and strangers. I thought he was, to use Graham Greene's phrase, "a burnt-out case," determined to maintain his dignity despite the aura of betrayal, failure, and disappointment that surrounded him. He was not a man to blow his own horn or call attention to one of his books, and he gave the impression of being above commerce or possibly unaware of it.

I mentioned the book to Bob, who was inclined to view the books of other editors as impediments to his own, but he had a certain respect for Joe Barnes, perhaps because Barnes was so clearly not a threat to him and perhaps also because he was a man of old-fashioned culture, integrity, and learning, whose taste in literature, though very different from Bob's own, Bob respected. Bob came back the next morning with the galleys in a paper shopping bag, aglow with enthusiasm, certain that he was carrying a major best-seller. "Of course, the jacket has to go," he said. "And the title."

Despite a volcanic eruption on the part of Frank Metz, the art director, the jacket was scrapped. Nina Bourne, challenged to come up with a new title, took one look at the old jacket and said, "Why not use the subtitle for the title?" Shortly afterward, with a black jacket bearing a swastika, a stroke of genius on Metz's part, and the title *The Rise and Fall of the Third Reich,* the book was relaunched and went on to become one of the greatest (and longest-running) successes in publishing history. A last-minute problem arose when bookstores all over the country protested displaying the swastika and threatened not to stock the book. The problem had to be taken all the way up to Max Schuster, whose dislike of the swastika was outweighed by his reluctance to be told what to do by booksellers.*

Like so many of the crises that occur between publishers and booksellers, this one proved to be a tempest in a teacup and soon died down—indeed, the swastika, which had hitherto been deemed unusable on book jackets soon became so popular, particularly on the covers of mass-market fiction, that the sight of the average mass-market display would have pleased Goebbels.

"It's better to be lucky than smart," a future president of S&S was to take as his motto, and it's true enough, though it is probably better still to be lucky *and* smart. Certainly, it's typical of the publishing in-

---

* Booksellers had threatened not to carry the first crossword-puzzle book with which Simon and Schuster had launched their company, on the grounds that because it had a pencil attached to it on a string it was a novelty item, not a book, something Max had neither forgotten nor forgiven.

dustry that a book that was long overdue and that might easily have been canceled for lateness—and that was rescued from obscurity only by luck and Bob Gottlieb's shrewd, last-minute repackaging—should have brought S&S a huge profit, enviable publicity, and every possible award and honor. Everybody was delighted by this enormous and unexpected success, except, ironically, Shirer, who in order to avoid what were then very high taxes had insisted on putting a "limitation clause" in his contract, stipulating that he would not receive more than $25,000 a year in royalties. Infuriated that S&S was soon sitting on millions of dollars of his money without having to pay him any interest, he spent much of the rest of his life trying to undo it.

I HAD my own unhappy authors to deal with. The Durants, who had hitherto remained in Los Angeles, communicating by letter, were descending on New York, and Max was working overtime to ensure that they got star treatment from everybody at S&S. The party to greet the Durants was held at the Schusters' New York apartment. The lone Chagall that constituted Max and Ray's claim to be art collectors and connoisseurs hung above the fireplace, but for the most part the walls were covered by handsome bookcases, filled with stately S&S books, all of them arranged neatly in some order of Max's devising. Among the many sources of frustration for S&S's art director was the fact that the first thing Max did with a book was to take its dust jacket off and dispose of it. All the books in Max's shelves showed only their bindings.

During the course of editing *The Age of Reason Begins*, volume seven of *The Story of Civilization*, I had corresponded a lot with the Durants and spoken to them often enough on the telephone to feel that I knew them, though they appeared to treat the telephone with suspicion. As a rule, neither of them took telephone calls alone. They spoke on separate extensions, Will's voice ghostly, polite, and distant, Ariel's louder and more aggressive. She often disagreed with her husband, and he often deferred to her. When he did not, she was in the habit of calling later, surreptitiously, as if afraid that he might overhear her, to instruct me to ignore his wishes. "Pay no attention to what Will told you," she would whisper urgently. "He doesn't know what he's talking about."

Their persons matched their telephone voices. Although both of them were diminutive, Ariel was clearly the more dominating presence and therefore seemed to loom larger than Will. Durant wore a well-worn, professorial blue suit. He had a good head of silver hair, a pink complexion, a neat little mustache, and a rather nervous expression, his eyes constantly darting toward Ariel as if in fear. He rather resembled a ferret. Mrs. Durant had the broad cheekbones of a Russian peasant woman, a fierce, prominent nose, dark, penetrating eyes, and large, mannish, ink-stained hands. She wore her gray hair in a kind of page-boy that looked as if she had done it herself at home with nail scissors, and her clothing seemed to have been made from woolens woven at home by a not particularly gifted weaver—they were basically shape-less and made up of many very heavy layers. Since it was warm in the apartment, I found it hard to imagine how she could bear to be so heavily dressed, but she never took a layer off. Both of them wore health-faddist "space shoes" that were molded to their feet, giving them ungainly duck-footed appearances.

Will's handshake was warm but a little tentative. The Durants and I had clashed mildly from time to time during the editing of *The Age of Reason Begins*. Will saw history as the story of humanity's constant struggle against ignorance and barbarism and preferred to write about art, philosophy, architecture, and poetry—i.e., "civilization"—than about warfare, battles, and diplomacy. I conceived it to be my duty to balance this and was constantly urging him to add more about the military and political side of history and correcting him on the subject of battles and armaments. He looked me up and down. "I was expecting somebody quite different," he said. "More like the elder von Moltke."

I apologized for not wearing my monocle, and we both laughed. Mrs. Durant did not. Her handshake was fierce, and her expression bellicose enough to satisfy Field-Marshal von Moltke himself. "Isn't it disgusting?" she said in a gravelly stage whisper, audible, I felt sure, to Ray Schuster, who was standing a few feet away, Max at her side looking as if he had wandered in by mistake. "My poor Will labors away, half blind, year after year, for a pittance, mere *pennies,* while *they*"—she tossed her head in the direction of the Schusters—"live like kings on his sweat."

"There, there," her husband said, patting her hand. She withdrew it sharply, not to be mollified. "If they think giving us a party will make up for it all," Ariel continued, her voice rising steadily in volume, "they can *forget* it."

Her voice was low and guttural and her expression that of Madame

Defarge and her *tricoteuses* friends demanding the guillotine for an aristocrat. "You should *see* him," she said, "working until midnight, *past* midnight often, sitting in his chair with a pad on his lap, writing, writing, writing, while I look up the references for him. . . . And *they* go on world cruises in the meantime. . . . They suck his *blood*."

I was about to point out that the Durants had earned formidable amounts of royalties over the years, which, to judge from the way Ariel dressed, they must be hiding in their mattress, but it seemed wiser to humor her. Neither Durant drank, nor did they touch the hors d'oeuvres, Will because he was a vegetarian and Ariel because she would rather have put molten lead in her mouth than the Schusters' miniature Swedish meatballs and tiny wieners on toothpicks.

We chatted about history for a while—Ariel's view of it was darker and more Manichean than her husband's, which possibly explains the tone of pessimism that crept into the later volumes of the series as she took on a more active writing role and won her place as coauthor—until Ray Schuster, apparently determined to play out her role as hostess, offered to take us on a tour of the apartment.

Ariel submitted to this unwillingly, her expression one of furious resentment, which reached its peak when we paused to view the Schusters' Chagall. "Bought with our sweat and blood," she hissed loudly, at which point Ray wisely decided not to continue the tour. (God knows what Ariel would have said at the sight of Ray's dressing room or her closets.) Shortly, word came back that Mrs. Schuster wasn't feeling well and that I should take the Durants out to dinner, together with whatever S&S personnel I might think it appropriate to invite, and the cocktail party ground to a merciful end.

Perhaps because I had taken them to dinner, the Durants came to the conclusion that I was on their side. They found me frivolous, insufficiently attentive to details, and reactionary in my view of history and made no secret of it, but all of this they could and did forgive so long as they could grumble about the Schusters to me and count on me to get Shimkin to release their royalty checks a few days early. Had I known that this relationship was destined to continue for another decade, I might have tried to correct their opinion of me, but I let it go and thus became stuck with my role.

Occasionally, over the years, they came to New York, but the cocktail party in their honor was never repeated. Ray absolutely forbade it.

CHAPTER 9

*T*HE REAL NEWS in book publishing wasn't about books. In fact it passed most of us by, probably because we were looking in the wrong direction.

In October 1959, a revolution of sorts had occurred when Bennett Cerf and Donald Klopfer took Random House public at $11.25 a share (it rose to $14 the next day and was soon selling for $45), setting off a boom in publishing stocks that quickly drew other companies, including S&S, into the stock market. It is probably coincidental (though ironic) that the moment when book publishing became the darling of Wall Street, ushering in a long period of mergers and acquisitions which is not yet over nearly forty years later, began with the death of Dick Simon.

Dick Simon, *The New York Times* noted with a rare touch of irony in its obituary of him, had persuaded a *Reader's Digest* writer to turn an article of his into a book called *Sudden Death and How to Avoid It,* sold over 260,000 copies of it, and was now dead himself at the age of sixty-one. The age of the entrepreneurial publisher, whose drive and personal taste was enough to make a publishing house grow and thrive, was over.

Dick was, in fact, a victim of the same forces that had persuaded Cerf and Klopfer to turn Random House public, a combination of success and undercapitalization that had led Schuster, Simon, and Shimkin to sell S&S to Marshall Field III in 1946. By 1957, when Max and Leon bought the company back, Dick was too ill and too depressed to join them. He had become a rich man, at the price of his own health, sanity, and vitality. Cerf eulogized Dick in the *Saturday Review*: "He talked vaguely of starting another publishing house of his own," Cerf wrote, "but his heart wasn't in it . . . and he retreated into a cheerless world of his own. He spent his last days huddled in a heavy topcoat in an over-heated room, pulling down the shades on the windows and locking the doors. He had hit upon this method of shutting out death."

There was going to be a lot of this sort of sadness going around shortly in the publishing world, though thankfully not always of the tragic sort that engulfed poor Dick Simon. Shortly afterward, the Los

Angeles Times-Mirror Corporation bought New American Library; Macmillan bought Crowell-Collier; Western Publishing, Harcourt, Brace, and Holt, Rinehart, and Winston went public; Times Books and Bernard Geis Associates were founded; and, most significant of all, Random House acquired Alfred A. Knopf for about three million dollars in Random House stock.

The Random House/Alfred A. Knopf merger astonished everyone in book publishing. H. L. Mencken had called Knopf "the perfect publisher," and while that might have been going too far, there is no doubt that the Knopfs' pursuit of perfection and elegant taste made their house very special. Alfred Knopf had never bothered to disguise the mild contempt in which he held other, lesser publishers, including Cerf and Klopfer, which made it all the more surprising that he and Blanche sold their firm. One reason was that their son Alfred Knopf, Jr. ("Pat"), had felt obliged to leave in 1959 to cofound a new publishing house of his own, Atheneum, at which point his father, who had never paid much attention to his heir, began to brood darkly over the fact that he now had none. Knopf was reported to have been deeply grieved by his son's departure, although he seemed to most outsiders to have done everything possible to bring it about.*

The Random House acquisition of Knopf made it clear that from now on the real money in books was going to be made not by writing or publishing but by buying and selling the publishing companies themselves. Although Cerf remarked that he "had every intention of continuing to publish books that lose money," Knopf, in his Olympian way, caught the spirit of the merger better when he remarked "that the level of American publishing [was] already so low that the journey to Wall Street will make no difference." Hardly was the ink dry on that deal than Random House also acquired Pantheon, which had been founded in 1942 by Helen and Kurt Wolff and was the most "European" of New York houses, with an enviable reputation for literary quality.

Less than four years later, Random House itself was acquired by RCA, partly in the belief that there was some kind of synergy between radio and television broadcasting and the book publishing business, setting a pattern for the future acquisition of S&S by Gulf and Western (which owned Paramount) and of G. P. Putnam by Universal-MCA. Of

---

* It is a measure of things to come in the publishing industry that Atheneum was later acquired by Macmillan, after the latter firm was taken over by that leviathan of corporate crookery Robert Maxwell, and vanished altogether as an imprint after S&S acquired Macmillan in the wake of Maxwell's mysterious death.

course, it was not show business that was driving these acquisitions at first—no movie studio has ever been foolish enough to buy a publishing house merely to get a crack at novels that they could see anyway and for the most part wouldn't want. Instead, there was a starry-eyed belief in the future of educational publishing as a growth industry (the syllogism was "more children—more schoolbooks"), mixed with a hefty dose of good, old-fashioned greed.

It was clear that the book-publishing business was about to undergo a process of radical change at just the moment when unprecedented paperback sales such as those of *The Caretakers* and deals such as the one for *The Carpetbaggers* were raising the stakes dramatically for authors as well. Irving Wallace's departure from Knopf over *The Chapman Report* was, in fact, a sign of the times. He came to S&S and Pocket Books in a deal that raised eyebrows throughout the publishing business. If the publishers thought they were going to get rich courtesy of Wall Street without the authors demanding their share, they were much mistaken.

B OOK PUBLISHING before the early 1960s was a remarkably stable industry. People often worked at the same company for years, often for a lifetime, while most authors tended to remain loyal to the house that published them. Both Hemingway and Fitzgerald were published by Scribner's for decades, while their editor, the fabled Maxwell Perkins, spent his whole career at Scribner's. Nobody in the book-publishing business in the 1940s or 1950s could have predicted that authors and editors would soon be switching from house to house with such rapidity that *Publishers Weekly* would find it hard to keep up with them, while the companies themselves changed hands almost as quickly.

Clearly, if book publishers were going to take their companies public for big bucks or merge with each other in pursuit of market share (a hitherto unknown concept in the book business), both their employees and their authors would soon be looking for better deals. Book publishers had always been inclined to tell young job-seekers, with a certain amount of pride, that this wasn't the right business to be in if you wanted to get rich—publishing wasn't about *money,* it was about *books.* You had to love doing it, and most people did.

One reason why publishing had remained a kind of upper-class WASP enclave for so long was that you really needed an independent income to live a decent life on the kind of salary most publishers were still paying in the 1950s. For years, secretaries had traditionally been hired from the ranks of well-off friends' daughters, as if a few years as a publishing assistant after Wellesley or Radcliffe or Smith was a kind of finishing school. Editors did not fare much better.

The word *exploitation* would have shocked people like Dick Simon or Bennett Cerf, but in fact the wage patterns of the book business bore some resemblance to those of the sweatshop, with the difference that since the book business wasn't supposed to be about money, the owners actually claimed that better salaries and benefits for employees or better advances for authors would destroy whatever it was that made producing books different from producing other, less exalted articles of trade. The subject of money was felt to be unseemly, the kind of thing that a gentleman ought not to think or talk about, let alone a lady. If publishers could be said to believe in anything, it was that book publishing was "an occupation for gentlemen," so much so that one book publisher even used the phrase as the title of his memoirs.

If the "new," mostly Jewish, publishing houses shared anything in common with their WASP predecessors and rivals it was the genial assumption that people who worked in the book business did it—or *ought* to do it—for the love of books. Since few white-collar workers in the book industry are unionized, there was no particular pressure on publishers to raise salaries or increase benefits. Furthermore, so long as most of the big firms were privately owned, nobody knew exactly what anybody else was making, let alone what the owners were taking home in profits.

The Random House decision to go public inadvertently put an end to this cozy tradition of silence. A company that is traded publicly has to list what it pays its directors and senior corporate officers, as well as its principal stockholders. The owners of the major publishing houses had always lived well, though usually with a certain discretion, since none of them was anxious to stimulate greed and envy among their employees and authors. Most publishers carefully avoided such obvious displays of wealth as chauffeured limousines and private dining rooms. Indeed, the only person who ever parked a Rolls-Royce in the courtyard of the Random House mansion at Madison Avenue and Fiftieth Street was the author John O'Hara, on his annual visit to his publisher.

Now, with publishers getting rich overnight by selling their companies or going public with them, the sense of embarrassment about money that people in publishing circles had always affected vanished just as quickly. Contrary to what had always been believed, it appeared there *was* a pot of gold at the end of the rainbow, and everybody wanted a share of it.

MY OWN regular salary review was invariably an occasion very similar to that of asking a headmaster a question about sex, and it produced a similar combination of embarrassment and evasion, along with a long and self-pitying account of how disappointing the results of the previous year had been and the sad state of the book business in general. I was lucky, Henry Simon (or later, Peter Schwed) would tell me sorrowfully, to be getting a raise at all, and small as it might seem to me in financial terms, it represented a real vote of confidence in my future at S&S. Max Schuster, it goes without saying, was protected from having to talk about money at all, and Leon Shimkin, to whom this distasteful task was usually delegated, had been known to cry real tears when describing the firm's financial affairs and the state of the industry to those who came to him seeking a raise.

At about the same time as the Random House/Knopf merger made the headlines, however, Paul Gitlin made his appearance at S&S and changed the hitherto even course of my life.

Previously, literary agents had played a fairly small role in the publishing business, as they were resented deeply by the older generation of publishers. Even the more powerful agents, such as Harold Matson or Paul Reynolds, were reasonable enough when it came time to negotiate a contract for one of their authors and more likely to counsel their clients toward patience and compromise than greed and threats. Far from attacking the publishing establishment, they felt themselves to be part of it and behaved with a certain self-conscious dignity, as if to make it clear that literary agenting was a respectable profession, like being a lawyer or a clergyman. Theirs, too, was a WASP profession, apart from a few newcomers such as Scott Meredith, and they looked down with undisguised contempt on the kind of vulgar "10 percenters" who proliferated in Hollywood. Even so, there remained among publishers of a certain age a certain suspicion of agents, however Ivy League their origins, rather resembling that which has surrounded snakes ever since Eve's unfortunate slip in the Garden of Eden. Besides, a good many authors, Hemingway and the Durants among them, managed to do without one.

Into this cozy world swept Gitlin, a partner in a firm of literary-minded lawyers, Ernst, Cane, and Gitlin. Short, rotund, stocky, Gitlin tended to lean forward on the balls of his feet, like a man walking into a powerful wind, and somehow gave the impression that he was on a collision course with you, and possibly the rest of the world as well. His voice was an aggressive growl, usually sharpened with impatience and, when opposed, a large measure of rasping, scalding contempt. Gitlin was tough and smart and made no effort to hide it, nor was he a man to mince words or take fools lightly.

He had approached the world of book publishing indirectly. The founder of his law firm, the late, great Morris Ernst, had been a formidable advocate of free speech, and his partner, Melville Cane, a man of great learning and refined literary taste. Gitlin's personality was more that of a street fighter than a civil libertarian or an aesthete—though he concealed a certain intuitive good taste—but he enjoyed the company of writers and had a profound respect for the written word, to whatever purposes his clients were to put it. Having taken over the job of looking after the Thomas Wolfe estate, as well as that of counsel to the Matson Agency, Gitlin soon found that there were no great mysteries to agenting. Indeed, he developed a certain contempt for agents who negotiated without a lawyer's eye and who had to rely on him to point out unacceptable or contradictory language. Most of them, he felt, were timid souls, unwilling to bluff or threaten publishers and unable to see the big picture.

It was then still usual to sell hardcover rights to one book at a time and to let the publisher handle the mass-market paperback rights for half (or in the case of a major best-selling writer, slightly less than half) of the proceeds. Gitlin was the first to see that if you sold a publisher three or four books by a major author and made it pay for the mass-market rights and the foreign rights at the same time, you would come up with a very substantial amount of money. With the right kind of legal and tax structure, a really successful writer might become *seriously* rich, instead of having to live from book to book, anxiously waiting for the next royalty check.

A glance at the correspondence between Hemingway and Perkins is enough to demonstrate that Gitlin was onto something. Hemingway never took advances against his novels and was forever pleading with

Perkins or Charlie Scribner to transfer relatively small amounts of money to his bank account. The notion that a writer should have to beg for money—*his* money—from his publisher, as if he were a child trying to wheedle an advance against his allowance out of a reluctant and all-powerful parent, was deeply repugnant to Gitlin. He was determined to put an end to that sort of paternalism.

GITLIN ENTERED my life as the agent for Cornelius Ryan, a successful war correspondent and writer for *Reader's Digest* who had just been finishing his classic account of D-Day, *The Longest Day,* when I arrived at S&S. Since I happened to be a fanatic student of military history, I was eventually drafted by Peter Schwed, Ryan's editor, into the small group of people who struggled to keep pace with Ryan's remarkable capacity for infinite military detail. Ryan's previous career as a writer of books had been modest—he had written, among other things, a ghosted autobiography of Wernher von Braun, the German rocket engineer, called *I Aimed for the Stars,* which Ryan, who had a wicked Irish wit, joked ought to have been called *I Aimed for the Stars—But Sometimes I Hit London.*

Unlike some people at S&S, who found him overbearing, I *liked* Ryan, who under a veneer of charm and a remarkably thin skin was in fact an acute historian and a man of very considerable courage. We were to grow much closer over the years—particularly since my father was the art director and one of the animating spirits of the all-star movie of *The Longest Day* that helped make Ryan an international celebrity and, by the standards of magazine journalism, a rich man. My main task, however, with Ryan grew to be that of a kind of British aide-de-camp, advising him on the many illogical and eccentric points of British military rank and organization (I was perhaps the only person in American publishing who knew that in the Household Cavalry, sergeants, for reasons lost in the mists of time, are called "Corporals of Horse," or that the rank of Field-Marshal is never written without the hyphen or with two *l*'s), helping out Frank Metz, our art director, with the transformation of his military maps into four-color endpapers, and fact-checking German military nomenclature. Schwed remained his editor.

Since Ryan saw no reason why Gitlin could not do for him and military history what he had done for Harold Robbins and popular fiction, Gitlin's attention was inevitably drawn toward me. I picked up the telephone one day to hear a rasping, low-pitched voice, full of menace, say, "Listen, kid, Connie says you're being helpful to him—I just want you to make goddamn sure that he's your first fucking priority, whatever anybody else tells you." Gitlin always referred to his writers as "clients," perhaps to emphasize his status as a lawyer instead of a mere agent and that his bark was, at least in my case, considerably worse than his bite.

In any case, he invited me out to lunch (ordered me, actually) and I found myself sitting next to him a couple of days later at the Café Louis XIV in Rockefeller Center, then his favorite hangout, being helped to a slice of Gitlin's wisdom of life as he knocked back a scotch on the rocks. "How much are they paying you?" he asked. When I told him, he snorted, eyes squinting like a bull's about to charge a tourist at Pamplona. "That's bullshit," he said. "I'm going to talk to Leon, put him straight."

Gitlin's care for his clients was all encompassing, and later came to include me and my family. Loyalty he prized above all other virtues (actually, he had a certain contempt for the others), with the result that I was to work with Ryan (alongside Schwed) until the very end, taking the last pages of his final book away from him as he lay dying of cancer at Memorial Sloan-Kettering.

GITLIN'S PURPOSE—apart from deciding if I was friend or foe—might have been to see if I was suitable material to edit Harold Robbins at some future point. Apparently, in the elaborate organization that had been handcrafted to publish Robbins, this was the only element that had not been engraved in stone. Not, Gitlin assured me quickly, that Robbins *needed* a lot of editing, the man was a natural writer, whatever people said of him, but from time to time it was necessary for somebody to pass a sharpened pencil over his prose.

Did Robbins take well to being edited? I inquired. Gitlin shot me a look of pure fury. Harold was no fucking prima donna, he told me. Besides, Robbins would do whatever Gitlin told him to do, and I should never fucking forget it. I had a dim perception even then that by merely lunching with Gitlin I was doing the equivalent of signing on for a voyage before the mast, with Gitlin as my Captain Bligh. "So long as all this doesn't backfire on me," I said, knowing that nothing was more likely, given the state of relations between Schuster and Shimkin. Gitlin looked at me as soulfully as he could manage. "You have my word, kid," he said, and he would prove to be true to his word, as he always was.

Having settled that (it would be some time before it took effect, since Robbins would be edited for several books more by Cynthia White of Pocket Books), he leaned closer to me. "I hear you're going to be helping out Peter Schwed with Irving Wallace's new book," he said. It was news to me. Wallace was a former Knopf author and screenwriter who had written a book about P. T. Barnum, which I had read more or less by accident, and whom Peter Schwed was trying to bring to S&S, which would be a major coup for him.

"What's the book about?" I asked.

Gitlin gave me a roguish wink. "Sex."

AND THUS I turned another corner. My career, which had been moving toward fairly serious nonfiction (the Durants, plus all of Max Schuster's friends), Dariel Telfer's novel notwithstanding, now suddenly moved toward mainstream best-selling fiction. I was also being drawn into the no-man's-land between Schuster and Shimkin. Each of Gitlin's deals had Pocket Books publish the mass-market edition of the book and S&S the hardcover edition, with the author getting 100 percent of both royalties, instead of splitting the paperback royalty with his publisher.

Gitlin and I soon became close friends, though I was careful not to be sucked into his social life, which seemed to consist largely of sitting around in restaurants or hotel suites and drinking with his clients or flying to L.A. or Cannes to hold Harold Robbins's hand while he gestated another novel.

As for the stories about Robbins's writing habits, I soon learned that they were, if anything, less dramatic than the reality. Robbins invariably waited until the last possible moment before beginning a novel, usually a couple of months before the finished book was supposed to be shipped. To this psychological burden, he added the fact that he always spent his income, substantial as it was, the moment it was received, without putting anything away for taxes. Thus, when he finally sat down to write, Robbins had given himself not only an impossible deadline but the added pressure of IRS liens—not to speak of the expenses of keeping houses full of servants in L.A. and Acapulco, plus the yacht, with its crew of four, in Cannes, and his wife, Grace. Once the wolf was at the door, Robbins would sit down reluctantly, often in a bungalow at the Beverly Hills Hotel, and start typing. Only after he had passed a certain number of manuscript pages under the door would Gitlin allow room service to send a meal in. Even then Robbins had been known to escape out a window to Palm Springs or Las Vegas unless Gitlin watched him like a jailer.

Compared to this, Irving Wallace seemed normal, although the subject of his novel raised eyebrows at S&S, except for those of Peter Schwed, who was hugely enthusiastic. *The Chapman Report* was based on a sex survey very much like that of Dr. Kinsey, a subject which seemed shocking at the time.

Whereas most agents make a point of spreading their major authors over a number of different publishing houses, Gitlin made a deliberate decision to put Ryan, Robbins, and Wallace in the same place and even, in time, in the hands of the same editor. He calculated that having three best-selling authors at one place would give him more leverage—it might even, in the long run, make the house dependent on him, so that he could pretty much get whatever he asked for. But no large publishing house can ever really become dependent on one or two authors, however many copies their books sell, and very few authors go on writing best-seller after best-seller forever. Anyway, if you publish two or three hundred books a year, other best-sellers are almost certainly going to come along sooner or later. Successful as, say, James Michener and John O'Hara were, Random House would have survived the loss of either or both of them, just as S&S and Pocket Books would have survived the loss of Robbins, Wallace, and Ryan. Publishers are, on the whole, more likely to tie themselves up in knots over the writers they don't have but want than over those they already have, particularly when it's a question of multibook deals spread over several years.

PART THREE

Nice Guys Finish Last

CHAPTER 10

"TELEVISION IS THE best thing that's happened to kids since the invention of mother's milk," Bennett Cerf, ever the optimist, announced ebulliently to an audience of librarians in the summer of 1960. The librarians had been indulging in that pastime common to all those involved in books since the invention of movable type: the prediction that culture is about to go belly-up once and for all and that the next generation will be, or already is, functionally illiterate.

Considering that Cerf would shortly sell Random House to RCA, which owned a TV network, his enthusiasm for television might not have been entirely objective. He himself was not always immune to the pessimism of those who make their living from books. A few years before, struck by the fact that booksellers were always predicting that the bookshop would one day go the way of the village blacksmith, Cerf had commissioned some research into the subject that produced the alarming information that not only did blacksmiths greatly outnumber bookstores in America but the per capita purchase of books by Americans was less than that of Thailand.

By 1961, however, the age-old pessimism of book publishing had been erased by a sudden burst of confidence, prompting *Life* magazine to devote a long, yea-saying piece headlined, NO MORE A HEADACHE, BOOK BUSINESS BOOMS! According to *Life*, publishing stocks were soaring, the proliferation of mergers was a sign of the industry's growth, and the founding of new publishing firms such as Atheneum and Bernard Geis Associates pointed to a rosy future. (Hardly any of the new firms founded in that era survived.)

Book publishing, "the business that capitalism forgot" in *Life*'s words, was suddenly glamorous, along with such businesses as "electronics [and] vending machines" and was being revolutionized by the use of some "mechanical brain" that could predict or create best-sellers. Indeed, Doubleday, *Life* reported, was already experimenting with an ambitious new sales program that would take the guesswork out of the book business. Doubleday salesmen were to be "armed with portable dictating machines" and sent out to take continuous inventory of the Doubleday titles at bookstores across the nation. These reports would be airmailed back to New York, where Doubleday's executives would be able to plot how many copies of each title had sold and how many were still on booksellers' shelves. "With uncanny accuracy," *Life* marveled, Doubleday statisticians would then be able to predict the sales of a book and identify a best-seller, "just as an election night statistician can predict the outcome of an election from the early results of a few scattered precincts."

Since Doubleday's ratio of best-sellers to failures was about the same as anyone else's throughout the sixties, it can be presumed that this futuristic scheme failed to pay off. It was, however, typical of the sudden optimism that overcame publishers and investors at the time. Wacky ideas proliferated as share prices rose: instead of editors choosing which books to publish by reading them, "sales experts" would determine the right "product mix" for each list; "books would be sold through the mail to people who read magazines" (as if the book club had not already been invented); and publishers would strive for market share, since "the only way to get more books read is to put more on the shelves," in the words of Doubleday's then-chairman Douglas Black, who had apparently not been told that they were returnable.

The Wall Street Journal, too, commented on the "book boom," though more cautiously, noting that book publishing was now "a growth industry." But it pointed out that many of "the perplexing problems" of the business—like picking the winners from the losers—had yet to be licked and described the process as "a gigantic dice game."

Publishers have always been eager to eliminate the risk factor, either by branching out into what might seem to be more "secure" businesses, such as textbooks or "information" (dictionaries, encyclopedias, et cetera), or by concentrating on "staples," such as cookbooks, auto-repair manuals, and the like. As Wall Street beckoned, they became even more concerned to show that theirs was a fundamentally sensible, predictable, feet-on-the-ground business, not a crapshoot—a business for grown-ups, not one dominated by spoiled children in the form of editors and authors. Interviews and articles tended to emphasize marketing and merchandising, as if the editorial side of the book business didn't exist. About this time, a business expert called in to evaluate S&S came to the conclusion that we would be better off if we published only best-sellers—advice that was passed on to us with a straight face by Leon Shimkin, whose pained expression made it seem as if we were stubbornly resisting the obvious. He had charts drawn up to show how much better off we would be by not publishing books that didn't sell and concentrating our energies on those that did. Just think, he would whisper hoarsely, how much *work* we would save if we published only best-sellers!

IF THERE was one thing I had learned after almost two years in book publishing, it was that the amount of work invested in a book seldom bears any relationship to its success. Most editors, in fact (I am no exception) spend a lot of their time on the literary equivalent of rescuing stray animals. Every editor has a list of projects that looked compelling when they were bought but have since become proverbial albatrosses around one's neck: novels that have grown out of control, the pages multiplying crazily like kudzu beside Southern roads; nonfiction projects that have taken sharp turns away from the original premise of the work; books that have been delayed far beyond their deadlines until nobody can remember why they were bought in the first place or even who bought them.

To this day, I dread going over the "inventory" of my undelivered books, since it never fails to reveal projects I have forgotten about altogether or which were bought when the current managing editor was still in school. No matter how late an author is with a book, it's my tendency to say, "Oh, don't worry, he's working on it," rather than pull the plug and terminate the contract for lateness.

It's not just a certain sympathy for writers, being one myself, or a degree of optimism, without which one would never become an editor in the first place—it's also that in my first years as an editor I gravitated naturally toward "problem" books and authors, or they toward me. Having bought a book, I hadn't the luxury of writing it off or letting it fail, as older, more successful editors can do. I felt myself responsible for getting it in and making it publishable, however late, off course, or unreadable it might have become over time.

This can be a positive, character-building experience, but it might also derive from a stubborn determination not to admit to a mistake. In either case, I became something of a specialist in the long-term resuscitation of doubtful projects that most editors would have left to die merciful deaths. I simply could *not* let them go and was willing to spend hours beyond counting to make them as readable as possible, only too often over the objections of the author—the worse somebody writes, the more they are likely to cling to their prose.

Early on in our friendship, I remember Bob Gottlieb handing me a badly written and unnumbered manuscript, heavily etched with laborious, inked revisions and second thoughts in an unreadable hand. "See if you can get this to the point where it's not a shame before the neighbors," he said—a *shondeh*, to use the Yiddish. It took almost twelve years before the novel saw the light of day, only to sink like the *Titanic*. By the time it was published, Bob was no longer at S&S, and during that long period the author's own life became as melodramatic as the plot of his book. All the while, every six months or so, another package of badly typed manuscript would arrive on my desk from him, together with a long letter chronicling yet another round of disasters, and pleading for something, *anything* by express mail, even if only fifty or a hundred dollars, to keep his head above water. "*My life is in your hands!*" one letter ended dramatically. Each time, I faithfully trudged down to the office of Shimkin's latest financial watchdog to beg for a check, despite the facts that the novel was equally out of control and nobody had read it but me.

In these circumstances, it is easy to persuade oneself that one is dealing with a work of genius, if only to justify the amount of time and energy spent on it or the endlessly growing file full of ill-spelled, single-spaced, stream-of-consciousness letters. Once a writer is far enough from shore, his or her editor invariably takes on something of the nature of a life buoy thrown to a drowning man—a relationship that is at once deeply flattering and profoundly wearisome for the editor, who can neither pry loose the kind of money that might help nor guarantee the eventual success of the book. This is not always an easy cross to bear. It is hard enough to be responsible for what happens to somebody's work—very often their lifework at that, in every meaning of that word—but being responsible for their *life* is something else again.

With age and experience, one learns to avoid playing this role, but in 1961 it was still a heady challenge to which I responded only too eagerly. I became involved in the rescue of a would-be novelist who had descended from job to job until he was living in a tar-paper shack in Northern California, reduced to the point where we had to send him typing paper so he could continue an interminable novel that we eventually published with one of the lowest net sales in S&S's history. Then I became entangled in the darkly comic life of a self-taught historian and respected businessman whose apparently prim and proper suburban marriage went adrift when his white churchgoing wife, the mother of his two children, ran off with a black dope dealer from Newark. A pioneering student of animal psychology persuaded me to buy a book he proposed to write about his attempt to make wolves in Alaska bring up his infant son as one of their pack. This was not exactly an original idea, but having spent a part of my own childhood watching my Uncle Zoltan and my father on the set of *The Jungle Book,* I was interested enough to persuade S&S to put up $2,500 to send him on his way to Alaska, where he promptly disappeared into the tundra with the boy, never to be heard from again, leaving me to many years of difficult correspondence with the boy's mother. Another of my authors, an old friend from Oxford, fled to a Tibetan monastery with his advance; another, apparently driven to a suicide attempt by writer's block, wound up in a padded cell at Payne-Whitney, where I visited him almost daily in the hope of rekindling his interest in his book.

I seemed to have a magical attraction for writers with ambitious, crackpot plans and foundering personal lives. Of course, some of this is inevitable when starting out—the big, easy books by established authors are unlikely to come one's way, and it would be a poor editor indeed who failed to be moved by a challenge while still earning his spurs. Besides, just about the only things a young editor has going for him- or herself are enthusiasm, a willingness to work harder than anyone else, and a certain naïveté. Book publishing, like most businesses, provides ample opportunities for cynicism over the long haul of a career, but it pays no dividends to start out a cynic.

I made any number of mistakes in those days—not the simple kind, which I still make, such as suppressing one's doubts about a book or persuading oneself that what is patently second-rate is really first-rate, or might be made so with the right kind of editing. I made the kind of mistake that involves the heart: buying a book because the author is so desperately needy, sincere, or wistfully appealing—the literary equivalent of a mercy fuck, in short. Learning to say no is the first, hardest, and most important lesson for a fledgling editor. The only thing harder to learn is when to say yes.

In any event, *no* was a word that I seldom used then, both because I found it hard to say and because I desperately needed books. This had its downside, of course—a lot of them were unsuccessful and took up an inordinate amount of time—but there was also an upside: I gained broad and unspecialized experience. Most editors stay with a well-defined area of interest and for good reason: It's usually easier to do what you know and what you want to do than to venture into uncharted waters. Thus, literary editors stick with what they conceive to be literature, nonfiction editors with nonfiction, and so on. I was willing to do pretty much anything. It wasn't that I didn't have preferences or tastes of my own, but I was determined not to be fussy until I could afford to be. I found myself editing books on mathematics and philosophy, memoirs, fiction, translations from the French, politics, anthropology, science history, even an illustrated encyclopedia of technology translated from the German. In my determination to cast my net as wide as possible, I subscribed to numerous French literary journals as well as the Russian *Literaturnaya Gazyeta,* which the FBI came to inquire about. In those days, a letter or a package with a Soviet postmark was held up mysteriously by the post office for weeks and arrived showing the telltale signs of having been opened and clumsily resealed.

What they found to interest them in *Literaturnaya Gazyeta* I cannot imagine—it certainly produced slim pickings for me, though I did many years later pick up a novel called *Faithful Ruslan,* a very sad story about a guard dog in a Soviet prison camp who, after the camp is closed down, is retired and can't adapt to freedom. It was clever, touching, and very convincingly told from Ruslan's point of view—much more effective, I think, than Richard Adams's *The Plague Dogs*—but for all my enthusiasm, it sank into oblivion, despite the cold war theme. Other editors seemed to have an enviable facility—or was it just plain luck?—for plucking best-sellers out of foreign waters, but my Hungarian, German, Russian, Italian, and Japanese writers, however highly praised by those in the know, never won the Nobel Prize or became best-sellers. I did have slightly better luck from time to time with French books, but then I don't really regard French as a foreign language, and many American readers and critics are, in any case, under the impression that they ought to take French writing seriously, even if they don't like it much.

Fortunately for me, the idea of worrying about whether a junior editor's books were making a profit had not yet occurred to anybody at S&S (or anywhere else), except perhaps Leon Shimkin. In book publishing, the motto for survival might have been that of academic life: publish or perish. The more books you bought, irrespective of any possible merit, the more seriously you were taken, and since there is very often a long gap between the signing of a contract and the delivery of a manuscript, it was possible for months or even years to go by before anybody knew whether one was buying best-sellers and works of genius or complete duds. Many a successful editorial career was launched by buying everything in sight, thus building up a long and impressive-looking list of acquisitions, then switching to a new job at another publisher before the manuscripts began to flood in. Some people did this several times in rapid succession, rising swiftly to positions of serious responsibility, while leaving behind them a flood tide of ghastly books and authors that would haunt other houses and editors for years.

Whatever *Life* might suppose, the truth was that book publishing at the beginning of the 1960s was still very much a business run by amateurs who took a certain pride in their fecklessness. Accountability was looked upon as an infringement upon an editor's right to follow his or her instinct. Given the general inefficiency with which the business was run, it would have seemed pointless to subject the performance of the editors to intense scrutiny, even had the machinery for doing so existed. The system of accounting itself was so slipshod as to be risible, in those halcyon days before the computer made numbers king. Whole rooms full of white-haired old ladies labored with pencils and adding machines to produce royalty statements that hardly ever reflected any kind of financial reality, since the books, which were returnable, drifted back from the bookstores for years, like flotsam and jetsam on the tide. Royalty statements were regarded with deep suspicion by authors and agents, with some reason.

THE LAID-BACK inefficiency of publishing in New York paled when compared to publishing in London, where monstrous lunches accompanied by a variety of wines were the rule, followed shortly afterward by tea. The shipping room was very often to be found under the stairs in a kind of cupboard, as at the august premises of Jonathan Cape, where a few wizened old men in brown coveralls wrapped parcels when they were not boiling the water for tea. Many if not most American publishers looked toward London with envy. There, the Anglophiles (who ranged from such hearty philistines as Simon Michael Bessie and Peter Schwed to aesthetes like Bob Gottlieb) would say, is where publishing is done *right,* at a nice leisurely pace, with plenty of room on everybody's list for first novelists and less vulgar obsession about profit. The difference between the two sides of the Atlantic was, in fact, one of scale. In the United Kingdom, book publishing was not only a well-regarded and honorable profession but one that loomed large in people's minds. London is a big city, but England is a small country, and most of it looks to London for news. Book news was treated with the same interest as every other kind, even by people who didn't read books.

Quite the reverse was true of America, a big country, in which New York is only one of many major cities, albeit the media center, and in which people were most interested in local news. News of book publishing seldom reached the hinterlands. Even today, there is no fevered national speculation about who will win an American Book Award, unlike the interest that surrounds, say, the Booker Prize in the United Kingdom, or the Prix Goncourt in France.

Much of this was about to change and in a big way. As Wall Street became interested in publishing as "a growth industry," there were people who actually thought that it might be made profitable as well and who observed its present arrangements with a cold eye. And even bigger change was in store with the rising popularity of television talk shows. The *Today* show had been going on for years, spawning imitations, before it occurred to anybody that authors were a cheap way of filling up time—in fact, they were *free* and only too happy to talk about their books. Television, which everybody had expected would destroy book publishing, in fact saved and reinvented it. Until television, the only way that publishers could get their books noticed was to advertise or pray for good reviews. Now, at last, they could do an end run around the reviewers and put the author in direct contact with millions of people at one time.

. . .

FEW PEOPLE guessed at the time how significant these changes would be. Among them was one of America's most successful novelists, whom I was at last to meet, when circumstances made it necessary for me to work with Harold Robbins personally, and I was summoned to the great man's hotel suite by a call from Paul Gitlin.

Gitlin, not a man easily awed, talked about his biggest client in a relatively hushed voice, as a cardinal might talk of the Holy Father. Harold wanted to meet me, he said, but I should be careful. Harold could be pretty rough, especially if he thought he was being bullshitted.

I had no reason to bullshit Harold Robbins, I said. My job, like that of my predecessor, Cynthia White, was simply to tidy up his prose and to point out holes in his plot and suggest ways of filling them. The larger questions, such as how much was going to be spent on advertising, how many copies we were printing, or what television shows he should appear on were, after all, not in my province. On these matters, Robbins was known to be sensitive. Gitlin had long since secured for him "most favored nation" treatment, meaning that if anybody else should ever get a bigger first printing, advertising guarantee, or promotion budget, Robbins's would automatically be raised to match the new terms. The same applied to his royalty rates and almost anything else Gitlin could think of.

Harold didn't like to be talked down to, either, Gitlin went on. And Harold did not like snotty people—I shouldn't forget that for a moment.

"I don't talk down to people," I protested. "And I'm not snotty."

"He might think you are because you're a Limey," Gitlin said.

"For God's sake, what's he got against the English?" I asked. "He's a huge best-seller there."

"He knows they like him. But that don't mean he likes them."

On that cheerful note, Gitlin hung up. I was to meet Robbins at noon, and we would lunch together, the three of us, at his hotel.

I had my own doubts about the meeting on the grounds that it represented an argument lost on my part. I have always had a real dislike of editorial discussions held outside my office. I had already found that things usually went much smoother and faster on my own turf, however cramped and unglamorous. Off it, some element of authority seemed to be missing. Later on, I mostly managed to get my way about this—in fact, I took to saying that I didn't pay house calls—but I was in no position to do so at that time with Robbins. Still, this was a compromise of sorts, since Gitlin's original suggestion was that I should fly to France and spend a week or so on Robbins's yacht at Cannes.

Gitlin had been both surprised and angered at my refusal to join Robbins's yachting party. Other editors, he snapped, would have killed for the chance to spend a week on Harold's yacht. Harold was a lavish host, he pointed out, who made sure that all his guests had a good time. My heart sank at the very thought of it, and to my own astonishment I dug my feet in and absolutely refused to go.

If there was one thing I already knew, it was never to accept that kind of hospitality from a major author, since you could never argue as an equal thereafter. Besides, like my father, I preferred to pay my own bills and decide for myself where I wanted to go and what I wanted to do, whenever possible.

Robbins's first words to me were "I hear you pissed on my fucking invitation."

Robbins was a muscular, compact man, with the battered face of a middleweight fighter who had seen better days. The corners of his mouth were permanently turned down, as if he had just finished sucking a lemon, and he hid his beady, suspicious eyes behind thick, wraparound dark sunglasses, of the kind then favored by Aristotle Onassis and Darryl F. Zanuck. His handshake was firm but moist, and his voice gravelly, rough, and full of suspicion and aggression, as if he had taken elocution lessons from a loan shark. Robbins's skin was deeply, expensively tanned, and his sandy, graying hair was sparse and combed artfully across his scalp to hide a growing bald spot. He wore a silk shirt, open to the navel, exposing a thick mat of chest hair and several gold chains. His hairy wrists were adorned with chunky gold bracelets and a gold watch, so that every time he moved them he clinked and clanked. The hands, I couldn't help noticing, were those of a working man, with short, stubby fingers, except that they were soft to the touch and well manicured, the nails apparently finished with several coats of polish. He wore black silk trousers and pointed, woven huaraches, of the kind favored by Hollywood producers in the 1940s. There was something anachronistic about Robbins, as if at an impressionable age his ideas about class and success had been forever fixed by exposure to studio czars such as Harry Cohn and Jack Warner when he had first gone west to work as a publicity man and would-be screenwriter in Hollywood after his enthusiastic reception as the author of *A Stone for Danny Fisher*. By the early 1960s the people Robbins had modeled himself on had vanished, leaving him behind as a kind of caricature of a bygone age.

Although Robbins had something of a reputation for generosity and unexpected acts of kindness, he usually faced the world with a grumbling snarl and a tough-guy attitude, as if he had a monumental chip on his shoulder, despite his enormous success as a writer, or perhaps because of it. Certainly his sales were in the millions—he was the world's most widely read living novelist—but that did not appear to give him much satisfaction, except for the money. At first, I assumed that this was because the critics either ignored him or attacked his books as perfect examples of what was wrong with American culture, but I was soon to discover that Robbins was indifferent to all that and even took a certain amount of perverse pride in it. Robbins positively *laughed* all the way to the bank. He said he "didn't give a shit" about reviews; he wrote for money, and as long as the money kept pouring in, he was content.

The truth of the matter was that Robbins didn't like writing and resented every moment that he was obliged to spend at the typewriter. These were not circumstances, to put it mildly, that led to the creation of great literature—not, of course, that great literature was what Robbins or his readers had in mind. Still, Robbins was no ordinary hack. He had begun as a writer of promise but quite deliberately sold out by writing ever more heavy-breathing potboilers about money and sex. In a real sense, Robbins delivered what his readers wanted, which explains his success. The scene in *The Carpetbaggers* when Jennie, the whore with the proverbial heart of gold, persuades the big movie producer, Maurice Bonner, to let her shave his body, after which she gives him a massage, a puff of marijuana to prevent his coming too quickly, then sex in a bathtub full of champagne, followed, in the morning, by breakfast in bed, remains, for countless men of a certain age, the best-remembered sex scene in American fiction and just possibly the most popular fantasy. Like most people who have sold out, Robbins was bitter about having done it and felt that he had sold out for too little. In interviews, he always sounded cocky and quick to defend his books against the critics, but the truth was that he despised his readers and despised himself for catering to them.

I explained to him that I hadn't pissed on his invitation. I simply didn't have the time. In any case, I wasn't sure my wife would enjoy the thought of my being at sea with a yachtful of broads.

Robbins smirked. "The kid is pussy-whipped!" he growled. Gitlin, who was seated beside his client on a sofa, gave a low, throaty laugh— more of a growl, in fact. Both of them were drinking scotch on the rocks. It was noon. The living room was dense with cigarette smoke— Robbins was one of those nonstop smokers who seem to keep several cigarettes going at once, lighting each of them with a heavy gold lighter. He stared at me aggressively through the smoke, like a Cape buffalo bull about to charge an intruder. It occurred to me that there was no reason for his hostility—after all, we were on the same side. Then it dawned on me that it was nothing personal; Robbins simply liked to present a surly face to the world, perhaps as a way of testing other people. If you reacted with fear or took it personally, he felt he had won. Since I had been to several boarding schools where the same was true, I smiled pleasantly, refusing to be drawn. The truth was, I hadn't even *mentioned* the invitation to my wife, since I had no intention of going.

I poured myself a cup of coffee from a silver thermos jug on the side table and sat down, my bulging briefcase beside me. The reason for my presence here was simple. Robbins took very little interest in the editing of his books. Once he had finished a novel, he was ready to play, and it was possible to make quite substantial changes without consulting him, once he trusted you—indeed, he got testy when he *was* consulted. *His* job was to write the details of fucking, he would say, not to worry about the fucking details. Any attempt to make him look at a manuscript again or even read the proofs was met with sour anger.

This, in fact, made the editor's job fairly easy. All you had to do was to fix the manuscript up as best you could without bothering the author and leave the rest to Gitlin. It was Gitlin's job, after all, to put Robbins's nose to the grindstone when the bills finally had to be paid, to get his hands on the royalty checks before Robbins could, to hold the IRS at bay, and to protect Robbins from all the people who might want to ask him questions in the normal course of publishing. It cannot be said that Gitlin did not earn his commission, every penny of it.

Usually, once the manuscript was delivered, Robbins's connection with it ended until it was time for him to promote the book, at which point he emerged into the limelight, led by his own personal publicity man, a heavyset Hollywood flack of the old school who made sure that Robbins traveled like minor royalty and threatened to cancel the tour whenever even the slightest thing went wrong. In this particular case, however, a small snag had developed with the manuscript itself, thus explaining my reluctant presence in Robbins's suite. According to the terms of his contract, the advance against royalties was paid out to Robbins as he delivered each chunk of the manuscript. In desperate need of a payment, he had written the first half of his new novel at a white-hot pace and had taken off for the south of France in a party mood. When, a few months later, he ran out of money again, he sat down and wrote the second half of the manuscript at an even more furious pace, but without rereading what he had written before. The result was that the two halves simply didn't match up. The events in the second part seemed to have little or nothing to do with what had taken place in the first half of the book, and the characters had changed both their names and their appearances so completely that they appeared to be different people altogether.

Undaunted by this—I guessed that Robbins's attention had simply wavered, as opposed to his having mistakenly given us two halves of separate novels—I had worked out a fairly simple way of stitching the two pieces together that involved my writing a few scenes in Robbins's all-too-imitable style and changing a few dates.

None of this need necessarily have involved Robbins himself, who was perfectly happy to leave this sort of thing to his editors, but the names of the characters and their physical characteristics—I mean the color of their eyes and hair, for example, since the men's penis sizes and the women's breasts sizes were always extralarge in Robbins's novels—posed a problem about which I felt Robbins should be consulted. After all, we could make the characters consistent with the first half of the book or with the second, and I felt that on something as fundamental as this, the choice should be his. Gitlin, when the question was posed to him, had agreed. He could not decide for Harold about something like that.

Neither Robbins nor Gitlin seemed eager to get down to brass tacks. They were apparently determined to use me as a punching bag for a long litany of complaints about S&S and Pocket Books, most of them things which I had not only no control over but no knowledge of, involving people I hardly even knew or had never heard of. Despite his success, Robbins harbored a long list of grudges. I defended my team weakly and without conviction, which of course only increased the volume of their complaints. Eventually, to my relief, Robbins announced that he wanted to eat. The sooner, the better, I thought, since Robbins was knocking back the Dewars at a pretty steady rate. Drinking merely made Robbins more monosyllabic and sarcastic—he was a master at the quick, unexpected dig, delivered in a hoarse whisper. Food, I thought hopefully, might soothe his savage breast.

Gitlin went off to whisper into the telephone, as if the luncheon order were an important state secret. He did not ask me what I wanted to eat.

Robbins fixed me with a baleful stare. "So what's the problem with the fucking book?" he rasped.

"Well, nothing much, really," I stammered. "I mean, it's a fast read, there's a lot of sex, and so on. . . ."

He nodded wearily. Praise seemed as wearisome to him, apparently, as criticism, or perhaps he simply felt that as a Brit and an intellectual, I couldn't have an opinion worth hearing.

Lunch arrived—a curious meal consisting of pastrami sandwiches and plates of salad, accompanied by a large can of Beluga Malossol caviar, surrounded by crushed ice.

"Since you're paying," Gitlin said, "we're having Harold's favorite dish."

"Goddamn right," Robbins said. He stuck a spoon into the caviar and covered the salad with a thick layer of it. Then he ate it silently, waving his hand to indicate that we should follow his example. Despite a certain feeling on my part that caviar ought not to be used as a salad topping, like the bacon bits you get at salad bars in diners, I had to admit that the combination was pretty good. You couldn't fault Robbins on getting what he wanted, and what he wanted was the best of everything.

When he'd eaten half his sandwich, he wiped his mouth and stared at me. It was clearly my cue to get down to business. I took the two halves of the manuscript out of my briefcase and placed them on the table, then explained the problem. Robbins listened unblinkingly, his face totally devoid of expression or interest, his head cocked to one side like a lizard waiting for its prey to wander into range. Every so often he glanced toward Gitlin as if to ask, Do I really have to listen to all this shit? Gitlin shrugged, What do you want me to do about it?

I finished and sat back, waiting for Harold to decide which way he wanted to go.

He blew two plumes of smoke through his nostrils and glared at me through it. "Let me get this straight," he said. "You're telling me that I fucked up? I got the names wrong in the second half of the book?"

I nodded. We could make the necessary changes, I hastened to add, since his impatience was unmistakable—nobody was asking *him* to do it. We just needed to know whether he wanted to go with the people in the first half of the book or the ones in the second half.

Robbins nodded. His expression was dark. "I don't have to do a fucking thing, that's what you're telling me? You'll do it all? You just want my decision?"

"Right."

Robbins stubbed out his cigarette. "My decision is leave it alone."

"Leave it alone?"

"You heard him," Gitlin said.

"But readers will think it's a mistake of some kind."

Robbins was unmoved. "Fuck 'em," he snarled.

I was so surprised that I didn't know what to say for a moment. Robbins lit another cigarette and decided to explain himself. "I've been working my ass off to write these books for years, trying to figure out plots and characters," he said. "Let the readers do some work for a change."

"But—"

"You heard the man," Gitlin said, in his deepest growl.

"We'll get thousands of letters complaining about it—"

"Who gives a fuck?"

Robbins stood up and held out his hand. The audience was over. As I picked up my briefcase and left, I could see Robbins and Gitlin sitting side by side on the sofa. They looked remarkably like Tweedledee and Tweedledum.

CURIOUSER AND curiouser, we received, in the end, not a single letter of complaint about the errors. Was it because many of Robbins's readers skipped over the parts between the sex scenes, or did they simply have faith in Robbins as a storyteller? Certainly they were loyal—and widespread. Years later, when I was traveling in India, I found myself running out of books to read—a catastrophe for me. I was then staying at a lakeside hotel in Srinagar, in Kashmir, and when I explained my predicament to the hotel concierge he gave me an encouraging smile. There was no problem, he promised me. He would have me guided to an English-language bookstore by one of his staff.

My guide was a tall, fiercely bearded Kashmiri of martial appearance and bearing, who wore a black lamb's-wool hat like a cossack's and carried a long stick with which to brush beggars out of my way. We set off for the Srinagar bazaar, a mazelike warren of tiny covered alley-ways, dense with wood smoke, the sharp odor of cattle droppings, and the smell of spices. We walked for what seemed a very long time, up and down steep stairs, in and out of darkened hallways, until I was hope-lessly lost. All around us was the deafening noise of India: animal cries, the shouting of store owners hawking their wares, prayers, the ringing of bells, and the wails and clanging that pass for music.

After what seemed like an eternity, we arrived at a tiny, dark hole in the wall in which lay a very old man, heavily bearded and wearing a tur-ban and white robes. He was smoking a hookah, which was tended lov-ingly by a boy of about ten, dressed only in a loincloth.

"English book shop, please, sahib," my guide said proudly.

I stared into the gloomy recesses of the hole, behind the old man. I could see no shelves or books. The old man rose to his feet and bowed. We bowed back, then sat on our haunches around the carpet solemnly, while the boy went off and came back with a brass teapot and poured us each a tiny cup of boiling hot tea. My guide cleared his throat, spat into the dust, and explained the purpose of our visit.

The old man beamed. From deep within the folds of his robes he produced a massive, rusty iron key, secured to his person by a string. He put a pair of steel-rimmed spectacles on his nose, untied the key with trembling fingers and gave it to the boy, who plunged into the interior of the cave and dragged out a big, old, brass-bound wooden chest. The boy unlocked the chest, inside which was a bundle wrapped up in a brightly embroidered piece of cloth. He placed this on the carpet before us.

With careful, loving hands, the old man unwrapped the bundle and pulled the cloth to one side. "Behold!" he said grandly. "The most fa-mous writer in English in all India." There before us lay the complete works of Harold Robbins, in torn and battered paperback editions that had been passed from hand to hand, no doubt from continent to conti-nent, and lovingly repaired with tape where necessary. The boy brushed flies off the books with a whisk, as if they were sacred objects.

After spirited bargaining, I bought *The Carpetbaggers* to see me through to Delhi and *The Adventurers* to read on the plane to London. They were pretty good, too. The famous bathtub sex scene in *The Car-petbaggers* still held up. I toyed with the idea of sending the books to Robbins when I got back to the States, but I decided he probably wouldn't be surprised that he was the most famous author in the English language in India, or anywhere else, either.

Since then, I have found copies of his books in a remote game lodge in Kenya, on a Nile steamer, and at an oasis in Morocco. A friend found one in a yurt in deepest Mongolia.

And there's still not been a single complaint about the one in which the characters are all mixed up. Maybe Robbins was right—his readers *don't* mind doing the work for him!

LIKE ROBBINS, Irving Wallace, whose sizable oeuvre has survived rather less well than Robbins's, was another novelist whose success was widely believed to be threatening Western civilization. Like Robbins and Sidney Sheldon, Wallace was a Hollywood screenwriter turned novelist. Screenwriting, however much it might be looked down on by the literati, was remarkably good training for writing fiction, particularly in the old days, when every script had to be approved by people like Irving Thalberg or David Selznick. Screenwriters knew exactly how to do all the things that puzzle many novelists: how to cut to the chase, how to maintain a consistent point of view, how to work out motivation for every action and to prepare the reader for sudden changes of plot, how to avoid flashbacks and, worse still, flash-forwards. A strong story line, divided into clear scenes, was what mattered in the movie business; it is also exactly what works for most readers of fiction.

Of course, there are plenty of writers who know this without having spent years on the old MGM lot. Tolstoy was a natural storyteller (if you don't believe me, go read *Anna Karenina* again) and so was Dickens, and it is no accident that much of their work has been filmed. Still, the twentieth-century division of fiction into two artificial and opposing camps—"high culture" and "low culture"—left a lot of people who liked novels with a real story having to content themselves with "lowbrow" fiction, a trend that became institutionalized as the book clubs and mass-market paperbacks entered the picture. By and large, the novels that reviewers and the intellectual elite took seriously were ignored by people who read fiction for entertainment and vice versa, although a small number of writers—usually European—occasionally bridged the gap with books that were both entertaining (i.e., conventionally plotted) and critically acclaimed, perhaps because neither they nor their critics were in pursuit of that elusive leviathan of American letters, "The Great American Novel."

Every successful fiction writer develops his or her own approach to the novel and always has, but in the increasingly merchandise-oriented world of popular fiction, the most successful ones needed, in the words of the showstopper from *Gypsy*, a gimmick. Following in the footsteps of Edna Ferber, James Michener perfected (if that is the mot juste) the gargantuan travelogue novel, which provided the whole history of a country or an area (more or less in the spirit of John Gunther's relentless piling up of facts), along with a strong plot. Harold Robbins provided a strong story, plus heavy-breathing sex and a light dose of the traditional roman à clef. (*The Carpetbaggers*, for instance, is loosely but recognizably based on the life of Howard Hughes, while the hero of *The Adventurers* resembles Porfirio Rubirosa, the famous Latin playboy.) Irving Wallace, drawn into the fiction game by Robbins's example and tired of taking orders from producers, directors, studio heads, and actors, invented the novel that is at one and the same time a strong story and an encyclopedia, with some sex thrown in to keep the reader's pulse going.

A famous piece of advice to writers is, "Do tons of research, then throw it away and start writing." Wallace reversed this piece of folk wisdom. He did (or caused to have done) tons of research and incorporated it wholesale into his novels. Ungainly as the results were, they worked, perhaps because it is part of our Puritan inheritance to want to believe that we are being instructed, that we are *learning* something, anything, even while we are being entertained. Thus, although Wallace titillated his readers with sex scenes (none of them quite as hot as those of Robbins, a source of great envy to Wallace; in Robbins's view, Wallace tended to write about sex as if he had never actually experienced it), he also gave them an opportunity to atone for their lascivious pleasure by reading what amounted to a whole travel book about whatever city the plot was set in, including the dimensions of every significant monument or work of art. It was like reading in alternate bursts from *The Joy of Sex* and a Baedeker's travel guide.

Wallace had had a relatively tame career as a nonfiction writer at Knopf and had then published a fairly unsuccessful and undistinguished novel with a minor publisher before being brought to Paul Gitlin's attention (though for a while, oddly, his agent was the stuffy and conservative Paul Reynolds, while Gitlin was his lawyer). Wallace had a positive mania for just those parts of publishing a book that bore or irritate most writers. He loved correcting proofs, indulged in deep, obscure arguments with the copy editors over knotty questions of punctuation, spelling, and accuracy, and rejoiced when he could prove them wrong. A loyal graduate of the Kenosha, Wisconsin, school system, he actually kept his old high school English teacher, Elizabeth Kempthorne, on his payroll to go over his manuscripts and proofs.

I was, in fact, drafted to work with Wallace by Schwed precisely because Wallace dearly loved the whole experience of being edited. The more pages of detailed notes Schwed and I threw at Wallace, the happier he was. "Don't skimp!" he would plead—I was to play devil's advocate to the hilt, without any respect for his feelings. Unfortunately, Wallace was so hypersensitive to criticism that he sometimes cried when contemplating a list of suggested cuts. Moreover, he invariably turned down every suggestion, however minor. His replies to editorial notes were usually two or three times the length of the notes themselves, full-blooded, single-spaced rebuttals, point by point, page by page. The first time this happened, I called Gitlin and asked him if he knew what happened and could explain what my role was intended to be. "Sure, kid," he said affably. "Your job is to make Irving feel good by doing a really thorough edit of his stuff. Then he gets to prove that he's smarter than you are, even if you did go to Oxford."

"It seems like a waste of time."

"What waste of time? It keeps you busy, it makes Irving happy. That's why I asked for you to work with him. I figured the more he turns your stuff down, the more you'll do. You two are made for each other, *bubbi,* trust me on that."

This proved to be true. For years, I continued to send Wallace long, detailed, persuasive, carefully thought-out memoranda about his books, which he continued to rebut. On the rare occasions when I slacked off— on the sensible grounds that nothing I suggested would ever make the slightest bit of difference, since Wallace would merely explain at even greater length why I was wrong about every point—he complained, usually to higher authorities through Gitlin, that I didn't love him or his work anymore.

Wallace had come to S&S with a novel that nobody else wanted to publish called *The Chapman Report,* about a Kinsey-type sex survey and the effect it has on a comfortable suburban community, which aroused Schwed's immediate enthusiasm. There was a lot of sex in the book—it was about sex, after all—but most of it was more informational than tit-illating. Still, as anaphrodisiac as Wallace's novels may have been to me, *The Chapman Report* stirred up a good deal of controversy, much of it within S&S itself. Unlike the books of Harold Robbins, *The Chapman Report* bore the S&S colophon—a small reproduction of Jean-François Millet's *The Sower*—on its spine and was indubitably "ours." S&S had always had something of a reputation for publishing novels that repre-sented, or perhaps predicted, social change, particularly the kind that couldn't be talked about. Laura Z. Hobson's *Gentleman's Agreement* had brought home the survival of old-fashioned anti-Semitism in postwar America, just as Sloan Wilson's *The Man in the Gray Flannel Suit* was the first to explore the corporate commuter of the early 1950s as a new species of American.

Publishing a novel that more or less prefigured the sexual revolu-tion was something else again, of course, and there was a lot of opposi-tion to doing it, despite Schwed's urging. I found this hard to understand; the real problem with *The Chapman Report* was that it was boring, not that it was pornographic. Still, the mere mention of the sub-ject was enough to give Max Schuster cold feet, and the manuscript had to be submitted to his son-in-law, Ephraim London, S&S's house coun-sel, for a legal reading.

Fortunately, London was a difficult man to shock. A crusading First Amendment lawyer, London had been battling censorship successfully for years, and there was nothing in *The Chapman Report* that was likely to surprise him. London swiftly gave his approval, though not with any particular enthusiasm. Since Ray Schuster was a one-woman fan club for her sons-in-law, there was no way Max could oppose the book. Max, however, was an expert at Nelson's trick and turned a blind eye to *The Chapman Report,* simply pretending that it didn't exist.

The Chapman Report swiftly rose up the best-seller list, establishing Wallace as a new superstar, comparable to Robbins and at least as pro-ductive. Unlike Robbins, Wallace seemed to live only to write. When he wasn't writing a book, he was writing endless, single-spaced letters that soon filled my small office. From time to time, they had to be gathered up, carefully packed, and sent to some university in Texas or Wisconsin. There was grumbling about the amount of work that was involved in keeping track of all this paperwork, most of which, in the normal course of events, would have been disposed of or lost.

. . .

I HAD managed to avoid going to Cannes to work with Robbins, but there was no way I could wheedle my way out of going to California to see Wallace. Besides, having grown up in Beverly Hills from 1941 to 1943, I had a soft spot for L.A. and was not altogether unhappy to be going there at the expense of S&S. Unlike Robbins, Wallace didn't show any signs of wanting to take over my life, so I booked myself into the Beverly Hills Hotel, where as a child I had once lived in one of the bungalows, and arranged to have Casey meet me there after I'd finished my business so we could take a leisurely drive up the coast to San Francisco.

At the time, a visit to L.A. was almost unimaginably rare among book publishers. Publishers traveled to London frequently, in pursuit of books or to sell their own wares, or to southern Florida or the Caribbean islands for sales conferences, but L.A. was alien territory, home of the movie industry and of an indigenous, sprawling, and exotic West Coast culture in which the book seemed to play no role at all; indeed, from the East it seemed hostile to books and everything they implied.

The age of movie tie-ins and TV miniseries had not yet arrived; in New York and Boston, publishers still regarded "the entertainment business" as the enemy, luring prospective customers away from the healthy pastime of reading books into the unthinking illiteracy of moviegoing and television watching. The notion that some connection might profitably exist between book and movie, or that television might be used to sell books, had not occurred to anybody, let alone the possibility that book publishing itself would one day become an integral part of the entertainment business, with many of the major publishing houses actually owned by movie companies.

In a fairly sluggish and suspicious way, the major studios competed to buy the movie rights to best-selling novels. They maintained "scouts" and "spies" in New York to tell them about the latest hot books, but hardly anybody in the movie business had any direct dealings with book people. It was all done through shadowy go-betweens, as if the movie and television people were afraid of rejection at the hands of the Brahmins of East Coast high culture, while book publishers and editors were aghast at the thought of being contaminated by the vulgarity and crass commercialism of the movie business. There was, in short, no good reason for book people to journey all the way across the country to see with their own eyes something they already despised, and even less reason for movie people, when visiting New York, to cultivate those who despised them.

IRVING WALLACE was a short, stocky fellow, then in his mid-fifties, with a massive leonine head of graying hair and small, rather pudgy hands. Wallace was never without a pipe, and everywhere in his house there were racks of them to hand. He and his wife, Sylvia, showed me around their home as if I were proposing to buy it—a curious custom of Los Angeles—and I was able to admire the full-size and fully stocked soda fountain they had built for their two children, complete with large glass bowls filled with miniature candy bars.

With even greater pride, Wallace led me to a small separate building in which he had his office. Air-conditioned, as silent as Proust's cork-lined study, equipped with every modern device from dictating machines to electric typewriters, Wallace's writing room had the look of a corporate headquarters, fluorescent lit and sleekly decorated in pale colors and blond wood, with a staff of eager, attractive secretaries. Around the walls were smooth metal filing cabinets full of research.

Through a heavy door, like that of a bank, was a kind of vault, arranged as a library, with one copy of every edition of Wallace's books, in every imaginable language: Urdu, Finnish, even pirated English-language editions printed illegally in Taiwan. The shelves and cupboards were all handmade by old-world master craftsmen out of rare woods. It looked rather like the cigar humidor at Dunhill, on Fifth Avenue, but lacked the deep, rich aroma of Havanas. As someone with an ambition to write myself, I felt a stab of envy at this floor-to-ceiling, wall-to-wall display. This, I felt, was fulfillment of a kind. Wallace seemed to feel it, too. He stood, slightly humble and bowed, his hands in a prayerful position, as if before a shrine. A silence fell over us, except for the faint hum of the air-conditioning system and the hiss of whatever system kept the place humidified. Finally, in a soft voice, Wallace said, "It's bombproof." Well, it made sense, he said, between puffs on his pipe. This was his life's work. His scripts were here, too, in fact everything he'd ever written, even his term papers from high school.

There was no way that he could risk having all this destroyed. The vault was guaranteed by the builders to survive anything short of a direct nuclear hit.

I nodded dumbly. The notion that Wallace foresaw some nuclear Armageddon in which all of Los Angeles would be destroyed except this room seemed too lunatic to comment on. He opened one of the cupboards to show that each script was contained in a gold-embossed, leather-bound box. One of them, in red morocco, was labeled, in fourteen-karat-gold letters, *Additional dialog for Francis the Talking Mule.* I wondered what some future generation would think when they found this strange time capsule among the glassy remains of a long-forgotten nuclear holocaust. Would they sum up all of mid-twentieth-century letters with *The Chapman Report* in Dutch and Francis the Talking Mule? Would learned papers be written about *The Sins of Philip Fleming*? What would the scholars of the future deduce from that dim tale of adultery and sexual longing that had so shocked Alfred and Blanche Knopf that they turned it down, forcing Wallace to look for another publisher?

These were questions that I couldn't very well ask Wallace, who was busily showing me how much more space was available for his future works. The entire structure had been designed in the grand spirit of American optimism, on the assumption that Wallace's output would be prolific and extend over a long, productive lifetime. There was ample room here for many more novels and nonfiction books, even should the Iron Curtain be raised and that many more languages opened up to him.

We stepped back through the door into the office. He opened another door, and there—Proustian indeed—was a small room lined in cork, with an old-fashioned table and desk chair. On the table was an antique typewriter. It was, Wallace said reverentially, the typewriter he had bought with his savings in Kenosha, where he had delivered newspapers to buy it. On it, he had written his first stories, which he had sent out to every magazine that published short stories. It was on *this* typewriter that he had composed all his books. Wallace stared at the typewriter, his eyes misting over, a cloud of pipe smoke drifting over his head, toward the concealed grille of the air conditioner. Here was where the act of creation took place, he whispered, in this very room, and on this very typewriter, beside which I could not help noticing a thick stack of fresh white paper, no doubt soon to be turned into yet another two-hundred-thousand-word novel.

Wallace shook his head, as if in awe. "Quite something, isn't it?" he asked in a husky voice.

I nodded.

"I thought you'd like to see this place," Wallace said. "This is where I got the idea for writing *The Chapman Report*—right here!" He touched the desk gently.

I stared at the clean, shining desktop, the rows of pipes, the glass humidor full of Wallace's favorite tobacco. The emotion of the moment was evident on Wallace's face. At any moment I expected him to ask me to take off my shoes, as if we were on holy ground, but fortunately he came out of his trance and took me off to admire his new Bentley.

THE MORE a writer is held in contempt by the reviewers, the more seriously he is likely to take himself. Harold Robbins was a notable exception to this rule, but Irving Wallace was more typical. In any case, life in L.A., particularly in those days, virtually forced writers to take themselves seriously, since nobody else did. In a society where money and beauty were the only things that mattered, it was hard for a mere writer, however successful, to compete. In the movie industry, screenwriters were at the bottom of the totem pole; on the other hand, a certain guarded respect, not unmingled with contempt, was accorded to what were described as "real" writers, the ones who actually wrote books that were published by major New York publishing houses. But they were still not taken altogether seriously by their neighbors in "the industry." Writers who lived in the shadow of the movie business, like Wallace, tended to suffer from massive inferiority complexes, since at every party, PTA meeting, and visit to the supermarket, they were surrounded by people who considered them impoverished dilettantes who wrote books only because they couldn't make it in the "real" world— that is, the studios. Hence, no doubt, Wallace's Bentley and Robbins's yacht.

Of course, L.A. was full of writers who *didn't* live in the shadow of the studios and didn't care whether they were invited to parties or not, who were there because they had always lived there, or because they liked the climate, or to escape from the presence of other writers, or out of some obscure combination of sun worship and natural living that was as deeply embedded in the city's culture as the entertainment business. The Durants, needless to say, were in this category and ignored the movie people—to the extent that they were even aware of them—as much as they were ignored by them. Whatever had brought them to the West Coast from New York in the first place, they lived in resentful seclusion among the ravines and steep, wooded hills of North Hollywood, unfindable without elaborate directions and a map. Back in the day of silent pictures, this had been a fashionable neighborhood, though its aspect was sinister and strangely dark for L.A.: winding, narrow roads, high walls with dense shrubbery concealing grotesque houses and huge, overhanging trees, all combined to produce an atmosphere that was more Transylvanian than Californian. Unlike Brentwood, where the Wallaces lived amid flat, manicured lawns, stately palm trees, and cheerful houses, the Durants' neighborhood was more in the spirit of Norma Desmond's gloomy mansion in *Sunset Boulevard*. Their home, what could be seen of it behind high stone walls and fiercely overgrown vegetation, was in the 1920s Hollywood Spanish Gothic style, with much wrought iron, heavy wooden doors, gargoyles, tiny barred windows, and carved oak shutters. It looked more than capable of holding off an assault by armed pikemen or the angry peasantry, if necessary. Innumerable parapets and towers vaguely suggested a medieval castle, while the rusting wrought-iron gate in the wall that faced the street resembled that of a prison, so that one half expected to be taken immediately to a dungeon. Had Erich von Stroheim appeared in livery to announce a chimpanzee's funeral, I would not have been surprised.

After I had vigorously rung the old-fashioned bell, Ariel Durant appeared from out of the dense shrubbery that covered the flagstone pathway and shuffled out to open the gate for me. Her home attire was even more eccentric and bulky than what she had worn in New York. She greeted me in a hoarse, gravelly voice and warned me that I was about to see something to which few people had ever been granted entry—she squeezed my arm sharply—Will's workplace, the place where he had researched and written his books. Max and Ray Schuster had never been here—a lot *they* cared for the Durants' labors; all that mattered for them was money, money, money. But I, Ariel confided, seemed to her—though she was prepared to be disappointed—to have a finer sensibility and a real love of history, despite my having been brought up in wasteful affluence and having chosen an odious profession that was based on exploiting honest, decent, hardworking writers and scholars and stealing bread out of the mouth of genius.

But the house into which she ushered me was not exactly the West Coast equivalent of a Left Bank garret. It would, in fact, have been luxurious, had the Durants cared to give it some thought and attention, and must have been built by or for a star. The library had big French windows overlooking the garden and the empty pool. The overgrown trees around the house made it dark and cool, but it was the books that gave it a certain dusty, mildewed air, rather like that of Miss Havisham's dining room in *Great Expectations*. I felt a little like Pip, when he returned from London dressed as a gentleman, except that there was no Estella in sight, worse luck.

The Durants' working arrangements, unlike those of Irving Wallace, seemed jury-rigged and primitive. Will worked in an old wooden armchair covered in ratty-looking rugs, writing in longhand on a pad placed on his knees, with lots of spring clips to hold cards bearing his handwritten notes, lit by a shaded lamp like that of an accountant. His pages were laboriously typed up by Ethel, the Durants' daughter. All around him were books, piled to the ceiling, covering the floor, even stacked in the fireplace. Ariel worked beside him, on a smaller chair, handing him the quotations and historical references he required.

Affable as ever, he rose and shook my hand. His movement scattered dozens of file cards and slips of paper. Ariel got him seated again, covered his shoulders with a blanket, and put all the cards and slips in order again. He did not thank her. He did not even seem to notice her presence, in fact, his mind, no doubt, fixed on the firm, upward march of progress.

Ariel dragged me out into the garden, clutching my arm. "You see what he's like!" she hissed.

I nodded sympathetically, though it seemed to me that Will was much the same as ever, caught up in his work to the exclusion of the rest of the world.

"He's getting worse and worse," Ariel said. "He pretends to be working just so as not to have to talk to me."

I murmured calming phrases. If Will had in fact developed a way of shutting himself off from Ariel's ceaseless rancor and complaining, I thought, he was a lucky man, and a smart one, too. I recognized the symptoms easily enough. My father had always been stone-deaf to the voices of his wives, though in fact his hearing was acute when there was something he wanted to listen to. He could hear a whisper from across a soundstage if it concerned his work, particularly if it was in Hungarian.

"Perhaps Will should have a hearing aid?" I suggested, though hearing aids, I knew, were no cure for that kind of deafness.

"He won't have one," Ariel said lugubriously, in her strange, guttural baritone.

That seemed to me proof of real common sense on Will's part. Ariel's grip was rendering my arm numb, but I could think of no polite way to escape from it. "I have to do everything," Ariel went on. "Whole passages of the book are my work, you know."

This was news to me. That Ariel busied herself with footnotes and hunting for the exact quotation or fact that Will needed I knew well, if only because Ariel never failed to mention the fact in her letters, which usually ended with the handwritten warning, "Don't mention any of this to Will!" (Will's letters often ended with a quick note from Ariel at the bottom, reading, "Pay no attention to what Will has written above.") But it had never occurred to me, nor to Max Schuster, that Ariel might be doing any of the actual writing.

"I do my share of the work," she said. "Don't you think it's wrong that I don't get any credit?"

I had no opinion one way or the other, but I knew that publishers had an almost superstitious dread of changing a winning formula. After nearly thirty years of publishing Will Durant's books, I doubted that Max would be overjoyed at the idea of adding Ariel's name. It seemed impolitic to suggest this to Ariel, who was still clinging to me fiercely. Indeed, I had the impression that unless I agreed, she might never let go, so I nodded encouragingly until she released her grip.

We were standing in front of a sizable swimming pool, empty and overgrown with weeds. The Durants' garden, a fairly narrow and pinched space between the house and the wall, had the look of a set for *Rain*, a tropical jungle that threatened to engulf us from every side. One thing that can be said in favor of Los Angeles is that it is usually light and sunny, but here there was a dark closeness like that which so dismayed the Roman troops in the Teuteborg Forest before they were massacred by Arminius's Germans. I am not normally afraid of plants, but there was something aggressive and claustrophobic about the garden that made me edge my way gingerly back toward the house, careful to keep my feet on the narrow flagstone path, not that the house itself was very much more cheerful.

All the same, it was with a certain sense of relief that I regained Will's library—partly because Ariel had gone off to get tea. There was an atmosphere that seemed in some way familiar, like that of my grandparents' house north of London in the years after the war—a certain overheated stuffiness that I associate with age. I experienced the same depressing and slightly guilty feeling that overcame me on those Sunday afternoons in Hendon—the sense of performing a slightly tedious obligation, coupled with a desperate desire to get away. Just as they had in Hendon, the minutes seemed an hour long, and every time I looked at my watch, I thought it must have stopped. I could not help feeling, too, that my visit gave the Durants as little pleasure as it gave me. I could hear Ariel banging pots and muttering in the kitchen, presumably infuriated because I had said yes when Will asked if I would like a cup of tea—for Ariel was ahead of her time in rejecting all forms of domesticity as unnatural impositions on womankind—while Will, however serene his smile, occasionally glanced surreptitiously at his watch. No doubt I was keeping them from a brisk afternoon spent producing five or six thousand words on the ideas of Hume or Hobbes, followed by a nut burger and a glass of herb tea, then early to bed with Pascal's *Pensées*.

Will and I sat companionably for a few moments. He had a tendency to go blank from time to time, perhaps as he contemplated the vast stretch of history still left to him to cover, with or without his wife's help. In the seventh volume of *The Story of Civilization* he had reached the seventeenth century. True, that only left him with three centuries to go, but since he planned to devote a whole volume to the age of Louis XIV, another to Rousseau and the French and American revolutions, and a further one to Napoleon, the work before him must have weighed heavily on his shoulders. I chatted with him about the nineteenth century and suggested it might be called *The Age of Victoria*, but he gave me a kindly smile of reproof and shook his head. He did not think he would live to reach the nineteenth century, he said, but felt it would probably require two volumes: The first might be named after Darwin and the second after Marx or Freud. He was not an admirer of Victoria. But if he reached Napoleon, he would be content. (He did, but only just.)

He wanted to be very frank with me, he said. It was of course a pleasure to see me, but there was a purpose to my being here, a small problem that needed to be dealt with between himself and S&S, which I might be able to raise with Max on my return. There were beads of sweat on his forehead. He wiped his brow with a handkerchief and fell silent again.

Might the subject be that of joint authorship? I asked, hoping to put him out of his misery, for he was clearly having a great deal of difficulty bringing the subject up himself. A look of immense relief appeared on his face, and he glanced in the direction of the kitchen, where the kettle could be heard whistling. "Ariel talked to you then?" he asked. I wondered what he had supposed we were doing in the garden. "Do you think Max will mind?"

I suspected that Max would hate the idea, but of all people he should understand that Will wasn't going to stand in the way of whatever Ariel wanted. After all, however scared Will might be of Ariel, it could hardly exceed Max Schuster's fear of Ray. All the same, it didn't seem to me that Will was all that happy about the idea himself. He had the look of a man who has given in to overwhelming pressure and was determined to put the best face on it. I guessed that in his own quiet, passive-aggressive way, Will had been resisting this change for a long time.

There might be problems, I told him. The sales department would probably raise all sorts of objections, as might the Book-of-the-Month Club. But I didn't think the general public would be affected one way or the other. What mattered most was his own comfort and peace of mind. It might even be a good opportunity to get some publicity for the Durants, who complained constantly that Will had never been on the cover of *Time* or a guest on the *Today* show and that Max had failed to procure the Nobel Prize for his work. I said I would talk to Max as soon as I was back in New York.

Tears welled up in Will's eyes, and he grasped my hand. "Thank you," he whispered.

Shortly afterward—I could not help suspecting that she had been listening at the door—Ariel arrived with a tray on which were three mugs of steaming herb tea and a plate of stale Fig Newtons. The tea was something special, she said—very good for the health. She and Will were great believers in it and drank several cups a day. It was without caffeine and absolutely unstimulating. The mugs were odd, heavy, gnarly things, cast by some amateur potter and glazed in a kind of jungle green. Was their daughter an amateur potter? I wondered. The taste of the tea was distinctly medicinal, with a bitter, unpleasant aftertaste. I drank mine quickly, anxious to get back out into the sunshine and tawdriness of Sunset Boulevard, as far away as possible from the Durants' glum and Sisyphean struggle with world history. I made a mental note to myself to seek out the most trashy double feature I could find and spend the evening as unculturally as possible; unfortunately for me, Ariel's tea had a pronounced laxative effect, and instead I spent most of the night in my hotel bathroom. I was still there the next morning, when Casey arrived from New York, and suffered off and on from severe stomach spasms all the way up the Pacific Coast Highway to San Francisco.

Perhaps for that reason, we did not enjoy the second honeymoon that we had discussed somewhat wistfully in New York. We visited San Simeon, stopped to have a hamburger at Nepenthe in Big Sur, stayed the night in a hotel where it was possible to bathe in a warm natural spring. Despite all this, the romantic mood was lacking.

By the time we had reached San Francisco, we had decided to take what was in those days the inevitable step toward healing a marriage: to have a child.

It is hard now, almost thirty-seven years later, to remember that period before the sexual revolution and the rise of feminism when married couples who didn't have children were looked upon with some combination of suspicion and pity and felt not to be really grown-up. Casey was ahead of the curve when it came to sex and feminism, but she too felt that a child would put everything right between us, as well as validating her adulthood in the eyes of her mother and grandmother. No doubt it would do the same to me, I thought, in the eyes of my father.

On the flight back, we discussed the future. I would cut down working every night and weekend, we would take vacations like civilized people, I would put S&S in proportion. . . .

It all made sense. Or would have, had I not been flying back to a series of events that was to change S&S—and ultimately the rest of the publishing industry—beyond recognition.

CHAPTER 11

"BIG THINGS FROM small acorns grow." Truer words have never been written. In 1961, S&S was lurching along much as it had for several years, undisturbed except by the minor, everyday fracases and turf wars of office politics and the growing split between Leon Shimkin and Max Schuster. There is no law that says partners have to feel about each other like Damon and Pythias. Bennett Cerf and Donald Klopfer at Random House were umbilically linked in friendship and sometimes took vacations together; Alfred and Blanche Knopf were married, if not happily then certainly successfully. No doubt it would have been nice had the two remaining owners of S&S followed that pattern, but it need not have been fatal that they did not. After all, even before Shimkin became an owner, Dick Simon and Max Schuster were beginning to drift apart. As young men they had been partners in the most exciting adventure of their lives, but whether they had ever really been *friends* is open to doubt.

I mention all this only to explain that S&S was by no means the simple, happy place about which old-timers were later to reminisce—no place ever is. There was a certain amount of jockeying for position among those who felt themselves qualified for higher office. Some attached themselves to Shimkin, who seemed the person most likely to end up in control of the company—nobody assumed that Max Schuster could go on running it for very long. Others merely sought a better, more secure foothold.

I was in an ambiguous position myself. On paper, I still worked for Henry; however, Bob was my friend, and I was also doing a lot of editing for Peter Schwed. Not for the first time in my career, I was obliged to steer a middle course between people whom I liked but who disliked each other. I consoled myself with the fact that I was welcome, for the moment, in every camp and that everybody—Schwed, Simon, Gottlieb, even Max—wanted me to work on their books. Perhaps because I had nothing at stake, I was the first to notice that the power structure had changed insensibly, as if an invisible hand were shaking it from below.

Which, in a way, was the truth.

. . .

IN THE meantime, however, everybody's attention at S&S was diverted by an ice swan.

The ice swan is a relic of a past age of opulent display, when the great international hotels of the world had five-star restaurants, and the summit of luxury was still the transatlantic liner. In those days, any self-respecting hotel kitchen or ocean-liner galley had a sous-chef whose task it was to carve sculptures out of huge blocks of ice, often gleaming fantasies of vaguely nationalistic appeal. These sculptures, by definition ephemeral, usually four to five feet high, were carved in bulk and stored in the freezer, to be brought out to form the centerpiece in the first-class dining saloon at dinnertime. Caviar was usually presented in a life-size ice swan, its back hollowed out to hold about a kilo. On the big Cunard liners, smaller ice swans were also used for caviar at cocktail parties, either the purser's, to which all the more important and distinguished first-class passengers were invited on the first night at sea, or at ones given by the more social passengers in their own staterooms during the voyage. On my mother's side of the family, I actually had a distant relative who was chief purser of the *Queen Mary,* and I remember him taking me down to see a big, brightly lit freezer compartment stacked with ice sculptures, like an Aladdin's cave of frozen treasures, in the center of which a heavily dressed and gloved member of the kitchen staff, his breath condensing in clouds of vapor as he chipped away with a mallet and chisel, was carving a swan out of a block of ice about five feet long and four feet across, to add to a whole row of swans, lined up neatly like a ballet chorus, on the floor.

It was therefore with some surprise that I found an ice swan in the shower stall of the men's toilet at Simon and Schuster late one morning, its elegant, curved beak coldly mimicking that slightly supercilious smile that swans have as it dripped on the floor. The hole in its back was empty, so I surmised that the can of caviar it contained must have been removed before it was parked here to drip to death. It was a spectacle that produced a certain melancholy—so much effort, melting away so fast and unseen—as well as inevitable curiosity.

It soon transpired that I was, unfortunately, neither the first nor the only person to have seen the swan. It had been delivered on a trolley by two men earlier in the morning, and, as fate would have it, they had brought it up to the twenty-eighth floor in a passenger elevator with, of all people, Ray Schuster. At that time, the caviar was still in place, as was a card suspended from its beak.

There could have been no greater sign of the kind of hanky-panky that Ray most feared was taking place behind her back, so, to the great indignation of the two deliverymen, she ripped the envelope off the bird's beak and, bursting into Max's office, slapped it down on his desk. "Explain *this*!" she cried.

Poor Max bumbled and mumbled, his confusion no doubt passing for guilt in Ray's eyes, but when he at last had worked out the whole story, he discovered that the swan was destined for Phyllis S. Levy, Bob Gottlieb's assistant. Tall, thin, svelte, with the high-cheekboned, long-necked beauty of a model, Phyllis was the antithesis of the grubbiness that usually defines book publishing. Perfectly dressed and coiffed in the style that Jackie Kennedy was already making famous, Phyllis maintained a small cubicle that was as elegant and carefully tended as she was. Bob had more or less inherited Phyllis when Jack Goodman, then the publisher and the heir apparent of S&S, died unexpectedly. Both of them had worked for Goodman, whom they had worshiped, Bob as an editorial assistant and Phyllis as a secretary.

The best friend and college roommate of Rona Jaffe and instrumental in bringing *The Best of Everything* to S&S, Phyllis had a shrewd eye for popular fiction, great charm, a wicked sense of humor, a sharp intelligence, and a small but steady flame of ambition. The swan had, in fact, been sent to Phyllis by Aubrey Goodman, a first-time author whose hand she had been holding on behalf of Bob. Goodman's book, *The Golden Youth of Lee Prince,* was a flagrantly autobiographical novel about the New York *jeunesse dorée* that Phyllis had brought to Bob's attention. At Phyllis's urging, the book had been given a dust jacket made of metallic gold foil, an innovation that failed in the stores, since all the jackets wrinkled and tore in shipment. Nevertheless, Goodman wanted to express his gratitude, and since an ice swan was mentioned in the book, he sent one to Phyllis.

He could not have imagined that the swan would get Phyllis fired, nor could she, but it did. The problem, as it transpired, was not so much the swan itself as the fact that Phyllis and Ephraim London, Ray's favorite son-in-law, had been having a long, passionate affair—one that was to go on, in one form or another, and with many ups and downs, until his death. No doubt Ray, who could hardly have been unaware of it—who knows about Max?—had been looking for years for an opportunity to punish Phyllis, and the swan inadvertently provided it, or at least a pretext for firing her.

The immediate consequences of Phyllis's firing caused no more than a temporary inconvenience to Bob, as well as a sense of dismay at the departure of an old friend, but it was interpreted by many as a sign of Max's weakness. After all, everybody knew that it had been Ray who had asked for Phyllis's head, and Max who had meekly acquiesced.

As it happened, it was just the kind of misfortune that was calculated to make Leon Shimkin's day, since he was looking for signs that Max was incompetent. Though he did not harbor any strong sympathy toward female editorial assistants in general or Phyllis in particular, Shimkin felt that the matter had been badly handled. Shimkin himself was—ostentatiously—a humble family man, whose idea of an exciting time was counting the mail-order coupons as they came in and whose only known diversion from the work of increasing his fortune was a couple of martinis at lunch. Caviar and iced swans were not his kind of thing, nor beautiful editorial assistants; still, he had a sense for how to handle personnel problems, and by his standards Max had failed. Shimkin believed in doing this kind of thing *quietly*, above all.

Several people who had seen Shimkin at meetings or at the little tête-à-tête lunches at the Rainbow Room he favored reported that he had expressed sadness at the way things were going. His dear old friend Max was slipping, he would say, shaking his head solemnly, his opaque, dark eyes tearing as he sipped his martini. Max wasn't the man he used to be, anybody could see that.

What S&S needed was a strong manager, somebody who could pull the place together, the way he himself had done when he became business manager, a Young Turk, somebody who knew how to keep his eye on the ball.

Shimkin had not yet chosen his man; he preferred to bide his time and let the right man fight his way to the top. Shimkin made no secret of the fact that he didn't believe in *giving* anybody a job—no, no, *his* way was to give a man an *opportunity*, to see how he overcame obstacles, to find out just what kind of stuff he was made of. If you wanted to feed a man, you didn't give him a fish, he would say, you taught him how to catch fish, then he would never go hungry again.

It was not for nothing that Shimkin had been the discoverer of Dale Carnegie, whose lectures he had attended with results that changed both Carnegie's life and his own: *How to Win Friends and Influence People* became the biggest best-seller in S&S's history. Whether Carnegie's teachings brought Shimkin any friends was open to question, but he very often sounded in conversation as if he were reading directly from Carnegie's book. These homilies did not conceal a certain predatory quality in Shimkin's gaze, but he rather fancied himself as the voice of reason and usually had a Carnegie phrase ready for any occasion, at any rate before lunch—after it, his conversation was more unpredictable.

Most people beyond his cadre of loyalists had a good deal of difficulty understanding Shimkin, who first of all talked in a low, husky whisper and approached everything in a roundabout way, and second, preferred ambiguity to a straight answer whenever possible.

It didn't pay to make things easy for people, Shimkin believed—after all, nobody had made things easy for *him*.

CHAPTER 12

*L*IKE THE REST of the heads of the major American publishing houses, Max took a London trip once a year. Sometimes he and Ray went on to Paris, where they were lavishly wined and dined by the heads of the major French houses. Since most French publishers knew no English and the Schusters knew no French, little or no business was done in Paris.

London, of course, presented graver dangers. Given the common language, it was always possible that Max *might* buy a book, if only by accident. The heads of the major British houses were regarded as a particularly wily lot, by no means above pitching a book to an American visitor after offering him a stultifying meal in which three or four different wines had been served, followed by mighty snifters of brandy with the cigars. Many an American publisher had woken up with a hangover in his bedroom at the Connaught or Claridge's to find that he had bought a book that he couldn't remember a thing about and which, in the cold, gray light of a London morning, seemed to have no relevance at all to American readers.

Senior editors who had acquired the right to make an annual London trip were expected to be more discriminating, of course, and to work harder, but it was still basically a perk and a much coveted one at that. In my case, of course, going to London from time to time was normal—I was born there, after all, my family was there, and I was a British subject—besides which Casey was a devoted Anglophile, so determined to absorb British culture that she taught herself to speak with a distinct English accent.

Since I had to be in England from time to time for personal reasons, it was only natural that I should arrange to see a few British publishers while I was there. Thus, I dipped my toe into the waters of London publishing without having been authorized to do so, much to the annoyance of those whose prerogative it was. I didn't care—S&S wasn't paying for my trips to London, my father was.

The first British publisher I called on was George Weidenfeld, who, like my father and my uncles, was a Central European Jew who had prospered in England and become, in some ways, more English than the English. I had met him many years ago in his Belgravia flat, when my Aunt Alexa took me to one of the parties for which Weidenfeld was already famous. For an Oxford undergraduate, Weidenfeld's parties were something of an eye-opener—heady mixtures of writers, artists, important foreigners, celebrities, beautiful women, and even royalty, presided over by a host who combined charm, cunning, and chutzpah to a degree that I had rarely encountered outside my own family.

My first impression of Weidenfeld was that he was not exactly a prepossessing figure. He was short and rotund, with a blunt, hooked nose, a balding head circled by a narrow, tonsorial circle of graying black hair, plump jowls, and a double chin covered with dark-blue five-o'clock shadow. There was a fine sheen of sweat on his face. His hands were small, plump, blunt fingered, the nails short and carefully manicured. In one of them he held, with surprising delicacy, a half-smoked cigar, its aroma dominated by that of his cologne, sharp and powerfully sweet, like overripe fruit in the tropics.

His accent was curious—a thin, surface layer of fluent upper-class English over a foundation of other, more guttural languages. The effect was in some ways more foreign than if Weidenfeld spoke English badly, like my father. The elegance of his appearance was marred slightly by the fact that he shaved carelessly, leaving several patches of stubble on his plump cheeks—clearly, his good fortune did not yet extend to a valet.

In fact, he was, even then, a man of many achievements. He had fled Vienna just ahead of the Nazis, then made his way to London, where, without money or connections, he soon founded a literary magazine, *Contact*, from which his publishing house, Weidenfeld and Nicolson, eventually emerged and prospered. In 1949, he was invited to be personal assistant to Chaim Weizmann, the first president of Israel, and managed to hold on to that post while remaining a British subject and continuing to run *Contact*.

"I'm a great admirer of your father's," Weidenfeld said, the first time I met him. The mobile, expressive face moved close to mine, the voice dropping to a whisper. "*The Four Feathers* is one of my favorite films."

"That was my Uncle Zoli's film, actually. My father is Vincent, the art director."

"I'm a great admirer of his, too," Weidenfeld said blandly, his eyes already searching over my shoulder for bigger game. "You must come here again, please."

When I saw him again after nearly nine years, George had invited me to breakfast at his house in Chelsea. The day before, he called to ask what I would like for breakfast. I said bacon and eggs would be fine. Anything I liked, George said expansively—eggs, bacon, sausages, tomatoes: a real English breakfast.

The next day, I turned up exactly on time and was greeted by a foreign manservant in a white jacket who looked astonished to see me. He reluctantly showed me into the living room, where the debris of a party was still in evidence. From somewhere nearby I could hear the sound of a shower, followed by a murmur of conversation. I heard the sound of toothbrushing and prolonged gargling. About half an hour later, George appeared, beaming with goodwill, as if I had not disturbed him in the middle of his toilette. We chatted about publishing until the manservant came back to say that breakfast was ready.

We sat down in a small but beautifully furnished dining room. The manservant, holding a pot of coffee, his face a picture of gloom, leaned over to whisper in George's ear.

"It appears that there's no bacon," George said.

"Eggs will do just fine."

"Ah, splendid." The manservant leaned over to whisper again. George frowned. "There are no eggs, either," he said.

It was now clear to me that George had forgotten all about our breakfast date. "Toast will do fine," I told him, conscious of the fact that I was becoming increasingly hungry.

"I'm afraid there's no bread in the house, for some reason," George said. "I could send him up to the King's Road to buy a loaf?"

I said not to bother, and we contented ourselves with coffee. Now that the crisis was over, George relaxed and offered me a job, which he was to do every time we met over the next twenty years or so. I said that I would rather be his friend than his employee, which pleased him, though he answered, "But my dear boy, you could be *both*!"

By the time I was back on the street and looking for a taxi, I had committed myself to buy one of George's books—I was already wondering how I was going to explain it to S&S—and accepted an invitation to one of his parties, which was taking place in two days' time.

I had altogether forgiven him for having forgotten that he had invited me.

"DID YOU realize that it's a *costume* party?" Casey asked me when the formal invitation arrived in the morning post.

I shook my head. George hadn't mentioned that detail at all, but there it was in cold print—or, to be more accurate, in raised italic engraving: *"Costume de rigueur."* My first thought was one of relief—we didn't have costumes, so we couldn't go—but I could tell from the expression on Casey's face that she was determined to go. After a day of unrelenting improvisation, aided by a quick visit to Berman's, the famous theatrical costumer near Covent Garden, we were able to turn up for George's party as Gypsies, Casey in a revealing dress with many necklaces around her throat, and myself with a sash, the kind of shirt a Gypsy violinist might wear in a Central European restaurant, and a bandanna tied around my head, à la Douglas Fairbanks, Sr., in *The Private Life of Don Juan.*

The whole world seemed to have congregated in George's house. It was rumored that Princess Margaret was coming later on—it was not true, but it made everybody even happier to be there. It was obvious at once that most people had gone to a lot more trouble than we had. I was mildly startled to see Victor Weybright, the publisher of New American Library, a man with a heroic paunch, appear as a red-stained Native American in a brief loincloth, deerskin moccasins, and a feathered headdress. There were the usual Pierrots, Mephistopheleses, and Napoleons, several slave girls and Cleopatras, even a few visiting American publishers, including Jim Silberman of Random House, who had ignored the instruction and turned up in business suits. To my surprise, Cornelius Ryan was there, dressed in a domino, presumably as a Venetian nobleman, holding a mask close to his face as he talked earnestly to a man dressed as a New Orleans riverboat gambler, complete with a waxed mustache and a velvet waistcoat. I went over to say hello. "Thank God," Connie said. "Someone who looks as out of place as I am." He introduced me to the riverboat gambler, who turned out to be a distinguished historian. Connie's wife, Kathy, was there somewhere, he said, dressed as a Greek goddess. Which one? I asked. Connie grabbed a drink from a passing waiter and tossed it down. "Jesus Christ, boyo," he said, "how the hell would I know? You're the one with the education in classics." I began to move away—Connie could be edgy and aggressive when he'd had a few drinks, and I didn't want to be around if things got ugly—but before I could put any distance between us, an apparition bore down on us that silenced even Connie.

It was our host, dressed in Middle Eastern regalia, either as the vizier of some exotic Arabian court or possibly Ali Baba. He wore a black-and-gold floor-length robe, a high gold turban with a big fake diamond and an ostrich-feather plume, gold sandals with curled, pointed toes, and a sash, in which he carried a great curved sword. With his dark, predatory eyes, his curved nose, his plump, beringed hands, and his knowing smile, George looked as if he would have been right at home in the streets of old Baghdad. At any moment, he seemed likely to produce a flying carpet for sale.

Connie lit a cigarette—no easy task in a mask—and leaned close to George. "There's something I've always wanted to ask you, George," he said, his soft Irish voice blurred only slightly by drink.

George waved his cigar like a magic wand, as if granting permission.

"Tell me," Connie went on, "how it is that a man like you is always surrounded by beautiful women?" Connie gave George a good look, from turbaned head to slippered foot. "I mean, let's be frank, boyo, you're fat, you're bald, you don't exactly have a handsome puss. What is it they see in you?"

This was a question that many people had asked themselves over the years. George had even managed to actually marry several very wealthy women, without whom it is doubtful that neither Weidenfeld and Nicolson, with its otherwise slim resources, nor George's own lifestyle, which was princely, could have been kept afloat.

Charm, of course, was one answer. Attention was another. With George, listening was a fine art. And George not only listened—in four or five languages—he *remembered,* and as a result he was a repository of gossip about everybody who mattered, so that he could always keep a woman amused.

George seemed to be running through his abilities in his mind, but then he gave a seraphic smile and beckoned Ryan closer to him. "My dear Connie," he said pleasantly, "it's very simple." He spoke clearly and slowly, as one might to a child. "You see," he said, "in certain circles I am known"—he paused dramatically—"as the Nijinsky of cunnilingus."

It was the one thing I hadn't considered.

Whether it was true or not, George had trumped Connie, who gave a forced laugh and crept off to get drunker as the evening wore on. I looked at George. He gave me a knowing wink, then stepped back into the crowd of friends and hangers-on, as splendid as Harun al-Rashid, leaving behind him a fragrant trail of cigar smoke and cologne.

You couldn't help admiring a man like that, even if he *had* just sold you 25,000 copies of a book you didn't want.

WHEN I told this story to someone at lunch the next day, she nodded gravely, as if to confirm that this was a well-known fact in British publishing circles. The London publishing world was (and still is) far smaller than ours, and people in it much more closely knit, "clubby" in a way that ours is not. That perhaps explains a certain bawdiness that is largely lacking in New York publishing circles, as well as numerous eccentricities of personal behavior, so beloved to the English mind.

It was impossible not to envy the British publishers. They seemed to be having a far better time than their American counterparts, and while they undoubtedly made less money, they often had more interesting or controversial lists, in those innocent days before the American houses bought up so much of the British book-publishing industry.

It was easy enough to understand why senior American publishers clung to their prerogative of making the London trip. In the various power struggles that had taken place at S&S since the death of Jack Goodman, this gradually became the jealously guarded privilege of Peter Schwed, who had risen from manager of the rights department to publisher, though in fact he was a busy and prolific editor, specializing at first in sports books.

Schwed, a wisecracking man, with a wide knowledge of sports and a good head for numbers, had more or less elbowed aside the somewhat more literary and less aggressive Henry Simon, not without some residue of bad feelings on both sides. Henry was a Columbia graduate and a scholar turned editor, while Schwed was a Princeton man (and vocally proud of the fact) who had worked at the Provident Loan Society (basically a genteel pawnbroker) before becoming a decorated artillery officer in World War Two and then joining S&S. Henry was gray-faced, melancholy, tall, rail-thin, and stooped, while Schwed was deeply tanned, assertive, short, stocky, a fiercely competitive athlete whose passion was tennis. Henry Simon was on his third marriage, while Schwed was outspoken about the happiness of his marriage. They were opposites in every possible way.

Schwed made his annual trip to London a kind of public event, in the nature of a royal progress, with an elaborate hour-by-hour, day-to-day itinerary, distributed in advance to everyone of note in the company. So far as it went, this was OK—one could ignore it or not. More difficult to ignore was the Dictabelt full of notes he mailed every day, which was typed up by his faithful secretary and circulated. These transcripts ran to many pages, from blow-by-blow accounts of Schwed's tennis games to the menus of his dinners with authors and publishing luminaries. Since, in those days, British agents invariably used an American counterpart to sell their books in the United States, those of us who had remained at home were obliged to call the American agent for every book or book outline that Schwed mentioned. We then had to read and report on whatever it was with scrupulous attention because Schwed, who had a statistical kind of mind and reveled in lists and numbers, kept elaborate records, as he was determined to show Schuster and Shimkin that his trips were worth what they cost.

I have no idea what Shimkin made of these reports or if he even read them, but they were, of course, just the kind of thing that Max loved. He annotated them in thick blue Chinagraph writing, adding his own comments, demanding further reports and readings, and circulating them throughout the company, often to people who had little or no idea what they were about.

It was as a result of this that I was drawn more directly into Schwed's orbit. He needed somebody to help him with the editing of his list, now that it was growing in size. I was not at all sure that I wanted to move from reporting directly to Henry to reporting to Peter, who would doubtless make more use of my time, but my doubts were as nothing compared to his about me.

If I wanted to work for him, he told me, I would get far more to do. He was happy to leave much of the editing to me, except with those authors whom he couldn't delegate, such as P. G. Wodehouse. He would square things with Henry, and of course I would continue to work with Max and to do whatever I was doing with Bob. The only thing that gave him pause, he said, looking at me intently, was whether I was altogether trustworthy.

It had not occurred to me that my trustworthiness was an issue. I had been conspicuously loyal to Henry, which was more than anyone else in the company could say, and so far as Max was concerned, I had been not only loyal but discreet. Others might make fun of Max, but I did not.

Perhaps because of his background at Provident Loan, Schwed was one of the few executives at S&S who favored the banker style in office furnishings. He sat behind an enormous varnished-wood desk with a dark brown leather top, tooled in gold, on top of which was a fake colonial brass lamp of the kind favored by bank vice presidents in those days, and a whole array of matching leather desk furnishings—blotter, in tray, out tray, calendar, as well as a pen set on an alabaster base—so that one felt about to be turned down for a mortgage. To one side of him was an impressive array of pipes, which he smoked nonstop. From time to time he knocked the ashes out of his pipe and fieldstripped it before lighting it again.

In what way, I asked, did he find my loyalty questionable?

Schwed rammed a pipe cleaner down the bore of his pipe and drew out a thick wad of brown goo. I had to understand something, he muttered, examining the results of his probe, unlike a lot of guys around here, he was a straight shooter. He was the kind of guy who always called the shots as he saw them.

I nodded vaguely. Sports metaphors have never meant much to me, and I have always had a tendency to distrust those who use them, a prejudice that was by no means limited to Americans. Englishmen who refer to any kind of difficulty as "a sticky wicket" leave me just as cold, if not colder. Besides, I am a born skeptic. The moment someone tells me how honest and straightforward they are, I find myself mistrusting them.

I had a certain reputation, Schwed went on, for being a Machiavellian type, rather than a team player. That wasn't his way of operating at all. He was open, up-front, honest, outspoken, blunt. Did I think I could live with that? And did I think I could play a straight game with him?

I looked him in the eye as firmly as I could and said yes, upon which we both stood up and shook hands, leaning across the big desk. Schwed's handshake was of the kind that feels as if you've just put your hand in a rock crusher. I continued to smile while he squeezed my hand in his. Once he let it go, I slipped it in my pocket, hoping to regain the use of it soon. Schwed waved his pipe at me from behind a self-created fog bank of tobacco smoke. "Welcome to the team," he said.

THE TEAM, as it turned out, was strikingly modest—no larger, really, than Henry's. Whereas Bob did, in fact, have a substantial team (though it would not have occurred to him to apply that word to his loved ones, admirers, and supporters), Peter's team consisted of himself, his charming and faithful secretary, Nelle Haber, his former secretary, Mildred Marmur, who was now running the S&S rights department and in the process of declaring her independence from Schwed, and now me—and I was not by anyone's definition a team player, as Schwed had rightly guessed.

As things turned out, no big change actually occurred to me. My salary was not increased significantly, and I stayed in the same small office. But I could not complain that I was being left without work to do, and certainly I was spared that most frustrating of experiences for most neophyte editors: staring at a bare desk, waiting for manuscripts to come in.

CHAPTER 13

*B*Y THE BEGINNING of 1963, I felt—albeit with a certain in-
nate caution—that I was a full-fledged member of the S&S "family." I
had expected that S&S would be a good place to work until I finally discovered what it was that I really wanted to do, but the thought was gradually entering my mind that I might have already found it. To an
extraordinary degree, I felt I had, at last, a *stake* in S&S, not in the form
of ownership, of course, but in the sense that I had joined it as one
might have joined a regiment in the British Army: for life.

I was confident enough to move with Casey into a larger apartment
and to accept the news that she was pregnant with a calm I would not
have felt a year or two earlier. When I called my father to give him the
news, I heard him sigh deeply, followed by a long silence. "My poor
Miki," he said, and that was that. It was not, I realized, that Vincent had
anything against bringing another child into the world—within reason
he was in favor of that—it was that he did not think that Casey and I
were even remotely ready for parenthood.

It goes without saying that he was right.

THERE HAD been rumors of change on the floor below us, where
Shimkin and his cronies (no other word will do) ran Pocket Books. New
blood was said to have been injected into the company, Young Turks
were reported to be making their force felt, particularly in the marketing
department. Since our own marketing department was not run on anything like scientific, efficient lines, it was felt, no doubt chiefly by
Shimkin, that it would do S&S no harm to receive a little advice and
help from downstairs.

Shortly afterward, though I was increasingly preoccupied with
Casey's pregnancy, which was turning out to be a difficult one, I began
to hear a name repeated over and over again, with various degrees and
types of emotion. I did not pay much attention. Editors, by definition,

are more interested in what is happening in the lives of their authors and agents than in the other departments of a publishing company, which in part explains why they are seldom chosen for higher management positions and so often fail when they are chosen. Editors should be looking *outward*, not inward.

With this in mind, it is hardly surprising that I had paid no attention to the name Dick Snyder, which was usually prefaced by, "You'll never believe what this guy said!" It was apparent that Richard E. Snyder, whoever he might be, was a man of action, and that anywhere he appeared, things changed quickly, if not always smoothly. It did not diminish the awe that surrounded him that nobody knew what his job actually was or even by what authority he appeared mysteriously from time to time at S&S.

Although invisible to most of us, Snyder was reported to have shaken up the Pocket Books sales department, to have breathed new life into Golden Books' marketing, to have turned up at meetings of the S&S sales department uninvited. He seemed determined to learn all about the hardcover-book business, and he was, by all accounts, a fast and impatient learner. Those who had met him commented on his high level of energy, his quick intelligence, and his sharp temper. He was not, it seemed, a patient or unassuming fellow, and a few bruised feelings were said to have been experienced among the sales and marketing people. This did not cause much grief in the editorial department, where life went on as usual and where change of any kind was frowned upon. Nobody worried or even gave the matter much thought—other brash young newcomers had come and gone over the years or stayed on to become sedate middle-aged executives who knew the importance of the old adage, "To get ahead you have to get along."

It was some time before I finally collided with this new phenomenon myself. Schwed had returned recently from one of his London trips, and, as was his habit, he called a large meeting to go over all the books he had mentioned in his many missives to S&S. We assembled in Schwed's office, each of us carrying a yellow legal pad, as if we were about to be examined—which was literally the case for most of us, as Schwed would not end the meeting until he knew exactly what had happened to every book and outline he had mentioned from London. Under the circumstances, it was no easy task to have to report that a book had been unreadable or, as was very often the case, simply wouldn't travel across the Atlantic, usually because the subject was simply too English to survive the journey.*

The room was crowded enough so that I did not at first realize that there was a stranger among us, sitting comfortably on the brown leather sofa facing Schwed's desk. Schwed himself, busy with his lists and his pipe, had perhaps not noticed the newcomer himself. I noted that the young man, who appeared to be about my age and height, was not carrying a yellow legal pad and looked so at ease that one might have thought it was *his* office. He was slender but with a solid build that suggested strength, and the rather protuberant eyes behind his glasses had a boldly purposeful, steely glint to them, as did the firm, dimpled chin. His complexion was on the reddish side, and his brownish hair was cut short. He wore the standard American businessman's uniform of the time: a gray suit, a white shirt, a neat tie, and shiny shoes with blunt toes and thick soles. There was nothing particularly elegant about his clothes, but they clearly identified him as a businessperson of some kind, not an editor, for even in those days editors were somewhat bohemian in their dress. Even those few who wore suits did so with a certain donnish flair or eccentricity, as if their ideal was to resemble a Harvard professor rather than a successful banker or advertising executive. Schwed, for example, usually wore a sports coat and favored a French beret on rainy days, while Bob wore corduroy trousers and open-necked shirts.

Not having noticed the interloper, Schwed plunged into his list. He began with the books that he had actually bought while he was in England. I sketched on my yellow legal pad. These books were no concern of mine at this point. I would read them later, if I had to draft the flap copy or do any editing to Americanize them or to compensate for the

---

* This is a loaded subject, even today—the work of some English writers travels perfectly well, while that of others, for no very discernible reason, doesn't at all. Some English best-sellers—Dr. Herriot's *All Creatures Great and Small*, for example, or the novels of John le Carré—go on to become huge best-sellers in the United States, while others sink without a trace into the Atlantic. Much English literary fiction, and almost all French and European fiction, doesn't travel at all, like certain kinds of cheese, but every once in a while there will be a startling exception, like Salman Rushdie or Martin Amis. The situation is complicated by the immense hunger for American books of all kinds in England, and, for that matter, in the rest of the world. Like Big Macs and blue jeans, American writing is by and large welcome everywhere, which tends to make the transatlantic traffic more or less one way. Thus, the novels of Mary Higgins Clark invariably top the French best-seller lists, whereas it is hard to remember the last time that *any* French novel, literary or otherwise, even appeared at the bottom of *The New York Times*'s best-seller list. The French complain bitterly about American cultural hegemony, while the British, who experience it much more severely, don't seem to care.

fact that English editors seldom do any editing at all and in general tend to regard the whole process as one of those odd American obsessions, like putting ice in whiskey or going to the dentist regularly.

Lost in my own thoughts—mostly having to do with prospective fatherhood, about which role I didn't have as yet a useful clue—I only half heard Schwed enthuse over an English novel about two tramps who tried to rescue small animals, rodents, pets, birds, and so on that had been hit by cars. It occurred to me vaguely that this very slight work of fiction might be difficult to sell to the mass of American fiction readers. Of course, it's hard to guess what will appeal to more intellectual American readers, who have hailed many a foreign oddity as a masterpiece; still, sentimentality about animals, while a more or less universal emotion in England (Graham Greene once said that while you could probably get away with beating a child in Trafalgar Square at high noon, you would be lynched for hitting an animal), didn't seem to me likely to win praise from the more serious literary critics here. All the same, I didn't feel it was my place to argue about something that Schwed was already committed to and about which he waxed fervently, his face shining with enthusiasm. This, he would have us know, was the real thing, the most talked-about novel in London. Every American publisher in London had been after it, and when Simon Michael Bessie heard that Schwed had nabbed the book right from under his nose, he almost cried, right there in the bar at Brown's Hotel. If he did say so himself, Schwed said, it was a coup, something to be really proud of, and proof that all his wining, dining, and tennis playing in London paid off in the end. Why, the biggest agent in London, Gerald Pollinger, though it wasn't his book, had called him at the hotel to congratulate him on buying *the* novel of the season. Of course, we were going to have to get behind the book, that went without saying.

At some point during this peroration, Schwed must have noticed the stranger on his sofa, because he stopped and stared at him. The stranger stared right back, one leg crossed confidently over the other, his expression inscrutable but not, one would say, convinced. Schwed cleared his throat noisily, and said, "Ah, excuse me . . ."

He didn't challenge the intruder, no doubt because the intruder's eyes were fixed unwaveringly on his, and nothing on his face showed even the slightest trace of self-doubt.

"Dick Snyder," the young man said pleasantly. His voice was a deep, husky, basso profundo growl, by far and away the deepest register I had ever heard in a white man's voice (as a child, I had once heard Paul Robeson sing "Ol' Man River" for my father at home).* Snyder's voice was harsh, rather than melodious, the accent was curious and hard to place—a combination of Brooklyn Jewish and Harvard that hesitated, from syllable to syllable, between the two.

"Did I send you a copy of this memo?" Schwed asked, holding up a thick sheaf of paper.

"No," Snyder said, pleasantly enough, but with the air of somebody who couldn't be moved by a bulldozer and wasn't about to explain his presence to anyone.

Schwed puzzled over this briefly, then decided to get on with his agenda. He continued to sing the praises of the novel he had bought in London, while Snyder doodled, lips slightly pursed as if he were tunelessly whistling. The more he thought of it, Schwed said, warming to his subject, the more sure he was that twenty thousand copies was the right number—maybe more.

Snyder waited for Schwed to pause, then spoke in a voice that dominated the room. "How do we *know* this novel is that good?" he asked.

"I just told you," Schwed snapped.

"That's all we have to go on, to set a first printing of twenty thousand? That you liked it?" Snyder smiled. He had big, square, even teeth, very white, and when he smiled they seemed to fill his mouth. At this moment, however, his smile conveyed no particular humor—it was more of a grimace, in fact. He did not look indignant, merely interested, as if his only reason for his presence was so he could learn more about the mysteries of hardcover-book publishing.

Schwed bit down hard on his pipe stem. "It's all we had a lot of times before, and they've all worked out just fine, goddamn it. Now let's move on."

But Snyder had pulled out of his pocket a list of his own, which he unfolded slowly. "Not all of them," he said agreeably, looking it over.

It was one of Schwed's boasts that his books never lost money and that he had the facts and figures to prove it. Nobody had ever challenged him on this point, to my knowledge, if only because nobody cared enough to do it. Besides, it was a patently absurd claim. *Every* ed-

---

* He was playing the role of an African chieftain in my Uncle Zoli's film *Sanders of the River* at the time, and that remains for me the stump puller of all voices.

itor has failures, and it was unlikely that Schwed had been spared them. As in the movie business, anything better than a 50 percent rate of success made you a genius. In book publishing there is no such thing as R and D. The only way to find out if a book is going to sell is to publish it. Most editors (and almost all agents and authors) invariably base their estimate of how well a book has done on the *gross sale*, before returns (sometimes six months or a year after publication) have come in, thus ignoring the fact that returns can turn an apparent success into a dismal fiscal failure. Since the lifeblood of book publishing is enthusiasm, it is easy to be misled—and to mislead oneself.

There was a certain tension in the air between the two men. Everybody else in the room was silent. Then the meeting resumed at a much faster pace. Schwed's only ambition now was to get us all out of his office. Snyder kept his mouth shut during the rest of the meeting, merely scribbling an occasional note from time to time on his piece of paper.

At the end of the meeting, Snyder left before anyone could talk to him, creating—as he no doubt intended—the impression that a new power had arrived on the scene. Schwed may have been tempted to complain about being second-guessed by a young man he didn't even know, but since he was very quiet about the results, it was possible to guess that somebody—probably Shimkin—had told him this was the way it was going to be from now on, like it or lump it, though knowing Shimkin, he was perfectly capable of wrapping up the message in mumbled flatteries and promises to control young Snyder, so that Schwed may have regained the twenty-eighth floor more cheerfully than was warranted. But the writing was on the wall for all to see, and shortly afterward Snyder took the first of the many jobs and titles he was to hold until he eventually became CEO of a much larger S&S.

Soon his initials were cc'd on almost every significant memo, and people were straining their eyes to interpret his almost unreadable handwriting, a powerful, hurried, energetic scrawl that was usually demanding more information right away.

I had not had a real opportunity to meet this wunderkind. For the moment, he was busy elsewhere and seldom appeared in the editorial department. (His office was still "downstairs.") From the area of sales and marketing there came rumors of firings, reorganizations, coups, and new alliances, like news from a Renaissance Italian city-state. These departments, which were hard for an outsider to separate in the first place, had always been run like feudal fiefdoms, and like most publishing houses we had one person, Tony Schulte, whose job it was to act as the liaison between all these vital services and the editors, who were either too busy or too lost in their own precious little worlds to involve themselves in the grubby business of actually *selling* the books.

Schulte was forceful, clean-cut, cheerful, handsome, and athletic. Reputedly heir to a cigar-store fortune, he was one of those rare people who actually understand the whole publishing process, not just one small part of it, and was as much at home perched on Bob's sofa in the evenings, talking about books, as he was downstairs, schmoozing with the guys in sales and marketing.

Snyder, as I was soon to discover, also had the ability to fit in anywhere he wanted to, together with a truly remarkable gift for not getting stuck in any one department or at any one level. His promotions and moves from one department to another took place at such a dizzying rate that it was hard to keep up with him, with the result that his business cards were always out of date. He seemed to soak up useful knowledge like a sponge, according to Schulte, who was at once admiring and dismayed, perhaps because he already saw in Snyder a potential and formidable rival.

The truth was, however, that they were oil and water. Schulte was laid-back, calm, and good-humored, a kind of New York Jewish patrician who did not as a rule take the trials and tribulations of publishing too seriously. Snyder was fiercely concentrated and totally focused on what he was doing, with the kind of steely determination that comes precisely from *not* having anything to fall back on. He could be very funny and enjoyed a joke as much as the next person, but it could not be said that he was calm or good-humored by nature. On the contrary, he was like a tightly wound spring, and to those who knew him he seemed often to be holding himself back from an explosion of temper by sheer willpower. One guessed, too, that his bark and his bite were likely to be equally unpleasant, especially when it came to ill-prepared or sloppy work or a reluctance to go the extra mile.

He himself went the proverbial extra mile almost every day, and his working hours were already legendary. He was in early, he left late, and he didn't go home until he had cleaned off his desk, according to Schulte, who was no slouch himself.

I was absent for a good deal of this time—Casey's difficult pregnancy, during which she was confined to bed for several months—ended successfully with the birth of a son, and I soon found myself plunged unprepared into the world of first-time parenting, made even more traumatic by the fact that Casey appeared to have no relatives to rely on except for her mother, whom she regarded as naive and unrealistic, and her grandmother, a difficult old woman. Since my family was in London and Casey would rather have died than ask hers for advice or assistance, we were without the safety net that most young parents have.

Once we had returned to some kind of routine, however different it might be from our previous way of life, my attention returned to S&S—it was a lot more rewarding to think about books and authors than about diapers, formula, and middle-of-the-night feedings. To my surprise, I was asked to attend the annual convention of librarians in Atlantic City, a request that was puzzling, since I could think of no very good reason why librarians would want to meet me, nor I them. Clearly this assignment was not a plum—Bob Gottlieb, I learned, had already turned it down—but I was in no position to be fussy. In those days, of course, Atlantic City was not Las Vegas East, as it has now become. It was a 1920s seaside town slipping ungracefully into terminal decay, its once elegant seafront hotels declining into single-occupancy rooming houses for the poor and the old or worse, its famous boardwalk now a haunt for drug addicts and muggers. It was a place that no sensible person would have chosen to visit, not even the librarians, who, I thought, could surely have picked better.

A COUPLE of days after I had written this into my calendar and more or less forgotten about it, I received a call from Snyder, saying that he, too, was going to the librarians' convention, to represent sales and marketing. He suggested that we join forces. I said that sounded like a good idea and a chance to get to know each other. He offered to rent a car, so we could drive there together.

It did not occur to me at the time that being sent to Atlantic City was S&S's way of putting us in our places—Snyder for making too many waves, me for expressing my opinion too often and too loudly. Nor did it occur to me that Snyder might have included me deliberately. The one area of the company about which he had little knowledge was the editorial department of S&S. I might have seemed like his best bet to get a foothold there, however small—after all, we were almost exactly the same age and both struggling to get ahead of numerous layers of entrenched and more senior people. I was more or less content with my position, but Snyder was not. He positively glowed with ambition in a company—indeed, in an industry—in which it was crass to admit to personal ambition.

In those days, the renting of a car was by no means the easy and everyday transaction it is now, nor was S&S particularly liberal when it came to that kind of thing. The best we were able to do was a yellow Rambler of uncertain vintage, which Snyder had picked up from some discount rental place known only to the S&S business department. He was, however, happy to leave the driving to me.*

Dick—we were on a first-name basis at once—lived only two blocks away from me, in an apartment on Fifty-seventh Street, where he and his wife, Ruth, were soon to have their first child. Far from being the fearsome personality that most people at S&S believed him to be, he could not, in fact, have been more simpatico. He was better at asking questions than at answering them, with the result that by the time we were in New Jersey, he already knew everything he wanted to about me. I had picked up only a few facts about him. Despite the broad Harvard intonation, he had gone to Tufts and was drafted into the army. Following the army, he had expected, without much enthusiasm, to go to work in his father's successful clothing business, but his father surprised him, saying, "I'd rather have a son than a partner."

Dick ended up as a trainee salesman at Doubleday, having chosen the business of book publishing as casually and accidentally as I had. Perhaps for that reason, we got along well from the very first. Almost everybody in the book business says that he always wanted to be involved with books, and perhaps it's true, but Dick and I were alike in never having given the matter any thought at all. Disappointment is a well-known spur to ambition, and it seemed to have worked in both our cases.

It is a curious fact that one makes the really significant friendships of one's life in much the same way as one falls in love, with one sudden, fell swoop—*un coup de foudre,* as the French say—and almost never by

---

* Years later, on our first trip to the Frankfurt Book Fair, before Snyder had graduated to chauffeur-driven limousines, I remember our renting a car at Frankfurt airport and driving in circles through the pouring rain and early morning rush-hour traffic of a strange city. Snyder read the map in a state of growing dismay as I got into the wrong lane or missed a crucial exit. We could actually *see* our hotel as we sped past it in the wrong direction again and again, apparently unable to approach it. "You are *never* going to do the fucking driving again," he growled in a deep voice, and I never did.

small degrees. It takes a lot of time and shared experience to make a friendship permanent, to *harden* it, but in my life the friendships that matter have been made instantly, and nothing afterward has ever changed or diminished them. Somehow, there formed between Dick and me in that claustrophobic little car a friendship that was to last through the decades, despite the fact that we had very little in common. In some ways, in fact, we appeared to be opposites. Dick was a born businessman, with a head for numbers and a real thirst for confrontation, whereas I was a born editor, happiest alone with a book or a manuscript, and in business matters, as in everything else, a natural compromiser. I do not think either of us realized how valuable these different qualities might be if they were wielded together, for a purpose. But that, of course, was in the future.

As we entered Atlantic City, the view became more and more depressing. Beyond the deserted boardwalk a gray sea met an equally gray, damp sky. Most of the old hotels were closed, their windows boarded up with plywood, their facades moistly crumbling with decay. The hotel we were booked into did not look any better, though it did have glass in the windows instead of plywood. A wizened old man dressed in a threadbare bellboy's outfit took us up to our suite in a trembling, clanking old elevator, which looked to have been the first one Otis ever made. "You guys come here for the convention?" he asked. I signified that we had. He sighed deeply. "Tell you one thing," he went on, in a lugubrious voice. "The librarians don't tip worth a damn."

The suite itself had ancient maroon curtains laced with dust and cobwebs, the beds were creaking and lumpy, the bathroom a nightmare of cracked, yellowing tiles and wheezing pipes. Having dragged our luggage into the suite with great difficulty, the bellboy stood forlornly at the door, a pillbox hat perched ridiculously at a slant on his bald head, the sleeves of his tattered bum-freezer jacket shiny where he had rubbed his nose on them, his gnarled hand extended for a tip. Dick palmed several bills into his hand and sent him off for a bottle of scotch and some ice. The only thing that cheered Dick up was the fact that there would be several hundred women downstairs at cocktail time, with practically no men. "We'll wash up," he said, "have a drink, then check out the talent."

But when we went downstairs to the hotel ballroom, the talent was disappointing. It was basically a room full of middle-aged women, intent on talking about books, especially literary novels and poetry, and even Dick's enthusiasm for the opposite sex soon melted. The lights dimmed, and we all trooped into the banquet room, where Dick and I found ourselves at a table with six pleasant but rather elderly librarians from Cleveland. Since my wife had often sung the praises of Cleveland's library system, I, at least, had something to talk about—perhaps the only time in my life when a familiarity with the cultural institutions of Shaker Heights was to prove a useful asset. Dick was not so fortunate. Although he knew more about library discounts than I did (no great feat since I knew nothing), it was not a subject calculated to keep his spirits high. Bravely, he held to it, through three execrable courses, but by the time coffee was being served he was rolling his eyes toward me in supplication. I quickly pleaded a headache, and we returned to our dismal suite, with its peeling wallpaper and forty-watt bulbs. Dick sat down and took his shoes off. Despite his ruddy complexion, he looked worn out.

"Cheer up," I said. "Tomorrow may be better."

He looked pensive. "Do you think anybody would miss us if we left?" he asked.

I didn't think so, but it seemed like deserting one's post under fire. On the other hand, anything seemed better than staying. What if somebody at S&S found out that we hadn't stayed? I wondered. What would happen to us?

Dick shrugged. "Nobody will care. Anybody asks, we'll tell them it was a great learning experience." He spoke, as he always would over the coming decades, with absolute confidence.

Quietly, as if stealth was called for, we sneaked downstairs, checked out, and got back into our rented Rambler. Dick's spirits rose as we hit the highway and put some distance between ourselves and the librarians. Through the mist, we could see the glow from the lights of New York. "Where do you see yourself in ten years' time?" he asked solemnly. "What's your ambition?"

I was silent for a few moments. I didn't have a clue about where I wanted to be *next* year, let alone in ten years' time. The truth was that I didn't really have a specific ambition. Fatherhood or not, my mind was still full of unrealistic or mutually contradictory ideas about the future, a well-stuffed cloud-cuckoo-land: I dreamed vaguely of going back to England, or taking up photography, or even of going into the movie business, the very thing I had run away from in the first place. To have a lot of different ambitions, I realized, was to have no ambition at all.

At S&S, where ambition might have made some sense and even done me some good, I really had none. Above me there were layers of people more senior than myself, who showed every sign of staying there for the rest of their lives (or mine)—starting with Bob Gottlieb, Henry Simon, and Peter Schwed—although it did occasionally occur to me that I might be able to leapfrog over one or two of the lesser ones without great difficulty and perhaps had already done so. With the appropriate modesty, I suggested to Dick that my ambition was to go on doing pretty much what I'd been doing but at a higher rate of pay.

"Bullshit," he said firmly. He lit a cigarette. "You're as ambitious as I am."

I denied it. "You're full of shit," he went on in a cordial tone, his deep voice rumbling. He sounded sincere and well intentioned rather than argumentative.

He pointed his cigarette at me in the dark. "Look at the facts," he said. "You joined the company as Henry's goddamn assistant. Then what happens? You look around, you see that Henry's not going anywhere, so you start editing manuscripts for Bob, who *is* going somewhere. As if that isn't enough, you jump ship from working for Henry to Peter—who, by the way, is going to eat Henry *alive*. You even get to work with Max and go to editorial board meetings." He chuckled knowingly. "Somebody looking at your career at S&S so far just *might* think you were pretty ambitious for a goddamn Oxford man, that's all I'm saying."

Seen from Dick's point of view, perhaps Schwed had been right to see me as Machiavellian after all. I laughed. "It's nothing I planned. It all just *happened*."

Dick snorted. "Nothing *just happens*, my friend." He puffed on his cigarette contentedly. "Listen, if all this comes naturally to you, you're way ahead. The best way to get ahead is not to be obvious about it, believe me." He was silent for a moment. Dick's ambition, it must be said, was unconcealed—far from being bashful on the subject, he was proud of it. This was one of his more appealing traits. You could call him a lot of things, but Machiavellian wasn't one of them, then or later.

"What's your ambition?" I asked, as much to get him off the subject of me as out of curiosity.

He didn't answer for a very long time. Out of the corner of my eye, I could see him slouched against the door, one arm slung over the seat back. He was gazing ahead, at what? I was reminded of Gatsby's green, orgiastic light at the end of Daisy's dock, but in this case there were only the twinkling lights of the oil refineries and chemical plants on either side of the highway, blinking mysteriously in the dark. There was something of Gatsby in Dick, I thought, as there is in every American who wants to rise above his father's station and dreams of gaining wealth, class, or both. Dick had already begun that process long ago, I guessed. His eagerness to learn was voracious, passionate, sometimes a little frightening. He was not just a fast learner but an *instant* one, soaking up what he wanted to know deftly. Already, in the few months since he had made his first appearance on the twenty-eighth floor, he had changed. The thick-soled shoes with blunt toes had given way to elegant English wing tips, his suits already showed signs of hand tailoring, the button-down shirts had been replaced by English ones with elegant, hand-sewn collars and showing just the right amount of cuff. Some time later, he admired one of my shirts and asked where it came from. I told him I had bought it at Pierce, Hilditch, and Key in London. A couple of weeks later, I noticed that he was wearing a similar shirt, having had his secretary call the London shirtmakers and give them his measurements. It was not just clothes—like Gatsby, he absorbed what he wanted to, adapted it effortlessly to himself, and soon knew more about it than you did. Even his Harvard accent had become more pronounced, now that he had one elegantly shod foot in the hardcover-book world, for it was clear that his immediate ambition was to become a hardcover publisher (*Peter Schwed, watch out!* I thought) though equally clear that his ambitions went beyond that, into some stratosphere that only he could see or imagine.

"I want it all," he said.

"*All?* Money? Fame? Power? A limo? Beautiful women? That kind of thing?"

He laughed, but I could tell that he was being serious. "Something like that," he said.

"Do you think book publishing is the right profession? It sounds to me as if the movie business might be a better choice."

Dick shook his head emphatically. "Nah," he said. "This is the one I'm in. Books have class. And look at the people who are running the goddamn book industry! Most of them don't know what they're doing. I mean, look at S&S. You and I could run it a hundred times better than it's being run now. A *thousand* times better! We'd make a good team, too."

If Dick wanted to team up with an editor, why hadn't he picked Bob, who was already successful? I wondered. But then I realized Bob already *had* a partner of sorts in Tony Schulte. Also, Bob would always want to be the star, and Schulte was willing enough to let him have the limelight. Dick would never be comfortable in *anybody's* shadow. He was picking a dark horse in me, certainly, but at the time he didn't have much of a choice.

"You know what I've left out?" he asked. Answering the question himself before I could, he said: "We're going to have a lot of fun, whatever happens."

We shook hands on that.

CHAPTER 14

*H*AVING FUN HAS always been an integral part of the book-publishing business—indeed, one of its main attractions. Bennett Cerf, whose enjoyment of life was so well known that it actually became one of Random House's main assets, boasted frequently about how much fun he was having. This caused a good deal of puzzlement and anxiety among Wall Street types, since most of them took a more conventional, Puritan view of business; they assumed that anybody who claimed to be having fun during office hours wasn't working hard enough. Even in such relatively unconventional businesses as television and the movie industry, few people would admit to having fun. On the contrary, people such as Jim Aubrey, who ran the CBS television network, worked hard to be seen as deadly serious, and so did his competitors and the men who ran the major movie studios. Aubrey was, in fact, known as "the Smiling Cobra," not because he had a sense of humor but because his thin, narrow-lipped smile always portended the dismissal of some major executive who had failed to please him. Motion-picture executives strove to present more serious appearances than bankers. It is hard to imagine any one of them being carried out of his office in his own chair, a broad grin on his face, as Cerf did the day Random House moved to its new building, or telling an audience of Wall Street analysts that publishing was the most fun you could have with your clothes on.

There was something about many of the new, predominantly Jewish book publishers that made them want to combine business and pleasure and enabled them for the most part to eat their cake and have it too. Dick Simon and Max Schuster, too, had always stressed the importance of having fun—and for the most part, they *did* have fun, each in his own way, as did the Knopfs, with rather more dignity. Alfred Knopf, an enthusiastic amateur photographer, took the portraits of many of Knopf's authors for the jackets of their books.

Although Dick Snyder came out of the Doubleday farm team—nobody at Doubleday had any fun except Nelson Doubleday, who had too much—and the circle around Leon Shimkin (who was no fun at all), he instinctively understood the relationship between personal pleasure and publishing that made it a different business from most. In no other area of the media is it possible to take a flier on something you like with as small a risk. Movies cost millions to make, television pilots are not only expensive but seldom lead anywhere, the content of most magazines is predetermined by editorial policy, but the investment in any one book, provided it's not by a big, best-selling author, can be measured in thousands—very often the low thousands at that. Moreover, every once in a while one of these long shots pays off. Successful self-help books, for example, are very often self-published (and self-promoted) until they reach the mainstream.

People who work in publishing houses, and by no means only editors, are always throwing off ideas, some of which get turned into books. One S&S employee's dance lessons led him to suggest Arthur Murray's book on how to dance that became a staple best-seller, year after year, just as Shimkin's knowledge of bookkeeping led him to the discovery of J. K. Lasser, whom he persuaded to write an annual income-tax guide that has been a best-seller for many decades. Cerf turned a taste for corny jokes into a succession of hugely successful joke books (some of them published by S&S), while Alfred Knopf's passion for good wine and food led him to the creation of countless books on the subjects and Dick Simon's fondness for cards led him to publish book after book on card games, including Charles Goren's best-selling bridge guides. The line between self-indulgence and commerce is nowhere thinner than in publishing. Fun made money.

. . .

IN THE meantime, book publishers were missing the biggest change in American culture since the twenties. The age of rock and roll had begun, and the big party of the sixties was under way, with London as its swinging capital. Nobody, not even Bob Gottlieb, whose antennae for trendiness were reputed to be tuned so finely, seemed to notice what was going on across the Atlantic, nor, increasingly, even under our windows on Fifth Avenue. Teen culture was about to take over the world, while book publishers on both sides of the Atlantic continued to worry about "high culture" and to publish books aimed at the parents and grandparents of the people who were making news and having fun.

I was very slightly ahead of the game because I genuinely *liked* the music, which was anything but fashionable to admit in publishing circles in the early 1960s, where most people were busy circling the wagons to defend "traditional" culture (of which the book was thought to be a bulwark) against the onslaught of sex, drugs, and rock and roll led by crazed and presumably illiterate teenagers. The notion that they not only might be literate but might even buy books if we took the trouble to publish any that interested them had not yet occurred to anybody.

The thought that the new youth culture was going to change most of our lives in all sorts of unforeseen ways had not yet penetrated either. We were still living the great middle-class dream, unaware that the ground was already shifting beneath us.

OF COURSE, the future did not seem clear at that time, not to me nor to Dick. It never does. One thing, however, *was* clear enough to me: So long as major agents weren't sending me books, I was going to find it hard to build up a personal list of authors important enough to make the company take me seriously—more seriously than as a hardworking book doctor and jack-of-all-trades. This clearly wasn't going to happen by combing the fringes of the listings for agents in *Literary Market Place* or cultivating the Jacques Chambruns of the world.

The major agents (nearly all men) in those days were hard to reach and notoriously capricious. But a few women, themselves the survivors of countless battles on the publishing front of the war of the sexes, were more tolerant of newcomers, more adventurous, and themselves contemptuous of the older male agents. Some of them had come out of the tough world of major movie-studio story departments, such as Phyllis Jackson and Helen Strauss. Both of them were—no other phrase will do—"tough broads," more than capable of holding their own with the movie moguls who had once been their bosses, let alone with easy prey like book editors and male literary agents. Jackson, in fact, when she had been a movie company "scout" in New York, had been the first person to bring *Gone with the Wind* to David Selznick's attention—it was still in manuscript—and urge him to buy it. She brought to the book business some of the flair, toughness, and drama of the movie business.

Phyllis was passionately loyal to her authors in a way that would have seemed excessive and in poor taste to men such as Paul Reynolds and Harold Matson—she took *everything* personally and looked, above all, for the kind of real enthusiasm and personal devotion in an editor that she felt herself. Her favorite editor, not surprisingly, was Bob Gottlieb, but perhaps because of my movie background she occasionally sent me a manuscript, and gradually we became pals. Through her—and because Colin Turnbull's *The Forest People* was being made into a play—I met Kay Brown, the famous theatrical agent, and through *her* Robert Lantz, who specialized in the theater and the movies but sometimes handled books and who had known my uncles and my father in Berlin before the Nazis.

There were plenty of younger agents to get to know too, among them Candida Donadio, whose authors included most of what was then the Jewish *nouvelle vague:* Joseph Heller, Wallace Markfield, and Bruce Jay Friedman, a close friend of Bob's. There was also Lynn Nesbit, somewhat easier to approach, then working for the urbane and dapper Sterling Lord. Nesbit combined not only brains and beauty but also taste and energy and was already building a list of remarkable writers. She lived in a garden duplex downtown, and the party she gave there for her friend and English counterpart Deborah Rogers was the first publishing party I had ever been to that wasn't dull and stiff (except for those in which one waited breathlessly for Ray Schuster to say something awful). In fact, Lynn gave me hope—she was elegant, witty, and to all appearances self-assured—that publishing didn't have to be a dowdy business. When I finally worked up the nerve to take her to lunch at the Italian Pavilion, then the mecca of the younger publishing set (the meccas of the older publishing set were "21" and the Café Louis XIV), she was absolutely certain that I was going to publish a lot of her authors and become her client myself.

"What makes you think I want to write books?" I asked.

"I can tell," she said, with characteristic impatience. "The sooner you start, the better."

ACCORDING TO the hallowed tradition of book publishing, it was necessary to have lunch with all these people, and many more, as often as possible. For editors, in fact, having lunch is regarded as a positive, income-generating, aggressive act, and a certain suspicion is extended toward those few who can be found eating a sandwich at their desk more than once or twice a week. Publishers have been known to roam through the editorial department at lunchtime to catch editors who are "not doing their job" in the act of unwrapping a tuna sandwich from the nearest deli. A large expense account is very often perceived as proof of ambition and hard work. Publishing might, in fact, be the only business in the world in which it is possible to be criticized for expenses that are too *modest*.

There were some exceptions, of course. Bob Gottlieb later became famous for not going out to lunch. Agents who wanted to see him had to come to his office for a sandwich. Everybody else in the world of book publishing, at least at what we in the British armed forces called "the sharp end of the stick," could be found from twelve-thirty to two-thirty at some midtown restaurant with a napkin in his or her lap.

Nobody has ever done a poll to see whether the agents—the putative beneficiaries of this largesse—really *want* to be taken out to lunch every day of the workweek. It is simply one of the basic assumptions of book publishing that he or she who lunches with the most agents gets the most books. In the fifties, and even the early sixties, such lunches used to be preceded by a couple of cocktails and often dragged on well past three o'clock, leaving both parties with bad headaches and tendencies to nap during the rest of the afternoon. In those days, editors did indeed give their all for their company—cirrhosis of the liver and cardiovascular failure only too often went with the profession and were assumed to be work-related illnesses. By the mid-sixties, as younger agents who limited themselves to water or one glass of white wine came to the fore, lunches tended to become more spartan. Still, drunk or sober, the average editor faced five lunches a week for the sole purpose of trying to charm comparative strangers into sending him or her manuscripts that in all probability would turn out to be no good, thus calling for another lunch to apologize for rejecting it—for not every agent takes rejection well, particularly if that agent has spent two hours rhapsodizing over the manuscript in question during lunch, while the editor nodded away as if agreeing with every word.

As if they didn't have to lunch out enough as it was, editors even formed their own lunch club that met once a month, though many avoided it on the grounds that no editor had anything much to gain from having lunch with another, and anyway, it was full of fossils and has-beens. For the latter reason, I rather liked it—some of the older members *were* certainly curmudgeonly and fossilized, but I found it interesting to talk to people such as John Farrar (one of the founders of Farrar, Straus and Giroux) or Ken McCormick, the editor in chief of Doubleday, both of whom had been editors for at least fifty years at that point. What struck me most was that while neither of them was rich—it's always been hard to get rich as an editor—they still had a certain joie de vivre and a keen interest in what was going on. Here, at any rate, was a profession in which age, if it was not treated with respect, was at least tolerated. Besides, allowance being made for Farrar's extreme testiness, they both still seemed to be having fun, thus proving Dick Snyder and Bennett Cerf right.

FUN WAS about to enter my life on a grander scale than that, however, and was to remain in it for over thirty years in the person of one remarkable (and diminutive) agent.

West Coast agents had long been an unknown quantity to most East Coast publishing people, who tended to look down on them as mere "10 percenters," knuckle draggers of no culture and no interest in books, who made their living peddling flesh and something called "screen treatments" and who appeared in the offices of New York publishers only from time to time in sweaty pursuit of original stories that could be made into movies. There had been a very few exceptions over the years—there was Myron Selznick, David's brother, a flesh peddler if ever there was one, but also a sophisticated and well-read man, and Leland Hayward, whose urbanity and sophistication had made him welcome on both coasts, as well as in those parts of Europe that mattered. Hayward was a man of taste and charm. Supremely elegant and something of a celebrity in his own right (he married two international social stars, Pamela Churchill and Slim Keith), Hayward was more interested in serving as the link between Broadway and Sunset Boulevard than in books, but when in New York he paid his respects to the more socially acceptable publishers, chiefly Bennett Cerf, who moved—or yearned to move—in the same social circles as Hayward, and the Knopfs, who were celebrities in their own way.

Hayward seemed at home almost everywhere except Los Angeles, although he lived there for years. He went out of his way to build a New England–style house in Beverly Hills, complete with clapboards, shutters, and a shingled roof—even a barn that would not have looked out of place in rural Connecticut or Vermont, except that it contained, among other luxuries, a completely equipped, lilliputian soda fountain for his children, the countertop low enough that they could serve themselves and their friends.

There was yet another West Coast agent, one who had modeled himself to some degree in Leland Hayward's image (except for the soda fountain), and that was Irving Paul Lazar. Lazar had been around, it sometimes seemed, since year one, a more or less permanent fixture in international society, the movie business, and, since the 1950s, the book business. He handled a good many writers who were all major celebrities. As a rule, he dealt only with heads of houses, mere editors being beneath him.

I had never met Lazar, but I had been hearing his name since 1950, when I first saw him, at Eden Roc on the Cap d'Antibes. Lazar was then in his forties, I suppose, and already something of a legend. My Aunt Alexa and I had been swimming and had been joined by Uncle Alex for lunch. Looking across the pool, Alex shaded his eyes with his copy of the Paris edition of the New York *Herald Tribune* and waved. "It's Irving Lazar," he said to Alexa. "We must ask him to dinner. By the way, nobody who matters calls him 'Swifty.' Bogart gave him the name after Lazar made three deals for him in the same day, on a bet," Alex explained.

The person in question was standing on the other side of the pool, an incongruous, diminutive figure among all the half-naked, oiled, and bronzed bodies. He was totally bald, and his face—what could be seen of it below huge, glittering, gold-rimmed Ray-Ban aviator sunglasses—was tanned, like his pate, to the color of a well-cared-for crocodile handbag. He was wearing tiny white shoes, a blue blazer with gold buttons, and white trousers pressed so perfectly, despite the heat, that he looked like a shiny, expensive beach toy that has just been unpacked by some lucky child. He was shouting into a telephone.

He was shouting into a telephone some thirteen years later when he called me, out of the blue, at S&S. "Lazar here," he said, as if there were none other. The voice was unknown to me and difficult at first to decipher. He seemed to be affecting a rich, even plummy, upper-class English accent, of the Lord Haw-Haw type, with every syllable accentuated, and for a moment I thought he was making fun of me. "Have lunch with me, dear boy," he went on grandly. "I want to pick your brain."

In what area, I asked suspiciously. "I'm not doing any business with your shop," Lazar said, still apparently aping a toff's accent for my benefit. "I do a lot of business with Bennett Cerf at Random House. I do a lot of business with Tom Guinzburg at Viking." He paused, perhaps for breath. "I don't know why I'm not doing any fucking business with Simon and Schuster," he snapped suddenly, as sharply as the crack of a whip, his voice changing to what I presumed was his natural accent, a grainy, impatient Brooklyn Jewish growl.

"Yes, all right, where?" I asked.

" '21,' for chrissakes, where do you think?" Lazar said. "One o'clock. Don't be late."

At "21," where I arrived a good ten minutes early, I had only to mention Lazar's name to be treated like royalty. I was swept to a red-checked table downstairs, opposite the bar, and given a bowl of celery and olives on ice and a basket of rolls. From time to time, as I ate the rolls, a captain arrived bearing bulletins of Lazar's progress. Mr. Lazar called to say that he would be on his way shortly. Mr. Lazar's secretary called to say that Mr. Lazar was just leaving his apartment. Mr. Lazar's secretary called again to say that Mr. Lazar was actually out the door. Mr. Lazar's California office called to ask Mr. Lazar to phone as soon as he arrived. Three quarters of an hour later—by which time I had emptied the basket of rolls—there was a bustle at the entrance of the bar, and Lazar appeared, dressed faultlessly, as ever, in a checked suit of the kind worn in England for attending the more fashionable race meetings. I waved to him, but he was busy scanning the room like a theater manager counting the house before raising the curtain. He plunged off to shake hands with everybody he knew, moving around the room in a slow, counterclockwise semicircle.

What I was witnessing was table-hopping as an art form. At some tables he paused for only a few moments, at others he stayed for a few minutes, at one or two he actually sat down to chat. There was hardly a table in the room at which there wasn't somebody Lazar recognized or from which somebody didn't wave to him. It was two o'clock when he sat down next to me, glanced at the table, and snapped at the captain, "Why aren't there any rolls on the table, for chrissakes?" He shook my hand. "You don't look like your uncle," he said, eyeing me. "He was a big fellow."

I didn't think a conversation about height with Lazar was likely to lead anywhere—and I was sensitive about the fact that I was the shortest member of my family—so I said nothing.

Lazar picked up the menu, took off his glasses, removed a gold-rimmed monocle from his breast pocket, put it in place, and studied the menu, holding it an inch or two away from his nose. "I want breakfast," he said. "Scrambled eggs with smoked salmon." He turned to me and said, "I got a late start this morning." I wondered whether this was his way of apologizing for being late, but nothing in his manner suggested that it was. "I mixed up my pills," he explained. "I took my wake-up pill last night and my sleeping pill when I got up this morning."

He turned toward the captain, who was hovering beside me. "He'll have a '21' burger, medium," he said, dismissing him with a wave while I was still looking at my menu. Lazar, as I was to learn, hated people who can't make up their minds about what they want to eat (or anything else), and was very likely to order for them if they weren't quick enough to suit him.

He settled himself down, sipped his virgin bullshot—the first time I had ever heard of this drink—and looked at me warily, as if he was wondering who I was and why I was sitting there. Behind thick glasses, his eyes were shrewd and penetrating, with the kind of beady stare that a macaw might bring to bear on you just before lunging to bite your finger. His head was completely bald—I wondered if he shaved it every day. It also looked as if he polished it, perhaps with something like Butcher's Wax. "You're younger than I thought," he said, the corners of his mouth turning down suspiciously, as if I had somehow deceived him on that score. "Do they let you make deals over there?"

I said they did, though they weren't deals of the kind that Lazar was famous for.

He nodded, then leaned conspiratorially toward me. "I'm going to give you a piece of advice you'll thank me for the rest of your life, kiddo," he said. It was the first time anybody had ever called me *kiddo*—a word I had until then associated only with tough-guy movies.

I stared back at him, eager for any piece of wisdom.

"Never forget this," he told me, his expression making it clear that I was not to take his advice lightly. "The first couple of million bucks you make—put it away! You don't ever touch that, you hear me? That's your 'fuck you' money. That way, anybody ever tries to make you do something you don't want to do, you can tell 'em, 'Fuck you.' "

Since at the time I was making a couple of hundred dollars a week and had zero in my bank account, Lazar's advice seemed of doubtful utility, though it clearly represented a deeply felt credo on his part. Over the years, he was to give me much more advice from his personal experience, ranging from "Always try to have fun, kiddo" to "Be a mensch when you tip." This last I received at that first lunch, when Lazar rose from the table at the end of the meal to continue table-hopping and, forgetting that he had invited me to lunch, left me with the check.

In some mysterious way, however, I must have passed some sort of test, for our lunch together placed me firmly on Lazar's daily list of people to call, and I remained there for thirty years. Once a day, I picked up the phone and heard him rasp, "Lazar here. What's cookin', kiddo?" or "What have we got going, kid?"—followed by a bewildering series of high-speed sales pitches. These, too, were sometimes interrupted by advice or reflections on life, my favorite being "Sometimes I wake up in the morning and there's nothing doing, so I decide to *make something happen by lunch*."

This, in fact, is as close as anyone has come to explaining Lazar's way of doing business. The moment he awoke, he got on the phone and proceeded to make something—anything—happen, mostly by trolling a series of celebrity names until whatever editor he was speaking to took a nibble at the bait. One learned early—I did, anyway—that these names might as well be picked out of a hat, since Lazar seldom bothered to inform celebrities and stars before offering up their names to publishers. "How about Cary Grant?" he might say. "Cary could write a great book. Give me, oh, say a million, and he's yours, I won't even mention him to anybody else. Well, better make that a million and a half. He's big in England, and he's dying to do it. . . . Greg Peck, how about him? Gene Kelly? I saw Gene last night. Give me half a million right now and he's yours."

This was basically Lazar's way of getting his day started, very often from the breakfast table by his pool in Beverly Hills—the equivalent of finger exercises for a concert pianist. Only if he got a good, solid bite would he actually *call* Cary Grant or Gregory Peck or Gene Kelly—or, later, Madonna, Cher, Sharon Stone, or Jessica Lange, for Lazar always kept up with the rise and fall of stars. If nobody bit, the names shuffled to the bottom of his list for the next day's calls. Only large, round numbers were mentioned, and one also learned that, as at auctions, it was dangerous to express polite interest. Lazar was only too likely to interpret anything less than an emphatic "not on your life!" as agreement and would then angrily insist that you had made an offer and hold you to your word.

When I began, tentatively, to make a few deals with Lazar—Garson Kanin, Larry Collins and Dominique Lapierre—I learned that his client list apparently included everyone, even people who had other agents—Oscar Levant once remarked, "Everybody who matters has two agents: his own and Irving Lazar." But Lazar did not consider himself an agent at all; he described himself as a deal maker and thus did not feel bound by the normal rules of agenting. Lazar would make a deal for anyone and later on work out a more or less amicable arrangement with the agent. Sometimes he took his 10 percent from the buyer, sometimes from the seller—sometimes, it was rumored, in the old days, from both. He frequently offered me authors who, to the best of my knowledge, were happily placed with rival publishers and were represented by more conventional agents.

"Truman Capote," Lazar said. "Wanna do a deal with him?" At the time, Capote was one of the bright stars at Random House, while I was an editor at a house not then famous for fiction. It seemed to me unlikely that Capote would want to leave Random House or that Random House would let him go, and I said so. "I can see you don't have the guts for this kind of thing, sonny," Lazar sniffed—he always called me *sonny* when he was pissed off—and he hung up, no doubt to offer Capote elsewhere. (Capote was a Random House author until his death.)

I learned that such offers often came about because Lazar was having a feud with a certain house or editor. If he wasn't happy with Random House, he would offer Capote around, probably without telling Capote; if somebody at another house had offended him, he would try to steal Vladimir Nabokov away. This practice didn't change over the years; it gave Lazar a chance to test the waters and check the market value of an author—a tactic that drove more sedate agents wild, since Lazar often told their clients that he could get them a better deal.

Capote was the accidental centerpiece of one of my more memorable lunches with Lazar some years later. I had made a date to meet him at the Grill Room of The Four Seasons at one o'clock and begged him to be on time, since I had a meeting at two-thirty. "Sure, sure," he said, with the slightly offended tone of a man who is never late. "One o'clock on the dot, kiddo." Needless to say, at one-thirty I was still waiting for him, while bulletins of his progress were brought to me. Finally, he arrived, did his tour of the room, sat down, and looked at me. "You ought to relax more," he said. "A young guy your age, you shouldn't look so stressed."

I was about to point out to him that he was the cause of my stress, but just as the captain was handing Irving a menu, Truman Capote, wearing a purple velvet jumpsuit and a matching purple hat, appeared at the table, looking like nothing so much as an aging pixie. "Hello, Irving," he said.

Lazar looked up impatiently. "I'm not speaking to you," he said.

Capote sat down. He looked as if he was about to cry. "Don't be angry with me, Irving," he said. His voice was as high-pitched as a bird's.

Lazar glared at him unforgivingly. "You turn up late for a sit-down dinner at my house. You bring along some piece of rough trade you've picked up from a gas station along the way as your date. I don't want to see you anymore."

"I *said* I was sorry."

It was beginning to dawn on me that I might as well not be there. Lazar did not introduce me to Truman Capote. Capote ignored me completely. It was nearly two o'clock, and we still hadn't ordered.

"All right, all right," Lazar said gruffly. "I forgive you, but it's the last time."

"I promise. Let's get together while you're in New York." The two men pulled out identical Hermès pocket diaries and Cartier gold pencils, put on their reading glasses, and peered at the week ahead, where, it turned out, neither of them had a free moment.

"Lunch with Jackie, cocktails with the Paleys, dinner at the Bombolanas—you know them, Irving, surely. That's it for Tuesday," Capote said.

Lazar studied his own diary as if it were the Rosetta stone. "Lunch with the Princess Borbón y Parma, cocktails with Marietta Tree, dinner at Lenny Bernstein's—that's it for Wednesday."

At last, after spirited negotiation, they managed to settle on a date for dinner and, with even greater difficulty, on a place, and Capote finally took his leave. Lazar sat back contentedly. I guessed that he felt his social schedule had one-upped Capote's, though the two seemed to me equally star-studded. "You know who that was?" he asked. "That was Truman Capote."

"So I gathered."

Irony was wasted on Lazar. He leaned close to me and whispered. "I'm going to tell you something about Truman that not many people know," he said. He paused significantly. "Truman's a fruit."

THERE WAS, I discovered over the years, a curious innocence about Lazar, despite his cynical exterior—a romanticism that came to the surface by fits and starts. It was not just his occasionally old-fashioned slang—surely nobody had used the word *fruit* to describe a homosexual since the thirties—but a certain innocent attitude toward his friends. He refused to believe the worst about anyone he knew. People who everyone else agreed were totally loathsome, Lazar professed to like. Couples who were on the brink of angry divorce he stoutly maintained were devoted to each other. Eventually, I came to understand that Lazar simply refused to believe that people close to him could be upset or miserable or unpleasant. Like the Sun King, he believed that his presence made people happy and therefore took unhappiness as a kind of lèse-majesté.

Lazar was a famously generous host, his generosity exceeded only by his unpredictability. He once invited me to a black-tie dinner at his home—a sit-down dinner for sixty people, many of them the kind of stars about whom it's often said, "You're kidding, I didn't know he was still alive!"

"I've got a surprise for you, kiddo," he said to me. "You'll never guess who you're seated next to."

My heart sank. Francis X. Bushman, maybe? Was he still alive? Just as we were about to sit down, a glamorous woman appeared and sat down on my right. Lazar called for silence and said, "This is a special moment, because Merle Oberon is going to be sitting next to her nephew, Michael Korda, and they haven't seen each other for years!"

Poor Merle stared at me in horror as everyone applauded, not so much because we didn't like each other as because the notion of having a thirty-year-old publisher as a nephew hardly fit in with her youthful public image.

For a long time, I thought that Lazar had a taste for practical jokes and that my reintroduction to Merle after twenty years might be one, but I eventually came to the conclusion that it was part of his innocence. Because he never remembered the bad things about people, he was very likely to seat ex-wives next to ex-husbands, or old enemies next to each other, having no exes of his own. He also appeared to have no enemies, unless you count germs.

Dirt was Lazar's only fear and his legendary obsession. If there is any truth to the Freudian notion that people who suffer from a germ phobia and wash their hands constantly are afflicted with unbearable feelings of guilt, Lazar must have been the guiltiest man on earth, yet guilt was absolutely foreign to his spirit. Once when he was being driven to East Hampton for the weekend by his hostess, he surprised her by producing a carefully typed list of the hospitals along the route— not, as she supposed, because he was afraid of having a heart attack, but in case he had to go to the bathroom. Hospitals, he explained, had clean bathrooms; he couldn't use a bathroom in a gas station. It's said that in the forties Lazar was discovered one night trapped in the men's room of Chasen's with Howard Hughes, another germphobe. They had both washed and disinfected their hands and were waiting for someone to come along and open the door; neither one of them was willing to touch the handle.

Oddly, it never occurred to me that Lazar was old, even when he reached his eighties and began to gallop toward his nineties. Since in his view I was either "kiddo" or "sonny," our relationship was a constant— he the grown-up, I the child. As I became more successful, Lazar's attitude toward me never varied. He was delighted for me, but I was still "kiddo" and always would be. Nor did Lazar seem to age. His energy was phenomenal, even frightening. No number of parties, including his own, could exhaust him or blunt his appetite for sociability.

I had always thought of Lazar as a kind of finished product—born somehow already wearing his Savile Row suit and gleaming handmade shoes—so it came as a surprise to me when I was having a sandwich with him at his house in Beverly Hills one day and saw in his den a framed photograph of him as a boy, with a full head of hair, standing in front of a 1920s delivery truck and looking remarkably self-possessed.

"Is that you?" I asked.

Lazar glared at me. "Yes, it is," he said. "Now sit down and eat."

There was also a photograph of Lazar as a brash young MCA agent, already bald but pudgy, not at all the trim figure I was accustomed to; one of Lazar in uniform, a serious expression on his face; and even one of him as a baby. Of course, one knew he had *been* a baby, but over the years he had so cocooned himself in legend that his past had become almost indecipherable. His father was a relatively prosperous Russian-Jewish butter-and-egg wholesaler in Brooklyn (who did a little modest loan-sharking on the side). Lazar seems, in fact, to have had a happy childhood—three brothers, a doting mother, and a father who served as a role model.

In his later years, Lazar looked back on his childhood with the kind of nostalgia that successful self-made men always develop for their roots. He had a whole repertoire of childhood anecdotes about how he had to learn to be tough, because he was the smallest boy in school; about how he fought full-grown teamsters for the best parking place at the market every morning for his father's truck; about how he learned to dress elegantly from the neighborhood gangsters in the era when guys such as Abner (Longie) Zwillman, Jake (Greasy Thumb) Guzik, and Legs Diamond controlled the streets and the rackets. Two themes dominated all of Lazar's stories about growing up: fighting back and standing out from the crowd, and a longing for a richer, more genteel way of life, apparently inspired by summer visits to more prosperous relatives who lived in the country.

Lazar was obsessed by class. I sometimes flew out to California and back the same day, and once I stopped off at Lazar's house before catching the red-eye home. On this particular occasion, I had apparently overdone things, and even Irving noticed that my eyelids were drooping. (Never tired himself, he was not usually aware of fatigue in others.) "Why not take a nap?" he suggested, and I gratefully bedded down on a sofa in his dressing room. I awoke to find the room in darkness. Stumbling to the nearest door, I opened it and realized that I was looking at Lazar's closet. Row after row of clothes were hanging there—yachting outfits, dinner jackets, blazers, sports clothes. At my feet, tiny shoes were lined up, each pair with its own wooden shoe tree. There seemed to be hundreds of pairs, for every possible social and sporting occasion. In glass-fronted cupboards against one wall, Lazar's shirts were arranged by color and pattern—hundreds of them. I felt like an intruder, but I was also reminded, inevitably, of Gatsby, and especially of the scene in which Daisy bursts into tears at the sight of his shirts.

It is no accident that the very worst thing Lazar could say about anyone is "he's got no class." This was invariably said more in sorrow than in anger and with a certain judiciousness, as if Lazar were the final arbiter in the matter. *Class*, of course, meant more than making *una bella figura*. Class in Lazar's eyes was an attitude and usually centered on lavish generosity, coupled with being a man of one's word. His house was full of symbols of that special lavishness that passed for class during his heyday as a Hollywood agent. Every surface was covered with silver cigarette boxes engraved with effusive messages of thanks and affection from Lazar clients, and there were enough desk fittings and clocks to stock Asprey or Tiffany. Then, autocracy and largesse were the rule. Lazar dealt as an equal with titans such as Sam Goldwyn, Louis B. Mayer, and Darryl F. Zanuck: men who not only were worthy opponents but could make their own decisions and didn't mind paying for what they wanted; men who were not, in a favorite phrase of Lazar's, "nickel-and-dimers." Those days, as Lazar never ceased to lament, were long gone, and he had to deal with book editors and movie executives who reported to committees, bid cautiously, and never sent anything to celebrate a deal.

It was probably a yearning for class that prompted Lazar to go to law school instead of joining the neighborhood gangsters or staying in the family business. He graduated from Brooklyn Law School in 1931, but he soon figured out that as the lawyer for vaudeville star Ted Lewis (Mr. "Me and My Shadow") he made a hundred dollars a week, whereas M.C.A. was taking 10 percent of Lewis's ten thousand dollars a week. When he was faced with lawyers, he seldom failed to point out that he was a lawyer himself, and he did practice bankruptcy law for a few years after law school. But, like Billy Rose, he seemed to have made his mark mostly as the quick-witted and ambitious assistant to older men, taking shorthand (a man's job in those days), running errands, establishing a name for himself as a bright young man around the courthouse. A good head for numbers and an already legendary amount of chutzpah brought him into the talent business when it was still in its infancy and consisted of booking musicians and acts in the Catskills, on the still flourishing vaudeville circuit, and in the mob-owned nightclubs, speakeasies, and jazz joints of New York's East Fifties. Lazar might have regarded all this as a step toward some more respectable profession, but it didn't take long for him to discover that he was good at what he was doing—for already he was fiercely competitive, unhappy at being a subordinate, and absolutely fearless. In later years, people wondered at Lazar's ability to stand up to studio heads, publishers, and difficult clients, but the fact is that his early experience was with people who were perfectly willing to have him beaten up or killed—and, in fact, he *was* beaten up and even stabbed in the course of business, yet he never felt intimidated. In an industry in which it has become fashionable for agents and executives to flaunt tough-guy talk, though, Lazar rarely indulged in gangsterisms—he had done business with guys who never said that kind of thing unless they meant it.

Lazar made his first trip to the West Coast in 1936. He claimed that it was by accident, but there were no accidents in Lazar's life. It's true that he accompanied two vaudeville clients out there because he didn't trust them to pay him his commission—he preferred to divide up the take at the end of every day himself—but it's likely that he had been looking westward for some time. In New York, show business took a backseat to the bigger, more serious worlds of finance, media, old money, and society. In Hollywood, show business was everything; society, class, and finance all revolved around the studios. Still, there was never any question of Lazar's becoming a 10 percenter. Lazar's roots remained in New York, and he kept them there. What's more, he cleverly avoided becoming a mere flesh peddler. He made deals for such people as Noël Coward, Tennessee Williams, Cole Porter, Clifford Odets, Maxwell Anderson, Lillian Hellman, Garson Kanin, and Ernest Hemingway. He sold books, plays, ideas, and people by going to the top from the very first—a feat made possible not only by his toughness and determination but by the simple fact that he was an outsider, a New Yorker.

Lazar understood instinctively that the prevailing ethos of West Coast movie people was then (as it is now) fear and envy of New York. New York was where the money came from; it was where the *owners* of the studios were—the bosses to whom men such as Mayer and Zanuck actually reported. New York was, above all, where talent, ideas, culture, and fashions came from, and in the days when it took nearly four days to cross the country, a person arriving from New York was greeted the way a traveler from Saint Petersburg was hailed upon arriving in some remote provincial town in nineteenth-century Russia.

In the late forties, Lazar decided to move to Los Angeles permanently, and he quickly established himself as the connection between New York and Hollywood, first imitating, then replacing, Leland Hayward. Not a reader himself (he was notorious for not bothering to read the books he was selling), he cultivated writers, publishers, and playwrights and brought the studio heads projects they could never have found by themselves, for prices they would never have dreamed of paying to anyone else. In New York, Lazar became known as the man who could get you bagfuls of money from Hollywood; in Hollywood, he was known as the man who could bring you the hottest properties before anybody else on the Coast had heard of them. In the days when a transcontinental telephone call was a big deal, Lazar was in touch constantly, perfecting his peculiar blend of gossip, news, and sales pitch, and a lot of people didn't know whether Lazar was speaking to them from his poolside in Beverly Hills or from around the corner on Fifth Avenue.

Lazar once half jokingly promised to grant a publisher not "world rights" but "universe rights." A certain grandeur was part of his manner, and Lazar rapidly became more famous than most of his clients. Even total strangers who knew little or nothing about book publishing and the movie business picked up the party trick of raising one trouser leg above the knee and putting a pair of horn-rimmed glasses against the kneecap to simulate Lazar's physiognomy.

Early on, Lazar hit upon three rules that stood him in good stead for over fifty years. The first was that he could always reach anyone, anywhere, any time. His secret weapon was the world's largest address book, full of the private, unlisted numbers of people whom nobody else can reach. The second rule was always to go directly to the top. His last rule was to insist on a quick answer, as I was quickly to learn.

MY FIRST lunch with Lazar at "21" did not lead to any immediate results, but he soon called with a new proposition: "Garson Kanin," he said. "How would you like a book by him? I'm giving you the first crack at this, so don't let me down, kiddo."

Fortunately for me, I was not obliged to ask who Garson Kanin might be or express amazement that he was still alive, since nothing was more certain to infuriate Lazar. Oddly enough, the name not only rang a bell, it chimed a whole chorus of them, for Gar Kanin was an old friend of my mother's, having directed her on Broadway in at least two plays. In addition, his wife, Ruth Gordon, had worked with my mother in Katharine Cornell's Broadway production of *The Three Sisters* in which my mother had played Irina, the youngest sister, and Gordon the awful sister-in-law. I said that I'd be interested.

"*How* interested?" Lazar asked sharply.

That would depend, I said, on what Gar planned to write.

"He'll write anything you want him to," Lazar snapped impatiently. "What I want to know is how much you'll pay."

This was my first experience of doing business with Lazar. I didn't want to disappoint him by seeming like a timid small-timer, but on the other hand I wasn't used to putting down money on anything quite as slim as this—usually an agent sent over at least a few chapters of manuscript or, if the writer was well known, an outline. Lazar was asking me to buy a pig in a poke, and I hadn't a clue what to say. Besides, there were people I'd have to talk to before making an offer, and most of them would certainly ask what it was that Kanin planned to write about.

Could Gar not be persuaded to put a few words on paper? I asked.

He would put as many words as I liked on paper the moment we had a deal, Lazar said abruptly. First, he needed a number.

There was no way of faking my way past this, I decided. I explained how interested I was, pointed out that I knew Gar of old, and promised to call Lazar as soon as I had talked to my colleagues.

"I can see you're not interested, sonny," Lazar said, more in sorrow than in anger. "I'll try Bennett. He's dying to have Gar on the Random House list." With that, Lazar hung up, leaving me feeling as if I'd made a fool of myself and perhaps lost a great opportunity. Only later did I discover that Lazar hadn't called me about Kanin until Cerf—and practically everybody else in publishing—had already said no.

At the time, of course, I assumed that Lazar was so disappointed in me that he would take me off his call list, but the very next day I heard the familiar voice say, "Lazar here," and he was off and running on someone new—Fernando Lamas, perhaps, someone else from his B list, or Gene Kelly, who was on Lazar's A list but bored everybody else because he was such a nice guy that people feared he'd have nothing to say in his memoirs. Before the week was out, he had tried me on Gar Kanin again as if he had never mentioned the subject before. Many years later, Lazar actually *did* persuade me to buy a novel by Kanin, *Moviola,* which turned out to be a million-dollar bomb, setting something like a new record for expensive failure in the high-powered fiction stakes, so perhaps the gods were watching over me the first time he was offered to me.

WITH LAZAR, I felt somehow that I had reached the big time, because if Lazar was anything it was big-time. He had the ability to make one feel that simply by being on his call list one was an important person, because Lazar wouldn't call anyone who *wasn't* important. I took it as a good sign that Lazar had singled me out for his attention, however eccentric—he wasn't a man to waste time on young people with no future. Besides, at S&S, Lazar talked only to me. Most important agents spread their business out among several editors or executives at the same firm, but Lazar was, if nothing else, absolutely loyal. "I dance with the person who brought me," he once said, and even if it wasn't completely true in his personal life—he had a notorious roving eye—it was always true in his business life (not that the two were easily separated). Once you were his friend, he did business with you and you alone, and that was that.

CHAPTER 15

*I*T WAS NO thanks to Lazar that I once met Fannie Hurst. An old friend of mine from school in Switzerland, Peter Wodtke, then on his way to becoming a major figure in the financial world, had called out of the blue to ask if I was interested in meeting a famous writer. Since that was, after all, my profession, I said I was indeed interested. Fine, he said, we'll meet at Fannie Hurst's, tomorrow at seven.

I had a moment of panic as I agreed. I hadn't a clue who Fannie Hurst was, though the name sounded familiar, and I hadn't wanted to sound like a schmuck to my friend, particularly since it involved something to do with my own profession. What kind of editor doesn't recognize the name of a famous author, after all? Somewhere in the back of my head was the idea that Hurst might be the author of *Stella Dallas*, but I wasn't even sure that it had ever been a book before it became a movie. Whoever she was, I knew she was not young, so I called Irving Lazar and asked him what he knew about her.

"Forget it," he said. "She's dead."

I objected. She could hardly be giving a cocktail party in her apartment from the grave.

Lazar was not convinced. "Trust me, kiddo, she's been dead for years."

I asked if he could remember any of her titles. "She was a journalist," he said. "Wrote for William Randolph Hearst, I think. They were big pals. She did books too, though. . . . Something Street . . . *Easy Street*? Nah. Wait a minute, I've got it: *Back Street*. Big best-seller, way back in the twenties, I think. . . . Got made into a movie." There was a pause, while he switched gears. "Listen, how about Gar Kanin?" he asked. "I'm not getting what I want from Bennett. Give me two-fifty and he's yours. No, make that three-fifty, and I'll throw in foreign. They love Gar in London."

I did not have an opportunity to read any of Hurst's works before her party, so when I met Wodtke in the lobby of her building I was still ignorant of her. Everybody *recognized* her name all right, but that was it. Most people, like Lazar, assumed that she was dead.

The Des Artistes is one of New York's most famous apartment buildings, a spectacular, towering Gothic fantasy on West Sixty-seventh Street just off Central Park West, where the lobby looks as if Count Dracula was about to descend in the elevator, and the exterior of the building makes you look up expecting to find Quasimodo perched among the stone-carved spires, buttresses, and gargoyles. Constructed during the 1920s as a kind of artists' cooperative because of the shortage of studio space in New York, the Des Artistes had its own restaurant, with sprawling murals by Howard Chandler Christy of naked nymphs cavorting in the woods, perfectly embodying the spirit of luxurious bohemian decadence and contempt for the bourgeoisie in which it was built, in the years before the Crash wiped out most of the people who had intended to live, paint, and sculpt there.

The ancient elevator bore us up to Hurst's floor at a glacial pace, as if rising from a crypt. It creaked and groaned like a ship under full sail. An ancient majordomo ushered us into a dark vestibule as if he had just risen from his coffin to answer the bell and showed us into a big, glassed-in living room–studio, two stories high, dimly lit by twenty-five-watt bulbs (in what had once been ornate gas fittings) and enough candles for a major funeral.

The windows were immense—two stories tall and filling one whole wall of the room—but they were draped in many square yards of black velvet, trimmed in faded gold, that came all the way to the floor. Against the other wall was a minstrel's gallery in dark wood, with a narrow carved-wood stairway leading up to it and false windows in stained glass. Everywhere, standing in sheaves in tall vases under the dim light, were calla lilies, hundreds of them, giving off a sickly, sweet, cloying odor.

Swimming in the gloom were our fellow guests, dwarfed by the furniture and, for the most part, even older than the butler, who announced us in a low, croaking whisper, like a rusty iron gate swinging in the wind. It was difficult to believe that only a few floors below us was contemporary New York City. It was as if we had stepped straight out of the elevator into the gloomiest of haunted castles, peopled by ghosts. The men were small, ancient, dressed with a certain old-fashioned elegance not at all of this epoch; the women lavishly, if eccentrically, sported long evening dresses in dark, velvety fabrics, richly patterned, old-fashioned material that might have served as the upholstery in a nineteenth-century Venetian gondola. Their jewelry was on the heroic scale: many strands of beads, massive gold chains, much amber. Several of the women carried gloves. Almost everybody was smoking with a cigarette holder as they stared at us. One elderly woman was actually peering in our direction through a lorgnette.

An elderly waiter appeared out of the darkness, like a fish rising out of the depths of an aquarium, and offered us champagne from a silver tray. The flutes were green and shaped like the calla lilies.

There was a buzz among the guests, and they parted for a small, slim, elderly woman with imperious features and an aura of energy. She was wearing one of the most extraordinary dresses I had ever seen, a floor-length, skintight, high-necked garment of black velvet, rather like that worn by Jane Avril in Toulouse-Lautrec's famous poster, around which curled embroidered calla lilies, the stem of one of them curling around her slender neck like a noose. Her complexion was not just pale, it was white, like that of Pierrot, against which she had slashed, with reckless abandon, scarlet lipstick and much eye shadow. This, clearly, was our hostess. My friend introduced himself and explained who I was, at which Hurst fixed her gaze on me intently. Did she understand, she asked, that I was a book publisher? Modestly, I assented. Her voice was penetrating, but despite her curious costume there was nothing particularly formidable about it. If one had heard it on the subway, one would not have thought twice about it. It electrified the other guests, however, who seemed to have been brought back to life by simply hearing Fannie Hurst speak. Hurst put her arm in mine and led me through her living room, introducing me to a few of her friends, who looked very jealous indeed that she had singled me out for contact.

Would I like to see the rest of the apartment? she asked. I was dying to, of course—who could resist the offer? Hurst took me into the dining room, where a lavish buffet was laid out on a rough-hewn table, like that in a monastery. The food was displayed on elegant silver platters, a presentation spoiled only by the presence of a bottle of ketchup. The dining-room chairs looked as if they might have been designed by or for trolls or dwarfs. And indeed, the whole room itself was like something out of *The Lord of the Rings:* narrow, windowless, and very low ceilinged, the walls covered in dark, carved wainscoting, such illumination as there was coming entirely from candles. At the table sat three elderly women, one of them wearing what appeared to be a velvet, hooded cape. Hurst ignored them and drew me back through the living room to a stairway that was uncommonly narrow and steep and lit by elaborate lanterns clenched in fists at the end of muscular, patinated bronze arms fixed at intervals along the wall. I could not help staring at them. "A present from Mr. Hearst," she explained, as we ducked through a low doorway into a gloomy passage.

"I'm only showing you this because you're a publisher," Hurst said enigmatically. Now that I was alone with her in the dark, I was beginning to feel sorry that I had accepted the house tour. The atmosphere was certainly sepulchral downstairs, but here it was thoroughly eerie. I was to experience much the same feeling of claustrophobia and apprehension many years later when, on a visit to Egypt, I climbed the steep, narrow passageway inside the pyramid of Cheops to visit his burial chamber. Here, Hurst's presence, pressed up against me in the dark, was strangely disconcerting. Her perfume may have had something to do with it. It carried a certain odor of calla lily—everything in the house did—but it was at the same time sweet and sharp, so that it brought tears to one's eyes.

We groped our way to the end of the passageway, where Hurst

threw open an ironbound oak door that could have held off a determined attack by Saracens. "This," she announced, "was my husband's bedroom. It's kept just as it was when he was alive."

It was a large though gloomy room, with the drapes shut tightly. On the dresser were her late husband's toiletries—silver-backed hairbrushes, a manicure set, various expensive masculine bits and pieces in tortoiseshell, ivory, and morocco leather, as well as an ornate silver-framed photograph of Hurst, taken at a considerably earlier point in her life. On the floor were his slippers, neatly placed, as if he might appear at any minute to put them on. The most noteworthy thing in the room—indeed, it was impossible to take one's eyes off it—was a large bed covered in black velvet, at each corner of which burned a big candle on a tall, wrought-iron pedestal, like those in a Spanish cathedral, as if a body was lying in state. But the bed, thankfully, was empty. Or almost so, for I noticed that it was covered in envelopes, a whole pile of them, as if somebody had dumped their mail here every day, except that all the envelopes looked similar. On the pillows rested a sheaf of calla lilies.

Hurst seemed lost in contemplation, then recalled my presence. "I come here every day," she said. "Just to say hello."

"I see. . . . And the—ah—letters?"

Hurst looked up at me, her large eyes filling with tears. She took out a lace handkerchief embroidered with—what else?—calla lilies and dabbed at her face. "What letters?" she asked.

"The ones on the bed."

She looked at them as if they had only just appeared there. "Ah," she said, "*those* letters. Well, every day I write to him, you see, and then I come up here and mail the letter to him by putting it on his bed."

I was touched. Here, surely, was a love that rivaled that of Queen Victoria for Prince Albert—after his death, she had his evening clothes laid out on his bed before dinner every night for the rest of her life. I looked at the bed again, and slowly an entirely irreverent thought crossed my mind. "Ah, how long has he been dead?" I asked, in as tactful a tone as I could manage.

Miss Hurst frowned at the word *dead*. I wondered if she was a Christian Scientist. "He passed over," she emphasized gently, "many, many years ago."

I stared at the pile of envelopes. It was large certainly, but it could not have contained more than a few hundred letters. If he had passed over many, many years ago, there should have been thousands of them on the bed. I pointed this out to Hurst, as gently as I could.

She nodded. "Of course you're right," she said briskly. "Every year or so, my editor comes over from Doubleday and gathers them up, then we take the best ones and make a book of them."

She mused about this for a moment. "They do pretty well, too. *Reader's Digest* loves them. The foreign rights aren't bad either."

She moved me out of the room and closed the door firmly behind us. "Well, you're a publisher," she went on, all business now, "so you know how it is with writers. It never pays to waste anything you've written, does it?"

I HAVE often wondered what it must have been like to be the editor assigned to the macabre task of collecting Hurst's letters to her late husband at regular intervals. Of course, every editor knows that the most important task is to get your hands on the manuscript. It is astonishing how much time an editor spends coaxing pages out of the author's grip or listening to reasons why the manuscript "isn't ready to be shown yet." Of course, in many cases this is intended to conceal the fact that nothing exists on paper, but more often it is a sign of the author's panic. Most writers work in isolation and seldom show their work in progress to anyone. So long as nobody has actually *read* the manuscript, the writer can imagine the success, praise, and money that will be lavished on him or her—hence the reluctance to bundle it up in wrapping paper and send it off to the publisher, where, the author may assume, an editor will read it with a cold and fishy eye and demand all sorts of inappropriate changes or even, God forbid, deem it unsatisfactory and ask for the advance back.

In 1963 and 1964, I was sent off on a number of wild-goose chases to persuade various authors to surrender what they had written—if indeed they *had* written anything. This task was a kind of punishment, akin to bill collecting or process serving, and was invented for me by Henry Simon, who still smarted over what he saw as my defection, and was no doubt intended to strengthen my character. It reached its lowest point when I found myself sitting in a New Jersey roadhouse with the bandleader Paul Whiteman and his agent. Whiteman had been a big man in his heyday, broad shouldered, stout, and beaming as he stood in front of his band, but age had shrunk him, and his clothes—tailored in the garish colors and shiny fabrics that had once been the mark of success in the big-band era—hung off him loosely, like deflated balloons. He had sunk to the point where he was conducting a very much reduced version of his band in shady-looking nightclubs, to audiences whose grandparents had danced to his beat, playing medleys of Cole Porter for kids who really wanted to hear the Beatles or the Rolling Stones. He still had the pencil-thin mustache and the toothy, gleaming smile of the showbiz professional, but his eyes were resentful and at times bewildered. Once he had played for kings, queens, movie stars, and millionaires; now he was doing one-night stands on the outskirts of Paramus. My presence—reminding him that he had a contract to deliver a book—did nothing to improve his day. We sat at a table near the bar in the stygian gloom of the roadhouse—What, I asked myself, is more depressing than being in a nightclub at noon?—with a tray of stale Danish pastries and a thermos of coffee provided by the management in the person of a swarthy, blue-chinned gentleman who might as well have a sign pinned on him that read, "Member of an Organized-Crime Family." Whiteman was determined to give me each and every one of the anecdotes with which he had sold Henry Simon on the idea of his writing an autobiography, while my instructions were to return with pages of manuscript.

I finally interrupted the flow and asked if I could see some of the book. No problem, Whiteman said. He nodded to his agent, who produced a stout briefcase, from which he took folder after folder. I leafed through them. They were all photographs, meticulously captioned, showing Whiteman in happier and more prosperous days, most of them with his arm around some celebrity. "These are just photographs," I said. "What about the text?"

Whiteman sighed and stared into the middle distance, his eyes avoiding me.

"Paul doesn't respond well to pressure," the agent whispered to me.

"*What* pressure? He's years late. Nobody's bothered him until now."

"We figured that was because you guys didn't care."

"Of course we care," I objected.

Whiteman held his hand up for quiet. He gave me a smile. "Listen to me," he said slowly, even impressively, enunciating every word carefully. "It's written, don't worry." He tapped a finger against his bald head. "You go back and tell them that it's all here, every word of it. The hard work has been done. Now it's just a question of getting it all down on paper."

Sidney Kingsley's very words.

THE NUMBER of times I heard this, or some variation of it, is incalculable. I heard it from Orson Welles—*his* book was already written, within that massive head, just waiting to come pouring out onto paper any day now. I heard it from Irving Lazar for nearly thirty years on the subject of *his* autobiography, and I have heard it from a wide variety of people over the years, ranging from Cher to Ronald Reagan. For some reason, celebrity authors always assume that the hard part of writing is the *thinking,* whereas the truth, as every professional writer knows, is that the actual writing is what hurts—thinking comes easy, by comparison, and nothing exists until it has been put down on paper.

That period, 1963 to 1965, saw a lot of celebrity books, as well as an increasing sense that if you paid out money to an author, however famous he or she was, you ought to get something back in the way of a manuscript—or at least enough pages to prove that work was being done, if only by a ghostwriter. This was a novel idea in most publishing houses and by no means a welcome one. Publishers had always shied away from asking for their money back, partly because gentlemen didn't do that sort of thing and partly because most publishing houses weren't efficient enough to do it on any reasonable scale—besides, the thinking went, the sums of money were usually relatively small, and most authors stoutly resisted repaying.

Public sympathy, moreover, was usually on the side of the writer in such cases. This was an attitude largely shared by editors, most of whom were quite used to waiting for years for a manuscript to come in and to treating the delivery date on a contract as infinitely elastic, fiercely resisting any attempt on the part of "the business people" to go after authors for late delivery, however much water had flowed under the bridge since the contract was signed. Bob Gottlieb, for instance, leaped to the passionate defense of writers whom he himself accused of being deadbeats at the first sign of interest in them from the business department.

The gap between "us"—editors, intellectuals, people of a certain *sensibility*—and "them"—suit-wearing *apparatchiki* who went around turning off the lights and didn't read books—was nowhere greater than at S&S, where the slightest intervention of the business people in editorial matters was seen as part of Shimkin's long struggle to gain control of S&S and deprive editors of their cherished privileges and independence. Even those who did not like Max Schuster—or dismissed him as a henpecked figure of fun—preferred him to the alternative, which was Shimkin.

IT IS the misfortune of most men that they achieve what they have always wanted at the point when it is too late for them to enjoy it or make good use of it, and Shimkin was no exception. Shrewd and patient, one of the rare figures in publishing who was a businessman first and actually preferred going over the account books to reading the books the company published, Shimkin was to secure complete control over S&S long after his energy and vision had already been eclipsed.

By the time that Shimkin and Schuster were equal partners in S&S (they rotated the offices of president and chairman of the board on a yearly basis), Shimkin was in almost as much danger of becoming a caricature of himself as Max was, despite the fact that he was by many years the younger man. Max's many eccentricities were equaled by Shimkin's endless financial homilies—the summit of his wisdom was "Fifty percent of something is better than one hundred percent of nothing," which he managed to work into every conversation at least once—not to speak of his unconvincing (and undependable) facade of Pickwickian good humor, his unflagging attention to unimportant details, his struggle with depression, and his growing drinking problem. To see the two men together was to be exposed to such a catalog of tics, quirks, manias, idées fixes, and compulsive behavior as to call for the talent of Dr. Oliver Sacks.

By the early 1960s, though Shimkin was in sight of his goal—as Max's deterioration and declining health began to be obvious—he was an angry and embittered man, no longer in complete control of himself. Already, it was well known throughout the company that there was no point in seeing Shimkin about anything that mattered after lunch, when two or three stiff martinis would have ignited his suspicion and his temper to a white-hot glow. His motherly secretary kept a pitcher of martinis ready in a thermos bottle for the late afternoon, when the ones he had drunk at lunchtime were beginning to wear off. By the end of the day, when he left for home, he was rolling unsteadily on his feet as he stood on Fiftieth Street looking for his car and very often looking for a fight as well.

CHAPTER 16

*T*HE MID-SIXTIES WERE a troubled and uncertain time for everybody at S&S, as they were, by and large, for the rest of the publishing industry. Although on the surface it might have seemed that at S&S the real question was how long Max could hold on to his half of the company, Shimkin's eventual ascendancy led to the sale of the company to a total stranger—a kind of Pyrrhic victory for Shimkin. In much the same way, Cerf, having brought off an astonishing coup with the purchase of Knopf and having taken Random House public shortly afterward, sold his beloved company to RCA. What had been unleashed throughout the industry was a kind of Gadarene rush to exchange the ownership of publishing houses for stock as fast as possible, before the game was up—a game that is still going on today as many of the bigger houses, themselves the result of numerous acquisitions and mergers, are put on the block for sale by their corporate owners, most of whom never wanted to be in the book-publishing business in the first place.

Shimkin was to be one of the first victims in the early stages of this game of corporate dominos. He *could*, no doubt, once he had rid himself of Max, have arranged to pass the company on eventually, by gradual stages, to his son, Michael, who had already demonstrated his interest in the business by opening a successful bookstore; or he could have chosen to preserve the company's independence by other means; instead, no sooner had he secured 100 percent of it than he was trying to sell it—an odd reaction to the culmination of a forty-year-old ambition.

Beyond the fact that Cerf, Shimkin, the Knopfs, and any number of others wanted to cash in their chips, there was no real reason for the wave of mergers and sales that began to hit the publishing industry in the sixties and continued through the seventies and eighties at an accelerating pace. Once the process had started, it was impossible to stop. The bigger publishing houses became, the more they enjoyed "economies of scale"—the ability to buy paper in larger quantities at lower prices, for example, or to share the cost of the sales force and the accounting department between a number of different imprints. In theory, the larger a publishing house became, the more profitably it could be operated—hence the logic of Random House's acquisitions of Knopf, Pantheon, Fawcett, Ballantine, and, eventually, innumerable British publishing houses, or S&S's eventual acquisitions of Prentice-Hall and Macmillan (which had already acquired Atheneum and Scribner's). All this lay far in the future in the mid-sixties, but the seeds were already sown for the stronger houses, with more powerful financial backing, to swallow the smaller and weaker ones.

Shimkin could read the writing on the wall, but he was not in any position to take advantage of that ability. Schuster was still his partner, and the last thing Max wanted to do was expand S&S or acquire other houses. On the contrary, Max's sole ambition was to hang on by his fingernails for as long as possible—or, perhaps, for as long as his health would permit him to do so. There were days when it must have seemed to Shimkin that Max's health was better than his own—say what you like, at least Max wasn't immobilized by episodes of depression.

Max's deterioration, by contrast, was undramatic and by small degrees. Those who worked close to him noticed, for example, that the shaking that had always affected his hands was growing more severe, that he often left large patches of his face unshaved, presumably because he could no longer hold a razor steadily enough to reach them, that his gait was more and more unsteady, so that in motion he resembled a windup toy—one had the feeling that a gentle push would send him backward out of control until he fell over. These were the signs, I recognized, of Parkinson's disease, from which my maternal grandfather, Octavius Musgrove, had suffered during his last years, and the one thing I knew about Parkinson's was that it didn't get better.

I have no doubt that Max knew it too, but he never mentioned his illness and took great pains to ensure, even more than before, that nobody saw him coming or going in the halls by arriving early and leaving late. Seated behind his desk, all one noticed was the trembling hands, and Max tried to hide that by clutching the arms of his chair as if he were holding on for dear life—as in a sense he was.

Given this weak and divided authority at the top, it is hardly surprising that there was a certain amount of not very discreet jockeying for power below. This resulted in the resignation of Henry Simon, ostensibly for reasons of health but actually because he had been badly outmaneuvered by his peers. As Max declined, Henry must have had every expectation of getting—at long last—a chance to wield some kind of power. But by the time Max got around to relinquishing some of his powers, Henry was old, cranky, embittered, and simply too tired to take on a real fight against younger, hungrier men. Peter Schwed was promoted over him to become de facto publisher, while Bob Gottlieb made his peace with Schwed and became managing editor.

What this meant, in practice, was that the two people who most disliked Henry Simon were now running exactly those parts of the company that affected him most closely. The bottom line was that his books were neither exciting enough nor profitable enough to reward him with the kind of position he craved. Bob had brought in a whole roster of new talent, while Schwed was responsible, despite his London trips, for a solid list of sports books and fiction and nonfiction best-sellers. In the final analysis, in book publishing nothing really matters but the books, and Henry had simply been outpaced by his rivals.

I had long since switched, with whatever pangs of conscience, to the winning side, and Henry knew it—and he wasn't about to forgive my defection. When I said good-bye to him as he was leaving his office, he shook my hand limply, an ironic smile on his gaunt face. "Good luck," he said. Then, with a bitter expression, he added, "but I don't think you'll need it."

Shortly afterward, Bob moved into Henry's corner office, I moved into Bob's, and Dick Snyder moved upstairs to join us on the twenty-eighth floor.

I was perfectly content and assumed that there would be no more changes for a long, long time. In fact, they had only just begun.

PUBLISHING, DESPITE a lot of humbug to the contrary, is a *reactive* business—which is to say that publishers and editors do not as a rule make taste or determine people's political opinions or effect major social changes. In the final analysis, they adapt, however unwillingly or hesitantly, to the demands, taste, and opinions of the marketplace or they go under. That is not to say that there are no exceptions. From time to time a book published in a spirit of stubborn contrarianism—written and published against the flow, so to speak—will become a major best-seller, but in retrospect this has often been because it accidentally tapped some nascent change in public opinion. To take a famous example, *Uncle Tom's Cabin,* one of the biggest best-sellers in the history of American publishing, is often credited with having created in its many millions of readers a revulsion against slavery that led directly to the Civil War—even Abraham Lincoln, on meeting Harriet Beecher Stowe, remarked that she was the little lady who had written the book that had begun the big war—but the truth is that the book capitalized on feelings that were already there. The success of *Uncle Tom's Cabin* merely signified that there were more people opposed to slavery—and to any compromise on slavery with the Southern states—than politicians, including Lincoln, had hitherto supposed; indeed, had the best-seller list existed in the mid-nineteenth century, Southerners might have viewed the success of Stowe's novel in the rest of the country—and the civilized world—as a good indication of the overwhelming number of people ranged against their cause.

To take another example, Wendell Willkie's *One World,* which S&S published in extraordinary numbers in 1943, did not convince the public that the United Nations was a desirable idea—the public had already formed that opinion and were therefore in sympathy with Willkie's book when it appeared. Despite the huge success of Laura Z. Hobson's *Gentleman's Agreement,* her novel did not change most Americans' feelings about social anti-Semitism—on the contrary, it succeeded precisely because the war and the Holocaust had made most literate people uncomfortable with anti-Semitism, even of the mild, social kind, and therefore willing to read a book condemning that kind of behavior. Books *follow* events, they do not cause them.

Most publishers are slow to pick up on change, in part because they are merchants, in part because they have a vested interest in the status quo. If they put an ear to the ground, it is usually to listen to what the bookstores are saying (via the sales reps), rather than to learn what is going on in the streets. Then, too, the more successful publishers are part of the "establishment" (the less successful ones merely aspire to be) and tend to share the opinions of those who are, or fancy themselves to be, like themselves: wealthy and powerful. Max Schuster and Bennett Cerf were somewhat more liberal in their politics than their WASP competitors, but they were not by any means radical or inclined to make waves. They held the more or less middle-of-the-road liberal opinions of their social group, which is to say that they voted Democratic, had admired Franklin D. Roosevelt and the New Deal, had preferred Truman to Eisenhower, supported (cautiously) Israel, had their doubts (even more cautiously) about Alger Hiss's guilt, and believed in the First Amendment without necessarily wanting to publish, or even read, *Lolita* or *The Story of O* themselves. Their spiritual center, as it were, was *The New York Times,* and few of their opinions differed from those expressed on its editorial page, which is not by any means the worst thing one can say about somebody.

As a consequence they were caught flat-footed by the violent social changes that engulfed the nation in the sixties, at just the point when it seemed to most people of fifty and above that after the Depression and the war things were pretty good and only going to get better. Then the pace of events speeded up dizzily, moving too fast for the usual leisurely pace of book publishing, in which it takes a year or two for somebody to write the book and nine months to a year for somebody to publish it. Before the returns were even in on the various panegyrics to Camelot, publishers were rushing out illustrated souvenir books on JFK's funeral, always one step behind the weekly newsmagazines and two steps behind television. The civil-rights crisis caught them not only unprepared but undecided and embarrassed. Book publishing, as an industry, was pretty much a white man's business, and while it gradually and with many delays and complaints began to accept women in positions of executive authority during the sixties, it was hard to find a single black person outside the mailroom in most publishing houses. This left book publishers in the uncomfortable position of being in favor of civil rights and racial equality everywhere but in their own offices (a position that has not changed noticeably some thirty years later).

The order of things, which had seemed so settled through the 1950s, was suddenly bewildering to those in charge, who were facing simultaneously the growing anger of women, the sea change in American culture, the revolt of youth (very often among their own children, not just in newsmagazine profiles and nonfiction outlines from authors), the civil-rights movement, and the first signs of widespread public disenchantment with the war in Vietnam. The last was a special problem, since many editors, most academics, and a large percentage of authors were speaking out against the war with increasing passion and expecting publishers to take a stand on it. This was something new. Book publishers had hitherto considered themselves to be under a kind of self-imposed obligation to publish both sides of most issues more or less impartially, rather than to take the moral high ground. There were exceptions, of course—few publishers would have been comfortable with a pro-Nazi book, and in general publishers have always tried to avoid books bearing unmistakably incendiary or subversive opinions, preferring to stay within the mainstream as much as possible. Those who had come of age in or before World War Two and who for the most part believed that you could trust the U.S. government and accepted the morality of the cold war (if not necessarily that of nuclear weapons) found it hard to adjust to the increasingly heated and partisan debate; in many publishing houses, the management hunkered down against the editors and vice versa. The confusion of the era was perhaps typified by the fact that at the same National Book Award ceremony (then in the midst of one of its many doomed attempts to make the giving of prizes to writers and poets seem glamorous and newsworthy) a streaker ran across the stage, followed shortly by a good third of the audience standing up and walking out of the hall in protest at the appearance of a member of the Johnson administration. Those who stayed were thus hit square between the eyes with both barrels of the counterculture—the sexual revolution and the antiwar movement—leaving many of them indignant and confused.

Neither at S&S nor at Random House was there any serious attempt on the part of management to throttle dissent, but that is not to say there was no friction as the war escalated. Before, there had always been plenty of young editors (more than there were jobs for, as a rule), but they tended to do much the same kind of books as other editors, perhaps on a less exalted plane, while waiting for their elders to die, retire, or change jobs. Now, for the first time, publishers actively sought out young editors who could bring them a different *kind* of book—for perhaps the first time since the invention of movable type it became an *advantage* to be young, and young editors with the right kind of hip and defiant attitude were briefly in demand. The years when S&S was to publish books by Jerry Rubin, Wavy Gravy, and Jill Johnston (among others) were still ahead, but already some of us were moving into uncharted waters. My small contribution was a book by the Venceremos Brigade—American college students who had volunteered to harvest sugar cane in Cuba—which caused a certain amount of heartburn at S&S.

Max had once turned down the memoirs of Albert Speer, when they were on offer to S&S. I had read much of the manuscript and thought that for all its evasions and self-deception, it was a unique and extraordinary book, one that provided a portrait of Hitler and the higher echelons of the Nazi leadership that nobody else could match, whatever one thought of Speer himself. I also thought it would be a huge success. Max listened intently to what I had to say, nodding his agreement. I was right, he told me, when I had finished. He had no doubt the book would be a big best-seller, and he, too, thought it was an extraordinary and valuable document and a major publishing opportunity. Then he leaned back in his chair and let out a sigh. "There is only one problem," he said, "and it's this: I do not want to see Albert Speer's name and mine on the same book."

You couldn't argue with that, I thought then and still think now. Max was broad-minded, but there were limits to his tolerance, and who was I to argue with him? Besides, I agreed and used much the same argument many years later to argue against publishing a book by Louis Farrakhan. I didn't think Max would have wanted his name on that book either. As Dick Snyder was later to say, "A publisher has an obligation to believe in the First Amendment but not to publish everything that's sent to him."

THE MID-SIXTIES changed publishing radically. Sex scenes in fiction became permissible almost overnight, as did the use of obscene expletives. Even the book clubs, which had long advocated a certain artificial purity in the fiction they chose for their readers, gave in to the relaxation of the old standards (all except the *Reader's Digest* Condensed Book Club, which to this day does not take books in which the characters swear or have sex out of marriage). Arguments like those between Hemingway and Maxwell Perkins over how to suggest the use of the word *fuck* in dialogue without actually printing it were no longer necessary or even thinkable. I remember with what trepidation I approved the use of the word *fuck* for the first time—in a Harold Robbins novel, of course—and with what indignation it was received by S&S and the printer, both of which tried to remove it and predicted dire consequences if it was kept in. I did not think the sky would fall, myself, and it didn't, though Max didn't like it a bit and put up a rather feeble rearguard struggle on the subject.

Max, however, was becoming an increasingly feeble presence at S&S. Most of what was being published was now done without his knowledge or, perhaps more important, interest. He was not alone in this. Except for the Knopfs, who despite having sold their company to Random House maintained strict control over their list, the sixties was the period in which many of the founders of the "new" publishing houses willingly or unwillingly began to surrender editorial control.

Publishing had once been a placid stream in which it was common for publishers to go on working well into extreme old age, since the public taste in books didn't change much; now, it was increasingly part of the media business, linked to television talk shows and movie companies, supplying not only popular entertainment but trendy advice for upwardly mobile readers. In this atmosphere, trends were hard to spot and seldom lasted long. The publisher almost *had* to be part of the generation he was publishing for, to share the same tastes and needs, to be able to turn on a dime, and, above all, to have a certain *Fingerspitzengefühl* for the popular culture. It was not an art that could be practiced successfully from the ivory tower, nor from Max's home in Sands Point. Besides, the growth of the industry was turning the founder publishers, one by one, into businessmen, however reluctant they might be. Bennett Cerf now had to deal with stockholders and Wall Street, and later with the directors of RCA and General Sarnoff himself, not just with importunate editors and prima donna authors; Max had to deal with Shimkin and the ever-present demand for increased capital outlays. Given their temperaments, it was natural that Cerf should come to enjoy his new role as Wall Street's publishing guru and that Max should hide himself away, revising endless drafts of letters to the Durants and to Madame Helen Kazantzakis, the formidable widow of the author on whom Max had staked his claim to cultural immortality. In neither case were they looking for new talent—they had reached the age (and the positions) where, increasingly, the old talent looked just fine to them.

Under the circumstances, the post of editor in chief (or its equivalent) was bound to become more and more important. He or she was to soon come to be a combination of rainmaker, intellectual gadfly, and live connection to the popular culture—roles that the owner-founders in simpler times had been able to fulfill themselves. What had once been an honorific became, almost overnight, the hottest position in publishing. Hitherto, there had been star authors, of course, but now, for the first time, there were about to be star editors, some of them bigger stars, in fact, than their authors. Even the best known of editors had been, in the old days, essentially bureaucrats and subservient to the owner or owners of their publishing house. Certainly, they neither sought nor were given fame. Maxwell Perkins in his own lifetime was very much an éminence grise, careful not to steal the limelight from his owner-boss Charles Scribner, let alone from his major authors. It is notable that when Perkins died, Hemingway neither recognized the immense value of Perkins's suggestions, enthusiasm, loyalty, and support to his work nor wasted a moment in suggesting to Scribner that somebody else could take on the role. The deep bond between author and editor that was to actually make writers leave their publishers en masse when their editor changed jobs only came later, with the demise of the owner-publisher and the advent of the publisher-businessman—for by that time the editor was the only person with whom the author had any meaningful contact, except perhaps for the publicity director. Perkins's fame was posthumous (alas for Perkins). In his own lifetime he worked in the shadow of his own authors and in that of Charles Scribner. He would not have recognized Bob Gottlieb, say, as his successor.

But it was, in fact, Bob who set the pattern that still holds in book publishing, in which the major editor or editors of a publishing house are generally believed (rightly or wrongly) to be capable of miracles by turning a manuscript into a successful book if they want to—the editor as a miracle worker. And not just miracle worker, for Bob was a father figure, even to people far older than himself, an analyst, always willing to delve into other people's problems, a father-confessor, on call twenty-four hours a day, as well as the fastest and most sensitively tuned reader on the block. Almost single-handedly, Bob managed to turn what had hitherto been thought of as a somewhat stuffy job into a glamorous one.

It might have been a power base, had Bob *wanted* a power base, but he showed no desire for one as yet, being for the moment content to create what amounted to a publishing house within a publishing house and to surround himself with faithful admirers—his "loved ones," as he liked to refer to those closest to him. Bob's publishing style was in part based on the new English model—in the sixties, many of the older English publishing houses, tottering on the brink of insolvency or irrelevance, sought new leases on life by bringing in as editorial directors young men whom the owners would never have tolerated in their houses or clubs in more normal circumstances. The members of the new breed were the publishing equivalent of the "angry young men" who changed the British theater in the late fifties. Sharper, tougher, rougher edged, borderline scruffy, openly ambitious (never a popular thing in England), and eager to change things, they came from outside the stuffy, middle-class background of most British publishers and were often openly contemptuous of their good manners, lack of passion for books or ideas, and banker's hours.

PERHAPS THE most admired of these new brooms was Tony Godwin, a former bookseller, whom Sir Allen Lane, the founder of Penguin, one of England's most respected cultural institutions, brought in to sweep clean his editorial office. Godwin, with his wiry, bushy mop of hair, his narrow body dressed in casual clothes, his very un-English gift of enthusiasm, and his even more un-English dislike of bullshit, was a man determined to have his own way and absolutely certain of his taste and judgment (characteristics that were to lead him from Penguin to Weidenfeld and Nicolson, and finally, fatally, to the United States). Even more charismatic was Tom Maschler, who had improbably been picked to revitalize the august and revered house of Jonathan Cape, Ltd., perhaps England's most distinguished publishing house. Maschler was as abrasive and impassioned as Godwin but with a darker charm that was very different from Godwin's engaging candor and with more unconventional and ambitious literary tastes. It was hard to find anybody who did not like Tony Godwin, even among those who thought he was a fraud, and even harder to find anybody who would admit to liking Tom Maschler, but the two of them provided Bob with a sense of what could be done if one combined a powerful personality and a willingness to take publishing risks with some real degree of control over the publishing process.

Because S&S was so much larger, Bob was never to gain the complete independence that Godwin enjoyed for a time at Penguin (until Godwin published a collection of fierce anticlerical cartoons by Siné, the author of *The French Cat*, at which point Sir Allen fired him) or that Maschler, always more subtle than his rival, was to have at Cape for many decades, until it passed into the hands of that Great Accumulator of publishing properties, S. I. Newhouse, making Maschler, at last, a rich man. Nevertheless, within the limits of what was possible at S&S,

Bob Gottlieb set out to acquire similar status for himself and did so very successfully.

Part of his strategy was to work closely with Maschler and Godwin, and with such younger and more unconventional agents as Candida Donadio or Deborah Rogers. At first, a remarkable number of Bob's books came from the Cape and Penguin lists, but very soon the tide began to flow in the other direction, as Bob's own well-developed personal taste was increasingly reflected in his list. It became clear that Bob was by far the strongest personality among these competing enfants terribles, with the surest sense of what would sell and the amplest resources. Eventually it came to seem that Maschler was somehow imitating Bob, or that he was merely a lesser British version of him, and the friendship between the two men, while it remained close, was fraught with competition and anxiety, at least on Maschler's side.

Still, for all the angst, a certain style had been found, and Bob was soon the first book editor to become a celebrity in his own right, much as he claimed to be embarrassed by the phenomenon and shunned the limelight. The story of how he had edited and renamed *Catch-22* became publishing legend, as did his clever promotion of Rona Jaffe with *The Best of Everything*. What made Bob formidable was that he combined a refined literary sensibility with first-rate commercial judgment. He was not an intellectual snob. *Crass commercialism* was not a phrase that frightened him, and he enjoyed a bad book as much as a good one, provided that it was, as he said with delight, "a *good* bad book." What he meant by that seemed mysterious to a lot of people in publishing (and most people at S&S) and even hypocritical, but in fact, I soon discovered, it was really very simple. A novel had to be written with *sincerity* and out of some genuine passion; if it was, then it didn't really matter at what level it was written, so long as it was honest. Deliberate, plodding attempts to construct long-winded production-line best-selling fiction, like the books of Irving Wallace, or fiction written with fake feelings and deliberate, empty sensationalism (like most of Harold Robbins's novels after *The Carpetbaggers*) bored Bob. He had a nose for the real thing, an authentic vision or view, whether it was "literary" or not. He could enjoy Jacqueline Susann's *Valley of the Dolls* or Grace Metalious's *Peyton Place* just as sincerely as he could Jane Austen—for what they all had in common, from Bob's point of view, was that they were *sincere* writers, trying as best they could to show the world as they understood and lived in it. Of course, Jane Austen was doing it in better

English and with a more refined sensibility, but the quality of the writing or the sensibility was not what mattered.

This was a controversial opinion at the time and remains so for many people, who tend to simplify this into a battle between crass commercialism and serious literature, as if there was not some common gray area into which the two merged—and have merged, more or less, since the beginning of the written word. In any case, it was Bob's stroke of genius to understand this, right from the beginning, and to approach the manuscripts he read with a far more open mind than the vast majority of his colleagues—and with higher standards, too.

Beyond this, Bob was a gifted *reader*. It might seem strange to suggest that reading is a talent, since most people assume that almost everybody can and does read every day, but Bob read as a great music critic might listen, with attention, pleasure, a high degree of discrimination, and a sense of perfect pitch. A sentence off balance, a few lines that could be cut, a wrong note, caught his attention, but he did not read, as so many editors do—as poor Henry Simon had, for instance—for the sole purpose of finding flaws. He read for and with pleasure, yet at the same time he could imagine, in his mind's eye, as he was reading, how the book might be reconstructed, how intricate changes might bring out the best in it, how cuts might get the reader to where he or she wanted to go faster.

It is conventional in publishing to divide good line editors, who can blue-pencil a manuscript in detail, from editors who are more concerned with the big picture, but Bob was good at both, and watching him work one soon learned that it is no good doing the one if you don't do the other, that sometimes the big fix was needed, sometimes every line had to be corrected, and on occasion both. You did what you had to, and that was that.

But no editor, no matter how good, can turn a bad book into a good one, so an editor ought to work only on those books he or she loves, for whatever reason. Loving the book makes the work worthwhile and makes it at least possible that something useful will be accomplished by working on it. Working on a book you hate, dislike, or are indifferent to accomplishes nothing at all.

Beyond all his other abilities, Bob was a great teacher, the kind who teaches without being aware of it, and for a period of about four years, during which he reigned as S&S's editorial star, he turned the editorial department into a kind of school, almost rabbinical in its method of instruction and entirely dominated by his firm but gentle insistence on getting everything right. Perhaps Bob's only weakness was that while he himself was a remarkably shrewd businessman and seldom overpaid for a book he wanted, he was determined to prevent the business people from intruding into the decisions that mattered to him: which books to publish and how to publish them. These were precisely the decisions, however, that the business people were determined to control, or at any rate to subject to some process of decision making more quantifiable and objective than, say, Bob's instinctive feel that this or that book was worth publishing and called for a printing of twenty thousand copies. This eventually became a serious problem for him in later positions at Knopf and as the editor of *The New Yorker*. At S&S, however, these problems did not arise. Fortunately for Bob and his authors, Shimkin's attention was fixed on getting Max out, while Max's attention was fixated on staying put.

For a time, no doubt, it might have passed unnoticed by Schuster and Shimkin that S&S was in the process of becoming something it had never been before: a "hot" literary house, putting out a remarkable list of new writers, one after another. The discovery and launching of Heller was followed by innumerable launches of new stars, whether from the United Kingdom, like Edna O'Brien, Len Deighton, and Doris Lessing, or from the United States and Canada, like Bruce Jay Friedman, Mordecai Richler, James Leo Herlihy, and Charles Portis. Unexpectedly, improbably, Bob had transformed S&S, with its reputation for nonfiction and self-help best-sellers, into the hottest fiction house in New York. The smart, irreverent, wisecracking Jewish black-comic novel, exemplified by books such as *Stern* and *A Mother's Kisses*, was virtually his invention and led to many anxious discussions with Max. Max was of the generation that did not think there was anything particularly funny about being Jewish—rather the contrary—and was made nervous by the fact that this new school of fiction tended to portray Jews as whining, complaining, neurotic, sex obsessed, and burdened with hellishly dominating mothers and weak fathers. In *A Mother's Kisses*, the hero's monster-mother begs and threatens a counterman, "I want you to cross your heart and swear to Christ that my son's patties aren't greasy," and most of these books prefigured the "self-hating" Jews of Philip Roth's later fiction (*Portnoy's Complaint* and after), caricaturing the urban Jewish family in ways that Julius Streicher himself might have envied.

It was not only Max who was sensitive to this kind of thing. Even Peter Schwed, who hardly admitted to being Jewish at all, expressed his doubts about Bob's new wave of young Jewish writers (the old wave included writers such as Meyer Levin, who wrote about being Jewish with glum seriousness). Shimkin also occasionally chimed in with complaints from rabbis in Larchmont or Westchester, none of whom, of course, had read the book in question but were merely passing on the unease of their congregations in the face of these new assaults on their faith. Jews poking fun at Jews—worse yet, at the fact of being Jewish—was still a controversial phenomenon in the 1960s, and to those whose minds were still on the Holocaust (which had not yet acquired that name) it was deeply shocking. It was one thing for Gentiles to hate and ridicule Jews—there was nothing new in *that*—but quite another for Jews to hate and ridicule themselves and, most sinister of all, for other Jews (Jewish publishers, for instance) to make money out of it.

It is to Max's credit that whatever his own doubts (and whatever pressures may have been put on him by Shimkin and many of his own friends), he did not prevent Bob from taking the S&S fiction list in a direction that cannot have pleased him. Of course, it helped that Bob was successful and increasingly famous—the Schusters might not necessarily *like* the books he was publishing, but they knew success when they saw it. Besides, Ray, though she was not much of a reader of new fiction, had a wicked sense of humor and was, in this area at least, comparatively unshockable. "So *nu*, what's so terrible about all these books?" she once whispered to me at the yearly office outing, which took place at the Schusters' Sands Point house. "Jews can't be funny?"

This was the occasion when Ray first announced (to her neighbor W. Averell Harriman) that Bob was "my Max's new young genius," a role for which Bob would have been well suited, with his Napoleonic lock of hair and his disheveled clothes, had it not been that he took none of this seriously; indeed, Bob at the Schusters' looked as if he were slumming far more than former governor Harriman, and in a way he was: Harriman, for all his wealth, was just a politician, whereas Bob was an intellectual.

For a brief time, Bob made S&S, by the sheer force of his personality, intellectually chic, a house very much in his own image, at least on the surface, for S&S was not nor could ever be a Farrar, Straus and Giroux or a Knopf—it was simply too big. Like its chief rival, Random House, it might, for a time, acquire a conspicuous frosting of avant-garde literature, but the cake itself remained made of self-help books, "inspirational" books, business books, big-time popular fiction, and middlebrow nonfiction, as well as such tried-and-true publishing staples as mysteries, puzzle books, income-tax guides, and books on gardening, cooking, bridge, poker, stock-market investment, and almost every known human interest. However much attention Bob's books might get in the New York literary world, the financial stability of S&S rested on its backlist and on its continued publication of relatively humdrum titles. Stability and profit in book publishing are more likely to come from *What to Name the Baby* or income-tax guides than from the latest new novel, however critically acclaimed.

A publishing house can only be so big if it is to represent the taste and vision of one person, even of one person's clique; above that size, if it is to survive, it must be more of a supermarket than a boutique. That is not to say that a publishing house doesn't need a trendy or famous editor who follows his or her distinctive taste; a house without such a person rapidly becomes dull and sooner or later begins to lose authors. For a good many years during the fifties, sixties, and seventies, Doubleday, then the largest American trade house, was financially successful while producing a seemingly endless flood of solid, safe, middlebrow books without any strong editorial figure. By the early eighties, however, Doubleday went into a sharp decline, and authors no longer wanted to be published there. A sensible publisher knows that any major house needs books that will be talked about, books that will create a sensation, books that represent a certain literary style or view of the world, not because these are necessarily profitable but because the attention they receive lends a certain cachet both to the rest of the list and to the reputation of the company itself. In much the same way, in the world of fashion the profit is no longer in the dazzling creations of famous couturiers, whose work is reported on in breathless prose by the media, but in the huge merchandising empires to which the couturiers have lent (or, rather, sold) their names. The dazzle surrounding this or that latest collection makes sense only when you take into account that it is being used to sell perfume, handbags, sunglasses, pens, watches, luggage, and jeans all over the world at outrageous prices. An editor who becomes a celebrity might or might not be profitable the best are, of course but lends glamour to what might otherwise be a fairly ordinary list. How much this is worth is hard to estimate, but it's worth *something*, and Max knew it. In Bob's case, most of his books were either modestly or outstandingly profitable, so the literary glamour he provided was not, in fact, costing S&S anything, but it is never easy when a young editor becomes better known than the owner of the company. It is to Max's credit that he managed to give up the limelight with a certain degree of grace and good humor.

By 1965, however, his health had begun to give way. He had always *seemed* like an old man, and a rather feeble one at that, but now he was clearly faltering. He saw fewer people, and those whom he saw could hardly fail to notice that his Parkinson's symptoms were far more pronounced, that he tired easily, that even his sense of humor, however peculiar, was going, giving way to an uneasy sharpness, as is so often the case with men who know they are coming close to the end of their careers. He had seen the future, and it did not include him. It was not just a question of age or health, however; Ray and her son-in-law Ephraim London both knew that the tax laws favored the sale of Max's share in the company while he was still alive, and they urged him to get out while the going was good. In these days, when even comparatively small companies are acquired and sold for immense amounts of money and when CEOs are commonly given huge stock options and golden parachutes, it seems ludicrous that Schuster's half of S&S was valued at only two million dollars, but in the 1960s it was the equivalent perhaps of twenty million or more today—enough to give Ray a sense of security for her own future. Whatever Max may have felt—and it was clearly a long and painful decision—he was unable to resist the urgings of his wife, his son-in-law, and his partner. In 1966, it was announced that he had sold his half of the company to Shimkin.

Max's departure was arranged with a remarkable absence of fanfare, perhaps because it was a humiliating surrender on his part, perhaps simply because he had no desire to put a good face on it. Like so many men—indeed, like Dick Simon, and, eventually, Shimkin—Max's retirement from the company he had helped to found was a death sentence. He talked of writing a book, of continuing his labors on the Inner Sanctum Library of Basic Books, of traveling, but without conviction. To nobody's surprise, least of all, I suspect, his own, he was dead within four years.

By one of those transactions understandable only to the business mind, Shimkin, having gained the 50 percent of S&S that he had coveted for years, merged the company with Pocket Books, of which he then owned 46 percent, and ended up owning more than 50 percent of the new, merged corporation, thus not only revenging himself on Max and posthumously on Dick Simon but also right royally screwing his partners in Pocket Books out of their control of that company.

IT WAS hardly to be expected that Shimkin would look with favor on the increasing independence and fame of Bob Gottlieb. A more far-sighted and generous man might have seen how important it was to S&S to encourage and reward him, but Shimkin was of that school of management which is essentially hostile and prides itself on *not* giving people what they want or, in this case, have earned. The harder you pressed him for what you wanted, the more he retreated into a defensive posture and found reasons why it couldn't be done. This was not a spirit that was likely to nurture talent nor to satisfy Bob, who, despite his disheveled appearance and an aura of unworldliness, was beginning to show recognizable signs of ambition.

At some deep level, Bob was beginning to know his own strength and to chafe at having to remain under the control of people he made no secret of despising. Yet seldom had I ever met anybody who found it so necessary to deny his own ambition. Bob believed—*had* to believe—that everything he wanted was in the best interests of the company, of his friends, of his authors. Promotion, more power, a bigger office, he maintained, had been thrust upon him. He had accepted them unwillingly, humbly, because he had the best interests of S&S at heart. Nobody had worked harder (which was true), nobody cared as much (which was almost true), nobody loved S&S more or was loved with such intensity by almost everybody who mattered at S&S.

The truth was that Bob's character disguised not only his ambition but a certain steely authoritarianism. He wanted to run things by himself, in his own way, but in spite of this need to dominate he always wanted to be loved. His was altogether the spirit of a benevolent monarch who both craves and needs his subjects' love. It was at all times evident to him that he knew best and that his opinion was formed out of his love of S&S, of literature, of other people, and with no selfish motive in mind. All, in short, was for the best in the best of all possible worlds—or would be, if only Schwed would stop interfering and if Shimkin finally saw the light and let Bob run the company.

What Shimkin saw instead was that Bob had a shrewd eye for com-

mercial success, a kind of natural instinct for "good trash," and that it
was therefore worth humoring him, but he had no intention of putting
Bob or his "fan club" in charge of S&S. Shimkin believed in doling out
small raises and bonuses, spoon-feeding a bit at a time, always encouraging the employee to believe that what he or she wanted was just
around the corner, and in this way he strung Bob on for longer than
anyone could have imagined, mostly because Bob was perfectly sincere
when he said that S&S was his home and his family. It had not yet occurred to anyone that he might be able to take those of his family he
needed most to a new home—it had probably not even occurred to him.
It was as if he could not even conceive of working anywhere else. S&S
was where he had come of age, where the most important and productive years of his career had taken place, where he turned himself from a
penniless student into the loved and admired arbiter of literary fashion.

Nor could any of those of us who were Bob's friends imagine working elsewhere or without him. To an extraordinary degree, he inspired
loyalty, affection, even love. Despite the fact that he did not enjoy the
autonomy he coveted, he was unfailingly supportive of those he liked.
He did not confine his support or his interest to the group around him,
however. He involved himself in *any* S&S book that caught his attention or seemed to have some possibility of success, whoever the editor
might be.

Bob's hand reached far and wide through the S&S list. Although he
was not much interested in history himself, he spotted such original
books as Peter Tompkins's *A Spy in Rome* and encouraged me in my effort to add more books on history to the list. Whether it was the rise of
the Zulu nation, in Donald R. Morris's *The Washing of the Spears,* or the
mutinies in the French army in World War One, in Richard M. Watt's
Dare Call It Treason, Gottlieb was as undaunted by long, fact-filled
books with lots of notes and pictures and a whopping great index as he
was by first novels. Provided you could show him genuine enthusiasm
(from both the editor and the author), Bob was always happy to let you
take a risk and never complained if it failed. Without perhaps intending
to become one, he was a great publisher—a rare feat for an editor, for
most editors are only interested in their own books to the exclusion of
everyone else's. With some exceptions, the better the editor, the less
likely he or she is to succeed as a publisher—indeed, one of the major
problems in book publishing for years has been that the only way an editor could be promoted and rewarded beyond a certain limit is to make

him or her a publisher, a perfect example of the Peter Principle in operation, in which a person with a certain set of skills is promoted to a job in which a totally different and contradictory set of skills are required (and usually lacking). Most good editors fail as publishers because they find it hard to be objective about books, tend to take the author's side in any dispute, and usually despise other editors. Bob was an exception. He made no secret of his contempt for certain editors, but he was generally objective about the books of even those editors he most disliked. Once, years later, when he had reached the status of a publishing god at Knopf, I bumped into him at the annual American Booksellers Association convention in Washington, where he was cruising the stands and coolly examining the competition. It had been a long time since we had seen each other, and I suddenly realized, seeing him there, carrying a shopping bag full of catalogs and freebie reading copies, how much I missed him—and owed him, too. He gave the S&S display a careful appraisal and sighed. "Yes, well," he said dismissively, "but how are *you*, Miki?" (Bob was the only person in publishing who called me Miki, which, as he knew, was what my parents always called me.) Busy, I replied. I had been working hard on a book that seemed to me to have the makings of a best-seller. Bob nodded. "Do you love it?" he asked. I said I didn't exactly *love* it, no, but I thought it might sell a lot of copies. Bob looked at me darkly and shook his head. "Shame on you," he said, and vanished into the crowded aisle.

IT WAS not to be expected, in the normal order of things, that two men as different as Bob Gottlieb and Dick Snyder would get along well under one roof, but in fact they developed a certain distant, wary respect for each other. Dick had a clear-cut picture of the future—he would run S&S and Bob would be one of his major assets—but it almost goes without saying that Bob did not share this vision. In Bob's view of the future, *he* would be running S&S, leaving the things that didn't interest him to Schulte, Snyder, or both. He recognized Snyder's extraordinary combination of energy and sheer competence—these were traits he shared himself—but he thought of him mostly as "Leon's man," somebody to be kept at arm's length from the faithful friends and the decisions that mattered about books. In later years, when Dick had become something of a publishing god in his own right (an angry one, many people said), he would affect a kind of gruff comradeship with Bob, as if they had been close at S&S, and Bob, with a certain noblesse oblige, allowed him to do so without, however, joining in. Dick, revealingly, always referred to Gottlieb as "Bobby" and was the only person to do so. A Snyder-Gottlieb alliance would have been a formidable combination of publishing talents, and Dick knew it, but there was never a prayer of it happening. For all his dedication to his "loved ones," Bob was an autocrat at heart, albeit one with a genuinely sincere belief that he was a *benevolent* autocrat; it was not in his nature to share power with anyone. Bob had no difficulty in recognizing a wolf when he saw one, and much as he admired Dick's sharp intelligence he was not about to put himself in the service of another person's ambition. Nor was he eager to see Schwed, a relatively benign figure, replaced as publisher by somebody with real teeth and his own agenda, as was clearly Dick's ambition.

All of this, of course, was passing beneath the surface, largely because Bob was the kind of person who could never have admitted, even to himself, that he was capable of playing office politics. It was impossible to imagine that Bob would ever leave or that anything would ever change, but, in fact, we were on the brink of changes so big and dramatic in our small world that they were literally unthinkable.

CHAPTER 17

*I*N THE MEANTIME, my own life was about to change. I was about to become, of all things, a writer, just as Sidney Kingsley had predicted. I got there by a curious twist of fate.

Years before, when I was still living in London, I became friends with Milton H. Greene, the glamorous photographer of high-fashion and show-business celebrities who had himself leaped into international celebrity of the most sensational kind when he made a deal with Marilyn Monroe to become her business partner and her producer.

Milton was a small, darkly handsome man, with an open, boyish smile of considerable charm that contrasted oddly with his brooding eyes. Though nobody could have guessed it at the time, his celebrated partnership with Marilyn was at once the zenith of his career and the be-

ginning of his downfall. It resulted in one of Marilyn's worst pictures—
The Prince and the Showgirl—and one of her best, *Bus Stop,* but in the
end Milton was no more capable of controlling Marilyn (or saving her
from herself) than Twentieth Century–Fox had been.

It was typical of Milton's charm that he had seduced Marilyn Monroe in one instant, right on her own doorstep. He had been sent out by
Look magazine to photograph her, and when she opened her door and
saw Milton, he looked so young that she said, "Why, you're just a boy!"
Milton looked her up and down slowly and carefully, taking in all of that
lush figure, and said, in his quiet, gentle voice, "And you're just a girl."

Milton not only charmed her, he somehow managed to *soothe* her—
no easy task, given her high level of anxiety, her pill taking, and her
mind-numbing hysteria. He persuaded her that he could help her break
away from the tyranny of the studio   with which she had had a love-
hate relationship since she was in her teens—choose her own roles,
make her own movies, and become a serious actress in New York. The
ink was not even dry on the contracts that linked them before Milton realized that he had bitten off more than he could chew, but by that time it
was too late.

In these unhappy circumstances, Milton spent a good deal of time
sitting in the small mews house he had rented just off Grosvenor Square
during the shooting of *The Prince and the Showgirl,* around the corner
from the elegant apartment building where my Aunt Alexa was living.
Milton and Alexa met and became friendly, and since I was often at
Alexa's, it was inevitable that I met him.

Against all the odds, Milton and I became friends, despite the difference in age. Milton, it transpired, loved to play chess, and since this was
one of my skills—my father had taught me to play on a tiny, folding,
pocket-size board during a train trip across the United States when I was
eleven—I took to coming over at odd hours, in case Milton was free.
Mostly, he was. Neither Laurence Olivier, who was costarring and di-
recting, nor Marilyn wanted him on the set, and as producer there was
not much for him to do but sit at home while other people spent his
money. Occasionally, Marilyn wandered through the house, dazed and
distracted, with a shopping list of complaints for Milton.

Soon after I had become a more or less permanent guest at Milton's
house, his wife, Amy, arrived from their home in Connecticut. Amy
Greene was a diminutive, exquisite woman, something like a high-
fashion model in miniature, whose energy surrounded her like a bright

aura. Unlike Milton, who could sit for hours without saying a word, perfectly content, Amy was as bright and restless and chatty as a parrot, forever in motion and determined never to be bored—the complete opposite, in some ways, of her husband. The last thing Amy wanted to see was Milton and me sitting around the house playing chess, but she wasted no time in finding out everything there was to know about me, and we soon became close friends.

Eventually, *The Prince and the Showgirl* was completed, for better or for worse, and the Greenes sailed for home. I lost sight of them until I myself went back to America, at which point I became a regular visitor to Milton's penthouse studio on Lexington Avenue and to their house in Wilton, Connecticut, on weekends.

By then, Milton's attempt to transform himself into a movie producer had failed. He had to go back to taking photographs because his experience at producing movies with Marilyn had plunged him into debt, but his heart was never in it. He was always looking for a way back into movie production or to Broadway. "I'm putting something together," he murmured mysteriously if asked what he was doing.

In the meantime, he did magazine work, while Amy, much to Milton's surprise, took a job as an assistant to the beauty editor of *Glamour* magazine. There, she quickly proved to be surprisingly ambitious and successful and soon became something of a gadfly at the magazine.

A great many unsuspected talents had worked at *Glamour* at one time or another, including Andy Warhol, who drew shoes and handbags for the magazine before his artistic career took off; Cybill Shepherd, who got her start as a cover girl; and Gloria Steinem. *Glamour*'s offices were full of people whose aspirations went beyond evaluating lipstick colors, so I should not have been surprised when Amy asked me to write a piece for the magazine. In 1962, *Glamour* was going through one of those crises typical of fashion magazines, in which the management begins to question the content of the magazine and wants it made more "relevant" to its readers. While *Glamour*'s readers wanted to know how to dress well and look pretty and were quite happy with the magazine as it was, the editors were forced to start looking for writers who could make contemporary trends and issues "relevant." Thus it was that Amy asked me if I could write a piece on rock and roll.

I said that I thought I could. Pop music was hovering out there, hard to avoid, but without yet having much impact on traditional culture. People who read books or edited magazines were aware of music that was then usually lumped together as rock and roll but regarded it as a noisy teenage fad, connected inextricably with mobs of screaming girls, greasy ducktail haircuts, and a generally surly and rebellious adolescent attitude. Everybody had heard of Elvis, of course, but he was usually dismissed as another of those weird Southern phenomena, like "snake-chunking," gospel revivals, and speaking in tongues. Bob Gottlieb, with his instinct for popular culture, was the only person I knew who actually *listened* to rock and roll, and he even owned some of Elvis's albums. From him, I had developed an interest in pop music myself, though I made no claim to be an expert—still, I enjoyed the music (had, in fact, ever since being introduced to Eartha Kitt and Bill Haley and the Comets while I was at Oxford) and at least knew more about it than *Glamour*'s editors, who thought it was trashy and preferred Frank Sinatra and Perry Como. I agreed to write the piece—five thousand words—and sat down at my portable Hermes typewriter (a purchase made in the days when I still saw my future as that of a foreign correspondent in a trench coat, writing my dispatches at a café table) to do it.

Very shortly, I was writing pieces for *Glamour* at a fast clip, one after the other. From time to time, I asked myself if the writing might eventually interfere with being an editor, but there seemed no good reason why it should—other men had hobbies like golf or stamp collecting. But the truth was that having two simultaneous careers *did* have a downside. Like a lot of other men, I was working at the expense of my domestic life. One could argue that working hard and making more money was good for everyone, but I knew better. I would probably have spent hours every evening editing manuscripts even if I had been obliged to pay S&S for the privilege and continued to bang away at my portable typewriter on the weekends. Workaholism, like alcoholism, has its own logic and invariably justifies itself. Anybody who can crank out a readable piece about almost anything is always in demand, and pretty soon I was writing for all sorts of magazines. It was not the kind of work that was likely to make me rich, but it *was* writing, and the sight of my byline meant more to me, for the moment, than the size of the check. I took pleasure in seeing my words in print to the extent that I even agreed to write the copy on the labels of Sherry-Lehmann's house brands of liquor.

The great thing about magazine writing is that you start ahead of the game, with somebody else's idea. Magazine editors, unlike book editors, mostly know what they want and have a fairly clear idea of who their average reader is. As a freelance writer, I never truly became a member of the *Glamour* family, but I gradually began to develop a feel for what might interest the *Glamour* reader, though without the cast-iron certainty that the editors had about the tastes and limits of their subscribers. Shortly after my debut, *Glamour*'s editor in chief, Mrs. Kathleen Aston Casey (it was then almost mandatory for the editors of women's magazines to have three names), expressed an interest in the fact that more and more women were engaging in dangerous sports. Like most topics seized on by magazine editors, this nugget of information reached her from a fellow guest at a dinner party—in the world of women's magazines at the time this constituted serious research. Mrs. Casey conceived an issue dedicated to the clothing necessary for the pursuit of these dangerous sports, whatever they might be—her fellow guest had not been clear on their exact nature—to be introduced with a feature article by me.

I took on the assignment happily enough, fairly confident that I would find women doing all sorts of unlikely sports. This indeed proved to be the case. Over a period of a few weeks I talked to women rugby players, a woman jockey, women scuba divers, women rock climbers, women hockey players, and even an embattled, if privileged, team of women polo players. The women's movement as such had not yet even begun—Gloria Steinem had yet to go underground as a *Playboy* "bunny," Betty Friedan and Germaine Greer had not yet written their books—but already it was apparent that women were eager to "push the envelope," as test pilots say, and confident that anything men could do they could do as well or better. I even met the first woman telephone lineperson, who had attracted national attention when she was photographed climbing a telephone pole in her overalls, work boots, and hard hat, but of course repairing telephone lines was not exactly a sport. All this was interesting but failed to satisfy Mrs. Casey's vision of danger.

Eventually, I made contact with a group of women sky divers in New Jersey who were willing to be interviewed and photographed. After several drinks, dinner, and a couple of bottles of wine, I felt the atmosphere was loose enough to enable me to ask just what they got out of parachute jumping. Was it excitement, the thrill of danger, a sense of liberation—what, in short, made them jump out of an airplane once a week when the weather was right? We batted this back and forth, but no answer was forthcoming, at least none that I thought would satisfy Mrs. Casey. Eventually, late in the evening, a schoolteacher, blushing prettily, leaned close to me and confessed that while excitement, danger, and liberation were all part of it, she, personally, always had an orgasm on the way down, right after opening her chute.

This, it seemed to me, was something to bring back to Mrs. Casey. Women's magazines were at that time just beginning to take the plunge into the deep end of the sexual pool that eventually resulted in Helen Gurley Brown's triumph in resuscitating the moribund *Cosmopolitan* with the "*Cosmo* girl," who was as outspoken about her sexual needs as she was insecure about her weight, manicure, and fashion savvy. *Glamour* was a long way from that but moving ever more quickly in that direction. The days when its readers could be satisfied by articles on accessorizing, fashions for office wear, and what to say on that first, crucial date were long since gone, and the word *orgasm* was off the list of taboos—indeed, half the articles seemed to be about sex, and one had the feeling that the magazine was running as hard as it could to catch up with its readers. Still, with any magazine, it's hard for an outsider to gauge the prevailing, generally unspoken moral code. It was clear that Mrs. Casey ran the magazine with an iron fist, but since we had never met, I wasn't sure just where and in what areas her limits lay. Sometimes I got away with things that I thought she would never print; on other occasions, things that seemed to me perfectly harmless produced a flurry of anguished calls from Amy and Karlys Daly, the beauty editor. One thing was clear: There was no appeal. Like most women's magazine editors, Mrs. Casey was an unapologetic tyrant. In my mind's eye, I thought of her as the Queen of Hearts in *Alice in Wonderland*, ready at any moment to shout, "Off with his head!"

The schoolteacher's experience, it turned out as the evening went on, had been mirrored by the others in the group. One of the older women confessed that it beat anything she had ever experienced with her husband, and another remarked, with a shy smile, that she sometimes made two or three jumps a day and came every time, "as regular as clockwork."

The parachute ladies had another thing in common: They could drink me under the table. I returned to New York with the beginnings of a fierce hangover but happy to have a lead for my story—so happy that I actually decided to present it to the formidable Mrs. Casey in person.

An audience was arranged, and I arrived ahead of time, feeling rather like a Roman summoned to the Temple of the Vestal Virgins. Far from providing a threatening atmosphere, however, Mrs. Casey's sanctum sanctorum was a riot of yellow and black: Every square inch that could be covered in fake leopard skin was. The walls, the carpets, the upholstery, the pillows were all done in leopard skin, and a profusion of leopard statues of various sizes, as well as drawings of leopards, made it clear what animal Mrs. Casey admired most. Even her signature pens were made of plastic formed to resemble a leopard's skin, as was her wastepaper basket. I half expected her to have whiskers, fangs, and a snarling countenance, but in fact she was an attractive woman of a certain age with gray hair and a no-nonsense manner.

Tentatively, I outlined my article, then approached the lead. I described my afternoon and evening with the women sky divers and explained their startling confession. The word *orgasm* did not frighten Mrs. Casey. She stared at me, her expression ambiguous, nodding slightly to indicate that the subject was neither taboo nor unfamiliar to her. It would, I suggested, be a terrific way to begin the piece—a real attention grabber. (An "attention grabber" was a constant demand from the advertising department.)

Mrs. Casey looked thoughtful. She fiddled with one of her leopard-skin pens for a while. There were three or four other women in attendance, including Amy and Karlys, but none of them said anything. It was rather like being in the headmaster's office at a boys' school, after some awful infraction of discipline, or perhaps the Mother Superior's at a convent. I half expected Mrs. Casey to lunge at me with a ruler, demanding that I hold out my hand. Finally, she spoke. Why, she asked, did I think these women experienced an orgasm while parachuting?

I had come prepared for this question, with a full Freudian answer. It was, I said, fairly obvious. First you had the physical excitement of the flight, then you stood up and a handsome young jump master put his hands on you—physical contact—and helped you leap into space. The Freudian elements were, surely, all there? Height, speed, adventure, the male touch that sends you spinning into space, the connection between sex and death, for there was always a risk involved when you jumped out of an airplane . . . I went on, quoting Jung and Reich and drawing on my knowledge of the orgone box.

Mrs. Casey was silent—by no means hostile but ever so slightly indicating with one elegantly raised eyebrow a certain impatience. When, at last, I paused for breath, she gave a small, ladylike snort of derision. "Nonsense," she said firmly. "It's the way the harness fits around the crotch."

· · ·

THE STORY on dangerous sports ran without the parachutists, I'm sorry to say, but it taught me the lesson that the simple, functional answer is usually the correct one, even (and perhaps especially) when it comes to sex. It also taught me that women's magazine editors, ranging from Helen Gurley Brown to Grace Mirabella, have a toughness of mind all their own. From then on, I avoided the *Glamour* offices but continued to contribute regularly to the magazine and even started to get fan mail. After a couple of years of writing long feature articles, Amy Greene asked if I would like to be *Glamour*'s movie reviewer. It was not something I had ever imagined myself doing—since almost everybody in my family was in the movie business, reviewers had always seemed to be the enemy, even (perhaps especially) when they were literate reviewers. My Uncle Alex had begun his career at the age of seventeen as the film critic for a Budapest arts weekly, and when he stepped behind the camera as a director for the first time, at the age of twenty-one, he remarked on how much easier it was to criticize a film than to make one. His attitude toward critics did not change over the years. My father's comment on movie critics was simply, "Vat the hell do *they* know about it?" Still, it was too good an offer to refuse—not just a regular monthly income, but getting to see movies before everyone else and for free!

Movie reviewers, I soon discovered, are courted fiercely by the major studios. In those lavish days, every movie company maintained a glamorous, plush screening room in midtown Manhattan, most of them furnished comfortably with big easy chairs or sofas and a staff of people whose only job was to see that reviewers got to see each movie in the most comfortable circumstances possible.

It was apparent to me from the beginning that *Glamour*'s readers were not looking for reviews of meaningful foreign films that would, in any case, never play in their towns, nor were they anxious to read slashing intellectual attacks against major movies, still less cleverness for its own sake. Basically, they wanted to know which of the current movies was worth seeing—it was a service column, in short. Gradually, over the months, I hit my stride, and my fan mail, most of it positive, increased sharply—an important fact, since *Glamour* had an elaborate month-by-month system for determining how many readers there were for each feature and column in the magazine, as well as their age, income, and so on. Fan mail played a part in scoring each writer's work, so the more letters you generated, the better.

It never occurred to me that I would go on reviewing movies for nearly ten years—at three movies a week, about fifteen hundred movies—until, in fact, I could hardly even *remember* a time when my evenings weren't taken up by screenings. I began by writing a review of each movie I'd seen, but before long it became like the obligatory essay at Oxford: something that was easy to put off until a day or two before the deadline, at which point there was nothing to do but cancel everything else, make a pot of strong coffee, and sit down with clenched teeth to *do* it. Doing it this way, the hardest part was trying to remember what movies I had seen, since most of them tended to run into a blur. Penelope Gilliatt, the formidable critic for *The New Yorker,* actually had a tiny flashlight in her purse so she could make notes during the screenings, but I relied on my memory, only to find, by the time two or three weeks had elapsed, that I couldn't remember a thing except dim recollections of plots. Time after time, the approach of *Glamour*'s deadline produced panic in me, followed by a late-night session at my typewriter—then it was time to start all over again with another month's worth of movies. The fact that I had taken on what some people might have considered to be three full-time jobs never dawned on me. I was a successful editor, with increasingly serious responsibilities for major authors, a monthly movie reviewer, and a freelance magazine writer. At the end of the day, I was making enough money to rent a house in Maine for the summer, and to dress fashionably, but I was working more or less constantly without noticing.

Though writing itself was a pleasure, seeing my own name at the top of what I had written was the ultimate thrill. I loved opening a new magazine and finding my name in it, even though some of the magazines I found myself writing for were very odd and "special" indeed— I seem to remember doing a piece on fetish clothing (God knows for whom) that brought me into what was then the fairly unknown bondage and S&M underworld of custom leather shops around Christopher Street, and another (possibly for *The New York Times*) on people who kept their own horses in New York City, which eventually led to my becoming one of them for over a decade. I had, it seemed, the dangerous habit of becoming part of my pieces. A piece on people who swam and surfed right through the winter led me to buy a wet suit, diving goggles, and gloves, and I can vividly recall swimming out to sea from the deserted beach at Robert Moses State Park on a cold and windy Thanksgiving Day—an experience that one day was instrumental in securing the English novelist R. F. Delderfield for S&S. Looking back on it, I seem to have been willing to try anything, including all-night dinners with Gypsies camping out for the winter in the Coney Island amusement park, and swimming in a pool full of dolphins with a woman who was part of a U.S. Navy experiment in communicating with them (an experiment that was later the subject of a best-selling novel by the French author Robert Merle, which I published, which was later made into a movie by Mike Nichols). I went fishing with Paul Newman and target shooting after dinner at an Italian club in the Village with its own pistol range. At one point, I even went to the top of the Verrazano Bridge to watch Mohawk steelworkers perform miracles of balance as they completed the span and learned, in case I had ever doubted the fact, that there are harder professions than editing books. I was, to put it mildly, game for anything, which is a good thing for a magazine writer to be.

I must have written tens of thousands, perhaps hundreds of thousands, of words, without ever once thinking that I might some day write a book. Writing books was something my authors did, not me. So long as I was merely writing for magazines, I did not have the feeling that I was competing with the people I edited or embarking on a new profession. I told myself that I wrote for magazines as a kind of hobby, except of course that I got paid for it; writing *books* would be a whole different story. Besides, if you're used to writing five-thousand-word pieces, a book seems like a monumental task. There was nothing I admired more than the *Sitzfleisch* required to write a book of 100,000 words or more. I shared Bob Gottlieb's combination of sympathy and awe for people who could do this. It seemed to require more courage than I had, so I put any desire to do it firmly out of my mind.

CHAPTER 18

As THE SIXTIES passed by, lost to most of us in hard work, S&S was increasingly divided by the question of succession, most of which hung on the question of what exactly Bob Gottlieb wanted. Even those who thought of themselves as Bob's friends, like myself, were in the dark. He continued to edit his books, extended his hold over much of the company, and seemed willing to accept the status quo, even though he wasn't exactly happy about it. Essentially, S&S seemed to consist at the time of two separate entities: the old, traditional S&S, run by Schwed, and the new, more contemporary S&S, orchestrated, if not run, by Bob. Typically, I had a foot in both camps.

But this was an illusion. S&S was still owned by Shimkin, and in the final analysis, he was to decide what happened. In some ways, the situation pleased him. If he was good at anything, it was at setting one faction against the other and allowing each of them to believe that he favored their side. He feigned sympathy to Gottlieb and his followers (particularly Nina Bourne, the advertising director, and Tony Schulte, who dealt with marketing), and let it be known that they were the future of S&S; he was equally sympathetic toward Schwed, and let him know that he represented the solid, day-to-day financial reality of S&S, which was what really mattered in the long run. Both sides had his ear, and both sides might have thought, from time to time, that they had his backing, but in fact Shimkin merely hoped to buy time by keeping Bob at S&S for as long as possible without having to give up much, if anything, in exchange. He was a master of retreat by small, slow stages, the Marshal Kutuzov of book publishing. One came away from him with a tiny raise, possibly a new title, some small concession—anything that would keep one from asking for major changes or a big raise. He was always happy to give away what he didn't mind losing in the interests of peace. His expression at such times was that of the Buddha, serene and benevolent, but it was deceptive. The truth was that Shimkin, having eliminated most of his partners, was for the first time in full control of both Pocket Books and S&S and not at all sure what he wanted to do with it all. He talked about taking the company public and dropped hints both to Seymour Turk, his chief financial officer, and to Dick Snyder that they were being groomed to succeed him. No Ottoman sultan ever divided his court with more subtlety or better ensured that his son and heir remained powerless.

Since all this was being played out against a background of trendy publishing successes and at a time when Wall Street's interest in book publishing was raising even the most second-rate of publishing houses to the level of interesting investments, Shimkin had good reason to be cheerful. All he had to do was make sure nobody rocked the boat.

The boat, however, was about to be rocked more severely than anybody could have guessed by Bob Gottlieb. As the sixties passed by, Bob's reputation as a wunderkind had grown by leaps and bounds. He seemed capable of anything, from securing, via Tom Maschler, the U.S. rights to John Lennon's book *A Spaniard in the Works* to publishing a whole string of "commercial" best-sellers. Then he announced the news that nobody—least of all me—had expected: He was leaving S&S to go to Knopf.

Pledged to secrecy during his negotiations, the news that he was leaving was a bombshell that rocked not only S&S but the industry. There were those who saw it as a crippling blow to S&S, particularly since he was taking Nina Bourne and Tony Schulte with him, and others who felt that it would spell the end of Knopf as a kind of icon of quality publishing. As it turned out, neither of these predictions was correct, but certainly for a moment it seemed as if S&S had been torpedoed and was fast sinking.

I felt, perhaps more sharply than most, a certain wistful sense of betrayal. Bob was my friend. We had been close, both at work and away from it, and although we were very different in many ways, we shared a great many things: We were both omnivorous readers (Bob was better read in literature, while I had read more history), we shared the same kind of sense of humor, and much the same view of the world. I was deeply apprehensive about what life at S&S would be like for me without Bob and also felt hurt that he had not asked me to join him at Knopf. This clouded our relationship during the transition period, since it seemed to me that I had been judged and found wanting. Bob, to be sure, broke the news to me with infinite tact and rightly pointed out that his departure offered me a great opportunity and that it was time for me to take on more responsibility and succeed on my own. I was quite incapable of taking this in, however, and for the longest time simply felt a numb resentment at having been left out.

Fortunately for me, the hysteria surrounding Bob's departure soon swamped my regrets. It is hard to describe the furor that his move created. Until that point, editors tended to stay with the same publishing house for their whole career—Maxwell Perkins, who stayed at Scribner's until he died, was fairly typical. What is more, frequent job changing was discouraged—a lingering effect of the Depression in the minds of those who remembered it or whose parents had lived through it. Nothing was more precious than keeping the job you had, however green the pasture might look on the other side of the fence, and loyalty to the company that employed you was assumed to be both owed and rewarded. The notion that a job was simply a stepping stone to the next (and better) job, or that the company might regard its employees, even the key ones, as essentially dismissable and replaceable cogs in the machine had not yet penetrated to the publishing business. In the circumstances, the fact that Bob was transferring himself and his key collaborators to Knopf (and by extension, to the rival Random House camp) was as if a Cambridge don had defected to Oxford or the admiral commanding the Naval Academy at Annapolis had put on an army uniform and taken command of West Point.

Of course, the more praise was thrown at Bob, the more S&S seemed to be lost without him, and very soon it became apparent that unless we acted quickly and carefully those of us who were left behind might be stranded. It was a strange and rapid change of mood. At first, people were overcome by the sense of loss, and wished Bob well, but almost overnight the tears and lamentations gave way to outright fear, as agent after agent called to say that this author or that one wanted to go to Knopf with Bob. Worse, they threatened never to send S&S another book if we made a fuss about it.

The extent to which Bob himself stirred up this incipient exodus is hard to guess, and it is perhaps a measure of the strength of his personal relationships with his writers that so many of them wanted to jump ship. Still, the effect it had on S&S was dispiriting and alarming.

Nobody was more shaken by Bob's departure than Peter Schwed, though his emotions on the subject seemed to me conflicted. Schwed was an intensely ambitious man, with a prickly pride, and it can hardly have escaped his attention that Bob and his followers were mildly dismissive of the kind of books he liked, and in general thought him better suited to run the rights department than to take on the role of publisher. So long as Bob was there, Schwed, whatever his title, was overshadowed by Bob's mere presence and undercut by Bob's feline wit. On the other hand, Schwed was a sentimental man, with generous impulses and strong, old-fashioned loyalties, and he felt a great debt to Bob, who had been at S&S almost as long as he had. Though Schwed was fiercely competitive on a personal level—indeed, it was the dominating charac-

teristic of his personality—he had a certain ancien régime attitude
when it came to publishing, perhaps the legacy of a youth spent at
Lawrenceville and Princeton, where competition was reserved for the
playing fields and gentlemanly behavior was encouraged off them. For
whatever reason, Schwed was determined to behave like a gentleman at
this first major test of his authority, as if what he sought from authors
and agents—and perhaps from Bob—was some kind of recognition
that he acted like the Princeton man he was. Fond of Kipling, whose
work he could recite in large chunks, Schwed set out to keep his head,
when all about him were losing theirs, and thereby made the mistake of
his career.

It was, needless to say, Dick Snyder who brought my mind sharply
to bear on the realities of the situation, a day or so after Bob's decision
had been announced, by plunking himself down beside my desk and
opening his mind to me. He looked tired and irritable.

"Nice guys finish last," he said, by way of greeting.

I agreed that this was certainly what most people believed in the
United States. The general opinion in England is the reverse, but I saw
no point in mentioning that.

"I blame Shimkin most," Snyder went on. "He should have given
Bobby what he wanted. Shimkin nickel-and-dimed him instead and look
what happened."

I agreed that Shimkin was penny-wise and pound-foolish, and not
only when it came to Bob. However, I found it difficult to believe that
money was the only reason why Bob was moving to Knopf. There he
would be, in effect, his own publisher as well as editor in chief, the heir
apparent and chosen successor to the Knopfs. At S&S, Schwed was publisher, and it was not a marriage made in heaven, despite Schwed's belief
to the contrary.

Snyder grimaced. His facial appearance seemed to change so often
that it was something of an adventure seeing him at intervals. At one
point his hair was short, and the frames of his glasses dark, thick, and of
executive caliber; at the next, his hair was transformed into a thick, wild
tangle of curls, like Medusa's, while he sported tinted aviator glasses. He
even grew a mustache for a while. It was as if he were trying out different personae in the hope of pinning down the one that would take him
to the top. "Who would you rather have running things?" he asked.
"Schwed or Bobby? Shimkin should have bitten the bullet and made the
choice between them. Still, it's lucky for you, isn't it?"

I must have looked puzzled and naive. "Come *on*," he snapped. "Don't tell me you haven't worked out that his job is yours if you go for it. You don't have any competition. There isn't anybody else here who can take the job, and just at the moment nobody in their right mind wants to come here. They all figure we're done for, going down for the fucking third time, *losers*. . . . You may not know it yet, but you've got S&S by the balls."

I thought about this, and it gradually dawned on me that Dick might be right—indeed, when it came to this kind of thing, he was almost always right.

Of course, even then Dick, like most people, credited me with Machiavellian deviousness, fueled by fierce ambition, a misunderstanding of my character that I had always found puzzling. Bob, trying to explain his own success at S&S, had once told an interviewer that although his was a competitive nature, he was too busy to have time left over for ambition, a statement that was widely ridiculed as naive and self-serving by those who didn't know him well but seemed to me right on the mark, not only about himself but about me. A person who is compulsively busy is unlikely to have much time left over for plotting his or her rise. I was often in the right place at the right time, but I had made no particular effort to find my way there, so I was momentarily baffled and even frightened by Dick's assumption that I not only coveted Bob's title but was planning how to get it. The idea had simply not crossed my mind.

Now that it had been placed there, it was hard not to think about it. In ten years, I had gone from an assistant editor to executive editor (one step below editor in chief on the publishing totem pole, at least theoretically) and was doing more books than any other editor except Bob—too many, in fact. My immediate reaction was that nobody else at S&S seemed any better qualified for the job than I was—whatever the job might be, for the truth was that the very idea of having an editor in chief was something of a puzzle. Max had assumed the title for most of the company's history but in the past had delegated it briefly from time to time to such varied personalities as Quincy Howe (later to find greater fame as a writer of popular history), Wallace Brockway (who went on to become a noted anthologizer), Clifton Fadiman, Jr. (who gave it up to become a book reviewer and book-club judge), Jerome Weidman (who resigned from S&S to write a long list of best-selling novels, the best remembered of which was *I Can Get It for You Wholesale*, a book that was rejected by S&S because it made Max uncomfortable but ea-

gerly acquired by Cerf for Random House), Joe Barnes (who gave up
the title almost as soon as it was conferred on him), and Jack Goodman,
who was best remembered for having hired Bob. Max reclaimed the title
after Goodman's untimely death and relinquished it reluctantly, first to
Henry Simon then to Bob, who liked to pretend that he had never
wanted it.

No recognizable duties or benefits came with it. In theory, the editor in chief was merely *primus inter pares,* first among equals, with no
particular authority over the other editors. Henry had wisely never attempted to exercise any such authority, and while Bob did, he managed
it with such delicacy and grace and by such exquisite indirection and
subtlety that, except for the end results, it was seldom visible. A managing editor performed the onerous task of keeping track of every book
S&S had under contract and trying to pry out from the editors the truth
about exactly what the state of progress was of each title on their list; an
executive editor (myself at this time) dealt with the paperwork necessary to put through contracts and such routine housekeeping as the assistants' raises; and a secretary of the editorial board (also myself) kept
the minutes of the weekly editorial meeting and drew up the agenda.
What the editor in chief did was unclear, and at times the title had been
allowed to fall into abeyance, since that seemed simpler (and less con-
ducive of bad feelings in the editorial department) than to let one editor
lord it over the others.

Even though the time had not yet arrived when Dick and I were to
get together in the evenings over a drink in his office to invent meaningless titles in order to lure senior editorial talent from other houses to
S&S ("Vice president and associate publisher?" "Chairman emeritus of
the editorial board?" "Senior editor and corporate vice president?"),
nobody with their head screwed on tight could possibly believe that an
editor's title held any genuine significance. Then, as now, editors were
judged by the books they acquired, the authors on their list, and the
number of best-sellers they published every year. Whereas titles in the
corporate world usually defined not only a person's function but his or
her place in the pecking order—one knew, after all, what the treasurer
or the vice president of human resources or manufacturing *did,* in principle, and who reported to whom—titles when given to editors usually
mean nothing and are likely to have been awarded either in lieu of a
raise or to stave off some crisis of self-doubt on the part of the editor.
Occasional attempts were made at S&S, as at most publishing houses, to

bolster the self-esteem of those editors who had titles by giving them, for example, engraved business cards and stationery, as opposed to the ordinary printed kind, but most people regarded the whole business, quite rightly, as something of a swindle, which explains perhaps why the idea of being editor in chief wasn't a burning ambition of mine at the time.

Still, the idea of somebody else being editor in chief wasn't something I wanted to see, particularly since a high-powered person coming to S&S from elsewhere might either regard me as a threat or expect me to report to him or her—something that had never been the case between me and Bob.

Gradually, it dawned on me that this was a case in which symbolism was all. The moment Bob left, his office was left empty, the door shut and locked, as if it were a shrine. Since it was by far the largest and nicest editorial office, I staked my claim to it by arguing that whatever the company chose to do about Bob's title, I was certainly next in line for his office and that it was both foolish and depressing to the staff to leave it empty. To my surprise, they gave in (although they made it clear that it was only for the time being and that I might have to move out if a new person was hired to replace Bob), which might not have been the case had I demanded the title or a significant raise. I moved into it immediately and soon had it painted light blue; I ordered a blue office couch and blue wall-to-wall carpeting and even a blue IBM Selectric typewriter, thus reinforcing my claim to occupancy. Either because of that or out of sheer inertia, the search for a successor to Bob fizzled out. I was sitting at his desk and in his office, and very soon I was given his title without having to threaten to leave or even bring the subject up.

It was thought at the time better to make as little fuss over this promotion as possible, since it could only draw more attention to the fact that Bob had left S&S for Knopf. No celebration took place, therefore—indeed, seldom has anybody received a promotion with less fanfare or amid a greater sense of gloom—and as Shimkin assured me, the title itself was a more than ample reward and would not, for the moment, be accompanied by any change in my salary. Had anybody told me that I would still be editor in chief of S&S thirty years later, I would have been amazed and perhaps disconcerted.

In the meantime, we were besieged by agents as their authors jumped ship. Almost immediately we received calls asking for the release of Joseph Heller, Robert Crichton, Chaim Potok, Mordecai Richler, Charles Portis, Jessica Mitford, Bruce Jay Friedman, Rona Jaffe, Doris Lessing, Sylvia Ashton-Warner, and many others—almost everybody, in fact, whom Bob had under contract or option. This was a difficult and delicate problem, but what made it worse was that it represented the more or less unanimous judgment among agents that those of us who remained at S&S were going to fail and, perhaps worse still, that we weren't worthy of their clients. It was rather like being kicked in the stomach once you've been knocked down in a fight. A small number of Bob's authors announced their loyalty to S&S and elected to stay, though I could not help noticing with a sinking heart—since they would be my responsibility—that at least two of them, Meyer Levin, the litigious author of *Compulsion,* and S. J. Perelman, were so notoriously difficult that Bob might almost have persuaded them to stay.

Curiously, the fact that we felt ourselves to be legally in the right made the literati even angrier. After all, none of the contracts gave the authors a right to leave simply because their editor had left (such "editor's clauses" came into being after Bob's departure but remained limited to a very small number of major writers and invariably contained any number of complicated loopholes); the writers had signed a contract with S&S and taken S&S's money. Nothing obliged us to release them, especially under threat, and indeed it seemed to both Dick and me that a mass release of Bob's authors to Knopf would create such an atmosphere of failure at S&S and seem such a confession of inferiority and defeat that the company might never recover its self-confidence or momentum. As I was going down in the elevator one evening, Dick got on at the twenty-seventh floor, looking tired and glum. "They're going to hand it over to you and me just as it crashes," he said. "No authors, the agents hate us, and everybody's waiting to see us fail." His face suddenly lit up with a broad smile. "It's a great way to start," he said. "We can only go up from here."

This optimism was soon overshadowed by real anger, however, first of all at the "literary community," which Dick perceived as being out to get us and as having written us off in favor of Bob. Dick saw it as a simple problem. Those who owed us a book should be made to deliver it, and that was that. After that, once we had published it, if they still wanted to leave us and go to Knopf, fine, but first they had to live up to their contractual obligation. A contract was a contract. If a writer could unilaterally cancel it, pay back the money, and leave for another publisher, why have contracts at all or option clauses? To this, the agents replied that writers are not indentured servants or slaves, they were artists. They couldn't be treated like inanimate objects. If they were prevented from following their editor, their ability to write might be impaired. Did we want to be responsible for destroying their creative ability? Were we aware that many of them had said that if they couldn't go with Bob, they wouldn't write a word for S&S? Both Dick and I were well aware of these threats, resented them bitterly, and didn't believe a word of them. Both of us were in agreement that this kind of emotional blackmail was at once ridiculous and unlikely to last. If we kept up a firm front, refused to let anybody go, and above all refused to make exceptions, sooner or later the fuss would die down. If there is one thing that's true about writers, it's that they need to write; it would not be long before even the most adamant of them sat back down at the typewriter. In the end, we might gain more respect from having toughed it out than from giving in. Certainly, so far as Dick could see, we had nothing to lose.

Peter Schwed, however, did not altogether agree. Persuaded that S&S would gain in the long run from behaving in an honorable and decent way, he let a couple of the writers who were closest to Bob go (most of them Candida Donadio's clients, for she was the most vociferous in her demands), thus undercutting Dick's position. After all, Dick argued, if we were willing to let Joe Heller go, what argument could we make for keeping, say, Wallace Markfield?

This was to be a fateful difference of opinion in many ways. In the first place, it confirmed Dick in what was to become his "us against them" view of the literary world and thereby set the tone for much of what was to follow; second, it led to a certain enmity between Dick and Schwed, with the result that in the very moment when Schwed's career seemed to have been capped by assuming complete authority over S&S, Dick was already determined to take his place.

I HAD a stormy drink date with Candida Donadio that to this day stands out in my mind as one of the more unpleasant and demeaning social occasions of a lifetime. I don't remember where Candida and I met—probably the Italian Pavilion. Bubbling over with enthusiasm and gossip, sharp-tongued and endowed with a wicked sense of humor, Candida resembled a Sicilian Earth Mother, her heavy frame wrapped like an untidy, bulky package in yards and layers of black *schmatta,* her enormous handbag weighted down with the manuscripts of her clients. A one-woman fountain of publishing news, she spent her life on the telephone. If you were about to get fired or lose a major author, Candida was likely to know about it before you did and spread the news from one end of publishing to the other before you'd had a chance to digest it yourself. In the days of the blockbuster paperback auctions, when rights sales were the big news, the rights managers of the major publishers were the source of every rumor, leak, and gossip item, their phone lines glowing red-hot from use. Candida was one of the few non-rights people plugged into their network and reveled in being the first to know whatever the hot secret of the day was.

She had a way of dismissing those she thought unimportant that made her no friends, and she was not shy about letting editors know that they didn't come up to the standards of her clients. Her loyalty to her clients was unquestioned, though not a few of them may have found it suffocating, which perhaps explains why some left her as soon as they had succeeded. She was also endowed with that rarest of commodities in the world of book publishing: a sharp, shrewd, sure taste for interesting new fiction. Whatever her other faults, you had to admire her judgment about books. When she really liked something, she was never halfhearted about it and almost always right.

Candida was, in short, exactly the person you wanted to have on your side if you were a publisher or editor, which made it all the more aggravating that she wanted to pull her authors away. We sat at a small table near the bar and ordered a drink. Now that we were here, I realized that I had made a mistake. Almost everybody in the bar was in publishing, and it must be perfectly clear to them why I was having a drink with Candida and equally clear from her body language how reluctant she had been to come. I told her, with as much optimism and enthusiasm as I could manage, that Dick and I had great plans for S&S and that we would go out of our way to do everything we could to make her clients happy.

She smiled, a little condescendingly I thought. I had the impression, perhaps mistaken, that Candida enjoyed watching me squirm. Snyder, always the optimist, had sent me on this mission with the warning to be tough. I was to take no prisoners, he advised, and not to retreat an inch—military metaphors had worked their way somehow into his mind, now that "the crunch" was on. But Candida showed no signs of surrendering. She heard me out, patiently enough, pausing from time to time to wave to people she knew as they came in or out, then shook her head decisively. She had no doubt that we would do well, even without Bob, but she could not think of S&S as a place for her clients anymore. They needed a sympathetic publisher, somebody who understood what they were doing. Peter Schwed liked sports books and writers like P. G. Wodehouse. Nothing wrong with that, but he couldn't replace Bob Gottlieb. I was probably a perfectly good editor, but not for the type of book her clients wrote, and Snyder, while he already had a reputation for energy and sales acumen, didn't appear to be somebody for whom literature was a first concern. She wished us nothing but good, but her clients had to go where they would feel comfortable, and that was that.

She wasn't giving us a chance, I said.

Candida fixed her dark eyes on me implacably. It wasn't her job to give us a chance. There were plenty of books and authors out there. When one came along that was right for us, she would send it over. In the meantime, the best thing we could do was to expedite the release of her clients from their contracts.

And if we didn't? She shook her head. I had to understand. All writers were like children, but her writers *were* her children. She felt about them as if she were their mother. If we forced the issue, she would fight tooth and nail to defend them.

We were only trying to protect our contracts, I explained. Once those who owed us a book had delivered it, they could go, but not until then. She—and they—owed us no less.

They don't owe you anything, she said. You can't stop it. And if you tried, there isn't an agent in New York who will send S&S a manuscript. She gave me a benevolent smile, with the air of a woman who has just delivered a piece of good advice to somebody too dumb to take it, gathered up her belongings, and left.

The next day, I waylaid Dick in the hall—he was in the process of moving upstairs from his digs at Pocket Books and slightly overwhelmed by what seemed to be a stroke of luck: He was where he had wanted to be for a long time, with a watching brief over S&S on behalf of Shimkin and a position that would give him as much power as he could amass for himself. I told him about my meeting with Candida. He nodded glumly. He had been going out to meet with agents, too, for the first time, and had been disappointed to find that most of them weren't even willing to listen to our side of the story.

He took me off to his new office, which was still only partially furnished. It was not particularly large or impressive, in view of what was
to come, but was equipped with a small refrigerator and a neat bar. It
took no gift of prophecy to guess that this was where anybody who
mattered at S&S was going to be after five o'clock, now that Bob was
gone, especially since Schwed, always the family man, usually left by
five or five-thirty and would therefore not even notice that Snyder was
mobilizing his forces for a takeover. There was a comfortable sofa and a
clear desk. Dick was perhaps at that time the only executive at S&S who
didn't have a typewriter near at hand, it being still the fashion in those
days for publishing executives to prove that they were basically editors
at heart and eager to bang out a few pages of well-chosen words with
their own fingers at the drop of a hat. Dick, no sentimentalist or fol-
lower of traditions, didn't bother. He made no secret of the fact that he
couldn't type and didn't even like dialing his own telephone. He was an
executive, the spoken word was his area of expertise, the decision his
specialty, to command and order was what he did best, and wherever
possible he tried to do it face-to-face for greater effect. You got a sense
of the man from his telephone conversations, but it was in person that
you got the full picture, and it was above all one of a man in charge, confident, energetic, and determined to get his way. Even the style of his
secretary, the only one on the floor who was from the outer boroughs
instead of the Seven Sisters or Convent of the Sacred Heart (and the
only one who brought coffee without making a face or a scene), proclaimed that this was a man of action, not a dreamer.

"Fuck 'em," he said.

He sat down and put his feet up on his desk—a trademark posture,
I was beginning to learn—and briefly admired the shine on his shoes.
Among the changes that followed his ascent to the twenty-eighth floor
was the arrival every morning of an elderly black man with a shoeshine
box. Never one to hog his perks, Dick had signaled the availability of
the shoeshine man to the more senior S&S editors, but I was the only
one to take advantage of his daily presence, the rest having some qualms
about being seen with him crouching on his knees before them on the
floor at a time when the civil-rights struggle was at its height.

Dick took off his glasses for a moment and stared out the door of
his office, as if taking in the reality of what he had been left to deal with.
He had been given the opportunity of a lifetime, he believed (and so it
turned out to be), only to find himself second in command on what

seemed to be a sinking ship—sunk, in his view, by its captain. Still, though he was unsentimentally clear-eyed, he thought he could make it work and was determined to use whatever assets he found. If he didn't have Bob, he would make me his editorial partner; if he had lost Schulte, he would take over marketing himself; if Nina Bourne had gone he would find a replacement who could at least mimic her style. Unlike Shimkin, who ran the company like a man driving a car with his eyes closed, Dick looked ahead. On a clear day he could see, if nothing else, where he wanted to go and sometimes even a hint of how to get there.

"Well," he said, putting his glasses back on and focusing on me, "what's done is done. We're not going to get any help from agents like Candida. Why should we? She doesn't respect weakness. Nobody does. If we'd put up a fight . . ." He shrugged. "The hell with that." His voice turned brisk. "We need to make a big splash, something to show that we're still in business, that we can still outpublish anybody, something that will be *noticed*." He put his arms behind his head and tilted his chair back as far as it would go. "Did you know," he asked, "that Bobby was thinking about bringing Jacqueline Susann here?"

I had heard rumors of this, but it was one of the very few subjects on which Bob had been closemouthed. Susann, who had vaulted to fame as the author of a successful book about her dog, *Every Night Josephine!*, and a subsequent number-one best-selling novel, *Valley of the Dolls,* was eager to leave her present publisher and come to S&S for what was then an unprecedented amount of money. This was not Bob's usual turf, and in the aftermath of his departure, there were those conspiracy theorists who wondered if it had been a signal of his intentions. Some suggested that Bob had involved S&S with Jacqueline Susann as an act of revenge, forever stamping the S&S fiction list as a home for schlock; others thought it might have been Bob's last great contribution to S&S, exactly the kind of big-time purchase that was needed to liven things up. The likelihood is that none of this was true—it was simply a question of timing. Bob had opened discussions with Jackie Susann, her husband Irving Mansfield, and their lawyer, Artie Hershkowitz, before he had made up his mind to leave; once he made the decision, it simply became one of the major pieces of unfinished business he left behind.

"She doesn't seem like Bob's cup of tea," I said.

Snyder laughed. He had two kinds of laugh—one was without humor, the other with. This was the former. "Bullshit," he said. "It would have been a good move. Jazz up the list. It's been a long time since S&S had a big number-one fiction best-seller. He'd have been a hero to the sales reps." His eyes took on a faraway look. "It's still not such a bad idea," he said, musingly.

"How far advanced was the negotiation?"

"I don't know. There was quite a way to go, I think." He scribbled a note on a pad in front of him. "I'll get the details," he said.

He sat upright and took his feet off the desk, back in action again, eyes sparkling. "Keep it to yourself," he warned. "Don't tell anybody. The only way to make this fly is to keep it a surprise." He waved me out of his office. "If we bring this one off, everything else will be easy," he predicted.

And as usual, he was right.

PART FOUR

Isn't She Great?

CHAPTER 19

*I*N SOME WAYS, my previous experience suited me well for taking on Jacqueline Susann—after all, when it came to commercial fiction, I had already had an apprenticeship that included Harold Robbins, and so far as "difficult" or "demanding" authors were concerned, who could be more difficult and demanding than the Durants? I had no reason to doubt my ability to deal with Jacqueline Susann and Irving Mansfield, nor was I among those who had been shocked by the success of her previous books, which did not signify to me, as they did to so many others, the beginning of the end of Western civilization.

In book publishing, however, vulgarity was still frowned upon. Bad taste frightened publishers. Bennett Cerf might flutter around the edges of show business, a Broadway groupie, joke anthologist, and panel member on *What's My Line?*, but when it came to his publishing persona, he expected to be taken seriously and worried about books "in bad taste." Max's ambition as a publisher was to load the S&S list with works of philosophy, history, and great literature, and he put his ears back and shied at the idea of anything that might be in bad taste carrying his name.

It was simply understood that one did not stoop to a certain level of vulgarity; in fact, one of the reasons why people went into book publishing in the first place was in order to avoid the vulgarity, celebrity worship, and indifference to bad taste that were all too clearly the norm in the movie business, the television industry, and the tabloid press.

Then, in 1966, came Jacqueline Susann's *Valley of the Dolls*, a huge best-seller that for the first time brought the worlds of Hollywood, TV, tabloids, and Broadway press agentry together to sell a novel in which they were all the subject. Jackie, then forty-eight, with her spiky false eyelashes, her gravelly chain-smoker's voice, her glittery dresses, her thick pancake makeup, and her feisty, tough-broad image seemed to many of the old guard of book publishing like the beginning of the end, Hollywood vulgarity at the door of the temple of culture.

Jackie herself was in many ways a much more lively creation than her novels, hugely successful as they were. She had arrived in New York from her native Philadelphia with show-business ambitions in 1936 as a high school beauty-contest winner. She emerged from a family in which her father, a successful if somewhat flashy society portrait painter, was a handsome, high-living, charming womanizer, while her mother was a hard-driving, long-suffering perfectionist who wanted Jackie to go to college.

Although Jackie talked about her childhood in Philadelphia as if she had been a princess there, it does not seem likely that with a painter and part-time art teacher as a father and a Russian Jewish schoolteacher mother, Jackie could have found acceptance even among the wealthy (and stuffy) German-Jewish aristocracy of the City of Brotherly Love, let alone among the daughters of Main Liners.

Jackie's family life, if she was to be believed, was a curious mixture of decadence on her father's side and prim rectitude on her mother's, though both parents traced their ancestry back through countless generations of upwardly mobile and deeply religious Eastern European Jews, none of whom, one guesses, would have been pleased to have a fast-living and highly assimilated portrait painter as a descendant, let alone a best-selling popular novelist.

From Barbara Seaman's biography of Jackie Susann, we learn that as a child Jackie's favorite book had been *Rebecca of Sunnybrook Farm*—surprisingly, in view of her adult success as the author of torrid roman à clef potboilers—but although Jackie always claimed to have had writing ambitions even as a child, in fact she came to authorhood late in life, after a checkered career as a stage actress, a model, a disk jockey, and a television personality.

Jackie adored her father and never stopped talking about him. In Barbara Seaman's biography of her it is alleged that when Jackie was a teenager she actually saw her father "humping" another woman on his studio couch—if true it would explain a lot about the way sex is treated in her fiction—but if so, the incident made her father only more attractive to Jackie. He seems to have treated his gawky, adolescent daughter as if she were a date, taking her to the movies, to fashionable restaurants, and even to speakeasies. One senses a certain collusion between father and daughter that reached its peak when Robert Susann, picked to be a judge at a beauty contest that was to choose the most beautiful girl in Philadelphia, not only encouraged Jackie to enter but made sure she won. Apart from a silver trophy that she held on to for the rest of her life, winning the contest carried with it a trip to New York City and a screen test—opportunities that Jackie was not about to waste and that were shortly to make the college plans her mother had for her superfluous.

She wanted to be an actress (or failing that, a model), but she never quite made it as either. What she got, however—and it was probably what she wanted most—was a chance to lead an independent life in New York City, as a single girl on the fringes of show business, instead of going to college.

Showbiz, as she always called it, attracted her like a magnet; she was an unapologetic star fucker—even in the literal sense: She had an affair with Eddie Cantor, for which she never forgave him, getting her revenge by turning him into the loathsome comedian Christy Lane in her second novel, *The Love Machine*. It was her passion for Broadway that brought about her marriage to Irving Mansfield, a press agent, promoter, and "producer" (of what, it was somewhat hard to say, or find out), who talked and acted as if he were a character straight out of *Guys and Dolls*, and was comfortable only at places like Lindy's, the Stage Delicatessen, and Sardi's (although late in life he managed to settle into the West Coast equivalent: a bungalow and a cabana at the Beverly Hills Hotel and a table at the Polo Lounge).

Jackie was around celebrities so much that she *became* a kind of celebrity herself, relentlessly plugged by Irving and the various Broadway gossip columnists of the day. The only thing she didn't have for full-scale celebrityhood was a talent or even a "gimmick," but this problem was solved, as if by miracle, in 1953, when she saw a poodle in the window of a Lexington Avenue pet shop. She bought her, named her Josephine, and a star was born—two stars, actually, for Josephine became America's most famous dog in 1963 when Jackie published *Every Night Josephine!* Jackie had discovered, after so many false starts, what she could *do*. Irving Mansfield finally had something to promote.

Between the two of them (or *three* of them, if you include "Josie," as Jackie called her, who was very much part of the promotion), they put Jackie's first book on the map, then went on to make Jackie's next book, *Valley of the Dolls,* a brilliant combination of soap opera, show-business gossip, and tearjerker, a worldwide number-one best-seller in hardcover and mass-market paperback and later a successful movie. Jackie had invented her own unique brand of fiction: shopgirl romance, brought up to date with lots of dirty talk, the suggestion of some pretty rough sex, and an unsentimental view of men. Jackie's fictional men were not modeled on Heathcliff but on her father: They were tall, handsome, sexy, and as emotionally tough as nails, and her heroines broke their hearts over them. (Amanda, in *The Love Machine,* was not untypical in that she carried Robin Stone's soiled face towels around in her handbag.) Jackie had uncovered a deep well of emotional masochism in American women, and far from exploiting it she simply shared it. She also understood, as if by instinct, that her readers were ready for the raw side of love, for abortions, suicide, and crass male behavior. (Christy Lane, for example, talks to his mistress while sitting on the toilet defecating noisily, with the bathroom door open.) She brought to her novels the equivalent of the case histories of Sacher-Masoch (whom she had never read) and a whole lifetime of familiarity with the seamy side of show business and blended it all with the more traditional elements of women's fiction. As Irving Mansfield liked to say, she "cried all the way to the bank."

Perhaps more important, Bernard Geis (her publisher), Jackie, and Irving created a new way of *selling* a novel, a shameless blend of column plants, celebrity appearances, and Hollywood gossip that was new to book publishing but was old hat for the theater and movies. You couldn't pick up a newspaper or turn on the television set without hearing about Jackie and her novel. Irving Mansfield put the book's cover in subway advertisements, something that had hitherto been thought more appropriate for hemorrhoid remedies than books, while Jackie actually got up at dawn to visit the warehouses from which her books were shipped to shake hands with the men who put them on the trucks and with the drivers themselves.

Publishers lusted after her sales but hesitated "to get into bed" (a favorite Irving/Jackie phrase) with the Mansfields—so much so that while Random House, somewhat shamefacedly, distributed both *Every Night Josephine!* and *Valley of the Dolls,* the books were actually published by Bernard Geis, himself something of an outsider. Geis's indifference to what was then thought of as good taste had been demonstrated to most of the more conventional publishing hands when he came up with the title of Helen Gurley Brown's first book, *Sex and the Single Girl,* in 1962 and shocked the old guard by making a huge best-seller of it.

Geis had a distribution deal with Random House that predated Jackie, so the Random House sales force sold his list. Random House's honor was saved by this semitransparent fig leaf. The only person who wasn't satisfied by this arrangement, though nobody knew it at the time, was Jackie herself, who fretted at not being given the same treatment as other best-selling authors, particularly Truman Capote, with whom she had traded insults on TV talk shows. Capote had likened her to "a truck driver in drag"—strong words for the time—and said of her skills as a writer, "She doesn't write, she *types*"; Jackie—who had a way with words (she had remarked of Philip Roth, then tasting fame as the author of *Portnoy's Complaint* and popularizer of masturbation, "I don't mind reading his book, but I don't want to shake his hand!")—had made savage fun of Capote's lisp.

Still, Jackie envied writers like Capote, and it was her ambition to be the star author on a major publisher's list that swept her into my life, changing it forever, not to speak of the industry in which I worked. Of course, I wasn't the magnet that drew Jackie to S&S. First of all, she wanted money, a ton of it, and a deal that would be the envy of other writers. Above all, she wanted status, the number-one place on a big-time publisher's fiction list, with first-class treatment all the way. As Irving Mansfield put it, "She just wants her publisher to love her, that's all."

Class mattered to her a lot, which was why the Mansfields approached Bob Gottlieb in the first place. They might not spend their evenings reading literature, but they were avid readers of *Publishers Weekly,* and they knew class when they saw it. Bob was erudite, brilliant, probably unavailable, and therefore exactly the editor Jackie wanted. His departure for Knopf almost ended the Mansfields' interest in S&S, particularly when it became apparent that Jackie was definitely not on the list of writers he wanted to take there. Eventually, Dick Snyder managed to make contact with their lawyer/agent, Artie Hershkowitz, and get things moving again.

It did not hurt that, when I was proposed to them as a replacement for Bob, they discovered that my uncle was Alexander Korda and my aunt Merle Oberon, for though they pretended otherwise, they were snobs and suckers for showbiz aristocracy. It was not for nothing that Jackie's motto was "too much is not enough," and her passion for upper-crust brand names was such that when one reporter eavesdropped on her conversation at a party, all she could hear, she said, was "Gucci-Gucci, Pucci-Pucci."

Dick and I negotiated laboriously with Hershkowitz, for whom the words *fine print* were the Holy Grail, and eventually a deal was concluded, on terms that left Shimkin breathless and shaking. Now it only remained to meet the author. It was thus that I first went to meet Jackie Susann in her apartment at the Hotel Navarro on Central Park South. I was accompanied by Jonathan Dolger, another S&S editor, Dick's theory being that we had spent so much money—and agreed to such onerous terms—to acquire *The Love Machine* that everybody involved needed an understudy.

Our mission was a delicate one: We were the first people at S&S to have actually read a portion of the manuscript, for Mansfield and Hershkowitz had sold us Jackie's novel without providing a page of manuscript to read, something of an innovation at the time. It was Jackie—and the sales curve of *Dolls*—that Irving was selling, not, as he put it indignantly when challenged, "some goddamn pile of paper." Once the ink was dry on the contracts, we received, after much prodding on our part, about a hundred pages of what Irving referred to as "rough draft," for once only too accurately.

The prospect of turning these pages into publishable prose in the time allotted to us had rendered us briefly speechless. Jackie wrote on pink paper, and despite Truman Capote's insult, typing was not her forte. Although she had two best-sellers to her credit, it appeared she had not yet discovered the shift key on her pink IBM Selectric, since she wrote everything in caps, like a long telegram, revising in a large, forceful, circular hand, with what looked like a blunt eyebrow pencil.

Neither the plot nor the structure was readily apparent, despite numerous "notes to the editor" written on cocktail napkins from the Beverly Hills Hotel and Danny's Hideaway, a show-business bar and steak house in New York City. Once Dolger had read the manuscript, he called me late at night in panic and asked, "What are we going to tell Dick Snyder?"

Dick's instructions to us the next day were simple and Napoleonic: "Just turn it into a goddamn book somehow, that's all I ask," he said, and that was that.

. . .

THE PURPOSE of our visit, though ostensibly social, was in fact to see if we *could* turn Jackie's pages into a book—or rather *how,* for Dick had made it clear that failure was not an option. Too much was at stake: his career, mine, and the whole question of whether S&S could make a go of it with high-stakes "commercial" fiction.

Dick, though he had no objection to solid nonfiction—if anything, he preferred it, since it was less of a gamble—had seen the future, and it included Pocket Books, movie tie-ins, and hype. He was already working night and day to launch *The Love Machine* with an unprecedented promotion campaign, every detail of which was subject to the Mansfields' approval. Plans for everything were being made on a scale exceeding even that for *Dolls:* sales dumps, displays, posters, Jackie's book tour, promotional material for the sales reps, a publication party to be "hosted" by gossip columnist Leonard Lyons and his wife, Sylvia, a party at the ABA convention for five hundred booksellers (at which they would be served a *Love Machine* cocktail, specially invented for the occasion by the bartender of Danny's Hideaway), giveaways, even a theme song, to be written by Sammy Cahn and sung by Tony Bennett. The one small, missing element of the enterprise remained the book itself, which Dolger and I had to squeeze out of Jackie (and rewrite) in a matter of weeks.

This was our mission, made more difficult by the fact that the Mansfields, schooled in the Hollywood art of holding out until the very last moment, both as a matter of prestige and as a way of extorting every last concession and advantage they could, however minor, resisted every attempt on our part to pin them down on such matters as when, exactly, Jackie intended to finish the book, or whether she would even *listen* to our suggestions for revisions. All Irving Mansfield said, with the chuckle that was a trademark of his conversation, was that we shouldn't worry, Jackie was a pro. In the meantime, would I remind Snyder that Jackie's "publicity girl," Abby Hirsch, flew first-class, the same as Jackie and Irving (she accompanied them everywhere, carrying Jackie's wig box), that Jackie always got a stretch limo, *not* a sedan or normal-size limo, that the driver had to be dressed in a black suit, *wearing* a chauffeur's cap, and that she expected the presidential suite in any hotel we sent her to. This was all minor crap, Mansfield said, hardly even worth mentioning, but I should understand that if Jackie thought we were going to nickel-and-dime her over chickenshit stuff like this, the way Bernie Geis had, she might conclude we didn't really love and respect her, and her unhappiness would inevitably slow up her work on the book ("heh, heh"). I had to bear in mind that Jackie was a very sensitive human being.

I bore it in mind all the way through the lobby of the Mansfields' building—in which there was a fountain with fresh gardenias floating in it, the first of its kind I had seen outside Beverly Hills—and up the elevator to their apartment, where Jackie herself opened the door. My first thought was that Truman Capote was onto something: She *did* look a bit like a truck driver in drag, or at least there was something very mannish about her appearance. She was tall, broad shouldered, large bosomed, with the deep, husky voice of a longshoreman, and she wore stage makeup that looked as if it had been put on with a trowel and then baked. Her face was an improbable dark tan, her lips a glossy bloodred, and her spiked eyelashes, striking on TV, were truly alarming close up. Her eyes were dark, bright, and very, very shrewd and tough. She offered her cheek, and I kissed it. "Irving's out walking Josephine," she said. She appraised me carefully. "Christ, I thought I was going to get a top editor," she said. "You look just like a kid."

"And you look just like a girl," I said, stealing Milton Greene's line to Marilyn Monroe.

It had worked for Milton on Marilyn, and it worked for me on Jackie. She gave a big grin and took us into the tiny kitchen. She opened the refrigerator and took out a bottle of Dom Perignon. I was interested to see that except for a can of dog food and an empty jar of cocktail capers, the refrigerator was bare. The Mansfields were not homebodies. She handed me the bottle and said, "Pop it, kid."

I popped it—a European education pays dividends sooner or later—and the three of us sat down in the living room, where glasses were already waiting on the coffee table. I noticed that they were from the Beverly Hills Hotel, as were the cocktail napkins. The Mansfields, as I was to discover, expected to be comped everything. When they stayed in a hotel, they left with a supply of soap, toilet paper, and Kleenex.

I struggled to sit upright while I poured. Jackie's upholstery—mostly some kind of shimmery gold fabric with a nubby weave—was protected by transparent plastic slipcovers so slippery that it was hard not to slide off the furniture. We were just toasting each other when the door opened and Irving came in with Josephine on a leash. Mansfield was a promoter and hustler and prided himself on being a tough guy, though all he was, in fact, was Jackie's spokesman—*she* was the tough one, not him. His ambition in life was to be a Broadway "character," to which end he had mastered the gruff voice, the sharp clothes, the hat cocked at a rakish angle, like Walter Winchell's, the "don't fuck with me" stare and the shameless chutzpah of that vanishing breed. He never quite brought it off, however—in some hard-to-define way he always looked like a small-timer, though he was deeply suspicious of being taken for one. I had the impression, then and later, that most of his life consisted of hanging around with his hands in his pockets telling people, "Jackie will be down in five minutes."

"Did Josie do her business, honey?" Jackie asked, with genuine concern.

"Yeh, yeh," Irving said, with the look of a man who hadn't noticed. He put Josephine in the bedroom, came back, and poured himself a glass of champagne. "So what do you think of Jackie?" he asked. "Isn't she great?"

As we were soon to discover, this was Irving's refrain. Whatever Jackie said or did, Irving chuckled and, as if he were her impresario, said, "Isn't she great?"

Great or not, it soon became apparent that as far as her books were concerned, Jackie *was* a pro, just as Irving had promised. The pink paper was not a whim. She typed each draft of her manuscript on a different color paper—pink was for her first, rough draft. What is more, though Irving liked to insist that she never needed nor accepted editorial advice, Jackie herself was a realist—she took what seemed useful to her and understood perfectly what her special strengths were. "I write for women who read me in the goddamn subways on the way home from work," she explained. "I know who they are because that's who I used to be. Remember *Stella Dallas*? My readers are like Stella. They want to press their noses against the windows of other people's houses and get a look at the parties they'll never be invited to, the dresses they'll never get to wear, the lives they'll never live, the guys they'll never fuck." Jackie—a chain-smoker—exhaled out of both nostrils like a dragon. "But here's the catch: All the people they envy in my books, the ones who are glamorous or beautiful or rich or talented, they have to come to a bad end, see, because *that* way the people who read me can get off the subway and go home feeling better about their own crappy lives and *luckier* than the people they've been reading about."

"Isn't she great?" Irving said with a chuckle.

In fact, I soon decided, in her own way, Jackie *was* great. Leavis could not have put it better in all the volumes of *Scrutiny*. She understood exactly what she was doing. In those days, when the TV industry was still glamorous, she had elected to write a novel about television, to this day the only successful one and the best. "The love machine" was not only the nickname for Robin Stone, the fabulously successful television executive who was the book's hero (and who was based on Jim Aubrey), but was also Stone's name for the television set itself. Jackie already understood that the television set was like a kind of lover, always present in the bedroom, available twenty-four hours a day, establishing a new kind of intimacy with the viewer. She didn't need Marshall McLuhan to teach her that. It was one of the reasons she was such a good promoter on television: She was, as she herself described it, "a natural on the boob tube."

Dumb she wasn't. She even had a theory about popular fiction that, so far as I am concerned, has yet to be bettered and that, if followed with a certain amount of energy, can hardly fail: a love story with a heroine every woman reader will identify with (in those days a pretty victim), a powerful man torn between his work and his love, and a cast of characters who are almost identifiable as celebrities.

She was also a phenomenally hard worker. She absorbed our notes and, with a total lack of prima donna behavior, carved out, with our help, a plot and structure that sounded pretty damned good and with any luck might even sound OK the next morning. I was impressed and relieved.

(Years later, at an ABA convention in Washington, D.C., I mentioned this to Bob Gottlieb, and he sighed. "Yes," he said, "it's true. Jackie *was* a pro. But you must be wary of thinking that's a good thing for a writer to be.")

I asked Jackie if she thought she could meet our deadline. She looked at me through narrowed eyes. "You bet your fucking ass," she said.

"Heh, heh," Irving said. "What did I tell you? Isn't she *great*?" Did we know that Jackie could also sing? Irving wanted to know. We shook our heads. He produced a tape and played a recording of Jackie singing "(Love Is) The Tender Trap" in a flat, harsh, totally tuneless baritone. It was, apparently, her theme song. We heard it twice, in awe, while Irving kept time with his right hand, clearly having the time of his life. Later on, people were to tell me that Irving used Jackie, but I knew better. No man ever loved a woman more than Irving loved Jackie. Only love could explain his listening to that recording for the umpteenth time with unfeigned pleasure.

"Am I right, or am I wrong? Isn't she great?" he asked. He gave us each a copy of the tape as a souvenir. "Let's go eat."

Dolger, eyes rolling, pleaded another engagement and went home with a bundle of manuscript, his notes, and his tape of Jackie singing, but the Mansfields were not about to let me escape that easily. I was to have dinner with them—they would hear of nothing else, otherwise Jackie's feelings would be hurt. Abby Hirsch, Jackie's publicity assistant, whose salary had been a source of endless kvetching during the contract negotiations, since the Mansfields were determined that S&S should pay it, turned up from the bedroom, where she had presumably been baby-sitting Josephine, and booked a table for us at Danny's Hideaway. Abby bore a remarkable resemblance to a younger and prettier version of Jackie—it was rumored that she wore the same dress size as Jackie and could therefore try on clothes for her, saving Jackie the trouble of shopping.

Before we left, however, Jackie was determined to change my appearance. At the time, in keeping with what was then the publishing tradition, I wore an old tweed hacking jacket from my Oxford days, with suede leather patches on the elbows. Jackie looked at me critically. "You're a big-shot editor," she told me, "but you dress like a bum." Irving was wearing a brand-new dark blue cashmere blazer, cut in the Hollywood, Sy Devore style, with dramatic wide lapels and gold buttons engraved with an ankh. The ankh, an ancient Egyptian good luck symbol, was Jackie's latest obsession. It was to play a major role in the plot of *The Love Machine*, and we created ankh pendants on gold chains for important lady booksellers and ankh rings for men, and we put gold-stamped ankhs on everything in sight. Some people involved with the book soon wore so many ankhs that they clanked and jingled like Gypsies at every step. We eventually came to refer to the ankh as "the ancient Egyptian symbol for schlock," though never within Jackie's hearing. She took the ankh seriously and made Dick Snyder spend thousands of dollars of S&S's money at her favorite L.A. jewelers for ankh items.

"Give him your blazer, honey," Jackie told Irving. For once, Irving rebelled. The blazer had just arrived from his tailor that morning, he was devoted to it, it had eighteen-karat gold buttons—all to no avail. Over his protests (and mine, for it was the last thing I wanted), Irving was forced to relinquish it. As I tried it on, I noticed that the lining was embroidered with ankhs too—the Mansfields never did things by half. I wondered in whose promotion budget the cost of Irving's blazer had been buried, the movie company's or ours? Unfortunately, Irving and I were different shapes. He was much bigger around the waist and had long arms, like those of a chimpanzee, I thought, as I surveyed myself in Jackie's mirror, draped in folds of blue cashmere. With some relief, I pointed out that it didn't fit.

Jackie was not to be contradicted, however. "It fits fine," she said, bunching the material up behind my back. "It looks great on you, doll. Maybe you should get the sleeves shortened a bit, but it'll do fine for tonight." I protested that I couldn't take it from Irving. "He wants you to have it," Jackie said firmly. And poor Irving, tears in his eyes, recognizing defeat, said, this time sadly, without the chuckle, "Isn't she great?"

DANNY'S HIDEAWAY was one of those quintessentially dark New York steak boîtes that cater to celebrities. By the time we sat down to dinner, our party consisted of Jackie, Irving, Abby Hirsch, myself, Myron Cohen (the borscht belt/Las Vegas comedian), Peter Lawford, and Lawford's date, a stunningly beautiful young woman whose eyes were thickly glazed, like homemade pottery. Lawford himself was drunk and seemed to have been captured by the Mansfields without knowing who they were. At times, he slept, noisily, his face on the table. At other times, he was rude and hostile. He alternated between quarreling with his girl and sticking his hand under her dress or his tongue in her ear, while she tried feebly to fend him off. "I could use a piece of that," Cohen said wistfully—he too seemed to be unsure what he was doing at the table, but like most comedians he wasn't about to refuse a free meal.

By now it was late, at any rate for me—well past ten o'clock—and I was starving. Every time the maître d' came over, bearing vast, gold-tasseled red velvet menus the size of doors, Jackie shooed him away and ordered another round of drinks. I had consumed the entire basket of breadsticks and rolls and was feeling queasy before Jackie finally allowed us to have menus. I didn't even look at mine. I ordered a steak and a baked potato and prayed for its swift arrival. In the meantime, Irving Mansfield had been regaling us with the story of his shoes: He had gone to his shoemaker in Beverly Hills and ordered a pair of slip-on loafers in alligator hide, the most expensive shoes he had ever owned. How much had they cost? Cohen asked. Two hundred and fifty bucks, Irving replied. Cohen shook his head. He had a pair of shoes that cost more than that, made for him in Vegas in baby Cuban caiman hide. He took one of them off and passed it to Irving, who examined it with envy, then passed it around the table so each of us could examine it in turn. When it got to Lawford, Lawford glanced at it with contempt, took off one of his shoes and banged it down in the center of the table. "Unborn baby turtle," he said. Five hundred dollars a pair and worth every penny. You didn't even know you had shoes on, they were so comfortable. Myron Cohen and Irving Mansfield looked as wistfully at Lawford's shoe as they had at his girl. Each of them carefully wrote down the name of Lawford's shoemaker as the food was served.

I was reminded of the Mad Hatter's tea party, but my hunger was so great that I didn't care. I picked up my knife and fork and prepared to eat my steak, but Jackie, noticing what I had ordered, was upset. I could get a steak any fucking where, she said. Danny's was famous for its lobster *Fra Diavolo,* which she had ordered, or its calf's liver *Veneziana,* which Irving was having. I could not eat at Danny's without giving them a try. She took a big spoonful of her lobster and dumped it on top of my steak, then put some of Irving's calf's liver on top of that. I glanced sadly at the mess on my plate, while Irving said, cheerfully again this time, "Isn't she great?"

I decided to go home and raid the refrigerator. I made my good-byes, pleading work to be done, my wife's health, a sick child, a headache. Luckily, by this time, neither Jackie nor Irving tried to stop me.

As I was collecting my briefcase from the hatcheck girl, the maître d' came running after me, anxiety written large on his face. I was afraid that Jackie was demanding my return. Instead, he handed me the check. "Mr. Mansfield says you're the publisher, so you're paying," he said. I glanced at the bill. It was the largest restaurant check I'd ever seen. I signed it boldly, added a humongous tip, and told him to send it over to S&S. A few days later, when somebody from the accounting department called to ask if I was out of my mind, I told him to charge it to the Mansfields' promotion budget.

S&S, like all publishers, was mildly conservative about expense accounts. Nobody made much of a fuss on the subject, but it was understood that you didn't splurge or spend more on a meal than Max would have spent, and he was a cautious spender, except where Ray was concerned.

That was about to change, along with much else. We were in show business now.

SHOW BUSINESS had swept into the S&S promotion and publicity departments with a bang. Where, formerly, a spot on the *Today* show and a modest cocktail party at the Schusters' apartment had been about par for the course for launching a book, we were now orchestrating huge parties on both coasts, sending out gift ankhs in plush-lined leatherette presentation cases shaped like books (accompanied by a personal note from Jackie on special *Love Machine* stationery), and ordering cakes in the shape of the book, with the cover to be reproduced in icing. For the first time in publishing history, the author's photograph seemed to be as important as the contents of the book, and hitherto unheard-of sums were spent on brand-name photographers and, inevitably, retouchers. While much of this did not concern me—I was busy transforming Jackie's scrawl into prose and engaging in a daily "story conference" to work out the plot—I was soon thrust into the role of S&S's ambassador-at-large to the Mansfields, since almost from the word go they had quarreled violently with Dick, whose role in the enterprise was to say no to their more extreme demands. *No* was not a word Jackie was accustomed to hearing, and while Irving had heard it often enough in *his* lifetime, he was reluctant to pass it on to Jackie. "You go back and tell Snyder that this is a deal breaker," I heard several times a day.

Of course, plans for the cakes had to be placed on hold until we *had* a dust jacket for the bakers to copy. This was no easy task. The Mansfields had strong ideas about what they wanted. Poor Irving came to jacket meetings with color swatches Jackie had given him, from which it was apparent that pink was her favorite color. Most authors, even major ones, took very little interest in their book jackets in those innocent days. In the case of very important authors, the publisher might show him or her the sketch for the jacket, but there was seldom any question of the author's approval. The Mansfields had it written into their contract and took it seriously; packaging, a concept that had not yet come into widespread use among book publishers, *mattered* to them, a lot. They sent every jacket suggestion to Hollywood, where, as they put it, there were people who really knew packaging, pros at the game instead of amateurs like us. Eventually, however, after much argument, angst, and innumerable flare-ups of temper by our art director, a *theme* was decided upon. The cover of the novel would resemble a movie poster (surprise, surprise!) featuring a man's hand touching a woman's, each of them wearing—what else?—gold ankh rings. Irving instructed us to get the best hand models in New York for the shot, which Frank Metz, our art director, did. When Jackie saw the proof, though, she didn't like it—she thought the hands were ugly. We explained that we had hired the best hand models in New York, just as Irving had instructed us. Jackie didn't miss a beat. "Get me the two *second-best* hand models in New York," she snapped.

"Heh, heh," Irving chuckled. "Isn't she great?"

"I WANT the name of the girl who put me on hold," Jackie screeched at me over the phone one day. "I want her fired! *Nobody* puts Jacqueline Susann on hold!"

There were tears at S&S whenever Jackie didn't get what she wanted or was made to wait even for a moment. This was a new experience for most of the employees. Book publishing had always prided itself rather self-consciously on being a profession in which good manners prevailed. People in book publishing did not, as a rule, raise their voices or shout insults at each other. Above all, they didn't shout at people who couldn't shout back. It simply wasn't done, not on either side of the Atlantic.

Most of the young women who worked in book publishing ("editorial assistants," never secretaries) were college educated (often from one of the Seven Sisters) and drawn to publishing by either a genuine love of books or the desire to become an editor or a writer. Shamelessly exploited, they were paid miserable salaries and allowed in compensation to read all the unsolicited manuscripts—the famous slush pile. Many of them were the daughters of publishing executives or well-known authors, unaccustomed to hearing a voice raised at them in anger.

The Mansfields were deaf to these social niceties. So far as Jackie was concerned, the assistants were the help, and therefore she took her anger out on them, if only because they had the least chance of shielding themselves. It was not just being put on hold that made her angry: She didn't like being told that someone was unavailable or in a meeting or out to lunch, and God help the assistant who didn't know the answer to any question she might ask, even if it wasn't her job to know or even her department. When angered, Jackie's voice rose to the sound of a buzz saw at full throttle—worse yet, she often complained about the assistants to their bosses or even to the top management. She was always asking for people to be fired, and we found the simplest way of handling the problem was to tell her they had been and move them out of sight.

Nor did she always confine her anger to the underlings. According to Barbara Seaman, Jackie once called poor Bernie Geis at three in the morning to complain there weren't enough books in the stores. When he pointed out the time to her, she replied: "You son of a bitch, I can't sleep, so why should you?"

No doubt the Mansfields cannot be blamed for the erosion of manners in the book-publishing business, but they certainly heralded a new era in which the old-world charm of publishing, admittedly always a little self-conscious and bogus, gave way to the kind of behavior that had always characterized the movie business. Jackie Susann's success unintentionally coincided with the decline and fall of the ancien régime and the rise of modern publishing, with its gargantuan mergers, its pretensions to big-business status, its impersonality, and its abrasiveness.

Jackie, to paraphrase Talleyrand's comment on the Bourbons loosely, neither forgot nor forgave anything. During the planning of the parties accompanying the publication of *The Love Machine,* Jackie had puzzled us all by warning Dan Green, the S&S publicity director, that no cripples were to be invited. I probed for an explanation. It wasn't that Jackie had anything against the people now called "the handicapped"— she simply felt that the sight of them depressed people and was therefore counterproductive to good promotion. In vain did Green protest, with a smile, that he wasn't about to turn one of her parties into a scene from the Cour de Miracles in front of the Cathedral of Notre Dame de

Paris, as described by Victor Hugo in his novel of the same name. Jackie was not amused, and she never forgave anybody for putting her down with a reference she didn't understand. "I don't care what they do in Paris," she snapped, staring at him suspiciously with narrowed eyes. Jackie had a sense of humor but not about herself, and she thought that Green was having fun at her expense. "No cripples," she said firmly. "You heard me."

We put this down to unamiable eccentricity on her part, but as usual she meant business. Toward the end of the Leonard and Sylvia Lyons party, the first of many (held in their apartment but for which S&S footed the bill), a distinguished older publishing figure arrived late, on crutches, having broken a leg. Jackie flung herself at Dan Green in fury, her talons bared (she favored enormously long and pointed bright red false nails, like those of the Dragon Lady in *Terry and the Pirates*, so that both Green and I feared for his eyes), and, pointing at the puzzled guest, cried: "Get him *out* of here!" She grabbed Green's tie as if to strangle him. "I *told* you, you son of a bitch! No cripples at my party!"

Many years later, she and I briefly chatted about old times. I mentioned Dan Green's name and her eyes blazed. "He's the one who tried to ruin Sylvia and Leonard's party for *The Love Machine*," she said fiercely. "He invited a cripple just to spoil the mood."

"Heh, heh," Irving chuckled from the background. "Isn't Jackie great? She never forgets a thing."

To an outsider, the curious thing about Jackie was that she and Irving seemed to have no private life. The Mansfields were totally wrapped up in keeping Jackie famous. They were always on the telephone, Jackie selling her book, Irving making deals.

The truth was that Jackie's big secret *was* her private life, and her success was in part a way of concealing it and in part a way of escaping from the pain of it. Far from being invulnerable and tough, as she liked to portray herself, she was a woman of great passion with a deep capacity for friendship, both supportive of her friends (most of whom led lives pretty much like the women in Jackie's novels) and dependent on their support. The secret was that in 1962, the year Jackie wrote *Every Night Josephine!*, she had been diagnosed with breast cancer. A mastectomy had failed to halt the spread of the cancer, and Jackie led the rest of her life in secret pain and on painkillers, struggling with a disease she refused to share with the outside world. Perhaps more painful still, the Mansfields' son, Guy, was autistic, a fact that they also managed to conceal from the world at large.

That perhaps explains the feeling that their lives together appeared to be a kind of facade, put together artfully for the purpose of being photographed. To be with them was to have the feeling that these two people existed only for the outside world, but it was an illusion. Jackie and Irving were living out a tragedy as painful as any in her books and putting on a show to cover it.

"Jackie is a trouper," Irving once told me, when she went on a talk show suffering from laryngitis, but it was far more true than he or Jackie ever revealed. She was a woman of her time, who not only believed that the show must go on but also felt that the public wanted celebrities to show happy faces, whatever might be going on in their private lives. Today, of course, the public expects to hear about all the sordid details of people's private lives, but in Jackie's day that wasn't so, and she lived in fear that her public would find out she *wasn't* just rich, happy, and successful. "I hear he's got cancer," I once heard Irving say about someone in show business, then, totally without irony: "When they hear about that in Hollywood, he's dead."

Jackie feared the same. The truth simply wasn't an option.

THE MANSFIELDS were, as far as I know, the first people to plan a whole new wardrobe as part of the campaign (plum-colored sequins were a memorable feature of Jackie's formal wear) and try to get the publisher to pay for it all, right down to the shoes. Their attention to detail was incredible. They lived and breathed "launch," as they called it.

The launch—another concept new to publishing—of *The Love Machine* was accompanied by incredible ballyhoo. The Mansfields might have their comic side, but when they moved into high gear it was impressive to behold. It was Jackie, after all, who virtually invented the idea of forging deep, personal connections between an author and the people who actually sold books. Hitherto, bookstore managers, let alone bookstore clerks, had been ignored, by both publishers and authors. An author visiting a store might shake their hands, while his publisher's sales rep whispered their names in his or her ear ("That's Faith, that's

Angela, the one with the thick glasses and the pens in his shirt pocket is Ted"), but that was about it. Jackie had been around stars long enough to know that wasn't enough. If these people were going to sell her book, she loved them, and she would make *them* love *her*. She not only remembered their names without coaching, she had a huge Rolodex, lovingly kept up-to-date by Abby Hirsch, with their birthdays and the names of their mother or husband or cat. On their birthdays and at Christmas they received loving, personal notes, handwritten by Jackie, and well before publication they got signed books, gift-wrapped and boxed, each with a personal message, not to speak of all sorts of ankh jewelry, ranging from pendants and rings to tie clasps and cuff links.

What she was doing, of course, was making the booksellers part of her team, to be used if necessary against her publisher, for she was not above mobilizing the booksellers to lobby for a bigger printing, a lower retail price, more ads, or further printings. She brought grassroots activism to the formerly staid business of selling a book, in some ways a more important contribution than the dazzle and the hype she also introduced.

Irving Mansfield was a master at the arcane art of "column planting," almost unknown in book publishing and now a vanished art. In those days there were still plenty of important columnists, not just Liz Smith, and even those outside New York counted for something, like Herb Caen in San Francisco or Irv Kupcinet in Chicago. The Mansfields were always busy planting items. Anything one said to them was fair game, however innocently it had been shared, since the rules of column planting were simple: In return for you supplying gossip about other people, the columnist would run your own plug. The Mansfields plugged *The Love Machine* relentlessly, and it paid off. The book soared onto *The New York Times*'s best-seller list and stayed there for months.

Perhaps the high point of the whole campaign was reached at the party given for the booksellers at the ABA convention in Washington, D.C. This had been carefully designed by the Mansfields to capitalize on the affection the booksellers felt—or were purported to feel—for Jackie. Dinner was to be served at intimate little candlelit tables for ten in the big ballroom of the Shoreham Hotel, and each table was to have one empty chair, rather like that reserved for Elijah at a seder, so that Jackie could move from table to table throughout the meal. The lighting was kept low, the orchestra played romantic music, and the booksellers filed past Jackie and Irving in the receiving line, where Jackie displayed her phenomenal memory, greeting each of them by name, not to speak of remembering the names of their dog or cat. "Heh, heh," Irving whispered to me. "Isn't she great? She could run for president!"

The only fly in the ointment was that each bookseller, as they left the receiving line, was served a "Love Machine" cocktail, a potent, sweet concoction involving, among other things, curaçao, Pernod, vodka, crushed ice, and a lot of fresh fruit, served in big tumblers. Snyder took one look at it and growled to a waiter, "Bring me a scotch," a wise decision, which I followed. The Love Machine was the kind of drink that is served in Florida resorts in a coconut shell or a hollowed-out pineapple, and it was predictably lethal. Very shortly, we had several hundred booksellers in various stages of inebriation, and the noise level was out of control. Dan Green, aghast, slipped up beside me and whispered, "What are we going to do?"

"Serve dinner?" I suggested.

Green nodded. We had the lights dimmed and brightened to signal that it was dinnertime. Nobody paid any attention except Jackie, who was furious.

We finally persuaded the waiters to start serving, and gradually, with many falls, bumps, and the crash of tipped-over chairs, the guests started to sit down.

"Look on the bright side," I told Green. "At least there are no cripples."

Nevertheless, it was touch and go. Jackie had envisioned a perfect party—a kind of Kennedy White House state dinner, with her as Jackie Kennedy and her book as the center of attention. There were copies of the book on each table, with pens, so that she could sign them. Each table also had a huge, gold ankh, designed so that a bookseller could stick his or her head through the loop and be photographed with Jackie standing next to him or her holding up the book. A drunken brawl was not what she had in mind.

The menu had been chosen, perhaps mistakenly in retrospect, with flamboyance in mind, and included a lot of flambé dishes, which Jackie, who wasn't interested in food, liked because of their drama. Great bursts of flame lit up the room, with the occasional smell of singed hair, illuminating, as in hell, Jackie, as she made her way from table to table. Booksellers were making paper airplanes of the promotional material and sending them flying through the room. Amoretti di Sarono, the small, round Italian biscuits wrapped in tissue-thin paper that had attained, at the time, a certain chic, had been placed on each table, and people were setting fire to the wrappers to watch them float slowly in flames to the ceiling. Jackie could be seen smiling fiercely, while attempting to shield her wig from flames in only partially disguised terror. At any moment, I expected the fire marshals to arrive. Green, wisely, I thought, was keeping well out of her line of sight. Setting fire to Jackie's wig would be a lot worse than inviting a cripple.

At last, the meal dragged to an end. There was a rousing fanfare. The lighting dropped from dim to dark. A hired singer sang *The Love Machine* theme, while four waiters descended a flight of stairs bearing a spotlit cake in the shape of a giant copy of the book. The whole room stood—unsteadily—to applaud as the cake moved slowly toward Jackie, but before it arrived, disaster occurred. One of the publicists slipped and fell into the cake.

One look at Jackie's face was enough to tell me what the right thing to do was. I went back to my hotel and told the operator not to put any calls through. The next morning, I got up at dawn and took the train back to New York City.

I never regretted it.

STILL, I remained friendly with Jackie, who fell out with everyone else at S&S until she had nobody else but me to talk to. Some time after she had finished touring for the book, she invited me to dinner at Danny's Hideaway again, just to say good-bye, for the Mansfields were leaving for Los Angeles the next morning to work on the screenplay for *The Love Machine*.

Jackie was in a benevolent mood; even she could not deny that the book had worked, though it was already apparent to me that nobody else at S&S was up to doing another book with Jackie, however many copies it was going to sell. About halfway through the dinner, she glanced at my wristwatch and shook her head. "You know," she said, "for a kid who's going places in this business, that's a pretty crappy-looking watch."

I shrugged. It was an old Rolex, which I had worn through the Royal Air Force and the Hungarian Revolution. It had belonged to one of my father's assistants in the art department at London Films, Philip Sandeman (of the sherry family), who had been instrumental in getting me into the Royal Air Force in the first place and had left it to me after being killed in a flying accident. I was mildly attached to it and said so.

Jackie dismissed all that. I should have a look at Irving's new watch.

Somewhat nervously—I think he was afraid that Jackie was going to give away his watch as she had his blazer—he took it off and passed it to me. It was a Cartier tank watch, with his name spelled out instead of numbers—"I-R-V-M-A-N-S-F-I-E-L-D"—and a small gold ankh beneath the Cartier signature. The *deployant* buckle had an ankh engraved on it. I admired it and, to Irving's great relief, handed it back.

"You know," Jackie said thoughtfully, "your name would fit. It has twelve letters."

I hadn't thought of that, but she was right, as usual.

"You ought to have a decent watch," she said. "Like Irving's."

I demurred. I liked Jackie, but I had no desire to be in her debt for a gold watch. Soon, however, we were in a shouting match, with Irving accusing me of turning down Jackie's gift out of ingratitude and Jackie accusing me of having insulted her. The more I thought about it, the more stupid and puritanical my resistance seemed. God knows I had *earned* a Cartier watch, with or without my name on it. Why should I not accept one when it had been offered to me? I caved in as gracefully as I could, and we embraced and parted company, the Mansfields for their cabana at the Beverly Hills Hotel, me for home.

The next day, as I was sitting at my desk, my assistant buzzed me on the intercom to say that there was a man on the telephone who had to speak to me about a watch.

Expecting that it was Cartier on the telephone, asking for my address, I took the call. A rich, deep, vibrant voice, gravelly, hoarse, with a distinct Brooklyn accent, told me it wasn't anybody from Cartier. "You Mike Korda?" he asked. "Irving and Jackie's friend?"

I acknowledged both facts and asked who he was.

"This is Sol," he said. "I'm down on Forty-seventh Street. It's about your watch."

"My watch? I don't get it. Isn't it coming from Cartier when it's ready?" In those days Cartier still delivered jewelry by hand on request, with a solemn messenger wearing a gray chauffeur's uniform, with breeches and leggings, and bearing the pale blue Cartier box. I had expected my watch, eventually, to arrive like that.

Sol snorted with impatience. "Hey," he said, "it has to be hand lettered. I got to put on the whatchamacallit? The fucking ankh."

"You do this for Cartier?"

"Cartier, *Shmartier.* You're getting a real Cartier watch, with the dial hand lettered—are you ready for this?—at wholesale! How do you like them apples, *bubbi?*"

There was a silence while I worked this out in my head. However I juggled them apples, what I was looking at was that *I* was apparently buying the watch, not the Mansfields. How much was this going to cost me? I asked.

I could tell from Sol's rasping voice that he was offended. "Cost? What are you talking about, cost? They asked me to give you the best deal I could. You tell me where you can beat wholesale on a Cartier watch?"

"Yes, but what are we talking about in numbers? Ballpark figure?"

A long, resentful sigh. "One large," he said. "With the lettering and the whatchamacallit maybe a little more. Say twelve hundred."

I tried to think of a way that I could explain to my wife why I had spent $1,200 on a gold Cartier watch I didn't need, with my name painted on the dial and an ankh. I couldn't do it. "Keep the watch," I said.

There was a long silence at the other end. "Make it nine hundred, I'll throw in the dial," Sol said. "You pay cash, and we forget about the sales tax."

"No." Even $900 was out of the question, I explained. It was a point of honor. The watch was supposed to be a gift.

"What am I going to do with the watch?" Sol asked, panic in his voice now. Sell it to someone else, I suggested. "Someone *else?* My boy already lettered your first name on the goddamn dial! Who I am going to sell a Cartier watch to whose first name is Michael?"

"Somebody whose family name has five letters," I said and hung up.

I was not out of the woods yet, however. The next day, Irving called me from Los Angeles. Jackie was in the bathroom crying her heart out, he told me accusingly, all because I had rejected her gift. I pointed out that it *wasn't* a gift. I was going to have to pay for it, after all.

"She thought you were different from the others," he said. "She thought we were *friends.*"

"We *are* friends," I said. "I just don't want the watch. Tell her company policy prevents me from accepting it."

Irving thought about this. He was not an unreasonable man when he was treated like an equal partner. "I'll explain it to Jackie," he said, in his best, confidential, man-to-man voice. An hour later, he called back and said, in a conspiratorial whisper, "Heh, heh, you're in the clear."

And I guess I was. Jackie and I stayed on a friendly basis, even though she left S&S rancorously before her next book, *Once Is Not Enough,* causing Dick to send her a single rose on the publication day with a note that read, "For us, once *was* enough." From time to time I met Irving Mansfield on the street, outside "21," or on Central Park South, waiting for Josephine to do her business. In a strange way, I was grateful to them: They had taught me, after all, that books could be merchandised, just like anything else, something that a lot of publishers have still to learn.

I must have been on Jackie's list of friends, too, for I continued to receive PR releases and even birthday cards. Years later, one night at home, the telephone rang at some ungodly hour. My wife picked up, listened for a moment, and, holding her hand over the mouthpiece, whispered: "There's a drunken woman on the phone asking for you."

I took the receiver groggily and at once recognized Jackie's voice, not drunk but hoarse and inarticulate with grief. "I just wanted you to know," she said haltingly, "Josephine is dead."

And in some strange way I felt sad—though I had never known Josephine in her prime. To tell the truth, Josephine had never much liked me. I had the impression, in fact, that she didn't much like men in general, not even Irving, though it was possible that she merely resented being relegated to the background. In the old days, Josephine had been the star, not Jackie, and went everywhere with her owners: restaurants, nightclubs, talk shows. Then, as Jackie herself became the star, Josephine was eclipsed, left behind, loved perhaps but no longer in the limelight, which probably explained why she sulked and occasionally snarled at Irving. Still, with her death, it was as if a chapter of what Jackie liked to call "the book of life" had come to an end, though I couldn't have guessed Jackie's own life would end so soon, in 1974.

In her own way, she changed the course of popular fiction, a prophet without honor to whom John Grisham, Robert James Waller, Judith Krantz, Jackie Collins, and Danielle Steel all owe a debt. Jackie, after all, reinvented the woman's novel, the mainstay of popular fiction, opened it up to a franker sexuality, to a tougher kind of story, to romance with tears *and* oral sex, to heroes with good looks and icy cruelty. She introduced readers of fiction to a rawer kind of sensation than had hitherto been acceptable to members of the Literary Guild and fiction buyers at the Doubleday bookstores, while, at the same time, introducing into the genre the first big dose of celebrity worship that was to blossom into the full-scale celebrity cults of the eighties and the nineties.

Jackie was ahead of that curve. More important, she taught everybody in book publishing a lesson: not just that books are merchandise and that nobody who wants to be a good publisher should ever forget that, but also that what most people want to read more than anything else is, quite simply, a good *story*. The rags to riches, poor little miss nobody in love with her all-powerful boss, the understudy who gets her chance to strut the stage in the star's role and becomes a star—these are not just clichés, as reviewers would have us believe, but part of the very reason why people buy novels in the first place: to get out of their own lives and troubles by reading about other people's.

Maybe Jackie picked that up from her mother, a great reader, or maybe she picked it up from being around her father, in what passed for the Philadelphia Jewish version of *la vie de bohème*, or maybe it was just all those hours as a kid reading *Rebecca of Sunnybrook Farm*, but wherever it came from, she knew it better than anyone before or since.

CHAPTER 20

*T*HE LOVE MACHINE sold more copies than any work of fiction S&S had ever published and even garnered some good reviews, including perhaps the most selling review ever to appear in the staid, stuffy, and august *New York Times Book Review,* in which Nora Ephron called it "a long, delicious gossip column" and summed it all up by writing that "it shined like a rhinestone in a trash can." Perhaps for the first time in publishing history, a book's editor was quoted in a *Times* review (up until then, editors, like valets and tailors, remained silent). "You have to push this book beyond regular book buyers," I said (correctly), "to people who haven't been in a bookstore since *Valley of the Dolls* was published." Ephron noted that we had paid $250,000 for the book (a fortune in those days) and that Twentieth Century Fox had offered a million dollars for the movie rights (which the Mansfields turned down)—the first time that the grubby subject of money had been raised there—and also brought up the hitherto taboo subjects of masochism, nymphomania, and incest. She also quoted me as saying, in regard to the competition between Philip Roth and Jackie Susann for first place on the best-seller list, "It's wild! You have these two books out at the same time, and their merits aside, one of them is about masturbation and the other is about successful heterosexual love. If there's any justice in the world, *The Love Machine* ought to knock *Portnoy* off the top simply because it's a step in the right direction." (This comment was to cause me untold grief when the wheel of life turned and cast me, years later, as Roth's editor.) *Newsweek* compared Jackie to "an Egyptian love goddess," called the book "an engaging sex-power fantasy," and compared her (unfavorably) to Thomas Wolfe.

There were two immediate consequences. The first was that Dick and I were proven right. We had gambled big and won, and there could henceforth be no doubt that I belonged in the editor in chief's office or that Dick's ascent to the top would be seriously delayed, least of all by Peter Schwed. The second was that having been quoted again and again in the press on the subject of Jacqueline Susann, I glimpsed, for the first time, the possibility that an editor need not necessarily be mute and invisible—that he or she might become as much of a celebrity as the best-selling authors were. Reporters, reviewers, professional deep thinkers called, one replied to their questions, and lo and behold, the next day there were one's words, appearing in print all across America and, for that matter, around the world. That this might turn out to be a two-edged sword had not yet occurred to me, but in the meantime Jackie Susann and Irving Mansfield had dragged me all too willingly into the limelight, and I was reluctant to fall back into the shadows.

In a curious way, *The Love Machine* sharply changed the stakes for both Dick and me. In the first place, we had proven ourselves as a team—a fact of more importance to us than to the rest of the world—and in the second place, perhaps more important, Dick had demonstrated his skill as a publisher in conditions of extreme stress. Successfully articulating the publication of a big book is the test of good publishing, involving the ability to keep in one's head not only the numbers and their daily fluctuation but the harmonious synchronizing of publicity, manufacturing, advertising, and sales—departments often run as independent fiefdoms. Dick established immediate control over the whole process and won universal respect (if not affection) by his ab-

solute recall of even the smallest bit of information and by the fact that
he was usually a step ahead of everybody else. Whatever the subject
was, he knew the right questions to ask and also knew when he wasn't
being given a straight answer. When a book is selling fast and in big
numbers, the publisher has no option but to go back to press blindly for
more printings of the book for fear of running out of stock, with the result that when sales start to slow down or stop, there is still a torrent of
books coming in from the printer. Many best-sellers end up *losing*
money for the publisher because of overprinting, while, of course, un-
counted best-sellers that might have been fail to happen because the
publisher prints too cautiously or fails to respond quickly enough to demand. (The adoption of the computer was supposed to cure this problem but has made no difference at all—returns of unsold hardcover
books still run at a crippling 35 to 40 percent—which is proof that it is
really a question of *Fingerspitzengefühl* rather than lack of information.)

Dick had the guts to go for a major reprint when he thought it was
the right moment and—far harder—to risk going out of stock rather
than reprinting when he felt that the sales curve was descending. The
latter strategy drove the Mansfields wild with rage, and they called at
every hour of the day and night, threatening, cursing, begging, and demanding for more printings. The book was number one on the *Times*
list, they saw it running out of the stores, and the possibility that we
might run out of books petrified them. But Dick, a cooler player by far,
could sense that sales had peaked and also understood that there were
plenty of books in the pipeline, even if they were invisible to the Mansfields or to S&S's own sales department. There were books at the jobbers, books in trucks and in transit all over the United States, and
cartons of books in the storerooms of bookstores that could be moved
to stores where the demand was stronger. Dick was determined not to
give back the profit S&S had made by ending up with a warehouse full
of returns or, worse still, of overprinted books.

When the Mansfields complained bitterly to Shimkin, Dick still refused to give in, with the dual result that we had very nearly a "clean
sale" of *The Love Machine* and that the Mansfields never forgave him.
"If I could say no to Jackie and Irving, I could say no to anyone," he
said later, summing up a crucial learning experience, but what in fact
mattered even more was that Dick gained absolute faith in his own ability and the sense that he could control the process, as well as the loyalty

of everybody at S&S who had been involved. He always argued that it was better to be lucky than smart, but for the moment he was lucky *and* smart—a hard combination to beat.

We had taken S&S from the shame and ignominy of defeat to a dazzling position of success. We were suddenly a hot house, with the number-one best-selling novel and, simultaneously, the number-one best-selling nonfiction book, *The Last Battle,* Cornelius Ryan's account of the fall of Berlin in 1945. Many of the agents who only a few months previously had been doubtful about sending us manuscripts at all were now on the telephone offering us their major clients.

It was a curious time. In keeping with his familiar techniques of personnel management, Shimkin had not as yet rewarded us in any significant way for bringing S&S back from the brink. Apparently having failed to learn from Bob's departure, he seemed to feel that the excitement of working long days and nights was all the reward we needed and would serve as an incentive to work harder still. In a sense, of course, he was right. Dick often said (though not to Shimkin) that he would have paid for the privilege of working at S&S in those days, and it was not much of an exaggeration. To be in one's mid-thirties and suddenly successful is heady stuff—there is probably no other period in life when success means as much or when it is so much fun, before one's lifestyle makes success mandatory, before one gets old enough to feel the hot breath of younger competitors, before the price of all those long hours and easy temptations has to be paid in failed marriages and broken promises. All that was still ahead, and in the meantime, for one glorious moment, we had grabbed the brass ring. Everything we did seemed to turn to gold, and if we did not have the big salaries or stock options or bonuses that were later to assume such importance (life expands inevitably to absorb income, however high), we were working hard, the office was full of pretty girls (at a time in which it was not yet a provocation to use the phrase), and every moment of the day seemed exciting and full of promise.

With what little could be pried from Shimkin in the form of raises, the Snyders moved to a large apartment on Central Park West, while Casey and I moved to an apartment near Sutton Place. Between the hours and the temptations of the workplace, the Snyders' marriage was beginning to unravel, and, though it was not immediately as apparent, so was mine. At this long distance it is hard to assign blame—and hardly necessary—but like so many of our contemporaries we were paying for a whole slew of mistakes: of marrying too young, of giving more thought to work than to marriage, of sowing wild oats once one was married rather than before, of being perhaps the last generation to look at marriage in the old, conventional way. It had not dawned on any of us as yet that this was an arrangement that guaranteed that the woman felt stifled, while the man felt he was being taken advantage of, and that offered the maximum opportunity to both for resentment and infidelity.

IN THE meantime, there was no sitting on our laurels, such as they were. The main disadvantage of success is that it has to be repeated. I had the good fortune to have inherited from Bob the English writer R. F. Delderfield, whose enormous multigenerational family sagas, set for the most part in the English countryside, suddenly acquired great popularity in the United States. This started a vogue that lasted for more than a decade for huge novels in the Trollopian mode, usually wearing on their dust jackets wraparound paintings in full color of the English countryside, with a pair of riders cantering along a country lane on the front. God only knows why Bob had not taken Delderfield with him to Knopf—perhaps, for once, he had merely guessed wrong and underrated the potential of this hitherto obscure writer, who seemed able to dash off a thousand-page novel almost overnight and whose productivity was alarming. In addition to other works of his, we published *The Green Gauntlet* with enormous success—a perfect example of being lucky rather than smart, since nobody had predicted that the book would sell—and went on to do *God Is an Englishman,* which established Delderfield as such a major best-selling novelist that it was thought necessary for me to go to England to meet him, lest he decide to follow Bob to Knopf now that he had vaulted onto the best-seller lists. R. F. Delderfield (Ronnie, as he was known to those close to him) lived outside Sidmouth, a small English seaside resort between Torquay and Lyme Regis, and indicated that he would be delighted to see me.

I flew to London, rented a car, drove down to Sidmouth and checked into the Hotel Victoria Regina, a vast red-brown nineteenth-century brick structure that combined the potted-palm grandeur of the late Victorian age—it actually had an all-girl string orchestra playing in the palm court at lunchtime—with the pervasive odor of furniture polish, mildew, and Brussels sprouts peculiar to English provincial hotel keeping. The empty promenade and the shingled beach on this gray afternoon in late October were windswept and wet with rain, even the seagulls huddled miserably for cover beneath the empty band shell on the pier. Through rain-lashed plate-glass windows I could see the English Channel busily demonstrating why Napoleon and Hitler had hesitated to cross it—slate-gray swells several feet high, crowned with plumes of wind-driven white sea spray, came pounding in one after another to crash on the rocks and shingles of the shoreline. This was familiar country to me. Not far from here was the school to which I was evacuated at the beginning of the war, when it had been assumed that London would be reduced to rubble overnight by the Luftwaffe. As it turned out, my school was one of the first places in England the Germans bombed, and I can still remember the excitement of watching the bombs fall one by one onto the beach, sending up plumes of sand, until the last one blew up the school's brick gardener's shed with a satisfying bang. During my national service, I had taken the same road to go back and forth to London on weekends from my training camp at Bodmin, riding the motorcycle my Aunt Alexa had bought me over my father's strong objections.

Having been invited for tea, I arrived at the Delderfields' cottage just before four in the afternoon and was greeted by Mrs. Delderfield, who led me into the sitting room, where we sat on either side of the much-needed fire. The cottage was just what I had imagined the home of the author of *The Green Gauntlet* would be like: low, timbered ceilings, mullioned windows, dim, old, chintz-covered, cozy furniture, dogs and cats everywhere, a grandfather clock ticking away, the sound of a kettle boiling in the kitchen. May Delderfield was a bulky woman wearing a purple cardigan that she appeared to have knitted herself, who spoke with a gentle North Country accent, entirely unaffected by her husband's success. Ronnie, it appeared, was still working in his study but would be out promptly at four. The grandfather clock whirred and groaned, chimed four times, and on the fourth ring Delderfield appeared, rubbing his hands jovially, to greet me. He was a big man, close to six feet tall, and broad with it, with the build and the hands of a manual laborer. He had a bluff, honest countryman's face, red cheeked and contented, and an engaging shyness, as if he still couldn't believe his good fortune. Clad in a heavy sweater and corduroys, he sat down in an armchair and lit his pipe, while May bustled after tea. Delderfield apologized for keeping me waiting, but he always worked until four on the dot, he said. He believed it was important to treat writing like any other job and put in a good day's work. He was particularly happy to see me here today, he went on, because it was something of a red-letter day. In what way? I asked. Delderfield beamed. At exactly three o'clock this afternoon, he said, he had finished his new novel. I congratulated him as May poured tea and passed around plates of biscuits and cake. I nerved myself to ask, If Delderfield had finished a new novel at three, what had he been doing from three to four? Ah, Delderfield said, just what he always did. As soon as he ripped the last page of the novel out of his typewriter, he put a fresh piece of paper in, typed page one, chapter one, and started a new novel. Time and tide, he said, in his soft countryman's voice, waited on no man.

Dick, sending me off to England, had given me strict instructions that I was to win Delderfield over, heart and mind. Whatever he wanted, I should do. He was not to even *think* about Bob Gottlieb from now on. After dinner at my hotel, as we sat over our port and cigars, Ronnie, as I now called him, had asked if I would like to join him in the morning. Sure, I said, imagining a brisk walk over the downs, followed by an English country breakfast. But not at all. It turned out that Ronnie began every day with a swim in the sea, winter or summer, rain or shine. It was to that which he attributed his ruddy good health and his ability to write ten thousand words a day. Remembering Dick's words, I agreed to join him and found myself at dawn clad in borrowed swim trunks, stepping gingerly into the same slate-gray sea that I had seen yesterday from the hotel. Viewed close-up, it was even more uninviting. Ronnie, who had driven down in his new Jaguar, the first fruit of his new success, accompanied by a black Labrador, took off his dressing gown, breathed deeply a few times ("Every deep breath is a penny in the bank of health!"), and strode slowly, majestically, and without hesitation into the water. The Labrador, I noticed, was too smart to follow him.

I knew there was no earthly way I could get into that water slowly—the only way was to plunge in as quickly as possible. I took a deep breath, closed my eyes, and ran as fast as I could on the slippery shingle—there was a thin coating of ice on the larger stones—then, as I felt the water come up to my knees, I dived headfirst. I thought for a moment that the water was so cold that I had been knocked out—and, indeed, it *was* cold, cold enough for me to remember that pilots who parachuted into the Channel during the Battle of Britain often died of hypothermia before they were picked up by rescue boats. The reason that I had been knocked out, however, was that the shingle at Sidmouth extends a good way out to sea. I had supposed that the water was getting deeper when I plunged in, but instead I had landed headfirst on the rocks. Fortunately, I was floating, but I was quite unable to move. Not far from me, as my vision came back into focus again, I could see Ronnie sporting about in the freezing water like a whale, his breath forming clouds of vapor. He waved at me cheerfully. "Grand, isn't it?" he called out. By now my teeth were chattering, my fingernails had turned an ugly purple color, and I could feel a warm trickle running down my forehead that was surely blood. I gave a hoarse bellow, and Ronnie swam over with a stately breaststroke to investigate. "Bloody 'ell!" he said, as he caught a closer look at me, and hauled me ashore. In a moment, he had me wrapped in his dressing gown, and before long I was back at the cottage, drinking tea with rum. Whether it was from the guilt of having nearly killed me or because we became, in fact, really good friends, Ronnie Delderfield remained an S&S author until his death, many years and many thousands of pages later.

When I told Dick the story on my return, he was delighted. For a long time afterward he told it himself, as an example of just how far an editor ought to go to keep an author happy. He always added at the end, "They say Bobby Gottlieb's a great editor, but let me tell you *this:* he doesn't have the balls to go swimming in the English Channel at dawn, the way Korda did."

PERHAPS AS a reward for service above and beyond the call of duty in England, Dick shortly afterward encouraged me to go to Los Angeles, partly to mend fences with Irving Wallace, Harold Robbins, and the Durants, partly in the belief, common to all those who live on the East Coast, that California is full of interesting new writers who don't have a New York agent. In those days, before the advent of the chain stores, I considered it part of my job to visit local bookstores and schmooze with the owners, a breed only slightly more pessimistic than dirt farmers, who blamed the publishers for most of their misfortunes, despite having the only product that can be returned unsold months, even years, after they have received it and for full credit. Given this, it has always been hard to understand how it is possible to *lose* money selling books, but most booksellers skated on the thin edge of bankruptcy. The visit of a book publisher always brought out the gloomiest side of them— here, after all, was, in their eyes, the person responsible for all their woes—so I usually approached any bookstore with a sinking heart. I usually asked if anything was selling, in the hope of at least hearing *something* cheerful, and this time, from bookstore to bookstore throughout Beverly Hills and Brentwood, the surprising answer was that something was indeed selling like crazy. Needless to say, it wasn't an S&S book, nor a book from any of the major East Coast publishers that had brought a ray of sunshine to the lives of the booksellers of Southern California— it was a paperback from the University of California Press, and it was selling so fast that they couldn't keep it in stock. Intrigued, I tried to buy a copy, but the booksellers were not exaggerating for once: There were none available. In the end, I managed to borrow a well-thumbed copy from one of the clerks at the Pickwick Book Store on Sunset Boulevard and took it back to the Beverly Hills Hotel, where I read it in one gulp, with absolute fascination.

The book was *The Teachings of Don Juan* by a UCLA professor of anthropology named Dr. Carlos Castaneda, and it purported to tell of his initiation into a peyote cult by a Yaqui shaman named Don Juan. In the drug-obsessed culture of the late sixties and early seventies, it was hardly surprising that Castaneda's doctoral thesis should have broken out of the academic world to become a local best-seller, though it was very possibly the first (and last) doctoral thesis in history to do so.

In later years, when Castaneda had become a kind of guru to a whole generation of college kids and his books had sold in the millions of copies, he was to take on a kind of mystic significance—indeed, when *Time* did a cover piece on him (albeit with a smudged and unrecognizable portrait of him, since he refused to be photographed or drawn), they portrayed him, perhaps inadvertently, as a mystery man and tried in vain to pin down his exact identity, as if it mattered. By that time, there were false Castanedas appearing on campuses all over the country, like false czars in Russia, and Castaneda was being sighted in all sorts of improbable places by people who swore that he was tall or blue-eyed or a kind of hippie god, with long hair and fringed clothing. Nobody laughed harder at this deification than Castaneda himself— Carlitos, as he often referred to himself slyly, as if he were the modern equivalent of the sorcerer's apprentice, which was not, in fact, too far from the truth and which explained a great deal of the literary appeal of his early books. On one level, at least, they formed a kind of bildungsroman in which Don Juan played the cunning sorcerer-teacher and Carlitos the bumbling, naive, and eternally hopeful apprentice. There was a side to Castaneda's work that appealed to the same needs in young people as J. R. R. Tolkien's *The Lord of the Rings* and T. H. White's *The Sword in the Stone*. The elements were all there: adventure, sorcery, the hard path to knowledge on which a young man risks everything to learn wisdom from his teacher. Castaneda was a kind of real-life hobbit, following the path laid down by the mysterious sorcerer Gandalf, or, in another context, the young Arthur seeking the wisdom of Merlin. Perhaps without knowing what he was doing, Castaneda had touched upon a surefire theme for a best-seller, even without the peyote lore, which was to give his work an extra allure of the forbidden and dangerous.

That Castaneda was a real person and not, as some suspected, a literary invention was apparent the next morning, when I called the university and was connected directly to his office. The voice that greeted me was rich, modulated, and had a slight Hispanic accent. I expressed my enthusiasm for his book and my desire to meet him. He chuckled. "I would be happy to," he said, "but first you ought to talk to my agent. You see, I am a *pushover,* but *he* is really fierce and mean, so I have to be careful not to anger him." I asked who his agent was. To my surprise, it was Ned Brown, whom I knew. Brown was a diminutive man with a choleric red complexion and a white mustache who had modeled himself somewhat on Irving Lazar. No spring chicken himself, Brown had been an agent for decades and was one of the few in Los Angeles who handled book writers, as opposed to screenwriters. He was Jackie Collins's agent at the time, and the fact that Castaneda had somehow found his way to Ned Brown seemed an indication that he was not as unworldly as his book made him out to be.

I contacted Brown immediately, who told me that his desk was piled sky-high with offers, but if I wanted to meet with his author, it was OK with him. He had already talked to Castaneda (who was either quick on the phone or possessed Don Juan's telepathic powers), and I was to wait in the parking lot of my hotel at eight tonight. How would I recognize Castaneda? I asked. Brown gave a mirthless laugh. "Don't worry," he said. "He'll recognize *you.*"

At the appointed time, I stood in the parking lot, scanning the people in arriving cars for anyone possibly resembling Castaneda. Most of the cars were limos, disgorging plump, middle-aged men escorting young starlets—hardly Castaneda's style, I guessed. A neat Volvo pulled up in front of me, and the driver waved me in. He was a robust, broad-chested, muscular man, with a swarthy complexion, dark eyes, black, curly hair cut short, and a grin as merry as Friar Tuck's, displaying perfect teeth. I got in, and we shook hands. He had a firm handshake. The hands, I noticed, were broad, strong, with blunt fingers, although the clothes proclaimed him to be an academic: a light brown tweed jacket, a neat shirt and tie, tan trousers, well-polished loafers. I asked him how he had recognized me. He laughed. "I'm a sorcerer," he said mischievously. "How could I miss you?" He turned down Sunset Boulevard. "Of course, it didn't hurt that Ned described you to me."

I had seldom, if ever, liked anybody so much so quickly—a feeling that remains undiminished after more than twenty-five years. It wasn't so much what Castaneda had to say as his presence—a kind of charm that was partly subtle intelligence, partly a real affection for people, and partly a kind of innocence, not of the naive kind but of the kind one likes to suppose saints, holy men, prophets, and gurus have. Castaneda's spirit was definitely Rabelaisian and ribald, and he had a wicked sense of humor, but nevertheless he gave off in some way the authentic, potent whiff of otherworldly power, to such a degree that I have never doubted for a moment the truth of his stories about Don Juan or of the miracles he says he witnessed and, later, participated in.

Something of this was borne out by his choice of a restaurant, a small, elegant steak house off Santa Monica. I had vaguely supposed that he might be a vegetarian, but he ordered rack of lamb and, when it arrived, ate it with gusto. There was, in fact, nothing at all of the vegan, sandal-wearing, ascetic, California crank about him. That his mind was on this world as opposed to the next was evident from the glint in his eyes whenever an attractive woman entered the room. Celibacy, it was clear, was not part of his belief system, nor was he opposed to drink, for he ordered wine with a discriminating judgment and drank it with obvious pleasure. Smoking, however, was against his principles, for reasons of health and wind—the sorcerous path, he made it clear, called for *physical* strength. It was not just the mind that had to be trained but the body.

Carlos, as I was already calling him, was not only a good talker in a town where good talkers are a dime a dozen, but, far rarer, a good listener. He transformed listening into a physical act, his dark eyes fixed on me, his mobile, expressive face showing, like a good actor's, a combination of attention, sympathy, and warm amusement. Chunky and solid as he was—he was no beauty—Castaneda had an actor's physical grace and an exact sense of timing, together with the ability to convey, by small subtle gestures and changes of expression, a whole range of emotion. I wondered if he had ever actually *been* an actor, but he laughed and denied it. Since, however, everything he said about his early years was open to dispute and he often contradicted himself, I was not convinced. But then, the truth is that all successful shamans and holy men are performers, and none more so than Don Juan, who combined the gifts of a stage magician with a great actor's gift for the dramatic moment. Perhaps Castaneda had acted on stage at school, in Brazil, or Argentina, or wherever it was that he had grown up (a matter that was never altogether clear), but his natural gift for acting would have made him a successful student at the Actors Studio. Nevertheless, I believed every word of his book then and still do. Behind the sly tricks—the Garbo-like seclusion, the deliberate obfuscation of his biography, his delight in leaving false clues to confuse journalists—Carlos Castaneda was the real thing. More real, in fact, then even his most devoted readers supposed him to be, for he had a kind of earthy, peasant common sense that is sometimes missing from the bumbling and innocent academic whom he describes in his books and at whose embarrassing antics he often laughed.

He ate with a certain delicacy—there were many signs that Castaneda had been brought up with a considerable degree of gentility—but great determination. What did I think of the book, he asked, between mouthfuls. I was bowled over by it, I said. At one level I thought it could be read as a straightforward adventure story, in the doughty Lawrence of Arabia tradition—city boy goes to the desert and learns how to survive there; at another, it was an anthropological classic, like Colin M. Turnbull's *The Forest People*. Turnbull, who was to become one of the few orthodox anthropologists who was an enthusiastic supporter of Castaneda's work, portrayed himself similarly as a fool among the Pygmies of the Iruti. Some readers were certain to see Castaneda's book as a how-to manual for hallucinogenic drugs, which at the time more or less guaranteed the book considerable success, but oddly enough I saw it as containing many of the elements of Machiavelli's *The Prince*, without, of course, the political context. What Don Juan was proposing, it seemed to me, constituted a way of looking at the world objectively, of breaking life down into acts—big and small, important or unimportant—each one of which had to be performed as well as one possibly could. Carlos nodded, beaming. "*Impeccably!*" he said. "Everything you do has to be impeccable." (It was one of his favorite words, as I was to discover.) His expression was wry and self-mocking. "It isn't easy," he said. "Half-assed doesn't count." He paused. "There is an impeccable way of doing everything," he said. He popped a piece of lamb into his mouth, with evident satisfaction, chewing powerfully. "Even eating lamb."

So it's a code of conduct? I asked. Carlos nodded thoughtfully. It could be. Yes, perhaps. You had to submit to discipline—that was what the kids who came to his lectures didn't get, of course. "They thought the book was about freedom, about doing whatever the hell you wanted, about smoking *pot*!" He laughed. But this was a mistake, he went on. Drugs were an initiation, a way of going deeper, no fun at all. Above all, they were part of a way of looking at the world and a way of ordering one's life. A code of conduct, yes, that was very good. He finished his lamb, and we ordered coffee. He drank his sweet and black—caffeine did not seem to cause him problems. He slept, he said, like a baby. Don Juan was firm on such matters. There was a time for sleeping, and you slept. There was a time for waking up, and you woke up. No complaints, no whining, no saying "I can't sleep" or "I'm so tired, I don't want to get up." Don Juan, he said confidentially, was a hard taskmaster. Much worse than the nuns in school.

How had he come to pick Ned Brown as his agent? I asked. "Don Juan found him for me," he said, laughing hard. "He told me to pick the meanest little man I could find, and I did." He paid the bill, and we stepped outside into the warm night. I told him I would walk back to the hotel, and he nodded approvingly. Carlos believed in walking. The body had to be healthy or what use was the mind? Besides, Don Juan always walked, straight across the desert, moving so fast that it was hard to keep up with him, never getting lost. Carlos breathed deeply. "He told me you would come too," he said, shaking my hand. " 'Somebody will come along who's interested in power,' he told me. You'll see."

"*Am* I interested in power?" I asked.

He gave me a crushing hug; then, as he tipped the parking attendant and stepped into his car, he smiled at me and said, "Do bears shit in the woods?" and was gone.

. . .

THE NEXT morning, I called Dick and told him I wanted to buy the rights from University of California Press for the doctoral thesis of a UCLA professor of anthropology. Dick grumbled a bit, but that was merely his way. By now, we had learned to trust each other's instincts. He always backed my hunches, even when he thought I was crazy, and never, ever second-guessed me. "Anybody in this business who is right more than fifty percent of the time is a genius" was one of his favorite sayings. The truth was that for a man who boasted about being "a numbers guy," Dick was in fact just the opposite. When it came to buying books, he had no patience with numbers, which he knew better than anyone could be skewed to prove anything. If you prepared a careful financial analysis for him on a book you wanted to buy, he was likely to glance at it, crumple it up, toss it in his wastepaper basket, lean back in his swivel chair, and say, "Now tell me why you want to buy the fucking thing." Dick enjoyed a daring gamble and had no respect for people who weren't willing to take a plunge on instinct. "Go with your gut," he liked to say, and, unlike most people, he believed it. If I wanted to buy some professor's doctoral thesis, it was OK with him.

I told him why, as quickly as I could. I could see him in my mind's eye, feet on his desk, leaning as far back as his chair would tilt, the way he always did when he wanted to think. "Anthropology's a good category," he said at last. "And all the kids are into drugs and Indians these days. Is anybody else after it?" I told him that Ned Brown had claimed his desk was piled high with offers, but that even if this was true, I was the only publisher who had actually met Castaneda. "Brown is probably lying," Dick said, "but you never know. Find out what he wants and give it to him. No point in nickel-and-diming him." He paused. "Don't come back without it," he said gruffly, his usual way of wishing me good luck, and hung up.

I called Ned Brown and after a spirited round of bargaining—Don Juan's recommendation had been spot on, for Ned was not only mean but tenacious, like one of those small terriers with big jaws that can hang on for dear life—I ended up owning the hardcover rights to Castaneda's book for about twice what I had wanted to pay. I returned a day or two later to New York to try to convince a skeptical sales force that we should put a major effort behind it.

Fortunately for me, Dick did not believe in democracy. His view was that the sales department existed to sell the books they were given, and he was not interested in opinions from the floor at sales conferences. When, on rare occasions, the sales director or one of the reps offered an opinion about the merits of a book, he was liable to snap, "Are you an editor? No. Just sell the goddamn thing." In this case, his confidence in my judgment (or, more important, in his judgment of me) was well justified. Our edition of *The Teachings of Don Juan*, despite a certain skepticism at S&S, pole-vaulted onto the best-seller list, and for the next ten years, Castaneda, in book after book, became a staple in our lives, one of the props on which the success of the new, post-Gottlieb S&S rested.

As the years went by, Carlos's view of sorcery became darker and more complex, particularly after he finished his apprenticeship and became a full-fledged sorcerer himself, but he remained, personally, as cheerful as ever, and we became close friends. He had an uncanny knack for guessing when I was in trouble or needed help, and at such moments called from a telephone booth in Flagstaff or, sometimes, downstairs in the lobby, "Michael! It's Carlos! Are you feeling *powerful* today?" His voice was enough to cheer me up, even at the worst of times, and did, indeed, have the effect of making me feel more powerful, or in control of events, so I had no doubts about Carlos's sorcerous abilities. Many years later, when a friend of mine from New Mexico, Rod Barker, insisted on taking a set of galleys of his first book up to Shiprock, at the heart of the Navajo reservation, "The Big Rez," and having a medicine man cast a spell over them with different colors of pollen, I was not surprised when the book was greeted with good reviews. Carlos had taught me, if nothing else, the importance of getting on the good side of the spirit world.

In the material world—what with Jacqueline Susann, Ronnie Delderfield, and Carlos Castaneda—we had made enough of a recovery for Shimkin, however ungenerous and suspicious his nature, to reward Dick by giving him, at last, firm and complete authority over S&S. He swiftly set about reconstructing it in his own image. Schwed found himself shorn of authority, Dick's office was enlarged and glamorized, and the long hunt for the right combination of tough, vigorous, ambitious, well-connected editors, which was to consume the next twenty-five years of Dick's publishing career and give S&S a reputation as a kind of roller-coaster ride for senior editors, began. Dick wanted an all-star team, and he was willing to pay for it—in salary, perks, inflated titles, and liberal expense accounts—but not everybody understood that he expected them not only to produce but to stand up to him. Person after person came to S&S, introduced as "a miracle worker," only to fail Dick's intimidating psychological obstacle course. Most of them left looking back on S&S as the worst experience of their professional career. Some were so shaken by the experience that they left publishing altogether. At other houses, editors were treated with respect. At S&S they were flung into the trenches from the first day, expected not only to acquire books at a tremendous rate but to hold their own vigorously against Dick's criticism and his demand of perfectionism.

It was not so much a question of Dick's bark being worse than his bite—his bark was certainly menacing, but he could bite fiercely, too—as it was of dealing with his naturally combative nature. He expected people to put up a fight and relished it when they did; at the slightest sign of fear or timidity, he bored in relentlessly, seeking the weak, vulnerable spot, going instinctively for the soft underbelly. What nobody understood is that he had an essentially Darwinian view of the world: People ought to fight for what they wanted or believed in and fight hard. Those who fought back for what they wanted to do gained his respect; those who didn't, he lost interest in.

Nobody in the industry would have put S&S high on the list of places that were fun to work at, but the odd thing was that those of us who made the grade were happy and wouldn't have wanted to work anywhere else. Like the Marines, people at S&S were proud of themselves for working under conditions that elsewhere were thought barbarously harsh. As one graduate of this trial by terror said, "If you can survive this, you can survive anything."

Dick worked harder and longer than anybody, setting the pace by example. Those who thrived did so because they gave 100 percent to the job and cared about doing things right; those who failed failed because it was a tough, unforgiving environment, very unlike the "loved ones" atmosphere of S&S under Bob Gottlieb, when Bob had played the indulgent and wise papa bear to an adoring circle of acolytes that shared his views and lived for his praise. The reward for the members of Dick's inner circle was to have passed the test.

. . .

SINCE SCHWED was still doing his London trip, largely as a reward for having acquiesced to Dick's taking his place without a fight, and since I was still unwilling to sit around waiting for agents to send me manuscripts, I devoted myself for a while to traveling around the United States in search of books. Next on my agenda was Texas, a state I had always liked, ever since visiting my mother in Dallas, whence she had moved from Chicago when my stepfather took over one of the major hotels there. I was at a stage of my marriage when travel seemed an interesting alternative to staying at home, and I developed a passion for the West. During the time I spent in Hollywood in the 1940s, my father, partly out of guilt at being absent so often, partly to escape from domestic difficulties, had taken me to the desert, to the Grand Canyon, to Yosemite, and to ski at what were then pretty backwoodsy and primitive ski resorts in the Rockies, hardly more than miners' camps in the early stages of becoming tourist attractions. I learned how to ride, and horses became a part of my life. Even in New York City, I managed to ride as often as I could and on my own horse. I became the only member of the New York book-publishing community to be a paid-up member of the Rodeo Cowboy Association (whose permanent secretary, I was later to discover when I met him on a trip to Montana, had been the young boy for whom Hugh Lofting wrote *Dr. Dolittle*) and subscribed to their newspaper. I joined the American Quarterhorse Association and even rode in the rodeo in Madison Square Garden, cantering into the arena on a chunky palomino in the opening parade behind Monty Montana and his Wonder Horse Rex. I carried, prophetically, for I was to one day build a house there, the state flag of New Mexico.

I was thus understandably interested when an agent I knew only slightly, Dorothea Oppenheimer, called to tell me about a new novel by a young writer from Texas. Larry McMurtry, she explained, had published three novels, two of which had been made into very successful motion pictures, *Hud* and *The Last Picture Show,* which was gratifying in its own way, of course, but had not led to any real sales of his books.

In a world of agents who make more money and get more publicity than their clients, Dorothea Oppenheimer was perhaps the last of a dying breed. That she was an Olympic-level kvetch cannot be denied, but beneath all that was a woman endowed with extraordinary taste, courage, humor in the face of adversity, and loyalty. She was completely devoted to her clients' interests, but once she knew that you shared her enthusiasm for an author's work, she was fair and never asked for the impossible. Shy, retiring, and always apologetic for not asking more for her clients, Dorothea shied away from conflict, but she more than made up for that by sheer stubbornness and patience. In one of those odd twists of fate that are so common in publishing, Dorothea had chosen Irving Lazar, of all people, to handle her movie rights (most East Coast authors' agents find it expedient to use a West Coast agent to sell movie rights for them), and Lazar criticized her endlessly for not being tough enough. Dorothea had few clients, but they were all real writers. "She's sitting on a gold mine, but she doesn't know what to do with it," Lazar said about her, implying that he did, which only made her more nervous. Most people complained that Dorothea drove them crazy; she drove *me* crazy, too—the mere sound of her voice was enough to transform me into Lazar, shouting, "You don't know what you're *talking* about!" to her over the telephone, while she sniffled gently, but I liked and respected her, and at the end of every conversation, we always made up and reverted to friendly banter again. If Dorothea said something was good, it was worth taking seriously, which was more than you could say for Lazar.

I quickly read McMurtry's first novel, *Horseman, Pass By* (the novel on which *Hud* had been based), *Leaving Cheyenne*, and *The Last Picture Show*. Though in later years I sometimes jokingly referred to McMurtry as "the Flaubert of the Plains," he was already an unusual phenomenon in American writing. He came out of the gate (to use rodeo terminology) with a remarkable ability to write about women and an absolutely sure eye for the bleak landscape of small-town Texas and the isolated ranches of the Panhandle, as well as the history of the West. You can count on the fingers of one hand (and still have a lot of fingers left over) the number of male American novelists who can create believable, sympathetic women characters—or who really *like* women, for that matter. In most of American fiction, the women are cardboard cutouts, not living human beings, reflecting the prejudices or the fears of the author. You can read the whole of Hemingway's work without finding a single really convincing woman character or the slightest hint that the author knew or cared what made women tick, and much the same can be said of every other male American fiction writer from Melville to Mailer. McMurtry, it was apparent, liked and understood women and wrote about them sympathetically and intelligently. He came with a perfectly developed sense of place, which gave all his fiction a deep, solid bedrock, but he was able to put women into that landscape as no other Western writer ever has, and he did it in his very first novel with the sure touch of a mature artist.

Unfortunately, as Dorothea Oppenheimer made clear, East Coast reviewers just didn't get McMurtry. It was, she thought, a question of urban prejudice—they simply couldn't take seriously a novelist who had been born in Archer City, Texas, was raised as a cowhand, and wrote about life in Texas. There was some truth to this, I thought. Most reviewers were urban or had come to New York City anxious to leave their rural or small-town upbringings as far behind them as possible. Not a few of the reviewers had come from places where there were cows, never wanted to see or hear of a cow again, and McMurtry's novels were full of cows. Besides, the prevailing tone of American fiction at the time was urban, Jewish, and Eastern—the West was seen, in the eyes of the literati, as "a colossal mistake" (to quote Freud's famous remark about America), a land given over to violence, deprived of culture, and essentially rednecked—a view that was not improved by the experience of having had Lyndon B. Johnson in the White House. McMurtry, Dorothea said, did not feel he had gotten a fair shake from the reviewers, nor did he think he was likely to. The fact that his books had been made into movies made the reviewers only that much less likely to take him seriously, of course—if there is one thing New York reviewers can't stand it's an author getting rich despite them. McMurtry's feelings on the matter were strong enough that he often wore a sweatshirt bearing a dismissive phrase often used about him by East Coast reviewers: "Minor Regional Novelist."

The reason why all this mattered was that McMurtry had just finished a huge novel (his earlier books had been quite slim), on quite a different scale from anything he had done before. It was called *The Country of the Horn* (cows again) and was the first (and perhaps still the only) big American novel with a rodeo background. McMurtry's present publisher had showed no enthusiasm for the book, and he was looking for a new home with an editor who not only understood what he was doing but might even take on the New York critics.

As it happened, I have never had the slightest respect for critics or any degree of interest in their opinions, despite my own sideline as a film critic. In most areas of artistic endeavor, film and theater, for instance, the major reviewers have at least some conception of and respect for popular taste and do not simply ignore anything that might appeal to it. Any theater reviewer of *The New York Times* who limited himself or herself only to off-Broadway productions of avant-garde plays and utterly ignored or automatically condemned anything with popular appeal, such as a big musical, or who judged a big musical by the standards of avant-garde theater, would be fired. Book reviewers for the *Times*— and, alas, not only the *Times*—however, get away with completely ignoring the vast majority of books that people actually buy and read, and on the rare occasions when they *do* review such books, they judge them by the literary standards of the esoteric books that nobody reads *except* critics. That the New York reviewers had not paid sufficient attention to McMurtry did not surprise or dismay me.

When I told Dorothea Oppenheimer this, she was in ecstasy. I must read McMurtry's new book immediately—she would get it over to me at once. I read it that night, and it was love at first sight. I found it difficult to conceive that any reader, even a *Times* reviewer, could dislike the heroine, Patsy Carpenter, around whose marriage to a young graduate student the whole book revolves. As for rodeo, here it was. If the American public wanted the *Moby-Dick* of rodeo, McMurtry had provided it. I called Dorothea the next morning and said I had to meet McMurtry.

She had been about to suggest that herself. McMurtry had developed something of a suspicion toward Eastern editors as well as Eastern book critics—toward anyone, in fact, who might think of him as a minor regional novelist—and a meeting might not be a bad idea, just to dispel any fears he might have that I was in this category. Would I fly down to Houston to see him?

I was eager to go. I called Snyder and explained what I was doing, which was fine with him. He liked action and would have been happy to have the entire editorial staff flying around the country in search of books. It was the sight of them sitting in their offices that provoked him.

I had arranged to meet McMurtry in the lobby of a downtown hotel, and it was only once I was there that it occurred to me that I hadn't the slightest idea what he looked like, nor, presumably, he me. The lobby was jammed with people, mostly tall, well-dressed Texans of a certain age with their equally tall wives. I could see nobody who resembled a minor regional novelist.

I paced the lobby until the crowd began to disperse—it was dinnertime—until there were only two people in it except for the staff; myself and a very tall, lean, serious-looking fellow, dressed in a sports jacket. He did not, at first glance, look like a Texan to me. He wore glasses and had a thick head of black hair, emphasizing his pallor. He was staring hard at me, which I thought was odd, since I had dressed, with Texas in mind, in jeans, my best pair of cowboy boots, handmade for me in El Paso with custom sharkskin bottoms and my initials in multicolored stitching, and the same pearl-colored Stetson I had worn in the Madison Square Garden rodeo. Instead of a tie, I wore a silver bolo of a cow's skull, which I had picked up in New Mexico. Eventually, the tall young man made his way over to me and coughed discreetly. "You wouldn't be Michael Korda," he asked, "would you?" I said I was, and we shook hands. "I was expecting somebody who looked a little different," he said warily.

I explained my interest in rodeo as we walked to his car. "Uh-huh," he said. He said "uh-huh" a lot, I was to discover, and it conveyed many meanings, from approval to outright disagreement, if one listened carefully. His accent identified him as northwest Texan (or southwest Oklahoman) to any amateur Henry Higgins, but he spoke in flawless, carefully articulated sentences, not at all those of a country boy, and didn't swear—a noticeable omission from his speech pattern, since most people at S&S laced even the most ordinary and innocent remarks with swear words. I did it myself, having fallen into the habit in the RAF, and those around Snyder did it because he did it, and also because, at least among the younger members of the staff, the Berkeley Free Speech Movement had won them the right. Now that the shock value of swearing had worn off, it was surprising—and pleasant—to note its absence. There was a grave, old-fashioned courtesy to McMurtry, which put me immediately at ease.

I told him how much I liked his work, especially the rodeo novel, although it turned out that his own interest in rodeo was rather less than mine. He had seen plenty of rodeo in his life, and he could take it or leave it alone. He did not share my enthusiasm for horses, either, having spent his full share of time on them as a teenage ranch hand for his father. So far as he was concerned, he had seen as much of horses as he ever wanted to. Still, we had a lot in common (our sons were the same age), and we got on well (so well that we are still close friends nearly thirty years and many books later), and I returned to New York as his publisher, carrying with me a carton of Diet Dr Pepper, to which McMurtry had converted me and which was at that time unobtainable in the Northeast.

My only reservation about *The Country of the Horn* had been its title. That was not the result of any prejudice about cows on my part—in fact, I had at first associated the title with the horn of plenty rather than with cattle—but simply because it didn't sound to me like a best-seller. McMurtry himself was not passionately attached to the title. When my wife suggested calling it *Movin' On,* a thought inspired by a recent country-western song, he was not exactly enthusiastic but acquiesced after the *g* had been reinserted. He seemed resigned to the fact that people always wanted to change the titles of his books. The movie people had insisted on changing *Horseman, Pass By* to *Hud,* on the grounds that the book's title made it sound like a Western, and now I was insisting on changing the title of *The Country of the Horn* to *Moving On,* on the grounds that our sales reps would like it better. McMurtry was willing to give us a sporting chance with the new title, but I could tell his heart wasn't in it, and looking back twenty-nine years later, I suspect he was right. *The Country of the Horn* had a certain dignity to it that *Moving On* lacked, although whether dignity would have made a difference is another story.

The problem, as I discovered the moment I was back in New York, was not the title, it was Patsy. This came as a surprise to me. I had expected to be told that there was too much rodeo in the book and maybe too many cows but not that there was too much Patsy. Every woman who read the book, however, complained that Patsy cried too much. Of course, Patsy had a lot to cry about—none of the men in her life was right for her—so it seemed to me perfectly natural that she should do so. It seemed that way to McMurtry too, who pointed out that most of the women he knew—and certainly all those on whom Patsy was based—cried pretty much all the time. There was certainly plenty for them to cry about in Texas, he pointed out, a place that was notoriously hard on both women and horses.

We had struck, it seemed, a basic difference between the East and the West, or at any rate between Texas and New York City, and there was nothing much we could do about it, since trying to stem the flow of Patsy's tears would have meant totally rewriting the novel, which McMurtry wasn't about to do, and I wasn't about to ask him to. As a kind of counterpunch, I had buttons made up to give away at the ABA convention along with an advance reading copy of the book that read "I'm a Patsy" (they probably should have read "I'm a Patsy for Patsy"). The booksellers wore them all right, but the ones that read the book came back to the stand to say how much they liked the book except for Patsy's crying. In the end, *Moving On* did OK—a lot better than McMurtry's previous books had—and was even taken by one of the major book clubs, but it wasn't the big blockbuster breakout book I had thought it would be. We had to wait fifteen years until *Lonesome Dove*, a book in which there are remarkably few tears, finally gave McMurtry the attention and reviews he had deserved right from the beginning. Still, we gave it our best shot in every possible way, which was more than you could say for his previous publisher, and to this day *Moving On* remains one of my favorite books.

COUNTRY MUSIC had been on my mind when I flew down to Houston to see McMurtry, in part because I had received in the mail a manuscript from *Atlanta Journal* columnist Paul Hemphill about the country-music business. Our sales rep in Georgia, a gentleman of the old school named J. Felton Covington, Jr., perhaps the most charming book salesman who has ever lived, had buttonholed me at a sales conference and made me promise on my mother's grave (though she is still very much alive) to read Hemphill's book myself. Since I not only liked Covington but had long since learned never to say no to a sales rep, I gave it my full attention.

If there was any subject less likely to cause enthusiasm at S&S than country music—except perhaps rodeo, cows, and crying women—I didn't know it. The point of the book was that country music was no longer a peculiarly Southern phenomenon and was going mainstream. This has certainly happened with a vengeance, but at that time it hadn't yet reached New York book-publishing circles, where if it was noticed at all it was regarded with disdain. The only person I could find who shared my enthusiasm for country music was a tall young woman named Julie D'Alton, at that time Schwed's assistant, who seemed to know the words to every country song. As it turned out, she was one of five similarly tall and beautiful sisters who could have, had they wished, formed a country group all of their own, though they were born and bred New Yorkers, educated at Convent of the Sacred Heart.

Encouraged by Julie's reaction to the manuscript, I called Hemphill in Atlanta and told him how much Julie and I liked his book and how hard it was going to be to sell it to anyone else at S&S. Even my own assistant, who was up on every aspect of the rock-and-roll scene, turned up her nose at the corniness of country music.

Hell, he could understand all that, Hemphill said, everybody up north still thought of it as hillbilly music, he knew that, but those who had doubts were just plain wrong, that was the long and short of it. Country music was sweeping the nation. Hemphill suggested that we ought to see what he was talking about firsthand. He asked us if we would like to join him on one leg of a bus trip he was making with Bill Anderson and the Poor Boys, a country group that was then fairly hot and beginning to acquire a certain reputation among country fans in the North.

This was an offer that was hard to resist, and it was another opportunity to wear my Stetson. Rationalizing this pleasure trip by saying that I couldn't edit the book without knowing more about the background from which the music came, we met Hemphill and the band in some godforsaken parking lot in New Jersey. Short of the moment when I had plunged into the bright lights of Madison Square Garden at a canter on a palomino while the band played "California, Here I Come" and thousands of kids twirled little blinking flashlights in the audience, nothing had struck me with such an instant rush as standing onstage behind the Poor Boys in whatever New Jersey town we were visiting.

When Hemphill suggested that we really ought to go to Nashville and see the Grand Ol' Opry before it moved out of its home in a former church, we flew down and joined him there. I had a whirlwind insider's tour of Nashville: Tootsie's Orchid Lounge on Broadway, the Recording Barn, in which the top country singers cut their records, and the odd experience of standing on the Opry stage next to the legendary bluegrass duo Flatt and Scruggs, and Ernest Tubbs, the grand old man of country music, while a chorus sang a Goo-Goo Candy Cluster commercial and fans fired off cameras with electronic flashes in the faces of the performers.

"It sounds like a joyride," Dick said, not without reason, when I got back, but eventually I was to end up publishing the memoirs of Tammy Wynette, Minnie Pearl, and Willie Nelson. It was just a question of going there, after all.

ALL THE same, I was all too familiar with the fact that *celui qui est absent a toujours tort*. I put away my Stetson for the time being and decided to stay put for a while. As it happened, fate was about to throw a celebrity of a very different kind in my path. "Celebrity publishing" was then in its infancy, and the era in which millions of dollars were spent by publishers to persuade major celebrities to put their name on an autobiography they hadn't written or even read and then go out and promote it was yet to come. "Lazarland" (since this kind of book was his specialty) was on the cusp of overwhelming publishers with what seemed at first like an easy way of buying books, since the book itself was in most cases the least important part of the equation. What the publisher paid for was the celebrity—the central, glittering attraction who got the big money. The next most important thing was the amount of money targeted for promotion and advertising. The person who got the least money, inevitably, was the writer—in most cases nobody except the editor ever expected to have to actually *read* the book. No better way to lose large amounts of money quickly in book publishing has ever been invented—you could publish hundreds, perhaps thousands of unsuccessful first novels, after all, for less than it costs to produce one celebrity autobiography—or pursued more zealously. It's not that publishers are stupid, nor even that they don't learn by experience—it's that people who don't much like reading books are always more interested in buying something that *doesn't* have to be read than in something like a novel that *does* (hence the ease with which agents sell books from a two-page outline instead of a whole manuscript).

The celebrity autobiography was well suited to the growing symbiosis between books and television. The critical question was no longer whether the book itself would be any good, but how many weeks the celebrity would tour for it and how many talk shows could be counted on to book him or her. It took a long time before it finally dawned on most publishers that the quality of the book did indeed matter and that not every celebrity was guaranteed to sell books. Even in the late nineties, publishers still made the same costly mistake of supposing that because, say, Whoopi Goldberg was a big star, people would necessarily buy her book. (Of course, in the beginning, the big amounts were in hundreds of thousands of dollars, not in millions, as they later were.) Some celebrities sold books; some didn't. It was a crapshoot, for high stakes, and the only person who never lost money doing it was Irving Lazar, who took home his commission of 10 percent and never looked back.

CHAPTER 21

*O*F COURSE, THERE are *celebrities* and CELEBRITIES. In our age, the biggest celebrities are movie stars, but even among movie stars there is a pecking order. I started off at the top, when in 1970 an agent called me to ask if I would be interested in publishing a book by Joan Crawford. If I was, she would like to meet me. We agreed upon a date for a drink at Crawford's apartment.

Of course I was not just interested—I was *fascinated*. It's not, mind you, that I was a fan of Joan Crawford's. "*Nourri dans le sérail, j'en connais les détours*"—having been brought up in the movie business, I'm inoculated against making a cult of any movie star, though if I *was* going to make a cult of any star, it would be Vivien Leigh or Catherine Deneuve, rather than Joan Crawford. Still, except for Lillian Gish, hardly anybody covered such a vast stretch of movie history, and very few people have been bigger stars for as many years. Besides, I had always been interested in Joan Crawford ever since my Auntie Merle told me, over her dinner table at the Malibu Colony, a story about Crawford. Having just announced her retirement, Crawford was coming out of a restaurant in Hollywood when a young girl ran up to her as she was getting into her limousine on Sunset Boulevard. "Oh, Miss Crawford," she cried out, holding out her autograph book, "you're my favorite star! Could I please have your autograph?"

Joan Crawford looked at her, her big eyes focused on the young girl's like those of a falcon about to swoop on its prey, and with an icy smile, in her deep, silky voice, she said: "Go away, little girl. I don't *need* you anymore."

As it turned out, Joan Crawford needed all the fans she could get, once she staged the first of her many comebacks, and by the time I met her she was no longer turning away fans in the street. She had made a kind of camp comeback in movies such as *The Best of Everything*, in which she played a corporate-executive equivalent of Mel Brooks's Nurse Diesel, then retired from the screen again but returned to achieve full-camp stardom in *What Ever Happened to Baby Jane?* In search of the kind of financial and emotional stability that had always eluded her, she had some years before married Alfred Steele, the swaggering CEO of Pepsi-Cola. For a time she gave a compelling and successful performance as a corporate wife and Pepsi spokeswoman, but this was cut short by Steele's death. The directors of Pepsi, whom she had supposed to be loyal to her late husband and fans of hers, turned out, to her surprise, to hate her guts and hardly even waited until Steele's body was cold before stripping her of her corporate perks and contesting the provisions Steele had made for her. Their behavior was to embitter Joan Crawford's last years, and her decision to do a book was an attempt to strike back by proving that she was still a star. It was not just a case of television appearances helping the sale of a book: The whole *purpose* of the book was to rack up television appearances so that every time the directors of Pepsi and their frumpy wives turned on the TV set, they would see Joan Crawford on the screen, telling *her* side of the story.

Joan Crawford had fallen on bad times since her days as the Queen of Pepsi-Cola. She was living in one of those featureless, postwar, modern apartment buildings made of white brick, like giant lavatories, in the East Sixties of Manhattan, near Bloomingdale's, with a bland lobby, low ceilings, and paper-thin walls bereft of moldings. She and Steele had spent most of their marriage living in the presidential suites of hotels, as he preached the Pepsi-Cola gospel around the world to anyone who would listen, from heads of state to the pope, so on Steele's sudden death she had been obliged to find a place to live in a hurry. Steele and Joan Crawford had made a dynamic team, which perhaps explains their success in the Soviet Union, where Pepsi-Cola became the first major American corporation to build its own plants, and where Steele also persuaded the Russians to let Pepsi-Cola become the exclusive distributor of Stolichnaya vodka in the United States.

Crawford's apartment was reached via a cramped elevator and a narrow, dark corridor, lit by recessed fluorescent lamps, that had rows of identical painted metal doors on each side. There was nothing to distinguish Joan Crawford's apartment from the other dozen or so on her floor. It had the same blank peephole, a little plastic plate bearing the apartment number, and a bell. A maid opened the door and ushered me into the living room. It wasn't at all what I would have expected of Joan Crawford. The walls were standard New York City landlord–issue white, there where white plastic venetian blinds on the windows instead of drapes and curtains, and the furniture seemed to have been salvaged from somebody's pool, that of the Beverly Hills Hotel, perhaps—lots of white-painted wrought iron with green plastic-covered cushions and white wicker. The tables were glass topped and so shiny that one hesitated to touch them for fear of leaving fingerprints. The familiar pink ashtrays with turquoise script actually *did* come from the Beverly Hills Hotel. I could imagine that Joan Crawford might have taken the ashtrays home with her, but I didn't see how she could have taken the *furniture*.

On the coffee table was a large ice bucket containing six bottles of Pepsi and a full bottle of Stolichnaya vodka—Joan Crawford apparently remained loyal to the Pepsi-Cola company, or perhaps to Steele's memory, despite everything. In each ashtray there was a full, carefully opened package of Pall Malls, with one cigarette sticking out exactly one inch, and a book of matches, folded back with one match sticking up. At various strategic locations, there were *un*opened packets of cigarettes and matchboxes, a reserve supply of Pepsi, and a generous supply of paper napkins. This, I was soon to discover, was only the tip of the iceberg when it came to Joan Crawford's need for order.

When she appeared, I was instantly won over, not only by the warmth of her greeting—most stars can pull that off when they need to—but by the fact that she was direct, cheerful, and very clearly a bundle of energy. She asked me what I wanted to drink, and I tactfully asked for vodka. She poured us two stiff ones and took the exposed cigarette from the nearest pack and lit it with the bent match.

The first thing she had to tell me was that she was not a prima donna, whatever anybody said. She had her faults, God knew, but she was a pro through and through. She had worked for the studios in the old days, when stars were expected to work their butts off and smile about it, and when you didn't say no to any demand the publicity department might make, however damned tired you were after getting up at five in the morning to be in makeup at six, and even if you were hungover, or sick, or suffering from the goddamn cramps. She just wanted me to know that S&S could count on her to go out and sell the book, that was number one. She had put Pepsi-Cola on the map all over the world, after all, so she understood a little bit about publicity. As for the book, I should know that she had never been one of those actresses who fought directors. She took direction and was grateful for it. She just didn't understand the new breed of actors and actresses, who went around looking like slobs and ignored their director on the set. Well, just look at Marilyn Monroe, for chrissake. In *her* day, Joan Crawford said with a snort of contempt, Marilyn would never have gotten through the door, however much she wiggled her ass and put out on the studio couches. Marilyn just hadn't been a professional, that was all, she had ignored directors, kept the whole cast waiting for hours because she was late, phoned in sick for every little sniffle. She, Joan, had told poor Marilyn, the director was God, that was all, and you did your best to do what he told you to—a strong director was your best friend. A lot of good it had done, sweet Jesus, in one ear and out the other.

I nodded. The feud between Marilyn Monroe and Joan Crawford had been no secret. Crawford had complained that she had been upstaged by Monroe's low-cut dress at some Hollywood function and remarked, rather too loudly, that *she* had tits too, but she didn't let them hang out over her plate for everybody to see. Monroe, who greatly admired Crawford, heard about it and was crushed, or pretended to be, and most people in Hollywood took Monroe's side, to Crawford's dismay. As for strong directors, I thought, if she wanted to think of me as the publishing equivalent, so much the better, though I guessed that Joan—for we were instantly on a first-name basis—would be something of a handful, in fact.

Joan exuded movie-star charisma, despite her age, which was unfathomable. The famous eyes had not lost a bit of their sultry, intimidating glare; the face, though weathered, was still glamorous; and her figure would have been the envy of most women thirty years her junior. She still had great legs and knew it, but the eyes were her strongest features, as they always had been, at once imperious and deeply sad, so that it was possible to be frightened of her and feel sorry for her at the same time. She was small, not nearly as tall as I had expected, but she made up for it in sheer dynamism. Even sitting, sipping her vodka, she was in motion, fingers drumming, feet tapping, like a thoroughbred in its stall. Eventually, as if she couldn't stand sitting for a moment longer, she stood up with the perfect grace and straight posture of the dancer she once had been and offered me a tour of the apartment.

I was not loath—this is, after all, an old form of Hollywood hospitality. The apartment, I instantly realized, was bigger than it had seemed to me at first, as if two adjoining apartments had been opened up into one. I admired Joan's spotless kitchenette, her narrow terrace, a gleaming but not particularly luxurious or glamorous bathroom, a smallish bedroom, pretty much filled by a big bed and a television set, with a window that looked out over brownstone rooftops toward Bloomingdale's. Joan flung open a walk-in closet to reveal row after row of shoes. Each shoe had a shoe tree inserted into it, and all the shoe trees matched and bore tiny labels that identified the shoes they were in. Above them hung several rows of coats, most of them in plastic zipper bags. There were, needless to say, no wire coat hangers to be seen.

We walked through Joan's dressing room into what must have been the living room of the next apartment. To my surprise, it contained countless pipe racks of clothes, arranged in neat rows. Each dress or suit was contained in a zippered transparent plastic bag, which was meticulously labeled. On the labels, Joan pointed out with pride, were recorded where she had bought the dress, the date and price of purchase, and all the significant occasions when she had worn it, together with the accessories that she had worn with it. There were hundreds—perhaps thousands—of dresses in the room, and more in what had been the bedroom of the next apartment. She had probably not worn some of them for decades. It was hard to work out her priorities. There was more room in the apartment for her clothes than for herself and she must have been paying a substantial amount of rent in order to house them. The walls were mostly bare, the furniture looked as if it belonged beside a pool, and the parquet floors were either bare or covered with cheap fiber matting. On the other hand, her hatboxes, each apparently specially made, took up enough room for a good-size family to live in.

We returned to the living room, having looked at every closet and storage space in the house, to talk about the book. What she wanted to do, she explained, was to give other women, perhaps less privileged than she, the benefit of her experience in managing a successful career and a busy family life. People admired her for her glamour and her energy, but they didn't see the hard work that went into looking good or appearing upbeat and cheerful however you were really feeling inside. The book would have beauty hints, tips on how to dress, advice on how to keep a husband happy and entertain his boss, all of it interspersed with anecdotes from Joan's own life.

I found it hard to see how the average woman was going to put Joan Crawford's helpful hints to use in her own life—they included the right way to serve caviar and how to train your maid to pack your clothes so they don't get wrinkled or crushed—but it is not in the nature of book publishers to harbor negative thoughts (the lifeblood of publishing is enthusiasm, after all, not caution), and in any case Joan, whatever her other talents, was a great saleswoman for her own cause. The great eyes

were mesmerizing, and even at her fairly advanced age she fairly radiated sex appeal. She was not then or ever an easy woman to say no to, as
countless people before me had discovered.

She envisioned — as most celebrities do—a book with a lot of pictures of herself, a strong can-do attitude, and a solid core of useful information, a book that would not only be useful but would give her
many faithful fans all over the world a glimpse of Joan Crawford's
world. "Your way of life?" I suggested, and her eyes went misty. That
was it, exactly, she said, clutching my hand so hard that I feared she
might actually break my fingers. Her book should be called *My Way of
Life*, that was exactly the title she had been looking for without knowing it, and I had produced it out of thin air. She could tell that we were
going to work well together and do great things. She was never wrong
about that kind of thing. Did I like caviar? she asked me. I admitted that
I liked it very much indeed, especially with vodka. She clapped her
hands together happily. She wanted to know what people *liked—really
liked*—then she would make sure they got it every time they visited her.
Mi casa, su casa was her motto—I should feel at home here, always.

I extricated my hand, finished my vodka, and went home a convert.
The very next day, I bought Joan's book, despite Dan Green's anguished prediction that she would be hell to tour.

Since Crawford's apartment was on my way home from work, I
took to dropping in from time to time to see how the book was going,
and, true to her word, there was always caviar for me to have with my
Stolichnaya. Every writer has his or her own method of working, of
course, but Joan's was singular and involved, as did much of her life, a
certain unreality. She dictated her ideas into a dictating machine, and the
tapes were then transcribed and rewritten by her ghostwriter and reappeared neatly typed up in a binder for Joan and me to go over. The only
problem was that Joan resolutely denied the existence of the writer and
insisted on treating every word of the typescript as if she had typed it
herself, improbable as this was, given the perfection of her fingernails.
This is not uncommon—lots of celebrities who want to have a book
hire a ghostwriter but won't admit to it—but Joan carried it to extremes.
Quite often, the ghost was *there,* in the apartment, typing away, while
Joan went on pretending that the apartment was empty apart from ourselves. While it's not unusual to conceal the existence of a writer from
the public (though I happen to think it's usually a mistake to hide the
fact), it's almost unknown to hide it from one's editor. When it comes

to their books, most authors have no secrets from their editor, who sees the manuscript, and very often the author, at its worst.

In fact, Joan's book was an even more remarkable exercise in denial than are most autobiographical works. A whole section, for example, was devoted to her experience as a mother—admittedly this was before her daughter Christina turned herself into the poster girl for abusive motherhood and elevated the humble wire coat hanger into a symbol of parental cruelty, but even then the stories about Joan Crawford's treatment of her adopted children were familiar. (Indeed, they had sometimes been used to make us movie brats of the forties mind our p's and q's.)

Joan, however, was rather proud of being a disciplinarian and boasted that she had made her children take a nap every day, even though they hated it as they grew older. Not many women noted with pride, as she did, that they made their children stand on a stool at the sink at the end of every day to "wash out their shoelaces and polish their little white shoes before putting them away." Needless to say, the little white shoelaces had to be removed from the little white shoes first, then washed until they were spotless, laid flat so they dried unwrinkled, and put back into the shoes when they were dry in exactly the right pattern—*not* crisscrossed. Seen as a task for, say, a tired six-year-old, this seemed to me to approach cruelty, but Joan felt that she was merely giving her children the benefit of her own harsh upbringing and that it would make stronger persons of them. The children were taught to ignore any weakness and be perfect at all times. Although Cathy had an allergy to horses, she was made to take regular riding lessons, with her eyes streaming and her face swollen. "I was strict when I thought it was necessary" was all Joan could be made to say on the subject. She saw herself as the perfect mother, and that was that.

Her view of children was perhaps best defined by the paintings in her bedroom: Margaret Keane portraits of children, sorrowful waifs with huge, sad, dark eyes that seemed to follow one around the room. Her choice in art was at once mundane and bizarre—enough so to have caused a famous scene when the director Jean Negulesco criticized her "lousy taste" in art before the entire cast of *The Best of Everything*, sending Joan into a rare burst of tears. Pride of place in Joan's living room was held by a large, three-quarter-length painting of herself wearing a clinging silver evening dress that left her shoulders bared and was cut so low in front that most of her breasts were revealed. It showed her, very oddly, with the face of a mature woman and the lush, nubile figure of a nineteen-year-old *Playboy* centerfold. Was this the way she saw herself? If so—and it certainly seemed to be, for she was determined to put the painting on the cover of the book—it was another piece of self-delusion, like her notion of herself as a good mother, offering tips on child rearing to other women, or her belief that she had brought the children up in an ordinary happy family, despite her four marriages and the fact that the children were always being made to pretend, against the threat of dire punishment, that the current man in their mother's life was their loving daddy.

In other ways, too, Joan's manuscript came increasingly to represent what she had wanted her life to be and bore less and less resemblance to the truth—or, at any rate, to the known facts. She described in detail how hard she had to work to juggle "film offers," despite the fact that she had not had such an offer in a very long time. She noted how hard-pressed she was to cope with the constant demands on her time by Pepsi-Cola, although the Pepsi people had been trying to get her off their backs ever since Steele's death.

Her recipes for a happy marriage were equally strange, particularly as they came from somebody who had three divorces to her credit. She recommended a blood-sugar pick-me-up for husbands, served at drink time, consisting of peanut butter and bacon on black bread cooked in a grill until it sizzled. Her cooking—she was inordinately proud of her ability as a cook, though the only time she served me dinner she ordered in from Casserole Kitchen—was of a kind that might be construed as murder in the first degree: She favored cream soups, pork chops, pot roast, lobster Newburg, and, of course, caviar, a veritable cholesterol binge that perhaps went a long way to explaining Alfred Steele's sudden death. To those of her women readers who couldn't afford to serve caviar to their husbands, she advised skipping the hairdresser a couple of times or giving up a hat they didn't really need. Nothing I could say convinced her that this advice was similar to Marie Antoinette's remark on the subject of the breadless: "*Qu'ils mangent de la brioche!*"

She strongly advised having afternoon sex and making men talk about their work. To the question of how a woman could take an interest in her husband's work if, for example, he was a cashier, Joan suggested asking him (presumably before or during afternoon sex): "Any holdups today?" For those nights when the husband *isn't* in, Joan recommended putting on a face mask of mayonnaise or pureed vegetables or a mixture of unflavored gelatin beaten with witch hazel, baking soda, and a raw egg. (At the last suggestion, Evelyn Gendel, the S&S editor who was going over the recipes for me, remarked, "She's *got* to be kidding!") But Joan took it all seriously, from brushing her hair one hundred strokes every night then pulling it hard (which she also did to her daughters until there were tears in their eyes) to teasing a husband out of his bad moods.

Gradually, it dawned on me that Joan's how-to book was in fact a kind of autobiography, not of the life she had lived but of life as she would *like* to have lived. All her marriages had been happy, her childhood, despite its up and downs, had been a happy one. Her children were perfect, happy, well adjusted, and loved her; Alfred Steele had been a kind of corporate Prince Charming (though photographs showed a plump, stolid man with an impatient expression, apparently eager to get away from whatever photo-op Joan created to show them as a happy couple). In short, in Dr. Pangloss's words, "In this best of all possible worlds, all is for the best." No blemish, however small, was allowed to tarnish this shining picture of perfection. *My Way of Life* was the equivalent of the kind of historical photographs that were once so common in the Soviet Union, in which all the faces were retouched and everyone who had failed to follow the party line had been carefully painted out.

In some ways, it was as scary a book as I've ever read, and the scariest thing was that it worked. In the days before the *Cosmo* girl, Joan was defining that nebulous ideal of "total femininity," the woman who knew how to be submissive to her husband, playful in bed, a terrific mother, and a busy, successful working woman. She could cook up a gourmet dinner for ten people at a moment's notice (in case her hubby brought his board of directors home on a whim), clean spots off the white carpet with her own blend of ammonia and soap, pack the children off to bed happy and clean, study up on the subjects guaranteed to get the dinner party moving in case conversation faltered, clean up after dinner (nothing must ever be left to the next morning), slip into a fabulous negligee that caters to whatever his particular idea of "sexy" is, and get up the next morning to go to work and be a killer competitor. Joan Crawford had no patience at all with women who didn't want to follow her example and, say, roll a Pepsi bottle around the floor under their instep to make their calves sexier for their husbands while reading the morning paper so as to have something to talk to him about when he comes home at night. Who but Joan Crawford would have instructed her readers to "get their shoulders back where God meant them to be," or to say "yes" to themselves over and over again in front of the mirror for a more youthful, positive expression?

Long before the book was complete, Joan's mind had turned to promoting it. She even took me out to her favorite restaurant, "21," to fill me in on her requirements for the tour, which were contained in a leather-bound loose-leaf binder in which each page was tucked neatly into a transparent plastic cover. This document was, Joan explained, to be "the Bible" for the people in the S&S publicity department who were organizing her tour. It was written in the third person, in an imperious tone of voice, with the more important points underlined. Miss Crawford, I read, must always have a black limousine (*not* a sedan). The chauffeur must wear *a black uniform*. He must not smoke in the car or talk to Miss Crawford. I read on. Miss Crawford must have a suite in each hotel along the way. The exact temperature of the suite was specified. The suite was to be provided with the same array of Pepsis and Stolichnaya vodka as she had at home, as well as the exact same placement of cigarette packets and matchbooks. There were to be flowers in each room, in pastel colors (*No white flowers!*). The refrigerator in the suite was to be stocked with fresh, unopened packets of Ry-Krisps and melba toast, *plain* cottage cheese, raw carrots and celery sliced lengthwise, on ice. There was to be an ironing board and a steam iron in the suite for the use of Miss Crawford's faithful German maid (whom she always called, strangely enough, "*Mamacita*"), and *a full hour* must be provided before departure to ensure that Miss Crawford's trunks and hatboxes were downstairs in time and packed into a *second* vehicle. The hotel manager or assistant manager must be in the lobby to greet Miss Crawford and take her straight to her suite, so she didn't have to check in.

As the tour began, Joan Crawford of legend reappeared, effacing the image she had created for herself of the calmly efficient, reasonable career woman. She became, to the horror of everybody directly involved in her tour, a star again, in the full meaning of the word.

That, perhaps, was the reason why she wrote the book in the first place, it now occurs to me.

Not long after Joan departed for the hinterlands to sell her book, my wife and I were woken out of a deep sleep late at night by the telephone.

I lifted the receiver and heard the familiar voice of Joan Crawford but raised in decibels to the level of a Boeing 707 leaving the runway. It was, by a strange coincidence, exactly the same level of anger and barely controlled hysteria that I was to hear many years later when I took a call from an unhappy Faye Dunaway, who actually *played* an angry Joan Crawford in *Mommie Dearest* and got the wire-hanger scene exactly right. "I'm in Cleveland," Joan howled. *"And there are white flowers in my room!"*

I'm not sure how I managed to get the situation straightened out. I think I called the night manager and had him replace Joan's flowers with others. Somehow I got Joan calmed down enough so that she could at least hear my apology, but the truth was that I had been badly shaken. Joan's voice was the very distillation of female rage.

Years later, I happened to mention Joan's horror of white flowers to my Auntie Merle. She nodded, as if it made perfect sense. "In Hollywood, white flowers are for funerals," she said crisply. "Joan knew that better than anyone."

I told her of Joan's late-night telephone call to me, and Merle laughed. "Rage was what she did best, that's all, darling—her specialty, like Fred Astaire's dancing or Jimmy Stewart's shyness. You're lucky to have heard it."

And I suppose I am.

ONE WRITER who had *not* followed Gottlieb to Knopf was S. J. Perelman, the sharp-tongued star humorist of *The New Yorker*, whom I had first met when he was hired by Mike Todd to write the script for *Around the World in Eighty Days*, for which my father did a good part of the art direction. Like most humorists, Perelman was a misanthropic and embittered man at heart, suspicious, jealous, touchy, and quick to take offense. But he was just about the only writer I know whose manuscripts made me laugh out loud uncontrollably. In person, he was a curious blend of Savile Row and Moskowitz and Lupowitz, a stylishly dressed figure, just short of being a full-fledged dandy, with a rakish little military mustache and steel-rimmed glasses with tiny lenses that made his eyes look like those of the little bon vivant who used to be *Esquire* magazine's trademark. The eyes were prominent, piercing, and showed no trace of good humor. The old Hollywood adage "Dress British, think Yiddish" might have been coined with Perelman in mind—might even have been coined *by* him, now that I think of it. He walked around New York in spiffy tweeds, a jaunty green hat, a loden cape, and handmade brogues, as if he were deer stalking in the Scottish Highlands. His home life—not that he ever discussed it—was reputed to be tragic. His wife, Laura, the sister of Nathanael West, was an alcoholic; his son was hostile; like most of the long-term *New Yorker* writers, he nursed endless grievances and feuds against other members of that narrow and all too often uncharmed circle. In short, he was not a happy man. Perelman took his writing more seriously than his public did, and he yearned to have his work celebrated as literature. He was not consoled when the reviewers merely praised him to the skies for being funny, and therefore he bore a grudge against even the best and most generous of reviewers. He was not pleased by his sales, either. He wanted to be a major bestseller, on the scale of Harold Robbins, but while his sales were respectable, they remained comparatively small, partly because most of his books were collections and most of his fans had already read the pieces in *The New Yorker*. He had left Random House after many years, out of disgust for his low sales, and was beginning to feel the same way about S&S. Low sales were not the only bone he had to pick with Random House. Bennett Cerf fancied himself a humorist and a punster and was the author of numerous collections of jokes. He was a fervent Perelman fan, but on some deep level he was also a competitor, determined to prove that he was funnier than his own author. Perelman's sense of humor did not extend to other people's jokes—in any case, what he wanted to hear from Cerf was glowing reports of sales, not jokes—and the relationship between the two men was inevitably frayed.

Unfortunately for Perelman, Max Schuster prided himself—improbably—on his ability as a humorist and a punster. A sample Schusterism was that when he was asked about whether he exercised, he replied, "At S&S we start every day by exercising our options." Max labored under the misapprehension that Perelman lived to hear other people's jokes, and he actually kept a file of fresh ones on his desk just in case Perelman should turn up. At some point, Schuster had taken to greeting Perelman by saying, in a loud stage whisper, "The jig is up!" whenever he sighted him, until Perelman complained that Schuster was deliberately persecuting him. Wherever he went, there Max was, waiting to rush up to him. In Paris at the Hôtel Georges V, in Venice on Saint Mark's Place, in New York in the dining room of the Algonquin Hotel, there was Max, lying in wait, as if he were playing blindman's buff, to rush out and say, "The jig is up!" at the first sight of Perelman. "He's following me around," Perelman complained wildly, eyes full of indignation and anger behind his steel-rimmed glasses. "Who needs that kind of craziness from a publisher!"

Perhaps the only benefit from this misunderstanding between author and publisher was that Perelman was unusually reluctant to appear on the premises of S&S, for fear that Max would be waiting to leap out at him and utter the dreaded line. Eventually, Bob had managed to calm Perelman, keeping him away from Max and treating him with great courtesy as the touchy man of letters he was, instead of the comedian he was not, and it fell to me to continue the job.

I had always thought that Perelman was a genius and once took *The Most of S. J. Perelman* on a week's vacation in Montana and read nothing else—in fact, I laughed so hard every night at pieces that I had read a dozen times before that my wife threw a pillow at me.

All the same, nothing I could do seemed to increase poor Perelman's sales, and eventually he left to live in London, where his boulevardier presence was more appreciated and where there was a certain respect for him as a literary exile, though he complained bitterly of the rye bread without seeds. There, he improbably formed a liaison with a much younger woman (his wife, Laura, had eventually succumbed) and set about the task of writing his autobiography, *The Hindsight Saga*. Alas, funny as Perelman could be at the expense of other people, he was unable to be funny about himself, or even frank, and the book was never completed, perhaps mercifully. Further embittered by this, he eventually quarreled with me and announced his departure from S&S by publishing a piece about me in *The New Yorker* called "Under the Shrinking Royalty the Village Smithy Stands," in which my fondness for horses and riding was caricatured brilliantly. I was none too gently lampooned as Mitchell Krakauer, editor in chief of "Diamond & Oyster," wearing riding breeches to work and hammering out horseshoes in a leather apron before my very own forge in my Rockefeller Center office. Seldom has an author expressed his unhappiness with his publisher more clearly.

> The oval anteroom of Diamond & Oyster, my publishers, had been refurbished since my last visit with a large bas-relief plaque of their logo, a diamond-studded oyster bearing the motto *"Noli unquam oblivisci, Carole: pecuniam sapientiam esse"* ("Never Forget, Charlie: Money Is Wisdom"), and under it a blond, oval-shaped receptionist strikingly reminiscent of Shelley Winters. As thirty-five minutes ticked away without any

word from Mitchell Krakauer, the editor I was calling on, I began to develop paranoid symptoms. Heretofore there hadn't been any hassle about seeing him; what was amiss now? Had some stripling in patched denim fresh out of Antioch whispered into his ear that I was *vieux jeu,* old hat, *nye kulturny?* Or had Krakauer learned in some devious way that Shelley Winters was in a 1941 play of mine, "The Night Before Christmas," and deliberately planted her double here to taunt me as a slippered pantaloon? I felt myself inflate like a blowfish at the veiled insult. Surely nobody could be so base, and yet in this carnivorous age of four-hundred-thousand-dollar sales and instant remainders worship of the bitch goddess Success overrode a decent respect for the aged. I got to my feet, cheeks flaming.

"Try Mr. Krakauer's line again, Miss. I can't understand why they don't answer."

DESPITE THIS portrait of myself, I was still trying to give the S&S list the commercial fiction that was rapidly becoming the lifeblood of publishing, as huge mass-market paperback sales provided a welcome new source of profits. Bob had been a master of gilding popular fiction with a literary veneer—thus making everybody involved feel good about it—but he had also recognized that to succeed a publisher needed to seek out fiction within the categories (or genres, as he preferred to call them) that mass-market publishers thought the public wanted. The genre that did best for them, apart from the big contemporary tearjerker like *The Love Machine,* was the romantic family saga (usually set in the spacious nineteenth century), with a strong, sympathetic woman as the heroine.

In this particular genre, most editors, then as now, don't really *like* this kind of fiction nearly as much as the public does—they looked down on it, in fact, and on those who read it. Most of the real enthusiasts for this kind of fiction were at the book clubs and the paperback houses or were buyers for the major bookstores rather than editors. The leading expert on the genre at the time was Barbara Bannon, the fiction reviewer for *Publishers Weekly.*

Barbara Bannon *loved* big romantic sagas and, perhaps more important, could tell the difference between the ones that were deliberately and cynically contrived to meet the demands of the market and the ones that were written from the heart. She was small, plump, emotionally needy, slightly disheveled, apt to drink too much at lunch, and resentful of the fact that she was unappreciated by her male superiors at *PW*, but she was fanatically loyal to her friends and to those authors who delivered the goods, always willing to go out on a limb for new talent, and, unlike a good many reviewers at more august publications, she genuinely loved reading fiction. Her excitement when she found a novel she liked was undisguised and unaffected, completely genuine, and totally unstoppable. She would not rest until she had gotten the word out to the right buyers (such as Faith Brunson at Rich's in Atlanta, or her equivalents at Higbee's in Cleveland or Kauffman's in Pittsburgh), the major paperback editors (such as Fawcett's Leona Nevler), and of course the ladies at the Literary Guild and *Reader's Digest*. Together, these women constituted a powerful support group for a certain kind of fiction and could turn the right kind of novel into a major best-seller.

The agent who more or less specialized in such books was Claire Smith, of the old and very respected Harold Ober Agency. One of the first things an editor ought to learn is that there are certain agents whose enthusiasm can absolutely be counted upon. One might not always *agree* with them, it goes without saying, but their enthusiasm is always genuine and sincere. Claire's enthusiasms—like Dorothea Oppenheimer's for Larry McMurtry—were transparent, passionate, and fierce. The very reverse of a high-powered or high-pitched agent, Claire was quiet, witty, clever, good company, and often startlingly frank and outspoken about her clients, toward whom she was, however, entirely loyal. She had been one of Bob Gottlieb's admirers, and it was therefore a surprise important enough to communicate to Snyder when she called out of the blue one day to announce that she had discovered a wonderful book. Was I, she inquired, afraid of long novels? I said I wasn't (which was true) and mentioned my qualifications as Delderfield's editor. This one, Claire said, was even longer than Delderfield's novels. Except for *War and Peace*, no such book came to mind. I would have to read the manuscript overnight, she warned me—other people were interested, and she might receive a blind offer at any moment. Undaunted, I asked her to send it over.

It proved to be very long indeed—three huge boxes full of typescript, under the unpromising title of *The Standardbearers*, but no sooner had I begun to read it than I knew it was the real thing. I read on and on until my eyes were weary. Sustained by many cups of coffee, I finished the book at four in the morning and called Claire as soon as I reached the office to tell her that I wanted to buy it. I had mentioned it to Dick in the elevator that morning and tried to convey my enthusiasm to him. He waved me to silence. "Don't tell me the fucking plot," he growled, "just buy the goddamn thing." Claire was a little surprised—I suspect she had invented the need for an overnight reading to add drama to the submission and had not expected that I would really read the book in one night—and perhaps for that reason accepted what seemed to me a rather modest offer. The author, she told me, was Susan Howatch, a young Englishwoman who had actually written the novel at the kitchen table of her house in New Jersey while looking after her infant daughter.

It is a frequently stated basic belief of book publishing that somewhere in the country at any given moment some unknown woman is writing a major best-seller (usually referred to as "the next *Gone with the Wind*") at her kitchen table while looking after her baby, but this was the first time I had experienced the phenomenon in real life. Susan Howatch had written her massive novel with one hand on the cradle and the other doing the typing, but, like most authors who succeed, she had never doubted that her book would be a best-seller.

When we met, Howatch turned out to be a serious and attractive young woman with intense, soulful eyes, partly concealed by bangs, and a determined chin. She was open to editorial suggestions and quickly agreed to change the title of the novel to *Penmarric* (the name of the great country house at the center of the book), but that firm chin made it clear that she took her writing in earnest and was not going to be a pushover when it came to changes. It was apparent, too, that she was a serious student of literature and something of a moralist, as well as a student of philosophy and religion. She seemed uneasy about writing popular fiction and needed to be reassured that it was worthwhile. Good as she clearly was at it, her heart did not seem to be in it. At the end of lunch—we became instant friends and have remained so ever since—I felt emboldened to ask a question about the plot. Although the book was set in nineteenth-century Cornwall, there was something very familiar about the story, I said. Was there not a certain uncanny resemblance to the life of Eleanor of Aquitaine, wife of Henry II? Susan Howatch blushed prettily. Yes, she admitted, she had in fact borrowed the plot directly from history, but after all, Shakespeare had borrowed most of *his* plots from somebody else. Did I think anybody would notice?

I wasn't sure, but I decided there was nothing to be gained by worrying her. After all, the book was written—she could hardly change or obscure the plot at this point. Time passed, and everything good that could happen to a book happened. The S&S sales reps loved the book, Dick decided to go for broke with a big printing, Barbara Bannon not only loved it but adored the author, once she had met her, and the buyers at the major stores predicted huge sales.

They were right, too. *Penmarric* launched Susan Howatch on a career as a major worldwide-best-selling novelist. At intervals of two years, one big novel followed another, each of them hugely successful—*Cashelmara, The Rich Are Different, Sins of the Fathers, The Wheel of Fortune*—each of them based on either the plot of a Shakespeare tragedy (*The Rich Are Different,* for example, though set in America in the 1920s, follows the story of *Antony and Cleopatra*) or the life of a major historical figure. The parallels were absolutely clear-cut, and yet never from 1971 to 1984 did any reviewer ever notice! Some readers did, though they were not disturbed by the fact.

With each success, Susan seemed to become more uneasy about what she was doing. It wasn't that she didn't enjoy the fruits of success up to a point, it was as if the kind of popular fiction she was writing simply didn't satisfy her own intellectual and moral needs. Indeed, with every new book we fought a well-mannered tug-of-war over the packaging and the flap copy, with Susan pulling for seriousness and me, needless to say, pulling for commercial appeal. "Tell her she's not Dostoyevsky, for chrissake!" Snyder instructed me when I reported to him Susan's concerns and misgivings, but even if I could have told her that it wouldn't have helped. She *knew* she wasn't Dostoyevsky, but she *yearned* to be, or rather an English, Anglican equivalent of him, dealing with serious moral issues as opposed to simply entertaining people. This resulted in an unfortunate paradox: The more copies we sold of her books, the more unhappy she was with us. We were treating her as a big commercial best-seller, not a "serious" writer, she complained, perhaps unable to recover from *The New York Times*'s curt dismissal of *Penmarric* as "a leaden lump of a novel," written in "early Prince Valiant style." There is no angst like that of a best-selling novelist who yearns for good reviews and doesn't get them, and nothing more sure than that she (or he) will blame the publisher.

Eventually, Susan's serious side simply won out over the side of her that was very ably writing entertaining romantic family sagas, and she moved on to religious novels, in a spirit of expiation for the frivolity of her previous works. She thus became the only best-selling novelist in my experience to walk away from her own success or to leave her publisher because he had sold too many copies of her books.

CHAPTER 22

By 1971, THREE years after Bob's departure, Dick had made good the loss and then some. He had proven we could publish big commercial novels (*The Love Machine*), we had acquired a string of best-selling fiction writers who delivered a book every year or two (Delderfield and Howatch), and we had acquired a lot of important celebrity books. Snyder was soon to prove his own instinct for the big nonfiction best-seller with a single stroke of genius: the acquisition of Bob Woodward and Carl Bernstein's *All the President's Men,* which among many other things, was to bring Dick out of the obscurity of being a first-rate manager and businessman and into the limelight as a kind of impresario and publishing celebrity in his own right.

Despite hiring endless numbers of distinguished literary editors, most of whom left before they had made any impact on the S&S list, the one area in which we remained deficient was serious literature. Dick liked to pretend that this didn't matter, and of course in a way it didn't, but it still annoyed him, and he yearned for an author of Nobel Prize potential.

Unexpectedly, one fell into our laps in the shape of Graham Greene, whom I had known—and loved—since I was a teenager and whose difficult, convoluted personality and wishes it soon became my job to interpret for Dick over the next few years.

THERE WERE always three separate and distinct Graham Greenes—the writer, the public figure, and the private man—so it is hardly surprising that his character seems to have eluded his biographers, both Professor Norman Sherry, whose definitive, authorized, multivolume biography idolizes Greene, and Michael Shelden, whose revisionist biography, *Graham Greene: The Enemy Within*, reviles and demonizes him. Greene himself was an acerbic, contradictory, and complicated man. He had a wry sense of humor and a schoolboy's taste for pranks and practical jokes, and he loved making a mystery of his life. Apparently, he took a malicious pleasure in leading both Sherry and Shelden down the garden path.

The Graham Greene I knew best was the private man, and on my part it was love—or at any rate besotted admiration—at first sight. I met him for the first time in 1948, at the age of fifteen, in Antibes on my Uncle Alex's yacht *Elsewhere*.

Greene had—as I was soon to discover—an intuitive sympathy for young people, together with a sly, subversive determination to help them break the rules, the result, no doubt, of his own unhappy childhood as the son of an English public-school headmaster, from which he attempted to escape by playing Russian roulette with a revolver. I, somewhat overwhelmed by a party that included Carol Reed, Vivien Leigh, Randolph Churchill, and his about-to-be ex-wife, Pamela, was doing my best to hide when a tall, lean Englishman with thinning sandy hair and the most alarmingly penetrating bright blue, protuberant eyes—rather like intelligent gooseberries, I thought—appeared beside me and handed me a cocktail. I looked at it suspiciously. My father had encouraged me to drink a glass of wine at dinner, but I did not think he would have approved of a cocktail before lunch. "Drink up," the stranger said. "You look as if you need it."

He had a curious way of speaking, very English, clipped, precise to the point of being old-fashioned and high-pitched, with a slight trace of a speech impediment and a tendency to turn every sentence into a question—a very donnish voice, as I was to discover when I eventually went to Oxford. I sipped the cocktail gingerly.

"Go on," he said. "It's a martini. It can do you no possible harm. I'm Graham Greene, by the way."

We shook hands rather formally. I had heard of him, of course. He had cowritten the script for *The Fallen Idol* (based on one of his stories, "The Basement Room"), and my father, who had done the art direction, spoke of him with great affection.

Despite Greene's promise, I felt that my lips seemed to have become anesthetized, not a bad thing under the circumstances, since Alex's view was that teenagers should be seen only if absolutely necessary but certainly not heard. I had no idea how I was going to get through a long luncheon with these people, all of whom were shouting at one another at the top of their voices about friends whose names meant nothing to me. Randolph Churchill's face loomed before me, gross, red, puffy, prominent bad teeth, a caricature of his father's. He had a laugh that hurt my ears and seemed drunk before lunch.

"The great advantage of being a writer," Greene told me, staring at Randolph as if he were an animal on display in the zoo, "is that you can *spy* on people. You're *there*, listening to every word, but part of you is observing. *Everything* is useful to a writer, you see, every scrap—even the longest and most boring of luncheon parties."

His voice dropped to a husky, confidential whisper. "Even Randolph," he added. "How fortunate for Pamela that she's never been faithful to him." He turned toward me with a schoolmasterly look. "There's always something a writer can use, later on. Nothing is wasted." (He took his own advice, too—the cruise on Alex's yacht he turned into a masterful piece of ironic comedy in *Loser Takes All*.)

I told him that I thought Pamela Churchill was the most beautiful woman I'd ever seen—a thought that had occurred, as I was to discover, to a lot of men already.

Graham stared at her. "Yes," he said thoughtfully, "one can see that it would be possible for a young man to think that. She looks rather like an expensive tart, and there's a certain attraction to that. But the main thing is to have a *lot* of women, then you'll discover that looks aren't even the half of it."

I don't remember what my ambitions had been before that moment, but I decided on the spot that I wanted to be a writer. Any lingering doubts I might have had were dispelled the next morning, when Graham allowed me to observe at a distance the writer at work. An early riser, he appeared on deck fully dressed at first light, placed himself in the shade of an awning, and took from his pocket a small black leather pocket notebook, of the kind sold in expensive English stationery shops, and a black fountain pen, the top of which he unscrewed carefully. Slowly, word by word, without crossing out anything, and in neat, square handwriting, the letters so tiny and cramped that it looked like an attempt to write the Lord's Prayer on the head of a pin, he wrote over the next hour or so exactly five hundred words.

He counted each word according to some system of his own, and when he reached exactly five hundred, he stopped, screwed the cap back on his pen tightly, stood up, and stretched. "That's it, then," he said. "Shall we have breakfast?"

I was later to discover that Graham's self-discipline was such that he stopped at five hundred words even if that left him in the middle of a sentence—it was as if he brought to writing the skill of a watchmaker or a miniaturist, or perhaps it was that in a life full of moral uncertainties and confusion, Graham simply needed one area in which the rules, even though they were self-imposed, were absolute. Whatever else was going on, his writing, like a daily religious devotional, was at once sacred and completely in his control. Once the daily penance of five hundred words was achieved, he put the notebook away and did not think about it until the next morning. It seemed to me then the ideal way to live, far better than my father's, which required him to work from dawn until late at night at the studio—and he brought his work home with him as well.

Graham and I breakfasted together companionably at a small café at the far end of the port of Antibes not far from where he would later have a small, spare apartment, almost monastic in its simplicity. From time to time, he would look suspiciously at people who passed us by, or sat down nearby for coffee and a croissant. Spies and informers were on his mind at the time. Much to his annoyance, he had recently been denied a visa to enter the United States, he informed me, because the FBI had revealed the fact that he'd joined the Communist Party briefly while he was an Oxford undergraduate. That he had done so as a student prank cut no ice with the U.S. government. The FBI, he said, had a dossier on him, and were now adding to it at every opportunity. He had no doubt that his telephone calls and mail were being monitored. Needless to say, this aura of political persecution made him even more glamorous in my eyes.

After breakfast, I stopped at a stationer and bought a small notebook and a fountain pen. I followed him everywhere, like a faithful dog, and as long as I was quiet, he didn't seem to mind being shadowed by a teenaged companion. It was the same relationship, I later realized, that young Bobby Henrey had with Ralph Richardson, the philandering butler in *The Fallen Idol*. Despite the difference in our ages, we became friends—though it was Graham whose spirit was that of a mischievous, daring schoolboy, not me. It was Graham who took me to a lushly furnished brothel in Nice, just off the Promenade des Anglais, on the grounds that this was a side of life to which every young man should be exposed as early as possible. It was Graham who encouraged me to drive Alexa's little Simca sports car and act as his chauffeur, despite the fact that I didn't have a license. I took to smoking English cigarettes in imitation of him and soon got used to a martini before lunch.

Of the private side of his life, I knew nothing. Youthful, even childish, as his behavior sometimes seemed, I was at the age when I still thought of all grown-ups as old, even ancient. Of the fact that he had left his wife and embarked on a long affair with a married woman, Catherine Walston, whom he had encouraged to join the Catholic Church, I was as yet unaware, though I was later to meet her. In the absence of his mistress—Catherine was unable to leave her complaisant husband for the summer—Graham visited brothels and flirted gently with Alexa, apparently content.

Even at the age of fifteen, I could tell that he was attractive to women, both because he genuinely enjoyed their company—rare for an Englishman of his age and class—and because there was, beneath the charm and wit and superb intelligence, a feline love of gossip and an unmistakable, unapologetic interest in sex. Graham was fascinating on the subject of sex, as a matter of fact, in that respect rather resembling the great British explorer and erotic adventurer Sir Richard Burton, whom he much admired. Like Burton, Graham was a mine of lore about the brothels and geisha houses and opium dens of the East, and also like Burton, he did not take a romantic view of women. Besides, he made no secret of the fact that he was a Catholic, living apart from his wife and involved with a married woman, which gave him a certain daredevil-damned quality, as if he believed in the fires of hell and was perfectly willing to risk them for, as he would have put it, "one good fuck." Since this was exactly what made Don Juan himself attractive to so many women, it is hardly surprising that it worked for Graham: Few women can resist a man who is willing to risk damnation for them.

During the course of the summer, Graham took over the role of sex adviser where I was concerned, having rightly concluded that my father was unwilling to bring the subject up at all. If I wanted to go to bed with a woman, I should ask her directly, he told me, and not beat about the bush—"Just tell her you want to fuck her. It's usually the best way."

While I was grateful for his advice, I was not yet in a position to try it out. Years later, I was to see it oddly echoed in a passage in *The Quiet American,* where the journalist Fowler, modeled after Graham himself, is talking to Pyle, the American whose childlike innocence and good intentions cause so much trouble. Pyle is in love with Phuong, Fowler's mistress, whom he intends to make an honest woman. After comparing Pyle's innocence to leprosy, Fowler savagely dismisses Pyle's claim to have Phuong's best interests at heart: " 'If it's only her interests you care about, for God's sake leave Phuong alone. Like any other woman she'd rather have a good . . .' The crash of a mortar saved Boston ears from the Anglo-Saxon word." The Anglo-Saxon "f word" was one that Graham used rarely, but precisely and with pleasure when he did.

Gradually, with an ever-changing guest list, our yachting party made its way slowly down the coastline. In Genoa, where we put in to take on fuel and supplies, Graham, who loved low dives, took me to a rough sailors' bar that was full of men in drag. A cruise-ship purser, dressed in a blond wig, a clinging red gown, and a feather boa, gave a convincing rendition of Sophie Tucker singing "Some of These Days," except for his five-o'clock shadow under the pancake makeup.

The journey was not all pleasure, of course. Alex was anxious for Carol Reed and Graham to repeat their successful collaboration on *The Fallen Idol.* The three of them often sat together on the bridge in the afternoons, Alex smoking a cigar and playing solitaire, while Graham smoked a cigarette and suggested ideas and Carol appeared to doze. Most of the time Alex shook his head wearily. One day, Graham read aloud a few lines he had written on the back of an envelope: "*I had paid my last farewell to Harry a week ago, when his coffin was lowered into the frozen February ground, so that it was with incredulity that I saw him pass by, without a sign of recognition, among the host of strangers in the Strand.*"

At this (which was, of course, the genesis of *The Third Man*), Alex smiled, but gloom soon settled back on his face when Graham explained that he hadn't a clue where the story went from there. Despite pleadings from Alex and Carol, despite offers of unprecedented amounts of money, the story seemed destined never to get beyond the first four lines.

We arrived at Capri just in time to see the sun set over Anacapri. Graham was in a reflective mood as he sipped his drink. "I should give anything to own a villa there," he said, not exactly *to* Alex, but in Alex's hearing.

We dined onboard that night, eating on deck, and Alex retired early, pleading fatigue (which was unusual for him), while his guests played chemin de fer. In the morning, when we sat down to breakfast, Alex joined us instead of taking his breakfast in bed, as was his habit.

Graham unfolded his napkin, and out dropped an old-fashioned, rusty iron key that looked suitable for a dungeon. "What on earth is this?" Graham asked.

Alex smiled. "It's the key to a villa in Anacapri," he said. "Quite a nice one. I had myself taken ashore late last night in the motor launch. I bought a villa. It's in your name, dear boy. Now I want the rest of my story, please." Even Graham was startled and impressed by this instant generosity. He pocketed the key, and within a few days he and Carol and Alex had worked out the story of *The Third Man*, which became one of the most successful movies ever made and which Graham turned into not a bad thriller novel as well. For the rest of Alex's life, the zither theme from *The Third Man*—a tune he hated—was played in his honor, while to Graham's great annoyance the story Alex had coerced out of him became more famous than any of his more ambitious books.

As for me, it merely increased my admiration for Graham, with whom I continued to correspond during the many years in which I finished school, served in the Royal Air Force, went to Oxford, fought in the Hungarian Revolution, and eventually emerged in New York as an editor at Simon and Schuster. The first letter I wrote on S&S stationery, in 1958, was to Graham, announcing my new job to him (he had been a publisher and an editor himself, at one time), and expressing the hope that one day, in the far future perhaps, I would have the honor of publishing *him*. He wrote back to say that he hoped so too, and wished me well, and there the matter rested until late in 1971.

Graham had been published for many years by Viking Press. They did well for him, and there seemed no reason that he would ever move. I was therefore surprised to receive a telephone call from Monica McCall, his agent, asking whether I would like to become Graham's publisher. Of course I would, I replied. Graham was both commerce *and* literature, a serious writer of international stature whose books sold in best-seller quantities. It could be argued that he was, in fact, the most eminent of living writers in the English language, and had only failed to receive the Nobel Prize—much to his private chagrin, though in public he put a good face on the matter—because one member of the Swedish Academy, offended by Graham's combination of Catholicism and reputed left-wing sympathies, blackballed him every year.

I was astonished and delighted at the prospect of adding Greene's name to the S&S list, but of course I wondered what had caused him to change. "It's quite a story," Monica said. She was an elderly English-woman whose formidably starchy appearance concealed a heart as soft as a marshmallow, as well as left-wing opinions that had gotten her into hot water in the McCarthy era and earned her Graham's loyalty. Graham, it appeared, had recently delivered to Viking Press the manu-script of his latest novel, *Travels with My Aunt,* one of his rare ventures into comedy. Viking had sent the manuscript to *Playboy,* hoping to sell the first-serial rights, and *Playboy* had called back to say that while they loved the book, they didn't like the title much—it seemed too prissy. Tom Guinzburg, the head of Viking, decided on reflection that he didn't like the title much either, so he sent Graham a cable advising him to change the title for the U.S. edition of the book. He also suggested a number of titles dreamed up by the editors of Viking at a brainstorming session. Had Guinzburg gone to the trouble of getting to know his eminent but irascible author, he might have spared himself and his edi-tors the trouble. Instead, he received in reply a terse cable from Graham in Paris that read: EASIER TO CHANGE PUBLISHER THAN TITLE. GRAHAM GREENE.

IT WAS thus that I became Graham's publisher and editor at last, and for the next sixteen years we corresponded constantly, and saw each other whenever I was in Europe, often in the company of my father, Vincent, who had been the art director on *The Fallen Idol* and *The Third Man,* and of whom Graham was genuinely fond. My father was famous on three continents for his taciturnity, but Graham, normally the most talkative of men, seemed to enjoy endless dinners with him, in Antibes, or London, during which the two men sat facing each other for hours across a table laden with food and drink, never saying a word, appar-ently quite content with each other's silent company. Once, after a din-ner during which neither one of them had spoken more than a few words, and those about the weather and the food, Graham whispered to me as I took him to his waiting taxi, "Your father is the cleverest man I know!" As for Vincent, he maintained stoutly that "Gray-ham," as he pronounced it, was the only Englishman he knew whose conversation was worth listening to.

Since Graham hardly needed editing in the conventional meaning of the word, much of my work consisted in pouring oil on troubled waters. Here was an author who knew his own mind and did not take suggestions lightly. I was not spared the occasional sharp rap on the knuckles to remind me of Tom Guinzburg's fate. A cable about flap copy read: I HATE THE WORD "STUNNING." I ALSO DISLIKE VERY MUCH THE TITLE "BEST-SELLING AUTHOR" WHICH IS MORE APPLICABLE TO MR. HAROLD ROBBINS. Or, about the grandiose plans for a glitzy mass-market paperback advertising campaign: THEY FILLED ME WITH DISMAY. THANK GOD I DON'T LIVE IN THE UNITED STATES. Or, refusing a proposed interview: SORRY, BUT SAVE ME FROM MICHIKO KAKUTANI! A fairly harmless list of questions after a libel reading by the S&S house counsel produced the comment, COMPLETE NONSENSE!, together with the suggestion that if we at S&S were afraid to publish the book we should let his agent know so that she could find another, more courageous American publisher. My relationship with Graham, while deeply affectionate on both sides, at first remained that of a pupil to a master, and I found myself reverting to adolescent status.

Perhaps the most striking thing about Graham's relationship with his publishers worldwide was his infinite capacity for attending to details and his determination to get them right. Although constantly traveling on mysterious journeys to faraway places—Vietnam, Panama, South Africa, Argentina—he kept in constant touch via his devoted secretary and later, when she resigned, his sister. The easygoing author who wrote his five hundred meticulous words every morning was an illusion of my youth. Nothing was too small to attract his attention—the exact shade of red of the English telephone booth on the dust cover of *The Human Factor,* a snide remark by William F. Buckley, Jr., in the *New York Post* alleging that Graham had said *America* was the word he hated most in the English language (A LIE.), and not only misprints in *his* books but in other people's. He frequently sent for books from the S&S list and almost always read them carefully, listing any errors and giving me his often surprising opinions on other writers, such as his comment on a biography of H. G. Wells that Wells "is the best novelist on sex in the English language." He often commented on the FBI's pursuit of him and gleefully speculated on the size of his dossier and how much trouble it must have put them to over the years.

He was constantly in touch by letter and cable. A query from me inquiring whether he would allow *Penthouse* to publish a condensation of one of his books, given the kind of photographs that it was likely to appear next to, was answered almost immediately from Switzerland with a cable saying that he had no objection to naked girls but disliked the way the magazine had cut and edited his text. A cable announcing that he was number two on the *New York Times* best-seller list which in my excitement I, not knowing where he was, had sent to his addresses in Paris, Antibes, and Capri received an instant reply chiding my "extravagance" for wasting money on three cables and suggesting that it might have been better spent on more advertising. About his photograph on the cover of *A Sort of Life* he complained that it made him look like "a Chinaman," with narrowed eyes and yellow skin.

On the subject of jacket art, we almost invariably clashed. My very first attempt to please Graham in this area produced a cable from somewhere beyond Suez begging me to eliminate "the fancy lettering," which we promptly did. I replied, in the best tradition of *Scoop:* LETTERING PROMPTLY UNFANCIED STOP, but there was an unbridgeable gap between Graham's sensibilities about jacket art and those of the American book trade, as is so often the case with English writers. Generally, these could be solved by eliminating fancy lettering or, say, finding the correct windmill for the cover of *Monsignor Quixote* (WINDMILL SPANISH, NOT DUTCH), but when it came to the mass-market paperback editions of his works, Graham often lashed out in righteous anger. Graham liked the idea of cheap editions of his works—and of course what were, in those days, the big six-figure advances—but he hated the inevitable commercial packaging. Occasionally he approved them "in despair," complaining that he had no time to argue about them across the Atlantic, but time and again he protested against "ghastly designs" and "vulgarities," which had roughly the same effect on his reprinters as water on a duck's back. A cable from me about the jacket for our reprint of *Twenty-one Stories,* inquiring whether it was the illustration or the lettering he objected to, produced the single-word reply, BOTH, while another about our reprint of *England Made Me* objected strongly to the "disagreeable" faces and the appearance, for no discernible plot reason, of a large swastika.

It should not be thought that all of Graham's correspondence took place by cable, nor was it limited to complaints. Often his letters were long and full of fascinating detail, such as one in which he described in detail his horror at the "grisly sight" of seeing dictators in the flesh— Pinochet of Chile and Stroessner of Paraguay—or another in which he expressed his pleasure that the film rights to *The Honorary Consul* had been optioned by Orson Welles because there was no danger of his actually making the film. From time to time, he gave me advice about marriage and parenthood, warning me against ever developing a sense of guilt about either—"to look for guilt one would have to go back to Adam and Eve," he cautioned wisely, though it was no advice he applied to himself. My father's death in 1979—they were neighbors in Antibes—shook him almost as deeply as Alex's had in 1956, and if anything drew us closer.

Graham's output was constant but variable. Major novels such as *The Honorary Consul* and *The Human Factor*, which was originally called *The Cold Fault* (and which I mistakenly announced to the press as *The Cold Vault*, due to an error in cable transmission, much to Graham's amusement), alternated with smaller books that reflected his diverse interests and his travels. Graham's minor works produced occasional friction, for they became increasingly eccentric or hermetic, reflecting his involvement in causes and people unlikely to interest the American reader. For example, he edited the memoirs of his ninety-year-old neighbor, Dottoressa Moor, in Capri. He also wrote a pamphlet attacking the excesses of the criminal underworld, the police, and the politicians of Nice, *J'accuse: The Dark Side of Nice*, which took up with Zolaesque anger the case of a young Frenchwoman whose gangster husband had abused her and abducted her child. He took the failure or nonpublication of these books in the United States in stride, though I suspect it merely confirmed his already low opinion of America's interest in the world beyond her shores. As he grew older, his restless curiosity and almost childlike fascination with eccentric and larger-than-life figures—a characteristic that he captured so perfectly in the person of Monsignor Quixote, the priest who tilts at the windmills of modern Spain and who in so many ways resembles the older Graham Greene—increased. He had always sought sainthood in secular figures and prized in others a simplicity and an innocence he had been denied, and his later works are a kind of pilgrimage in search of a different kind of faith.

In writing the flap copy for the dust jacket of his autobiography, *Ways of Escape*, I had referred to him as "enigmatic, secretive, and elusive," and increasingly this rather romantic description, which he had accepted at first unwillingly, seemed true. He liked to feel he was living "on the dangerous edge of things," and his skill at writing cloak-and-dagger novels was more than matched by his own adventures and divided loyalties. He was at once a sentimental leftist (about Africa, Cuba, Panama, and Vietnam at any rate) and a man of old-fashioned Tory attitudes when it came to England, complaining that the only things he missed when he was abroad were the sausages and dinner at Rule's or Simpson's, old-fashioned London restaurants where he always ordered roast beef. He was a friend of Kim Philby's (and loyal to him to the bitter end), but continued to maintain his shadowy connections with the British Secret Intelligence Service (SIS), for which he had served as an agent during the war.

He traveled constantly and involved himself fearlessly—some would say recklessly—in politics, as if he was determined to add to the bulk of the FBI's file on him. "Just think of the *money* I'm costing them!" he liked to say, delighted at the thought of the documents and reports on his activities piling up in Washington. In one letter, he reported that he was just back from visiting Panama, Nicaragua, and Cuba (where he spent twenty-four hours with Fidel Castro) and expressed horror that bombs were being distributed by the CIA in Nicaragua in the shape of Mickey Mouse dolls that would explode when a child picked one up—a story that sounds as if it might have been passed on to him by Fidel. Still, he never made any claim to objectivity, particularly when it came to the U.S. government, and the murky world of guilt, betrayal, and ruthlessness that formed the background of so many of his novels also influenced the way he saw the real world beyond his fiction.

Having been an agent for the SIS, Graham looked for conspiracy everywhere and found it, partly because he liked to spend his nights with the kind of shadowy figures who might actually be spies—or, like him, enjoyed pretending to be—partly because it pleased him to suppose that the tentacles of the SIS or its rivals and enemies extended everywhere, embracing people who seemed on the surface quite innocent and ordinary, like the harmless vacuum-cleaner sales representative who becomes a spy in *Our Man in Havana*. Graham himself was quite capable of giving even the most harmless of activities a twist to thrill a naive listener, though very often with tongue in cheek. Thus, he hinted to his biographer that he and my Uncle Alex had "surveyed" for the SIS the waters off Yugoslavia during a cruise on Alex's yacht, although given the guest list (which included both men's mistresses), Alex's myopia, and the fact that there were no cameras onboard except mine, it is hard to imagine what kind of surveying they could have done, even if there was anything about the Yugoslavian coastline worth knowing or that the SIS couldn't have gotten out of a Baedeker travel guide.

In fact, with Graham it was always difficult to tell where the spy novelist left off and the spy himself began. From time to time they came together, as when Graham turned up unexpectedly in the White House in the guise of a Panamanian diplomat (complete with diplomatic passport) as part of the entourage of General Omar Torrijos, the leftist ruler of Panama from 1968 to 1981, during an official visit. He was photographed standing behind Torrijos and President Carter, without anybody in the White House or the press recognizing him—ironic in view of the fact that he was still unable to obtain a visa to visit the United States except by making a special application as "a former communist," which he was unwilling to do as a matter of principle.

Over the years, Graham's FBI file began to obsess him more and more. Ostensibly, his brief flirtation with communism, which he claimed was a student prank, was the cause of the U.S. government's refusal to grant him a visa. Behind that simple explanation, however, was a layer of misunderstandings about Graham among Americans who had never met him (particularly those who either made or supported American foreign policy), most of whom bitterly resented his portrait of Alden Pyle, the naive but deadly central figure of *The Quiet American,* whose love for Phuong does not prevent him from helping to plant a bomb that kills dozens of innocent Vietnamese.

Each brush with America made Graham more determined to track down this famous file, as if it were the Holy Grail. He saw it as the source of all his problems with America, possibly even as the source of his problems with the Nobel Prize for Literature committee; he assumed that he was being watched, his correspondence opened, his telephone calls recorded, while someone, somewhere deep in the bowels of the Hoover Building in Washington, D.C., gathered this information and misinformation and used it against him at every opportunity.

Early in 1981, when we met for a drink at the Ritz Bar in London, one of his favorite haunts, he asked me if I would be willing to do him a great favor. Anything, I said. He nodded darkly, his long, slim fingers touching as if in prayer. He glanced to either side and drew himself closer to me. He had read about the Freedom of Information Act, he said, and wondered if I could find a way of getting him access to his FBI file. I had no idea how the Freedom of Information Act worked and said so, but I promised to do my best. He confirmed it by letter, adding that given his views on America's involvement in Vietnam, it was likely to be a bulky dossier, possibly even sufficient material for a short book. He thought it would be particularly interesting to know who had informed on him in various places all over the world over the years. The only thing he really wanted at this point in his life was a look at his FBI file—and, of course, the Nobel Prize, which was still being withheld from him by one vote, from a man who seemed determined to outlive him.

When I got back to New York, I looked into the matter, which turned out to be amazingly simple—though I did not tell Graham this, since he would have been hugely disappointed. All I had to do was get a lawyer in Washington to make an application to the FBI, then wait. Time, it appeared, was the major factor, perhaps because the government hoped that some applicants would simply lose patience. In this case, time dragged on for months, while Graham inquired impatiently whether there was any news and wondered if the FBI was using the time to destroy or alter their records on him.

Finally, there arrived in my office a slim envelope containing the FBI's famous Graham Greene dossier. Though many of the names and some of the information had been carefully blacked out, my heart sank instantly at the sight of it—this was not at all the bulky package Graham had been expecting for all these years. One typical item was a clipping from Walter Winchell's column in the New York *Daily Mirror*, dated December 19, 1956, in which Winchell wrote: "Hollywood newspaper people are not happy about America's most-decorated soldier (Audie Murphy) taking the lead role in the film version of 'The Quiet American,' which libels Americans. The author of the book admits to being an ex-Commie." The clipping had been pasted carefully to a sheet of paper, at the top of which Clyde Tolson, J. Edgar Hoover's assistant, housemate, and reputed lover, had written his initials to indicate that Hoover had read it.

Another item, also bearing Tolson's initials, was a reply to a request for information from Marvin Watson in LBJ's White House, where apparently they wondered who Graham Greene was and why several antiwar groups were quoting him on the subject of Vietnam. The FBI memo explained helpfully that he was "a well-known Catholic British writer."

The only other document of note was a lengthy report on an International Congress of Intellectuals, held in Warsaw in 1948, in which

Graham Greene was listed as a delegate, along with Pablo Neruda, Jorge Amado, Louis Aragon, Le Corbusier, Bertolt Brecht, Lord Calder, Ted Hughes, Randall Jarrell, and Ruth Benedict. A note at the bottom of the document warns that John Rogge, a former assistant attorney general from the New Deal, "is bringing to the Congress an address from Henry Wallace." Apparently the worst the FBI could produce about Graham was that he might have listened to an address from the former vice president.

This was about the extent of the FBI's knowledge of Graham Greene. There were no glamorous spies, no records of telephone conversations, no record of his visit to Fidel Castro or his travels in Vietnam, no dark accusations of opium smoking or visiting prostitutes, no mention even of his having been a member of the SIS or a close friend of Kim Philby. Far from being a thorn in J. Edgar Hoover's side or the target of constant FBI surveillance, Graham had apparently hardly ever attracted Hoover's attention.

Graham brooded darkly on the possibility that the FBI file was a fake, that somewhere they had concealed the *real* file, with all the dirt, and from time to time he urged me on to further effort, but nothing came of further inquiries. The bomb had turned out to be a damp squib, and no book was to come of it.

Perhaps because of that, our relationship temporarily lost some of its warmth, and eventually, with a typically cutting comment, he went back to Viking, ostensibly because he was dissatisfied by the number of copies we had remaindered of *Getting to Know the General,* a book about the late Omar Torrijos that had been difficult, if not impossible, to sell.

We continued to correspond, and I continued to see him whenever I went to Europe—in some ways it was easier to think of him as a friend when I was no longer his editor, though I am not sure the reverse was true. I had thought of Graham as old when I was fifteen, but now he really *was* old, his eyes an icy blue, so pale that he seemed almost blind, his face puffy where he had once been gaunt, yet he continued to travel, to write, to involve himself in countless lost causes. In his last letter to me, he said he was well, "except for the incurable disease of age."

He never did win the Nobel Prize.

PART FIVE

Jesus Wants You to Be Rich!

CHAPTER 23

*B*Y 1972, I had written hundreds of thousands of words for magazines and newspapers without the idea of writing a book ever having crossed my mind. Despite having edited God knows how many hundreds of books—many of which, truth to tell, might better have gone unpublished—the book still seemed to me something of a sacred object, not to be undertaken in a light spirit. When I thought of writing a book, I thought of Graham Greene rather than many of "my" authors, who seemed to have stumbled into writing books more or less by accident and learned how to do it, to the extent they had learned at all, by trial and error. It might seem odd that after so much exposure to authors, I still held naive illusions about authorhood, but such is the fact.

After the New York *Herald Tribune* closed its doors in 1966, Clay Felker, then the editor of the newspaper's Sunday magazine, reconstituted *New York* as an independent enterprise and eventually made it a home for the practitioners of what was then called "the new journalism," including Jimmy Breslin, Tom Wolfe, Gail Sheehy, Nick Pileggi, and "Adam Smith." "The new journalism" was hard to define, but in practice it meant writing nonfiction as narrative, with a clear-cut story line, strong characters, and as much pizzazz as possible. In the "old" journalism, typified by the news pages of *The New York Times*, the writer was ideally invisible—he or she reported the facts as objectively as possible. In the "new" journalism, the writer bullied his way into the story, sometimes overwhelming the people he was writing about, and inevitably blurred what had once been the fairly rigid distinction between nonfiction and fiction—a distinction that had in any event been eroding under the influence of books such as Meyer Levin's *Compulsion* (which presented fact as fiction) and the nonfiction of Norman Mailer (in which fact and fiction were indistinguishable). In keeping with the zeitgeist, the new journalism was almost by definition overheated, full of sound effects, and occasionally shrill. The people who were good at it, such as Wolfe and Breslin, were journalistic exhibitionists, media stars whose specialty was making even the humdrum and the insignificant seem important and, above all, exciting. Even the restaurant reviews had to be written like narrative stories, with a beginning, a middle, and an end, which probably explains why the celebrity chef appeared as a culture figure then, since a writer could hang a story on him, as opposed to simply reporting whether the food was edible and the service good or bad.

The staff writers at *New York* constituted a small, clubby set; very much on the defensive, they were not exactly welcoming to outsiders or newcomers, and it was not then a place for which I thought of writing. When my agent Lynn Nesbit urged it on me, I was torn between reluctance—I feared being out of my depth—and enthusiasm, for I was getting tired of writing for women's magazines, with their restricting format and narrow range of interests.

Almost from the first, the pieces I did for *New York* were splashy successes, in the sense that they were controversial, lent themselves to being cover pieces, and stirred up a lot of talk. I attribute this far more to Felker's shrewdness—no magazine editor ever had a better sense of what would sell copies and start a buzz than Felker in his heyday—than to any skill or insight of mine. Indeed, the first piece I wrote for Felker came about only because none of the women's magazines (nor the *Times*) wanted it. Some months previously, my wife and I had been dining out at a restaurant where two rather drunken men seated near us began to make remarks about her fairly low-cut dress. I kept my temper for as long as I could, but when they continued, despite a complaint to the owner, I lost my temper completely, grabbed a heavy cut-glass ashtray, and flung it with a good deal of force at the larger of the two men, hitting him neatly on the forehead. Once the ensuing fracas was over, I was astonished to find that Casey was furious with me. I had been under the impression that I was defending her honor, and that she would be grateful for it. She, on the other hand, felt that she had been handling a potentially embarrassing situation gracefully and without a scene and that I had acted on her behalf without even asking for her opinion—

that, in fact, it was not *her* honor that I was defending at all but my own, as if she were chattel or a possession of mine.

As I thought about it later, I decided that she had a point. I had assaulted the man because he was making lewd remarks about my wife—it was my own amour propre that was at stake, not Casey's. I was not sorry to have thrown the ashtray at a rude and noisy oaf, but on the other hand I could understand that Casey felt the situation had been taken out of her hands.

Lynn Nesbit passed my account of the ashtray incident on to Felker, who instantly saw that it spoke to many of the questions that were beginning to trouble women about their relationships with men. Himself an unapologetic male chauvinist at the time, Felker nevertheless had an eagle eye for the kind of popular psychology that appealed to women readers, and he knew just what to do with the goods when he had them. My story appeared with a striking cover and was soon at the center of a fierce debate. For some time I had been writing, in *Glamour,* about the ways in which women were badly treated—or perceived themselves to be—in the workplace, using for examples the everyday evidence before my own eyes at S&S. S&S was not worse than anyplace else, but there was no shortage of horror stories about male chauvinism. Some men, then, felt that in the war between the sexes I had betrayed my gender.

With the piece in hand, Lynn Nesbit managed to persuade Nan Talese, then an editor at Random House, that she should commission me to do a book on the subject. With considerable misgivings, but won over by Lynn's enthusiasm and Nan's quiet confidence in her own judgment, I agreed. I did not ask anybody at S&S what they thought about my signing a book contract with Random House—the whole idea seemed to me so unreal that I didn't take it seriously. Editors sometimes wrote books, I knew—Hiram Haydn, then at Atheneum, had written a novel, and it was not unknown for an editor to write a book about a subject that interested him or her, stamp collecting, or photography, for instance. Mostly, however, when editors wanted to become writers, they resigned, as Justin Kaplan had done when he decided to write a biography of Mark Twain. The general feeling was that an editor should be one thing or another and not "play both sides of the street," as it were, but I couldn't see what harm it would do, and in any case, despite Nan's optimism, I took it for granted that the book, like most books, wouldn't go anywhere.

Of course, that was underrating both the subject and my own

nascent ability to attract media attention, which had so far been hidden under a bushel from everyone, myself included. No sooner was *Male Chauvinism* published than I was swept into a whole new world, about which my only knowledge was vicarious, gleaned from people such as Jackie Susann and Connie Ryan—instead of organizing a book tour, I was doing one. The subject of male chauvinism was hot enough to get me on *Today,* Merv Griffin's show, Irv Kupcinet's show in Chicago, and even *The Tonight Show* (then starring Johnny Carson), not to speak of radio talk shows that I hadn't even *heard* of. To my surprise, I did not suffer from stage fright—I was not my mother's son for nothing, it appeared. Fame, it turned out, was transitory—twenty-four hours after doing *Tonight,* total strangers in the street recognized me on sight; forty-eight hours after doing it nobody gave a damn or could remember my name—but it was heady while it lasted.

I had stumbled across the idea of writing about power, thus fulfilling Carlos Castaneda's prediction, because S&S was as fertile a ground for observation of the uses (and misuses) of power as it was for watching male chauvinism at work. The phrase "Nature, red in tooth and claw" could well have described S&S at this period, and it was no great leap to depict this in a book for the general reader. The book I had in mind was similar to one by the English humorist C. Northcote Parkinson, whose most famous book, *Parkinson's Law,* was a tongue-in-cheek business manual, full of clever observations but not intended to be taken with an entirely straight face.

Nan Talese, who loved this idea, had no sooner bought it for Random House than, in a crosstown shuffle that was to become familiar, she moved to S&S and handed me over to Jim Silberman (who would later follow her to S&S himself).

Silberman liked the idea of a book about power, too, but his intention was for it to be taken seriously, as a guide to getting ahead, in the American tradition of self-help books. Had he told me this outright, I would probably have refused to do it or claimed that I didn't know how. Very fortunately, he did not approach the problem frontally but merely led me by indirection (and by very clever editing and packaging) away from the fairly broad humor of Parkinson toward something that might be taken seriously by an ambitious junior executive. I thus found myself launched on the road again, this time in the role of an expert on power. Silberman had calculated shrewdly that the time was right for the subject. The self-help career-advice book, a staple of American publishing since the days of Benjamin Franklin, had reached a kind of temporary peak with big best-sellers such as *Don't Say Yes When You Want to Say No* and *Winning Through Intimidation*. The old tried-and-true message that had made Dale Carnegie famous (and Leon Shimkin rich) with *How to Win Friends and Influence People* had given way to more threatening and aggressive formulas.

Power! had seemed pretty funny to me when I wrote it, but it didn't seem to me to have the makings of a best-seller. That, however, was exactly what it became. Reviewed everywhere (often with outrage), *Power!* leaped onto the *New York Times* best-seller list just as Silberman had predicted. It was as if a blast-furnace door had suddenly opened, blinding me with the brightness within. *Male Chauvinism* had been a heady experience, but *Power!* was on an altogether different scale, a brief taste of what media celebrity is like, a ride on the uphill curve of a roller coaster. *Time* and *Newsweek* consecrated long articles to the book, media pundits wrote serious think pieces about what the book's success portended for our society, I was lampooned and parodied by countless humorists, bitterly attacked by Richard Reeves in *The New York Times Book Review*—my first experience of being savaged as a person, as opposed to merely having my work savaged—and caricatured by cartoonists all over the country, even in *The New Yorker* (fame indeed!). I appeared on every possible talk show—in one hilarious encounter, Johnny Carson tried to move his desk into the "power position" as we tried to psyche each other out. I had—rather cavalierly—chosen blue as the "power color," mostly because I have always been partial to blue when it comes to suits, shirts, and ties. If there was going to be a power color, I decided, why not blue? Soon after the book was published, people started having their offices painted blue and ordering blue carpets and upholstery, even at S&S and Random House, where one might have supposed people would know better than to take my word for it.

Men bought blue power ties, wore power shoes (four eyelets, plain toes, highly polished), and rearranged their office furniture overnight to produce the power look. Businesswomen went for their kind of power clothes, hired male secretaries (at that time the ultimate power symbol for a woman), and bought the right kind of power briefcase. As for *Power!* itself, it zoomed up the best-seller list to number one.

· · ·

NOT EVERYONE shared my pleasure at this unexpected success. A good many of my authors sounded very frosty indeed when they called me, and who can blame them? Who wants an editor whose book is number one when one's own book hasn't even hit the list? Some of my colleagues were equally distressed, even more so when I was attending a literary cocktail party and Mildred Marmur, formerly of S&S, then director of rights for Random House, arrived with the news that the mass-market paperback rights for *Power!* had been sold for $485,000, a sum that would probably have to be multiplied by ten to reach its equivalent today. "Well," Snyder said, giving me a bear hug as I looked at a lot of glum faces, "there's nothing like success for teaching you who your friends are." The same is true of failure too, as we were both to discover.

My feet hardly touched the ground—literally, for Random House kept me out on the road selling the book as long as they could, from city to city, until, finally, I reached some kind of apotheosis at a gathering of self-help stars in some huge arena in Dallas. The heavyweights of the self-help trade were there, so my appearance came rather late in the program, behind such stars as Robert Ringer, author of *Winning Through Intimidation,* and old troupers such as Og Mandino, Napoleon Hill, and Joe Girard ("The World's Number One Salesman"). There wasn't an empty seat in the house. The audience was mostly white males in their forties and fifties, with the slightly desperate looks of men who never quite made it in whatever job they had and believed passionately that there existed somewhere a formula that would change their lives.

I was already mildly uneasy at the thought that I was about to tell these people how to change their lives for the better when the speaker before me, a robust, red-faced cleric of some Southern fundamentalist offshoot church, wearing a suit that appeared to have been made from parachute silk, a white Stetson, and alligator cowboy boots, rose to his feet and approached the podium. He grabbed the mike, walked to the front of the stage, threw his Stetson at the front row, and in a voice that would have woken the dead had there been any in the audience, cried out, "Jesus wants you to be rich!"

There was an uneasy stir in the audience, while he repeated this, louder each time. "I mean *he* wants *you* to be rich, my friends. No doubt about it. But *you've* got to want it too. So I want each and every one of you to get on your feet right now and shout after me, 'Jesus wants me to be rich!' "

A few people stood and mumbled, "Jesus wants me to be rich," with rather shamefaced expressions.

The preacher cupped his ear. "I cain't hear you," he complained. "And if I cain't, he sure cain't. Heaven is a lot further away than this stage. You got to get to your feet and holler so he can hear you. You got to shout it out like you believed it. Now let's go!"

A group of attractive young women, rather like football cheerleaders in matching green sweaters and short but demure white skirts, appeared onstage behind the preacher, smiling with perfect teeth, and added their voices in chorus to the chant. By now, the audience was whipped into a kind of frenzy, shouting "Jesus wants me to be rich!" over and over again to shake the rafters, their faces suffused with passion and belief. It was beginning to dawn on me in a panic that I was going to have to follow this act with my little talk on power, which was bound to come as something of an anticlimax, when the preacher reached into his pockets and began to pull out thick wads of dollar bills, which he flung out toward the audience. Bedlam ensued as people struggled for the bills floating down in the hot, still air of the auditorium while at the same time keeping up the chant, accompanying it with pounding feet in time to "JE-SUS-WANTS-ME-TO-BE-RICH!" over and over again, with the ear-splitting, repetitive effect that had characterized French supporters of the Algerian colonists in the 1950s, who liked to sound out "*L'AL-GÉ-RIE-FRAN-ÇAISE!*" on their car horns all through the night.

By the time the preacher had finished, wiped off his face, and handed the mike over to me, I had already decided that this was not the profession for me. I had neither the shtick nor the passionate zeal that was called for if one wanted to make a living in the self-help trade, and perhaps more important, I wasn't myself a true believer in my own formula, nor quite cynical enough to go on selling it from city to city despite that. It was a relief when the dark night of the soul caught up with me at last, at midnight in the Albert Pick Hotel in Cleveland, during a Shriners' convention, with middle-aged men in funny costumes and gold-laced fezzes raucously chasing women up and down the halls as bells rang and the fire alarm pealed incessantly. I had finally had enough. I called Selma Shapiro, the Random House publicity director, and said, "For God's sake, get me home!"

. . .

IN YEARS to come, I have often met people (mostly, but by no means only, men) who tell me, often in terms of the greatest sincerity and gratitude, that reading *Power!* changed their lives. This happens not just in America, either, since the book has by now been translated into almost every conceivable language (and is currently having a new lease on life in Eastern Europe, where the fall of communism has made it necessary for a whole new generation of readers to learn where to put their desks or what the power color is). To this, I have always been able to answer, with perfect sincerity, that it changed mine too.

Not immediately, however. Because of the endlessly slow way in which authors receive money (they wait until the end of a six-month royalty period, only to find, as a rule, that rights income from a mass-market sale will be reflected on the *next* statement, so the money tends to trickle in over a long period of time instead of in a single gusher, like movie sales) I did not feel immediately rich, which was probably just as well. I *did* feel what the French call *dépaysé,* as if I had lost my bearings. For a brief, perilous moment it seemed as if I might actually have to choose between the two professions. Very fortunately, Dick Snyder told me not to even *think* about it. I could write as many books as I liked, he didn't care. Snyder still knew how to crack the whip, however—indeed, one reason for my dark night of the soul in Cleveland was that I had inadvertently missed an appointment with Paul Gitlin and Harold Robbins, obliging Snyder to fill in for me. I was still working for S&S, he had reminded me in a brief, curt message, and it was time to cut the crap and come home.

The real problem was not at work, however, but at home. While success was not the only reason for the slow deterioration of my marriage to Casey, it certainly didn't help. As is so often the case, the first person to become dazzled by fame was the person who had become famous. While I was to write later that successful people are generally nicer than those who are not, I'm not sure that I fit into that category. With so much of my attention focused on S&S and what remained of it directed toward writing and promoting my books, domestic life got short shrift. It was a condition I had observed often enough in my authors' lives, not to speak of my own family's, so I should have known better. My father and his brothers seldom came home from the studio until late at night, worked seven days a week, and were often on location for months at a time. They considered this normal and did not connect it to the domestic complaints and unhappiness that greeted them on the rare occasions when they *were* home.

In any event, my sudden and bewildering emergence as a self-help guru coincided with a period in which my marriage took a turn for the worse. It does not seem particularly surprising, in retrospect. As if there were a contagious epidemic of flu, everybody's marriage seemed to be collapsing in the early seventies, even those of people whose marriages had seemed to outsiders as solid as the Rock of Gibraltar—it was no doubt partly the logical aftermath of the sixties, when, for a decade or so, everything had seemed permissible.

There had been moments, in the sixties, when even the world of book publishing, outwardly one of the more conventional occupations, was touched by the craziness of the era. Sales conferences, which had usually been held in New York, began to take place in Florida or the Caribbean islands or the Georgia seacoast and rapidly developed a wild, permissive, anything goes tradition—at S&S and Random House, certainly. Once defined by heavy drinking, marathon poker playing with the sales reps, and an occasional bit of bottom pinching in the "hospitality suite," these twice-yearly events took on the appearance of a saturnalia, with rock music blaring at all hours of the night, the smell of marijuana drifting through the corridors, and an atmosphere of sexual license that shocked many of the older generation—not that sales conferences hadn't always caused a few knowing winks among publishing executives and editors and given heartburn to any number of suspicious spouses, but in the sixties the partying got serious the moment the last slide of the day had been shown to the reps and the torches were lit for the luau cocktail party in the hot, moist, tropic air. Some kind of peak was to be reached when an S&S all-girl singing group, composed of Joni Evans, Susan Kamil, assistant art director Judy Lee, and several other executives, fêted Dick with a rendition of "My Guy."

The American Booksellers Association convention, often held in Washington in the middle of the summer—surely the most hot and uncomfortable setting imaginable for a convention outside of hell—became another place for licensed play, perhaps because it was closer to New York and attended therefore by more people from the home office, particularly since most of them had nothing to do there except cruise the booths of rival publishers picking up freebies. I remember a party in the S&S hospitality suite in a Washington hotel when a young assistant editor, dancing in an abbreviated dress, did a high kick and accidentally sent a lamp shade flying, to land on the head of the wife of the then heir-apparent, Michael Shimkin. With the air conditioner overburdened in the August heat of Washington, the buckets of ice melting on the table, and half a dozen sales reps smoking cigars and playing cards in the bed-room, it was like dancing in a sweat bath, and shortly after the Shimkins left there was a nasty fistfight, quickly settled by Snyder, over the young editor. And that was *before* the fun really started.

It was a period when anything seemed possible. Dick Snyder's marriage had already faltered, Bob Gottlieb left his wife, Muriel, after God only knew how many years, to marry the actress Maria Tucci, beautiful daughter of one of his authors; Tony Schulte's marriage ended; Jim Silberman left his wife, mass-market publisher Leona Nevler, for Selma Shapiro, causing such a scandal that they were both obliged to leave, Selma to set up her own publicity firm and Jim to begin an imprint of his own at S&S.

In the early seventies, the publishing business was following in the wake of the country's flirtation with sudden social change. The old certainties seemed dead and buried, all hell had broken loose, and the ties that people had supposed were bound for life came suddenly undone.

People not only made strange (or at least unexpected) life decisions, they made even stranger career decisions. In a move that surprised everyone on both sides of the Atlantic (but was to set something of a pattern for the future), Tony Godwin, the mercurial and much-admired joint managing director of Weidenfeld and Nicolson, in London, came to New York to become editor and publisher of his own list of books at Harcourt Brace Jovanovich. One of the statelier and more ponderous old-line New York publishing houses, HBJ was then undergoing an ambitious (and ultimately unsuccessful) face-lift at the hands of its testy and demanding chief executive, Bill Jovanovich. Jovanovich, a maverick himself who wanted to control every aspect of his publishing house right down to the smallest detail (and considered himself qualified to do so in any area), had picked an equally maverick personality in Godwin, whose passion for detail was exceeded only by his determination not to be bossed around by anyone (including Jovanovich) and his total ignorance of the United States.

Godwin, who had left his wife and children and seemed to be beginning a whole new life virtually from scratch, had started as that rarest of creatures, an enthusiastic and unorthodox bookseller. He founded the famous Better Books store on Charing Cross Road just after the war, and later revived Bumpus, one of the more revered of London's book-shops. Picked by Sir Allen Lane, the founder of Penguin, to modernize Penguin's fiction line, Godwin's innovations astonished the London lit-erary world and eventually led to a clash with Lane, who was alarmed by the far-reaching changes Godwin was making in one of Britain's most respected cultural institutions, and more than a little jealous of the younger man as well.

From there Godwin went to Weidenfeld and Nicolson, where he swiftly acquired a reputation for commissioning large quantities of books on outline, always a risky way of building up a list quickly. As it happened, his boss, George Weidenfeld, had been doing just that for years, but he usually commissioned large, illustrated coffee-table books by titled celebrities, which were usually ghostwritten, and on which Weidenfeld usually made his money back by selling finished books at inflated prices to American publishers and book clubs before the manu-script had even been written. Godwin, on the contrary, was commis-sioning long books on serious nonfiction subjects by major writers and academics, many of which had a limited appeal to American readers. Those in the know thought he was lucky to have jumped before he was pushed, though not necessarily into Jovanovich's arms.

Small, rail-thin, sharp-featured, with an engaging smile, a full head of wiry gray hair—a kind of Anglo-Welsh "afro"—and bright, sparkling eyes, Godwin's greatest asset was his charm. He was a bril-liant talker, with an endless supply of lubricious anecdotes about every-one he knew, and the kind of infectious enthusiasm that other publishers envied. He had good taste, too: His authors in England had included Len Deighton, Edna O'Brien, Joan Didion, Eric Ambler, and Antonia Fraser, though he never managed to acquire that kind of stellar list for Jovanovich, perhaps because he was now competing directly against more powerful houses such as Random House and S&S.

He had a way with women, too. He managed to combine a lower-class defiance, then having been made fashionable by the success of movies such as *Alfie*, with a certain weary vulnerability, like a bantam gamecock that needs looking after, but despite the buzz that surrounded him, by 1974, a year or so after his arrival in New York, he seemed to have missed the boat and looked somehow diminished and sad. Perhaps the tide was running against him. Publishers were being acquired by corporations that didn't know anything about the book business and were more interested in the bottom line than in owning the hot new candidate for the Booker Prize or a 200,000-word work of history by a fashionable Oxford don. Jovanovich himself was already spending more of his time on educational publishing, which was less risky and far more profitable. He eventually bought SeaWorld and moved Harcourt Brace Jovanovich down to Orlando, closer to the seals and killer whales, which made far more money for the company than trade books.

Before that happened, Godwin was dead—he collapsed alone in his apartment from an asthma attack, a sad way to go for a man who loved company and disliked being alone. It was as if with his death the business on which he had scarcely made an impact suddenly changed. The age in which the editor was the center of things was over. The businessmen were taking over.

CHAPTER 24

FOR ME, ODDLY enough, this brave new age was ushered in by Jovanovich. For some time now, Leon Shimkin had been making no secret of his desire to cash in his chips and sell S&S. Naturally, he did a kind of fan dance, alternately attracting buyers and denying his intention to sell—probably no more than a natural attempt to get some idea of what the company was worth. The truth was that while on the one hand Shimkin wanted to sell, on the other he wanted the buyer to let him continue to run things. There had been so many false warnings that most of us had lost interest in the subject altogether, so it was with some surprise that I received a phone call from Snyder, saying that we must speak immediately.

We met in a hotel bar over the weekend, and it swiftly transpired that the person who had caused this degree of alarm in Dick Snyder was Bill Jovanovich, who had offered to buy S&S away from Shimkin. Paul Gitlin, Harold Robbins's agent, was also a board member and general counsel for Harcourt Brace Jovanovich. Learning of Jovanovich's interest in acquiring S&S, Gitlin called Shimkin, and discussions between the two principals began almost at once. With Gitlin pushing hard, there was a serious possibility that the deal might happen, despite predictable ego problems between the two men.

In the meantime, however, Dick had met Jovanovich—had been summoned to the great man's presence, actually—and learned almost immediately that trading Shimkin for Jovanovich would not be in his or my interests. Many of the things that people who didn't like Dick complained about were true about Jovanovich in spades: his temper, his ego, his impatience, his determination not to be upstaged and to have the last word. Jovanovich, Dick assured me, wanted to run things in detail and to have the last word on everything; he liked to cut his executives down to size; he was proud to run a "lean" company (that is to say, he was against corporate perks for his senior executives); and when it came to managers and editors with "inflated" reputations (i.e., Dick and me), he was from Missouri (metaphorically speaking, since he was in fact some kind of Yugoslav). Most important of all, although Jovanovich claimed to know everything there was to know about trade-book publishing, he didn't know his ass from his elbow—an amateur, in short, who would be telling us what to do.

Dick's ear for trouble was flawless, and I had no doubt that everything he said was true. Jovanovich wanted to talk to me, too, Dick told me, and I should take his phone call and be as noncommittal as possible. In the meantime, this was a deal that had to be killed, the sooner the better. Would I mind if he told Shimkin that we would both resign if the deal went through?

In for a penny, in for a pound, I thought—I had always trusted Dick and saw no reason not to now, though I had a certain queasy feeling in the pit of my stomach at the thought that I might have to leave a place where I had worked for nearly twenty years—so we shook hands solemnly, and Dick went off to do what he had to do. I received, as promised, a gruff call from Jovanovich, promising me that nothing would change, and a far gruffer one from Gitlin, who had guessed that something was going on. Jovanovich, he promised me, was a man of culture who would respect my opinions. At some point in the conversation Gitlin became aware, if he was not already, that I was not enthusiastic about the deal. What could I possibly have against Jovanovich, he asked? He was terrific with editors (I recalled that he had not been terrific to Tony Godwin) and looked forward to working with me. Dick, Gitlin went on, might have a few problems with Jovanovich, since they were both stubborn men, but I would have none, and if by chance one should arise, I only had to come to Gitlin and it would be taken care of.

But that was something I had been resisting for years, much as I liked Gitlin. Once Gitlin did you a favor, you were his for life, so far as he was concerned. I told him that I was flattered by Jovanovich's confidence in me, but Dick and I were a team: We went together, and if he wasn't happy about the deal, neither was I. I was making a big mistake, Gitlin said darkly. Shimkin had already made up his mind: S&S was going to Harcourt, and Jovanovich wouldn't forget anybody who had come out against him.

I didn't care. I had complete confidence in Dick's ability to kill the deal, and it was not misplaced. He made it evident to Jovanovich that he risked buying a publishing company without its major executives and evident to Shimkin that Jovanovich was unlikely to listen to a word he had to say. The deal fell through, and the only significant consequence of it was that Dick now decided that the sooner he found for Shimkin a deal we could all live with, the better for all concerned. Until now, Dick had been trying to prevent Shimkin from selling; now, he was determined to get Shimkin to sell as soon as possible to someone who took the same view of the future as Dick did.

It was against this background that, on a business trip to Los Angeles, Snyder met Robert Evans, the boy-wonder producer of *The Godfather*. He mentioned to Evans that S&S might be for sale, and Evans told his boss, Charles G. Bluhdorn, the conglomerateur owner of the Gulf + Western Corporation, whose purchase of Paramount Pictures had made him a power in Hollywood.

By reputation, Bluhdorn was the most ruthless conglomerateur of them all, the so-called "Mad Austrian." His violent temper, his many eccentricities (not all of them endearing), and his amazing volatility had made him a celebrity among a class of people rarely seen outside boardrooms. But while his fellow conglomerateurs preferred to remain invisible, Bluhdorn sought the limelight and apparently never shut up.

THE FASCINATION that certain artifacts of the sixties and seventies once had is hard to explain: white go-go boots, for example, or platform shoes for men, or Petula Clark singing "Downtown"—these things bring back not so much nostalgia as a certain wonder that they ever held our attention. The "conglomerate" is just as much a part of that increasingly remote past as bell-bottom trousers and Nehru jackets. Indeed, it is hard to conjure up a time when the word itself seemed to suggest to most people something new and threatening, a business corporation the only purpose of which was to maintain a dizzying rate of growth and which did so by the constant acquisition of other companies.

Not only did the companies acquired usually have little or nothing in common with the core business of the acquirer, very often the acquirer had in fact no core business to begin with—it existed merely for the purpose of growth, like certain parasitic amoebas. People feared that the companies they worked for would be acquired by a conglomerate—more often than not in an "unfriendly" takeover that resembled, to those who were acquired, the rape of the Sabine women—which would then proceed to fire employees wholesale, without regard to the years they had spent with the company or the importance of their work. Conglomerates were seen by most people outside Wall Street as bad things, manifestations of greed and long-distance management by strangers who didn't know a thing about your business. The word most often associated with them was *ruthless.*

What Gulf + Western knew of S&S they learned through Dick, and the first thing they understood was that Dick was their kind of guy, a tough, shrewd, practical man who could get things done and who thought big. What Gulf + Western was about, after all, was growth, expansion, a ballooning list of assets against which they could borrow more money to buy more assets, brand names that were—or appeared to be—gilt-edged, which made it even easier to borrow still more money and dazzle Wall Street. The only thing that was bad was standing still, since people might then begin to ask whether the company was really making any money at all.

For the first time since the Jovanovich deal had surfaced, Dick was relaxed, happy, smiling, though one saw him seldom, since he was in the middle of the bargaining. He poured me a drink one night in his office, and as we clicked glasses he said, "The good times are coming, trust me."

In a very short time, the deal was done, and S&S changed hands, becoming a part of what was known as "The Gulf + Western Family," to the horror of older executives, many authors, and most of the outside world. It was bad enough that Bennett Cerf had sold Random House to RCA, but now Simon and Schuster had been bought by the most rapacious and ruthless of conglomerateurs. Shimkin could hardly have gotten a worse press among those who cared for culture and literature if he had owned the *Mona Lisa* and sold it for kindling. Bluhdorn was seen as the Vandal at the gates, no doubt eager to fire literary editors, put a stop to the purchase of first novels, and restrict the S&S list to vulgar best-sellers such as Irving Wallace and Harold Robbins. Since I was the editor of both Wallace and Robbins, I did not think I had anything to fear, but at some point Dick told me not to worry anyway. "Trust me," he said, "nothing will change. We'll just make more money and get stock options, that's all."

As a matter of fact, nothing *did* change at first. We did not quit our home in Rockefeller Center for G+W's tower at Columbus Circle, nor were we told to stop buying first novels. Life went on much as before, except for Shimkin, who was swiftly replaced by Dick. The generous perks of a big conglomerate with a movie studio showered down on some of us, everything from our choice of leased cars to telephone credit cards, Simmons mattresses at discount, free health-club memberships, sales conferences in the Dominican Republic, first-class air travel, and unlimited movie screenings. More important, we had, for the first time, a sense of security. Bluhdorn *liked* books, much more than he liked mattresses, zinc, steam valves, or automobile bumpers.

Some time went by before I met Bluhdorn, partly because Dick was eager to protect what he regarded as my delicate sensibilities and partly because Bluhdorn's ramshackle corporate empire was run like a feudal kingdom. The CEOs of each of G+W's many components were like medieval barons, with unlimited power in their own fiefs. When Bluhdorn needed to talk to (or scream at) one of them, he sent for them; he did not need to meet their underlings. However, perhaps because of my family name—Bluhdorn was fascinated by the movie business—I was eventually invited to a pre-Christmas dinner in the G+W building.

As we milled about for cocktails, I got my first real glimpse of the diversity of G+W. I met executives from the movie business, the industrial-valve business, the truck-leasing business, the mattress business, the desk-lamp business, the zinc business—there appeared to be no end (or logic) to the businesses Bluhdorn had acquired, and of course there *was* none. G+W eventually contained divisions devoted to manufacturing, communications, foods, consumer products, agriculture, mining, and financial services, and included, among many other assets, New Jersey Zinc, Paramount Pictures, Desilu Productions, Merson Musical Products, Consolidated Cigar Corporation, Quebec Iron and Titanium Corporation, Madison Square Garden, Furniture City, Tool Industries, Bonney Forge and Foundry, Mal Tool and Jet Engineering, Collyer Insulated Wire Company, Simon and Schuster, Simmons Mattress, and a substantial portion of the Dominican Republic. Bluhdorn's real secret was understanding the simple fact that if you owned a business, bankers would lend you money to buy another one. So long as you kept buying companies, you could go on borrowing more money, like a giant Ponzi scheme. The trick was to keep moving; the one thing you couldn't afford to do was to stop and consolidate, even had that been possible, since the vital flow of money from the banks would then stop.

Shortly before dinner, Dick managed to steer Bluhdorn through the crowd in my direction. I was confronted by an energetic man in his early fifties, with a wild look in his eyes and the red complexion of someone whose blood pressure is off the scale and who doesn't pay any attention to diet and exercise. Bluhdorn's teeth seemed either too big or too many, like those of a shark. Huge and glistening white, they filled his mouth like bathroom tiles. I tried to shake his hand, but he gave me a bear hug, squeezing me so tightly that I thought his intention might be to break my ribs. "Dick tells me you're a goddamn genius," he said—he spoke quickly, with a faint, guttural Germanic accent, behind which there lurked the hint of some other language, Yiddish perhaps. I modestly deflected the compliment. "No, no," Bluhdorn cried, "if he says it, it's *true,* goddamn it to hell! I love geniuses! You're my boy!"

He let go of me and pinched my cheek, hard enough to bring tears to my eyes. I do not know if he had acquired this habit by reading about Napoleon, who often singled out one of his veterans on parade by pinching his cheek, but I could see that Bluhdorn was in fact Napoleonic in other ways. He had the same piercing eyes, the visible energy, the total self-confidence, together with the absolute certainty that he was your master and that you would do anything for him.

It was not a type likely to frighten me, having grown up in the wake of my Uncle Alex. Like Alex, Bluhdorn could radiate charm when he wanted to; also like him, Bluhdorn was an expert at telling people what they wanted to hear, then doing the opposite. He had, in fact, persuaded Shimkin to sell S&S by offering him an honored place on the G+W board, where he could serve as an elder statesman, only to pull the seat out from under Shimkin the moment his company had been bought, thus plunging Shimkin into well-heeled, but gloomy, retirement.

Bluhdorn was Napoleonic in more ways than one. He had the reputation of disliking anybody who was taller than he was, and certainly short people seemed to do better at G+W than the tall, which I took as a good augury for Dick and myself, who were about the same height as Bluhdorn. Unlike the emperor, however, Bluhdorn did not surround himself with a praetorian guard of very tall men to show his contempt for their height; on the contrary, Bluhdorn's bodyguard of assistants and PR flacks were short, nervous, and sweaty. Clearly kept on a tight leash by their master, they laughed when he did and cringed when he didn't, and clung close to him like remora around a shark.

Bluhdorn released my cheek, and made his way off through the crowd, embracing everyone he passed like a politician on the make. He had the gift, I could not help noticing, of remembering people's names, which in a company of G+W's size and diversity cannot have been easy.

I was seated at the dinner table next to the tallest man in the room, Michael Burke, former president of the New York Yankees, now president of Madison Square Garden, who had been shanghaied into the G+W family when Bluhdorn bought the Garden. I knew Burke slightly—he was a fellow equestrian—and he was what the Irish call "a lovely man," funny, brave (he had been a spy behind the German lines in Rome in 1944), and engagingly cynical about authority figures, including Bluhdorn, who suspected, correctly, that Burke made fun of him behind his back. Unfortunately for Bluhdorn, Burke was the darling of the New York press, and a beloved figure in the world of sports, so it was almost impossible to fire him.

Beside each place setting was a thin black box wrapped with a gold ribbon. We had been advised not to open our presents before Bluhdorn's speech, and the rumor was that each box contained a Christmas bonus check. Burke and I talked horses and hunting through the meal. There was a certain queasiness in the air, partly caused by proximity to power—most of the executives around the table were from out of town, and only saw Bluhdorn once a year, so they were like officials from the far corners of the Roman Empire invited to dinner by the emperor, and not sure whether the meal would end with dessert or their beheading— partly because the G+W tower was notorious for swaying in a high wind, producing a sensation not unlike seasickness in those who had delicate stomachs. If you looked at your glass closely enough, you could actually see the water moving.

As dessert was served Bluhdorn rose to speak. His voice was high-pitched and rasping, something between quacking and an angry bark, and his way of encouraging the troops was to single them out one at a time to be "roasted" with fierce humor. It was, in fact, an amazing sight:

thirty or so middle-aged men in blue suits (there were almost no women present), nervous smiles fixed on their faces, waiting to see who Bluhdorn would pounce on next. They didn't even know what to pray for—the natural thing was to pray that he would skip over you, but then again, being skipped over might mean that he didn't care about you because he'd already decided to fire you. Michael Burke sat through this remarkable performance with stony indifference—Bluhdorn apparently knew better than to give Burke the treatment—then, clearly bored with the proceedings, he took the ribbon off his gift package and peeked inside. A smile came over his face, as he pulled out of the box a pair of one-size-fits-all stretch black gloves—Bluhdorn had bought a clothing company that manufactured them. Burke pulled them on, then held up one black-gloved hand. A deadly silence fell over the room, and Bluhdorn, momentarily silenced, stared at Michael Burke suspiciously. "Yes?" he asked. "You have a question?" Burke nodded cheerfully. "I just wanted to know which one of these guys I'm supposed to strangle," he said.

Nobody laughed harder than Bluhdorn, but although the big teeth were clenched in a grin, there was nothing humorous about the way he looked at Burke. Right then and there I decided that Charles G. Bluhdorn was not a man to cross.

BLUHDORN'S LIFE was not exactly an open book, and the few facts tended to contradict each other, even in his "official" biographies, but it seems certain that he was born in Vienna, in 1926, of middle-class Czech parents. Whether or not he was Jewish was a question that was often asked, but never answered. The fact that his family moved from Austria to England in 1936, and that Bluhdorn was relocated to the United States as a refugee in 1942 certainly makes it seem likely that he was—not to speak of the fact that his speech, rapid, staccato, and sputtering as it was, was laden with colloquial Yiddish insults like *putz*, *schmuck*, and *nebbish*. Still, a lot of New Yorkers affect a familiarity with Yiddish, if only to make themselves sound like tough guys. All one can say is that Bluhdorn seemed to tread a careful line on the subject, allowing some people to believe he was Jewish, and others not.

His business career was in the Horatio Alger tradition. Having arrived in New York as a refugee, he went to work for a cotton broker at a salary of fifteen dollars a week, then switched to the commodities import/export business—a lifelong preoccupation with Bluhdorn, who bought and sold sugar futures the way other men play golf. By the time he was twenty-one, Bluhdorn had cornered the market in malt—his trading in that substance was, in fact, so hyperactive that it attracted the attention of the U.S. government, and brought about his first brush with Washington, though by no means the last. At twenty-three he was in business for himself, already a millionaire and something of a legend, but while he traded in almost everything from lard to pasta, he dreamed of something more stable, of an empire.

Bluhdorn's epiphany—his equivalent of Paul's vision on the road to Damascus—came in 1957, when he bought Michigan Bumper, a decrepit manufacturer of stamped replacement bumpers. It was not just that he saw his future in a more solid business than commodities, with their notorious fluctuations, nor even that he believed (wrongly) that the automobile spare parts business was the wave of the future and would survive every vicissitude of the economy—it was that with the purchase of Michigan Bumper he worked out the simple formula that would take him far beyond malt, lard, sugar, and bumpers into the financial stratosphere.

Michigan Bumper was an unglamorous, low-rent, rust-belt corporation, whose stock (and industrial expertise) was at the bottom of the barrel, but once Bluhdorn owned it, it did not take him long to discover that bankers were happy to lend him money to acquire another corporation. However decrepit Michigan Bumper might be, it *existed*—unlike most commodity deals. Somewhere in the wasteland of the industrial Midwest there was a real-life, Dickensian factory, belching smoke and turning out replacement bumpers for 1948 Fords and Chevrolets for sale to people who couldn't afford factory parts. Bankers, Bluhdorn discovered, love bricks and mortar, and in no time he was able to merge his new acquisition with Beard & Stone Electric Co., of Houston, another unglamorous manufacturer of replacement auto parts.

Since Houston is near the Gulf of Mexico and Michigan is in the Midwest, some clever soul came up with the idea of calling the merged corporations the Gulf & Western Industries (the idea of replacing the ampersand with a plus sign was to come later, as a symbol of the synergy that Bluhdorn sought, but never achieved, the idea being that the whole of the company was worth more than the sum of its parts).

From these grimy and humble beginnings, Bluhdorn set out on a bank-financed spending spree in 1960.

Each acquisition opened up possibilities for another; each acquisition financed the next. It was a recipe for rapid growth, and while it dazzled investors, it failed to enchant Wall Street, where Bluhdorn was regarded with deep skepticism, partly because of the helter-skelter nature of his acquisitions, partly because Bluhdorn himself never inspired the confidence of major Wall Street figures. There was something about him that set their teeth on edge, a demonic energy, a quality of bluster, a habit of superheated exaggeration and crazed enthusiasm—a simple inability, perhaps, to shut up and stop talking. He remained an outsider and a renegade, and resented the fact bitterly.

In 1966, however, Bluhdorn's fortunes took a turn for the better that was to turn him, from Wall Street's point of view—and perhaps the rest of the world's—from a frog into a prince. Paramount Pictures had been declining for years, its famous name weighted down with expensive failed pictures and a board of directors that consisted of timid old men. Although Adolph Zukor, the founder of Paramount, was still alive, approaching his centenary, and although the studio had once been Hollywood's greatest, the company had slipped far behind its rivals and was in danger of disintegrating. Always quick to recognize a company in distress, Bluhdorn snapped Paramount up.

There are a lot of reasons why wealthy businessmen choose to go into the movie business. One of them is that it can be enormously profitable (of course it is also possible to lose your shirt, as Joseph P. Kennedy and Kirk Kerkorian discovered); a more potent reason is social. By the 1960s Bluhdorn was a rich man, but how many people want to invite the owner of New Jersey Zinc to dinner parties, and how many attractive women want to hear about the automobile spare parts business from the man sitting beside them at the dinner table? Money is not everything, as Bluhdorn—like Marvin Davis and Rupert Murdoch, after him—discovered.

The purchase of Paramount transformed Bluhdorn overnight, however, as he must have guessed it would, from a megalomaniacal acquirer of rather dull companies, most of them on the verge of collapse, into a figure of mystery and power, a financier straight out of a Harold Robbins novel. The owner of a major studio is welcome everywhere; attractive women who aren't even slightly interested in the zinc business are as breathlessly fascinated by movie gossip as anyone else (or, if they're very beautiful, may even be looking for a way *into* the movie business). Bluhdorn suddenly became a *glamorous* person, rather than being merely rich.

What is more, despite the suspicion and hostility Bluhdorn's acquisition of Paramount caused in Hollywood, where it is an axiom that no outsider can understand the movie business or succeed at it, he was, in fact, made for the movie business, and it for him. To begin with, he loved taking risks; then too, although he constantly challenged and fought with the people around him, he recognized talent when he saw it, and was willing to back it—more, much more, than can be said of the proprietors of most movie studios. That he was a monumental pain in the ass, a full-time kibitzer, a tyrant, and totally involved in the process almost goes without saying, but these are just the qualities that are lacking in most studios, and that the old studio heads—Louis B. Mayer, Harry Cohn, Darryl F. Zanuck, and Jack Warner, to name a few—had in superabundance.

Bluhdorn's impatience, his histrionics, his boasting, his kinetic hyperactivity, and monumental chutzpah—in brief, all the things that made him a distrusted figure on Wall Street and in the financial press— were assets in Tinseltown. It was sheer chutzpah to pick Robert Evans, then best known as a smooth and handsome young suit-and-cloaker who became an actor and Hollywood man-about-town, to be Paramount's version of Irving Thalberg, a move that confounded everybody in the industry, including Evans himself, but with his usual shrewdness, Bluhdorn made sure that Evans was surrounded by tough businessmen with good heads for numbers, like Martin S. Davis. The mixture was enormously successful: Paramount's run of box office disasters was replaced by pictures like *Catch-22,* *The Godfather,* and *Love Story.* Bluhdorn's talent for knocking people's heads together and persuading them to do what they didn't want to do was a godsend for Paramount, whether it was getting a reluctant Walter Matthau to star in the movie of Neil Simon's *The Odd Couple* or talking Irving Lazar into accepting an offer for the screen rights to *Funny Girl.* Profane, tireless, crackling with nervous energy, it was as if Bluhdorn always got what he wanted, and since success breeds success, it was soon the case.

He loved Hollywood, and the glamour that went with it, the private jet whisking him off to L.A., the discreet bungalow at the Beverly Hills Hotel, the atmosphere of luxurious decadence combined with hard-headed deal-making and unbridled competition, the opportunity to spar with egos that were even bigger than his own. These were the late sixties, too, before the fear of AIDS and the abuse of cocaine took their toll of people's private lives in Beverly Hills and Bel Air. It was the time of Hugh Hefner's West Coast Playboy mansion, of nonstop partying at the home of disgraced financier Bernie Cornfeld, of parties at Bob Evans's home where there were always beautiful girls, dozens of them, some of them swimming tirelessly back and forth in the floodlit pool, hour after hour, just to give the guests something to look at. Whatever else Bluhdorn got out of his acquisition of Paramount, one of them was a reputation as a man who liked women, and expected to be provided with them—no big deal in the movie business, which has always been run in the spirit of a sultan's harem.

Stories were told about Bluhdorn's blossoming into a full-blown man of the world, one of them being that when Bluhdorn swept into the Plaza Hotel on his way to the Oak Room (then his favorite place for lunch, before he started using his own dining room at the top of the G+W tower), followed by his entourage, he saw a very beautiful young woman sitting on a taboret, and gave her the once-over. Turning to one of his PR men, he told him to invite the woman to lunch, then swept on.

A few minutes later, the PR man returned from his mission empty-handed. It wasn't his fault, he explained—she was waiting, in fact, for her husband, so there was no way he could have persuaded her to accept the invitation. Bluhdorn ignored the man and glanced at the table setting in front of where the PR man was to sit. "Take all that away," Bluhdorn told the maître d'. "He won't be eating with us."

Stories of abrupt dismissals like this were rife, but most of the people at the core of G+W were fanatically loyal to Bluhdorn and he to them. Once he had decided that you were "my boy" or "a genius" or both, he was endlessly supportive, though you had to be able to withstand his ferocious attempts to persuade you to accept his point of view. In truth, the quickest way to gain his respect was to disagree with him, if you had your facts right and were willing to stick up for them. "Goddamn Snyder," he once said, speaking affectionately of the head of S&S, "he *never* agrees with me!"

On occasions, it sometimes seemed as if G+W really was the heartless and monstrous mega-conglomerate trying to take over the studio in Mel Brooks's *Silent Movie*, in which the corporate motto was "Engulf and devour," and the inscription chiseled into the marble wall of the corporate bathroom read, "Our bathrooms are nicer than other people's homes." I remember a whole day spent in the Paramount movie theater (apparently sited below the G+W tower so that you could hear the rumble of the subway trains, by the same architect who put the sway into the building) in which each division's numbers were projected onto a screen, while the head of the division was spotlit in his seat so that Bluhdorn could praise or excoriate him, as the case might be, and another, at a time when he was incensed by a series of muckraking articles about G+W in *The New York Times,* written by Seymour Hersh, when Bluhdorn tore a copy of the *Times* into pieces and flung them out at the audience of G+W executives, the climax of a speech of self-justification so violent, frenzied, and incoherent that everybody was in a state of shock by the end of it.

That was the public man, of course, who rather cherished his reputation for tantrums and high drama. At closer range, he could be far more subtle.

I WAS drawn into Bluhdorn's circle of interest when in 1980 I published *The Fifth Horseman,* a novel by Larry Collins and Dominique Lapierre that foretold a terrorist attack on New York City by Palestinians using a smuggled atomic bomb. Collins and Lapierre were journalists, graduates of *Newsweek* and *Paris-Match,* respectively, and they therefore managed to give the book a certain scary realism. I do not know whether he had actually read *The Fifth Horseman,* but something in the book sparked him off in the spirit of Paul Revere. Over and over, with mounting passion, he held up meetings by explaining to startled and terrified financial managers how New York City could be blown to pieces—all of it, even the G+W tower, for chrissakes—by terrorists, and (his voice rising in pitch like an air-raid siren) NOBODY IN AUTHORITY WOULD LISTEN, NOBODY WAS PREPARED, NOBODY WAS TAKING THIS SERIOUSLY! It could be happening, he cried, at this very minute!

The only way to make people aware of the danger, Bluhdorn finally decided, was to make *The Fifth Horseman* into a movie, a *big* movie, which he figured would be a huge international box-office hit. It became his mission to get the movie made.

Unfortunately, there was one obstacle, even after Bluhdorn had managed to buy the rights from the authors' agent, Irving Lazar: Barry Diller, who was then running Paramount (and doing a brilliant job of it), didn't want to make it. Bluhdorn never stopped arguing with Diller about *The Fifth Horseman* (and the more Bluhdorn argued, the more Diller dug his heels in), but he would not, under any circumstances, *order* Diller to make the picture. Whenever things got out of hand, Diller, whose ability to handle his mercurial boss smoothly was legendary, would simply remind Bluhdorn that all he had to do was send a memo ordering him to make *The Fifth Horseman* and sign it. The picture would then be made.

But of course that was the one thing Bluhdorn couldn't, or wouldn't, do. He believed in delegating authority. Besides, if the project failed, he wanted to be able to say to Diller that it was *his* decision, not Bluhdorn's, that if he wasn't man enough to stand up to Bluhdorn, he wasn't man enough to run the studio. Diller was secure in the knowledge that however much Bluhdorn might rant and rave at him, his boss would never send that memo. The only people who didn't understand that were the authors, who assumed that when Bluhdorn wanted something done, it happened.

As the editor of the book, I was dragged into this imbroglio because of my knowledge of the story—I was, after all, the one person who could be certified as having actually *read* the book, unlike Lazar, who didn't even pretend to have read it.* Thus, I was summoned one Saturday to Bluhdorn's country home for a "story conference," the purpose of which, I soon discovered, was to persuade Milos Forman to sign on as the director of *The Fifth Horseman*. Bluhdorn figured that if he could get a treatment, a director of real stature, and a couple of stars committed to the project, Diller would find it harder to say no.

Bluhdorn's country home was vast, rambling, and handsomely landscaped, but its most notable feature was a parking lot big enough for a good-size motel. Bluhdorn's car and driver, Forman's car and driver, and the car and driver that had been provided for me were drawn up in it as I was conducted to the pool house, where Forman, casually dressed, and Bluhdorn, in the kind of matching short-sleeved pool shirt and shorts that men used to wear poolside in Miami Beach hotels in the 1950s, were sitting under an awning, lighting up cigars.

---

* Dominique Lapierre tested this by slipping a hundred-dollar bill into the copy of the manuscript he gave Lazar to read. Lazar returned the manuscript saying how great it was, the hundred-dollar bill still in place.

The pool itself was huge, glamorous, and empty. As I sat down, I remarked politely on what a nice pool it was.

Bluhdorn seemed startled. "Pool? *What* goddamn pool?" he asked. "We're not here to swim, goddamn it," he barked. "We're here to talk about the goddamn *Fifth Horseman*."

Having put me in my place, Bluhdorn gave Forman, who had probably heard it a dozen times before, his set piece on the dangers facing New York and the need to wake the country up—the whole goddamn world, in fact. Forman nodded at appropriate moments, his eyes half closed. He did not attempt to interrupt Bluhdorn, not so much out of deference but because Bluhdorn never seemed to pause for breath. Bluhdorn was the only man I had ever met who could talk while he was inhaling. Occasionally he stuffed his cigar in his mouth, but that didn't slow him down either.

Eventually, he finished, lit another cigar, and asked Forman to comment. Wearily, Forman proceeded to explain the many difficulties of turning *The Fifth Horseman* into a movie. He shared Bluhdorn's enthusiasm, of course, he said, with an expression so devoid of enthusiasm as to appear almost blank, but the ending was weak, a real letdown. The cop who is the good guy finds the bomb at the last moment and defuses it. It's predictable, Forman said.

Bluhdorn nodded. This was apparently not the first time he'd heard this criticism of his baby. He pointed his cigar at me, "What do you say to that?" he asked, as if the ending were my fault.

I shrugged. "The ending works in the book," I said. "Maybe for the movie you could do something different. After all, in all these books, like *Black Sunday* and so on, the terrorists' bomb always gets defused at the last moment. Maybe in the movie you should make the audience believe that's what's *going* to happen, then, at the very last second, you simply show an atomic bomb going off in New York City. The cop has failed. If that doesn't shock the audience, I don't know what will."

There was a long silence. "You mean, we fry eight million New Yorkers on screen?" Bluhdorn asked.

"Not *all* of them," I said cheerfully. "People in Queens, the Bronx, and Staten Island would probably survive. But that's not the point. Make the ending tough. Have the bomb go off."

There was a longer silence. Then Bluhdorn leaned over, rumpled my hair, and pinched my cheek affectionately. "No," he said, "that's a terrible idea. But at least you're trying. I want you to make this your number-one priority from now on."

It was nearly dark by the time we had finished and Forman and I were dismissed. I accompanied Forman back to his car. Did he really think the ending was the problem? I asked. "No," he said. "Forget the ending. Who cares? The movie is never going to get made."

"My father used to say half of making movies is wasting time."

He rolled his eyes. "He was a wise man. And an optimist."

Waste of time or not, Bluhdorn didn't give up. The next time I heard from him was by way of a telephone call from one of his secretaries. Bluhdorn wanted me to join him for dinner at the Saint-Tropez tomorrow night to talk about the movie.

I said I'd be delighted. Then I asked where the restaurant was, since I'd never heard of it.

"It's not a restaurant, it's a place. He wants you to join him for dinner in Saint-Tropez, France. Do you know where it is?"

Yes, I knew where it was, of course, and had been there often, mostly with my Uncle Alex, on his yacht. Did I have a place to stay there? the secretary wanted to know. Mr. Bluhdorn and his party were staying at the Byblos, which was one of the more glamorous hotels in the South of France, I remembered. Would I like her to book me a room there?

I was momentarily tempted—the last time I had stayed at the Byblos had been with my Uncle Alex and Orson Welles, after Welles had performed the astonishing feat, at La Mère Teraille's restaurant, in La Napoule, of eating two whole roast chickens before devouring a pot of her famous bouillabaisse that would normally have served four persons, with plenty left over for seconds—but then it occurred to me that by staying in the same hotel as Bluhdorn I would automatically become part of his entourage, and might find it difficult to escape. No, I said, I would look after myself, and called Larry Collins, who, together with Dominique Lapierre, was the real object of Bluhdorn's visit, and asked for a bed—at the time Collins and Lapierre had houses close by each other in the hills above Saint-Tropez. If experience had taught me anything, it was to make sure of your own accommodation and rent your own car.

I booked myself on the Concorde, then from Paris to Nice, where I would rent a car for the drive to Saint-Tropez—covering ground that was familiar to me from my childhood and youth. It promised to be a splendid trip, at once full of nostalgia and free—and, as Snyder pointed out, chargeable to the G+W corporate budget, rather than S&S's. I decided to rent a Mercedes at Nice—there was no point in economizing on comfort, I reasoned.

My trip was uneventful but punctuated by constant communications from Bluhdorn's staff: At both airports I was paged relentlessly. Mr. Bluhdorn was over the Atlantic now, together with Mr. Diller, and they would touch down at London, where I should join them for the flight to Nice. Then: They would land in Paris, not London. Then: They were no longer going to land in Paris but had decided to fly on to Amsterdam, instead, where I should meet them.

I ignored all these messages, turned a deaf ear to the loudspeakers calling out my name at the Nice airport, and drove on to Saint-Tropez, arriving at Larry Collins's house with hours to spare before dinner.

Collins had received no word from the Bluhdorn party, so I went down to the hotel Bluhdorn was to stay at—prudently taking a book with me—and waited until finally, after several hours, there was a bustle of limousines outside in the courtyard and Bluhdorn arrived at last. He burst into the suite like a rocket, apparently unfatigued by nearly twenty-four hours of travel on a small airplane.

He immediately made for the nearest telephone in the suite, one of those futuristic, streamlined ones that the French are so fond of, and struggled with it for a few moments, stabbing at the buttons and cursing—Bluhdorn was one of those men who seem unable to deal with any mechanical device. I put him out of his misery and placed a call to New York for him. Whoever was on the other end, Bluhdorn did not waste time on amenities. He simply started talking, asking for the prices of various shares, giving orders to buy or sell, and unloaded enough sugar futures to fill God only knew how many trains and ships, his eyes bright despite the time change, a fresh cigar held delicately between his blunt, well-manicured fingers.

Bluhdorn's two traveling companions were considerably less full of life than their mercurial chief. Barry Diller, the head of Paramount, looked so tired that his eyes seemed to have rolled up in their sockets, exposing only the whites, like two hard-boiled eggs. I asked him how the trip had been. Diller groaned. Bluhdorn, he said, had never stopped talking all the way across the Atlantic—even when he went to the bathroom, he left the door open a crack so he could continue talking. Although hotel suites had been booked for Bluhdorn and his party every-where along the route, they never left the airplane. Instead, so as not to waste time, people with whom Bluhdorn had business waited at the air-ports to come onboard the airplane. As soon as the meetings were fin-ished, the airplane took off again for the next city. The third man in the party was one of Paramount's European executives, a genial, plump man in his sixties, who had apparently been chosen because of his calm-ing effect on Bluhdorn. Though tired, he looked happier than Diller. I asked Diller why this was so. Barry nodded gingerly, like a man with a bad headache who doesn't want to make it worse. "He's learned to sleep with his eyes open," he said.

Bluhdorn finished his call and asked for the time—watches, appar-ently, had a way of going dead on his wrist, perhaps because of the waves of energy emanating from him, or perhaps it had to do with his mechanical ineptitude, whatever the cause he preferred to ask the time rather than glance at a watch. Of course the simple answer may be that since he was always surrounded by people who were paid, among other things, to do his bidding, he simply saw no point in wearing a watch, or making a phone call, or carrying money for tips. Other people could do all those things for him, leaving him free to talk and worry about the price of sugar.

I told him that it was eight o'clock. "Jezus Ker-RIST!" he howled. "We're going to be late for dinner."

Bluhdorn was in motion again, sending the Paramount executive to search his luggage for a resupply of cigars, briefing us about our host, ordering me to place one last call to New York. We descended to the lobby in a flying wedge, led by Bluhdorn. Collins and Lapierre were waiting for us in the lobby. Bluhdorn hugged them, pulled their ear-lobes, pinched their cheeks. They were his boys, he told them, the god-damn movie was going to get made if it was the last goddamn thing he did. People had told him that *The Godfather* was a mistake, but he hadn't listened, he had kept his faith in the book, in the young director, in the whole goddamn thing, and look what had happened. A huge fucking hit, one of the biggest ever! You had to believe, that was all, and he believed, he just wanted them to know that. This was said, I guessed, for the ben-efit of Barry Diller, who had made it very plain that he did not believe, but Diller was beyond arguing, putting one Gucci-clad foot in front of the other on the gleaming marble floor like a man who has just gotten out of bed for the first time since surgery.

Bluhdorn seated us in the limousine like a tour director, and we set off. We were having dinner at the home of Dino Fabbri, he explained, an Italian industrialist and printing magnate, who was both a close friend and a business partner of Bluhdorn's. Fabbri's house, when we arrived there, overlooked the sea, and was built in the style and on much the same scale as that of the Emperor Tiberius's on Capri. The approach was hilly and winding, past small guest houses and garages hidden among small, fragrant pine trees. Bluhdorn charged up a broad flight of marble steps to embrace his host, while we straggled behind.

Fabbri was tall, slender, elegant. He didn't seem to mind Bluhdorn's bear hug, but he didn't look as if he enjoyed it much either. He managed to extricate himself, shake hands with each of us, then led us through room after magnificent room, all of them in the somewhat cold and formal style of the lobby of a very expensive, but modern, grand hotel *de luxe*—the Baur Grünwald in Venice came to my mind. The floors were gleaming marble, and the furniture heavily gilded. Bluhdorn was on edge, trying to move as fast as he could, but Fabbri held him back, determined to show him the grandeurs of his *palazzo*, with a certain amount of pride. Clearly, he had gone to a great deal of trouble to put on this dinner. Spread out gracefully in the rooms were any number of very beautiful women in *couture* dresses, most of them showing a lot of deeply tanned skin, and a certain number of very sleek men wearing the kind of summer suits that can be had only from a Roman tailor, which never seem to crease or wrinkle. Under the subdued lighting, there was a sparkle and glare of gold and gemstones. Fabbri, in short, had produced a party of beautiful people for Bluhdorn, all of them attractive, wealthy, or both. Bluhdorn, however, despite his eye for a good-looking woman, walked right past them all without a word, until we were on the terrace, which was lit with blazing torchères. At the far end a huge buffet had been set up. There were piles of lobsters, displays of every imaginable kind of seafood, hot dishes, cold dishes, all presented with the kind of old-fashioned opulence and elegance that only the French can achieve when money is not a concern. Fabbri held out both arms in a gesture of hostly pride. "What do you think of that?" he asked.

Bluhdorn wasn't impressed. "Are we here to eat or to talk business?" he growled, and before we could even put a few *crevettes roses* with *ail* on a plate, we were whisked off to a small library, a few of the beautiful young women were pushed out, and we sat down to discuss all over again, at interminable length, the problems of making *The Fifth Horseman* into a movie. Tired Barry Diller may have been (when we finally did sit down to dinner, he instantly went to sleep at the table), but he was not so tired that he had forgotten how to say no.

Collins and Lapierre told him all their ideas for turning the book into a script, while he listened politely, shaking his head. In the end, even Bluhdorn got tired of the whole thing, and we were eventually allowed to sit down and eat. About midnight, I was told that I should spend the night, since Bluhdorn wanted to talk to me over breakfast. Too tired to be apprehensive, I allowed myself to be led away to one of the guest houses. I could not help noticing that while the rich often spend lavishly on their houses, they tend to economize on guest rooms. This one could have been a bedroom on the ground floor of any budget-priced motel in America. Clearly, some young woman had been displaced from it on my behalf, since her things were all over the room. I moved her lingerie off the rumpled bed and fell instantly asleep.

In the morning, I walked up to the main house and found Bluhdorn seated on a terrace, at the breakfast table, surrounded by flowers and birds, reading the morning newspapers in several languages. He was wearing an open sports shirt in a vivid pattern, a pair of shorts, and sandals, but there was nothing relaxed about his manner. We talked about the previous night's meeting as we ate breakfast. Did I think it had gone well? he asked.

I sipped my coffee. I saw nothing to be gained by avoiding the truth. No, I didn't think so, I said. Whatever the story problems were, it didn't seem to me that they had been solved. The truth of the matter was that it was all a waste of time and effort. The fact remained that either you wanted to make a movie about a Palestinian terrorist planting an atomic weapon in New York City or you didn't. If you did, there was more than enough material to make it, whoever wrote the screenplay. If you didn't, then no amount of ideas, however clever, would convince you.

Bluhdorn nodded. He was in a sunny mood—maybe it was the weather, maybe he was simply a man who enjoyed breakfast. He lit a cigar and looked out over the orange groves and pine trees to the sea. "What the hell," he said. "We tried, right?" No answer seemed to be called for. "What else do you have to do here?" he asked.

Nothing, I told him.

He raised an eyebrow. "Jesus Christ," he said. "You mean you flew over here just for this one goddamn meeting?" I nodded. He reflected on this and shook his head. "Then you'd better be getting back to New York."

I was back in New York the same day. The journey had been so rapid that a lot of people didn't even know I had been away, and, after a few days, I wasn't even sure myself.

PERHAPS BECAUSE the trip had been unsuccessful, I never came that close to Bluhdorn again. It is possible that he associated me in his mind with one of his rare failures, though I think it is more likely that his attention was already being drawn away by more pressing concerns.

The scene during which Bluhdorn had made confetti of the *Times* for our benefit was prophetic. Seymour Hersh's investigative reporting was the opening salvo in an attack on G+W, most of which was aimed personally at Bluhdorn—who took it personally, of course.

Hersh's charges stemmed from a defection that Bluhdorn regarded, perhaps correctly, as a personal betrayal, comparable to that of Judas—Joel A. Dolkart, a partner at Simpson Thacher & Bartlett, and G+W's chief legal adviser, had been indicted on many counts of fraud, including the theft of $2,500,000, in the face of which, being disinclined to spend several years in prison, he agreed to cooperate, providing the feds (and *The New York Times*'s Seymour Hersh) with a rich harvest of allegations with which to torment Bluhdorn. It was, one of Bluhdorn's advisers put it, "as if Henry Kissinger had defected to Moscow."

Increasingly, Bluhdorn began to resemble a Spanish fighting bull—snorting, angry, bloody, and unbowed, reacting to pricks from the picador. It was not that any of the allegations were, in themselves, all that startling—they included "questionable tax practices," "questionable corporate payments abroad," "unreported use of company resources for the private gain of company officials," the "mishandling" of the company's annual financial statements, "a pattern of transactions . . . designed to conceal the true financial condition of the company," and "inadequate public disclosures about the administration of [the company's] employee pension fund," but nevertheless the company's innermost financial secrets had been exposed, in an invidious light, by a long-term insider, something that happens rarely in corporate America.

Many of the charges were spurious, or exaggerated by the press, or made more dramatic in the telling by Sy Hersh; others were pretty much the norm in high-flying conglomerates like G+W. After all, nobody had ever pretended that G+W was AT&T or IBM; it was a company in which executives were expected to think on their feet, to take risks, and to do everything they could to keep the stock price going up. Certainly, it wasn't the kind of company in which people spent a lot of time worrying about whether X or Y was really entitled to use one of the corporate jets, or pause to ask whether the financial people should be spending their time working on Bluhdorn's personal taxes. It was understood by everyone—certainly by the shareholders and the executives—that in a certain sense Bluhdorn *was* G+W. When you invested in the company, you were investing in Charlie Bluhdorn's smarts, instincts, daring, and ambition. It was Bluhdorn who had collected this odd group of companies, Bluhdorn who bought and sold them, Bluhdorn who was not just the spokesman for the company, but its very reason for being. There simply was not, in his mind, a difference between himself and the company, they were one and the same thing.

This was not, alas, a position with which Sy Hersh sympathized, or Stanley Sporkin, the crusading chief of the Enforcement Division of the Securities and Exchange Commission. What seemed to most people within the G+W "family" that revolved around Bluhdorn merely interesting management idiosyncrasies, perhaps even lovable eccentricities on the part of the company's founder, appeared to Sporkin as gross illegalities. The truth, one suspects, is that Sporkin's ambition and Bluhdorn's clashed—for Sporkin was a deeply ambitious man, as ambitious as Bluhdorn himself, and in Bluhdorn he doubtless saw an opportunity for endless stories in the press for himself, as a crusader for corporate justice and responsibility. "This will be war!" ran one headline, quoting one of Bluhdorn's lawyers, which more or less set the tone for the dispute.

The endless wrangle and the publicity that surrounded it—for Sporkin turned out to be a master at getting his side of the story told in the press—ended in 1981, in a kind of draw in which the company basically agreed to stop doing what it had denied doing, and the SEC agreed to leave it alone. One consequence of the long struggle, however, was that Bluhdorn stepped out of the spotlight for a time. He no longer gave long, garrulous, and alarmingly frank speeches to financial reporters, and he spent more time than before at his house in the Dominican Republic.

At company functions, he began to seem almost benign. He set out to portray himself as the elder business statesman now, rather than as the hard-driving conglomerateur. He wanted people to see Gulf + Western as a successfully completed organization, not as a conglomerate that was constantly changing, unfinished, and fluid, and this was achieved, on paper, at any rate, by splitting it up into eight divisions. Paramount and Simon and Schuster, for instance, were lumped together in "The Leisure Time Group"; the grandly named "Consumer Products Group" was principally engaged in the manufacture and sales of cigars, and so on, until a total of some 850 different types of products and services were divided into eight "groups"—a Procrustean way of proving the company had arrived or matured. "Synergy," the magic word that was supposed to explain to shareholders and the other rubes outside the tent what the purpose of all this conglomeration was, now became a war cry within the company, as if there were really some link between auto parts, truck and auto leasing, mattresses, movies, resort hotels, sugar, zinc, and books.

Bluhdorn's energy remained undiminished, as did his notorious inability to relax. Once, visiting the Dominican Republic for an S&S sales conference (for a while, it became mandatory to use the G+W resort for sales conferences, despite the many difficulties of getting down there), I was invited by Mrs. Bluhdorn and her daughter to look at their horses—my interest in them having apparently been passed on through the company. Elegant, beautiful, and gracious, Mrs. Bluhdorn showed me over the ranch, where there were, indeed, a lot of horses, some of them pretty nice. I should come back one day, she said, when I had more time. Charlie loved going on horseback picnics up in the mountains. It was a wonderful way to spend a day—a long ride up into the mountains, a swim in a clear mountain stream, surrounded by wildflowers and birds, then a delicious picnic, and the ride back. . . . I nodded appreciatively at the thought of this idyll, until a certain skepticism intruded into the picture. I found it hard to even imagine Charlie Bluhdorn on a horse, let alone giving up a whole day to a picnic. Perhaps there was a side to him I hadn't seen? Did Mr. Bluhdorn, I asked, enjoy riding? Mrs. Bluhdorn laughed charmingly. "No, no," she said, "Charlie joins us for lunch in the helicopter, then he flies back afterwards."

As Bluhdorn became less visible, there were rumors of illness, even of cancer. In the end it should have come as no surprise when he died suddenly of a heart attack at the age of fifty-six, in February 1983, on a plane on his way to the Dominican Republic. He had lived his life at twice the pace of any normal man—even of the normal ambitious business executive. Forever in motion, talking, pleading, threatening, he was like a force of nature. Far from surrounding himself with "yes men," he thrived on argument, the angrier and more furious, the better. In an era of increasing corporate blandness, with CEOs who seem determined to behave as if all business were a kind of public service, Bluhdorn was the last of the great business eccentrics, a one-man band who made capitalism seem not only profitable, but fun. Always a trader at heart, he treated the American business world like a supermarket, rushing about in it like a demented shopper, picking up bargains without a shopping list to guide him. The last time I saw him, for a few brief seconds, in the dim light of the Top of the Tower restaurant, he looked pale and gaunt. He paused only long enough to say, "Cheezus Ke-RIST! You tell those boys I'm still going to get that goddamned movie made." The old, rasping self-confidence in his voice and the broad grin were still there, but the movie never did get made.

CHAPTER 25

$\mathcal{G}$ULF + WESTERN'S PURCHASE OF S&S took place at just the moment when Dick Snyder had engineered his greatest triumph and brought about the publishing coup of a lifetime. It was to transform him overnight into a major publisher and a celebrity in his own right.

I had thought it odd when he called me at home from Washington late one night, speaking in a deep, conspiratorial whisper. Can anybody overhear our conversation? he wanted to know. Only the cats, I told him, but he was in no mood for banter. "This is serious stuff," he growled. "Listen."

I listened. For some time, Dick had been traveling to Washington. I attributed this in part to a desire on his part to get away from New York and home and in part to his burgeoning friendship with David Obst, a beaming, bearded young agent who then specialized—insofar as he had any direction at all—in Washington political books. As the Watergate scandal heated up, this category, once tepid, had become red-hot. The focal point of public interest was no longer New York, nor even Hollywood, but Washington, and Obst, by a singular combination of sheer dumb luck, extravagant chutzpah, schoolboy charm, and shrewdness had managed to carve out for himself a special niche as the literary agent for political figures in trouble. It was said that what you needed to survive in Washington in the early seventies was a good criminal lawyer and a book contract, and Obst became the man you called the moment you were indicted.

Obst resembled a plump, Jewish Jimmy Stewart, if you can imagine such a thing, which is to say that his persona was that of a country bumpkin in the big city, but underneath that facade, he was fiercely ambitious. He suffered from neither fear nor shame. He would not have hesitated to walk right up to a widow at her husband's funeral and sign her as a client if he thought she had a story to tell. What he was *not* was disciplined, organized, or a businessman, and in Snyder he found at once the ideal purchaser of his goods and a kind of surrogate older brother, tough, demanding, smart, but willing enough to let his hair down and have a good time once the deal was done.

It was love at first sight on both sides. Dick had been looking for somebody to mentor, as well as a territory of his own. He could leave me to do big-ticket fiction and the occasional piece of nonfiction. He found in Fred Hills somebody (at last) who knew how to do lucrative self-help books. He eventually hired Nan Talese for quality and Jim Silberman for solid midlist books, but he himself, with the help of Alice Mayhew, made Washington his turf and the Washington political book his specialty. (The fact that all these people came from Random House did not stem from any vendetta on Dick's part after the defection of Gottlieb—it was simply that Dick believed in hiring the best people he could get, and Random House was full of them at that time.)

What he was calling me about in such secrecy was a book Obst had steered him to by two young reporters at *The Washington Post*. Knowing my lack of interest in politics, he did not bore me with the details. I had to believe, he said, that these two guys, whom he had just met, were onto the biggest story of the decade, maybe the biggest political story of the century. This would be a sensational book, one that might bring down the president, even change the country. I had never heard my friend sound so excited.

Did he want my opinion? I asked. If so, I would need to know a little more. No, he said, with a trace of impatience, he didn't need my fucking opinion. Politics was something he knew more about than I did.

This was a terrific story, and that was that. The question he wanted to ask *me* was whether I thought he should buy the book on the spot, before some other publisher got wind of it.

Up until this point, Dick had left the buying of books to other people—not that he didn't second-guess them or that he didn't reserve to himself the final decision about money—since that was, after all, their job. He hadn't ever stepped out of the careful structure by which books were reviewed and considered to make an offer for one himself. I divined that he wasn't seeking my approval—the idea would not have occurred to him—but wanted to cover his ass just in case the whole thing blew up on him—he could at least say that he had discussed it with me. After all, I *was* editor in chief.

"Well, given that I haven't a clue if it's worth buying," I said, "how much is Obst asking for?"

"Fifty thousand dollars."

"That's no big deal, Dick," I said.

"I *know* it's not a big deal. Should I do it, though?"

I thought for a moment. So far as I was concerned, Dick could buy anything he liked; besides, he was right—he *did* know more about politics than anybody else at S&S except Alice Mayhew, and his gut instinct about books, despite the fact that he did not always bother to read them, was impressive. "Listen," I said, "when I called you about Carlos Castaneda, you said the only thing that matters in this business is having the guts to back your own hunch when it really matters. So back your own hunch. I don't see how you can go wrong, frankly. And if you do, what the hell, it's only one book, right? Say Obst got you drunk."

Dick laughed. "I'm getting Obst drunk, as a matter of fact," he said. "I'm going to screw world rights out of him." It was the last time I ever caught that note of hesitation in Snyder's voice, at least when it came to political books, because what he brought back from Washington was Bob Woodward and Carl Bernstein's *All the President's Men*, which did indeed change America and played a major role in bringing down Nixon. More important, it transformed book publishing into a red-hot part of the media.

In the newspapers, in the weekly magazines, and on the television networks, journalists had always considered the book to be a kind of lumbering dinosaur, slow and irrelevant. Books contained history, not news. With surefire instinct, Dick made *All the President's Men* (and later *The Final Days*) not only newsworthy but *news*. This was publishing what the French call *les actualités,* news as it happens. The book was "embargoed" until publication day, there were no advance galleys for reviewers, the papers had to send people to stand in line at stores on publication day. In the meantime, every magazine and newspaper fought over the serial rights, the movie rights were bought, and nobody talked about anything else. Dick's bet paid off as never before in the history of publishing. It changed a lot of other things as well: for a time, our offices were bugged by who knows which government agencies; we became perhaps the first book publisher where certain offices had to be regularly swept for bugs; Woodward and Bernstein became major celebrities (even before they were portrayed so glamorously by Robert Redford and Dustin Hoffman that a whole generation of young Americans decided to go to journalism school); the newspaper business, which had been declared dead by television journalists, received a new lease on life; and Snyder's judgment about books, never tentative to begin with, became an article of faith at S&S.

As the decade wore on, S&S became *the* Watergate publisher: John Dean, Maureen Dean, John Ehrlichman, and John Mitchell all became S&S authors, David Obst was launched—briefly—into superstar orbit as an agent, and money poured in—very fortunately, since G+W was not the kind of company that would have wanted a "showcase" publishing house that broke even, however proud Bluhdorn might be of owning it. Indeed, it was Dick's peculiar genius that he at once understood that if growth was what Bluhdorn lived and breathed, growth is what he would get, and that the fastest way to grow was not to publish more books, but to buy up other publishing companies—in short, to make S&S a miniature version of G+W, by following the same methods. Watergate fueled a lot of this optimism about book publishing at the higher corporate levels of G+W—nobody paused to ask what we would do when the scandal finally ebbed. It quickly became the pattern to rely on some outside miracle to balance the books at the end of the year, an unfortunate pattern that was still followed twenty-five years later when the death of Princess Diana made many a publisher's numbers look good, including those of S&S.

Watergate made more careers than it unmade, though not everybody did well in the long run. Woodward went on to become a perennial best-seller and star journalist, Dick and Alice Mayhew rose in their separate (but linked) trajectories, but Bernstein eventually plummeted, and David Obst, who had begun the whole thing, ended up an S&S em-

ployee, representing the company in Los Angeles, and eventually sank
for many years into obscurity, outstripped in fame by his wife, who became a much talked-about movie producer. It was a melancholy ending
to a spectacular if short-lived career. The position of "West Coast editor" was in any case, at S&S as at most companies, a kind of elephant
graveyard, a sinecure without power or responsibility for those whom
the management hesitated to fire for one reason or another. Dick had
done his very best for Obst—he was conscious of the debt he owed him
and of their friendship—but the job itself was a dead end. (Later on,
when Dick was picked by the press as one of "the toughest bosses in the
country," this and many other acts of generosity were ignored, in favor
of constructing an image of meanness that was never a reality.)

That is not to say that life couldn't be difficult at S&S. Dick was determined to build up a strong editorial team, by which he meant a team
of what he liked to call heavy hitters. The truth was that he was only
really comfortable with those editors whom he had long ago learned to
trust. New ones were hailed briefly as "stars," given freshly redecorated
offices and inflated titles, then subjected to what must have seemed to
many of them a system of institutionalized hazing that few survived.
Nan Talese, though often miserably unhappy, survived, partly out of
saintly patience, partly because she was capable of looking Dick directly in the eye if sufficiently provoked. Stubborn defiance from
women he understood, and he usually backed off at the last moment.
Richard Kluger, now a distinguished nonfiction writer, was brought in
from the world of journalism under the impression that he was to have
carte blanche to publish his own list of serious nonfiction books, only to
find himself relentlessly criticized by Dick, who discovered that Kluger
couldn't—or didn't want to—fight back. Kluger eventually resigned
on the grounds that the job was making him blind. Patricia Soliman was
hired away with much fanfare from Coward-McCann, where she had
had a very successful career as a publisher and editor of popular fiction.
She was allowed to create for herself an office environment in which
everything was painted pink and mauve, given the meaningless title
of "associate publisher" (which was Dick's way of encouraging editors
to think of themselves as part of management without giving them
any power), then terrorized to the point where she could hardly perform. Some unhappy recruits, such as Erwin Glikes and Larry Ashmead,
went on to spectacularly successful careers after their experiences at
S&S (at Basic Books and HarperCollins, respectively) but looked back

at their time there, in the words of Ashmead, as "the unhappiest years of my life."

None of them was unhappier than Henry Robbins, whom Dick wooed away from his job at the distinguished literary house of Farrar, Straus and Giroux. Robbins was a man who took himself and literature seriously (he was inclined to confuse them) and had brought a steady stream of literary writers to Farrar, Straus, most of whom were devoted to him. It was Dick's hope that Robbins would not only bring with him a good many of his writers but give S&S the literary reputation that had mostly so far eluded it.

Unfortunately for Robbins, Dick's commitment to the cause of literary fiction was not only skin-deep but profoundly ambivalent. He wanted the kudos of publishing literary fiction but disliked the fact that most of it loses money. Besides, almost from day one Robbins seemed to him pugnacious, arrogant, opinionated, and self-righteous. It might have missed his attention, however, that Robbins, a classic type A personality, had an even shorter fuse than he did.

At first, Dick rather enjoyed the occasional spat with Robbins, under the impression that, like himself, Robbins enjoyed a good fight for its own sake, but gradually it dawned on him that Robbins *meant* it, that there was no way he would back off, shake hands, have a good laugh, and get back to work. On the contrary: He conceived of his role as that of the defender of literary values against the philistines, with Dick playing the role of philistine in chief. Every novel that Robbins brought to the editorial board was a sacred cause—not only did he not hear any criticism of it from other readers, but he did not even *tolerate* questions, however well-meant or harmless. He did not compromise. Reasoning with him, as Churchill complained about de Gaulle, was like trying to reason with Joan of Arc.

Things finally came to a head when Dick issued an invitation to Barry Diller to have lunch with the S&S editorial board. This was partly yet another attempt at "synergy" and partly to show Diller that we were professionals, not naive, wide-eyed literary enthusiasts. Dick lectured us seriously before Diller's appearance and warned us to be on our best behavior, like a headmaster getting his students ready for a visit by an important school benefactor. It is a pity that he did not notice the smoldering anger in Robbins's eyes on being told that a movie mogul was coming to lunch to hear us discussing books.

Diller, when he turned up, was as un-mogul-like as it is possible for a studio head to be—elegant, sardonically witty, charming, deferential, he went out of his way to fit in. Robbins, however, was a frightening spectacle. His face was contorted with anger, his eyes blazing, his hands clutching the silverware so hard that his knuckles were white. I tried to kick Dick under the table, but he was oblivious to any warning. The soup was being served as Diller, in a gentle voice, explained what Paramount could do to help us, and what we might be able to do for Paramount. Alas, no sooner was the soup plate placed before Robbins than he seized it and, in a burst of temper, flung it across the room toward Diller—luckily missing him. "I'm not going to sit here and listen to some goddamn movie person tell us how to publish books!" he yelled, then stood up and walked out of the room, slamming the door behind him.

There was a brief silence, interrupted only by a nervous giggle from Nan Talese, then Dick turned to Diller and said, with majestic aplomb: "Henry Robbins is a little . . . high-strung." He paused for a moment, as if looking for some better explanation. "Actually," he went on, "I wouldn't want to mislead you—not all our luncheons are as exciting as this."

Diller took the explosion calmly. He seemed, if anything, pleased and impressed, but the incident inevitably led to Robbins's eventual resignation. Except for the acquisition of Joan Didion, who had followed Robbins from Farrar, Straus (thus sparking off a major publishing feud between Dick and Roger Straus that still survives to this day), there was little to show for Robbins's time at S&S. If we were going to publish "serious" fiction, by major literary figures, we were going to have to do it on our own, Dick decided, not by bringing in an editor and hoping writers would follow him or her. Fortunately, just such an opportunity presented itself shortly.

GENIUS IN one form of the arts seldom extends to the others, so I was skeptical when a dear friend, Billy Barnes, then an agent at International Creative Management, suggested one night over dinner that I might like to become the publisher of Tennessee Williams's fiction. There is no American playwright whom I admire more than Williams, and at least two of his plays are masterpieces, but of course that was not necessarily a guarantee that he could write a novel or short stories of the same quality or that S&S could publish them successfully. Indeed, his previous ventures into fiction had been published, very quietly indeed, by a small press and without much impact. This was exactly the reason, Billy explained, that Williams wanted to come to a big, commercial publisher, who could put some muscle behind the books.

This would have normally set off an alarm bell inside my head. The notion that a big publisher can sell more copies of a book than a small one is widespread but doubtful. A book that is too "special" or hard to categorize might, in fact, do far better with a smaller publisher on whose list it will have a certain importance than on that of a big, mainstream publisher, where it might disappear. Also, a lot of small publishers can bring to a book of narrow appeal a personal enthusiasm and attention that no big publisher can duplicate. In this case, however, my admiration for the author was so great that Barnes did not even have to work hard to get me on the hook. By the time our main course was served, I had agreed to publish a novel and a book of stories by Tennessee Williams, with whom Barnes promised me a meeting in the near future.

Since Williams was then living at the Elysée Hotel on East Fifty-fourth Street, Billy suggested that we meet at one o'clock at Lutèce, which was conveniently close. Besides, he said, Williams would be pleased and flattered—his previous publishers had certainly never taken him to lunch at Lutèce.

A reservation was quickly made and the proprietress, Mme. Soltner, informed of the importance of my guest. The chef, André Soltner, himself was hard to impress—many of his clients were rich and famous, after all, and unlike most of his rivals in New York, he insisted on treating everyone who dined in his restaurant with equal courtesy—still, for the French nobody takes precedence over a distinguished man of letters. For Monsieur Williams, Madame said, Soltner would insist on preparing a special menu. I should not concern myself about the luncheon—each course would be a veritable work of art, in homage to Monsieur Williams.

On the appointed day, Billy Barnes and I met at Lutèce. Madame Soltner had given us the best table in the house and from time to time came over to bring bulletins from the kitchen: The *soupe d'écrevisses* in the manner of New Orleans was coming along famously; the boned quails would not go in the oven until Monsieur Williams arrived. At in-

tervals, small delicacies appeared from the kitchen to whet our appetites
as we sipped our kir royales. Barnes was a man of dazzling charm, as
unmistakably Southern as Tennessee Williams himself, which perhaps
explained the length and closeness of their relationship. Barnes was
good-looking, flamboyantly gay in both senses of the word, outrageously funny, and apparently had a rare gift for jollying his most important client along at those not infrequent moments when Williams
stubbornly dug in his heels and refused at the last minute to do something that Barnes had arranged for him. Tennessee, Barnes confided,
could be a *little* difficult at times and needed to be handled with kid
gloves. Despite a basically sunny disposition, he had dark, brooding
moments when he thought everyone was plotting against him, and he
suffered from a tendency to listen too carefully to people who were
close to him but didn't always have his best interests at heart, if I knew
what he meant, Billy whispered to me in his most conspiratorial fashion.

I nodded. No genius was easy to deal with or altogether predictable,
and there was no reason why Williams should be an exception. Much as
I enjoyed Billy Barnes's company, I had the sense that time was flying,
and, indeed, when I looked at my watch, I saw that it was already a quarter to two. I also noticed from the corner of my eye that Soltner was
leaning out of the kitchen giving frantic hand signals to Madame. Might
it not be a good idea, I suggested to Barnes, to give Williams a call, just
to make sure there had been no mix-up about the date. But no, Barnes
had telephoned him in the morning, and Williams had been eagerly
looking forward to meeting me. He was an artist, that was all, and like
all artists he was unpunctual. Not only that, Barnes whispered, as if he
was imparting a great secret to me, Tennessee was not exactly a morning person. He went to bed and got up late, so for him one o'clock was
early in the day.

I was about to ask why, if that was the case, Barnes had set the luncheon for one when the unmistakable figure of Tennessee Williams appeared. Madame Soltner rose from behind the *caisse*, while Soltner
himself, his face broadly beaming, emerged from the kitchen, wiping
his hands on his apron, to greet Williams. Williams, smiling shyly,
looked mildly confused, I thought, as if he was not altogether sure what
he was doing here or even if this was the place he was supposed to be.
He was dressed neatly in gray flannel slacks, a tweed sports jacket, and
a long wool scarf wound loosely around his neck over his shirt and
tie—not exactly the elegance of the average Lutèce client but altogether

the outfit of Sartre, say, appearing for lunch at the Café Flore, on the Left Bank. The one alarming note was that his thick horn-rimmed glasses were askew on his nose, tilted at a steep angle so that one eye was looking over the top of them and the other peeking out the bottom. "*Bonjour, cher maître,*" both Soltners called out to Williams at just the moment that he shuffled forward and, missing the fact that there were two or three steps in front of him, took a nosedive straight to the floor, landing in a heap just short of our table.

All of us, Soltner first, rushed to get him on his feet again. Williams seemed unhurt, though his glasses were more skewed than ever. Full of concern, the Soltners brushed him down, Madame removed his scarf, and he was gently guided to his seat. Would he take a little something to restore himself? Soltner inquired solicitously. Williams nodded in slow motion. Perhaps a dry sherry, Soltner suggested, or a glass of white wine? Williams thought about it for a while, eyes half closed, like a man listening to distant music. "Ah believe ah'll have a vodka," he said at last. He thought some more. "Better make that a double," he added.

Billy Barnes introduced me, and we shook hands. We chatted a while and were soon on a first-name basis. Tennessee was genial to a fault, and he apologized for being late. "Ah overslept, baby," he explained. "Ah woke up with this *sinus headache?* Ah think ah may be comin' down with this *cold?*" He rubbed his nose hard between thumb and forefinger, as if in pain.

He drained his glass and asked for another as the waiter brought the first course. Tennessee sipped his drink while we ate. Madame and her husband hovered over his shoulder anxiously, waiting for him to taste the soup, but Tennessee didn't appear to be hungry. Gradually, he became aware of their presence. He just wasn't up to eating today, he told them, it was all the cold medicine he had been taking. It cut the appetite, that was all. If he could have just a simple omelet? The Soltners masked their disappointment. But of course, Soltner said, beaming, as if making an omelet was the ambition of a lifetime, and went off to the kitchen. But when the omelet came, Tennessee didn't touch that either; he had another drink instead.

By now, it was becoming apparent that my newfound friend was drunk and determined to get drunker. It was apparent to Barnes, too, who was talking at a fever pitch to cover the long silences from Tennessee. By the time Tennessee had ignored all four courses of the meal, plus his omelet, and was calling for a postprandial cognac, he had slipped so far down in his chair that his face was close to the top of the table. Suddenly, in a kind of panic, he glanced at his watch (just like the White Rabbit, I thought, and I wondered if he was going to dip it in his glass), cried out, "I had no ide-ah how late it is!" and in an attempt to rise to his feet slumped to the floor instead.

Barnes and I, with the help of the staff, managed to walk him up the stairs and out the door to a taxi, into which Barnes bundled him briskly, while Tennessee wallowed in the back, eyes revolving, like somebody who fears they are being kidnapped but can do nothing to prevent it. Barnes leaped into the cab beside his client and slammed the door shut. "Don't you worry," Barnes shouted out to me, as the cab sped off. "He's terrific on the tube."

ACTUALLY, THE question of whether or not Tennessee Williams was terrific—or at any rate, would remain sober—on television was not my main concern. My first concern was whether he would stay sober enough to finish his novel, which was called, despite many attempts on my part to talk him out of the idea, *Moïse and the World of Reason*. The pages I saw at first made no sense at all, but I put that down to the fact that it was early days and that the ways of genius are not like those of ordinary men. It seemed to me that there was no plot as such in what I read, but whenever I brought the matter up in calls to Tennessee he simply chuckled and said, "I know, I *know,* baby, but it'll come, don't fret." Criticism, at any rate, did not disturb him. Genius or not, like most playwrights he was used to rewriting things at the request of the director or the actors and took it all in his stride, with a good nature fueled, I had no doubt, by his favorite cold remedy.

As we became closer, I began to appreciate more and more the genuine sweetness of Tennessee Williams. It is not a word I normally apply to anyone, but it seems the only one to describe him. Yes, Tennessee could be difficult, certainly he had a temper when he felt himself betrayed, but the core of him was one of essential simplicity and sweetness. There was a gentleness and a capacity for trust in him that comes out so strongly in the characters in his plays he clearly loved best: Blanche in *Streetcar,* Laura in *The Glass Menagerie*—indeed, in most of his women. Pursued as he was by his own demons—an unhappy childhood, an attachment to his unfortunate sister, Rose, alcoholism, pill dependency on a heroic scale (mostly Seconal, Nembutal, Doriden, and amphetamines), a desperate need to be loved, and a taste for rough trade—he remained a true romantic about people, always trusting them until proven wrong, and sometimes, with dismaying effects, long afterward.

Shortly after S&S acquired his novel, I attended a black-tie dinner in his honor at the National Arts Club, at which he was to receive an award. The dinner was an elegant and star-studded occasion—literally, for many of the stars who had appeared in the Broadway productions of Tennessee's plays over the years were present, as well as a glittering crowd of his admirers and various mandarins from the worlds of culture and high fashion. Tennessee himself sat on the dais, a shy smile on his face, his glasses again askew, and his black bow tie at an angle. To his left sat the mayor; to his right, smiling vacantly, a tiny, fragile-looking, elfin gnome of a woman in her late fifties, dressed in blue, with silver hair cropped short and a strangely unlined face like that of a china doll. As dinner was served, I noticed that Tennessee merely picked at his food, hardly eating a thing. From the expression on his face, I judged that he had been fighting off another cold with his favorite remedy.

Once dinner was over, the speeches began, each one more admiring than the one before. The mayor claimed Tennessee for New York City, various speakers from the National Arts Club claimed him for American culture, one after another actors and actresses rose to praise him or to relate intimate, affectionate anecdotes about him. The emotional temperature of the room was rising to a crescendo. Everywhere I looked there were people crying, by no means all of them actors. There were actual *civilians* crying—even my own eyes were moist with tears. Tennessee Williams was not just admired—he was *loved* as perhaps no other American playwright has ever been.

Throughout all of this display of emotion, Tennessee sat as motionless and gently smiling as a bronze Buddha, his mind possibly elsewhere, while his diminutive, silent companion—who had eaten all of her dinner and a good deal of his—stuffed herself on the petits fours. Tennessee's eyes were glassy. I wondered if he had prepared for the evening by taking Ritalin, the virtues of which he had preached to me once but for which he was a poor advertisement.

At last, the moment came for Tennessee himself to speak. With un-feigned shyness he stayed in his seat while everybody else—except the woman sitting next to him—rose to their feet applauding and calling for him to speak. Tennessee blushed modestly and finally rose to his feet, swaying slightly. He waved for silence, and, as the room grew still, he leaned toward the microphone. In his musical Southern drawl, enunci-ating very slowly, even hesitantly, but by no means quietly, he said: "I would like to introduce you all to mah beloved sister, Rose . . ." He paused to indicate the small woman seated beside him, who seemed to be totally unaware of the fact that he was talking about her. Tennessee smiled down at her, his expression full of sympathy but somehow puck-ish. He took a deep breath and went on: ". . . who had the first *pre*-frontal lobotomy in the state of Alabama."

With that, he sat down, still smiling benevolently. The room re-mained hushed while everybody contemplated this bombshell. Rose herself smiled on, as vacantly as ever, while the rest of us waited for Tennessee to say something—*anything*—else. But he did not.

A lady from the National Arts Club seated next to me gave a loud, disapproving snort. "I *told* everybody we should have given the award to Arthur Miller," she said angrily. "At least *he'd* have made a decent ac-ceptance speech."

ECCENTRIC BEHAVIOR is par for the course among writers of ge-nius, most of whom are solitary people who only come up for air for brief periods between books, at which point they are often embarrass-ingly determined to be the life of the party and the center of attention until the typewriter reclaims their attention, but Tennessee was a play-wright, quite a different creature, and although he liked to present him self to strangers as a shy and diffident country boy in the big city, a kind of gay Huck Finn, he was in fact, like most playwrights, intensely so-cial, for playwrights, unlike poets and novelists, are partners in a process that involves many other people, some of them with even bigger or more fragile egos than the playwright's own, such as stars, directors, producers, and investors. Tennessee knew everybody from Jackie Onassis down, had been everywhere, was at home everywhere, and usually seemed to know everybody's secrets, for he had an insatiable appetite for good gossip and was a brilliant raconteur. What was not so immediately apparent was the steel behind the charming, if eccentric, facade. A stranger, looking at Tennessee's life, might easily have concluded that Tennessee had given up writing, for his life seemed to revolve around drinking, making telephone calls, and going to endless parties, but somehow, in the middle of the uncontrolled chaos that was his life, Tennessee somehow always found time to write—indeed, for a man in poor health who had a drinking problem and who took a witch's brew of pills, his productivity was amazing, even alarming. I came to the conclusion that while he liked the chaos that surrounded him, he was somehow able to take refuge within his head. Every time I went over to see him in his dark, crowded, book-filled little suite—which looked as if it had not been cleaned or tidied since the days when Tallulah Bankhead lived there—I could not help noticing that Tennessee was seldom alone. There were always bottles and unwashed glasses everywhere, and often from the tiny kitchen came the noise of some unseen person, banging and crashing amid the china and the glassware, presumably in a rage at having been banished from the living room because of my presence. On such occasions, Tennessee would carefully pretend that there was nobody in the suite but the two of us. Very often he was suffering from what he called a sinus cold, though it looked to me as if what he meant was a bad hangover. Hungover or not, nothing deterred his meticulous perusal of the edited text of his book or his shrewd advice on how to merchandise it.

Moïse had begun as a novella, and Tennessee labored mightily to inflate it to the length of a full-size novel without losing its pace. At one point, he was so doubtful about the book that he offered to give the advance back (though by the next day he had changed his mind and called, early in the morning for him, to say, "You didn't tell Billy that, did you, baby?"). The story was about three people and their need for each other: Moïse, an impoverished and quixotic young woman painter with a gift for unfinished canvases, a character based on Tennessee's old friend Olive Leonard; the narrator, a young man from Thelma, Alabama, a self-styled "distinguished failed writer" who strongly resembles the young Tennessee; and Lance, a young man whose intensity, strength, and sexual energy held them all together while he lived and whose absence gives the novel its driving pathos. Set on the night Moïse gives a party to celebrate her retirement from "the world of reason" and the narrator loses the second love of his life, the novel is at once lyrical and puzzling, a kind of autobiographical peep show full of brilliant jeux d'esprit. The characters talk—and talk and talk—about the loss of innocence and the rekindling of desire, two of Tennessee's favorite themes, as the night goes by. He often said that he wrote all his work for Rose, but I think by that he meant that Rose's innocence and simplicity was what he sought to find and convey in his writing.

In the end, Tennessee rewrote it so many times, in so many different places—New York, Key West, Tangiers, Europe—and added so many new pages to it that even he was muddled by its intricacies, as was I. This was not just a function of complicated plotting: Tennessee's pages were typed on what appeared to be several different but equally ancient manuals, all with frayed, faded ribbons; each page was heavily revised in a shaky hand that Tennessee himself could not always decipher, and whole paragraphs were slashed out fiercely then partially restored. In my editorial notes, the questions "Where does this *go*?" "Who *is* this?" and "What does this *mean*?" recur with alarming frequency, along with such questions—which seemed pedestrian to Tennessee—as "Is there such a thing as a *square* camera lens?" and "What is a Blue Jay notebook?" (It turned out to be a lined school notebook with a mottled black-and-white pasteboard cover, in which Tennessee still liked to write and with which, as a schoolboy, he had begun his writing career.)

In the end, after several years of revising, *Moïse* was finally published, though its sales disappointed Tennessee, and me as well. Most of the reviewers seemed baffled by the book, with its stagy plotline and the unbridled lyricism of its dialogue. James Leo Herlihy commented fulsomely that it was "like a wild street song heard on the eve of a Doom's Day [*sic*] that is forever postponed," while Elia Kazan, rather more cautiously, responded to the book I had sent him by simply writing, "Tennessee Williams is a great man." The truth was, nobody knew quite what to make of the book, and there was a natural tendency to compare it to Tennessee's major plays, however unfairly. Myself, I thought it uncommonly courageous of Tennessee to have tried his hand at a novel, particularly one that celebrated the fatal decline of the characters' sexual and artistic powers.

In any event, the completion of *Moïse* was enough to persuade Tennessee to move forward with a collection of his later short stories. Even so fervent an admirer of his as Lady Maria St. Just, who was to become the devoted and fiercely protective literary coexecutor of his estate, has remarked that "[Tennessee] is not a great short story writer like

Chekhov." There is no denying that, though it was a form that suited him better than the novel. At any rate, Tennessee wrote immense numbers of short stories, many of which were unpublished, and was still writing them at a tremendous rate in the early 1980s. What he proposed was to gather together those he liked the best, from both the unpublished ones and the most recent ones, in a volume called *Fairy Tales,* a title that he was unable to mention without a fit of giggles.

I was of two minds about the title myself. That part of my brain that is devoted to publishing loved the idea. "*Fairy Tales* by Tennessee Williams" might well have been the first really successful collection of literary short stories in the history of book publishing, and the title would have all but guaranteed a storm of publicity and controversy, to which Tennessee looked forward with glee. The part of my brain that is *not* devoted to publishing thought that it was risky and in doubtful taste. Every time the subject came up at marketing meetings opinion was equally divided. However, Dick Snyder loved the title and told me to ignore the doubters. "It'll sell books," he said firmly, which was just what Tennessee thought, though in his case he was also anxious to shock those of his admirers who, in his opinion, took him too seriously. Like many another genius, Tennessee craved the support and protection of those close to him who felt it to be their business to look after him, but chafed at their concern at the same time. He liked to set them against each other—indeed the main reason why Tennessee had chosen Billy Barnes as his agent was that Barnes, with his sense of fun, his Southern accent, and spirited campiness (on those occasions when he chose to be campy, for he could be perfectly businesslike when he wanted to be) didn't seem serious enough to Tennessee's camarilla, who were, for the most part, *plus royalistes que le roi.* When I expressed my doubts about the title to Tennessee, he told me, "Loosen up and have some *fun,* baby," with a certain warning snap of venom in his voice, rare between us, and that was that.

"Don't worry about it," Billy Barnes said to me later. "He's just having his fun. He'll change his mind before the book hits the stores, you'll see."

A greater worry was the stories themselves, many of which were incomplete, impossible to understand, or simply bizarre. Some sense of them can be gained from their titles, which included "The Killer Chicken and the Closet Queen," "Mother Yaws," and "Tent Worms."

A note from my assistant John Herman, no mean judge of literary fiction, read, "For whatever it's worth these seem to me brilliantly written, humorous, but utterly outlandish and very hard to follow." That was putting it kindly.

One of the stories, "The Donsinger Women and Their Handyman Jack," seemed to have been composed by Tennessee in many different places and states of mind. Some of it was typed on yellowing writing paper, some of it on lined paper torn from a notebook, some of it on the back of writing paper from the United Nations Plaza Hotel. Changes were scrawled in various colors, some recent and bold, others ancient and scarcely legible. The Donsinger women are a large family of sisters occupying a crumbling mansion in what had once been a respectable neighborhood in some Texas town. Predatory, possibly cannibalistic, and unapologetically nymphomaniacal, the sisters are nightmare creations. They subsist by rummaging through the garbage cans of restaurants by night, and they spend their days in rocking chairs on the veranda of the house, making lewd conversation. One of them finds a young man named Jack in the street. Jack has been kicked off the family ranch by his father. She hides him in the unused henhouse, hoping he will serve as her handyman and stud, but it turns out that even though he is spectacularly well endowed, that is not on his agenda. He is a poet and has eyes only for beautiful young Oriental men delivering Chinese food. The sisters are eventually incarcerated in the state mental asylum, after much violence and bloodshed involving the police and the National Guard, but they escape from there only to self-destruct. Jack is eventually spurned by the Chinese youth he loves and is last seen sunk in grief on the porch of the decaying Donsinger house. The moral of the story is that grief, to the person of feeling, is a permanent wound, not a transient state. "It takes up residence in the human heart" and will last "as long as the heart endures." To which Tennessee added, perhaps as an afterthought, a moving and simple phrase that is Tennessee at his best (as much of the rest of the story is Tennessee at his worst): "And the heart is a stubborn organ."

"The heart is a stubborn organ" might also have served as Tennessee Williams's motto and was certainly the theme of each of these stories, whatever their merits (or lack thereof). By this time, in 1982, Tennessee was on a roller coaster of pills and booze, and his writing showed the consequences, and he knew it. Yet even in "The Donsinger

Women," there are flashes of the old lyricism, the occasional wonderful phrase, and the sense of a powerful imagination going hauntingly out of control.

Tennessee himself could tell that the stories needed work, and I spent a good many hours with him trying to make sense of them, but even with the best will in the world Tennessee's heart wasn't in it. He wanted the stories published, but he found it hard to concentrate on revising them and often toyed with the idea of giving up the whole project. Many of the older stories were in comparatively better shape, but by fits and starts he tried to revise those, too. A couple of years after we had signed the contract for *Fairy Tales,* and over six years since he had first broached the subject, Tennessee was beginning to have second thoughts, just as we were about to announce their publication in our catalog. He called me out of the blue one day, just as Billy Barnes had warned, to say that he didn't know whose idea it had been to call the collection *Fairy Tales,* but he couldn't allow it. "It's real tacky, baby," Tennessee said, despite the fact that it had been his idea from the beginning.

From an outsider's point of view, it was easy enough to guess that Tennessee's life was coming apart at the seams. He was hard to reach, restless, and plagued by ill health of an unspecified nature, complaining of headaches, personal problems, and the ubiquitous oncoming cold. A photograph intended for the jacket of *Fairy Tales* shows him wearing a neat straw hat and smiling seraphically, his eyes completely obscured by big dark glasses. The effect is to cancel out the smile or contradict it, and there is a kind of ghostly sadness to the picture, as if he had already guessed it would never be used and was mildly amused by the fact.

Indeed, *Fairy Tales* (now referred to more prosaically as "Untitled Collection of Short Stories") was postponed several times. By now, I had real concerns. Every time a book is postponed after appearing in a publisher's catalog, the orders are canceled. When new orders are solicited, they are invariably fewer, and after a number of postponements, the bookstores simply lose interest and decide the book is never going to happen. At that point, it falls into limbo, from which no amount of effort is likely to rescue it. This book was on its way there rapidly.

After considerable difficulty, I managed to pin Tennessee down to a meeting. I turned up on time to find him in his bathrobe, a towel wound around his neck. He did not look good: His face was puffy, sallow rather than tanned, and there was a noticeable tremor to his hands. The blinds were pulled in the living room, but we sat down there anyway, in partial darkness. Around us, covering every flat surface in the room, was the evidence of a party that must have ended only hours ago—bottles, glasses, overflowing ashtrays. Tennessee's legs were bare, and he was wearing red morocco slippers. He seemed baffled by my presence, despite several telephone calls to confirm our meeting. From time to time, he glanced uneasily toward the kitchen, where, as usual, somebody was crashing about in a rage. Tennessee pulled the towel around his neck a little tighter. He coughed gently. "A cold," he said. "I woke up with this *sinus* headache." He rubbed his thumb and forefinger down his nose, to indicate pain, knocking his glasses off. He replaced them and stared glumly into the middle distance.

I offered to come back another time, if he wasn't feeling well. Tennessee waved away the suggestion. He was feeling well enough. There followed a long pause, interrupted from time to time by somebody whistling "You Make Me Feel Like a Natural Woman" off-key in the kitchen, or possibly the bedroom, it was hard to be sure of the geography of the apartment. One sensed that there was a world beyond this room, but like characters on a stage in a play, we were cut off from it.

Had I had breakfast? Tennessee wanted to know.

I nodded. I was almost ready for lunch, in fact.

Tennessee sighed. "Ah have not," he said gravely, and picking up a glass he emptied the contents of several other glasses into it, swirled it carefully to mix it up, and took a gulp. I wondered what it contained. For all I knew he might have been mixing vodka, bourbon, and curaçao, or for all *he* knew, for that matter. He smiled. "That's better," he said. What were we going to talk about?

I pulled the manuscript of one of the short stories out of my briefcase, together with some notes that John Herman and I had made. Tennessee glanced at them with a combination of deep suspicion and alarm. He did not seem to be in any state to go over them.

The phone beside him rang. He picked it up and listened intently. "Uh-huh," he said, "uh-huh, uh-huh, baby." He listened some more. I could hear the voice on the other end—a thin, angry, electronic squeak. Tennessee closed his eyes, wincing. "I'm real sorry," he said. "Uh-huh . . . No, *real* sorry, baby . . . I mean it. . . ." He listened some more, then drew a card from the pocket of his dressing gown. He held it up close to his eyes, but was unable to focus on it. He held it as far away as he could, at arm's length, but still didn't seem able to read it. He turned it upside down, then, in a pleading voice, reading it as desperately as a man on television who had forgotten his glasses might look helplessly toward the TelePrompTer for the words of his speech, unable to make out a word on its screen, he said very slowly, "No, baby, I can't talk about it now, I'm in the middle of a meeting with . . ." He frowned, and tried turning the card the other way around. "With mah editor . . ." A long, anguished pause as he searched for the name, then, finally, with an audible sigh of relief, he thought he had it and gave it the old college try: "With mah editor Michael Kop-ta . . ." He gave me a questioning look over the top of his crooked glasses, and I shook my head. He put down the receiver.

"Michael Korda," I said.

He nodded. "I know, baby," he said softly. "It was on the tip of mah tongue."

He sent me a very nice letter a few days later, just to make sure my feelings hadn't been hurt by his lapse of memory, but, as I assured him, I didn't mind a bit. Tennessee was a sweet man, and now that I'm closer to the age he was then or past it, I'm having trouble remembering people's names, too, even without a hangover. About the confusion in the two stories I had come to discuss with him, Tennessee later commented: "Maybe [they] got mixed up a bit in your office. Offices do that to Mss., viz ICM . . . Sorry they didn't make your Fall list . . . Fondly, Tennessee."

He sent me a draft of a new story, "Old Sweetheart of the Keys," about two cousins who own a decrepit bar on Dry Bone Drive, one of whom sits rocking on the veranda. Toward the end of the story, Tennessee had added in his unsteady handwriting a warning from one of the cousins to the other: "You can't rock faster than death." It was an image that appeared in my mind, not long afterward, when I heard that he had died in that cluttered apartment in February 1983, from a lethal, and perhaps deliberate, overdose of pills and alcohol, during which he choked to death on the cap of a pill bottle he was trying to open with his teeth.

We never did publish *Fairy Tales*. Somewhere in the margin of one of his stories, he had typed: "I am being interviewed by Gayblevision and I think I am being quite indiscreet in some of 'y [my] disclosures, but then I think, 'When have I ever been othe 5wise%(and is not all art an indiscretion if it is true.' "

He had promised me one more story, "The Final Strategic Retreat of General Scronch," and to this day I'm sorry it never arrived.

CHAPTER 26

*O*NCE S&S WAS firmly established as part of "the G+W family," flying to the West Coast became more frequent. After all, Paramount, our "sister corporation," was there, and if any synergy was ever to take place, there would have to be some exchange of ideas on a person-to-person basis. Dick, who could take advantage of the G+W corporate airplanes, was frequently in Los Angeles and was soon on a first-name basis with everyone who mattered at Paramount. I was less enthusiastic about going there, but eventually Dick somehow managed to plant in Bluhdorn's feverish mind the notion that I was the key to the synergy he craved between S&S and Paramount.

Since synergy was the ostensible raison d'être for having bought us in the first place, Bluhdorn was determined to see it flourish, or at least to produce an example of it for the shareholders, and it was eventually decided that Barry Diller and I were to meet at regular intervals so that I could brief him on the books we had under contract, just in case one of them might sound to him like a possible movie.

For many reasons, these meetings never took place, the most important of them being that Diller didn't want to hear the plots of a lot of novels that he wasn't interested in. His interest was aroused only by the novels he *couldn't* get access to—those he could find out about simply by listening to me he automatically wrote off as useless. When he was in New York, he found innumerable reasons why he was unable to see me; when I offered—unwillingly—to see him in L.A., he also found reasons why that was impossible. Months, even years, went by, punctuated by angry memos and telephone calls from Bluhdorn, demanding to know when a meeting was going to take place. Eventually, Bluhdorn simply set the date himself, sent me over an airline ticket by messenger, and told me to go or else.

A limo picked me up at the airport and took me directly to Paramount, where I was to meet Diller for lunch in his office. When I arrived there, however, he wasn't there, though a lavish cold lunch had been spread out in his sunny, spacious office. He was in Palm Springs and would probably not arrive before three, his secretary informed me.

I had brought some manuscripts with me, so I helped myself to lunch and settled down to read. Eventually, reluctantly, Diller arrived, full of apologies, and sat down to listen, with the expression of a man who is about to undergo root-canal surgery.

I didn't blame him. Nothing is more boring than listening to somebody tell the plot of a novel. I resist listening to this kind of thing myself at all costs, even to the point of rudeness. My heart went out to Diller, but I had a job to do.

I promised Diller I would make it as quick and painless as I could. There was just one small point, I told him—traditionally, whenever somebody from outside the movie industry offers a movie person an idea or a story, he or she will listen politely—or as politely as anyone can listen whose only desire is to get on with the next appointment—then say, the moment their interlocutor pauses for breath, "Let me explain to you why that won't make a movie."

It doesn't matter what the story in question is—it could be *Gone with the Wind* or *Funny Girl*—it is in the nature of a fixed, knee-jerk response to anything coming from outside "the industry," or to the east of the San Bernardino Mountains. I explained to Diller that I had no vested interest in any of the novels I was about to talk to him about, that I was here only because Bluhdorn had made me come. I would do my number, he would listen, then I would go, and we could both report that synergy had taken place. The only thing, I begged him, was not to explain to me why none of these books could be made into movies, first of all because I didn't care, and second because, having grown up in the movie business, I didn't believe a word of it. Many of the things that "couldn't be made into a movie" *were* eventually made into movies, often with success. A large number of the things that were "naturals" as movies were made and turned out to be flops—there were no rules.

Diller nodded sagely and agreed. He leaned back and waved me to begin. I read off the first title on my list and quickly summarized the plot. Before I could finish, Diller had raised his hand to silence me. "Let me explain to you why that won't make a movie," he said.

I shook my head and tore up the list.

Diller raised an eyebrow, but he seemed pleased and relieved. "I'll let Charlie know that we had a successful meeting," he said pleasantly, rising to shake my hand. He saw me to the door, we both reported a major blow for synergy, and the meeting never took place again—

indeed, once it happened, Bluhdorn apparently took it off his checklist and never mentioned it again.

IT WOULD not have occurred to any of us in the 1970s that we would one day look back on it as a golden age, at least in terms of the publishing business. Admittedly, the period in which the majority of publishing houses were still privately owned had gone, and with it the close, day-to-day relationship that had once existed between ownership and the editorial staff. Except for a few cases—Farrar, Straus and Giroux, for example, or (hanging on by the fingernails) Viking—ownership was now more remote, in some cases so remote as to be invisible. S&S was an exception only in the sense that Bluhdorn occasionally took a personal interest in our affairs, partly because he liked books and partly because Dick Snyder had won his respect.

Still, even Bluhdorn was as remote as Zeus for most of the people who worked at S&S. One could not imagine him dropping by people's offices to share a joke with them, like Bennett Cerf at Random House, nor could one walk into his office to read him a couple of pages from a hot new manuscript, as people had often done with Dick Simon.

Management in the recent past had been a meaningless term in most publishing houses. At S&S management consisted of hardly much more than the treasurer, Sy Turk, and his secretary, whose job under Shimkin had been to urge caution when ordering office supplies. At Random House, Viking, Knopf, and almost every other major publishing house, the situation had been roughly the same. Management was basically housekeeping. "The chain of command," to use another term then unfamiliar in publishing, went straight from the owner(s) to the publisher (sometimes they were the same person) to the editors. The "business people" were on the sidelines, looking on in horror or, like Chicken Little, predicting disaster, but they were seldom brought into the meetings that really mattered. Their advice, if sought at all, tended to be sought after the fact, the usual question being some version of "This is what we've decided to do, now how do we pay for it?"

With publishing becoming a big business and the major houses increasingly owned by outsiders, the concept of management took on a whole new meaning and importance. The managers of RCA, which owned Random House, and Gulf + Western, though very different companies, both wanted their publishing asset run like a business, and at most levels were really at ease only when talking to businessmen like themselves. Dick realized this early on and began transforming himself from a successful publisher to a businessman/manager, though he never lost his publishing skills or altogether gave up his hold on the publishing process. Everywhere, though, however it was accomplished, management, hitherto despised, took on a new importance, with the effect that layers of management began to surround the editors and the publisher, who soon found themselves subordinated in the new pecking order. Instead of being at the top, those who actually published and edited the books found themselves gradually relegated to the bottom, reporting to managers who soon constituted a whole separate and more powerful element within the house. Rather than to books, these people were dedicated largely to proving to the owner that the publishing house was being run like a serious business and in compliance with the parent company's demands, rules, and expectations.

Forecasts—always nebulous in a business where a single unexpected best-seller can turn a poor year into a good one and where sheer dumb luck operates almost as mysteriously as it does in the movie business—became enshrined as "business plans," which were soon engraved in stone. Targets were set and had to be met, numbers had to be produced in huge quantity and ever-growing complexity to justify any decision. This soon required a large number of bureaucrats.

The one thing that had set book publishing apart from most American businesses was that the great majority of the people who worked at a publishing house were actively engaged in acquiring, editing, and producing the final product. There was no thick layer of management and bureaucracy, as there was in such supposedly "modern" businesses as car manufacturing or television, which is why a couple of really big best-sellers was all it took to produce a terrific year. The number of people involved in the process was small, and they were comparatively low paid, hence overhead was low and a sudden increase in profit instantly noticeable. Conversely, a bad year, one in which there were no surprise best-sellers, could be ridden out, often without letting anybody go, since the company was staffed leanly to begin with. Book publishing *looked* inefficient to the outside observer, but it in fact had all the advantages of a guerrilla army over a standing one: It could live off the land, change direction quickly, and needed no expensive and cumbersome general staff to guide it.

Now, however, without the actual business of buying and selling books having changed in any appreciable way,* publishing houses began to take on all the appurtenances of conventional big business. In short order, there were more people managing than there were actually publishing books, many of them basically managing the editors, who became, as it were, the smallest—or perhaps more accurately, the least powerful—cogs in the machine and certainly the most carefully scrutinized.

In the meantime, the direction of the major houses fell into the hands of people who "understood business" as opposed to books and who in general despised, or were at least deeply suspicious of, those who read books and dealt directly with authors. Authors were perceived, like actors and writers in the old Hollywood of the studio moguls, to be overpaid troublemakers, spoiled children. The word *creative*, always spoken with a certain sense of resentment by those in power, came to be a synonym for *unbusinesslike, improvident, irresponsible,* and *self-indulgent.* "The creative side" of the business was where the problems arose—books that lost money, books that were late, books that shouldn't have been bought in the first place, books that made trouble or the wrong kind of headlines, often infuriating the parent company. "The creative people" were writers—notoriously a sullen, difficult, and demanding lot, "navel gazers" who usually had an unrealistic and inflated view of what their work was worth—or editors who wanted to indulge their personal taste at the expense of the company, lived off their expense accounts, and often took the writer's side against the company. (Of course, writers complained in turn that most editors never stood up for their authors and yearned for the editors of some mythical golden age, who went to bat for their authors even at the risk of losing their jobs, something which was never really the case, as any reading of the Hemingway/Perkins correspondence will demonstrate.) It was always a common joke among publishing people that "this would be a

---

* More than sixty years after the Depression, unsold books are still returnable by bookstores to the publishers for full credit, an emergency measure that was intended to save booksellers from bankruptcy as the economy collapsed and remains in effect even though the big bookstore chains have long since become profitable giants, dwarfing all but the largest publishers, and have driven out of business just those small, independent bookstores that the returns policy was meant to protect.

great business if it weren't for writers," but by the mid-seventies publishing was beginning to be run by people who at heart believed that and included editors as well.

ONE REFLECTION of this growing attitude was the idea that people from outside the publishing world could do a better job of running it than those who were already infected with a taste for reading, a sympathy for writers, and the desire to have a regular table at "21" or the Italian Pavilion. This seemingly culminated in Dick Snyder's decision to hire the former president of a Fortune 500 medical-supply company to run what was now called the consumer division of S&S, on the grounds that his management skills and his knowledge of consumer sales would be invaluable assets. This was not as strange a hiring choice as it seemed—Dick was under some pressure from Gulf + Western to run S&S in a more "businesslike" way and therefore picked a man who, on paper, would surely seem about as businesslike as it gets and at least wouldn't go about trying to come up with ideas for new books or asking why we published so many first novels.

"He's going to run this like a *business*," Dick promised, though no sooner was the poor man onboard than Dick began to make fun of his ignorance about book publishing, and he was soon excluded from any of the meetings at which major decisions were made and relegated to a large, luxurious office many floors away from Dick's, where he had nothing to do. Once, when Dick and I were sitting in his office discussing the acquisition of a major author on whom we had our hearts set, I suggested it might be a good idea (or at least polite) for me to tell the man who was ostensibly the head of consumer publishing about what we were doing before he read about it in the papers. "Fuck him," Dick said cheerfully. Not every publishing house was so lucky—in many, the outside businessmen brought in were actually placed in charge, with calamitous results.

At every level, management people scrutinized what publishers, editors, art directors, and the manufacturing staff actually did and began to establish controls over the way it was done. The amiable chaos and anarchy in which books had hitherto been created gave way to a more orderly process, and accountability (another new buzzword) began to be established in the publishing process. Where people were lucky, as at

Random House and S&S, the movement toward efficiency was blunted by the fact that those at the top still preferred books to balance sheets. All the same, the Random House or the S&S of the mid-seventies was almost unrecognizable to those who had worked there ten or twenty years earlier, and classic editors were fast being replaced by people for whom books were "units" and "titles" were interchangeable. The tail was beginning to wag the dog.

Some of these changes were skin-deep. It had always been normal at every publishing house to prepare a financial estimate (known at S&S and elsewhere as a P&L) on each book that was being considered for publication, but this was usually prepared after the fact—that is, the decision to publish was made *before* the numbers were done, so the whole thing was more of a sop to good business procedure than a useful management tool. Now the P&Ls throughout the industry grew more complicated, requiring estimates that by their very nature were likely to be problematic. On the surface, the numbers were being worked out in enough detail to satisfy the financial people, but in fact, however impressive in appearance, they still represented guesswork.

What's more, when the book was considered really important, everybody ignored the whole process. If Dick wanted to make a two-book offer for a major best-selling author, he told the editor to go ahead—the numbers would be done later, to justify whatever the outcome was. "You can't make any money out of a book you haven't bought," Snyder used to say. If you wanted to be competitive, you had to go out into the marketplace and buy the hot books and the big-name authors and you could buy them only at the market price. It was one of his favorite sayings, the other being "If we own it, we love it"—once we had bought a book, we had to be committed to it heart and soul, no matter how awful it was. It didn't get you anywhere to complain (let alone admit) that Harold Robbins had been plagiarizing himself for years, or that most of Irving Wallace's novels could be cut by 25 percent without losing a thing.

This was partly an answer to Dan Green, the brilliant head of S&S's publicity department who was to one day succeed Snyder as publisher. Green was one of the few people whose publishing instincts were as sharp as Snyder's, though he lacked Snyder's pit-bull capacity to get things done. Green, like Snyder, could read the auguries, almost three-dimensionally. He looked at the daily sales reports from the major bookstores, skimmed the key reviews, went over the publicity schedule and compared the author's appearances with the sales (Was there a blip the day after he or she did the *Today* show?), closed his eyes thoughtfully for a few seconds, then decided to run an ad in *The New York Times* or the *Chicago Tribune,* go back to press for another ten thousand copies, and print jackets for a further ten beyond that. Conversely, he might say, despite enthusiastic reports from the reps in the field and lots of publicity, "It's all over—don't print any more, they're all going to come back." Somehow, he could weigh the intangibles—a drop in sales at Higbee's, in Cleveland, a reluctance to order more copies from a buyer in Pasadena—and tell that the book had peaked, even though it might still be number one on the best-seller lists and selling like crazy.

It was an art, developed in part by having traveled around the country and met the key players at the jobbers and in the stores, however small their jobs might appear to be, in part by the sheer ability to read the numbers and figure out what they *really* meant, and whether the tide was going in or going out. Long before computers made their appearance on people's desks, those who really knew their way around book publishing could figure out when to start the presses rolling on overtime and when to stop them dead, despite cries from all over the country (as well as from the author and his or her agent) for more books—a skill which is life and death in publishing terms and which the computer has done very little to improve upon, given the enormously high rate of returns today. Then and now, the bookstores were their own worst enemies—since they could return whatever stock remained unsold to the publishers, they had no vested interest in caution, or even realism, and were, then as now, inclined to take few copies of books they didn't understand and far too many of those they did.

Green, a man for whom worry was a permanent state, chewed the end of his pencil (sometimes the business end of his ballpoint pen, if he wasn't careful), wriggled around in his chair until his shirttail was hanging out, gnawed on the end of his tie, and came up with the right decision, time after time. It was a joy to see him do it. With Snyder, the physical contortions were missing, and the process was more inquisitorial, but the result was the same. The difference was that whereas Green had to argue for his conclusions with Snyder, Snyder didn't have himself to argue with. One way or another, however, the publishing industry remained a business in which the key decisions were made by the equivalent of spitting on one's forefinger and holding it up to the wind, a fact that was never fully understood by the conglomerates and big corporations that bought into the book business, nor by the outside businessmen who came in to make sense of it, perhaps in part because it was kept carefully concealed from them.

Outsiders, particularly from the West Coast, used to say how nice it must be to work in a business where people weren't crazy and where greed and ego were at least kept to rational levels, but by the 1970s they were wrong. The only major difference between the movie business and the book business by then was that in the book business the money was smaller.

PART SIX

Comme Ci, Comme Ça

CHAPTER 27

*T*HE MID-SEVENTIES BROUGHT about changes in my life that had nothing to do with publishing, as well as some that did. In 1974, Dick Snyder brought Joni Evans over from Morrow to run the S&S rights department. Joni had been a star at Morrow—she was sharp, bright, aggressive, and smart, in addition to which she was tireless, fiercely ambitious, and boiling over with enthusiasm. It came as no surprise to learn that she had been a cheerleader at Mamaroneck High, along with her sister, Joyce. The two sisters had between them enough energy to keep a whole football team going, and no sooner had Joni arrived at S&S than her enthusiasm was quickly noticed.

This was hardly surprising—the mid-seventies was the period in which the rights directors of the major publishing houses suddenly became stars. What had hitherto been a fairly low-profile job suddenly became glamorous as the prices paid for mass-market paperback rights escalated into the millions. In buying a book, it became essential to know what the paperback rights might go for. Rights directors were also in constant touch with their "customers"—any rights director worth his or her salt was on the phone all the time—and provided, among other things, a kind of industrywide hot line of news and gossip. If the book clubs thought a big novel needed a better title or if the major paperback editors said they might buy a book if certain changes were made, such opinions could no longer be ignored. Rights directors, if they were any good, began to play a role in the editorial process. They even became involved in publicity, advertising, and promotion, since the paperback publishers, having paid a lot of money for the rights to a book, were not unnaturally determined to have some say in how it was promoted or at least to make sure that the hardcover publisher didn't simply take their money and run. As foreign rights came under the control of rights directors, they soon learned more about what was going on among foreign publishers than any editor could and became just as familiar with the publishing gossip in Bologna, Paris, or Stockholm as with that of New York. They knew what was happening at the movie companies and among the magazines that competed for serial rights—they were, in fact, fountains of knowledge in an industry where knowledge is power. Finally, a company's income from rights very often made the difference between profit or loss at the end of the year, so rights directors usually had the ear of the publisher, to the consternation of older and more conservative editors.

Most of the rights directors were women, as were many of the editors at the book clubs and most of the major mass-market paperback editors and nearly all of the movie "scouts." Women such as Mildred Marmur, the rights director of Random House (who had been a secretary at S&S when I first came there and worked her way up to become rights director), or Joni Evans played major roles in opening up major executive jobs to women throughout the book industry, but, just as important, they also played a part in making editors and authors more conscious of the need to think about the markets for a book.

AFTER MY experience in Texas at the self-help convention, I had sworn to give up writing books that advised people to do anything. I had already signed a substantial contract for a book that was to be called "How to Be a Winner 100 Percent of the Time," and contemplated with resignation having to pay the money back, but Lynn Nesbit urged me not to worry about it. If I had to pay it back, I would, but why not try and come up with something else? My new editor, Jason Epstein, who had replaced Jim Silberman, might be interested in a book about my family, she said. I had written the first chapter of such a book many years before, at the urging of Bob Gottlieb and Nina Bourne, so I sent it off to Epstein to see what he thought of it. He loved it and simply transferred the contract from the defunct self-help book to the new one, an act of faith and generosity that I have never forgotten (and that probably wouldn't happen today). I wrote *Charmed Lives* quickly and with pleasure—here, at last, was a story I knew by heart—and to my delight, Epstein liked reading it as much as I liked writing it.

Shortly after I had turned in the manuscript, which was very long, Milly Marmur called me to tell me in confidence that the Book-of-the-Month Club judges loved *Charmed Lives* and might well take it as a Main Selection, except that they felt it was too long. In those days, a Main Selection of the BOMC was a very big deal indeed—they picked only eleven books a year—and made a real difference in sales. But the thought of going through the manuscript and cutting it one more time made my heart sink. "Listen, *bubbi*," Milly said firmly, "I'm ordering in, you're coming over to Random House, and we're going to cut this book together, every night this week if we have to, so they can have a clean, cut version back on their desks by next Monday. It's now or never. They need a selection, but something else could come up, and that's it for you. Are you on your way, darling?"

I was on my way shortly. Milly and I spent the next few evenings huddled on the floor of her tiny office, cutting, pasting, retyping, renumbering until we had a tighter, slimmer manuscript ready for the BOMC. The BOMC took *Charmed Lives* as a Main Selection, which set the tone for its success in hardcover, and later in paperback, but it wouldn't have happened if Milly had not intervened forcefully.

It was a bravura performance but not atypical of what was happening everywhere in publishing. Rights directors knew what was happening, and knew how to *make* things happen. "Ask Joni what Rights thinks about it," Dick said more and more often before making a decision on a book. It did not take long before Joni moved out of the rights department and began to acquire her own list of authors, for she had formidable editorial talents too. Not only that, it became apparent to those in the know that she and Dick were a couple, a change that not only had a major impact on S&S but, in its way, on the whole publishing business. A relationship between two strong-willed, ambitious people, both of whom lived, breathed, and talked publishing and worked in the same office was bound to be unusual. Further, he was her boss, and not an easy or forgiving one at that; once they were married, their private and their public lives became almost inextricable, which was not always a blessing. Dick began by boasting that he was never bored because they could talk about publishing all the time, but this attraction eventually palled and became a subject of complaint rather than satisfaction.

. . .

IN THE meantime, however, the Snyder/Evans relationship ushered in a new era in book publishing. Dick-and-Joni, as they came to be known once they went public—even to people who had never met them—or the Snyders, as they became once they were married, not only liked to live well, they liked to flaunt it. Their relationship made the gossip columns (albeit at first in harmless ways), partly because they liked to give large parties in their glamorous digs (first a duplex penthouse at the top of the St. Moritz Hotel, overlooking Central Park, then a town house in the East Sixties) and partly because they were publishing books that made news. At first, it was hardly noticed, but gradually it became apparent that book publishing was in the process of becoming glamorous. The Snyders, for a time, epitomized the change, indeed were in part responsible for it—the Prince Charles and Lady Di of the book business.

For the first time, book publishing became not just fashionable but chic. The National Book Awards, which, under one name or another, had schlepped on year after year, arousing no interest at all beyond a narrow circle of book publishers and authors who attended it, was transformed from a typical book-business get-together, in which men in tweedy suits and odd footwear and young women in off-the-rack dresses lined up at the bar in a fog of cigarette and pipe smoke and elbowed their way forward to clamor for drinks in plastic glasses, into a formal black-tie banquet with exactly the same people, needless to say, only now in dinner jackets and evening gowns. The black-tie banquet of the Literacy Volunteers, in part the brainchild of columnist Liz Smith, actually managed to mix book people and social celebrities at one yearly event, as if the book itself had become an object of fashionable charity. Journalists, credulous as ever, took all this at face value and began to treat publishing as a "hot" business. Book parties, which had once been equally tweedy and small-bore in social value, blossomed into full-scale extravaganzas, complete with celebrity guests and coverage in the newspapers and local television news. Editors, publishers, and writers who had hitherto labored in decent and often well-deserved obscurity were themselves presented as glittering celebrities, and their doings were chronicled in the gossip columns and in fulsome magazine articles. (I myself appeared on the cover of *New York* magazine, riding a motorcycle and smoking a cigar, and in *The New York Times Magazine,* riding a horse.)

Nothing could be more extraordinary than the way in which book publishing was swiftly transformed into a glamorous occupation—so much so that Irving Lazar, who had for years been considered a movie agent who dabbled in books, refashioned himself almost overnight into a book agent who dabbled in movies. The book business was where the action was, or at any rate where it was thought to be. Book deals, hitherto mostly of interest to the small circle of people who read *Publishers Weekly* on a regular basis, began to be reported on in the big-time media, and publishing news became a hot item, and book publishers, most of whom had hitherto eaten at rather modest restaurants, swiftly took over the new Grill Room of the very expensive Four Seasons restaurant, making it a kind of exclusive club. It is a measure of what was happening that when Random House regretfully gave up its old digs in the Villard Mansion, on Madison Avenue, it moved to a modern, glass-fronted skyscraper on the East Side. When S&S moved into its own building in Rockefeller Center, Dick hired a noted architect, James Polchek, to design luxurious new offices that included a private dining room, with its own kitchen, for the CEO, carpets with the S&S logo (Millet's sower, chosen long ago by Max Schuster to symbolize the dissemination of knowledge) woven into the design, hallways lined with floor-to-ceiling mirrors and decorated with valuable antique American quilts, and a conference room that doubled as a screening room. Dick's personal chef, his private dining room, his executive gym, the Mercedes with a chauffeur that waited for him downstairs, and his use of a G+W jet came to symbolize the ambitions and the freewheeling lifestyle of book publishing. When we flew down to Washington for John Dean's publication party, we did not take the shuttle as ordinary human beings did; we were driven out to Teterboro Airport in New Jersey in the Mercedes, then flew down to D.C. in a Learjet, with the refrigerator stocked with Dick's favorite brand of vodka, caviar, and black bread.

The expensive, glamorous surroundings seemed appropriate to the ambitious plans that were being made in the executive offices of publishing houses all over town. It is some measure of just how futile these ambitions were to prove to be that at both Random House and S&S dramatic hallways have been filled with secretarial cubicles, big offices have been partitioned into smaller ones, then partitioned again, palatial dining rooms and well-equipped professional kitchens are now filing rooms. The spirit that created these ambitiously designed premises has long since departed; the present is more spartan, utilitarian, pessimistic, the future uncertain.

Of course, nothing is more common among celebrities than making the mistake of believing their own press clippings. Those who were, however briefly, touched by the wand of glamorization in the mid-seventies not only believed they had earned it—and that it was going to last—but confused it with growth. That was the case in book publishing, where despite a thin layer of glamour at the top and a lot of hype in the outside world, the business was still pretty much the same as ever. People weren't reading or buying more books—the action was in buying up rival book companies and "consolidating" them into larger and larger companies. It was growth of a kind, to be sure, but forced rather than natural. The same authors were still writing the same kinds of books, which were still being sold in much the same quantities. The book itself was still a fully returnable item, so that nearly two books were printed for every one that sold, and its ultimate destination was either to be "remaindered" for sale at a dollar or less a copy, or "pulped" to make more paper products. Efforts were made to make this cumbersome and ancient process look well thought-out, streamlined, and efficient for the benefit of the shareholders of the big companies that now owned most of them, but most of it would have seemed familiar enough to Gutenberg. Add to this that the basic product of this particular slice of the media business was still being created in large part by people banging away at typewriters on kitchen tables and it is easy to understand why the glossy public image of the publishing business was so misleading.

NINETEEN SEVENTY-THREE was a crucial year for me. For years, I had been an avid horseman, though I contented myself with renting horses at stables all over New York City, until I finally settled down as a regular customer at a stable at Clove Lake, on Staten Island, where I rode every Saturday and Sunday, as well as on Thursday evenings, when my son, Christopher, and I practiced as part of their "parade team," doing figure eights at a canter and more complicated movements with twenty or so other riders, to the accompaniment of waltzes and marches over a loudspeaker.

I even took up fox hunting, having been introduced to the sport by Jane McIlvaine McClary, one of the doyennes of Middleburg, Virginia, horse society, whose novel, *A Portion for Foxes,* I not only published but presented to a sales conference while dressed in full hunting regalia, including boots, breeches, a white stock, a gold-buttoned pink coat, and a top hat. (The Warwick Hotel, greatly to my disappointment, firmly vetoed my plan to ride into the conference room and present the book from horseback.) Jane McClary was a foxhunter of international fame and was so pleased to have a horseman for an editor that she overestimated my skills by a considerable factor. On my first visit, she proudly informed me that she had secured permission for us to go over the Middleburg Gold Cup steeplechase course in the morning, and, despite my feeble and terrified protests, I found myself being carried over the biggest fences this side of Aintree on one of Jane's horses, my eyes closed, both hands grasping the horse's mane for dear life. The same horse carried me over immense stone walls and terrifying embankments on my first day with the Middleburg Hunt, until I was eventually neck and neck with the master, my stirrups flapping as I hauled desperately on the poor animal's mouth, while the master shouted indignantly at me to slow down and fall back behind him. (A valuable lesson is never to ride a horse you don't know who is named Black Devil, as this one was, or anything similar.)

As a result, I acquired an entirely unjustified reputation as something of a daredevil rider and was not only asked back many times but soon invited out to the kind of black-tie dinner where the gentlemen retire to the library after dessert to drink brandy, smoke cigars, and tell anti-Roosevelt stories.

It definitely wasn't my milieu, and if I kept at it long enough I was dead certain to break my neck, but once again it got me out of the house. In fact, between riding, flying down to Middleburg for the weekends to hunt, work at S&S, and writing my books and magazine articles, I was very seldom home, and almost always reading or writing something when I was. Having set out determined not to be like my father, I ended up doing the same thing.

IT HAD always been my ambition to have my own horse, instead of hiring one at a livery stable, and with the publication of *Power!* there seemed no good reason not to do so. I purchased a large, elderly gelding of uncertain breeding and temperament, whom I renamed Malplaquet (after the most famous of Marlborough's battles), and decided to keep him at the venerable Claremont Riding Academy, on West Eighty-ninth Street, near Central Park, where I had taken to riding early in the morning almost every day. It was thus that I first saw Margaret Glinn, the wife of the well-known and very successful Magnum photographer Burt Glinn. She was a blond, beautiful woman, with the grace of a born rider, extravagantly dressed, trotting a big, handsome chestnut Thoroughbred (Tabasco, whom she was later to purchase) around the Central Park reservoir. For a very long time she did not seem willing to look at me, while I glanced at her surreptitiously—which would have been hard not to do, since she was perhaps the most striking woman I had ever seen. A long period ensued in which we circled the reservoir every morning in opposite directions, saying "Good morning!" to each other as we passed, until finally, some months after our first encounter, we went around the reservoir in the same direction together for the first time.

Now that we were at least riding in the same direction, we were able to talk. It transpired that we were both English, though Margaret's Englishness, unlike mine, was of the pure, nonhyphenated kind—she was the only daughter of a Gloucestershire farmer and had ridden since the age of three or four. Sophisticated, glamorous, and alarmingly well-traveled, she retained an English country girl's dislike of the city, although she seemed to me to be the supreme example of a fashionable city-dwelling woman. She had married an officer in the Kenya police while in her teens, gone to live in Kenya, where the marriage swiftly dissolved, lived for a while in Paris in the motion-picture world, then met Burt Glinn and soon followed him to New York. Glinn had used her as a model, and initially they had lived together in a big apartment that he shared with his old friend Clay Felker. It was a typical bachelors' digs, which sounded, as she described it, like that in *The Odd Couple,* with layers of newspapers on the floor and the smell of cigars in every room.

Burt might have been happy enough to stay there forever—he liked the comradeship and the sense of *la vie de bohème,* but Margaret, who was tired of communal life and living out of unpacked suitcases, eventually got him to move into a glamorous apartment of their own, with big windows overlooking Central Park, where they entertained lavishly and frequently. Years of traveling around the world with her husband as he worked had taken their toll—Margaret had decided to stop traveling, an act of independence that baffled Burt and of which Tabasco and her morning rides were a symptom. Just as the young had cried out, "We ain't marching any more," Margaret had put her foot down and refused to travel, except during the winter, when she and Burt usually rented a house in Cuernavaca with the Halberstams, John Chancellor and his wife, JFK's favorite photographer, Stanley Tretick, and his wife, Mo, and other media figures.

It sounded like such a glamorous life, in fact, that I was at once envious and somewhat overawed. Admittedly, I had been brought up surrounded by glamour and I was used to moving in fairly glamorous circles as an editor, but Casey and I lived rather simply. For several years we had rented a succession of immense old summer houses in Dark Harbor, Maine, on an island in Penobscot Bay, but we tended to live quietly up there, too.

Dark Harbor was a curious and unlikely place to choose for the summer, and perhaps if my mind had been less fixed on my work I might have wondered why Casey had chosen this remote island, where most of the tiny community of summer people were far richer than ourselves.

Dark Harbor might have been a place in which to repair whatever differences had begun to pull us apart, but as is so often the case, it had the opposite effect. Rather like Margaret's travels with Burt, the more Casey and I were together, the further we drifted apart, and there didn't seem anything to be done about it. By the time I met Margaret in Central Park, the thing we had most in common—though I didn't know it then and resisted the notion for a long time—was that our marriages had drifted beyond the point of no return.

Oddly enough, the four of us became friends almost at once. Hardly a weekend passed that we didn't go out to dinner together. Casey and I became frequent guests at the Glinns' apartment, and we eventually even made plans to go away on a vacation together, renting a house in San Miguel de Allende, Mexico, with a third couple, despite the fact that Margaret and I had long since become lovers.

When Margaret's marriage finally exploded (the only word that can describe the event), followed a year or so later by my own (which was more of a collapse than an explosion), it was as if we had known each other for a lifetime. After all, our balancing act had gone on for almost five years before we were finally able to go downtown to City Hall and tie the knot, during which time I had nevertheless somehow managed to write two books and maintain a successful career, which is a tribute to either my single-mindedness or Margaret's patience.

Whichever, it was a period of great excitement and happiness for Margaret and me and for Dick and Joni, who had married before us. It seemed, for a time, as if anything was possible, not just in our personal lives, but at S&S.

CHAPTER 28

*B*LUHDORN LIKED GROWTH. It was the lifeblood of his em-pire, and he lived to make new acquisitions. Had Dick been content to sit around buying books and increasing the company's sales, Bluhdorn would have lost interest in him quickly and possibly in book publishing too. Fortunately, Dick saw his own future and that of S&S as one of growth by acquisition, so Bluhdorn was not disappointed. Shimkin had sold S&S to Bluhdorn in 1976 for $11 million, most of it in Gulf + Western stock, which wasn't bad for a company that had been launched in 1924 with capital of $25,000 and that was grossing about $50 million a year at the time of the sale. In 1974, when S&S celebrated its first fifty years, it was a major publishing house, but that was no longer enough. The outline of the future was easy enough to perceive, as one by one, with a few exceptions, some of the most famous and illustrious names in publishing—most of them, it was true, poorly managed and short of capital—surrendered their independence. The big fish swallowed the small, without it crossing the minds of the biggest ones that they too might eventually be swallowed.

Size, of course, does not protect a publisher from failure. On the contrary, the bigger you are, the easier it is to make expensive mis-takes—and to hide them. The late Ronald Busch, at one time publisher of Ballantine Books, which was bought by Random House in 1973, and later the publisher of Pocket Books, part of S&S, was quoted as saying that buying the big books got easier as the company got larger. "With all the conglomerate money today," he said, "it's like playing Monopoly. If we had to use our own resources, we'd think twice about bidding as much as we do. . . . But with a parent or a conglomerate that has annual sales of two or three billion dollars and up, with two or three million shareholders, what's the risk?"

He might have added "Who cares?" Inevitably, the atmosphere changes when the people who own you are far away and deal in billions instead of being just down the hall, counting every penny, and it doesn't always change for the better. Caution doesn't get you noticed—on the contrary, it is generally better to fail big than to think small.

THIS ALONE explains some of the larger failures in publishing, as does the belief that somebody who has written one successful book is likely to write another. In my case, the lesson that this is not necessarily—or even commonly—true came in the shape of a telephone call from Claire Smith, one of my favorite agents, who had first brought Susan Howatch to my attention and for years represented Ronnie Delderfield. A suggestion from her was one that ought to be taken seriously, so when she dropped a hint that one of her biggest and most famous clients, the English civil servant turned best-selling novelist Richard Adams, author of *Watership Down,* was thinking of changing publishers, I ran to inform Snyder of the news.

Watership Down had been a huge best-seller, winning a readership of millions of devoted fans, including myself and Margaret. It had gone unnoticed for ages by American publishers because very few of them were attracted by a long novel about rabbits, told from the rabbits' point of view. The few who took the trouble to read the manuscript thought it might work if it was drastically shorter and rewritten as a children's book, but most simply passed on the opportunity to read what was to become one of the most successful and acclaimed works of fiction of the decade.

This particular form of blindness is not by any means rare. Tolkien's *The Lord of the Rings* went unread by most American publishers, who found it too long, too demanding, and neither a children's book nor an adult novel. James Herriot's *All Creatures Great and Small* went unread, or was rejected, by visiting Americans for years, even though it was already a big best-seller in the United Kingdom. Fantasy and whimsy—particularly *British* fantasy and whimsy—make many

American publishers acutely nervous. There has always been a certain transatlantic fear that the English sense of humor doesn't "travel," still less the English fascination with small animals.

The tale of the rabbits eventually made its way to America and went on to become an instant best-seller on publication here. Like Tolkien's hobbits and their friends, Adams's rabbits captured the affection and the interest of all but the most hard-hearted, unsentimental, and obdurate of realists, even if there was about the book, on a second reading anyway, a whiff of sanctimonious and slightly self-conscious religiosity, together with the sense that the author might be too clever for his own good. Still, in its own way, the book was a work of genius, deeply imaginative and satisfying, though the author himself, once he had been brought over for a publicity tour, appeared to be something of a queer fish, and a fish out of water at that.

Of course, most writers who have produced a work of genius *are* queer fish. The deeper a person plunges into his or her own imagination and the stronger the hold of the invented world becomes, the less the writer is likely to appear "normal" to other people. Tolstoy was a very queer fish (or odd duck), even in nineteenth-century Russia, where odd ducks abounded, and English literature is full of even odder ducks. The writer is even more likely to be an odd duck when his or her great work of imagination is essentially childlike. To see the world's complexities with the simplicity of a child's eyes is a special form of genius, the Reverend Charles Dodgson being a perfect example of the type, and Adams had much the same curious, divided view of the world as the author of *Alice in Wonderland*. He was at once a serious adult, carrying a heavy load of religious and moral baggage, and a wondering child, able to imagine a whole rich world in a country hedgerow full of rabbits.

To a casual observer, Adams looked a little unhinged in his appearances on American television, but that might have been because most of his interviewers wanted him to be funny about rabbits, whereas he wanted to talk about morality and religion. He was also undergoing the equivalent of the deep-sea diver's bends, having emerged suddenly from a lifetime of obscurity into the limelight of celebrity and wealth.

It is possible that I read *Shardik* in something of a daze. *Watership Down* had seemed to me a work of real talent, totally convincing and entertaining, and *Shardik,* which I sat up all night reading, seemed far more ambitious and darker, almost like *The Lord of the Rings* in that it presented a whole imagined society, with all its history, folklore, and religion meticulously invented. At its center was Shardik himself, a great bear who is at once the object of a cult and a perfectly real bear, a kind of ursine equivalent to the rabbits of *Watership Down*.

This was a potent mix, and I was able to report the next morning that Adams had successfully avoided the dreaded "second novel" syndrome with a book that was as original as the first but richer. I was not alone in this opinion. Peter Mayer, then running Avon Books, a major paperback publisher, had been the U.S. paperback publisher of *Watership Down*, and was determined to keep Adams. When he heard that we were anxious to buy *Shardik*, he called immediately to propose that S&S and Avon copublish it. He had read the manuscript overnight as well and was overcome by it, though not rendered inarticulate—indeed, he talked to me about it for what seemed like hours, his voice trembling with enthusiasm, describing the plot in detail as if I had not read the book myself.

The next day, he repeated it all word for word on the telephone to Dick Snyder, who had *not* read the book, of course, but had already heard about it from me. Dick rolled his eyes and interrupted from time to time to say that he didn't want to hear another word about Kelderek, the lone hunter who discovers Shardik the great bear fleeing from a forest fire and believes him to be the avatar of the god of his people, or the cult of the virginal priestesses, or Genshed, the evil slave dealer who mutilates children, that he wanted to talk about the *deal*, not the goddamn *plot*— but Mayer was not to be stilled until he fell silent and hoarse from talking, at which point Dick wisely told me to negotiate a deal with Mayer, who would otherwise, he guessed, get him to give away points just to get him off the phone.

Dick had no objection to going into partnership with Mayer— "Fifty percent of something is better than a hundred percent of nothing" might have been Leon Shimkin's motto, but Dick was not above using it too when it suited his purpose, and felt that the amount of money involved—$550,000, which was *big* money then—made it sensible to share the risk. Further, when it came to Richard Adams, Peter Mayer knew what he was doing, and Pocket Books might not. Dick just didn't want to spend more time listening to how good the book was or being told how to publish it. Mayer positively reveled in details, so it took a very long time to get a contract drawn up, particularly since Mayer made a moral and personal issue out of even the smallest disagreement and was capable of talking about his feelings and the rightness of his position for hours, or even days, to make his point.

It was some time before I actually met Mayer, who was, until then, merely an impassioned, unstoppable voice over the telephone. As it turned out he was charm itself in person, a tall, exceedingly attractive man, about my age, chain-smoking like a chimney, and with the kind of furious, eclectic erudition that I recognized as basically European. His enthusiasm—not just on the subject of *Shardik*—was overwhelming and infectious, and it was very hard to resist him when he was in a good mood—he is perhaps the only person I had ever met about whom the old cliché "His eyes blazed with enthusiasm" was literally true. When he was *not* in a good mood, he was capable—though never with me—of becoming snappish and withdrawn, and in his own way he could be as difficult and imperious as Snyder. A gifted publisher, rather than an editor, Mayer rather perversely prided himself on his skills as a businessman, about which Dick, who regarded him, in this area, at least, as an amateur, was cautiously skeptical. "He falls in loves with books," Dick would say. "That's OK for editors, but not for publishers." In the long run, Dick would be proven right, when Mayer went on to become a major figure in world publishing as the CEO of Viking/Penguin, after a short and deeply unhappy stint as the head of Pocket Books with Dick as his boss, but at the time of *Shardik* it seemed to a lot of people that Mayer was emerging as the Renaissance man of book publishing, equally adept at high culture and low culture, at home with foreign literature to a degree remarkable in American publishing, and with a remarkable flair for both promotion and, as some pointed out enviously, self-promotion. Few other publishers would have spent their spare time running a small private press of their own, as Mayer did, or done it as well, come to that.

Egged on by Mayer—an active partner if ever there was one—we drew up an enormously ambitious plan for publishing the book, not just because we wanted to earn our money back but because it had been a high-profile purchase. The fact that Adams had moved to S&S for his eagerly awaited second book was major news, and not just in publishing circles. We would look, not to put too fine a point on it, like *putzes* if it didn't succeed. A big American tour was planned for Adams, specially bound reading copies, stamped with a gold-foil emblem of Shardik's head, were prepared (that had not yet become a staple of book PR), and every effort was made to whip up the enthusiasm of the S&S sales force.

• • •

IN THOSE days, sales conferences were still relatively modest events, and the sales reps were mostly middle-aged men, schooled in a certain weary cynicism about "the product" they were called upon to sell. They had heard it all before, and their eyes showed it—novels that were supposed to be number-one best-sellers that went down the drain, books that were hailed by the editor as if they were the Second Coming incarnate that were ignored or reviled by the critics; in short, theirs was not a happy lot.

In those days, the editor presented his or her own books, and there was therefore a premium on being a "good presenter." Bob Gottlieb's presentations had been justly famous—he was capable of making even the dreariest and least promising of first novels sound like potential best-sellers and Nobel Prize winners. While the sales reps knew better than to believe more than 50 percent of what he said, they admired his performances and were willing to follow his lead. The truth was that they were always more than willing to be seduced. Besides, Bob was right just often enough to have gained some credit in their eyes. He had been right about *Catch-22*, he had been right about Charles Portis's *True Grit*, right about Robert Crichton's *The Secret of Santa Vittoria*, right about Chaim Potok, Jessica Mitford, and James Leo Herlihy, so they could forgive the number of times he had been wrong. Track record counted with the reps, and they had an infallible nose for bullshit.

I had inherited Bob's mantle as the star performer at sales conference. I had learned from him to rise to my feet to present a book that was particularly important, to speak extemporaneously (very important, since most editors spoke from notes and droned on interminably, boring the sales reps to death with details they didn't need to know or the plots of novels), to convey as much enthusiasm and sincerity as possible, even at the risk of being thought corny, and to elicit the maximum audience participation. That is not to say that the reps actually believed me any more than they had Bob—the only person they truly believed was Dick, because he told them the hard, basic facts of life, such as that anybody who failed to get so many copies of this or that book into their accounts would be fired, or that their bonus depended on getting out twice as many copies of a book as they thought possible.

For my part, I sympathized with them and liked them. I had been out "on the road" briefly myself, as a very junior editor, when I was taken from store to store and jobber to jobber throughout Georgia by J. Felton Covington, Jr., one of our most senior sales reps, a Southern gentleman of the old school, whose laid-back manner, slow drawl, and deep courtesy were so appreciated by booksellers of his region that he was able to place some of Bob Gottlieb's most difficult first novels in stores that normally only carried Bibles. Cov's patience, his ability to sit for hours swapping stories with some small-town bookseller in order to get him or her to take half a dozen more copies of some book that Dick wanted pushed, or, not infrequently, some book that Cov himself fervently believed in, for like most sales reps, Cov was a big reader—there was not much else to do in the evenings, when you were on the road—his genuine interest in the lives of his customers, right down to the names and health of their dogs and cats, his inexhaustible good humor and bottomless stomach for coffee—no matter how many cups he had been offered and drunk during the course of a day, he always accepted another at the next or the last bookstore as if he hadn't had a cup since breakfast—all this was the part of the book business that editors and the people at the top tended to overlook, or simply accept as normal.

Dick knew better. He drove the reps mercilessly, but he understood how important their job was, and on the whole was more at ease with them than with the editors, most of whom expected all their books to be taken at face value. Most editors lacked the reps' fine, bracing cynicism and their hearty masculine hedonism. In those days, reps tended to be men's men who ate well, drank a lot (after hours), played poker, enjoyed a game of golf, and were happy enough to relax by the pool at break times, trading publishing gossip and watching the girls go by.

All the same, being a sales rep was just about the toughest job in book publishing—the hours were punishing, the demands imposed on them were often unreasonable, and they were routinely bullied, prodded, and threatened at the end of every sales meeting, after days of having had to sit for hours on end in stuffy conference rooms, glassy-eyed with boredom, feigning interest as best they could. It was little wonder that they cut loose after dinner in the hospitality suite. The truth was that the reps truly loved books—cynical they might be, but in the end the people who *really* believed in the list in any publishing house were the reps themselves, not the editors. There wasn't one of them who couldn't have made more money selling almost anything else, but season after season they went out with their sample cases full of galley proofs and catalogs, convinced that this was the best list ever and determined to convince the even more skeptical booksellers and book buyers of the same.

. . .

IN ANY event, the reps had to be convinced that *Shardik* was going to work. At Dick's suggestion, I sent each of them a bound galley with a personal letter, asking them to read the book before the sales conference and giving them my considered opinion that what we had here was a work of genius and a huge best-seller.

The presentation itself was considered by Dick to be so crucial that he sent me to bed early the night before, shooing me out of the hospitality suite by 10 P.M. "Tomorrow is the big one," he said, like a football coach. "Don't blow it! Take my advice—get some sleep. Tomorrow morning I want to see you knock their socks off!"

Somewhat resentful at being sent to bed early like a child (just as things in the hospitality suite were getting interesting—somebody had pushed the poker players into the bedroom and set up a tape player in the living room for dancing), I brooded on what I would tell the troops. There was no question about it, this would have to be the presentation of a lifetime.

The agenda had been arranged so that there were lesser books before my big moment, which was to come just before the coffee break, so the reps would leave the room on a high—this was the kind of thing that Dick was a past master at orchestrating, down to the smallest details. I rose to my feet, the jacket of *Shardik* flashed on the screen, complete with the twenty-four-karat-gold bear mask, and I launched into my spiel. I talked to them about *Watership Down,* reminded them of its huge success, tried to convey the richness and subtlety of the plot, acted out key scenes, key characters, and rose to a crescendo of optimism and enthusiasm. I was moved myself, and I could see that I had my audience in the palm of my hand, that they would go straight from here to put out the biggest number of advance orders that S&S had ever had for a work of fiction. For once, I could see, there was no doubt in their faces. They were with me 100 percent.

Shortly before the morning session, I had been in the men's room and overheard one of the reps saying to another that Hugh Collins, our Chicago rep, had read *Shardik* and loved it. Collins was perhaps the most prickly and curmudgeonly of the older reps, a hard-drinking Irishman with a hair-trigger temper who was not afraid of arguing even with Snyder. Collins was a difficult man to impress, so the fact that he was a fan of the book would mean a lot to the rest of the reps. As I reached the end of my presentation, I saw Collins in the first row, among all the heavy hitters of the S&S sales force, and caught his eye. He looked cheerful enough, so I took the plunge. Sweating, exhausted by the sheer force of my own enthusiasm, basking in the admiration of everybody on the dais, I finally finished my presentation, and in the complete silence that followed—the phrase "you could have heard a pin drop" came to mind—I pointed at Collins and said, "But you don't have to believe me. I know somebody else here who has read the book, and he'll tell you what he thinks." I paused for effect. "Hugh," I said, "you've read *Shardik*. What did *you* think of the book?"

There was another long pause, during which just the slightest trace of doubt crossed my mind, now that it was too late. Everybody was looking at Collins, and I could see on his face a curious mixture of expressions. Enthusiasm was not among them, I thought. Finally he spoke. Somebody had passed him a microphone, so his voice boomed out, filling the room. He waved one hand from side to side. "*Comme ci, comme ça,*" he said, with the look of a man who has just bitten into a lemon.

That did it for *Shardik*. In the laughter that followed Hugh Collins's comment—it turned out that whoever had said that he liked the book was thinking of somebody else—the book's chances wilted. Unfortunately, the rest of the world voted with Hugh Collins. *The New York Times Book Review,* in a front-page review, even speculated that Adams might in fact have written the book before *Watership Down*. "How else," the reviewer asked, "can one explain the amateurish quality which pervades so much of this book by a writer who has previously displayed such masterful gifts?" Most reviewers advised Adams to stick with rabbits, and *Time* made it clear to parents that *Shardik* was no children's story.

Even Adams's publicity tour did little to ameliorate the debacle. The truth was that his readers deeply resented the fact that he wasn't writing about the rabbits of *Watership Down* and were not much interested in anything else he had to say or write. In the end, Hugh Collins's remark was just about on the money.

Of course nothing lasts forever. In publishing there is always a new list, new books to enthuse about, more unforeseen failures and successes. Rather like farming, each new season cancels out the previous one and restores hope. By the time the disaster of *Shardik* was over (Mayer's hopes had been washed away, too—the public didn't want the book in paperback, either), we were on to new things, this time centered on a very different figure than Richard Adams, whose popularity never recovered from his novel about the great bear and who retired to his tax haven to become a rather fussy English man of letters of a rather conventional kind, as if the fairy godmother whose kiss had given him the genius to write *Watership Down* had kissed him off after one book, then relegated him to the ranks of ordinary writers.

CHAPTER 29

AT ABOUT THE same time as I was coming a-cropper with Richard Adams, I stumbled upon a different kind of literature, which would eventually bring me many friendships with people who were not part of the book world.

There was a time when nothing much was known about the Mafia, and few books were written about it, but all that changed dramatically when Mario Puzo turned it, overnight, into an enduring American myth. Books were soon as much a part of Mafia life as pistols.

Long before I acquired a reputation for publishing books by "wiseguys," I *knew* wiseguys. My son, Christopher, and I used to ride at Clove Lake Stables, on Staten Island, once or twice a week. On Thursday nights, the stable put on a floodlit "musical ride" for young riding students, in which up to twenty of them, mounted, performed intricate maneuvers in the ring, to the accompaniment of rousing martial-band music from loudspeakers. A lot of the kids were regulars, including one little girl, about Chris's age, who was always brought to the musical ride by her father, a tall, bulky, well-dressed man, who was driven in a big, black, shiny Cadillac.

One cool, dusty autumn evening, I was leaning against the side of my black VW Beetle, when a large man in a belted raincoat and hat à la George Raft came over to me and whispered hoarsely, "Mr. F. wants a word wid yez." He did not seem to be offering me a choice. He waved his thumb in the direction of the little girl's father, who was leaning against the side of his Cadillac and wearing a camel-hair overcoat with the belt knotted loosely around his waist, a silk scarf, and a homburg.

Mr. F. and I shook hands, and he offered me a cigarette. His voice was conspiratorial, even where no conspiracy was involved, and as gravelly as a trout stream. He had admired the way I brought my son out here to ride. No doubt I had noticed, he did the same for his daughter.

I nodded, wondering where this was going. Did I think that the fellow in the derby was a good instructor? Very much so, I said, happy to vouch for Paul Nigro. Mr. F. nodded. He thought so too. This Nigro fellow had told him that she would ride a lot better if she had her own pony—what did I think of that? I said I thought Nigro was probably right.

Mr. F. leaned closer, sharing his expensive aftershave with me. I should understand, he said, that he didn't know a goddamn thing about horses. He liked a good day at the track, you couldn't beat it, go with some good fellows, get some fresh air, win a few bucks. . . . He knew a lot of people in that world, but they weren't any help when it came to buying a kid's pony. Since I rode myself, did I have any idea where he might start?

I gave Mr. F. a couple of names, which he wrote down on the back of an envelope, and promised to make a few calls on his behalf myself. I made the calls, as promised, and shortly afterward heard that he had bought a pony, paying in cash.

A few weeks later, I saw him again. This time he came across to me himself, followed by his bodyguard, and shook my hand warmly. I congratulated him on his purchase. He took me by the arm and leaned close. "Listen," he said. "You did me a favor. I want to do you one."

I told him that wasn't necessary.

He shook his head impatiently. "I found out a little bit about you, my friend," he said. "Turns out you're some kind of big-shot boy wonder in book publishing. No offense, but if you're such a big shot, why are you driving a piece a shit like this?" He gave the left front tire of my VW a contemptuous kick. What kind of car did I like? he asked. Maybe a Chrysler, a Mercury? Or a Buick?

I was partial to Buicks, I allowed, maybe because my father had owned one when we lived in Beverly Hills.

"Al-*right!*" Mr. F. said with enthusiasm. "Now we're talking." How would I like a good-as-new Buick, leather seats, air, power windows, the works, for, say, my VW plus two grand?

Two grand sounded like a steal to me, I thought (but did not say), for it was beginning to dawn on me that if I said yes, Mr. F. would almost certainly send his bodyguard out to steal a late-model Buick off the streets for me. Besides, Mr. F.'s generosity was not only criminal, it was spurious. It would cost him nothing to steal a car, in exchange for which he would be getting a perfectly legitimate Beetle, with a proper VIN and registration, plus two thousand dollars in cash. I, on the other hand, would have a bigger, more glamorous car, for which I might go to prison the first time I was stopped by the police.

I managed to get out of the "gift" by blaming my wife and her sentimental fondness for the VW, though not before Mr. F., the bodyguard, and I had dinner together at a dark little Italian restaurant in deepest Brooklyn, where the bar was occupied entirely by wide-hipped figures straight out of *Guys and Dolls*. I was an object of considerable merriment, since Mr. F. introduced me to everyone as the man who had turned down a free Buick.

We remained in touch and on friendly terms for many years, until Mr. F. was eventually sentenced to life imprisonment. It is a measure of what the supposed good life in the Mafia was *really* like that when Mr. F. was arrested, among the many charges, including conspiracy to murder, was the one that he had neglected to pay sales tax on the purchase of the pony for his daughter.

Perhaps because my relationship with Mr. F. had been cordial, I was an easy mark when an old time Hollywood agent called to ask if I would read the autobiography of Mr. B.—as Joseph Bonanno was known to his associates. To his intimates he was Don Peppino, to his subordinates simply Mr. B. or The Don, and to law-enforcement people and the tabloid press he was Joe Bananas.

Under any name, Bonanno, then seventy-seven years old, was one of the most feared and respected figures in organized crime, the associate of Charles ("Lucky") Luciano, Alberto Anastasia, Carlo Gambino, and Joe Profaci (whose daughter Bonanno's elder son married), indisputably the boss of his own "family," and perhaps the highly controversial "Boss of Bosses" and head of "The Commission." It was widely rumored that Mario Puzo had based Don Corleone in *The Godfather* on the character and the career of Bonanno, and Gay Talese had written a much-acclaimed, best-selling book, *Honor Thy Father,* about Bonanno's relationship with his son Salvatore ("Bill") and with his contentious colleagues on The Commission.

Being the subject of a book, fiction or nonfiction, though bad enough, was one thing; writing one's own was quite another. No "godfather" had ever written a book or even been tempted to, and Bonanno's decision to do so was bewildering to his fellow mafiosi that the subject came up on countless FBI taped intercepts of their conversations. For example, at a meeting in the Staten Island home of Paul Castellano, the boss of the Gambino crime family, the FBI heard the family consigliere, Joe N. Gallo, remark to his don, on the subject of Bonanno's book, "It makes you wonder, is this son of a bitch senile, or is he a fucking nut?" Many of Bonanno's rivals doubted that he was a nut and assumed that the book was some form of plea bargain with the feds. It was certainly the most eagerly awaited book in Mafia history—a group of people not hitherto known for their interest in literature.

Even in a world full of colorful figures, Bonanno was regarded as something of an eccentric. While the other dons lived in the shadows, Bonanno was a public figure and courted the media. He was viewed by most of his colleagues with a combination of suspicion and bewilderment. In a world where most of the players were, at best, semiliterate, Bonanno read poetry, boasted of his knowledge of the classics, and gave advice to his cohorts in the form of quotes from Thucydides or Machiavelli.

Of course Bonanno's manuscript did not exactly spill the beans on the Mafia. It was, to put it mildly, an exercise in caution, almost written in code. While Bonanno wrote at length and in detail about The Commission (the existence of which other Mafia headliners had always denied), his point of view was that the whole thing was just an example of old-fashioned Sicilian patriotism, that *cosa nostra* consisted merely of men of honor and goodwill banding together to defend the ancient Sicilian virtues in a new and materialistic world.

Still, reading between the lines, the history of the Mafia in America was there, written by an insider and a participant. He described in great detail his own rise to power, the jockeying among the various factions, and the gangland executions by which "order" was maintained, often uneasily, among them. He gave a frank account of his attempt to machine-gun some of Al Capone's men, who had unwisely journeyed from Chicago to interfere in the affairs of the New York families. Bonanno described Capone (who was apparently not a sore loser, since he presented Bonanno with a gold and diamond watch) as "a rather jolly fellow," but he judged people and events by his own strict Sicilian standards, and seldom criticized those who, like Capone, had not been born into "the tradition," with its unforgiving code of behavior. Bonanno's admiration went to men such as his father-in-law, Don Calorio Labruzzo, a retired butcher, whose pride was so touchy that he carried a thick cane with which to beat anyone who insulted his sense of honor.

Although Bonanno had a literary agent, his real representative was in fact his son Bill. Tall, good-looking, conservatively, even elegantly, dressed, Bill Bonanno rather resembled Kris Kristofferson and did not show any obvious sign of following in his father's footsteps, except for the fact that he required his parole officer's permission to travel.

It was to him, therefore, that I expressed certain questions and reservations about the book, once we had bought it. In some areas, I felt, his father was being remarkably, perhaps even dangerously, frank, while in others I felt that he was holding back. Bill Bonanno did not disagree but did not want to suggest what his father might or might not add. He was being uncharacteristically cautious, I discovered, because his father had been outraged by *Honor Thy Father,* in part because Bill had cooperated with Talese rather too fully. The quarrel had since been patched up, but it had made Bill gun-shy of any direct involvement in literary matters concerning his father, quite apart from the fact that this book was intended to be a reply to Talese's assertions about the Mafia and organized crime. If we wanted changes, Bill said, we would have to go to Tucson and see his father.

Since it seemed like a good opportunity to escape from winter in New York, I made arrangements to fly with Margaret to Tucson, close to where Bonanno lived.

THE BONANNO home bore no relationship to the grandiose and funereal family compound of *The Godfather.* A modest brick house with a narrow patch of lawn, it resembled its neighbors and showed no signs of any special concern for security.

Bonanno had gone to a good deal of trouble to make our stay agreeable. He had flown his daughter Catherine in from California, to act as Margaret's companion, in case she wanted to go shopping, and laid on a lavish spread for the luncheon that celebrated our arrival. The don himself was a ruddy, cheerful man. Despite the heart attacks and an operation for bladder cancer, he seemed fairly robust, although one had the sense that age and illness had somehow shrunken him. For a man who had lived most of his life in the United States, his English was difficult to understand, first because he talked in a low, whispering (but by no stretch of the imagination menacing) growl, and second because his Sicilian accent was impenetrably thick. For a man of his age, he seemed astonishingly lively and energetic, but he was able to change himself into a mumbling, forgetful, harmless old man in an instant, with a skill that Laurence Olivier would have envied. At such times, his English deserted him altogether, his hands trembled, and he walked with his back bent. It is not for nothing that Mr. B. was a knowledgeable admirer of Italian grand opera. The opera, after all, is about the same things as the Mafia is: murder, passion, intrigue, and pride, together with the desire to cut, as Italians put it, *una bella figura*. As a boy, Bonanno had been a keen actor in an amateur theatrical group and fancied a career on the stage, but his father had been "a man of the tradition," deeply involved in vendettas and determined that his son should carry them on in the new world.

His generation of "godfathers" mostly kept to themselves and discussed business in Sicilian whenever possible. In his heyday, Bonanno, with his conservative, respectable, well-tailored business suits and far-flung business interests, had seemed the most assimilated of the dons, and indeed he had irritated members of The Commission by urging them to invest in legitimate American businesses. Bonanno's ambition seemed to be to succeed as an American businessman, out in the open, with a smile and a courteous handshake for everyone and an A-1 credit rating. He owned a controlling interest in two garment-center coat companies, a funeral home, and a cheese company in Fond du Lac, Wisconsin.

Bonanno took me on a tour of his home, accompanied by his dog, "Greasy" Bonanno, an elderly Doberman. Here was the brick barbecue pit, which had been badly damaged when somebody—"Clowns!" Bonanno said contemptuously—threw dynamite over the fence; here the "secret room," concealed behind a wall in the bedroom, where Bonanno could take refuge in an emergency; here the cork-lined basement office from which the FBI had taken his private papers and his arsenal when they raided the house; here the picture window through which the FBI had tried to film him from an unmarked van, so that lip-readers could try to transcribe his conversations with friends. That unmarked van, it appeared, was a more or less permanent presence on the street. Even Bonanno's garbage was the object of their scrutiny.*

---

* Bonanno's garbage produced enough evidence to persuade a judge to issue a search warrant and eventually led to Bonanno's conviction on a charge of conspiring to obstruct justice—a charge that Bonanno denied vehemently, pointing out with the pained air of a man whose professionalism is being attacked that if the papers in his garbage were *really* incriminating, he would have burned them.

The house was decorated in a homey, comfortable style, with plush velour furniture, lots of tourist-quality Sicilian wood carvings of donkeys and children, and a collection of porcelain birds. There was a big brick fireplace in the living room and much dark, heavy, formal furniture, which looked as if it had originated in the East—or perhaps even Sicily—and been shipped out to Tucson.

Bonanno showed us with pride framed photographs of his late wife, Faye, a ceramic tile with the Bonanno family crest, paintings of his birthplace in Sicily (a matter of some consequence, given the Sicilian habit of carrying ancient feuds from the old country to the new world, so that most of his trusted companions—and not a few of his most dangerous enemies—were from the same village as he), the Christmas cards he received from Dr. and Mrs. Billy Graham, and a huge framed photograph of his son Bill's wedding to Rosalie Profaci, the Mafia equivalent of a royal wedding, for Profaci was the head of his own Mafia family, one of New York's Five Families and an ally of Bonanno's—the wedding had attracted nearly three thousand guests and featured a wedding cake that towered over the bride and groom, and a guest list that included a congressman, a judge, several clergymen, and a newspaper publisher.

These, Bonanno said, his eyes turning damp, had been the good old days, before everything turned sour. First there had been Apalachin, and the accusation that Bonanno, who had advised against a "national meeting" of The Commission, had been present, when in fact he wasn't there at all, and had merely lent his driver's license to somebody else who presented it to the state police when they broke up the meeting. Then there had been the troubles with his cousin Stefano Maggadino, boss of his own crime family in Buffalo, New York, who may have masterminded the kidnapping of Joe Bonanno from the streets of New York, and possibly an attempt to kill Bill. Troubles rained down upon Bonanno's head after that. There was the problem of Bill's divorce from Rosalie, all the more difficult since it was at once a marriage and an alliance, then Gay Talese's book, with its defamation of the "traditions" by which Bonanno lived, his own failing health, the death of Faye, the government persecution that sent both his son Bill and his son Joe to prison, the FBI's endless attempts to send *him* to prison, and, as if all that weren't enough, the decline of his "tradition," supplanted by men who did not value honor as he did, who traded in narcotics, prostitution, and pornography, which he had forbidden in his family.

Mr. B. wound up our tour of his house and took us into the kitchen, where a big table was set for lunch, by a window overlooking the famous barbecue pit that had been damaged by a bomb thrown by unknown assailants. The assailants were only unknown to the *police,* of course; Bonanno doubtless knew perfectly well who they were himself. Here, his good spirits revived—he took his duties as a host seriously. We had an *aperitivo,* then a long meal of many courses, prepared by his daughter Catherine, with plenty of good wine.

In the privacy of his kitchen, Bonanno was more expansive. He was not willing to talk about current mob politics—he would not even admit that he was informed about them, though rumor had it that couriers arrived frequently from Brooklyn and took advantage of his cork-lined cellar to fill him in on what was happening and get his blessing for various decisions—but about the past he was less guarded. He chatted about Capone, the Castellamarese wars, the bootlegging connection between Joseph P. Kennedy and Frank Costello. Mr. B., it turned out, had met John F. Kennedy, and even FDR—his political connections had once been a priceless asset.

Bonanno explained at length that he, in his time, had been—still was, some might say—a don, but being a don had nothing to do with crime or even business. The term was a mark of respect to somebody who held a special kind of role in the community. A doctor might be referred to as "don so-and-so," as might a priest, or a pharmacist. A man might be the leader of a family following "the tradition"—what we would call "The Mafia"—yet still not be a don. The don made himself available to advise, to give justice, to help those in need. His neighbors who came to him in full respect never left empty-handed. In short, a don was a community leader, and the responsibilities of being a don were heavy and had to be taken seriously. The great men of his tradition had been dons, of course, as he was. Carlo Gambino, for instance—he had been a don, a real man of the tradition. His old friend Charlie "Lucky" Luciano had been a don, though being as Americanized as he was he did not take being a don as seriously as Gambino had, or Vito Genovese, for example. Gambino and Genovese were men to whom an ordinary person could bring his problems, who would listen gravely, and do whatever they could to help. Even his cousin Stefano Maggadino, rest in peace, a man of no culture or elegance, was, in Buffalo, the don, a man who understood the tradition, even if he did not always practice it.

What about Frank Costello? I asked. Had he been a don? Bonanno poured espresso from a metal pot for each of us. He shook his head sadly. "Frank Costello was merely a pimp," he snapped.

. After lunch, we were to work on the book. Mr. B. suggested that Margaret might like to go sight-seeing or shopping. He would get her a car, and Catherine would accompany her. I took Margaret out onto the patio and told her to use the car we had rented at the airport. Bonanno's offer was generous, and surely well meant, but who knew where the car came from or what might be in the trunk? Admittedly, this didn't seem likely, but reality in the Bonanno family was different from our own— after all, Bill Bonanno, despite the fact that he appeared to be prosperous, had been sent to prison for using a stolen credit card to buy an air ticket home to Tucson for Thanksgiving. True, he still denied the charge; true, the feds had been (and still were) looking for the slightest slipup to nail him; true, his father claimed that the whole thing had been a misunderstanding and that a subordinate of Bill's was responsible; still, it wasn't the kind of thing that happened to most of us, any more than most of us would have given our driver's license to an associate who would later present it to the state police as his own.

Smart as the Bonannos undoubtedly were, they tended to do things that the rest of us would regard as imprudent or even reckless, and when they got caught, they gave explanations that often seemed, on the face of things, either too convoluted to understand or simply implausible.

As we spoke, the two Bonanno sons were out on parole again, while their father was under indictment. Even allowing for the government's determination to make a case against the Bonannos and for the notoriety of their name, it appeared, to say the least, that they seldom approached even the simplest of business transactions in a straight line. The truth was that the old man did not see the world the same way as most of us. We may resent the law, but we accept it. He, on the other hand, rejected the whole concept of law, except as it was laid down by his own tradition and enforced by people like himself.

In the evening, Bonanno took us all to one of his favorite Italian restaurants, a dark, discreet place, hidden away in a fold of the desert. Inside, our large party was seated at the best table, while Mr. B. chatted to the proprietor at the bar. When he was done, he walked slowly down a shallow flight of steps into the restaurant, a dapper figure in his tailored blazer and tinted aviator glasses, not at all like the prince of darkness that the FBI swore he was. As he descended the steps, a small orchestra, hidden away in the gloom at the far side of the restaurant, struck up the theme from *The Godfather*. Mr. B. waved at them genially and sat down with a smile. His expression was shy, rather than proud, as if this musical tribute to his status, while deserved, was yet another part of the wearisome burden he carried as a don.

From out of the darkness, there appeared a succession of figures, most of them his age or thereabouts, who came to pay homage to him. They leaned over to whisper in Bonanno's ear, clasping his hand as they talked, their diamond rings sparkling in the candlelight.

The proprietor brought over a bottle of wine and uncorked it. Mr. B. tasted the wine and nodded benevolently. "I like wine more than I used to," he said, eerily echoing Don Corleone. "Anyway, I'm drinking more of it." He had never been a big drinker, he went on. A man had to know how to control his appetites. Habits too were dangerous. Never stick to the same schedule every day, for example. Poor Albert Anastasia had stuck to a schedule, and look what happened to him, assassinated in a barbershop. . . . The only habit he had kept to all his life, Bonanno said, was to drink one—and only one—shot of good cognac at night, before going to bed. It helped him to sleep, he said.

I asked if he had trouble sleeping. He sipped his wine, shook his head. No, he always slept soundly, like a baby. Why not, after all? He had a clear conscience, that's what really mattered. About his life, he had no apologies to make.

And second thoughts? I asked.

He sat silently for a moment, his big hands on the table. A few, he acknowledged at last. There were people he had trusted, and in whom his trust was misplaced. Yes, he went on with a sigh, perhaps he had been too trusting, too reliant on the old traditions of loyalty. Still, it had been a good life. He could not complain.

He took a drink of his wine as the antipasto was served and held up his glass to toast us.

"To *cosa nostra*," I thought I heard him whisper.

There was a long silence; then, after a pause, he added with a laugh, "I'm talking about our book, of course."

I T ' S   N O accident that the publishing of Mafia books has become a kind of subindustry in its own right. Americans have always yearned for a time and place in which a simpler, more violent justice reigned—hence the fascination with the cowboy, which has been going on for nearly a century and a half. That the real cowboys were "saddle tramps," underpaid, lawless, lousy, and generally despised and that most people who lived on the frontier yearned to duplicate the settled comforts of the East and replaced saloons with churches and schools as soon as they could, has been overlooked in the pursuit of a national myth. The Mafia, too, provides a myth in the national consciousness: a place where loyalties are absolute, where respect matters, and where problems are settled with a gun. Thanks largely to *The Godfather,* the phrase "I'm going to make him an offer he can't refuse" became a part of the language, and part of the enduring popularity of the movie (or movies) based on Mario Puzo's book comes from the suggestion that "the don" metes out rough justice to street punks and enforces his own morality with an iron hand.

Until the publication of *The Godfather,* most people were inclined to view the members of organized crime families as a dangerous nuisance, but, to the great surprise of the wiseguys themselves, they suddenly found themselves being taken seriously and even treated with guarded respect by ordinary citizens—or at least those ordinary citizens who didn't have to deal with them directly in their day-to-day business affairs. There had been hints of this before, as early as World War Two, when the government went to Luciano, then in prison, to secure the services of the Mafia in Sicily to prepare the way for the Allied landings, or during the Kefauver hearings on organized crime, when some of Mr. B.'s colleagues made their first appearances on national television, and thereby made the phrase "taking the fifth" part of the language.

After *The Godfather,* hoods grew used to being celebrities, and not a few of them, like Joe Colombo, actually went so far as to campaign publicly for more respect (a campaign that attracted so much attention in the media that Colombo's fellow dons had him shot while he was making a speech). Since the members of the mob were just as much against street crime as the ordinary citizen was, and since they mostly killed each other, it was not hard for them to achieve a kind of respectability, so long as they kept saying loudly enough that they were against narcotics and would kill anyone who sold drugs to children.

The truth, of course, was that they were only against selling narcotics to *their* children, not other people's. No matter how many times the big bosses like Paul Castellano, the boss of the Gambino crime family, claimed that anybody who dealt in drugs would be killed, drug dealing remained the most profitable business of organized crime—fast, easy money that no mobster was about to give up, whatever the boss said in public. Paul Castellano never tried all that hard to enforce a ban on drug dealing in the Gambino family, but such efforts as he made were enough to get him killed outside Sparks Steak House, in Manhattan.

The newfound fascination of Americans for the mob was, in its own way, as unrealistic as the transformation of Western gunfighters into national heroes. After all, Billy the Kid, a nasty little psychopathic killer in real life, was transformed into a national hero while he was still alive and killing, and that was back before television and the movies. Given this, it is hardly surprising that there exists such continuing interest in glamorizing the affairs of a bunch of people who specialize in breaking heads, committing usury and extortion, selling cigarettes without tax stamps, and beating up tavern owners who don't want to pay exorbitant fees for a jukebox.

I suppose I'm as guilty as anyone. My second venture in organized crime publishing was *Wiseguy,* a big best-seller by Nick Pileggi, which told the story of Henry Hill's rise and fall in the Brooklyn mob and was later made into the movie *Goodfellas.* This, as it happened, was something of a milestone in publishing, since New York State tried to prevent S&S or Pileggi from paying royalties to Hill under the "Son of Sam" law, written to stop criminals from participating in any profits from a book or movie based on their crimes. S&S contested the law, more out of respect for the First Amendment than out of any concern for Hill, and took the case all the way to the U.S. Supreme Court, which ruled in favor of S&S, thus establishing that a person doesn't have to be a good guy to make money out of his life story.

Hill and Pileggi's success set off a rush to acquire Mafia books among the major publishers. In this, S&S was fortunate to be ahead of the curve. As with any other profession, word of mouth was the key to success. In wiseguy circles, the fact that S&S had published Bonanno's and Pileggi's books was enough to make us, for some time, the favorite publisher of organized crime. From telephone booths all over New York City I received calls from gravel-voiced gentlemen whose names ended in vowels, eager to sell me their story of life in the mob.

Some worked, some didn't. A contract with a mob lawyer who promised to reveal where Jimmy Hoffa was buried didn't work out, nor did a book on the bloodletting in the Philadelphia mob by one of the principal bloodletters. On the other hand, a relapsed mobster named

Joseph ("Joe Dogs") Iannuzzi, after failing with his autobiography, hit one out of the ballpark when he conceived of *The Mafia Cookbook*. Joe Dogs, an amiable felon whose beating at the hands of one Tommy Agro encouraged him to become a federal informant and witness, was an expert cook, having in better days prepared food for Agro's crew in many a hideout. His cookbook became an instant success.

Joe had honed his skills while cooking for the marshals who guarded him and the FBI agents who came to question him about his former associates. In the end, it was partly due to Joe Dogs's testimony that the heads of the major New York families were eventually convicted. There was a certain irony in the fact that a mob hanger-on, not even a "made man," better known as a cook than as a criminal, had brought low such major organized crime figures as Tony Salerno, Carmine Persico, John Gotti, and Vincent Gigante, not to speak of the fact that Joe Dogs's revelations about the mob were the indirect cause for the assassination of the Boss of Bosses himself, "Big Paul" Castellano.

It was the kind of thing that would have brought a faint smile of irony to the lips of Joe Bonanno. He had always believed that his colleagues were letting the wrong kind of element into their world, and neither Joe Dogs, with his pots of sauce, nor Tommy Agro, an undersize enforcer with a ridiculous hairpiece and a hair-trigger temper, would have seemed to him altogether serious as men of honor.

Cosa nostra had descended in one generation from the sublime to the ridiculous. The world that Gay Talese had written about with such seriousness in *Honor Thy Father* and that Bonanno himself had described so lovingly in *A Man of Honor* was reduced to grotesque comedy, enacted by buffoons. The "men of honor" had once controlled the streets, enforcing what they thought of as justice (of a fairly predatory nature, to be sure) by their own brutal code. Then, they had lived in the neighborhood; now they had mostly moved to the suburbs, and came into the city like any other commuters: warily, unwillingly, complaining about the dangers of being mugged by black or Hispanic kids. Mobsters no longer went out in the streets to run the numbers game or deal in drugs or loan money—they were *afraid* to. They drove in from Staten Island, or Westchester, or the Island, and huddled in the safety of their Cadillacs, paying black and Hispanic kids to do the grunt work for them. Their sons—those who had not gone to college to become doctors or lawyers—knew they didn't own the streets anymore, that they had lost the neighborhoods to "the coloreds," that the Russian Mafia in Brooklyn was more violent than they were, that the Chinese, the Vietnamese, and the South American criminal organizations were carving away what had once been sacred Sicilian territory, even in "Little Italy." Of course, the Sicilians still had the garbage business, the labor unions, Fulton Fish Market, and so on, or would for a while, but it was no longer a growth business and was in the process of rapidly becoming folklore, a legend of the past.

Maybe it was in the cards the moment members of the mob started to write about their world. Maybe it had always depended on silence and secrecy. Maybe Bonanno himself, in his attempt to justify the world he lived in and set the record straight from his point of view, had helped to bring about the end of it by raising the curtain on what went on behind the stage.

The mob, it turned out, had been better served by *omertà* than by best-sellers, and in the end all that was left of it was a collection of recipes for people with hearty appetites who liked Italian food.

IT WENT largely unnoticed by those who criticized S&S for publicizing or enriching Mafia figures that we published even more books by cops and FBI agents—so much so that at one time when I was visiting One Police Plaza (headquarters of the NYPD), I remarked that everyone in the building seemed to be spending his time at a typewriter writing an outline or looking for an agent.

I began, as it were, at the top, by publishing the autobiography of Patrick Murphy, Mayor John Lindsay's controversial NYPD commissioner. Murphy was controversial, in fact, only within the ranks of the NYPD—elsewhere he was universally admired. His view that it was not sufficient for an officer merely to refuse graft and bribes, that he must actually *report* on fellow officers who were corrupt, was regarded as revolutionary in the 1960s and still is. Murphy always seemed to me to be a man who would have been more comfortable as a Jesuit than as a police officer, but we worked well together and produced a very good book, *Commissioner,* which dealt in detail with most of the problems that still haunt the NYPD today. This was no small achievement. Before Murphy (and for the most part after him), it was unthinkable for a police commissioner to actually admit in print that there might be anything wrong with the NYPD, and the reaction to *Commissioner* within the

NYPD was pretty similar to that of Bonanno's among the bosses of organized crime—a combination of shock and outrage.

Murphy was good-natured about the fuss. In his own quiet way, he was a pretty tough cookie, and being a cop himself, cops didn't scare him—nor mayors either, for he proved to be famously resistant to Mayor Lindsay, who had been under the impression that his police commissioner would take his orders from City Hall. Perhaps because we both enjoyed target shooting, Murphy and I became friendly, and I developed a certain interest in policing. At the time, Murphy had stirred up a lot of bad feelings in the NYPD by opening up more command positions to officers who weren't of old Irish police stock, and had even suggested that a black and a white officer might share the same police car, a notion so radical that mass resignations were threatened. Once, when I visited Murphy on the top floor of police headquarters, I pointed out to him jokingly that while big changes were being made at the precinct level, practically everybody on his floor, right down to the sergeants, was of Irish descent. It might well be Grabowski and Vitigliano in a prowl car, but on the way to the commissioner's office the signs on the doors announced an endless succession of sons of Erin among the chiefs, deputy chiefs, and their staff. Murphy was not amused. It had apparently never struck him as strange.

IT WAS because of my friendship with Murphy that I went out to Detroit to meet with an even more radical police commissioner. Ray Girardin was a reporter who had been criticizing the Detroit police department for years, until a reform mayor, in a move that surprised everyone, put Girardin in command of Detroit's police, with instructions to shake things up. In addition to the usual problems of a big-city police department—corruption, cronyism, antiquated equipment and methods—Detroit was saddled with a racial problem that made New York City look like the New Jerusalem. In Detroit, a predominantly white police force clamped down hard on an inner-city population that was mostly black and poor, in the interests of a white upper middle class that had long since moved out to the suburbs. Girardin became something of a hero—everywhere but in Detroit, needless to say—by rolling up his sleeves and forcing change on the Detroit police department. Many of those changes—"community policing," a civilian review board to examine charges of police brutality, nondiscrimination within the department—remain major and controversial issues in other American cities more than thirty years later. It was Girardin, largely forgotten, who first tried to put them into effect.

As it happened, Girardin's reforms were swept away by an unexpected event—although perhaps not entirely unexpected by Girardin, since he had predicted it—the Detroit riots of 1967.

Affable and soft-spoken, Girardin promised to have me picked up at the airport by a police car and taken straight to meet him, which sounded a lot better than a taxi. When I arrived, two cops were waiting for me. In keeping with the Detroit police department's well-earned reputation for macho policing, they carried huge amounts of extra ammunition on their belts, leather "slappers," weighted nightsticks, the kind of old-fashioned policeman's gloves that had strips of flexible lead sewn into the leather over the knuckles, and not one but *two* pairs of handcuffs. They looked at me stonily through dark Ray-Ban aviator sunglasses—anybody coming to visit Commissioner Girardin from New York was potentially the enemy, a liberal, a do-gooder, a bleeding heart, perhaps even a journalist. Wordlessly, they led me outside, as if they had just arrested me.

Inside their police car, two twelve-gauge Winchester riot guns were fixed in clamps to the dashboard and the floor, a sight not often seen in the Big Apple. I did not listen to the chatter on the radio as we drove into town from the airport, but I noticed a certain uneasiness in my two escorts, who were whispering to each other in the front seat. I asked if there was a problem. No, I was told, everything was OK, but they needed to make a slight detour, if I didn't mind. I said I didn't mind at all, at which point the siren and the flashing lights were turned on, and with a screech of tires we set off through the endless suburbs of Detroit, ignoring red lights and stop signs.

By now, the radio chatter had a certain hysterical tone to it, and even I could make out the word *shootings* and the phrase *officer in need of assistance.* We were driving through poorer neighborhoods now, and a number of black men in the streets looked at the police car with undisguised anger. From time to time I heard what seemed to me the sound of shots. At last the police car pulled to a sudden stop, my two escorts unclipped their shotguns, and they got out of the car. "Just stay put," one of them said. "We'll lock the doors. You'll be OK." I didn't much fancy sitting in a locked police car for who knew how long, while angry crowds roamed the streets, but the two cops didn't pause long enough to debate the point—besides, better inside the car than out on the pavement as possibly the only white civilian for miles around. From time to time, somebody threw a rock or a bottle at the police car, and a couple of kids spat on the windshield. It was not exactly comfortable, but I told myself that for somebody who had lived through the Hungarian Revolution, this was small potatoes. Soon, there was an odor of burning. Through the windshield, I could make out fires. From somewhere behind me came the noise of breaking glass. I hunkered down in the backseat and hoped for the best.

What seemed like hours passed, though it was probably not more than fifteen or twenty minutes. Eventually, my two escorts reappeared, unlocked the door, and got in. They brought with them an aroma that I recognized instantly from Budapest: a pungent combination of spent gunpowder, sweat, and soot. They were clearly in no mood for explanations. Wearily, they reloaded their guns, then we set off again. Two or three times more we stopped and repeated this little drama, until we headed back toward the center of Detroit, away from the angry mob.

"We'll have you there in a couple of minutes," the cop next to the driver said, swiveling around to look at me. His face was darkened with smoke, and his eyes were bloodshot. Looking at him, I was reminded of the duke of Wellington's remark on the first sight of his army in Spain: "I don't know what effect these men will have upon the enemy, but, by God, they frighten me."

"What's going on out there?" I asked.

"A riot."

"How bad is it?"

"Pretty bad."

"If they want to burn down their own neighborhoods, let 'em," the driver said, with a shrug.

His companion nodded. "Sure. But you got to stop them looting. And shooting at us."

They both fell silent for a moment. I had no difficulty in imagining what was likely to happen to anybody who was suspected of opening fire on a Detroit cop.

"You'll be OK at headquarters," the driver said. "I'll say one thing for Girardin. At least he was smart enough to take a few precautions. I mean he must have seen it coming. That's why he had all the manhole covers around headquarters welded shut. He didn't want them pulling the manhole covers, then breaking into the building from underground."

Even in Budapest, I reflected, nobody had taken this precaution. The idea that the manhole covers around police headquarters had been welded shut at the last minute gave me some sense of just what was taking place here—a realization confirmed by the sight of my destination, which was ringed by armored cars and floodlights.

As it turned out—and not surprisingly—Girardin was too busy to spend any time with me. His office had the look of the Smolny Institute, from which Lenin directed the 1918 revolution: heavily armed men trooping up and down the stairs, weapons stacked everywhere, people rushing back and forth with urgent messages, an almost palpable sense of urgency in the air, and the unmistakable scent of violence everywhere. At least half a dozen people told me that the manhole covers had been welded shut.

I flew back the next morning, having been driven to the airport by another silent pair of cops, through streets that were deserted and over which hung a thick pall of smoke.

Few of my subsequent books from the right side of the law led me into any similar adventure. I was taken on a tour of Chinatown by the precinct captain, introduced to the NYPD detective who specialized in art theft, and spent a good deal of time at One Police Plaza, meeting prospective authors. Since law enforcement is a small world, I soon had books by FBI agents and even by U.S. marshals. Just like the people in organized crime, every law-enforcement officer has a story to tell, and most of them are good raconteurs.

I've never done a police cookbook, though. Not yet. Probably somebody is writing one right now in the front seat of a patrol car.

THE SEARCH for a different kind of criminal, by a very different kind of cop, brought Peter Mayer and me together again briefly when I was presented with the opportunity to buy Ladislas Farago's *Aftermath: Martin Bormann and the Fourth Reich*, by his longtime (and long-suffering) agent, Maximillian Becker. Farago was the author of a best-selling biography of Patton and a kind of self-appointed expert on matters of secret intelligence. "Laci" (the Hungarian diminutive of Ladislas), as Farago was always called by his friends, was a rotund, bearded man, with an ingratiating smile and definitely uningratiating eyes.

In Farago, I instantly recognized a type completely familiar to me: the transplanted Hungarian with the deliberately mysterious background who knows (or claims to know) everyone and is so far beyond scruples as not to understand their existence. Farago embodied all those stories about the cleverness of Hungarians—"A Hungarian is a man who enters a revolving door behind you, and comes out ahead of you"; "The Hungarian recipe for an omelet begins, 'First, steal a dozen eggs.' "

Farago might have posed for the portrait of "the Hungarian on the make," with his soft, heavily accented voice, his gestures, his charm, his endless fund of anecdotes, his hypnotic self-confidence, and his total imperviousness to abuse, insults, or refusals. It was a waste of breath saying no to Farago—he simply bounced back like an inflated rubber beach toy and came at you from another direction. Once, later in our relationship, when I had learned to be cautious, Farago appeared in my office in distress, tears in his eyes, to ask for a further advance of $5,000 against the book he had been writing for many months, none of which I had as yet seen because it was "too secret and dangerous" to show me. He had spent so much money on research, Farago said, that he was broke. His house was about to be taken away from him, his beloved, patient wife was prostrate with fear and distress, he was a ruined man if I said no. Nothing less than $5,000 could save him. He would go down on his knees before me, if necessary. I said no anyway—after several such pleas, Dick Snyder had warned me to turn off the money tap until we saw some manuscript—but Laci, far from breaking down or getting angry, kept right on smiling. "Well," he said, "if not five thousand, how about five hundred as a personal loan, from one Hungarian to another?"

It was Farago's thesis that the Fourth Reich was in existence and flourishing in South America and that an active Nazi underground was thriving there. He had set out to document this, and in the course of his researches had come upon proof that Martin Bormann was alive and well and living in prosperity as one of the leaders of this movement. Of course, there was a grain of truth to all this, as everybody knew, particularly since the Israeli capture of Adolf Eichmann. Farago documented a whole subculture of escaped Nazis, with their social clubs, their own German villages painstakingly re-created in the Andes and on the rolling plains of Argentina. He even produced photographs of an annual beauty contest in which "Miss Teenage Nazi South America" was chosen in a beer hall draped in swastikas that looked alarmingly like the one in Munich from which the Führer had launched his movement.

All this was interesting, but what was sensational was the claim that Farago had found Bormann, not only alive and well but in control of a vast fortune in Nazi funds smuggled to South America in the last years of the war. Bormann, Farago alleged, had fled to Argentina with the help of the Vatican, paid over a substantial part of his fortune to Eva Perón in exchange for protection, then moved among half a dozen South American countries, and ended up in a convent-hospital in the windswept Bolivian Andes run by Redemptorist nuns, where "between freshly laundered sheets," he recovered from injections designed to prolong his life and awaited the return to power of Juan Perón. Farago had not only actually *seen* the ailing *Reichsleiter*, but in a complicated transaction, for which we had paid him another emergency transfusion of money to travel to South America again, had acquired a beer bottle that bore Bormann's fingerprints, as well as a photograph of Bormann taken as he crossed the Bolivian frontier on his way to the convent.

It was Farago's way to declare his own documentation "beyond dispute," without showing it, usually on the grounds that it was far too dangerous and explosive to let out of his hands. On those occasions when I insisted on seeing some proof, Farago went to the opposite extreme and produced cartons of documents, all of them in Spanish, German, or Portuguese, either in the form of blurred photocopies or retypings of the originals. Either way, there was nothing to be gained by plunging into them. Seldom has the truth that the publisher is at the mercy of the author been proven more amply. Farago could prove anything, given his hoard of documents, so in the end you either had to believe him or not. But where I was cautious, Peter Mayer, who bought the mass-market rights from us for Avon for a small fortune, was a confirmed believer, perhaps because he had not grown up surrounded by Hungarians, as I had. Mayer was convinced that *Aftermath* was destined to be the most important book any of us would ever publish, and he eventually persuaded Dick, who was initially a skeptic, that Farago had the goods.

In a rare burst of synergy, Dick managed to procure an audience for Farago with the executives of Paramount, who were bowled over when he produced the beer bottle for them to look at, and Paramount soon bought the motion-picture rights. Whatever else may be said about Farago, he was a brilliant salesman—at the time they bought the rights, Paramount had seen no more of the manuscript than Peter Mayer or I had.

As the manuscript, finally, did begin to come in, the S&S legal department raised all sorts of queries about Farago's "proofs," which he dismissed angrily. What, after all, did lawyers know? They were professional skeptics, trained not to be able to see the forest for the trees. Of *course* the documents were ambiguous and full of holes! Brave men had risked their lives to get him these documents. We were trying to expose a vast, dangerous Nazi conspiracy, well provided with funds and professional killers, with tentacles reaching to the highest levels of the Vatican, the CIA, and every South American government. Of course there would be gaps in the documents, ambiguous evidence, difficult puzzles—this was not a real-estate transaction, after all, this was living history, serious politics, the most explosive news story since World War Two. Certain assumptions had to be taken, certain risks accepted—this was not a book for the weak of heart to publish.

Since nobody wanted to be classed among the weak of heart—and since we had already invested a considerable fortune in Farago's book—we proceeded, eventually convincing everyone, including ourselves and the S&S sales reps, that *Aftermath* was going to be a huge best-seller that would make front-page news. Even Hugh Collins acknowledged that in *Aftermath* we had the real goods—he pledged to get the book into the windows of every major bookseller in Chicago.

WELL, WE *did* make front-page news, well before publication—and above the fold in *The New York Times* at that. Unfortunately, it was with a story that the presumed Martin Bormann whom Farago had discovered and photographed was in fact a harmless Argentinean schoolteacher named Nicolas Siri. Before long, the Germans produced Martin Bormann's skull and dental fittings, allegedly found in the rubble of Berlin, just where he had last been seen by Arthur Axmann, Baldur von Shirach's successor as head of the Hitler Youth, during their escape from the *Führerbunker* in May 1945. Not to be outdone, the Russians revealed Bormann's diary of his last weeks with Hitler, which he had left behind in the bunker. Although Farago argued that the skull was a fake perpetrated by reporters from *Der Spiegel* and the diary a forgery by the KGB (for what purpose it was not clear), the air was definitely out of his balloon. The distinguished English historian Hugh Trevor-Roper gave the book the coup de grâce in a long, devastatingly destructive review in *The New York Review of Books* that would have led anyone but Farago to hide his head in shame.

Needless to say, the idea of doing so did not occur to him—shame was not one of the emotions he was capable of feeling strongly—however, the news scuppered *Aftermath*. Farago's explanation that this was a simple and unfortunate case of "mistaken identity" that in no way reflected upon the rest of the book went nowhere, but did not dismay Paramount, since whatever they had in mind as a movie had nothing much to do with the facts anyway, nor with Farago's book, come to that.

Apparently loyal to the old Hollywood belief that there is no such thing as bad publicity, they proceeded with their plans for the movie. The signature of the contract had been delayed for months, but when it was finally ready, Max Becker, Farago's agent, a Central European with the sad face of a beagle and a quality of weary chutzpah, announced that rather than waste time sending it back and forth for signature, he and Farago would come to the Paramount office in New York to sign. There was a little personal request of Farago's that he also wanted to convey, Becker said. Farago was a sentimental soul, deeply stirred by the trust that Paramount had shown in him. It would mean a great deal to him if Paramount could make something of a ceremony of the occasion—perhaps a bottle of champagne and a toast, as between friends, while the check was handed directly to Farago.

The bottle of champagne was not a problem, of course, but the check was. Normally, once a movie contract has been signed by both parties, the check request is made out and circulates through the accounting department for ages. In many cases, the documents are sent from New York to Los Angeles for multiple signatures of people who are either too busy to sign or on vacation, then back to New York, until, finally, the check is issued by some bank in Des Moines or Oklahoma City and sent on from there by the slowest possible form of mail—yak mail, if it existed—the object being to keep the money earning interest in the movie company's account for as long as possible. The idea of actually handing a six-figure check to anybody struck at the very heart of motion-picture economics.

Still, under the monotonous drip-by-drip pressure of Max Becker, Paramount eventually caved in. Mountains were moved, miracles performed, as a gesture of faith and friendship the impossible was arranged. The check was to be handed to Farago as he signed the contract. Farago, Becker reported, had tears in his eyes when he heard the news, so moved was he.

On the appointed day, early in the afternoon, everybody involved in *Aftermath* gathered in a conference room at Paramount. Champagne was served, while Farago, dewy-eyed, made a small speech. He was a deeply sentimental soul, he emphasized, personal loyalties were what mattered to him more than anything. This was a vote of confidence that he would never, never forget. Even the hard-bitten film executives were moved as Farago went on about the Holocaust, his own experiences, the heavy weight of history. Finally, at about a quarter to three, he sat down and signed the contracts with a flourish. The envelope containing the check was handed to him.

Becker, it was noticed, had not taken a seat or drunk his champagne. He was, in fact, poised, like an Olympic runner in the blocks for the start of a sprint, overcoat on, hat wedged firmly on his head. Although he was the least athletic man imaginable—with the possible exception of Farago himself—he looked like a man determined to break some record, nostrils flared, hand outstretched, every muscle tense. No sooner had Farago received his check than he handed it to Becker, who ran, not walked, to the door, as if a starter's pistol had been fired, and left, so quickly in fact that it was impossible to ignore his hasty departure.

Farago gave a shy shrug and smiled, like the good confidence man he was, then, his voice dropping low, he apologized for Becker's haste. "You understand," he said, "we wanted to get the check deposited before three o'clock, when the bank closes."

He gave a gentle wink. "Just in case you should change your mind," he added, man to man.

PART SEVEN

Money for Jam

CHAPTER 30

ERY FEW EVENTS in my life as a writer have had more personal significance than writing *Charmed Lives*, the story of my father and his two brothers, and of the film empire they built. In the first place, it was the book I was born to write, as if I had been observing and storing up memories with just that purpose in mind for years. But it was also, in a way, a farewell to the people and events that had dominated my life for over thirty-five years, a kind of Oedipal exorcism, which may have been what was on my editor Jason Epstein's mind when he came up with a phrase of Freud's for the book's subtitle: *A Family Romance*.

Since I began *Charmed Lives* at just about the time when my marriage to Casey was breaking up (and when Margaret's already had), it was written under conditions of some stress—though the emotional complications of separation and divorce put me in the right mood, perhaps, for tackling the tangled lives of my father and his brothers; or at any rate, they gave me a greater understanding and tolerance for many things, including the feeling of abandonment I had experienced during my own parents' divorce.

When it was done and I had finished basking in the warmth of the unexpectedly positive reviews, I began to worry about what I was going to write next. Already, the thought of *not* writing a book—of sticking to my last like the proverbial shoemaker—did not cross my mind. By now, writing a book was a fixed part of my life. Without a book contract to fulfill, I felt like a man with too much time on his hands. Besides, although I was happy enough to have put my family behind me by writing about them, I was already beginning to miss them. The research for *Charmed Lives* had brought me closer to them, in some ways, than I had ever been in real life. In reading about them, I began, at last, to understand them, and many things that had hitherto been mysterious were clear to me. It was hard to give that up. Friends and acquaintances (not to speak of many of the critics) described *Charmed Lives* as the book of my lifetime, but I clearly couldn't write another book about my own family, even had I wanted to.

On the other hand, the dark background of anti-Semitism in Hungary, which I touched on lightly in *Charmed Lives,* fascinated me. I decided that the only way I could persuade anybody to read about this unhappy chapter in Central European history was by putting it into the form of a novel, and to my surprise, Epstein agreed. After all, I thought, why not? I had written a book that had become a number-one bestseller in hardcover, with *Power!*, *Charmed Lives* had been a Main Selection of the Book-of-the-Month Club, why should I not try a novel? I soon discovered that it is easier to tell writers what is wrong with their novel than to write one; still, I flattered myself that I eventually got the hang of it, and within a year *Worldly Goods* was written. It was chosen as a Full Selection of the Literary Guild, went to paperback for a lot of money, and sold more than enough copies to satisfy Random House—it was even optioned briefly as a feature movie.

I was more aware than most that for a first novel it was something of a triumph. It had the effect, however, for the first time, of attracting in-house attention to my second career. So long as I was writing nonfiction, however successful or highly praised, nobody at S&S or, more to the point, Gulf + Western, seemed to mind. Dick Snyder was delighted to have an editor who could actually write books and happy on my behalf when they were successful, while everybody else did their polite best to pretend that it wasn't happening. I had never felt that there was any conflict, and on the whole it seemed to me better from everyone's point of view for me to be a Random House author, rather than published in-house—which, in any case, nobody had ever suggested. Besides, I had a deep loyalty toward Random House, where I had been treated with great courtesy and genuine enthusiasm and recognized that my career as a writer of books owed much, if not all, to the efforts of Nan Talese, Jim Silberman, and Jason Epstein.

Perhaps because the movie rights to *Worldly Goods* were optioned, however (and perhaps too because I based the sinister billionaire hero of the novel on Bluhdorn), questions began to be asked about why an S&S employee was making money for one of our competitors. It looked bad to the corporate people, even disloyal, and pressure was put on Dick to do something about it. The last thing I wanted was a confrontation in which I had to choose between being editor in chief of S&S and writing books, and I could see that this was the direction we were going in.

DICK AND Joni had found it, perhaps not surprisingly, increasingly hard to work together now that they were married. Joni had risen to become publisher of S&S, and Dick was finding it difficult to defuse charges of nepotism. The press might ooh and aah over a marriage that seemed to prove that two ambitious people could make a good team at work and still be a romantic couple at home, but no doubt at Gulf + Western it didn't look that way. Nor, given the personalities of the two people involved, can it have been easy for Joni to be Dick's subordinate at S&S while being his wife at home. It was natural for those who were jealous of Joni to suppose that she benefited somehow from going home every night with the boss, though in practice it was rather the reverse, since Dick went out of his way to avoid showing favoritism.

Still, the relationship between the two of them had already led to a certain amount of unhappiness among the rest of the S&S executives. Phyllis Grann moved downstairs reluctantly to take charge of Pocket Books, reporting directly to Snyder. She had resented Joni's role and was not noticeably more pleased when Joni later traded her somewhat ambivalent position for that of wife. In effect, Phyllis went into exile on the floor below, and took on a host of problems that were not of her own making. This eventually led her to resign and move to Putnam, where her dazzling success as both an editor and a businesswoman was to serve as a permanent reminder to Dick that he had lost one of the brightest stars in publishing and made her a competitor. His boss at Gulf + Western, the caustic and sharp-tongued Martin Davis, who took Bluhdorn's place after the latter's untimely death, seldom failed to bring this to his attention.

Davis, whom a major magazine had named one of the hundred meanest bosses in American business, had once been in charge of publicity at Paramount. He was now Dick's boss and nemesis. Bluhdorn's demise had been followed by a brief but bloody struggle for power. The leading contender was Jim Judelson, an affable engineer-businessman, whom Dick had cultivated assiduously, and whose chief pride was a remarkable desk lamp designed like a giant articulated, stainless steel crane, on a marble base. Judelson had been, to outward appearances, though for no very obvious reason, Bluhdorn's designated heir, and on Bluhdorn's death, Dick had confidently declared his loyalty to him. Unfortunately for all of us, Judelson came out the loser to Davis.

Dick had made the mistake of a lifetime, the kind that, like the curse of the Fates in Greek tragedy, cannot be repaired or expiated. Davis took a certain grim pleasure in giving Dick orders that he knew would be difficult and personally painful to carry out. (This reached its apotheosis when Davis ordered him to change the name of Simon and Schuster to Paramount Publishing, a humiliation on a grand scale that involved chipping the company's name off the stone of its own building in Rockefeller Center, as well as reprinting all the company stationery.) It is very possible that the decision to move Joni from her job as publisher of S&S to an imprint of her own was in part inspired from above. Dick told those close to him that it was a move intended to save his marriage—in effect, to take Joni out of the chain of command and give her a place of her own—and he may have been right about that too. After all, he had reached the age when he wanted to sit back and enjoy his success, whereas Joni was still immensely ambitious and anxious to succeed. In any event, for all these and many other reasons, Joni's new imprint, Linden Press (named after the trees that bordered the drive of the Snyders' new country house in Westchester County), was announced and soon off to a rousing start with best-sellers by Mario Puzo, Jeffrey Archer, and Joseph Heller.

AGAIN SEARCHING for a new subject for a book, I had been drawn back to one of the major figures in *Charmed Lives,* whom I had been obliged to skimp on at that time. Merle Oberon had been my Uncle Alex's second wife, and her presence had loomed large in my childhood. The other Korda wives, all actresses—my mother; my Aunt Joan, Zoli's wife; and the dreadful Maria, Alex's first wife—nurtured something of a resentment against Merle, whom Alex had made an international star by giving her the part of Anne Boleyn in *The Private Life of Henry VIII* in 1933.

Her subsequent rise—despite many other contenders who pursued her, some of them successfully—to become first Alex's main romantic interest and then his wife aroused even stronger resentment among Alex's brothers—though, to be fair, they would have disliked any woman who deflected Alex's attention away from them. It did not help matters that Merle, a great beauty, developed a somewhat haughty attitude toward Alex's brothers and their wives or that her tastes were fabulously expensive. In the mid-thirties Alex had Cartier in London design for Merle a necklace of twenty-nine massive uncut emeralds suspended from a diamond and platinum *collier*, which became the most photographed Cartier necklace of all time and was to become the centerpiece of the Cartier show in 1997, this among many other gifts; while Alex's brothers didn't mind a bit when Alex spent a fortune on *himself*, they took a dim view of his spending money on Merle, particularly since Merle, in the mid-thirties, was keeping her options open and still accepting bids from a number of other men, as well as carrying on an affair with a handsome young actor named David Niven.

Perhaps as a result of this, I heard, even as a child, a great deal about Merle, much of it in the form of whispers that adults fondly suppose children will not overhear. It was thus that I learned that Merle had in fact been born not in Tasmania, the child of a dashing English jockey and his colonial bride, as Merle's official biography had it, but in Bombay as Estelle "Queenie" Thompson, a "chee-chee" (or Anglo-European or half-caste) girl of mixed parentage.

The Anglo-Europeans in British India were a breed apart, descendants of English soldiers or Welsh railway laborers who had married native women. Anglo-Europeans were "protected" subjects in the Raj, but had no right to a British passport or to residence in the United Kingdom. Ridiculed and looked down upon with undisguised contempt by the British, whom they imitated insofar as they were able to, despised as casteless by Hindus and as infidels by Muslims, theirs was a small, separate, and embattled community, entirely Christian (because of the Welsh railway workers, the Anglo-Europeans were mostly "Chapel"), in which social prominence, such as it was, depended almost entirely on skin color. The lighter the skin, the more chance a pretty chee-chee girl had to pass. (There was almost no chance for the boys to pass, of course.)

Queenie had passed so successfully that she became a feature of Bombay nightlife while still in her early teens and eventually made her way to England as the girlfriend of a wealthy young Englishman. She went on to become an "exotic" dancer in London's West End, eventually becoming the star attraction at the glamorous Café de Paris and the girlfriend of the expatriate black American jazz musician Hutch.

Her beauty was extraordinary and much admired by everybody from the Prince of Wales down. She had a heart-shaped face, dark, almond-shaped eyes—"bedroom eyes," as they were then called—gleaming black hair, a long, swanlike neck, wonderfully graceful, long-fingered hands, "like those of a temple dancer," as one admirer, stumbling rather too close to the truth for comfort, wrote in describing her, and full, perfectly shaped lips that curled up at the corners so that she always seemed to be giving a knowing, erotic smile. It was a face that promised a certain lush sensuality, too exotic to be English, despite the pale, ever so slightly olive complexion.

Already the toast of London, Queenie's beauty was her ticket to better things. Rather like Eva Perón, Queenie was good at getting men to give her an introduction she needed, a mention in the papers, her picture in the magazines, the next step up. It was not just her beauty, which was astonishing, but her manners and charm—for along the way, Queenie had learned how to please, without giving up a bit of her fierce desire to succeed or her equally fiery temper, an inheritance, most likely, of her Welsh blood. Each small step brought her wealthier and more suitable friends, with more influence—one of which was to lead her, eventually, to the tea line in the commissary at the studio where Alex, newly arrived in England himself, was about to start shooting *The Private Life of Henry VIII* in 1932.

Queenie had used up one of her markers to get into the studio, hoping for a screen test, but her luck was better than that. Alex happened to enter the room, with his soon-to-be-divorced wife beside him, the Hungarian silent screen star Maria Corda (the former Maria Farkas, she had substituted a *C* for the *K* in Alex's family name, since it looked more Christian), whose career and marriage both had fizzled in Hollywood, and Maria, catching sight of Queenie's face, dug her nails into Alex's arm and cried out, in her inimitable Hungarian accent, "There she is, you fool! Look at that face! It's worth a million pounds! *There* is your damned Anne Boleyn."

. . .

IT WAS ironic that the girl in the tea line was not only to play Anne Boleyn opposite Charles Laughton (in the first British film ever to be nom-
inated for the Best Picture Academy Award, and for which Laughton
won Best Actor) but was to supplant poor Maria in Alex's life and eventually become the first Lady Korda, when he was knighted—though not
before he had shrewdly changed her name from Queenie Thompson to
Merle Oberon.

Merle's real background was not by any means a well-kept secret,
and the more famous she became, the more it leaked out, and the harder
she strove to suppress it. Merle spent most of her life refining the story
of her origins, but from time to time the truth slipped out. Merle herself sometimes slipped up—once, when asked what her favorite food was
on a celebrity cooking program, she answered "Curry"—and when
she was tired or stressed her singsong accent became unmistakably
chee-chee, as Charles Laughton unkindly pointed out when she made
I, Claudius with him.

When I wrote *Charmed Lives*, I had been more than usually circum-
spect on the subject of Merle, but despite kid-glove treatment, her
lawyer, a gravel-voiced Hollywood heavyweight, called me less than
twenty-four hours after Merle had received the bound galleys I sent her.
Faced with the threat of a time-consuming and expensive lawsuit, I
wrote Merle virtually out of the book altogether, which didn't please
her much either, and we received no further invitations to dinner at Malibu—not necessarily a punishment. Merle's dinner parties were stately,
rather than amusing, and her home, in which almost everything was
white, was so perfect and spotless that her husband hovered beside you
as you helped yourself to caviar, just in case you dropped an egg on the
carpet. Rod Steiger, who was Merle's next-door neighbor, once complained to me that the guest bathroom was so obsessively clean he was
unable to urinate into the toilet bowl.

In any event, once Merle died, I became interested in telling the *real*
story of her life, not out of malice, for I liked and admired her, but because I thought the truth was more interesting (as is so often the case)
than the fiction she had concocted. You couldn't help admiring the pluck
of the little chee-chee girl who had managed to break out of the narrow,

constrained little world into which she had been born and go on to become wealthy, famous, and admired. Queenie had been a survivor, a
strong, passionate young woman determined to make it in the great
world with the weapons that were available to her. I decided that the only
way to re-create her was to do the research as if I were going to write a
biography, then write the book as a novel, trying to get inside her head.

I knew that I was going to call the novel *Queenie* before I'd written
a page, and unlike anything else that I'd written, I knew from the start
that it was going to work—Queenie herself was simply too strong a
character for the book *not* to work. Before that, of course, it needed an
enthusiastic publisher. This was complicated by the fact that Dick now
wanted me to be published by S&S, in order to put an end to the complaints he had been receiving from Gulf + Western. I had resisted the
idea, but the announcement of Linden Press resolved that difficulty—
Joni was her own publisher, and I could not have asked for a shrewder,
more skillful, or more enthusiastic editor. She shared my affection for
Queenie, and much as I regretted leaving Random House, nobody
could have worked harder for a book than Joni did for *Queenie*. Joni was
determined to make the book a best-seller and made the whole process
seem fun—no easy task.

In the end, *Queenie* succeeded even beyond our wildest expectations. It became an international best-seller, went high up the best-seller
list (and reached number one in paperback), and was eventually made
into a seven-hour television miniseries, with Mia Sara as Queenie,
Claire Bloom as her long-suffering mother, Kirk Douglas as my Uncle
Alex, and Joel Grey as the Irving Lazar character—an experience made
odder by the fact that Kirk Douglas had looked after me when I was ten
years old and used to spend the evenings in my mother's dressing room
on Broadway during the long run of *The Three Sisters,* in which she appeared as Irina, the youngest of the sisters, together with Katharine
Cornell, Judith Anderson, and Ruth Gordon. Douglas, who had only
just changed his name from Issur Demsky, had one small scene in which
he appeared in a white tunic to bring in the samovar for tea and therefore plenty of time to teach me to play chess. It was with some dismay
that I saw him play Alex, almost forty years later, with a vigor that
would have surprised poor Alex, always the most languid of men. Still,
even on the small screen, Douglas captured something of Alex's
spirit—a combination of charm and shrewdness that would have done

justice to a Renaissance cardinal, together with a certain indefinable melancholy, which was hugely attractive to women.

THE EXPERIENCE of actually *becoming* a best-selling novelist after having published so many was, of course, hallucinatory. Being one of the few people in publishing who actually knew what it was like to be a successful writer and who had been out on tour time after time promoting my books gave me a curiously mixed perspective. There is an Italian saying that the translator is a kind of traitor ("*Traduttore, traditore*"), and something like that applies to editors who moonlight as writers, particularly if they are successful. Throughout the publishing industry, the editor is widely viewed as suspect to begin with by those in management, and an editor who is also an author is doubly suspect. Whatever the difficulties, humiliations, and anxieties of the author's life—and there are a good many, not all of them the publisher's responsibility, to be sure—I have experienced them in one form or another. I have been bumped from major television shows at the last moment (I began one promotion tour on the evening Operation Desert Storm began, with the entire country glued to CNN), set up (I did an interview with Johnny Carson without knowing that Merle Oberon had died while I was in the greenroom; Carson mentioned it at the end of the interview, by which time I had been talking about her for five minutes), left stranded (with food writer Gael Greene and her mother in the empty cafeteria of a radio station miles outside Detroit in a blizzard), missed connections, even been flown from Boston to Toronto at the last minute for an interview only to discover that I didn't have any proof of citizenship on me and couldn't get back into the United States. I have actually sung a number with the Chipmunks on an early-morning television show while promoting a book and made chapatis during a demonstration of Indian cooking, so that I spent the rest of the day promoting my book wearing a suit covered with flour. I have been ill on tour, abandoned by my escort, taken to bookstores where they not only don't have my book in stock but have never heard of it, given lectures and readings to audiences of less than half a dozen who have drifted in merely to get out of the rain, and been mugged of my overcoat and scarf in below-zero weather on my way to a show. At the beginning, I loved every minute of it.

The great days of author tours ended with the escalation of airfares. Until then, provided the author was not determined to live like a Saudi prince, it paid to keep him or her traveling for as long as possible—the more cities, within reason, the better. Back in the 1970s and the 1980s, there were still plenty of important regional shows, many of them nationally syndicated. You went to Boston to do *Sonya*, to Dayton, Ohio (and later Chicago) to do *Donahue*, to Los Angeles for Carson and Merv Griffin, and so on. In time, the major shows tended to move to New York or Los Angeles (with the exception of *Oprah*, which remains in Chicago), while travel costs rose until it was no longer feasible to send the author from city to city flogging his or her book. In the meantime, the invention of the "satellite tour," in which the author sits in New York or Los Angeles and does show after show across the country without leaving the room has changed the author tour considerably. Still, the fact remains that the biggest revolution in the book business has been brought about by the curious symbiosis that established itself between television's need for free talent and the need of book publishers to reach the public.

Television rescued the book business from the marketing trough into which it was descending. Already by the end of the sixties, the decision about whether to buy certain kinds of books—self-help titles, diet books, exercise books, and so on—was being made on the basis of the author's appearance, telegenic appeal, and ability to get his or her points across convincingly on-screen, and authors in these categories were soon to find that a videocassette of their performance on television weighed more heavily with the publisher than an outline of their ideas. Charm, smile, appearance, energy, the ability to sell while looking natural and to sum up a whole book in a sentence or two became all-important in publishing certain categories of books, favoring those authors who were natural salespeople.

Those authors already in the public eye—whether actors or politicians—are usually astute at promoting their books, since it's just an extension of what they normally do every day. Nobody is better at it than Joan Collins, unless it is her sister, the novelist Jackie Collins, both of whom I once edited at the same time—an idea foisted on me by Dick Snyder, who had apparently never heard the phrase *sibling rivalry*. Among politicians, nobody was better at pitching his book on television than Richard Nixon.

Never a man to let the difficulties of something overwhelm him, Snyder saw no reason why S&S should not become Nixon's publisher, despite the fact that it had been books about Watergate that had put Sny-der's S&S on the map as a major publishing force. *All the President's Men* and *The Final Days* had not only done much to turn Dick into a celebrity but had begun the enormously fruitful friendship between himself and Alice Mayhew, the editor of both books, that would pro-duce almost two decades of brilliant and hugely successful nonfiction publishing and make S&S a key player in acquiring serious and impor-tant journalists and historians. The fact that these books, for the most part, had a certain liberal bias, at least so far as Nixon and the war in Vietnam were concerned, did not prevent Dick from responding enthu-siastically when I told him that I had heard Nixon was thinking of changing publishers. What was more surprising, it turned out, was that Nixon himself didn't have any reservations about being published by a company that had made something of a specialty of publishing books that were critical of him and that had played a part in bringing him down—I had assumed we would be the last house on his list.

That, of course, was to underrate the spirit of realism that governed Nixon's decisions, as I was shortly to discover.

CHAPTER 31

*T*LIKE TO think that I'm inured to famous people, having grown up in a family full of them. Still, no one is completely immune to a cer-tain kind of celebrity—not even celebrities themselves. The only time I ever saw de Gaulle close up, I had to keep pinching myself to be con-vinced that it really *was* the general. I felt the kind of awe that one is supposed to experience at one's first sight of the Grand Canyon or the Taj Mahal. All the same, he was just as I had expected him to be—immense, remote, austere.

Nixon was different. First of all, he had always fascinated me—as he did almost everybody—in a strange and inexplicable way. Far from being remote, like de Gaulle, whose memoirs I had published, Nixon was a familiar presence for so long that he seemed like a member of the family. Way back in the fifties, I remember, dinner parties were ruined by arguments when the subject of Nixon came up. Then, too, his tri-umphs and tragedies, his repeated rise and fall, his reputation for odd behavior, the contrast between his noble rhetoric and the public moments of mean-spiritedness, and, above all, his apparent view of himself as a kind of latter-day Prometheus, and the echo of failed greatness surrounding his political life always made him the most authentically Shakespearean of American presidents.

"You won't have Nixon to kick around anymore," he told the press bitterly after his defeat in the California gubernatorial election of 1962, but he was wrong: We *always* had Richard Nixon to kick around—even in exile and apparent disgrace (it was never perceived that way by Nixon), he remained part of our national consciousness, controversial even in forced retirement from the political scene.

I first met Nixon in the early 1980s at a luncheon at his town house in New York. The reason for my invitation was that I was Julie Nixon Eisenhower's editor—encouraged by Irving Lazar, she had written a book on famous people she had known who had "made a difference"— and she felt that it would be appropriate to introduce me to her parents. Lazar had sent me off to meet Julie and her husband, David Eisenhower, in Washington, where they had an apartment at the Watergate, by some strange coincidence. Julie and I had bonded immediately. It was one of those August days when the heat in Washington is unbearable, and the air-conditioning in the Watergate was strained, so that sitting in the Eisenhowers' sunny living room was like being in a sauna with one's clothes on. When David appeared, he was wearing a three-piece suit made of some kind of heavy tweed, rather like a Brillo pad, and sweat was pouring down his face. Fearing that he might collapse from heat prostration, I took the liberty of suggesting that he might want to take off his jacket and vest, or perhaps even change into a lighter suit. But that, Julie explained, was impossible. David's grandfather, President Eisenhower, had left David all his clothes in his will, and David felt obliged to wear them, once they had been altered to fit him. Apparently, Ike had not owned any summer-weight suits, or perhaps they simply hadn't reached David yet, but in the meantime he saw it as his duty to wear his grandfather's clothes. Naturally, it would be something along the lines of lèse-majesté for him to remove the presidential jacket and vest and sit in his shirtsleeves, so he gamely continued to sweat in the sweltering heat, out of respect for Ike.

Nixon, who would surely have approved of his son-in-law's behavior, was at the time in what amounted to exile in New York and beginning to build up his reputation as an elder statesman, foreign-policy guru, and political wise man in the long aftermath of his resignation. People reported sighting him from time to time at this restaurant or that. He was by no means in hiding, but there was still something mysterious and faintly unconvincing about his pose as an ordinary New Yorker, and not just because the bottom floor of the Nixons' house was full of Secret Service agents and their bulky communications equipment.

New York was Nelson Rockefeller territory, a place full of Democrats and liberal Republicans who, if they agreed on nothing else, shared a dislike of Nixon. In a city where great wealth, family and social connections, and glamour were what mattered, Nixon was not wealthy, socially connected, or glamorous, nor, with his famous need to control events, did he seem altogether at ease in the chaotic, uncontrollable big city, any more than Mrs. Nixon did. They remained small-town Californians who had ended up in New York only because they had been obliged to leave Washington. New York was their Saint Helena. Nixon's tan, Mrs. Nixon's stiff hairdo, the finger bowls on the table all seemed somehow un–New Yorkish, as did the decoration of the house, which was startlingly Oriental.

A taste for the Oriental in home decor is very Californian—after all, California is on the Pacific rim—but the Nixons seemed to have been carried away by it. Most of the art, the furniture, and the rugs were Chinese, or of Chinese inspiration; so, for that matter, were the servants and the food. I fantasized briefly that Nixon might have been a real-life Manchurian candidate—which would certainly have explained his conversion from a founding member of the anticommunist China Lobby to architect of rapprochement between Washington and Beijing. Were the servants, I wondered, in fact his controllers? Had his presidency been a carefully orchestrated Chinese plot?

Nixon had been delayed downstairs by some business, so that Mrs. Nixon, Julie, and I were seated when he arrived in the dining room. I stood while Julie introduced us. I fear that I stared at him rudely. My initial thought was that he was much taller than I had expected. For some reason, Nixon had always seemed to me *small*, but he was a good six feet tall, with the shoulders and bulk of an athlete and the brief, firm handshake of the professional politician. Cutting a formal, presidential figure even in his own home, he wore a beautifully cut dark-blue suit, a white shirt, and a sober tie. At close quarters—and the dining room was so small that they were *very* close quarters—he was a formidable presence, made more so for me by the simple fact that it *was* Nixon.

Most striking of all was his voice: a deep, rumbling basso profundo, rather like an avalanche in the distance, pitched an octave or two below even Henry Kissinger's. Nixon's voice was far warmer, deeper, and more human than it sounded on television. Television had done him no favors—in the end, this was perhaps his major political tragedy. His complexion, which seemed sallow on the screen, was in fact healthy and deeply tanned, and the scowl and the famous five-o'clock shadow were hardly noticeable. There is a theory that great men have large heads and prominent features—think of de Gaulle and his nose, LBJ and his ears, FDR and his jaw—and by this standard, if no other, Nixon had reached greatness. His head was enormous, his jowls and ski-jump nose were just as cartoonists had always portrayed them, his eyes were dark and penetrating. "Welcome," he said, rather formally. "Nice to see you."

I mumbled something appropriate and sat down. To my astonishment, Nixon went to the other end of the table, took Mrs. Nixon's hand, and said, "Nice to see you," in exactly the same tone of voice, then sat down, unfolded his napkin, and addressed himself to his soup.

I thought about this a lot at the time. I didn't doubt that Nixon and Mrs. Nixon were close, but he seemed to have some difficulty revealing the fact in front of a stranger. On the other hand, I thought I saw a look of pain in Mrs. Nixon's eyes, which made me wonder if Nixon had really noticed that she was there. I remembered John Ehrlichman telling me that he had once suggested to Nixon, early in the 1968 presidential campaign, that it would be nice if the Nixons could hold hands as they walked down the steps of the campaign plane upon arriving somewhere. Nixon, he reported, fixed him with a darkly fishy stare and said flatly, "We don't do that sort of thing."

Years passed, and I did not see Nixon again. I continued to publish Julie and to see her from time to time. Then, by one of those bizarre twists of fate so common in book publishing, I became his editor. Even in our author-editor relationship, Nixon remained an elusive, enigmatic presence. One did not telephone him—one telephoned a member of his staff, who passed the question on to the president (as he was always called) then called back with an answer. It was made clear that under no circumstances was there to be direct communication: a holdover, no doubt, from the White House days, when nobody was allowed to see the president with news that he did not want to hear—or, at any rate, that H. R. Haldeman and Ehrlichman didn't want him to hear. (Later on, when I published Ronald Reagan, I was surprised by the contrast. Reagan not only *liked* getting telephone calls but called himself, at odd hours, and I often had to wait while he and my wife discussed their horses or exchanged information about pig breeding, an interest they shared. They exchanged photographs of each other on horseback, and Reagan sent her an autographed photograph of himself with a prize pig at the Iowa State Fair.)

I had not expected that Nixon would take well to editing, but he did, albeit indirectly. No prima donna, he accepted editorial advice with good grace and turned out, unsurprisingly, to be very sophisticated about the publishing process. He approached book promotion with all the enthusiasm of a born campaigner. He discounted the major reviewers, whom he rightly assumed would write about his books with a liberal bias—"When they don't like a book," he wrote to me about the editors of *The New York Times Book Review,* "they pick a reviewer that shares their prejudices"—and went after the big television news shows, where he could appeal to his public over the heads of the reviewers.

Strangely enough, the postpresidential Nixon was as good on television as the old Nixon had been bad—perhaps because now he had nothing to hide. The role of elder statesman seemed to suit him better than the role of president. White House insiders had always complained of his uninterruptible monologues on foreign policy, but the monologues worked very well for him on the *Today* show and *Larry King Live,* where his pronouncements were treated with awe. Television celebrities, being as easily impressed by former presidents as ordinary mortals are, were unlikely to contradict him or ask tough questions. More important, television sold books.

The only problem in publishing Nixon came from Nixon's supporters. His loyalists, particularly in Orange County, where he was regarded in much the same light as Bonnie Prince Charlie used to be in Scotland, were apt to cruise the local bookstores to check that his books were properly displayed or, God forbid, out of stock, and they did not hesitate to make their complaints directly to the head of Gulf + Western, often attributing any absence of books to liberal bias or to sabotage.

In August 1989 I received an unexpected invitation to dine at the Nixons' house in Saddle River, New Jersey. (They had long since abandoned Manhattan for the friendlier Republican suburbs.) Nixon's staff presented me with careful instructions on how to reach the house but seemed a little puzzled that I was driving myself. I could see why the instructions were necessary. Within a mile or so of a New Jersey commercial strip full of minimalls and service stations, the Nixons' house was tucked away as secretly as Shangri-la: Behind high, dense growths of trees and hedges, it was impossible for any casual intruder to find—rather like any number of culs-de-sac in Bel Air, but without palm trees. The courtyard was a blacktop space big enough for a good-size motel.

The puzzlement of Nixon's staff became clear as I pulled up before the entrance—a kind of California-style porte cochere—in my silver Porsche cabriolet. A row of limousines to one side made it evident that Nixon's guests tended to be driven by chauffeurs rather than to drive themselves, let alone in foreign sports cars. The security people at the door seemed uncertain what to make of the car.

Inside, I found most of my fellow guests milling about in the entrance hall, looking suitably solemn. The only one I recognized was Robert Abplanalp, a large, jovial-looking man who had been much in the limelight as a Nixon backer and personal friend during the Watergate days. He and Bebe Rebozo had appeared in the press as the ultimate Nixon loyalists, *plus royalistes que le roi*. There were three Chinese gentlemen present, one of them clearly the senior, with the bland, inscrutable faces of professional diplomats. There were no women present—it was to be a stag dinner.

Before we could introduce ourselves to one another, Nixon appeared at the top of the stairs at exactly the moment we had been summoned for. He descended halfway, stretched out his arms just as he used to do when he was campaigning, and with a broad smile announced in his deep voice, "Gentlemen, the good news is—the bar is open."

We trooped into the living room and sat down in a rough circle around Nixon, while the butler took our drink orders. As I was shortly to discover, drinks in the Nixon household were not to be taken—or even *held*—lightly. They were served in immense, heavy tumblers, and every time a guest took a sip, Nixon, who had an eagle eye as a host, attracted the butler's attention and said, "You'd better freshen up that drink." Like the ever-replenished "Bottomless Cup of Coffee" that used to be the pride of Prexy's, the now-defunct New York City hamburger chain, glasses at the Nixons' were impossible to empty.

In homage to Nixon, I had asked for one of his famous daiquiris, made with almost no sugar, the recipe for which was said to be one of his more closely guarded secrets, and I can report that it lived up to expectations: The president's claim that his was the best daiquiri ever was no more than the truth.

What I was not prepared for was the odd formality that he imposed on himself and his guests. There was no conversation as such. One guest, Richard Solomon, who was then assistant secretary of state for East Asian and Pacific affairs, had just returned that day from Paris, where the Cambodian talks were going on. Nixon asked him to give us a report on the state of the negotiations, which he did, at some length, while we sat and listened. When he was through, Nixon gave us his views on the subject, during which absolute silence reigned, while the butler freshened up our drinks. Except for the drinks, it was rather like a tutorial. The three Chinese men—later introduced as Han Xu, the departing ambassador of the People's Republic of China, who had been chief of protocol at the time of Nixon's visit there in 1972; Minister Zhao Qixin, from the embassy; and Chen Mingming, the ambassador's principal secretary, who translated for them—were presumably accustomed to feigning interest at the interminable meetings of the Chinese Communist Party and gave these disquisitions their full, rapt attention, while most of the Americans slumbered gently, arms crossed in front of them, chins resting on their chests.

What kept my attention focused was not the subject of Cambodia but the fact that Nixon was in the habit of referring to himself in the third person, something I had never heard anyone do before—not even members of the British royal family. "When Nixon was president . . ." he said, in his deep, sonorous voice, his dark eyes flickering over his guests as if he expected one of us to challenge him. Even stranger, he often expanded his self-description, as in "when Nixon was president and leader of the free world," as if the latter were also an office to which he had been elected. It was as if Queen Elizabeth II, having abdicated the throne, referred to herself in the third person as "the queen and defender of the faith."

Roused from slumber by the announcement that dinner was ready, we filed into the dining room, where the first course proved to be a contribution from Abplanalp, who had branched out from manufacturer of aerosol valves for spray cans to entrepreneur of smoked fish—a kind of Gentile Barney Greengrass. While we ate our smoked tuna, smoked trout, and smoked salmon, the real purpose of the dinner became apparent. The massacre of the Chinese student protesters in Tiananmen Square had occurred only two months earlier, and Nixon was debating whether he should continue with his plans to revisit China. He was also deeply concerned that the reaction of "the liberal media" toward events in China might prejudice Chinese-American relations, on which he set great store as the major achievement of his foreign policy.

Han Xu had won Nixon's respect and friendship in 1972, and he was in a position to carry to the Chinese leaders an informal message that, despite the unfortunate events in Tiananmen Square, Nixon was still on their side. The role of the rest of us was, on the one hand, to flesh out the dinner party—surely orchestrated because a social occasion would be more palatable than a simple face-to-face meeting between Nixon and Han Xu—and, on the other, to provide a suitable audience of industrialists (Abplanalp, of the smoked fish, and Dwayne Andreas, CEO of Archer Daniels Midland), high-level mandarins (Solomon and Robert Ellsworth, a former representative and ambassador to NATO), and a media figure and/or intellectual (me).

A year or so later, when Nixon came to lunch at Simon and Schuster, his genial, good-natured aide, John Taylor, actually provided in advance a list of suitable questions for us to ask the former president. Each of us was allocated one question, to which Nixon then gave an articulate five-minute reply; to at least one editor's regret, though, Watergate was not on the list of suggested subjects. In his own home, Nixon followed much the same formula in reverse. He went around the table, introducing each of us in turn (when it came to my turn, the president chuckled wickedly and said, "He's a type we don't often get at this table, heh heh—a New York intellectual!") and asking us to give a short summary of the state of our business or concern. He listened intently—nobody was a more intent listener than Nixon—and then, for the benefit of the Chinese, gave his own views on what we had said.

Needless to say, the Chinese were not there to hear about the book-publishing business, agricultural products, precision valves, or smoked fish. Ellsworth brought up the key question—the pièce de résistance, as it were—which was how America was reacting to Tiananmen Square and whether Nixon should go to Beijing.

The Chinese came to full attention at this. I could not help admiring the way Nixon had managed to get somebody else to raise the question—surely the diplomats must have appreciated the subtlety of it, too—and the way he gave it careful scrutiny, as if it had caught him by surprise. Nixon, I seemed to remember, had done some acting at school and had put on amateur theatricals to amuse the troops when he was a naval officer in the Pacific; it occurred to me that if fate had called him to the stage instead of to the bar he would have made a fine actor. He knitted his brows and appeared to give the matter serious consideration. He believed, he said, that there was more to be gained by Nixon's going than not. *Some* people (he frowned darkly)—naysayers, pinko parlor liberals, professional skeptics—would doubtless criticize Nixon. Nixon was used to that. It had never stopped Nixon in the past.

The Chinese nodded.

Great powers, the former president went on, could not allow their foreign policy to be determined by the scruples—he chuckled—"or prejudices" of the liberal media.

A set of deeper nods, with a hint of puzzlement, from the Chinese, for whom media scruples were surely not a problem.

The interests and the good relations of two such powers as China and the United States were more important than transitory events, Nixon continued, warming to his theme. Ordinary Americans, he affirmed solemnly, his voice lowering to a confidential pitch, had a better sense of what really mattered than the media did. Ordinary Americans liked and respected China and were not dismayed by horror stories.

Nixon seemed to be distancing himself not only from the media but from the White House. He leaned closer to Han Xu, eager to explain to him the workings of the American mind. "When Nixon was president and leader of the free world," Nixon said, his voice rumbling, his eyes locked on Han Xu (who continued to eat methodically and with enthusiasm while the translator whispered in his ear), "we had troubles of our own here in the United States." He paused to let this sink in, while Han Xu's attention remained fixed on his plate. "We, too, had so-called student riots, protests, anarchy in the streets of Washington," Nixon said, just in case Han Xu was unfamiliar with the antiwar movement. "When you go home, you should tell your people that many of us understand." He paused dramatically. "When Nixon was president and leader of the free world, he found that—*firmness paid*. You tell them that."

The words *firmness paid* were uttered with the full force of Nixonian emphasis, familiar to anyone who remembers his television appearances at such moments as the Cambodian incursion: the frown, the steely focus of the dark eyes, the out-thrust jaw, the even deeper lowering of the voice, and the slow delivery, as if to say, "This is the important bit, so pay attention."

My fellow guests nodded, apparently all in favor of firmness toward student demonstrators. The Chinese smiled too, for the first time: Firmness had so far been a hard sell for them in the United States—even in the Bush White House, where running over students with tanks was seen as, at the very least, poor PR for the Beijing regime. Han Xu finished what was on his plate, put his knife and fork down neatly, and raised his glass of red wine—a gift from the president of France, we had been informed—in a gesture of gratitude, not quite a toast but by no means casual, either. He whispered something to the translator. "He is grateful for the president's understanding," the translator said. "He will communicate it at home."

"Good," Nixon rumbled.

It occurred to me that part of the problem in current Sino-American relations might be that the Chinese had simply been listening to the wrong Americans over the years. Not unlike European explorers of Africa in the nineteenth century, who stumbled into the uncharted interior and latched on to whatever self-proclaimed kings and chiefs they first met up with, without having the slightest idea of what these supposed authority figures might represent, what their real power might be, or what their people and their neighbors thought of them, the Chinese had been "opened up" by Nixon and accepted him blindly as representing American hearts and minds. Just as the English in Africa had backed native rulers long after it should have been apparent to them that the rulers' own people had abandoned them, the Chinese remained loyal to Nixon after his fall and seemed unable to accept the legitimacy of his successors. It was one of the odd paradoxes of Nixon, whose rise to power was driven by anticommunism, that he ended up being taken more seriously in Beijing (and, eventually, in Moscow) than in Washington. Indeed, he soon came to be a kind of lobbyist in Washington for the two mutually antagonistic Communist regimes.

He showed no discomfort at the thought; quite the contrary, he was proud of the faith the Chinese had placed in him. After dinner—at which, once again, each of the guests in turn presented the host with a little speech about the hopes and dreams of his own little segment of American capitalism (the Chinese were tactfully exempted from sharing their hopes and dreams with us), followed by a detailed *tour d'horizon* of the world situation from Nixon—I could not help wondering if there had been a little more frivolity when Pat Nixon was the hostess, and wishing for the presence of wives and/or girlfriends. Then we withdrew to a somber room, with a huge rough-stone fireplace, for coffee and liqueurs. While some of the other guests got down to the serious business of the evening—telling old political war stories from the

Nixon campaigns and drinking monster stingers—I followed Nixon, who had offered to show his Chinese guests around the house.

At first, nothing caught my eye. Most of the rooms had a certain formal, unlived-in quality, rather like an expensive hotel suite or, more to the point, the White House. The unlived-in feeling apparently extended to Nixon: He didn't seem familiar with the layout of the house himself. At one point, he opened a closet door, apparently thinking that it was the door to his study, then slammed it shut hastily, with a muttered oath. Like people lost in a museum, we circled aimlessly, it seemed to me, for some time, searching for a particular piece of art he wanted to show his guests, until he finally said, "Here it is!"—as if somebody had moved it, which was unlikely, since it was fastened elaborately to the wall, with a plaque underneath. As it happened, the piece was undoubtedly worth finding—a magnificent silk tapestry of a cat playing, a gift from Mao to Nixon. The Chinese seemed to me more interested in the plaque, on which Mao's name appeared, than in the tapestry itself.

Nixon did not seem particularly interested in his collection. Perhaps he had shown it to visitors too many times before: the screen from the Japanese government, the Philippine folk art from President Marcos, the endless ceremonial gifts that are among the perks of being a head of state. With considerably more animation, Nixon flung open the door of his study—lucky on the second try—and ushered us in. "This," he said solemnly in the third person, "is where Nixon works."

The Chinese assumed a reverential expression—one they had perfected, presumably, for the display of any of Mao's artifacts. All the same, it was difficult to imagine any work being done in this unused room: It had something of the quality of a stage set furnished with expensive new props. No doubt Nixon was a clean-desk man, but this particular desk, shoved uncomfortably into a corner, showed no sign at all of use. There was not a paper in sight, and the desktop, like everything else in the room, was polished, spotless, and apparently brand-new. The desk chair showed no signs that Nixon had ever sat in it. "This is the desk at which Nixon wrote all his books," Nixon said. He patted its shiny leather top affectionately, as if it were a horse.

I looked around the room, searching for a single sign of Nixon's occupancy, for a single personal possession. There was none to be seen. We stood uncomfortably around the empty desk, and then Nixon told Han Xu that he wanted him to have a souvenir of this visit—something that would convey some part of the American spirit. There was a man in the forties and fifties, he said, whom Nixon had always respected as a true patriot—a prophet without honor in his own country, a man who had made great sacrifices for the truth and had been martyred for his pains but had lived long enough to play an important part in Nixon's own career. That man wrote a book, Nixon continued, one of the most important books of the twentieth century, a book that every American ought to read, and not just Americans, either, for his message was universal.

We stood around Nixon, spellbound by his emotion, for he was speaking, it was apparent, from the heart, and his eyes, normally piercing, were humid. I racked my brain trying to think who this great American might be. Eisenhower seemed all wrong, and anyway I knew that the Nixons harbored a certain resentment toward Ike and Mamie, who seldom, if ever, invited them to a private dinner, just the four of them, during the eight years of the Eisenhower presidency. John Foster Dulles crossed my mind, but it seemed unlikely that his views on China would commend themselves to Han Xu. Then it came to me. Of course! Nixon was talking about J. Edgar Hoover. Probably nobody had been a more loyal Nixon booster than Hoover, from the very beginning of the young congressman's career, and Nixon, during his presidency, had once paid Hoover the supreme compliment of accepting an invitation to dinner in Hoover's house, with the smoked mirrors, the overstuffed easy chairs in which Hoover and Clyde Tolson used to sit companionably in the evenings watching television game shows while eating their dinners off TV trays. "Remind me never to do this again," Nixon was reported to have whispered to John Ehrlichman as they made an early departure from Hoover's dinner party. Yet there was no doubt that Nixon owed Hoover a lot.

But I was wrong. Nixon bent down and opened the bottom drawer of his big desk and withdrew a copy of Whittaker Chambers's *Witness*. I was fascinated to see that the drawer was full of hardcover copies of Chambers's book. Had Nixon bought up the entire stock? I wondered. Briefly, Nixon summed up Chambers's life for the politely bewildered Chinese. Had they heard about the Pumpkin Papers, about Alger Hiss, about the discovery of the typewriter on which Hiss committed treason? Succinctly, from long experience, Nixon filled the Chinese in on the Hiss case and Chambers's part in it, explaining to the three Communist bureaucrats the undoing of the Communist conspiracy in the United States and the way the liberal media persecuted all those who had tried to bring the truth to light, Nixon himself not excepted. Names emerged from the dim past: Helen Gahagan Douglas, Mrs. Hiss, Joe McCarthy—a whole chunk of American history, which now seemed as remote as the Long March probably seemed to the Chinese, and during which, as could hardly have escaped their notice, their own country had been billed as one of the principal villains. The Chinese nodded amiably—no doubt they were accustomed to hearing far more unlikely glosses on the past from their leaders, and at far greater length. Besides, they were not diplomats for nothing. Han Xu showed every sign of agreement with this view of history, and after Nixon autographed a copy of *Witness* for him he clutched it to his bosom as if it were the Holy Grail. Would he take it home? I wondered. Would scholars in China dissect Chambers's narrative carefully, looking for clues to understanding the United States, or to understanding Nixon? Would they puzzle over the Pumpkin Papers and write dissertations on the microfilm that marked the beginning of Richard Nixon's rise to power?

We returned to the fireplace, where the atmosphere, fueled with stingers, was getting boisterous. Nixon, I could tell, had had enough of the Chinese by now, and they seemed to have tired of him, too. They had what they had come for—a friendly signal from Nixon, a veiled assurance that he would not call off his visit—and a signed copy of *Witness* besides. I took my leave with them.

Nixon walked outside with us, to shake hands. He saw the Chinese into their waiting limo, then said good night to me. He looked across the blacktop at my Porsche, studied it carefully, and said, "What the hell is *that*?" He then went back indoors.

I left feeling like Dorothy leaving Oz. As I drove home, around me in the night was suburban New Jersey and behind me was a kind of magic world where the past was still alive, where the Wizard was still wise and all-seeing, and where Whittaker Chambers was still an American hero. It was a testimony to Nixon's power that he could make *his* world of exile seem more real than the world around him—that he could create, somehow, the illusion that he was still president, that Watergate had never happened, that the bombing of Cambodia or the shooting of the Kent State students hadn't really mattered.

At that time, the Richard Nixon Library and Birthplace had not yet opened, but I should have been able to predict what it would be like, even then, right down to the mail-order catalog offering a T-shirt showing a nervously smiling Nixon shaking hands with a befuddled and stoned-looking Elvis Presley. In fact, Nixon was his own monument, a kind of living, breathing Mount Rushmore—the one American president of this century about whom it is absolutely impossible to be indifferent.

I DOUBT whether any publisher has ever grown rich from books written by presidents. We did a good deal better with Nixon than we had done with Jimmy Carter, however, whose speeches I had published in a volume called *A Government as Good as Its People*. Patrick Anderson, a friend of Larry McMurtry's, then speech writing for "the Governor," as those who were close to Carter called him even in the White House, persuaded me to come down to Washington to discuss a book of Carter's speeches. When I got there, I was mildly surprised to note that everybody had a glass bowl full of peanuts on his or her desk, including Anderson. Our discussion about the speeches was so quick that it was over before it started, which I didn't mind a bit. What I *did* mind, as I told Anderson later, was that I never received a set of presidential cuff links.

In the Nixon era it was impossible to get anywhere *near* the president without being presented with a pair of cuff links enameled with the presidential seal, and I had admired them on many people's cuffs, including those of Henry Kissinger. Indeed, in Nixon's time, a whole drawer of the president's desk was reserved for such small mementos, and he passed them out to everybody who entered the Oval Office, as did his aides. Once, when a group of rabbis came by to ask for more support for Israel and were presented, each of them, with a box of cuff links, the last rabbi to leave the room, overcome by curiosity, opened his box and peeked inside, just before reaching the door. He stopped, turned around, and said to Nixon, "Mr. President, I hope your promises about Israel mean more than this present. My box is empty."*

When Anderson asked me how I had enjoyed my visit to the White House, I told him that I was disappointed not to have received the traditional cuff links. Anderson replied, with some embarrassment, that the

* Another drawer in Nixon's desk was filled with dog biscuits, since King Timahoe, the red setter that Nixon's aides had urged him to buy to make him seem more warm and human to the public, in fact hated Nixon and would growl and back away every time Nixon tried to pet him for the camera. John Ehrlichman, who had led the research group that decided that a red setter would have the most appeal for voters, came up with the idea of the dog biscuits, so that Nixon could surreptitiously palm one from the drawer and hold it out to King Timahoe whenever the president wanted to be photographed interacting with his dog.

president and Mrs. Carter felt that kind of gift giving had been over-done in previous administrations—in short, it was tacky.

I thought that very strange. The only reason any normal citizen wants to visit the White House on business, I told Anderson, is to get the cuff links, or whatever the equivalent is for women. After all, take away the cuff links, and who on earth would want to meet Jimmy Carter?

Anderson was not amused—at the time, he took the view that Carter was leading a moral crusade and was going to be part of a great moment in American history—but he managed to persuade the president to send me a handwritten letter of thanks when the book was finally published. To my surprise, Carter misspelled the title of his own book ("*A Goverment as Good as it's People*"). I had it framed and treasured it for many years, until somebody stole it off my wall, together with an angry letter from Lyndon Johnson about a book I had published that was critical of him.

I was therefore not as excited as Dick Snyder expected me to be when I heard that he was going after Ronald Reagan's memoirs. As it turned out, the book was to usher in the era of huge advances for ghost-written celebrity autobiographies that was to make Harry Evans famous at Random House and eventually help to bring his career there—as well as the era—to an end. Oddly enough, we at S&S learned our lesson sooner than anybody else, since even dedicated Republicans who had contributed hundred of thousands of dollars to the president's campaign chests could not be persuaded to buy the signed edition of the speeches or the autobiography, and the general public, which had twice voted Reagan into office, completely ignored his books. In short, it was a disaster, which we attributed at the time to the fact that too much time had elapsed between his departure from office and the publication of the books. It can be explained more simply by the possibility that while the public had a good deal of affection for the president, they had no curiosity to know more about him and were smart enough to guess that they wouldn't find out anything new from his book anyway.

ULYSSES S. GRANT was the last president in American history who actually sat down on his front porch with a pad of paper and wrote his own book—under difficult circumstances, too, since he was writing against the clock, dying of throat cancer and in great pain. Since then, however, books by presidents have been largely ghostwritten, sometimes completely, as in the cases of Dwight Eisenhower and Lyndon Johnson, sometimes with the more or less active participation of the president in the process. Nixon did a good deal of his writing himself but was aided by a staff of people who did research for him and drafted whole sections of manuscript that Nixon then rewrote and revised. This is a perfectly respectable approach to writing a memoir—Winston Churchill employed a large staff of people to feed him research and first drafts, but there is no question that the final draft sounded like Churchill, much as Nixon's final drafts sounded a lot like Nixon (minus the profanity). Johnson's prose, in contrast, had the unmistakable flatness of a ghosted product, and no president was ever more removed from his book than was Reagan.

The Reagan book had, as they say, a "history," which partly explained how it came into our hands. In June 1977, Bill Adler, a book packager and agent who specialized in celebrity authors and who was briefly testing the limits of conflict of interest by working at S&S as an editor at the same time, had signed up Reagan to do a book on politics in Hollywood in the 1950s—the blacklisting and the witch-hunt in the movie business in the McCarthy years as seen from the side of one of the chief witch-hunters, so to speak. Adler's enthusiasm was not contagious. Most of the staff of S&S thought of Reagan as a West Coast right-wing extremist, and dreaded having to publish the book. This, as it turned out, need have concerned no one, since it was never written. The advance was modest, but so long as S&S refused to accept the money back, Reagan owed S&S a book, which he cheerfully acknowledged. At one point, in 1987, Irving Lazar, who as an old friend and neighbor of the Reagans considered himself entitled to be the president's agent, wrote to Nancy Reagan offering to sell the president's memoirs to S&S, despite the fact that to all intents we already owned them, and had his knuckles firmly rapped by her—she not only said no, she told him to refrain from even discussing the possibility with S&S or anyone else.

Thus Dick Snyder was in the position of having an option on the president's memoirs, as Reagan's second term drew to an end, and made a deal that satisfied everybody. Reagan was to receive, after he left office, what was certainly the largest advance ever paid to an author to date, and S&S was to get what Dick would call in his press release announcing the deal, "the book of the century."

Dick was jubilant at this coup, which was to be kept secret until the president had left the White House, lest he be accused of making a record-breaking book deal while still in office. The president had been affable, charming, totally forthcoming, everything he was reputed to be, Dick said, and confided one thing more: He had promised Reagan that I would be his editor. The president and Mrs. Reagan had been delighted to hear that, and looked forward to meeting me.

There was, however, one small fly in the ointment. I brought up the fact that I was already Kitty Kelley's editor (I had published her biography of Elizabeth Taylor), who was then working on what was supposed to be a sensational, unauthorized kiss-and-tell biography of Nancy Reagan. Mrs. Reagan was known to be furiously apprehensive about the book. "I hope she gets hit by a truck," Mrs. Reagan was reported to have said about Kelley. How would the Reagans feel when they found out that I was Kelley's editor? I asked. And how would *she* feel when she learned that her editor was working with the Reagans?

All I had to do was to handle things firmly and everything would be fine, Dick replied. If necessary he would step in personally and help. Since I was only too aware of the fact that things had *not* been fine between S&S and the Collins sisters, I wasn't optimistic that they would be any better between S&S, the Reagans, and Kitty Kelley.

As it turned out, the person who objected most strongly to this arrangement was Kelley, not the Reagans, who took the whole thing in stride once it hit the papers. I could have understood the Reagans' objection to being published by the same house or having the same editor as Kelley; it was harder to understand why Kelley was so upset. Much to my dismay, she was moved to Alice Mayhew to solve the problem. I entered on the job of being Reagan's editor, therefore, in a glum and slightly resentful frame of mind, since it had cost me a major author and, for a time, a good friend. Such regrets as I had, however, were soon assuaged by Reagan himself, who was charm personified.

In the meantime, we moved forward to select a writer to work with the president and eventually settled on Robert Lindsey, one of Alice Mayhew's authors, a former journalist of some distinction, and the author of *The Falcon and the Snowman*. Lindsey was a Californian, which made it easier for him to spend time with Reagan, and, like everyone else, he succumbed quickly to the president's charm, although he noted with some concern that "Reagan is not a very introspective man and thus not easy to interview." (This turned out to be an understatement.) Alice Mayhew and I drafted a proposed outline of the book, in which we recommended, rather hopefully, that it should begin with a memorable opening line, like Nixon's ("I was born in a house my father built."), stress his humble origins, and achieve so far as possible the simplicity and dignity of Grant's prose.

The publication of the president's collected speeches took place rather quickly and caused a small tremor of alarm. Beautifully packaged, they failed to sell, despite a lavish marketing campaign that involved Charlton Heston as the spokesman. Of course it is a well-known fact that nobody wants to read speeches—I had only to recall Jimmy Carter's to remind me of that—but Reagan's popularity was so great that we assumed *his* speeches would be an exception to the rule, that his supporters would *have* to buy them, out of sheer loyalty. When they did not, a certain panic set in regarding the memoirs.

It had been supposed that since he was the most loved and admired president since FDR, his memoirs would sell like hotcakes, whatever was in them. They might not be *read* by large numbers of people, but they would be bought in vast quantities. Now that this could no longer be depended upon, the quality of the memoirs became an urgent concern, so my associate editor, Chuck Adams, and I went to California in haste to review the text and—frankly—urge the president to greater candor.

THUS, CHUCK and I found ourselves early one afternoon in 1990 in Beverly Hills, paying a visit to the president in his office in Century City, the vast, monumental neo-Egyptian real-estate development whose owner, Marvin Davis, has his office in the same building. I had visited Davis's office once, to have coffee with him—Irving Lazar had been trying to sell me his book, but it turned out, as was so often the case, that poor Davis had no intention of writing one and didn't have the slightest idea of who I was or why I had come to see him. Davis's office was in keeping with his size—he is a man of enormous height and girth.

Reagan's surroundings, by contrast, were restrained and modest, designed in the Williamsburg colonial style and staffed by clean-limbed, smiling young women and good-looking young men in suits. Both genders presented a perfect picture of wholesomeness. They all had perfect teeth. Many of the men wore red-white-and-blue patterned ties, while most of the women wore red-white-and-blue scarves. It wasn't exactly a uniform, but almost.

The waiting room contained a long, glassed-in cabinet, built against one wall, containing all the saddles with which Reagan had been presented during the years of his presidency, many of the Western ones gleaming with silver. (Interestingly enough, when actually on a horse, the president seemed to favor English saddles, field boots, and old-fashioned flared whipcord riding breeches.) After a short wait, I was taken into a small, handsome room, lined with bookshelves and carpeted in blue, where, from behind a large and perfectly clear desk, devoid of any sign of work, Reagan rose to greet me, his brow furrowed as if he had been deep in thought. He was dressed in a tan summer suit, and once he had me in view, he smiled as naturally as if we had been friends for life. He had the kind of suntan and presence that only movie stars possess, a bigger-than-life quality that is purely physical and that makes it hard to take your eyes off them even when they're not doing anything. His head was big, majestic, deeply seamed, his hands big, gnarled, sinewy, well cared for, but still a workingman's hands, the only part of him that seemed genuinely Lincolnesque.

Reagan walked to the middle of the room, grabbed my hand, shook it heartily, then pulled me carefully into the position he wanted. "Smile!" he said, and an electronic flash went off. One of the pretty girls with the Betsy Ross scarves was taking our picture with a Polaroid. I looked down at the carpet and saw that there was a small, neat little cross on it, presumably duct tape. It was the president's "mark," the place every movie actor has to reach exactly in order to be in focus for a scene. The president had hit his mark like the pro that he was, then placed me at just the right angle for a handshake photo. At the end of our talk I was presented with the photo, in a special frame, and Reagan signed it for me.

This, I realized, was not only routine for visitors; it was, in many cases, the only reason for the visit. People seemed to come to have their pictures taken with Reagan the way they might with Old Faithful or

Mickey Mouse, as if he were a kind of tourist attraction. He didn't seem to mind—on the contrary, he did it with genuine good nature.

Once we sat down, the president seemed to lose interest in the proceedings. He had done his part; now, it was time for me to do my part, which was to say thank you and go. Since I had substantive questions to ask him, however, I stayed, rather to his surprise, and we chatted briefly, as a kind of warm-up to the big meeting tomorrow, when we would all get together, the president, me, Chuck, Bob Lindsey, and the president's staff, to discuss the manuscript.

I apologized for all the press about the Reagans and Kitty Kelley, and particularly for an ill-advised interview with me in the *Los Angeles Times*, in which I had been quoted as saying, "Let's face it, Kitty Kelley's book is not likely to be too flattering, if the past is any guide." This comment had caused Mrs. Reagan great pain, and been reprinted all over the world, to the discomfort of Dick Snyder and Mort Janklow, the Reagans' agent—so much so that I had promised not to give any more interviews, despite the fact that I was on tour for my new novel *The Fortune*, a copy of which I presented to Reagan.

"Well," Reagan said pleasantly, his big, rough-hewn hands on my book, "it worried Nancy more than it worried me." These things happened, he said. He had worked for the big studios. You had commitments, and you had to fulfill them. You couldn't just renege on them. He understood that.

I told him that I had agreed to let Kitty Kelley go to another editor, so there would be no conflict of interest in having the same editor for both her book and his. He nodded, and thanked me. He would tell Nancy, and he was sure that it would please her. It would be a load off her mind. For himself, he didn't seem to care one way or the other. It would be hard to imagine a gentler, nicer, more natural, or more sincere person, now that he was no longer just a voice on the telephone— relaxed, easygoing, unhurried, although perhaps a shade *remote*, I thought, as if none of this really affected him at all. Lindsey's warning about his coauthor's lack of introspection had proven only too true. The president was genial, lavish with the anecdotes that were his familiar repertoire, and appeared never to have met a person he didn't like.

At one point, we had mapped out a beginning in which the president would relate his thoughts on leaving office, "perhaps what goes through his mind as he flies back across the country in Air Force One, after the inaugural of his successor, passing over this vast country, thinking about where he has come from, his roots, what he has achieved in these past eight years, what is ahead for those who lie sleeping or working below . . . as the president of the United States returns to California a simple citizen again." But no amount of prodding could get the president to reveal what his thoughts, if any, had been on that historic occasion or any other. Given that reticence, Lindsey had done a remarkable job, but there were areas where more was required, symbolized by the fact that Reagan had absolutely refused to even *mention* his first wife, Jane Wyman, in the book—an omission that I feared might make the reviewers question his willingness to face facts.

Encouraged, I took up the question of Jane Wyman, and while Reagan's benign expression didn't change, his eyes looked a little frosty. Bob Lindsey had already brought that subject up, he said, and he'd thought it was settled. There was no point in going into all that stuff at this late stage. Why, he himself hardly remembered a thing about his marriage to Jane. It was all water under the bridge.

But it *wasn't* quite all water under the bridge, I thought—he had a daughter from that marriage, after all, so he could hardly have forgotten it completely. I pointed out that reviewers were likely to pick up on this, and use it as a stick with which to beat him over the head. If he left out of his book something as simple and well-known as his first marriage— didn't even *mention* it!—they would conclude that he was leaving out even more important things.

"I never pay much attention to critics," Reagan said placidly. "Never have." The world was divided between two kinds of people, he said: those who *can* and those who *criticize*. The president looked pleased with himself, as if he had just thought this up.

Ignoring the critics was a sensible attitude, I agreed. I tried to pay no attention to them either, in my own small way. The problem was that what we had here was a big edifice, the integrity of which could be destroyed by concentrating on a single brick. Give the reviewers an excuse to dismiss the book, and they would. Why risk it? I wasn't looking for a whole chapter about Jane Wyman, after all. A couple of lines would do.

The president looked gloomy. Even the thought of a couple of lines about Jane Wyman made him uncomfortable. Long or short, it wasn't something he wanted to do. It occurred to me that it might not be Reagan himself who was being stubborn about this point but Mrs. Reagan. I made a mental note to ask Janklow to call her, who liked and trusted him, and see if he could persuade her.

With that, Reagan concluded business by standing up and taking me on a tour of his quarters to see all the photographs of his horses over the years. His affability returned as he described each one in detail. I had heard people criticizing his memory, but there seemed to be nothing wrong with it at all. He could even remember the names of Margaret's horses. It was, I decided, merely a question of whether he was interested in a subject or not. If he was, I was soon to discover, his memory was razor sharp; if he wasn't, he couldn't remember a thing.

I walked back to the hotel, and called Janklow, who promised to call Mrs. Reagan, and went off to dinner with Lindsey and Chuck Adams to prepare for the morning.

In the morning we met—Fred Ryan, the president's genial chief of staff, Bob Lindsey, myself, Chuck Adams, and a couple of staffers—in a large room, around a big coffee table. Promptly on time, Reagan arrived, carrying a brown paper bag and dressed this time in a golf jacket, casual pants, and cowboy boots—an outfit in which he looked ten years younger and even more the movie star—and announced that he had a golf date at noon. This came as something of a surprise for us, since we had been anticipating an all-day session. Lindsey looked particularly shocked, since he wanted to go through the whole manuscript, line by line. Reagan, however, was at his placid best. He would deal with the big problems, then go and play golf. We could settle the rest. He had thought things over during the night, he told us, and come to the conclusion that it would be all right to mention his marriage to Jane Wyman. We quickly inserted four lines in the manuscript, and that was that. I guessed that Janklow had succeeded in persuading Mrs. Reagan to drop her objection to the mention of her predecessor.

The idea of starting the book with the president's return home had seemed to him too negative. He had a different beginning in mind and sketched it for us from his big, reclining chair. Why not begin with the most important moment of his presidency? He had no doubt what it was. It was on November 19, 1985, during his first meeting with Russian premier Mikhail Gorbachev, near Geneva. Reagan had realized, he told us, that the summit meeting was going nowhere. The two leaders were surrounded by advisers and specialists as they discussed disarmament and were unable to make any human contact, so Reagan had tapped Gorbachev on the shoulder and invited him to go outside for a walk. The two went outside, and Reagan took Gorbachev down toward the shore of Lake Geneva. "You and I," he told Gorbachev, "are old men—

grandfathers." The peace of the world was on their shoulders. Why could they not simply sit down and talk things out, man to man, without advisers and "experts"? So they went into the boathouse, overlooking the lake, just the two of them alone, lit a fire, and at the end of a long, heartfelt discussion, Gorbachev agreed to take major steps toward nuclear disarmament and to come to two more summit meetings as well, one in the United States, one in the Soviet Union. It just went to show, the president said, his eyes moist, how important a person-to-person approach was.

Reagan told this story as if it were a scene from a movie, with vivid detail and real feeling—indeed, his sincerity was so plain that all of us were touched. He was obviously right—it was the perfect way to start the book. There was only one problem, I whispered to one of his aides. Since Reagan spoke no Russian and Gorbachev spoke no English, they could not have been alone for the discussion.

The aide nodded. "They *weren't* alone," he whispered back. "There were interpreters, security men, a whole bunch of people. That's just the way the president likes to remember it."

I nodded. This was a problem that had arisen before. Reagan's memory was selective. Rather like Woody Allen's Zelig, he had a tendency to place himself in events. He also was known to confuse fiction and reality. There had been the anecdote he had told Medal of Honor winners about the Eighth Air Force bomber pilot, who, when his B-17 was mortally hit by flak, ordered the crew to parachute out. Just as the pilot was about to jump from the flaming aircraft himself, he discovered that the ball gunner was trapped in his turret, wounded and unable to get out of the hatch above him, terrified of dying alone. The pilot took off his parachute, went back to the ball-turret position behind the wings and lay down on the floor so that he could put his arm into the turret and hold the dying boy's hand. "Don't sweat it, son," he told the gunner, "we'll go down together," as the plane plunged to the ground.

This brought tears to Reagan's eyes and to the eyes of the Medal of Honor winners. The only problem, as the press soon discovered, was that it had never happened. It was a scene from a movie, which the president had unwittingly transposed to real life.

He had the ability, rare even among actors, to convince a listener that something had happened the way he told it when it hadn't, and he believed it with complete sincerity himself. Thus, we had to argue Reagan, with considerable embarrassment, out of the story about how he had been the first American soldier to enter the German death camps and record the atrocities there (a story that he is said to have told to Yitzhak Rabin, bringing tears to Rabin's eyes), because it turned out that Reagan had never left the United States during World War Two—he spent the entire war in Hollywood, in fact, recruiting personnel for army film units. He had seen some of the first death-camp footage taken and somehow convinced himself that he had been there. There was no intent to deceive on his part, he was simply one of those born raconteurs who told the same stories over and over again until they *became* truth.

We moved on to other subjects. The title had long been a problem, since Reagan had clung to the idea of calling the book *Trusting the People,* which didn't even *sound* like an autobiography, but we managed to persuade him to accept *An American Life,* which he quite liked. On three other subjects he was intractable, however. He would not add a single word more to his rather hermetic account of the Iran-*contra* affair (in fact, it was the only subject on which I received a brief, stiff note from Reagan, via his chief of staff, declaring that while the president shared my goal of making the book "an open, frank account," he had made his decision on this matter, and we were to "move ahead promptly in accordance with his instructions"), nor did he wish to explain in any detail how he had formed his views on abortion or how the savings-and-loan crisis had begun.

I pointed out to him that most people regarded the savings-and-loan crisis as having occurred on his watch, rightly or wrongly, and that he should therefore address it somehow in the text. He shook his head patiently. A lot of people supposed that, he said, but it wasn't true. The problems with the savings-and-loan organizations had begun in California and Texas, had they not? I agreed. Well, the president went on, that was just the point. In both of those states, state law precluded federal intervention—there was nothing the federal government could have done. It simply wasn't his responsibility.

I got up to stretch my legs and was followed by the aide who had been sitting next to me. Surely federal law supersedes state banking laws, does it not? I asked him. The aide shrugged. "Well yes, technically," he said. "But he's always believed that, you see."

I saw all right. Reagan was so persuasive, so gentle, so convincing a father-figure, so *charming,* that nobody wanted to argue or disagree with him. Besides that, his ideas were deeply entrenched, and sincerely held. Even when he was wrong, it was easier to go around him than to face the fact head-on.

We returned to the table just as coffee was served. Reagan, whose mind was already on his golf game, gave the paper bag to an assistant, who came back a few minutes later with a handsome china plate on which were neatly piled some homemade cookies. The president took the plate and held it up so that we could admire them—for a moment I thought he was going to say that he had baked them himself, but no, they were chocolate-chip cookies that had been baked for him by the Reagans' Hispanic maid. He described with pride how she had risen at the crack of dawn to bake them and had given them to him to bring to the office as he was getting into the car.

I glanced at the plate. The cookies looked as if they had been baked by a child or somebody to whom the idea of a chocolate-chip cookie was basically foreign. They were lumpy, with a crisply burned crust, and rather thick for cookies. Still, Reagan was beaming at them as if they were culinary works of art, and it was impossible not to be touched by his pride and by his genuine gratitude that somebody who worked for him would go to this much trouble on his behalf. He took one off the plate, then passed it to the person on his right, and so on around the table. Chuck Adams, I noticed, put his in his pocket. I tasted mine, found it too sweet (but I totally lack a sweet tooth), and put the remainder in my pocket, where I was to find it later in the day. Lindsey took a cookie and put the plate back in front of the president, who repeated, with exactly the same degree of pride and emotion, that they had been baked for him by the maid.

Some minutes elapsed while we sipped our coffee and discussed various points—my notes include questions such as "*Why* did RR pick Haig (or the rest of his cabinet)?"; "What did RR think of Begin personally?"; and a mysterious one that reads simply, "Cut the nutmeg story?"—but it was becoming increasingly apparent to me that we no longer had Reagan's full attention.

At first I thought he was probably thinking about his golf date—as an outdoor man, he cannot have relished spending the morning indoors with a writer and two editors. Then it dawned on me that his gaze was fixed not on some far horizon visible only to him but directly on the plate with one cookie. His expression was determined but mildly guilty, as if he had been caught in the act of some misdeed. The truth struck me like a thunderbolt. What he wanted was the remaining cookie, but of course he couldn't take it. The lesson had been drummed into him during his childhood and was now ineradicable: You do not take the last cookie on the plate, you offer it around.

Every child is taught some version of that, of course, but I had no doubt in the poor-but-honest household in Galesburg (and later, Dixon), Illinois, where the Reagan family often made do with "oatmeal meat" (a mixture of oatmeal and hamburger, served with gravy), the lesson was drummed into him harder than most, for the family lived precariously on the knife edge of respectable poverty. Reagan's father was a shoe salesman who went on binges whenever things were going well for him, and while Reagan's descriptions of his childhood tend to be sentimental and affectionate, one has an underlying sense of just how important it was to his mother to keep up appearances and how seriously both parents took the teaching of good manners, which was the main thing that kept them in the middle class. There were a good many things that Reagan had done since his days in Illinois that must have surprised and discomforted his mother—getting divorced, for one thing—but he had remained, as she surely had wished, an essentially decent and truthful man who saw people as individuals and treated everyone with courtesy. Given who he was, taking the last cookie on the plate was out of the question, and he knew it; yet the more he looked at the cookie, the more he wanted it.

I was tempted to ask Chuck Adams to put his cookie back on the plate, but I didn't think that he would get away with it, and, being good-mannered himself, he would hardly want to admit that he had only pretended to eat his cookie, despite the fact that it had been made for a president. Mine had a bite taken out of it, so that was no use.

Eventually, it became evident that Reagan's mind was elsewhere and that nothing could be accomplished until it was returned to the matters at hand. I coughed and, once I had his attention, said how much I had enjoyed my cookie.

Reagan nodded vigorously. They *were* good, weren't they? They had been baked for him only this morning by the Reagan maid, who put them in a paper bag and handed it to him as he was getting into his car. Reagan's face was as full of emotion the third time he told this story as it had been the first, while Lindsey, Adams, and I smiled as if we had never heard any of it before. Only Reagan's aides looked glumly at their hands, presumably wondering how many more times they would hear about the maid before the end of the day.

Now that I had given Reagan a cue, he picked up on it instantly. Lifting the plate, he pointed to the remaining cookie. Would anybody like the last cookie? he asked. One of his aides took the plate from his hand and passed it on. The aides, I noticed, knew better than to reach for the last cookie. Chuck Adams passed the plate on to me, and I passed it on to Lindsey, the last man in the circle. I caught a glimpse of the president's face. His eyes were hopeful and bright, his whole expression that of somebody who has done the right thing and seen it pay off. He was already reaching for the plate when Lindsey, who had been bent over a copy of the manuscript, oblivious of the small drama taking place at the table, absentmindedly grabbed the cookie and bit into it without even looking up.

Reagan's face crumpled, his expression that of a man who has just staked the farm on one card and lost. His eyes turned humid, almost welling up with tears—I have seldom felt so bad for anyone. Then his stoicism returned. He took the empty plate from Lindsey's hand, placed it back on the table, and directed his gaze to the far horizon, leaving us to get on with the details.

It was hardly surprising that the question of who had actually written the book came up in the press from time to time. Everybody knew that Reagan wasn't writing it all by himself, but Bob Lindsey's name was not to appear on the jacket or the title page—even if it had been supposed to appear there, his taking the last cookie would probably have made the president want to take his name off it. I came up with a quick answer to such questions that seemed to satisfy everybody: "Of course the president wrote the book—it's his book—but with the editorial assistance of Robert Lindsey."

This seemed to solve the problem, so far as reviewers were concerned, and it did not erupt again until Reagan himself came to S&S for a press conference in October 1990, shortly after the book had been published. After being introduced to the people at S&S who had worked on the book, Reagan and I posed for photographers, each holding a copy of the manuscript and pretending to edit it, then Reagan stood up, walked to the door, and waved to the photographers jauntily. Pausing at the threshold, he called out to them cheerfully, "I hear it's a terrific book! One of these days I'm going to read it myself," and was gone.

. . .

I HAVE always remembered him that way, cheerful, upbeat, good-natured, and even when the book didn't sell—for by the time it came out it had, quite unfairly, become fashionable to put down Reagan, even among those who had been his supporters—I looked upon it as one of my happier publishing experiences.

Who else would tell the story of the dead goldfish at the summit? It appears that during the first summit meeting, when the president was staying in the home of my old schoolmate the Aga Khan, he was informed that one of the goldfish in his host's aquarium had died. Feeling responsible, Reagan sent the Secret Service out to search through Geneva for a replacement, and placed the dead goldfish in a matchbox in his pocket, which he then forgot to discard, so that during his initial meetings with Gorbachev, on which hung the fate of the world, he was carrying a dead goldfish in his pocket. From whom else, after all, would you get that kind of candor? What other president would have had that sense of old-fashioned good manners toward his host? And in an age of faked emotions in politics, how nice to look back on somebody who, whatever his faults, *genuinely* believed in what he was saying. Even when it was wrong.

CHAPTER 32

FEW PEOPLE IN book publishing ever learn much from experience—or to put it another way, almost everything that experience teaches them eventually turns out to be wrong. This is not because of stupidity or even stubbornness but because every book is a different product. Even when books fit (or appear to fit) within a given genre or category ("presidential memoirs," for example, or "women's novels"), books and authors differ. No sooner has somebody said that science fiction is dead than a science-fiction novel—the late Carl Sagan's *Contact*, for example, or Michael Crichton's *Jurassic Park*—proves the statement untrue. The reverse holds good, which is that any attempt to capitalize on successes like these by publishing similar books will invariably fail.

Historical novels were said to be dead until *The Clan of the Cave Bear* demonstrated that it was only necessary to find a new way of writing one; many people in publishing will look you in the eye and tell you that romantic fiction is dead, despite the fact that every book Danielle Steel writes is a best-seller, as are those by Anne Rivers Siddons. Many publishers believe that the glamorous, glitzy novel is dead, despite Judith Krantz. For that matter, hardcover mystery novels were thought by many publishers to be in such a bottomless decline that most of them got rid of their mystery imprints at just about the time when Mary Higgins Clark was writing her first novel.* (Mary would go on to write an uninterrupted string of twenty-one best-sellers and to become and remain one of my closest and dearest friends.)

A GOOD illustration of this—indeed, an object lesson—was the publication of Shirley Conran's *Savages*. Something of a name to conjure with in the United Kingdom, Shirley Conran became an overnight success in the United States when S&S published her first novel, *Lace,* in 1982. The book succeeded partly because of its eye-catching tag line ("Which one of you bitches is my mother?"), partly because it was a shopping and brand-name-dropping novel in the tradition of Judith Krantz's *Scruples,* and partly because it was brilliantly (and on Conran's part ruthlessly) promoted. There is a certain market, always, for a novel that combines sex, romance, and the address of the right shoemaker in Paris, and *Lace* was written to capitalize on this market.

Joni Evans and I bought *Lace,* in fact, precisely because it seemed to us that S&S had been slipping in this market since the days of *The Love Machine.* Of course, we had Jackie Collins, which was a very good thing, but we hadn't *made* Jackie Collins, since she had already been a very successful writer when she left Warner Books for S&S. We had built up her sales, but that isn't at all the same thing as launching somebody from scratch, which was the challenge when we agreed to pay a major amount of money after reading the first draft of *Lace.*

---

* Publishers were right to see that the hardcover mystery business was changing—the days when your local stationers rented out mysteries at a dollar a day (not so long ago—my ex-wife was still renting one or two a day even in the mid-sixties) went the way of the dodo—as mass-market paperbacks took the place of rentals, only to be supplanted, eventually, by the rental of videotapes. Things change, of course—the local stationer itself has been replaced by a convenience store owned and run by people who don't even speak English. Nevertheless, the appetite for mysteries remains.

Unfortunately, *Lace* was one of those novels that read better on the first read than on the second. I had been carried away by the bold first line, the sheer energy of the story, and all the extravagant descriptions of life in the world of haute couture. It was, as one woman reader said, "like eating M&M's while masturbating," and indeed there was something mildly sinful about the book, like overindulging in a good Swiss patisserie, a feeling of being unable to stop but slightly sick at the same time. A closer inspection of the manuscript once we owned it revealed certain flaws of logic, plotting, and even ordinary common sense. In addition, it was far too long and full of somewhat schoolgirlish passages, which work in the United Kingdom but read strangely to Americans. I girded my loins for battle and waded in, and pretty soon Shirley Conran herself was ensconced in an office next to mine, doggedly rewriting in a tiny hand, making out wall-size charts of the chronology and the interaction of the characters, in many different colors of ink, and driving a succession of typists mad. Early in the proceedings Shirley presented me with a sweatshirt that bore the legend SHOW, DON'T TELL! as a response to my constant advice to keep the book moving by writing scenes instead of narrative and description. On the whole, few writers have taken to criticism with more cheer and harder work than she did, and we soon became friends. Her determination was something of a force of nature and was, in its own way, infectious. The marketing plans for *Lace* became, for a time, the talk of the industry, for we were determined to make the book work, whatever it cost to promote it (and its author). No stone was left unturned. We had reading copies, contests, bookmarks, featured stories about Conran, giveaway lace garters embroidered with the title in gold thread, window displays—not just in bookstores but in the better shops on South Rodeo Drive in Beverly Hills—product tie-ins, every imaginable tchotchke.

Unlike most novelists, Shirley was a known factor to talk-show hosts, because of her self-help book, *Superwoman,* so we planned a full-scale publicity tour, for which Shirley planned her wardrobe with the care of a general organizing an assault and prepared herself, in the meantime, by going on a strict diet and visiting a health spa. In short, we gave it the full Jacqueline Susann treatment, and—no surprise—it worked. *Lace* bounced onto best-seller lists all over the country (and soon the world) and sold a ton of copies in hardcover, in paperback, and for the Literary Guild. It even got made into a trashy miniseries, always a sign of success. Actually, it passed my personal test for women's popular-fiction success, which is that substantial numbers of women could be observed reading it on the subway and on buses. (Airplanes were the place to test the success of men's action novels and self-help books.) Jackie Susann had used this as one of her tests to determine if we were reaching the real heart of the market for her kind of fiction, so it had been one of my happiest moments to ride the D train one morning and count the number of women who were absorbed in reading *Queenie*. *Lace* worked on the D train, which meant we were home free.

Naturally, her second novel, *Savages,* was eagerly awaited, and when she delivered an incredibly detailed outline, it seemed like a sure thing—it was to be the story of a group of glamorous young women who become stranded on a tropical island during a vacation trip and are forced to survive by their wits and their meager survival skills. We bought the book and went through the long process of getting it written—a group activity involving Shirley, her assistant, two editors (me and Joni), a freelance line editor, a researcher, and a staff of people doing roughly the same tasks on the other side of the Atlantic. Once again, Shirley moved into S&S with her wall charts and a chronology that unrolled on the floor, with every event in the book neatly marked off and described. By this time, Shirley was a known quantity to fiction buyers, but we did not scale down in any way our promotion plans. A lavish press kit was prepared, reading copies were printed, and we arranged a full author's tour; in short, everything was done to ensure that the book would sell like *Lace*.

Instead, it bombed, dismally, completely, absolutely, from the very first moment it hit the stores. The campaign was there, the ads were terrific, Shirley did her number on TV, the stores took huge numbers of the book, all the elements of success were present and accounted for. The one thing we hadn't foreseen was that even Shirley Conran's loyal fans hated the book.

It wasn't the reviewers who killed the book. The problem was that Shirley's readers evidently didn't want to read about women eating raw fish or building a raft or learning to kill with their bare hands. They associated Shirley with luxury, glamour, sex, and wealth, and somehow, as if by magic, they sniffed out the fact that this wasn't the mix that Shirley was selling in *Savages*. They walked right past the huge piles of it in the bookstores as if the expensive four-color jacket and the displays were invisible. It's one of those mysteries of the book trade, the way readers *know* when an author has failed them and how quickly the word of mouth spreads. The public knows the book is dead long before the stores, let alone the publisher, have worked it out.

As one of the older sales reps said about *Savages,* "It's *Shardik* all over again—you can spend all the money you want, you can't make 'em read what they don't want to read."

PERHAPS THE greatest mistake a publisher can make is to think in categories in the first place. Categories are the hallmark of mass-market publishing, in which it is necessary to stock the shelves with so many mysteries or so many science-fiction novels every month and in which the important thing is that the books themselves (and their covers) fit into a given category—the twenty-first novel in a paperback science-fiction series had better be as much like the previous twenty as possible, or there will be trouble from readers, jobbers, and retailers. In hard-cover publishing, almost the reverse holds true, which explains (with a few notable exceptions) why so few mass-market people become successful hardcover editors or publishers. What works in hardcover is generally what is different, unexpected, and new, and even when people seem to be writing the same kind of book over and over again—as many best-selling novelists do—they need to be reinvented from time to time, and they can't be imitated or cloned. Danielle Steel and Mary Higgins Clark write books that sell in the millions, but anybody setting out to create a stable of writers to provide books in their styles or following their formats would likely fail.

Doubleday was perhaps the only major hardcover house that succumbed to the notion of cranking out hardcover books in ever larger quantity, as if they were paperbacks. This might have been because Nelson Doubleday was more interested in his baseball team than in books, or possibly because Doubleday owned the Literary Guild, an enormously successful book club, and category publishing is the lifeblood of book clubs, or even because Doubleday owned its own printing plant, which needed to be kept busy. Whatever the reason, Doubleday became an unwieldy giant and for a time collapsed, until revived in a smaller form by a new owner—an object lesson, one would have thought, to everyone in the business.

But by the eighties, the prevailing opinion had changed. Big became better. What had limited the size of publishing houses was the sheer difficulty of obtaining information about thousands of different "products" and the amount of time it took for numbers from the field to work their way up to the desks of the people who made the decisions. Beyond a certain size, there was simply no way to keep track of things, and the publishing process either got out of control or had to be bound by so many rigid rules that it was unable to function, except when it came to the most obvious best-sellers.

The computer put an end to that concern. Information, such as it was—for the next step was to rationalize what people needed to know—was now almost instantly available, no matter how big the company was. The gray-haired old ladies with pencils in their hair gave way to casually dressed youngsters who knew how to run computers and get the numbers out of it in a form that a busy man could read and understand in an instant. As if by a magic wand, the gray-haired old ladies in accounting were fired and went home to Queens or Brooklyn or the suburbs of New Jersey, occasionally surfacing to write pathetic letters when something "their" company had done made news.

The computer changed everything, and the race for size—this time with management controls, *s'il vous plaît*—was on.

BY THE early eighties, Dick Snyder had hit his stride, and begun to move from the day-to-day grind of publishing books to the big time of corporate acquisition. In 1984, he acquired Esquire Corporation, buying everything except the magazine. He ended up with Allyn and Bacon, an educational publisher; a nontheatrical film company; a lighting company; a company that made storage cabinets; and what one of those involved in the purchase called "a few other dogs and cats." Within a year all Esquire's executives were history, and not long afterward so was everything Esquire had consisted of except Allyn and Bacon itself, which was to become the nucleus of S&S's educational and informational business, which fifteen years later was to be sold for over four billion dollars.

Dick was on a roll. Gulf + Western (which had changed its name to Paramount, after its most famous asset) was no longer in the synergy business—that word had died along with Bluhdorn. The company was now firmly in the entertainment and educational business; the zinc, the valves, the replacement bumpers, the gloves, the mattresses, all the *chaz-*

erei that Bluhdorn had acquired over the years on his demented shopping spree had been sold off, without sentimentality or regret, by Martin Davis, with the result that Paramount was awash in cash and looking for companies to buy. Needless to say, they had to be companies with some kind of coherence—Davis was not about to follow down Bluhdorn's path. What Wall Street wanted now was companies that made sense (or *appeared* to make sense, anyway), with some kind of rational plan for the future. Books, education, and movies looked like a sensible enough combination on paper to satisfy investors.

There were two key factors involved, both of which worked to Dick's benefit. The first was that education became a hot issue in the 1980s, partly spurred by the beginnings of the computer revolution, which seemed to demonstrate that if American kids were going to grow up and compete with Japanese, they would be better off learning mathematics and science than welding and home economics. The second was that book publishing as an industry was entering into the second stage of mergers and acquisitions that was to eventually lead to the creation of a small number of publishing behemoths, themselves eventually swallowed up by even larger corporations.

Once again, the pace was set by Random House, which had been acquired from RCA by S. I. Newhouse (together with Knopf, Vintage, and Pantheon)—a plus for all concerned, it seemed, since Newhouse, whose family-owned Advance Publications had a huge stake in the newspaper and magazine business, was at least interested in the book business. Newhouse, whose ambitious acquisition of magazines was to bring him, among many others, *Vogue, Architectural Digest, Vanity Fair,* and *The New Yorker,* set out to acquire publishing houses in much the same spirit. Random House was launched on a long period of growth by acquisition. Before the decade was out, it even became the dominant publisher in the United Kingdom, including among its imprints such old and respected houses as Jonathan Cape, Chatto and Windus, and the Bodley Head.

Snyder was not about to let S&S take a backseat to Random House. Much as Dick and Martin Davis disliked each other (a fact they scarcely even bothered to hide in public and in interviews), Davis was smart enough to rely on Dick's shrewdness and acquisitive skills, so long as his ambitious and assertive subordinate stayed within the area of educational publishing. They might quarrel, Dick might brood and curse about Davis, but Dick still managed to bring off deal after successful deal, as if he was determined to extract a word of praise from Davis, who was grimly determined not to give him one. Dick first sold Silhouette (a paperback romance publisher) to Harlequin, its chief competitor, taking home a lucrative twenty-seven-year distribution agreement, then bought the moribund Stratemeyer Syndicate (which included Nancy Drew, Tom Swift, and the Hardy Boys), and acquired Prentice-Hall for $700 million, thus turning S&S overnight into a major educational, informational, and reference publisher and something of an industry giant.

If Random House had moved decisively in an attempt to dominate the trade book business throughout the English-speaking world, S&S had set out to become the world's largest publisher of educational books and material. The rest of publishing jogged behind, in a protracted spasm of smaller-scale mergers and acquisitions that were mirrored in the book-selling business: Chains forced the independent stores out of business by deep discounting, then proceeded to gobble each other up and open new stores throughout the country at a dizzying rate, mostly in the shopping malls that were coming to dominate the retail world. In short, a new world was forming in which sheer size was the key to survival—or so it was believed at the time.

Dick moved ever higher into the stratosphere of corporate management but was still determined to call the shots when it came to trade publishing, which soon gave S&S the reputation of being a hot seat for publishers. This hardly mattered to those of us who were close to Dick, however, since he was always happy to plunge back into acquiring books rather than companies and never stopped thinking of himself as the publisher of S&S even when he had given that job to somebody else—Joni Evans, briefly, Dan Green, and eventually Charles Hayward. Nobody lasted long or enjoyed the experience.

IT WAS Dick's continuing interest in the S&S list that explains how we became involved with Jesse Jackson—that and the overbearing salesmanship of Irving Lazar. Lazar had called me one day to suggest that I should buy Jackson's autobiography before somebody else grabbed it. "He's hot, kiddo. Just do me a favor and give me a quick yes or a no, because I've got a lot of interest on this one," he said urgently.

Further conversation made it clear that Lazar had nothing to show— "You can read all about Jackson in the newspapers, for chrissake, why the fuck would you need an outline?" he said—and that it was very possible he hadn't bothered to tell Jackson that he was selling his book.

All the same, the idea seemed like an attractive one to me. Jackson was a national figure, highly visible and controversial without being *too* controversial, like Louis Farrakhan, for instance. Jackson was a gadfly, sure, but he was an *establishment* gadfly, who knew exactly how to play the black card in the white world. Besides, he was, in his own way, a genuine hero, whose childhood in the South and whose years in the Movement as the protégé (whether self-proclaimed or not) of the Reverend Martin Luther King, Jr., were of genuine interest. There was a story to be told in Jesse Jackson's life, and only Jackson could tell it, if he was willing to. Finally, if there was one area in which S&S—and the book business in general—was weak, it was in the area of books by and about blacks. There seemed to me everything to be said for publishing Jackson, and I immediately called Dick to tell him so, only to find him less than enthusiastic. Jackson's star, he felt, had faded; besides, he was a troublemaker. Random House had burned their fingers badly by publishing Muhammad Ali's autobiography, and if you couldn't sell Muhammad Ali to white book buyers, you sure couldn't sell Jesse Jackson.

I could tell that Dick was not about to be budged by argument, so I called Lazar back to say no, but Lazar wasn't about to take no for an answer—a sure sign that the other interested publishers didn't exist. Dick was dead wrong, Lazar said, he just hadn't been exposed to Jackson's charisma. Five minutes with Jackson, and Dick would be singing a different tune, I could bet on that.

I wasn't about to bet on it, but after a flurry of telephone calls I was able to tell Lazar that Dick and I would be happy to join the Reverend Jackson for the lunch at Lazar's New York pied-à-terre at Sixty-sixth Street and Fifth Avenue the next time Lazar came east. Dick thought it would be a waste of time, but he had a genuine affection for Lazar, who was just the kind of larger-than-life character Dick himself was intent on becoming, and some degree of curiosity about Jackson.

On the appointed day, we settled into Dick's limo for the drive to Lazar's apartment. I detected a certain amount of restlessness on Dick's part. He liked to be well briefed before any meeting, but he knew only about Jackson what he had read in the papers. He wasn't mollified when I told him that was all *anybody* knew about Jackson. What was he going to talk to Jackson about, Dick complained, although since I assumed that Jackson was going to be doing most of the talking—he was a preacher, after all—I didn't see that as a problem. Dick picked up a copy of *Time* from the pocket in the back of the driver's seat and leafed through it. "There it is!" he said, stabbing a page with his finger. What he had found was a story about teenage pregnancy in the ghetto, in which children of thirteen, twelve, even eleven were having babies. Here was a subject with which to break the ice in talking to Jackson, he said.

Lazar let us in and made the introductions. The Reverend Jackson—his followers, as I was soon to learn, referred to him, without humor, as The Rev—was tall, with the build of an athlete beginning to run to fat, beautifully dressed, sported a gold Rolex wristwatch, and gave the impression of a man in a singularly bad mood. This, as it turned out, was entirely due to our presence. Jackson had been persuaded by Lazar, very much against his own instincts, that he should write a book. Now that he was actually here with us, however, he felt a strong resentment against having to put on a show for us—or, as one of his associates later put it, "to audition for whitey."

Even Lazar's considerable reservoir of charm failed to produce a cordial atmosphere, nor were matters helped when it was discovered that The Rev suffered from a whole complicated series of food allergies of which he had failed to inform his host, so that there was virtually nothing that he could eat of the elaborate lunch that Lazar had ordered. A tuna-salad sandwich was sent for, while the four of us sat around the dining-room table making uncomfortable small talk. It was apparent even to Dick and Lazar that there was no chance at all of asking Jackson any questions about his life or how much of it he was willing to have committed to print. On the subject of anything more personal than the weather, Jackson put up a stone wall.

Finally, Dick decided to break the ice. On the way over here, he said, he had been reading a newsmagazine and had come upon a fascinating article about teenage pregnancy. Jackson leaned forward, his face blank, an expression of impatience on his face. His eyes—remarkably small and close together for such a broad face—showed nothing, except for a certain sullen suspicion. Dick, not always the most sensitive of personalities, plunged on with his analysis of the magazine story, despite a warning glance from Lazar. Here were girls of twelve, even eleven, for chrissake, having babies! It was an outrage, a really frightening thing, didn't the Reverend Jackson agree?

The Reverend Jackson nodded. He had not touched his tuna-salad sandwich, I noticed, as if he had decided he simply wasn't going to break bread with us, but he relaxed a little, now that he had a subject to discuss. He held up one neatly manicured hand to still the flow of Dick's eloquence. "I know where you're comin' from," he said, his voice low, deep, silky, soft, a voice born for the pulpit. "You are talkin' about *babies* having *babies*."

Dick's eyes snapped open behind his tinted aviator glasses (the power symbol of Paramount at that time). That was it exactly, he said. Nobody could have put it better. Jackson had come up with just the right phrase, one that said it all.

I was pleased, but not surprised. If there was anything The Rev was good at (apart from getting money out of the pockets of guilty white folks), it was coming up with the right phrase. Words, after all, had always been the power of black Southern preachers, eloquence their stock-in-trade, the Bible the only book that mattered. The Rev was the inheritor of a long tradition. He might not be able to stop teenage pregnancy, but he could define it in a phrase better and more quickly than any *Time* editor.

Now that Dick had found his subject, he was not willing to let it go. Teenage pregnancy was a terrible problem, he went on, it blighted lives, both of the mothers and of their children. It was exactly the kind of subject on which Jackson should be speaking out, loud and clear. "The thing is," he said, looking Jackson intently in the eye, "you ought to be doing something about it, because it's a problem for your people."

There followed a hush, broken only by a snort of alarm from Lazar, who had been contentedly eating his shrimp cocktail, his mind on other things. Lazar was not exactly race sensitive, but he had been around blacks in show business long enough to know that *your people* from the mouth of a white man was fighting words, almost as bad as the *n*-word, and in fact a euphemism for it.

Jackson's nostrils flared, and his eyes became very hard indeed— hard enough that Dick became aware he had overstepped the line somehow. Jackson leaned close to him, a broad smile on his face, and speaking very slowly, as if to a child, he said, "Dick, here's the way it is. *Your* people, they go to the good schools, colleges, they study hard, they come out they get the good jobs, lawyers, doctors, big business, all that stuff." Jackson's voice dropped even lower. "All my people got is—" Before he had finished the sentence, Dick had turned to me and said, "Buy the goddamn book."

. . .

ONCE WE had reached an accord, the atmosphere lightened considerably. Jackson was jovial, though he still did not touch his sandwich, and Lazar was in good spirits, having made a deal. Occasionally, Jackson glanced at his watch—he had to catch the shuttle back to Washington, and a car was coming to pick him up. He stood up, towering high over Lazar, and we all shook hands. The Rev put a lot into his handshakes—they were warm, firm, and prolonged, and for emphasis he used both hands. "We are going to be *partners*," he said, and it was possible to believe it. There was only one small thing on his mind, however, as we walked with him to the front door. "Where's the—ah—toilet, my friend?" he asked Lazar, and a look of alarm spread across Lazar's face.

"What time is your plane?" he asked sharply.

Jackson glanced at his watch. "I have about forty-five minutes to make the shuttle."

Lazar opened the door and endeavored to push Jackson out into the hall. "Traffic is terrible," he said. "You don't have time. Wait until you get to the airport, that's my advice."

Jackson thought about this for a moment. "I only a need a minute," he said.

Lazar shook his head. "You don't know what the goddamn traffic is like, this time of day. You go when you get there."

Jackson stood his ground, glaring down at his agent. "Irving," he said slowly, "I want to go to the damn bathroom, now! Where *is* it?"

Lazar gave way reluctantly and pointed toward the bathroom. Jackson went off, did what he had to do, returned in a moment, shook hands again, and was gone.

We were about to take our own leave of Lazar, but he asked us to wait—he had something urgent to do. He, too, went to the bathroom, but as the minutes ticked by I realized that he wasn't there for a call of nature. I could hear the sibilant hiss of an aerosol container, so I walked down the corridor until I could just see through the half-opened door.

Lazar's bathroom was mirrored, floor to ceiling, and had a marble floor. Lazar, grimly determined, was on his knees by the toilet with a towel and an aerosol container of lemon-scented Lysol, vigorously spritzing every surface in sight.

. . .

OF COURSE, Lazar's germ phobia was well known—likely he would have been just as alarmed if Dick or I had used his bathroom. In any event, I think Jackson would probably have been more amused than annoyed had he caught Lazar at it. Over the years that followed, in which The Rev tried out ghost after ghost (including, improbably, Ben Stein, a Jewish conservative), I had ample opportunity to observe that Jackson was tolerant to a fault. He was willing to give anybody a chance if he thought it might be in his interest to do so, and moral judgments on others did not come easily to him, despite the fact that he was an ordained minister.

His book never got written—I finally came to the conclusion that it was not so much the choice of writers that gave him pause as some deep inner doubt about the whole idea of putting his life down on paper. Jackson was a gifted teller of anecdotes, most of them having to do with his own life, and no doubt had embellished them over the years. He had used stories about his life to make points in sermons, in political speeches, and in conversations, but the idea of sitting down with somebody who was actually going to weigh his stories against the known facts was perhaps something he did not relish.

It was impossible to be around Jackson for any time and not like the man. My assistant Nancy Nicholas and I spent many, many hours together waiting for The Rev, who liked to set meetings at the last minute, usually late at night on weekends, and who was invariably hours late. We never held it against Jackson, and the pleasure of seeing him, when he finally arrived, was always genuine.

Short of Ronald Reagan, nobody staged arrivals better than Jackson—the long wait, often in hotel lobbies, or his suite, the arrival of messengers bearing news of his whereabouts and revised ETA, finally the bustle as the Reverend Jackson's advance staff swept in, the more important ones bearing cellular telephones, others his briefcase, raincoat, even his minister's robes, splendid in purple and black, in a transparent plastic garment bag, then, at last, Jackson himself, always on the run, surrounded by a few favored journalists and a couple of stout bodyguards.

His hotel suites contained all the chaos of a presidential campaign; indeed, Jesse Jackson's life was like a permanent presidential campaign—the rows of cellular phones charging on the floor, the serving tables piled high with food and soft drinks, buckets full of melting ice, the television sets all switched to the news, with the sound off, and at least a dozen people packed into the living room, while Jackson himself huddled behind a closed door in the bedroom with a visitor or took a nap. The atmosphere was always one of crisis, even when—*especially* when—nothing was happening. When he was in good form, Jackson's eloquence was formidable. He once came to S&S to talk to the CEOs of a couple of dozen major corporations about defense spending and what it was doing to the black community, whose needs were being sacrificed to the military-industrial machine. His audience, which began as hostile, was so mesmerized that it stayed an hour longer than intended and emerged—for the moment at any rate—converted to Jackson's view. When he was tired, however, or when things weren't going his way, he could be mulish, impatient, and monosyllabic, though never discourteous—his Southern upbringing prevented that.

The only time I ever saw them together, I was struck by how greatly he and Bill Clinton resembled each other, but by that time Jackson had assumed an elder-statesman stance, Clinton having preempted The Rev's role as the party leader and communicating with blacks for himself, much to Jackson's discomfiture. It was impossible to think of them as black and white—they were merely two Southern boys, spoiled by their mamas, gifted students who had made good just the way they were supposed to, each of them married to a woman considerably stronger than himself, and each of them sharing the same ability to charm, the same attraction for the opposite sex, and the same sense of entitlement. The only difference was that Clinton was president and Jesse Jackson wasn't, but Jackson had managed to carve out a role that transcended the presidency, with his own foreign policy, his own constituency, and his own blueprint for the future. Still, I could see in Jackson's eyes that he wasn't happy. If there was one thing about him that I learned during the many years of working on various versions of his book, it was that the Reverend Jackson liked to be the center of attention.

WELL, WHO doesn't? you might say. Indeed, in the eighties most of us fulfilled Andy Warhol's prophecy by becoming the center of attention briefly, starting with Dick Snyder and Joni Evans. Joni's career path took the shape of a neon zigzag. Dick decided that despite the difficulties, he needed Joni Evans as publisher of S&S again, so Linden Press (much to my regret as a Linden author) was closed down. After that, however, their marriage began to falter, and Joni left to run Random House, replacing Howard Kaminsky, a diminutive dynamo of a man. Kaminsky went to Morrow, while Joni was moved crosstown to head a new Random House imprint, Turtle Bay Books (named after the area in which the imprint's brownstone lay), which was soon closed down, leaving Joni jobless until she changed gears and reemerged as a William Morris agent.

From this one can deduce certain things, the first being that it's probably not a good idea for a husband and a wife to work together in the same place, particularly if they have high-profile jobs. (Ironically, Joni and I had collaborated to edit Mary Cunningham's book about herself and Bill Agee, the CEO of Bendix who had first mentored her, then had an affair with her, then married her, following which they both had to leave.) The second lesson is that almost no relationship can survive the kind of media scrutiny that was being given to book publishing. Perhaps most important of all, the old idea that job security was one of the benefits of publishing was, at last, definitely dead and buried.

THE ARGUMENT for working in book publishing had always been that while the pay was low and the perks consisted of nothing more than free lunches and all the books you could read, in most places you had to work hard at it to get fired. By the 1980s, that was no longer true. At the higher levels of book publishing, the pay was actually pretty good, and in those houses that were owned by big corporations or media conglomerates or movie studios, the perks began to include (at any rate for a lucky few) stock options, bonus plans, special retirement funds, a leased car, free parking, discounts on anything the parent company manufactured—all the bells and whistles, in short, of corporate America. At the very highest level, the cornucopia was tilted even more steeply and disgorged such goodies as private dining rooms, the use of corporate jets, and company-paid apartments.

While these benefits were limited to a very small number of people at the largest houses, the consequences went all the way down through organizations. When companies were merged and acquired, people got fired—indeed, that was one of the major reasons for merging and acquiring in the first place—and the need to make each year better than the one before in order to satisfy the corporate parent meant that more and more people got hired and fired as quick fixes. You didn't find your editors in-house anymore, nor your executives. You hired a headhunter to raid other houses for editors, tried them out, and if they didn't measure up quickly, you fired them and started all over again. Since, increasingly, the editors didn't expect to be at a house for very long, they left the moment they had a better offer elsewhere. Star editors were wooed and fought over by major houses, though all too often they turned out to be past their peaks when they moved or to have grandiose illusions about becoming publishers.

Job security had always had two faces—on one side, the loyalty of the company toward the employee and the promise that he or she would be kept there for the long haul, and on the other side, the employee's loyalty toward the company and his or her willingness to be patient and trust that long service would bring its own rewards. With companies being merged, bought, and sold, however, that kind of patience and trust was increasingly meaningless—the people who owned you had probably never heard of you, had no idea what you did, and couldn't have cared less anyway. This was all the more difficult in the case of editors because it is hard to measure what they do in any simple way: The next book of the author whose novel has just failed may be a huge bestseller; an editor switching jobs might inherit a list and thereby get credit for a surprise best-seller he or she had nothing to do with. In any event, the gestation of books (and of editors, for that matter) is a long one, requiring considerable patience and optimism, and the process of editing is not one that lends itself to dramatic color photographs in the parent company's annual report. The story goes that when Rupert Murdoch bought Harper and Row (which he was later to merge not very successfully with Collins, his U.K. book publishing acquisition), he walked down "editors' row" and, seeing a lot of people bent over the desks reading, asked what the hell they thought they were doing and when they were going to get to work. (The story is told about several people, but it fits Murdoch better than most.) All of this meant that while the salaries were climbing a little, job security plummeted.

So did prestige. Even as late as the 1970s, a publishing house was basically an organization built around its editors, and the connection between ownership and the editors was strong, personal, and direct. The rest of the company consisted of service departments that were in most ways subordinated to the needs of the editors. To the extent that there was any glamour to publishing, it was provided by the editors.

With the appearance of big, merged publishing houses, the picture changed. The glamour, such as it was, was at the top, where houses were bought, sold, and merged, new imprints created, and multimillion-dollar deals made. Slowly but surely, the editors were relegated to the status of pieceworkers. If they provided a steady flow of profitable books, they were rewarded—very often with bonuses instead of salary increases, since a bonus can be withheld the next year whereas a salary increase is forever—if they did not, they were fired, and new ones brought in. Both the power and the prestige of their position were stripped from them, as the decisions they once made unilaterally were assigned to others, and as layers of management were created to supervise and quantify the editors' work. The editors were no longer at the *center* of the company in a large publishing house, but on the periphery, at once part of a large and growing bureaucracy and the focus of its attention.

From the point of view of management, the editors are just about the hardest part of the publishing process to deal with, except of course for the authors themselves. It is hardly surprising that most publishing houses are now run by people who would just as soon climb Everest without oxygen as edit a book (or, in some cases, *read* one). If you want to know what's happening in the other departments of a company, you can get numbers, printouts, bar graphs, charts, the kind of thing that appeals to business-minded persons and is thought to make sense, but the editors deal not in numbers, which hardly ever prove anything when it comes to books, but in ideas, hunches, style, most treacherous of all, *words*.

Most of the really big mistakes in book publishing come from ignoring the importance of words in favor of numbers or personalities. Of course, it's easier to buy books by numbers, which explains why so many bad books by novelists at the tail ends of their careers still get bought for millions of dollars. It's a lot easier (and quicker) to make decisions by digging up the previous sales figures, calculating the royalty earnings, adding on foreign sales, and so on than to actually *read* the book. Most of the big writers who regularly grace the best-seller list are bought and sold without anybody going to the trouble of reading the manuscript—indeed, such deals are usually made *without* a manuscript, purely on track record and numbers. A lot of publishers are far more comfortable dealing with a P&L than a manuscript anyway—the numbers can be crunched, studied, fine-tuned, but they're *real,* as opposed to the author's words, which, even if available, merely produce more words, in the form of subjective reports from the editors.

As for celebrities, they too represent a way of buying a book for a lot of money without having to read anything. By definition, the celebrity isn't going to write the book—he or she is merely selling his celebrity. Here again, fame can be quantified: The number of people who have seen a star's movies can be counted, the sales of a singer's record albums are available, their worth as assets carefully assessed, which is a great comfort to people who would rather deal in numbers than in words, or have lunch with movie stars and politicians instead of writers.

FAILING ANYTHING better in the way of celebrity, murders will do, provided the case is sufficiently splashy. I myself published Flora Rheta Schreiber's book about Joseph Kallinger, the humble shoemaker of Philadelphia who went on a killing spree with one of his own sons. For many years, I received a Christmas card from Kallinger, who was in the state institution for the criminally insane in Pennsylvania, where he was unwisely placed in the shoe-repair shop at first, thus giving him access to the same sharp, curved shoemaker's knife with which he had carved up a number of people during his heyday as a serial killer, with results that would have been predictable to anybody but a psychiatrist. Still, it wasn't Kallinger or any of the other murderers whose books I published who brought me the most attention but somebody who, in the end, got off: Claus von Bülow.

To be more exact, it was von Bülow's then mistress, Andrea Reynolds, a Hungarian beauty with a background that read like the plot of an Ouida novel, who came to the attention of Joni Evans and me. Reynolds (who was eventually to soar to respectability as Lady Plunkett) was then at the height of her notoriety, having fled from life as a wealthy housewife to the defense of von Bülow, whom she scarcely knew, convinced of his innocence. She quickly became the Passionaria of von Bülow's legal tribulations, as well as his mistress. Since few other people, so far as one could tell, believed that von Bülow was innocent of having attempted to murder his fabulously wealthy wife, this caused something of a sensation. It was no doubt in part Andrea's sheer determination to prove the rest of the world (not to speak of a Rhode Island jury) wrong that helped get von Bülow through the second trial, in which his conviction was overruled.

The notion that Andrea was going to write a tell-all insider's account of what really happened in one of the most sensational criminal cases of the 1980s would be enough to attract any publisher, and it was considered a remarkable coup that Joni Evans and I managed to get to her before anybody else—indeed, my involvement was based partly upon the belief that as a Hungarian and the author of *Charmed Lives* I would be irresistible to Andrea Reynolds, while as an Oxford-educated Englishman von Bülow and I would have much in common. As luck would have it, I had recently been awarded the George Washington medal by the Hungarian-American Society for being the most distinguished Hungarian-American of the year. As a result, I knew plenty of people who were acquainted with Reynolds, most of whom, when asked about her, raised their eyebrows and shrugged expressively. Hungarians have a certain admiration for those of their countrywomen who achieve fame for their beauty or their abilities as seducers of men, which explains the national pride in the careers of the Gabor sisters and their mother, so I was thus not surprised, when Joni and I finally met Andrea Reynolds, to find that she was a vivacious, shrewd, and voluptuous woman, with that peculiarly Hungarian combination of beauty and a razor-sharp tongue that is perhaps only truly appreciated by Hungarian men and explains, perhaps, much of the melancholy with which they approach marriage.

At any rate, Andrea entertained us at lunch with gossip about the trial and convinced us that the book would be full of headline-making news. Snyder, perhaps because he was trying to keep Joni happy, authorized us to buy the book, for which he ended up paying a lot more money than we had anticipated, with a lot of it up front, since Andrea turned out—not very surprisingly, in retrospect—to be a sharp bargainer who recognized two eager marks when she saw them and employed a first-rate power lawyer.

Shortly afterward, Joni and I went to see Andrea and Claus in their Fifth Avenue apartment—or rather Sunny von Bülow's apartment, for her presence was everywhere, like that of a ghost, though she herself was still in a coma, as she remains to this day, across town in a luxurious hospital room, surrounded by some of her favorite pieces of furniture, with a manicurist and a hairdresser who visit her every week. The apartment was huge, taking up a whole floor, so that the elevator let one out into a hallway with only one door. It had high ceilings and big windows overlooking Central Park, but despite that there was something dark and gloomy about it—maybe a result of its sheer size and formality, the carved wood paneling, the antique tapestries, the dark, unidentifiable Old Master style paintings, the heavy drapes, or perhaps even the servants, who were silent, grave, and strangely glum. The dining room was enormous, but something about it suggested that it had been many years since it had been used, a feeling one had about most of the big rooms that we were led through.

Andrea greeted us in a small sitting room, slightly more cheerful than the rest of the apartment and crowded with antique furniture and expensive bric-a-brac and bibelots, like a Madison Avenue antique shop. There was a well-used backgammon board on the coffee table. Claus was a striking figure. Very tall, broad shouldered, once athletic, he was dressed casually in a sweater, tan trousers, and moccasins, and it was easy to see how he had charmed Sunny not so many years ago, when she had still been married to the dashing and notoriously unfaithful Prince Alfie von Auersperg.

Sunny had been something of a throwback (it was hard not to think about her as if she was dead), a tall, beautiful American heiress of enormous wealth, whose ambition, so far as one can tell, was to marry into the European nobility. A hundred years ago, this was common enough, when the daughters of the robber barons of New York and the meat packers of Chicago were shipped across the Atlantic with their mamas and trunks full of clothes to look for the right kind of husband: a duke, or a prince, with the right bloodlines, a castle, *Schloss*, chateau, or palace, and a need for ready cash. By the end of World War Two, however, this was already the stuff of musical comedies rather than real life. Sunny appeared, in this as in so many other ways, to be hopelessly out-of-date. Nevertheless, her ambition was to be part of the aristocratic European fast set and to marry into it, which she did twice, with all-but-fatal results.

Claus himself had belonged to this set only on sufferance. It was said that he had appropriated the *von* to his name, he wasn't rich, and, having read law at Oxford, he eventually found himself a job working for the eccentric American oil billionaire John Paul Getty in England, where Getty lived in self-imposed and splendid exile. What Claus actually *did* for Getty is not altogether clear, but it gave him ample scope to play the man-about-town and to move easily in the circle of the international rich, where a good-looking, charming, and well-dressed single man with the right kind of manners was always welcome. In a way, Claus was as much of a throwback as Sunny, with his unapologetic snobbery, his life of ease as the husband of a rich woman, his fin-de-siècle elegance, and his weary sophistication. How many men these days had no profession, no job, and apparently no ambition?

Indeed, Claus did not seem to have accomplished much in his life (though many people no doubt regarded his marrying Sunny as the accomplishment of a lifetime, given her fortune). Even his notoriety was of recent date, acquired only when he was accused, tried, and convicted of trying to murder Sunny. Marriage had enabled him to live like a rich man, and the accusation of attempted murder had made him famous.

His expression was that of a man who was amused by both fame and fortune. He had a good face for a villain (if he *was* one): a supercilious, slightly lopsided smile, a long, slightly crooked nose, a raised eyebrow, sharp little eyes for such a big, strongly featured face. Absent the Prince Valiant hairdo and the funny hat, he reminded me of Olivier's portrayal of Richard III, at once amused and gratified by the horror he inspires in other people. Claus, it was easy enough to see, hugely enjoyed his notoriety, which, like that of the Marquis de Sade, had an unmistakable whiff of decadence and sexual kinkiness to it. At his trial, his relationship to prostitutes and drug dealers was alluded to, and his former mistress, the beautiful Alexandra Isles, actually testified against him. It was even rumored that von Bülow practiced necrophilia, an accusation that he denied, but without any particular vehemence. I guessed that he would rather be accused of anything than of being middle-class. His strength, in fact, was that he not only was unshockable himself but rather enjoyed shocking people. I suspected that this might have been the reason why the charge of attempted murder was directed against him in the first place: He had made himself seem like just the kind of man who might do it.

We sat down and, while tea was served and Joni and Andrea exchanged gossip, Claus and I conversed about England. His voice was curious—upper-class English, with only the faintest trace of Europe buried deep in the background and a tendency to laugh loudly at his own jokes. We were very quickly at ease with each other, perhaps because so much of my early life was spent around people who were self-created. Claus seemed to have invented himself as a cynical dandy, cultivating a certain Byronic pose.

Claus was at pains to make it clear that the book was going to be Andrea's and Andrea's alone. He would not interfere or influence her; she should tell the story as she saw it. Andrea laughed. "It will be *our* story, darling," she said firmly—after all, she had sold the book to us on the basis that it would be as close as anyone could ever get to having Claus tell his story—and from the expression on her face it was easy to judge who the dominant partner was in this relationship. Claus lit a cigarette and smiled blandly. Whatever his relationship had been with Sunny, he did not argue with Andrea. He gave the strong impression, in fact, that he never argued with anybody, that he was always in agreement, which perhaps explains why people were puzzled and even angry when that turned out not to have been the case.

Would we like to see the apartment? Andrea asked. Of course, we were unable to resist, so we were taken on a brief tour. Along the way, we met Claus and Sunny's daughter, who said hello quietly then leapt into another room like a startled deer. It was beyond mere shyness—it was the involuntary flight of a girl who has been exposed to more tragic incursions than she can bear and for whom, perhaps, the idea that Andrea was going to write a book about her father was the last straw. We went through an enormous, old-fashioned kitchen, the kind that required a small army of servants, hardly a place in which a young girl could get a glass of milk and a few cookies for herself, then down a short flight into a plain-looking room full of metal garment racks hung with clothing. In the center of this sat an elderly lady behind a sewing machine, working away. I wondered if the clothes had once belonged to Sunny.

I thought of Sunny herself, dressed carefully every day in an expensive negligée, her hair and nails done, unconscious and kept alive only by machines, and all of a sudden I wondered whether the book was such a good idea after all.

Years later, when I saw Al Pacino play the devil in *The Devil's Advocate,* I realized to my surprise that the apartment in which he took up residence in New York looked exactly like that of the von Bülows.

. . .

WORK ON the book progressed quickly, according to Andrea, even though—against our advice—she had chosen to write it herself, without help. As time went by, we became more familiar with Claus. He had a slightly heavy-handed sense of humor, a kind of leaden German joviality, and his charm, while constantly on display, could wear through to reveal a certain snappish petulance and some impatience when things did not go as he expected them to or when he was bored. Andrea worked hard to keep him amused, but I was reminded of Madame de Maintenon's weary comment about Louis XIV when she was the mistress of his old age: "Quelle horreur d'avoir à amuser un homme inamusable" (What a terrible thing it is to have to amuse a man who is unamusable).

We took them to Rao's, where Claus was treated with the grave courtesy owed a man who had beaten a murder rap, for dinner with Irving Lazar, who was eager to meet them—he was furious that he hadn't signed up Andrea as a client and determined to get Claus to write a book of his own (an idea that Claus tactfully discouraged). During dinner, Andrea and I fell into a discussion about writing and editing (now that she was working on her book, she had taken on the airs of a writer and spoke of her new profession with grave authority), while Claus became increasingly bored, as was often the case when he was not the center of attention, at least of Andrea's. Eventually, during a pause in our conversation, he interrupted. "Well," he said, in his low voice, very slowly so that all attention was focused on him, "I'm an expert on comas, not commas."

There was a moment of silence, then Lazar said, rather loudly, "Jesus Christ, he *did* it!" The same thought must have occurred to everyone around the table at the same time, because after that the dinner broke up rather quickly—there was none of the usual sitting around over coffee and brandy.

Shortly after my belief, such as it was, in Claus's innocence was shaken, my confidence that we were going to get the book we wanted was also shattered when Andrea delivered her manuscript. We discovered that it was alarmingly reticent on the subject of Claus von Bülow and concentrated mostly on her own childhood, which, however picaresque, was not what we felt we had paid for. A tug-of-war followed in which we demanded more sensational newsbreaks and more about

Claus and his trials, while she dug her heels in, and eventually we turned down the manuscript and never got our money back, yet another example of the dangers of celebrity publishing.

CHAPTER 33

*A*s THE EIGHTIES drew to a close, publishing was beginning to go through another period of rapid change, as the book suddenly seemed to be the way in which major news was made. Of course, books had always made news, but for the most part indirectly. Rachel Carson's *Silent Spring* had made news by drawing the public's attention to environmental threats, but the material in the book had run in *The New Yorker* first, as had John Hersey's *Hiroshima* and Hannah Arendt's *Eichmann in Jerusalem*.

In the seventies, however, Woodward and Bernstein's *All the President's Men* and *The Final Days* not only made news but *were* news. By the time Woodward wrote *Wired*, his book about the life and death of John Belushi, the "embargo strategy" had been adopted by many publishers, sometimes for books where a premature leak might matter, more often just to give the impression that a book contained newsworthy material when it didn't. Books were thus not only an extension of journalism but a *subject* for journalistic scrutiny, as were, by extension, the people who published them.

This was something new. Books never brought people news. News was the business of papers or, later, radio and television. Now books, despite the slow, creaky, shade-tree-mechanic nature of producing them, which had not changed much since the invention of movable type, were becoming news carriers, even though it normally took nine months to go from a complete manuscript to a finished book, or perhaps three months if it was done on a "crash" basis, which required putting most of any publisher's production department to work on a single title.

The "instant" book had been created by paperback publishers to capitalize on a news event, like the many brought out immediately after the Israeli raid on Entebbe, in 1976, but "instant" books were now *making* news, which led, among other things, to a whole new relationship between book publishing and the press that was at once far more competitive and far more antagonistic. In any event, book publishing, so long as it remained small and relatively unprofitable as businesses go, had never been of much interest to the press to begin with—now that publishing houses had grown into major companies, often allied with even larger ones, as S&S was with Paramount, changes and events in the publishing business became legitimate news.

Until the eighties, most book publishers weren't big enough to have anything interesting to hide, and any gossip worth printing would have been about the authors, not the people who worked in publishing houses. From the eighties on, publishing houses were growing and acquiring so fast that they nearly always had something to hide, if only from the financial press, while many editors and executives were getting more press than authors. Part of the reason why journalists began to pay more attention to book publishing was that it was neither far away nor a world apart, the way the movie business is; book publishing took place on the Boston/New York/Washington shuttle axis, and most people in book publishing were accessible, rather than walled off from the press by PR people. So long as somebody like Lee Iacocca stayed behind his desk, he was hard to get to, and any interviews would be with company PR men present to ensure that nothing controversial was addressed, but the moment he wrote a book, he was out there in the open, eager to be interviewed by anybody, if he thought the interview would sell books. In short, he was just like any other author, and you could ask him questions you could never have asked him otherwise and get answers, too.

The book, after all, has a totemic significance, and not only to the ancient Hebrews. Even today, when the role of the computer in education is becoming ever more significant, children in the Judeo-Christian scheme of things have it drummed into their heads at an early age that the book is something special, that books in general are worthy of respect, a good thing. People might not *read* them, but they respect them.

Somehow, books have managed to keep something of their sacred aura—misused, ghostwritten, edited until they scarcely bear any relationship to the original manuscript, sometimes so denuded of meaning as to call for a special category called "nonbooks," shipped out by the truckload as "merch" (a category even lower than nonbooks), used as a political tool by aspirant or retiring politicians (the dreaded "campaign biography" being the lowest form of this category) and as a means of striking back at ex-spouses by celebrities, the book is nevertheless central to our culture in a way that nothing else—movies, tapes, newspapers, television, or magazines—can or, very likely, ever will be.

AS THE eighties gave way to the nineties, where once publishers had complained there were not enough stores in which to sell books, they suddenly became impossible to escape. The wholesale building of new stores in shopping malls put bookstores all across the country where few or none had existed before, and in just the place where people might be expected to buy them, if they were going to buy them at all. Soon superstores—close to the malls but in large buildings of their own—eclipsed the stores in the malls, while price clubs at major retailers offered best-sellers at enormous discounts.

The British and Europeans, who had always looked down their noses at American book-selling techniques and boasted that in France or Germany people bought far more books per person than in America, found themselves stumbling to catch up with the transformation of America's bookstores into book supermarkets with bright lighting, discounts, floor displays, shopping baskets, shopping carts, checkout counters, and hours that kept the stores open seven days a week until late at night, instead of being closed on just those days and at just those times when ordinary people might be free to buy a book, which had always been the traditional way of selling books. It was as if the American genius for merchandising, which had invented discounting and the supermarket in the first place, had at last been directed toward that most ancient piece of merchandise, the book, with startling results.

The immediate effect was not necessarily to enlarge the pool of readers (or to make the average American reader any more inclined than before to buy literary first novels or translations of European fiction) but to deal an almost fatal blow to the mass-market paperback business. Readers who had formerly been willing to wait a year to read major best-selling writers in paperback now "moved up" to hardcover books in droves, as discounting pushed the price of best-sellers down. In any case, it was not just the price of hardcover books that had kept many readers from buying them—previously, many bookstores had been hostile to the kind of people who bought big best-selling fiction in paperback. There was a certain snobbery to selling books, and many bookstores found it easy to make potential customers feel uncomfortable and out of place. The new bookstores solved this problem by emulating that most user-friendly of familiar (and classless) institutions, the supermarket. It worked so well that for a while it was hard to find mass-market books in any quantity except in major airports.

IN THE meantime, the computer—which in some publishers' doomsday scenario had replaced motion pictures and television as the invention that would bring the printed word to the end of its long run—turned out instead to offer publishers significant advantages, and not just as a business tool. The computer brought about a long-awaited revolution in the way manuscripts were processed. The illegible, intractable, smudged, and grimy pages that made up most manuscripts had always defied rationalization. It was a fact recognized with a sigh of resignation that the better a writer was, the more sloppy his or her manuscript was likely to be. Since the age of Gutenberg, copy editors and printers had gone blind before their time in the struggle to decode page after page of manuscript and render it correctly in type.

The archetype of the writing genius who wrote all his books in a crabbed, illegible hand was Tolstoy, whose pages were typed on a primitive typewriter by the unfortunate Countess Tolstoy, who alone could decipher his handwriting. Much corrected by him, these pages were then sent to Tolstoy's publisher in Moscow, where printers puzzled over each line and handwritten change, crossed themselves and hoped for the best, then set it all in type. Tolstoy then corrected and rewrote in galley proofs, not once but over and over again, his changes and additions circling tortuously round and round the margins of the galley sheets until they took on the appearance of the Dead Sea Scrolls or perhaps a black-and-white work by Jackson Pollock. When Tolstoy was completing *War and Peace,* he did this so many times that his exasperated publisher finally sent a telegram to him in Yasnaya Polyana that read simply: DEAR LEV NIKOLAYEVICH—IN THE NAME OF GOD, STOP!

Things had not changed much if at all in all the time since Tolstoy wrote *War and Peace.* The speed with which a manuscript could be turned into a book was still dependent on hand labor and good eyesight, and printers and copy editors alike were of necessity outrageously overeducated for their jobs. It was common enough for copy editors to be fluent in several languages and more knowledgeable about most things than the vast majority of the writers whose work they edited—indeed, most authors depended on the copy editor to make sure their dates were correct, their quotations in order, their notes properly done, and to save them in short from mistakes, ignorance, and carelessness. Given the amount of time this process took, and the fact that it had to be done over and over again in manuscript, in galleys, and in pages, the task was inevitably a slow one—it was possible to fly the Atlantic in under four hours and for a man to have walked on the moon, but manuscripts moved through the production process at the speed of a sharp pencil and no faster.

The computer—and its offspring, the word processor—changed much of that. It did not eliminate copy editors or printers, but at least it had the potential to speed up their work. The author could now hand his book in on a disk, the disk could be corrected and used to set type—the only reason for a hard copy (as the paper manuscript now came to be called) was so that the editor could read it, since the editors remained a nonelectronic link in the process, for the most part, still reading the old-fashioned way and making their changes in pencil. Indexing a book, for example, once a weary matter of reading every page carefully and noting each name down on a three-by-five card, could now be done electronically—and since time is money, the cost inevitably went down. Of course some writers and most editors remained stubborn holdouts, but it quickly became normal to demand that an author produce his or her book on disk, and that part of the business which had hardly changed since Gutenberg set his first Bible into type at last took a great leap forward.

These changes were symbolized, at S&S at any rate, by the appearance of a matte black laptop computer on the polished veneer console behind Dick Snyder's desk. It was not, to be sure, that Dick himself had any intention of learning how to use a laptop, but he recognized before most of his fellow publishers that the computer was going to change a lot of things in book publishing and that it was crucial to be ahead of the wave. His colleagues were surprised at—and mildly amused by—Dick's interest in computer technology, since it would be hard to find a man more technologically challenged in ordinary life, but the laptop behind his desk, though a prop, was the symbol of his determination to move S&S into the twenty-first century ahead of schedule.

Dick had always shown a certain interest in technology. Years before, when VCRs were still a novelty and the battle between the VHS and the Sony Betamax format was being fought, Dick had tried to persuade James Beard to do a cooking tape. It was his idea that the S&S sales reps would get a whole package to sell—a book by Beard, a videotape version of the book starring Beard, and perhaps even a line of prepared foods by Beard. (He had in mind a freezer in the trunk of every sales rep's car.) Nothing came of it (unless you count the fact that I had a delicious meal in Beard's kitchen while trying to persuade him that his future was on tape rather than in books), but Dick did not forget. In the eighties, he challenged industry wisdom by plunging into the videotape business after discovering to his rage that the people who owned the videotape rights to *Jane Fonda's Workout Book* were making even more money out of the tape than S&S was out of the book. Dick abruptly ordered his editors to get video rights every time they bought a book—no exceptions—and promptly set up a new division to exploit these rights. In the event, most agents refused to give up video rights, which went the way of movie rights in the twenties and thirties, and the S&S video division never got off the ground. It had spawned, however, almost as an afterthought, an audio division, which soon expanded into a major business; by the end of the nineties, S&S was the world's largest publisher of audiotapes.

Thus, it was only natural that Dick should have been fascinated by the computer and determined to makes S&S the leader in a field that had not yet even been defined. Without most of us paying much attention to what was happening, Dick advanced on two fronts, ambitiously as always. He set out, first of all, to integrate the computer into the daily work of everybody at S&S, an enormous investment that after considerable difficulties resulted in a computer terminal on every desk. At the same time, he set out to make S&S the industry leader in the field of computer books, in pursuit of which he set out on a buying spree that eventually led to the acquisition of Macmillan from the estate of that notorious rogue elephant of the English financial world, Robert Maxwell, known to the English tabloid press as "Captain Bob."

Dick had tried to do business with Maxwell before and nearly acquired Maxwell's scientific-publishing assets at a price that would have been the coup of the century, but Martin Davis rejected the deal, to Dick's anger and mortification. Fortunately for Dick, Captain Bob's ship was destined to hit the rocks in a storm of scandal a few years later after Maxwell died suddenly—the rape of the employees' pension funds was almost the least of the posthumous charges against him—and S&S

acquired large parts of Macmillan at a bargain price, becoming the biggest educational publisher in the world and far and away the strongest publisher of computer books. (S&S also ended up with the Free Press, Scribner, and Atheneum, all of which Captain Bob had managed to pick up while people still thought he was solvent.) The publishing house that Shimkin had sold to G+W in 1975 for $11 million in stock was now a multibillion-dollar publishing colossus in which the educational, reference, and computer business dwarfed the trade end. From Dick's perspective, the future was already here and about to pay off.

Nor was he alone. Out there beyond Rockefeller Center, vast changes were taking place throughout the publishing industry. Buying up distinguished English publishing houses one after the other, S. I. Newhouse had made Random House the biggest publisher of trade books in the English-speaking world, setting off a trend that made Random House Australia's leading publisher and placed S&S offices in such cities as London, Moscow, and Singapore. The German Bertelsmann group had already bought Doubleday, which itself had acquired numerous other publishing houses, as well as the Literary Guild. A different German publishing company was soon to end up with Farrar, Straus and Giroux, despite the many years Roger Straus had fulminated at the way big companies were buying up the publishing industry, Dick being his special target. The Pearson group, a U.K. publishing conglomerate, eventually picked up Viking, merged it with Penguin, then added to it Putnam to form a formidable international publishing company. The purchase of Time Inc. by Warner merged all of Time's book-publishing assets—including the formerly august Boston firm of Little, Brown, the Book-of-the-Month Club, and Time-Life books—with Warner's, creating yet another publishing giant.

Since the booksellers were following the same path—expanding at a furious rate while consolidating by purchasing the smaller or weaker chains—it seemed likely that there would soon be two major book chains plus a rapidly diminishing number of specialty and independent stores, the futures of which were, to put it mildly, uncertain. Typically, New York's Fifth Avenue, along the plush midtown strip between Fifty-seventh Street and Forty-eighth Street, which had once boasted two Doubleday bookstores (which stayed open until midnight), Scribner's landmark bookstore, the Rizzoli store that specialized in art books, as well as a B. Dalton and a Barnes and Noble store within a few blocks of each other, was quickly reduced to only one store. Across the country, famous stores and chains collapsed or were bought up—Pickwick, in Los Angeles, Kroch-Brentano and Stuart Brent, in Chicago, bookstores that had been part of the publishing scene for decades, simply vanished, replaced by superstores in the suburbs and by chain outlets in the shopping malls, themselves often swept out of business by the superstores and the price clubs.

Thus, the book-publishing industry seemed at last to have made the transformation from cottage industry to big business. True, it still rested on imponderables—little old ladies typing away at their novels on kitchen tables; the whims of writers; four-page outlines of books that were sold for hundreds of thousands of dollars, or even millions, on buzz alone—but most of the bigger publishers had covered themselves against these uncertainties by going into other, more predictable (and profitable) businesses, such as education. Besides, once you were beyond a certain size, you could absorb failures that might have sunk a publishing house in the old days, when a single best-seller could make the difference between wealth and bankruptcy. Insofar as any business whose foundations rest on such insubstantials as a writer's imagination and insight might be thought of as solid, book publishing appeared more firmly planted than it had ever been before.

Of course, that was an illusion.

CHAPTER 34

When your government talks of peace, your draft card is already in the mail.

—BERTOLT BRECHT

*T*HE EARLY 1990S may now be seen as the calm before the storm, but of course one could not have guessed that then. Looking back on it, there were warning signs of major changes to come, but I no more perceived them than I did the fact that I would be diagnosed with prostate cancer in 1994. I could not have felt healthier or in better shape and would have been astonished to learn that I was in for major surgery and the scare of a lifetime. I would have been just as astonished had some Gypsy soothsayer foretold many of the changes that were to sweep over book publishing before the end of the decade. It is just when we feel ourselves to be on solid ground that the ground opens before us.

The nineties were a time of success for almost everyone in book publishing—the proliferation of new stores drove sales up in almost every category of book except the literary novel, while discounting made the price of hardcover books—the best-sellers, at any rate—seem almost reasonable. Bookselling was no longer part of the carriage trade, and ordinary people were buying books in unprecedented numbers. Admittedly, a lot of them weren't the kind of books that would have pleased Henry Robbins, had he still been alive to complain, but among all the "merch" and dreck that cluttered up the aisles and the counters of the new bookstores, a surprising number of real books managed to sell. Perhaps the greatest miracle of the book industry is the way in which the public will, given the opportunity, home in on a good book by an unknown writer and make it a surprise best-seller (often surprising the publisher more than anybody). The nineties were to be extraordinarily rich in such books and continue to be as I write. The successes of *Longitude, The Perfect Storm, Angela's Ashes, Into Thin Air,* and *Cold Mountain* are each, in their own ways, perfect examples of the public's ability to discern a remarkable book despite all the attention directed toward bad or mediocre ones. If nothing else, this serves to remind us that even the most careful and expensive marketing plans cannot sell people a book they don't want to read. Hugh Collins is still right.

THE PACE of change in the world of publishing continued relentlessly in the 1990s. The eyes of publishers were now trained on all those English-speaking countries that had once been rendered on the world map as part of the British Empire and which were now accessible at last to American publishers, if only because the Americans had bought up so many English houses, or, as in the case of S&S, founded their own.

The old distinctions that had separated the English-speaking world into the United States (plus the Philippines and sometimes Canada), the United Kingdom and the British Commonwealth, and the "open market" (i.e., the rest of the world), which English publishers had defended fiercely for decades, collapsed almost as fast as the Berlin Wall and at about the same time. The new world market had no divisions. Books were sold wherever there was a demand for them or a place in the local bookstores. The bigger a publisher was, the more fit it would be to take advantage of the world marketplace—another reason for growth.

Publishing was now a hot international business, the favorite child of the information age. With the fall of the Soviet Union and its satellite empire, a whole new world opened up—one of readers who had been deprived of the truth for nearly fifty years, as well as being deprived of Western entertainment. The world was reading English—or busy learning it—and hungrily consuming books of every kind.

AND YET, behind the facade of prosperity, growth, and optimism, there was a certain unease to be felt, a kind of *après nous le déluge* feeling that it was all too good to be true and wouldn't last. For the simple truth remained that the old problem of book publishing hadn't changed: You shipped out a lot of copies, you were at the mercy of the big bookstore chains to get them displayed and sold, and the ones they didn't sell you took back for full credit.

Much of what had happened to book publishing since the 1960s would have seemed incredible or marvelous to Max Schuster, Dick Simon, or Bennett Cerf, but the retail end would have seemed depressingly familiar. It was merely, on a larger scale, the same old story that had been worrying publishers ever since the Depression. Now, of course, it was further complicated by the fact that there were only two major bookstore chains, which wanted to dominate the publishing process, insisting on changes in jackets, titles, prices, and so forth, before they agreed to stock a book in any quantity. The business had mushroomed far beyond anybody's expectations, but it still stood on feet of clay when it came to actually selling the product.

Snyder thought that he had found a solution: expand into textbook and informational publishing, which were more predictable businesses, and where the rate of growth and overseas expansion were far more favorable. Others thought that the solution might lie in pursuing market share. This was the "German solution" to the problem, based simply on the fact that in Germany, where the book business was dominated by a very few major players and where book clubs were far more important than in the United States, market share mattered as much in selling books as it did in selling refrigerators or any other kind of consumer goods. Newhouse had dabbled with the strategy, perhaps accidentally, as a result of simple eagerness to acquire more and more publishing companies, perhaps because to anybody in the newspaper and magazine business, market share is the Holy Grail.

The Newhouse organization, like the rival Gannett organization, had been adept at turning places with two or three newspapers into one-newspaper towns, on the sensible principle that the best competition is no competition, and transferred the same simple technique to the magazine business, insofar as possible. Thus, growth and sheer size were not simply a question of ambition, but of *strategy*. If you added together Random House, Knopf, Pantheon, Vintage, Villard, Crown, Times Books, Ballantine, and Fawcett, not to speak of innumerable London publishing houses, you could begin to think about dominating the market, in addition to which, if one of your imprints failed to pick up a major author, there was at least a good chance that one of the others would. Really, on paper, it looked like the answer to the problem—one or two major publishing companies confronting one or two major bookstore chains. Reduce competition, and you could minimize your costs by consolidating shipping, marketing, bookkeeping, and so on, eliminating much of the inherent wastefulness of traditional book publishing.

It looked to some like a reasonable idea, but in practice it didn't seem to make much difference, maybe because there were simply too many major players left and maybe because nobody at Random House took it seriously. In any event, people's attention at Random House as the nineties unfolded was riveted on the question of whether Harry Evans, the energetic and media-conscious former journalist, was a swashbuckling genius who had found at last a way to popularize books and authors or a loose cannon about to sink the ship.

To outsiders, it seemed that Evans was onto something—his media-genic publishing breakfasts at Barneys, his cheerful optimism, the big risks he took, his willingness to talk to the press, and his sense of humor and lack of self-importance, all had the feel of a fresh breeze in a stuffy room to people in other publishing houses but seemed to provoke the equivalent of class warfare among his colleagues. It is, of course, always risky to enter publishing late in life from another profession. Publishing people are by nature clannish and suspicious of outsiders, and Evans was a celebrity, a social figure, a famously expatriate Brit, the husband of the even more famous Tina Brown, a major figure in Fleet Street journalism, and an early victim of Rupert Murdoch (the last ought to at least have won him the sympathy of any right-thinking person in publishing). Evans, however, had not risen through the ranks as an editor or a book publisher and didn't seem much to care or think that it made a difference. As a result, one heard a lot about his failures and excesses but nothing about his successes—he was portrayed persistently as an amateur with a flair for self-dramatization and no interest in the details of publishing, even at times within Random House. Worse, to journalists, he was an apostate, having escaped from the newspaper world to the more glamorous world of book publishing, where his major interest might have seemed to an unkind and casual observer to lie in attending as many black-tie functions as possible. All the same, when Evans left Random House in 1997, it occurred to me that if there was no future for somebody as gifted as he in book publishing, it was a pretty bleak prospect for the rest of us. Here, after all, was a man of taste, judgment, proven editorial skills, a sense of the jugular for news and publicity and the courage to throw the dice, who had tried to make publishing fun, yet it was as if his departure, whether voluntary, or, as it was rumored, under pressure, was the first step toward the cleansing of the temple, a warning sign that it was important to take publishing *seriously* if you were going to survive in it. Having fun—particularly in public— was clearly no longer a good career move.

IT SHOULD have come as no surprise, however. He had been memorably preceded by Dick Snyder, who had been largely responsible for taking S&S from a company worth $11 million to a global corporation worth in excess of $5 billion and nevertheless had been unceremoniously fired by Viacom, shortly after they acquired Paramount.

It would be hard to imagine anything better calculated to demonstrate that the best way to survive in publishing is to not stick your neck out. Dick had been outspoken, quick to make enemies, hugely ambitious, and determined to continue S&S's rapid pace of growth. However, he had supported his friend Barry Diller when Diller tried to take over Paramount, thus adding further fuel to Martin Davis's dislike of Snyder, for Davis was determined to see Paramount sold to Viacom.

Thus Dick repeated the costly mistake he had made in 1983, when he had supported Jim Judelson instead of Davis. There was in Dick a streak of romantic loyalty, and it cost him dear, since he twice backed the loser in a major corporate fight. It cannot be said of him that he ever wanted to be on the losing side—that was not an element of his personality—but he liked a good fight and wasn't afraid of the odds against him. What is more, once he was *in* a fight, he didn't hold back or try to play both sides.

I had no idea at all of what had happened when I was called to his office, shortly after lunch, on June 14, 1994. By that time, Dick was far more involved in corporate management than in the day-to-day affairs of trade publishing. After a series of stopgap experiments, he had at last found a team whom he trusted—just barely—to manage S&S, and as a result I no longer saw him as often, though we still remained friends. Even so, like most people summoned unexpectedly to his presence, I quickly tried to imagine what mistake of mine had attracted his attention. When I entered his office, I could see that he was shaken.

When he told me that he had been fired, I found it hard to believe—Dick fires people, I told myself, he doesn't *get* fired!—and it took a few minutes for it to sink in. We sat there for a few minutes—we were joined shortly by Alice Mayhew, trying to make small talk, but there was really nothing to be said, except that it was going to be hard to imagine S&S, after so many years, without Dick. Then, gradually, the reality of it sank in. Later on that night, I remember joining him somewhere for a noisy dinner—Bob Woodward had flown up from Washington with his wife. Dick's third wife, Laura, was also there and a lot of other people whom I don't remember. But I do remember stepping out onto Madison Avenue with him after dinner, as we embraced in tears, and saying to him, "It's the end of an era."

And so it proved to be.

THE REMOVAL of two of the more interesting and ambitious figures in book publishing—albeit for very different reasons—in fact set the stage, had one but known it, for an even bigger series of events. In 1998, Random House was bought by Bertelsmann, while Putnam and Berkley Books had been acquired by Pearson in 1996 and merged with Viking and Penguin. The vogue for publishing giants seemed to have reached its peak—or, as some thought, was only just beginning.

Perhaps more ironic, Viacom eventually sold the educational and textbook empire that Dick Snyder had assembled at S&S for nearly five billion dollars and held on to the S&S "consumer unit" itself, thus reducing S&S back to the company that it had been in 1984, when Dick made his first big acquisition with Esquire. It was as if we had started small, grown to unimaginable size, then shrunk back to what we had been at the beginning—the reverse of the American dream.

IT IS possible to look back and see when and how this transformation began. When the Knopfs sold their beloved publishing house to Bennett Cerf in 1960 and Cerf then took Random House public, then sold it to RCA, the die was cast. After that, it was only a matter of time before publishing houses with whose names everybody was familiar— Macmillan, Harper, Atheneum, Scribner, Prentice-Hall, to name a few—fell one by one like trees to a logger's ax. Scribner, for example, the house that employed the fabled Maxwell Perkins and published F. Scott Fitzgerald, Ernest Hemingway, and Thomas Wolfe, was gobbled up by Macmillan, then Macmillan was bought by S&S, and Scribner became an "imprint" (albeit a successful one) of S&S, while its famous bookstore on Fifth Avenue, perhaps the most beautiful bookstore in the country, became (O shame!) a Benetton store!

Dick himself, by concentrating on acquisition as the quickest way to growth, had set in motion forces nobody could control, not even him. He made S&S so valuable that Viacom, in need of money to pay off the debt it had incurred to buy Paramount in a fierce bidding war, had almost no choice but to break up what he had so painstakingly built. He was—the ultimate irony—the victim of success.

ON THE other hand, the essentials of the profession haven't changed at my level. Only today, the florist in the small country town where I live handed me a manuscript—a novel—and asked if I would mind reading it, if it wasn't an imposition. No, I said, as I took it, it's never an imposition. It's how I make my living. My curiosity to open up a new manuscript and read it remains—strangely, after all these years—undiminished. Not that I'm a Pollyanna. I am prepared to be disappointed and very often am— this is in the nature of publishing. Last week, I received a vast manuscript from an agent, a highly touted contemporary novel about the West, and before I had read more than a few pages I knew it was merely ersatz

McMurtry, nothing like the real thing—a zircon, not a diamond. Probably somewhere out in the West, however, at this very moment, some kid with dirt under his fingernails from looking after his father's stock is sitting down at the kitchen table, or in his room, to write a novel—on a computer, no doubt, instead of an old manual typewriter. Maybe he'll be the new McMurtry, and maybe he won't, but this one wasn't. Still, I kept on reading to the end, out of duty. "Give the author a break," to paraphrase Dick Simon.

Sometimes, when I'm at home, I am interrupted by one of the many people who need to talk to me or simply want to pass the time of day— the gardener, the plumber, the man from Airborne Express with a package.

Very often, whoever it is will bang on the window of my study to attract my attention and, when I come to the door, say, "Sorry to bother you, but you didn't look like you were working—you were just sitting there reading."

But that *is* my work, I want to say. It's what I *do,* like gardening or plumbing or delivering packages.

And really, is there a better way to make a living?

Money for jam.

ACKNOWLEDGMENTS

I owe this book—and much, much more—to the gentle prodding and enthusiasm of my friends Lynn Nesbit and Morton Janklow, who overcame my doubts and pushed me toward writing it.

I owe a great debt of gratitude to Robert Loomis of Random House, whose wisdom, patience, and unerring eye truly make him "an editor's editor" (in this case literally as well as metaphorically).

I am deeply grateful to Tina Brown for giving me the opportunity, during her *New Yorker* days, to try my hand at writing profiles, some of which appear in edited and somewhat different form as part of this book.

I am indebted to Eric Rayman of Simon and Schuster for his help with the tangled history of S&S in the Dick Snyder era; to Rebecca Head, who not only lived through many years of this story with me but also remained constantly my dear and indispensable friend and loyal supporter; and to Carol Bowie, who dealt patiently with the many revisions of the manuscript.

Any errors and faults in it are all mine.

INDEX

ABOUT THE AUTHOR

MICHAEL KORDA is the author of *Male Chauvinism: How It Works; Power! How to Get It, How to Use It; Success!; Charmed Lives*, a memoir; *Man to Man: Surviving Prostate Cancer;* and the novels *Worldly Goods, Queenie, The Fortune, Curtain*, and *The Immortals*.

He was born in London in 1933 and educated in Beverly Hills, New York, and Switzerland. He served in the Royal Air Force and then attended Magdalen College, Oxford; his last year there was interrupted by the Hungarian Revolution of 1956, in which he actively participated. After returning from Budapest, he completed his studies, graduated from Oxford, and moved to the United States. He is the editor in chief of a major publishing house.

He and his wife, Margaret, live in Dutchess County, New York.

This book is set in *Fournier*, a typeface named for Pierre Simon Fournier, the youngest son of a French printing family. Pierre Fournier made several important contributions to the field of type design, pioneered the concept of the type family, and is said to have cut 60,000 punches for 147 alphabets of his own design. The Fournier typeface was released in 1925.